Literary Lectures

Literary Lectures

Presented at the Library of Congress

LIBRARY OF CONGRESS   WASHINGTON   1973

Library of Congress Cataloging in Publication Data
Main entry under title:

Literary lectures presented at the Library of Congress.

    CONTENTS: Mann, T. The theme of the Joseph novels.
—Mann, T. The war and the future.—Mann, T. Germany
and the Germans. [etc.]
    1. Literature—Addresses, essays, lectures.
I. United States. Library of Congress.
PN501.L47   809   72–14365
ISBN 0–8444–0084–X

For sale by the Superintendent of Documents, U.S. Government Printing Office
Washington, D.C. 20402. Price: $7.55, domestic postpaid; $7, GPO Bookstore
Stock No. 3016–0018

iv

Preface

Continuing interest in these out-of-print lectures testifies to their durability and prompts their reissuance in this volume.

Literary activities beyond those primary ones of storing and serving literature to readers began in the Library of Congress with the first appointment of a Consultant in Poetry, Joseph Auslander, in 1936. Poetry readings and literary lectures came later, supported, as was the consultantship in poetry, by various gift funds. Thomas Mann's lectures as Consultant in Germanic Literature, beginning in 1942, were the earliest of these lectures published by the Library.

Lectures presented under the auspices of the Gertrude Clarke Whittall Poetry and Literature Fund have accounted for most of those presented by the Library since 1956, although it has become customary in recent years for the Consultant in Poetry to deliver one or more lectures, represented here by Louis Untermeyer's "Edwin Arlington Robinson, A Reappraisal" (1963), and Reed Whittemore's "Ways of Misunderstanding Poetry" (1965).

It has frequently been the case that a group of lectures by several persons has been planned for delivery, as well as for publication, in a series. Thus the lectures by Irving Stone, John O'Hara, and MacKinlay Kantor appeared in the brochure *Three Views of the Novel* (1957); those by John Crowe Ransom, Delmore Schwartz, and John Hall Wheelock in *American Poetry at Mid-Century* (1958); those by Robert Hillyer, Richard Wilbur, and Cleanth Brooks in *Anniversary Lectures* (1959); those by Pierre Emmanuel, Alain Bosquet, Erich Heller, and Hans Egon Holthusen in *French and German Letters Today* (1960); those by Marc Slonim, Lin Yutang, Giose Rimanelli, and Arturo Torres-Rioseco in *Perspectives: Recent Literature of Russia, China, Italy, and Spain* (1961); and those by Ralph Ellison and Karl Shapiro in *The Writer's Experience* (1964).

Roy P. Basler
Chief, Manuscript Division

NOTE

The lectures in this volume are reproduced from editions published over a period of some 30 years and thus reflect a number of changes in Library of Congress editorial style.

Contents

Literary Lectures

The Theme of the Joseph Novels

Thomas Mann

Presented at the Library of Congress November 17, 1942

IT IS, perhaps, not a matter of indifference to those who listen to an address to know the inner circumstances and the feelings of the speaker standing before his audience: a word of personal acknowledgement may have precedence here over all factual discourse and account. Let me begin, therefore, with the statement that this is a precious and great, a festive and stirring hour for me. To speak here, not as a stranger or outsider, but, to a degree, in an official capacity, as a member of the staff of the Library of Congress; that is a great honor, a great joy for me: it holds the charm of the improbable and adventurous; a charm to which, as you know, artists and poets have at all times been particularly susceptible. They would not be what they are, if their view of the play of life was a sober, phlegmatic view, and not, rather, a marvelling and animated, deeply entertained, a *festive* view, which knows, just through the medium of art, how to turn life into spiritually sublimated entertainment, and into a festival for others as well.

It is a good and fortunate coincidence that the topic on which I want to speak—or, am to speak—is, in itself, a festive topic, not only because all art as such has, or should have, festive character; but because a literary work is to be discussed whose very object is the idea and the nature of the festival: more than that—it is, for its own part, a sort of festive celebration, an observance and visualization, a solemn action which playingly neutralizes time and depicts the past and the future, the timelessly existing, *the myth*, as the present.

You have been told, of course, that I am to speak about the book "Joseph and His Brothers," a tetralogy of novels, or epic in prose, whose final volume, "Joseph the Provider," is just about to be completed. Let me say first, that I was quite startled and disconcerted

1

when Archibald MacLeish suggested this book to me as my topic for tonight,—I was much rather inclined to refuse than to accept. Would it not seem terribly presumptuous, vain and egocentric, if I talked today, and here, about my own affairs, my own work, in other words: about highly personal and private matters instead of general and important ones, of the great cares and hopes of our time, of the war and its objectives? And yet, this is a time and a world where it makes almost no difference what we talk about—we always talk about one and the same thing. Categories crumble, the borderlines between the different spheres of human thought become unessential. Everything is connected with everything else—and, in truth, it has always been so: only, we were not conscious of it. Once, it was possible to distinguish between a "purely esthetic," "purely philosophic," "purely religious" sphere and the sphere of politics, of human society, of national and international community life, and to declare that we were interested in the one but not in the other. This is no longer possible. We are interested in the whole, or we are interested in nothing. "Totalitarian" is an oppressive word in its strictly political meaning; we do not like to hear it because it signifies the voracious absorption of all things human by the state. But, then, we are indeed living in a totalitarian world, a world of totality, of spiritual unity and collective responsibility, before which all sovereignties have to abdicate. Unity is the word of the historic hour. The world wants to become one, all the way, into practical reality, down to economic matters. It is a world of infinitely mutual *implications,* and to talk about belletristic literature, about a novel, is not necessarily insipid infidelity toward the great and burning concerns of our time, and toward the plight, the struggle, the longing of humanity. —Of course, it depends a little on the novel.

I have often been asked what it actually was that made me turn to this remote and out-of-the-way subject and induced me to transform the biblical legend of the Egyptian Joseph into a broad cycle of novels, requiring many years of work. In answering this question, there is little importance in the external and anecdotical circumstances which prompted me, almost a decade and a half ago when I was still in Munich, to re-read the story in my old ancestral bible. Suffice it to say that I was delighted, and that immediately a preliminary probing and productive searching began in my mind as to what it would be like to renew and reproduce this charming story in fresh narrative and with modern means—with *all* modern means, the spiritual and the technical ones. Almost immediately, these inner experiments significantly associated themselves with the thought of a tradition: the thought of Goethe, in fact, who relates in his memoirs "Dichtung und Wahrheit" how he, as a boy, had dictated the Joseph story to a friend and, in doing so, had

2

woven it into a broad narrative. However, it soon met the fate of destruction because, in the author's own judgement, it still lacked too much in "substance." As an explanation of this youthful and premature venture, the sixty year old Goethe observes: "This natural story is highly amiable: only, it seems too short, and one is tempted to carry it out in all its details."

How strange! Immediately, these words from "Dichtung und Wahrheit" came to my mind, in the midst of my reveries: they were in my memory; I did not have to re-read them,—and indeed, they seem most fitting as the motto for what I then undertook; they furnish the simplest and most plausible explanation for my venture. The temptation which the young Goethe had naively followed, namely to carry out the short legendary report of the Genesis in "all its details," repeated itself in my case at a stage of my life when the poetic execution could definitely obtain human and spiritual substance as well. But what does that mean: to carry out in detail what has been briefly reported? It is exactness, realization; it is to draw into proximity something very remote and vague, so that you believe you see it with your eyes and grasp it with your hands, and you think, that, finally, you learn the definite truth about it after having so long entertained very uncertain ideas on the subject. I still remember how amused I was, and how much of a compliment I considered it, when my copyist in Munich, a simple woman, brought me the typewritten copy of the first volume, "The Stories of Jaacob," and said: "Now we know at last how all this actually happened." That was touching—for, after all, it did not happen. The exactness, the realism are fictional, they are play and artful illusion, they are realization and visualization forcibly brought about by all the means of language, psychology, presentation and, in addition, critical comment; and humor, despite all human seriousness, is their soul. What, above all, is inspired by humor in the book is the analysis and scientific research, which are, just like the narrative and the descriptions, a means of establishing reality; and the command to the artist, to create forms and not to talk are invalid in this case.

The reasoning also is playful, it is not really the language of the author but of the work itself, it has been incorporated in its linguistic sphere, it is indirect, a stylized and bantering language, a contribution to the pseudo-exactness, very close to persiflage and, at any rate, to irony; for scientific treatment of wholly unscientific and legendary matters is pure irony.

It is quite possible that such secret charms played their part at the time of the earliest conception of the work. But this does not answer the question as to how I came to select this archaic subject-matter from the dawn of mankind. Different circumstances, some of a personal and others of a general temporal character, contributed to it, and the personal ones were also of a temporal nature; they had something to do with those years, with a stage of life that had been attained. The readiness is all. As a man, and as an artist, I must somehow have been in *readiness* to be productively attracted by such subject-matter, and my Bible-reading was not mere chance. The various stages of life have different inclinations, claims, tendencies of taste—as well as abilities and advantages. It is probably a rule that in certain years the taste for all purely individual and particular phenomena, for the individual case, for the "bourgeois" aspect, in the widest sense of the word, fades out gradually. Instead, the typical, the eternally-human, eternally-recurring, timeless, in short: the mythical steps into the foreground of the interest. For, after all, the typical is already the mythical, insofar as it is pristine pattern and pristine form of life, timeless model and formula of eld, into which life enters by reproducing its traits out of the unconscious. Definitely, the attainment of the mythical viewpoint is of decisive importance in the life of the narrator; it signifies a peculiar enhancement of his artistic mood, a new serenity in recognizing and shaping which, as said before, is ordinarily reserved for the later years of life: for the mythical, it is true, represents an early and primitive stage in the life of humanity, but a late and mature one in the life of the individual.

There the word humanity has been pronounced—in connection with the ideas of the timelessly-typical and the mythical it automatically made its appearance. I had been in readiness to feel productively attracted by a subject-matter like the Joseph legend, because of the turning of my taste away from the bourgeois toward the mythical aspect. But, at the same time, I was in readiness for it because of my disposition for generally human feeling and thinking,—I mean: a feeling and thinking in human terms,—a disposition which was not only the product of my individual time and stage of life, but that of the time at large and in general, of OUR time, of the historic convulsions, adventures and tribulations, by which the question of man, the very problem of humanity was presented to us as an indivisible whole, and imposed upon our conscience as hardly ever to a generation before us.

I believe, Ladies and Gentlemen, that the sufferings and stirring adventures, through which humanity has been going now for decades, will bring forth a new, deepened feeling of humanity, indeed a new HUMANISM, remote from all shallow optimism, but full of sympathy, which will be only too necessary for the work of reconstruction that will confront us after the tremendous moral and material devastations, after the collapse of the accustomed world. In order to build up, or at least lay the foundations for the new, better, happier and more social

4

world, freed from unnecessary suffering, which we want our children and grandchildren to have, the City of Man, as I should like to call it, we will need a binding and all-determining basic pathos, guiding us all the way to detailed and practical matters; we will need sympathy for it, and love. And with all this the mythical novel has something to do which was conceived in 1925 and of which I am speaking to you: it is by no means an out-of-the-way, evasive, extra-timely product, but inspired by an interest in humanity transcending the individual,—a humorous, ironically softened,—I am tempted to say: a bashful poem of man.

Rather, it turned out that way unintentionally; for the author was far from attributing it this quality in the beginning. Once again it came to pass that a work developed a much greater aspiration than was inherent in the rather skeptical and by no means ambitious nature of the one on whom it imposed itself, and from whom it exacted efforts far beyond all plans and expectations.

To begin is always terribly difficult: until one feels oneself master of a subject; until one learns the language it speaks, and can reproduce it; —much courting and laboring, a long inner familiarization is required. But what I planned was so new and unusual, that never did I beat about the bush longer than this time. There was the need of establishing contact with a strange world, the primitive and mythical world: and to "take contact," in the poetic sense of the word, signifies something very complicated, intimate: a penetration, carried to identification and self-substitution, so that something can be created which is called "style," and which is always a unique and complete amalgamation of the artist with the subject.

How much of an adventure I considered this mythical enterprise of mine, is indicated by the introduction to the first volume of "Joseph and His Brothers," "The Stories of Jaacob," which forms the anthropological prelude to the whole work. Entitled "Descent into Hell" it is a fantastical essay which seems like the cumbersome preparation for a risky expedition—a journey down into the depths of the past, a trip to the 'mothers.' The overture was sixty-four pages long—that might have made me suspicious in regard to the proportions of the whole, and did so to a degree—especially as I had decided, that the personal story of Joseph alone would not do, but that the primeval and original story, the history of the world demanded to be included, at least in perspective. The stories of Jaacob filled a heavy volume: in mingled order, anticipating and reverting, I recited them, strangely entertained by the novelty of dealing with human beings who did not quite know who they were, or who knew it in a more pious, deeply exact way than the modern individual; beings whose identity was open in back and included the past with which they identified themselves, in whose steps they tread and which again became present through them. "Novarum rerum cupidus"—this characteristic fits the artist better than anyone else. Nobody is more bored than he by the old and worn out, and more impatient for the new, although nobody, on the other hand, is more bound to tradition than he is. Audacity in confinement, fulfillment of tradition with exciting news, that is really his calling and his business, and the conviction that "such a thing has not been done before" is the indispensable motor of all his industry. I have always needed this spurring conviction in order to accomplish anything, indeed, even to begin anything, and it seemed to me that I had never experienced it more strongly than this time. "The Stories of Jaacob" and their successor, "The Young Joseph," were completed while I was still in Germany. During my work on the third volume, "Joseph in Egypt," the break in my outward existence occurred, the trip from which I could not return, the sudden loss of my life's basis: the larger part of "Joseph in Egypt" is work born in exile. My oldest daughter who dared to return to our already confiscated house in Munich, after the revolution, recovered the manuscript and brought it to me in Southern France; and slowly, after the first shock of my new, uprooted situation, I resumed the work which was continued and completed in the Swiss refuge which we enjoyed for five years, on the Lake of Zurich.

Now, then, the narrative entered into the highly developed and sophisticated cultural sphere of the Nile Empire, which, through sympathy and reading matter, had been familiar to me since the time of my boyhood, so that I knew more about it, than even the teacher who during Religion Class questioned us twelve-year-old boys as to the name of the holy steer of the ancient Egyptians. I showed that I was eager to answer, and was called upon. "Chapi," I said. That was wrong, in the opinion of the teacher. He reproached me for having raised my hand, when I knew only nonsense. "Apis" was the right name, he corrected me angrily. But "Apis" is only the latinization or hellenization of the authentic Egyptian name which I had given. The people of Keme said "Chapi." I knew better than the good man, but discipline did not allow me to enlighten him about it. I kept silent—and all my life I have not forgiven myself for this silence before false authority. An American boy would certainly have spoken up.

Occasionally I thought of this early incident while I was writing "Joseph in Egypt." A work must have long roots in my life, secret connections must lead from it to earliest childhood dreams, if I am to consider myself entitled to it, if I am to believe in the legitimacy of what I am doing. The arbitrary reaching for a subject to which one

6

does not have traditional claims of sympathy and knowledge, seems senseless and amateurish to me.

Due to its erotic content, the third Joseph volume is the most novel-like part of this work which, as a whole, had to make of the novel something different from what is generally understood by this term. The variability of this literary genre has always been considerable. Today, however, it almost looks as though nothing counts anymore in the domain of the novel except what is no longer a novel. Perhaps it was always that way. As far as "Joseph in Egypt" is concerned, you will find, that its novel-like erotic content, too, has been turned into the mythical by stylization, despite all psychology. That holds true particularly for the sexual satire which is centered around the figures of the two dwarfs: the asexual one in his kindly nothingness, and of Dudu, the malicious and procreative midget. In a humorous spirit, a connection is shown here between the sexual and arch-evil, a connection which must help to reconcile us to Joseph's "chastity," his resistance to the desires of his unfortunate mistress, as given by the biblical model.

This third of the Joseph novels grew under the constellation of my parting from Germany—the fourth grew under that of my parting from Europe. "Joseph the Provider," the final part of the work which brings its length to over two thousand pages, came into being entirely under America's sky, in fact, largely under the serene, Egyptian-like sky of California. Now Potiphar's demoted favorite slaves as a prisoner in a Nile fortress whose commander is a good man—so good a man, that Joseph later makes him his Major Domo, accepting him into the divine story as a helpful friend. In the fortress, Joseph is commissioned to act as a valet to the distinguished servants of the Royal Court who arrive one day as prisoners under investigation: the baker and the cup-bearer. Now the dreamer interprets dreams, and the day comes when he is taken from the prison in haste and stands before Pharao. He is thirty years old then, and Pharao is seventeen. This hypersensitive and tender youth, a searcher of God, like Joseph's forefathers, and enam-oured of a dreamy religion of love, has ascended to the throne during the time of Joseph's imprisonment. He is an anticipating, a premature Christian, the mythical prototype of those, who are on the right way, but not the right ones for that way. It is a widely ramified sequence of chapters in which Joseph gains the unlimited confidence of the young ruler, and at whose end he receives the ring of power.

Now he is Viceroy, takes the well-known measures of Providence for the coming famine and enters into a matrimony of State with Asnath, daughter of the sun priest of On-Heliopolis. But here, the story returns from the Egyptian soil to the theatre of the first and second volume, to Canaan, and a complete long short-story is interpolated which gives to

7

this volume its outstanding female character, as the first one had it in the person of the lovely Rachel, the third one in the fruitlessly desiring Mut-em-enet. It is Thamar, the daughter-in-law of Juda, a figure of grand style, the female paradigm of determination, whose spiritual ambition scorns no means that might help her, the pagan child of Baal, to get on the path of Promise and to become a forebear of the Messiah.

Now the famine assumes reality, and dramatically the well-known action takes its course, which is nothing but a precious childhood memory, and for which the curiosity of the reader can be captivated only by the most detailed presentation and visualization of every How and Why. The arrival of the brothers, the meeting with the prescient Benjamin, the play with the silver cup, the great scene of recognition, the scene in which a musical child sings to the aged Jaacob, that his son Joseph is alive and lord over the land of Egypt;—in minute detail we learn—and some day my Munich copyist, too, will probably learn, —how all that has really happened. The novel extends to the solemn passing away of Jaacob, the father, in the land of Goshen; and with the tremendous procession which brings home the body of the patriarch, so that he may rest in the twofold cave with his fathers, ends the whole work which through one and a half decades of outer stress was my steady companion.

Ladies and Gentlemen, some people were inclined to regard "Joseph and His Brothers" as a Jewish novel, even as merely a novel for Jews. Well, the selection of the old testamental subject was certainly not mere accident; most certainly there were hidden, defiantly polemic connections between it and certain tendencies of our time which I always found repulsive from the bottom of my soul; the growing vulgar anti-semitism which is an essential part of the Fascist mob-myth, and which commits the brutish denial of the fact that Judaism and Hellenism are the two principal pillars upon which our occidental civilization rests. To write a novel of the Jewish spirit was timely, just because it seemed untimely. And, it is true: my story always follows the dates of the Genesis with semi-jocular faithfulness, and often reads like an exegesis and amplification of the Tora, like a rabbinical Midrasch. And yet, all that is Jewish, throughout the work, is merely foreground, just as the Hebrew cadence of its diction is only foreground, only one style element among others, only *one* stratum of its language which strangely fuses the archaic and the modern, the epical and analytical. In the last book is a poem, the song of annunciation which the musical child sings for the aged Jaacob, and which is an odd composition of psalter recollections and little verses of the German romantic type. That is an example for the character of the whole work, which seeks to blend a great many things; and, because it conceives and imagines everything

8

human as a unity, it borrows its motives, memories, allusions, as well as linguistic sounds from many spheres. Just as all the Jewish legends are based on other, timeless mythologies, and made transparent by them, thus Joseph, its hero, is also a transparent figure, changing with the illumination in vexatory fashion: he is, with a great deal of consciousness, an Adonis—and Tammuz figure; but then he perceptibly slides into a Hermes part, the part of the mundane and skillful businessman and the intelligent profit producer among the gods, and in his great conversation with Pharao the mythologies of all the world, the Hebraic, Babylonian, Egyptian and Greek are mingled so thoroughly that one will hardly be aware of holding a biblical Jewish story book in one's hands.

There is a symptom for the innate character of a work, for the category toward which it strives, the opinion it secretly has of itself: that is the reading matter which the author prefers and which he considers helpful while working on it. I am not thinking, in this connection, about factual sources and material research, but about great works of literature which in a broad sense seem related to his own effort, models whose contemplation keeps him in the right mood, and which he seeks to emulate. All, that can be of no help, does not fit, has no reference to the subject,—is hygienically excluded,—it is not conducive at the moment and therefore disallowed. Well then, such strengthening reading during the last Joseph years was provided by two books: Laurence Sterne's "Tristam Shandy" and Goethe's "Faust"—a perplexing combination; but each of the two heterogeneous works had its particular function as a stimulant, and in this connection it was a pleasure for me to know that Goethe had held Sterne in very high esteem, and had called him one of the finest intellects who had ever lived.

Naturally, it was the humorous side of the "Joseph" which profited by this reading. Sterne's wealth of humorous expressions and inventions, his genuine, comical technique attracted me; for to refresh my work I needed something like this. And then, Goethe's "Faust," this life's work and linguistic monument developed from tender, lyrical germ-cell, this enormous mixture of magic opera and mankind's tragedy, of puppet-show and cosmic poem. Time and again I returned to this inexhaustible source,—especially to the second part, to the Helena scenes, the classical Walpurgis Night; and this fixation, this insatiable admiration indicated the secret immodesty of my own endeavors, they revealed the direction in which the ambition of the Joseph story pointed,—its own; for the author, as usual, had at the outset been quite innocent of such ambition.

"Faust" is a symbol of humanity, and to become something like that in my hands was the clandestine tendency of the Joseph story. I told about beginnings, where everything came into being for the first time. That was the attractive novelty, the uncommon amusement of this kind of fable telling, that everything was there for the first time, that one foundation took place after the other, the foundation of love, of envy, of hatred, of murder, and of much else. But this dominant originality is, at the same time, repetition, reflection, image; the result of rotation of the spheres which brings the upper, the starlike into the lower regions, carries, in turn, the worldly into the realm of the divine, so that gods become men, men in turn become gods. The worldly finds itself pre-created in the realm of the stars, and the individual character seeks its dignity by tracing itself back to the timeless, mythical pattern, giving it presence.

I dwelled on the birth of the Ego out of the mythical collective, the Abrahamitic Ego which is pretentious enough to assume that man should serve only the Highest, from which assumption the discovery of God followed. The claim of the human ego to central importance is the premise for the discovery of God, and from the very first the pathos for the dignity of the Ego is connected with that for the dignity of humanity.

At the same time, these humans remain confined in the mythical, the collective, to a large extent of their being. What they call spirit and culture, is just the conviction that their lives are the embodiment of the myth, and their ego detaches itself from the collective in much the same way as certain figures of Rodin wrest themselves out of the stone and awaken from it. Jaacob, weighty with stories, is also such a half-detached figure: his solemnness is still mythical and already individual; the cult which he devotes to his feelings, and for which he is punished by the jealousy of the Highest is the bland but proud assertion of an ego, which loftily feels itself the subject and hero of its stories. It is still a patriarchal and respectable form of human individualization and emancipation, and it grows far more bold and daring in the complicated case of his son Joseph. There is one, who has not discovered God, but knows how to "treat" Him; one who is not only the hero of his stories, but also their director, indeed the one who poetically "adorns" them; one who, it is true, still participates in the collective and mythical, but in a banteringly spiritualized and playful, purposefully conscious manner. In short, we see how the ego, in the process of its emancipation, soon becomes an artistic ego, attractive, delicate and—endangered, a tender concern for the respectable father, but with inborn possibilities of development and maturing, as have not existed before. In its youth, the artistic ego is of inexcusable egocentricity: it lives under the dangerous assumption that everybody must love it more than himself. But due to a sympathy and friendliness which nonetheless

10

it never renounces, it finds its way into the social, while it matures, and becomes the provider and benefactor of a foreign people and of its own: in Joseph the ego flows back from arrogant absoluteness into the collective, common; and, the contrast between artistic and civic tendencies, between isolation and community, between individual and collective is fabulously neutralized,—as according to our hopes and our will, it must be dissolved in the democracy of the future, the cooperation of free and divergent nations under the equalizing sceptre of justice.

A symbol of humanity—in a certain way my work was entitled to this secret opinion of itself. After all, from the original and simple, the typical and canonical it led to the complicated, involved, late: the way from Canaan to the Egypt of the New Kingdom is the way from the piously primitive, the God-creating, God-contemplative idyl of the archfathers to a highly developed and sophisticated culture with its luxuries and absurd snobberies, in a land of the grandchildren, a land whose atmosphere is so much to Joseph's taste because he is himself a grandchild and a late soul.

The feeling for the way, the advancement, the change, the development is very strong in the book, its whole theology is connected with it and derived from it: namely, from its conception of the old testamental "Bond" between God and man: from the conviction that God and man are mutually dependent upon each other in common aspiration for enhancement. For God, too, is subject to development, He, too, changes and advances: from the desert-like and demoniacal to the spiritual and holy; and He can do so without the help of the human spirit as little as the human spirit can without Him.—Were I to determine what I, personally, mean by religiousness, I should say it is *attentiveness* and *obedience;* attentiveness to the inner changes of the world, the mutation in the aspects of truth and right; obedience which loses no time in adjusting life and reality to these changes, this mutation, and thus in doing justice to the spirit. To live in sin is to live against the spirit, to cling to the antiquated, obsolete, and to continue to live in it, due to inattentiveness and disobedience. And whenever the book speaks about the "concern with God," it speaks about the just fear of this sin and folly. "Concern with God" is not alone the creating of God in one's thoughts, and determining and recognizing Him, but principally the concern with His will, with which ours must coincide; with the demands of the present, the postulate of the aeon, of the world hour. It is the intelligent listening to what the world spirit wants, to the new truth and necessity; and a special religious concept of *stupidity* follows from that: the stupidity before God, which does not know this concern, or complies with it as clumsily as Laban who still believes

11

that he must slaughter his little son and bury him in the foundation of his house, a custom which once was quite beneficial but is so no longer.

Must I add, Ladies and Gentlemen, that we owe the tribulations which we now have to endure, the catastrophe in which we are living, to the fact that we lacked intelligence toward God to a degree which had long become criminal? Europe, the world, was full of stale and outworn things, of evident obsolete and even sacrilegious anachronisms which had been clearly outdistanced by the world will, and which we permitted to continue, in dull mind and in disobedience to this will. It is understood, that the spirit is always ahead of reality, that reality follows it clumsily. But never, perhaps, had there existed before such pathological, such unmistakably dangerous tension, in the social, political and economic life of the peoples, between truth and reality, between things long reached and accomplished by the spirit and between things which still took the liberty of calling themselves reality; and foolish disobedience to the spirit or, religiously speaking, to God's will, is undoubtedly the true cause for the world explosion which stuns us. But explosion is equalization, and I think that here, in this hall, it is quite the right place to express the hope that after this war, we—or our children—will live in a world of happier equalization between spirit and reality, that we will "win the peace." The word peace always has a religious ring, and what it signifies is a gift of intelligence before God.

You understand, I am eager to prove, that it is not wholly vain and idle to speak about my private work at a moment like this, instead of general and important matters. I may tell myself that there are connections between my work and general and important matters, —indeed underneath all badinage, that is its secret motor. In a discreet and unpathetic manner, the case of mankind is tried in it, and therefore the manner in which this book treats the myth is so different from a certain contemporary manner of employing it: a malevolent and anti-human manner whose political name we all know. After all, the word "myth" has a bad reputation nowadays—we only have to think of the title of the book, which the "philosopher" of German fascism, Rosenberg, the preceptor of Hitler, has given to his vicious textbook: "The Myth of the 20th Century." So often, in the last decades, had the myth been abused as a means of obscurantic counter-revolution that a mythical novel like the Joseph, upon its first appearance, inevitably aroused the suspicion that its author was floating with the murky stream. This suspicion had to be discarded for at a second glance a process could be observed similar to what happens in a battle when a captured gun is turned around and directed against the enemy. In this book, the myth has been taken out of Fascist hands and humanized

12

down to the last recess of its language,—if posterity finds anything remarkable about it, it will be this.

In the idea of humanity, the human idea, the sense for the past and that for the future, tradition and revolution form a strange and, to my mind, infinitely attractive mixture. The slogan of the "conservative revolution" has played a pernicious part; fascism has seized it as it seized the myth, and has pretended to be the conservative revolution. Its nature is fraud. But what better formula than just this: "conservative revolution" could be found for the spirit and meaning of that famous speech which an American opponent of Fascism, Henry A. Wallace, Vice President of the United States of America, held before the members and guests of the Free World Association on the 8th of May of this year? This speech, "The Price of Free World Victory" is, I think, a beautiful example of the unification of tradition and revolution in the sphere of the Humane; the stirring proof that today the conserving and the revolutionary will are one and the same, are simply the *good* will.

May I say, that my composition is of a somewhat similar nature? It bases its concept of piety upon the idea of time, of change, of development, of advancement toward perfection, an advancement for which God and man ally themselves,—but at the same time the idea of tradition plays in it a thematic part of the first order. I related to you how a Goethe memory, a word of his about the Joseph tale, entered into my first reveries when I tried my hand at this subject; I also told you of the secret reference to Goethe's Faust which my work dared to take while it grew. That was playful boldness which sprang from the sense for tradition and succession and corresponded to the inner nature of my task, a mythical task. For what else is myth but succession and recollection, the forming and coining of the present with the past, the childlike identification with an admired idol—in short, tradition? Myth is tradition, and to live in tradition means to live in the myth.

An artist's life, Ladies and Gentlemen, is a life of *experience* in manifold ways: when it strives to follow the great, it also becomes a means of experiencing greatness,—not like the scientist, nor the historian: not objectively and from without, but in a subjective, practical, productive way. Three times, at different stages of my life, have I lived under the prolonged tension of tasks, which had a certain affinity to greatness: at the age of twenty-five, when I tried my hand at the novel of the German bourgeoisie Buddenbrooks, at the age of fifty, when in the Magic Mountain I made a friendly alter ego pass through the adventures of European intellectual controversies, and between sixty and seventy, when I told mankind's fairy tale of Joseph and his brothers. To participate playfully in the consciousness of great creativeness and to acquire, thereby, the right to a more familiar celebration of greatness than the wholly inexperienced and uninitiated possess, that is something, that is worth a life. "That a man entertains himself and does not spend his life like dull cattle," I have my Joseph answer a critic of his mythical temerity, "is after all what matters most; and what heights of entertainment he is able to reach—that is what counts."

And now, Ladies and Gentlemen, let me finally return to the fact which seems to me to have a certain symbolic value, after all, namely that the mythical play of Joseph and his Brothers, begun in Germany, continued in Switzerland, transplanted to America was completed here, in contact with the American myth. For there is such a thing; you, too, live in a tradition here, walk in footsteps, in paternal footsteps, which you call your "Way of Life." The pioneer-like optimism and hearty faith in man, the mental youthfulness, the benevolent and confident ideas and principles upon which the Union was founded by the fathers, amounts to the American myth, which is alive today. In his biography, Goethe speaks about an "alleviation for humanity" effected by the American war of liberation; and the European emigration to America (which finds its way into the final parts of the Wilhelm Meister), sprang from the constant desire to participate in this alleviation; it was the pilgrimage to a pure fountain of health. But the measure and the significance which this flight and migration has assumed at present, are something new. The diaspora of European culture which we are witnessing, the arrival of so many of its bearers, representatives of all categories of science and art, to these shores; their more or less involuntary decision, transformed, however, into an amor fati, to complete their work in the American air of life,—that is something very strange and unprecedented; it opens unexampled possibilities of exchange and equalization and may be supremely helpful in creating the new feeling of humanism of which I spoke. Our emigration thus assumes an entirely different significance from that of any former emigration, the significance of the coalescence of the hemispheres, of the unification of the earth. "Europe wants to become one" that is long obsolete; the *earth* wants to become one. "Unification" is the word and command of the world hour, and the future belongs to the union of knowledge *and* hope, of profundity *and* courage, of faith and labor in the face of all doubt, and despite all doubt.

14

The War and the Future

Thomas Mann

Presented at the Library of Congress October 13, 1943

NOWADAYS, it is not an easy but a rather oppressive situation to stand upon a platform behind the speaker's desk and see the eyes of an audience turned toward you with inquiry and expectancy. I say "now," but this situation which may be natural for the man of action and mass-persuasion, for the politician and party-man, has in truth always been strange and inappropriate for the artist, the poet, the musician of ideas and words, a situation in which he has never felt quite at home, for he becomes, to a certain extent, untrue to his own nature. The element of strangeness and uneasiness lies, for him, in the very nature of the task, in speaking, in committing himself, teaching, in stating convictions and defending opinions. For the artist, the poet, is one who absorbs all the movements and intellectual tendencies, all the currents and spiritual contents of the times and allows them to act upon him; he is affected by all of them, digests them all mentally, gives them form and in this way makes visual the total cultural picture of his times for his contemporary world and for posterity. He does not preach nor propagandize; he gives things a plastic reality, indifferent to nothing; but committed to no cause except that of freedom, of ironical objectivity. He does not speak himself; he lets others speak and even when he is not a dramatist, his conditions are those of the drama, of Shakespeare, wherein the person who happens to be speaking is always right. To speak on his own responsibility is foreign to him, burdensome and alarming. He is, of necessity, a dialectical nature and knows the truth that lies in Goethe's words: "Sobald man spricht, beginnt man schon zu irren" [as soon as a man speaks, error begins]. He agrees with Turgeniev, who said: "When I describe a man and say that he has a pointed nose, a long chin and white hair, or red cheeks, or long teeth, or that he is cross-eyed, or that his eyes have this color and that expression, it cannot be contradicted. It is a cheerful reality. There is nothing

15

to be said against it. But when I defend an opinion, a contradictory one can immediately be raised against it. It can always be assailed; the opposite can also be defended, and I must not only take into account that I will meet with external contradiction to my one-sided position but I also have the contradiction in myself internally, and, in denying this when committing myself to one point of view, I renounce my freedom."

That is true, and yet there are moments, historical conditions, in which it would prove to be weak, egoistic and wholly untimely to insist upon one's freedom of criticism and to shy away from a confession of faith. I mean THOSE moments and THOSE historical conditions in which Freedom itself, by which the freedom of the artist also exists, is endangered. It is reactionary, unscrupulous, and suicidal, and the intellectual undermines his own existence, if through his need for freedom, he plays into the hands of the enemies and assassins of freedom. These enemies are only too happy if mind considers nothing but the ironical attitude worthy of itself, if it despises the distinction between good and evil, and considers the preoccupation with ideas such as freedom, truth, justice as "bourgeois." In certain conditions it is the duty of the intellectual to renounce his freedom—for the sake of freedom. It is his duty to find the courage to affirm ideas over which the intellectual snob thinks that he can shrug his shoulders. I have had the experience in America when speaking on democracy and my belief in it, that some high-brow journalist who wanted to earn his critical spurs, would say that I had expressed "middle-class ideas." He was expressing a false and reactionary concept of the banal, a misconception with which I had already become all too well acquainted in Europe. I am thinking of Paris at a time when I was discussing Briand and his liberal European struggle to maintain the peace, with members of the "bourgeoisie" who were already strongly infected with fascism. "But, my dear friend," they would say, "Que voulez-vous avec votre Briand? That is the worst banality, d'une trivialite insupportable." What the high-brow journalist was characterizing with "middle-class ideas" is actually nothing else than the liberal tradition. It is the complex of ideas of freedom and progress, of humanitarianism, of civilization—in short, the claim of reason to dominate the dynamics of nature, of instinct, of blood, of the unconscious, the primitive spontaneity of life. Now it is by no means natural for the artist, for any human being who stands in any relationship to the creative, to be eternally talking of reason like some learned ass. He very well knows the importance to life of the sub-rational and super-rational powers of instinct and dream; and he is not at all inclined to over-rate the intellect as the guide and moulder of life. He is far from being an enemy of instinct. He recognizes that

16

the recoil from the rationalism of the eighteenth and nineteenth centuries was historically and intellectually justified, was inevitable and necessary, but it was crass and immoderate; and if one had the imagination to foresee how the irrational, the dark dynamics, the glorification of instinct, the worship of blood and impulse, the "will to power" and "élan vital" and "myth as cri de bataille," and the justification of violence—how all these ideas would look, when translated from the intellectual sphere, where they were very interesting and fascinating, to the sphere of reality, of politics—if one had imagination enough to foresee this, the desire speedily evaporated to sit upon this side of the boat, where all and sundry, anyway, down to the last petty scribbler and beer-hall demagogue were to be found. It is a terrible spectacle when irrationalism becomes popular. One feels that disaster is imminent, a disaster such as the one-sided over-valuation of reason could never bring about. The over-valuation of reason can be comical in its optimistic pedantry and can be made to look ridiculous by the deeper powers of life. But it does not evoke catastrophe. That is brought about only by the enthronement of anti-reason. At a certain period when fascism took over politically in Germany and Italy, when nationalism became the focus and universal expression of all these tendencies, I was convinced that nothing but war and general destruction could be the final outcome of the irrationalistic orgy, and that in short order. What seemed necessary was the memory of other values, of the idea of democracy, of humanity, of peace, and of human freedom and dignity. It was this side of human nature that needed our help. There is not the slightest danger that reason will ever gain complete ascendancy, that there could ever be too much reason on earth. There is no danger that people will some day become emotionless angels, which, to be sure, would be very dull. But that they should become beasts, which as a matter of fact would be a little too interesting, that, as we have seen, can readily happen. This tendency is much stronger in human beings than the anemic angelic one, and it is only necessary, through general glorification of instincts to set free the evil ones which are always ready to appropriate such a glorification to themselves, in order to bring the bestial tendencies into triumphant ascendancy. It is easy and self-indulgent to throw oneself on the side of nature against the mind, that is to say on the side which in any case is always the stronger. Simple generosity and a slight sense of humane responsibility should decide us to protect and nourish the poor little flame of mind and reason upon earth that it may shine and warm us a little better.

Freedom and justice have long ceased to be banal; they are vital; and to think of them as boring, simply means an acceptance of the fascistic pseudo-revolutionary fraud that violence and mass-deception are the last word and most up-to-date. The better mind knows that the really new thing in the world which the living spirit is called upon to serve is something totally different, namely, a social democracy and a humanism which, instead of being caught in a cowardly relativism, have the courage once more to distinguish between good and evil.

That is what the European peoples did. They refused to submit to evil, to Hitler's New Order, to slavery. And I should like to take this opportunity to say a word in honor of this now deeply depressed part of the earth. It may well be that we Europeans will only play the part of "Graeculi" in the Roman world of power that will arise out of this war, whose capitals will be Washington, London, and Moscow; but this diminutive role should not decrease our justifiable pride in our old homeland. How much easier, how much less arduous would it have been for the European peoples if they had accepted Hitler's infamous New Order; if they had reconciled themselves to slavery; if they had, as it is called, "collaborated" with Nazi Germany. They have not done so, not a single one of them. Years of the most brutal terrorism, of martyrdom and executions have not succeeded in breaking their will to resist. On the contrary, the resistance has only grown stronger and the most outrageous of all the Nazi lies is that of a united Europe defending its holiest possessions against the invasion of foreigners; the foreigners against whom these holiest possessions must be defended are they, the Nazis, and no one else. Only a corrupt upper-crust, a treasonous gang for whom nothing is holy but money and advantage, is collaborating with them. The people have refused collaboration and, as the victory of the Allies is more clearly outlined, the more confident does the opposition to oppression become. Seven million people have been deported to enforced labor; almost a million have been executed and murdered; ten thousand more are imprisoned in the hell of the concentration camp. Notwithstanding, the uneven, the heroic battle continues. I say: all honor to the peoples of Europe. They are fighting our battle. They are our allies and they deserve to be treated as our allies. Slowly, very slowly, freedom is drawing near, yet their tenacity is indomitable. They deserve our confidence; they should be allowed to have their way, to clean out the powers who have betrayed them and led them into misery. They deserve to be spoken to in a frank and friendly way so that their belief may not be shaken that the liberators are really coming as liberators and not to submit them to the power of the old, decayed, and despised order.

But in speaking of Europe, I cannot omit my own country, and I take for granted that you wish to hear from me about this problem, about its relationship to the world, about how it could possibly have got into the condition in which we find it today; the question of the common responsibility of the German people for the misdeeds of the Nazis. These are painful and complicated matters—experiences which one can scarcely communicate in words to those, who in these times live amongst their own people, in complete harmony with them, in unshakable faith in the cause of this people, and who are permitted to fight enthusiastically for that cause. This perfectly natural good fortune is denied us emigrés, not so the enthusiasm and the struggle for this cause. We also battle. But it is our destiny to carry on this battle against our own land and its aims, of whose corruptness we are convinced; against the land whose speech is the spiritual material in which we work, against the land in whose culture we are rooted, whose traditions we carry on, and whose landscape and atmosphere should be our natural shelter.

You will say to me: "We are all fighting for the same cause, the cause of humanity. There is no distinction between you and us." Certainly, but it is your good fortune to be able to identify yourselves with the cause of your people, of your fighting forces, of your government; and when you see the symbol of American sovereignty, the Stars and Stripes, you are perhaps not naïvely patriotic enough that your heart beats with pride in your throat and that you break into loud hurrahs, but you look upon this emblem with a feeling of home, with sympathy and confidence, with calm pride and heartfelt hopes, while we——. You can scarcely conceive the feelings with which we look upon the present national emblem of Germany, the swastika. We do not look upon it, we look away. We would rather look at the ground or at the sky, for the sight of the symbol under which our people are fighting for their existence, or rather delude themselves that they are fighting for that existence, makes us physically sick. You do not know how horribly strange, how detestable, how shocking it is for us to see the swastika-ornamented entrance to a German consulate or embassy. Now I have this experience only in the cinema; but when I lived in Zürich I often came into the neighborhood of the house of the German representative with the ominous flag upon it, and I confess that I always made a wide detour as one would about a cave of horrors, an outpost of murderous barbarism, extending into the realm of a friendly civilization under whose protection I lived. Germany—a great name, a word which carries with it hundreds of homely and respected, pleasant and proud associations. And now, this word, a name of terror and of deadly wilderness, into which even our dreams do not dare to transport us. Whenever I read that some unhappy person has been "taken to Germany," as recently the party leaders from Milan who had signed the anti-fascist manifesto, or as Romain Rolland who is said to have died in a German concentration camp, cold shudders run up and down my back. To be

19

"taken to Germany," that is the worst. To be sure, Mussolini has also been taken to Germany, but I doubt whether even he is happy under Hitler's protection.

What an abnormal, morbid condition, my friends, abnormal and morbid for anyone, but especially for the writer, the bearer of a spiritual tradition, when his own country becomes the most hostile, the most sinister foreign land! And now I wish to think not only of us out here in exile, I finally wish to remember also those people who are still there, the German masses, and to think of the cruel compulsion which destiny has forced upon the German spirit. Believe me, for many there the fatherland has become as strange as it has for us; an "inner emigration" of millions is there awaiting the end just as we. They await the end, that is the end of the war, and there can be only ONE end. The people in Germany in spite of their strangled isolation, are well aware of it, and yet they long for it, in spite of their natural patriotism, in spite of their national conscience. The ever present propaganda has deeply impressed upon their consciousness the pretended permanently destructive results of a German defeat, so that in one part of their being they cannot avoid fearing that defeat more than anything else in the world. And yet there is one thing which many of them fear more than a German defeat, that is a German victory; some only occasionally, at moments which they themselves regard as criminal, but others with complete clarity and permanently although with pangs of conscience, too. Imagine that you were forced, with all your wishes and hopes to oppose an American victory as a great misfortune for the entire world; if you can imagine that, you can place yourself in the position of these people. This attitude has become the destiny of uncounted Germans and I can't help feeling that this destiny is of a particular and uncommonly tragic nature. I know that other nations, too, have been put into the position of wishing for the defeat of their government for their own sake and for the sake of the general future. But I must insist that in view of the all-too-great credulousness and the desire for loyalty in the German character the dilemma in this case is especially acute, and I cannot resist a feeling of deepest resentment against those who have forced the German patriotism into such a position.

These people have been deluded and seduced into crimes that cry to High Heaven. They have begun to atone for them and they will atone even more severely. It cannot be otherwise; common morality or, if you wish, divine justice demands it. But we out here, who saw disaster coming, we who ahead of our compatriots intoxicated by a fraudulent revolution, ahead of all the rest of the world, were convinced that the Nazi rule could never bring anything except war, destruction, and

20

catastrophe, we see no great difference between that which these scoundrels have done to us and what they have done to our people at home. We hate the corrupters and we long for the day which rids the world of them. But with very few exceptions we are far from being victims of a wretched emigrant-hatred against our own land and we do not desire the destruction of our people. We cannot deny their responsibility, for somehow man is responsible for his being and doing; but we are rather inclined to speak of an historic curse, a dark destiny and aberration than of crime and guilt.

The case of Germany is for that reason such a confusing and complicated one because in it good and evil, the beautiful and the detestable are combined and blended in a singular way. For example, the great artistic personality of Richard Wagner has often been mentioned in connection with the phenomenon of national socialism, and Mr. A. Hitler's preference for his art has been pointed out, a preference against which one would like to protect Wagner and which, nevertheless, is not without significance and instructive meaning. The Wagnerian art revolution, though upon an incomparably higher plane, was a phenomenon related to the national socialist revolution. It cannot be denied that a work such as the "Ring of the Nibelung" is fundamentally directed against the whole modern culture and civilization in the form in which they were dominant since the Renaissance, and that this work in its mixture of primitiveness and futurity addresses itself to a non-existent world of a classless folk. The resistance, the indignation, which it aroused were directed much less against the revolutionary aspects of its form, or because it broke with the laws of operatic art, from which it obviously diverged. The opposition arose from a totally different source. The German Goethe disciple, who knew his "Faust" by heart gave utterance to an angry and contemptuous protest, a well-founded protest. It came from the still existing cultivated world of German classicism with which this work was a total break. The cultivated German burgher laughed at the Wagalawaia and all the alliteration business as barbarous nonsense, which can readily be understood. The extraordinary, one can say the planetary, success with which eventually this art met in the modern world, the world of the international bourgeoisie, thanks to certain sensual, nervous, and intellectual stimuli, was a paradox. For we must not forget that it was meant for a totally different public than the capitalistic burgher world, namely, for the romantic "Volk" which is also the ideal of national socialism.

The Wagner revolution was an archaic one in which reactionary and futuristic elements were mingled in the most peculiar way. He is always interested in the Ur-epic, the original and utmost simplicity, the pre-conventional and pre-social. Only this seems to him a theme suit-

21

able for art: his work is the German contribution to the monumental art of the nineteenth century which took the form in other nations, primarily, of great social-poetical novels—Dickens, Thackeray, Tolstoy, Dostoievski, Balzac, Zola. These monumental works that reveal a similar tendency toward moral grandeur were, par excellence, the European nineteenth century, the literary world of social critique. The German manifestation of this greatness knows nothing of society and does not want to know it. For the social is not musical and altogether not suitable for artistic productions. The only suitable themes for art are the mythical and purely human ones, the unhistorical, timeless Ur-poetry of nature and of the heart; and out of these depths the German spirit creates perhaps the greatest and most beautiful thing that the century has to offer. The non-social Ur-poetry is in fact Germany's own special myth, its typical and fundamental national nature, which differentiates it from the other European national minds and types. Between Zola and Wagner, between the symbolic naturalism of the Rougon-Maquarts novels and Wagner's art, there are many similarities. I am not thinking only of the "leitmotif." But the essential and typical national difference lies in the social mentality of the Frenchman and the mythical Ur-poetical quality of the German world. The complicated question: "What is German?" receives perhaps its best answer in the formulation of this difference. The German mentality is essentially indifferent to social and political questions. This sphere is utterly foreign to it. This is not to be understood merely negatively but we can actually speak of a vacuum, of a lack, of a deficiency, and it is probably true that in times when the social problem is dominant, when the idea of social and economic equality, of a juster economic order is felt by every alert consciousness as the most vital and urgent problem—that under such circumstances, this deficiency which is often so fruitful, does not make the happiest impression and leads to disharmony with the general will of the world. Faced with immediate problems, this deficiency leads to attempts at solutions that are evasive and carry the imprint of a mythical substitute for the genuinely social. It is not difficult to recognize in so-called national socialism, a mythical substitute of this sort. Translated from political terminology into the psychological, national socialism means: "I do not want the social at all. I want the folk fairy-tale." But in the political realm, the fairy-tale becomes a murderous lie.

Ladies and Gentlemen, it is horrible and humiliating to behold the civilized world obliged to fight to the death against the politically distorted lie of an aggressive folk fairy-tale, which in its earlier spiritual purity had given the world so much that was beautiful. In former times, it was innocent and idealistic, but this idealism began to be ashamed of itself and became jealous of the world and of reality. "Germany is Hamlet" it used to be said. "Tatenarm und gedankenreich," [lacking in deeds and rich in thought], Hölderlin called it; but it preferred to be rich in deeds, even in misdeeds, and poor in thought. "Deutschland, Deutschland über alles, that means the end of German philosophy," Nietzsche asserted. This jealousy of the world and reality, was nothing but jealousy of political action. And because this was so foreign to the German mind, politics were understood as a realm of absolute cynicism and Machiavellianism. The Germans were encouraged in this interpretation by the appearance of Bismarck, who, though not without a certain affinity to the type of the artist, was a man of violence who openly despised the ideological German liberals, who existed after all, considered him atavistic and reactionary. And yet, because of his "realism," he was admired as a political genius, although he was by no means as brutal as the Germans understood him to be, for Bismarck had a keen appreciation of the importance of moral imponderables. But, to his German fellow-citizens, every moral embellishment and justification of power politics seemed pure hypocrisy, and never would a post-Bismarckian German have been able to say, as Cardinal Manning did, "Politics is a part of morals." Ultimately, hypocrisy is a compliment to virtue. It implies the recognition of moral standards in principle. There is a difference whether the Ten Commandments are not kept, as is the case the world over, or whether they are dropped officially and solemnly. The German, when he wants to be political, thinks that all morality and humanity must be thrown overboard. A Frenchman said: "When a German wishes to be graceful, he jumps out of the window." He does the same thing when he wants to be political. He thinks that for this purpose he must de-humanize himself. We do well to see in national socialism an example of this jumping out of the window, an exaggerated over-compensation of the German lack of political talent.

Does this prove that the German character is fundamentally related to national socialism and that this German nature is inherently unchangeable? There may be some partial truth in this, but one must not forget how many humane and, in the best sense, democratic tendencies were active in German life—tendencies which it has had in common with the great world of Occidental Christian civilization and which were always opposed to nationalistic barbarism. We must not forget that the Hitler party never got a real majority of votes and that it came to absolute power only by intrigue and terror, by coup d'état. At the beginning of the present war, there were more than two hundred thousand people in German concentration camps, to say nothing of the many tens of thousands of victims of this system who were tortured to death in Nazi camps and Gestapo cellars. Even today announcements appear in the German press of executions of so-called national traitors whose real numbers we do not know as only limited numbers are published for purposes of intimidation. It is often said that German youth has been hopelessly corrupted by national socialism, but events that took place in the University of Munich, which created such a stir in America, prove that now, at last, after the experiences of years, German youth is ready to put its head on the executioner's block out of conviction that national socialism is a shameful aberration and that Hitler is the corrupter of Germany and of Europe. For the sake of justice these things must be put into the other side of the scales. Not that Germany and the German people should be relieved of guilt and of responsibility. Looked at from a moral, pedagogical point of view, after the appalling pride, the inexcusable superiority intoxication in which the country has lived for many years, its fall at first, cannot be too deep; and, after all that has happened, it does not become us emigrants to advise the victors as to how Germany should be treated. That the common future should not be too heavily burdened by their decisions is the hope of liberal America. Neither Germany nor the German people should be sterilized or destroyed. What should be destroyed is that fatal power combination, the world threatening association of the Junkers, the army generals, and heavy industry. The German people should not be prevented but should be helped to shatter forever the domination of these groups; to put through the already overdue agrarian reform, in short, to bring about the real, the honest, the purifying revolution which alone can rehabilitate Germany in the eyes of the world, of history, and in its own eyes, and open for her a path into the future—for this future, for the new world of unity and cooperation for which we hope the German spirit is by no means historically unprepared and unfit. We should be psychologists enough to recognize that this monstrous German attempt at world domination, which we now see ending catastrophically, is nothing but a distorted and unfortunate expression of that universalism innate in the German character which formerly had a much higher, purer, and nobler form and which won the sympathy and admiration of the world for this important people. Power politics corrupted this universalism and turned it into evil, for whenever universalism becomes power politics then humanity must arise and defend its liberty. Let us trust that German universalism will again find the way to its old place of honor, that it will forever renounce the wanton ambition of world conquest and that it will again prove itself as world sympathy, world understanding, open-mindedness, and spiritual enrichment of the world.

Wisdom in the treatment of the defeated opponent is desirable if only because of a feeling of shared guilt. The world democracies, which in 1918 were in possession of unlimited power, failed to do anything to prevent the calamity in which we are living today. The pacification of the world through reforms and the satisfaction of human need for justice, which now preoccupy the whole world, could have been realized at that time. This would have prevented the rise of the dictators and the whole dynamic explosive philosophy of hate; but fascism, of which national socialism is a peculiar variation, is not a specialty of Germany. It is a sickness of the times, which is everywhere at home and from which no country is free. Never could the regimes of violence and fraud in Italy and Germany have maintained themselves even for a month, had they not met with a very general and disgraceful sympathy from the economically leading classes and, therefore, from the governments of the democratic countries.

I certainly would flunk an examination in Marxism. But although I know that fascism has its ideological side and must be understood as a fatal, calamitous reaction against the rationalistic humanism of the nineteenth century, I must admit that I also visualize it as a political-economic movement, a counter-revolution pur sang. As such it is an attempt of all the old social and economic reactionaries to suppress the peoples and their aspirations for happiness, to prevent all social progress by attaching to it the frightening name of Bolshevism. In the eyes of Western, conservative capitalism, fascism was frankly a bulwark against Bolshevism and against everything that they wished to assail under this name. especially since the German purges of June 1934, in which everything that was socialistic in national socialism was destroyed and the old power combination of Junkers, army and industry was saved. This bloody act was cleverly aimed to gain international support of the Nazi regime. For it demonstrated to the West that a change of power had taken place in Germany but not a revolution that threatened the existing economic system. It indicated that fascism meant "order" in the established sense of the word. There was a little disgust with the atrocities committed, but no inclination to make the regime internally impossible by diplomatic isolation, a result which at that time could have been easily achieved. Here was the curious phenomenon of a so-called "revolution," which had the support throughout the world of every reactionary, of every "Comité des forges," of all enemies of freedom and of social progress, as well as of the aristocracy, of any "Faubourg St. Germain," of society people, of the nobility, of royalist generals, and of that part of the Catholic Church which sees in Christianity, above all things, hierarchy, humility, and devout adherence to the existing order.

Field Marshal Goering is the personification—the very voluminous personification—of this power complex of the Junker, the military, and industry, a grotesque mixture of the "miles gloriosus" bedecked with medals, and the big business man. He is the master of the German European industrial monopoly since the subjection of Europe, which came into being by undermining the moral resistance of the democratic powers and with the aid of a very general susceptibility to the fascist bacillus. The people are living or perishing in impotent revolt against the new order. Whatever "collaboration" exists is the collaboration of the rich, of the business-as-usual people all over Europe. These prosper; they make profits; buy in the black market; carouse at Monte Carlo, while the people are starving and become the sacrifice of Germany's planned conspiracy to weaken and to ruin them morally and physically.

I repeat: in the eyes of Western conservative capitalism, fascism was simply the bulwark against Bolshevism and against everything which was understood by the word. Every abomination which fascism perpetrated internally was accepted without the realization that its external correlate was war. Perhaps there was no objection even to that. In France, for example, war and defeat were the means of overthrowing the Republic and of bringing about the "national," or fascist revolution. The fascist regimes were braced by the foreign powers, for in the wildest chaos, in disregard of justice and destruction of culture, they professed to see order, beauty and security—security not for the people but from the people, security against all social progress. With a semblance of justice the dictators could shout: "What do these people mean? Why are they suddenly making war on us? Were they not openly or secretly our protectors and abettors? They placed us in the saddle and secured us in it, by financing us, praising us, flattering us: they offered us on a platter the external successes with which we annihilated our internal opposition. Surely they don't mean it. They have no intention of destroying fascism. Secretly, they wish to preserve it. They are fighting half-heartedly with indistinct aims, the indecision of their wills is our protection. To be sure, they are slowly getting the upper hand on the battlefield but, if only we continue the war as long as possible, the inner differences between the Allies will come to an open break and we shall profit by it. We shall play the East against the West and avoid an unconditional surrender."

They are mistaken and their hopes will be crushed. Certainly there are differences of ideology and world policy between Russia and its allies, but this war is amongst other things a means of conciliating these differences—a conciliation between socialism and democracy upon which rests the hope of the world. They are united in the battle against human degradation which is what the conquest of the world by fascism would mean. They are united in the battle for freedom and

26

justice. But a war for freedom and justice can only be waged with the people and for the people, and we sincerely hope that the same thing will not happen that happened after the wars with Napoleon. Those wars were called "wars of freedom" as long as they lasted, and the people, with their desire for freedom, were needed to do the fighting; but afterwards they were interpreted as "wars of liberation only from foreign oppression" so that the people might be robbed of the internal revolutionary fruits of victory.

At that time, in the year 1813, the princes and the governments were not fighting so much against Napoleon as against the revolution, whose sword-bearer the Emperor was, but the people were given to understand that they were fighting for freedom, and I wonder whether you do not feel, as I do, the abomination of this deceit.

In this connection, let me make a short remark about the idea of democracy. Democracy is of course in the first line a claim, a demand of majority for justice and equal rights. It is a justified demand from below. But in my eyes it is even more beautiful if it is good will, generosity and love coming from the top down. I do not consider it very democratic if little Mr. Smith or little Mr. Jones slaps Beethoven on the back and shouts: "How are you, old man!" That is not democracy but tactlessness and a lack of feeling for differences. But when Beethoven sings: "Be embraced, ye millions, this kiss to all the world"— that is democracy. For he could say: "I am a great genius and something quite special, but the people are a mob; I am much too proud and particular to embrace them." Instead he calls them all his brothers and children of one Father in Heaven, who is also his own. That is democracy in its highest form, far removed from demagogy and a flattering wooing of the masses. I have always subscribed to this kind of democracy; but that is exactly the reason why I feel deeply that there is nothing more abominable than deception of the masses and betrayal of the people. My unhappiest years were those, when in the name of a false peace, of appeasement, the people were sold out to fascism. The sacrifice of Czechoslovakia at the Munich conference was the most horrible and humiliating political experience of my life, and not only I felt so, but all decent people throughout the world.

In March 1932, a year before I left Germany, I delivered a lecture in honor of Goethe's centenary at the Prussian Academy of Arts in Berlin, a speech which closed with the words: "The credit which history today still grants to a free republic, to a democratic society, this rather short-term credit, rests upon the still maintained faith that what its power lusty enemies pretend to be able to do, namely, to lead the state and its economy over into a new world, democracy also can do." This warning, which at that time, was meant for the citizens of the

German republic, could today be directed toward the citizens of the entire Occidental world. If democracy has not the courage in this world and afterward to rely upon the popular forces, to see in it a real war of the people and strive toward a new, a freer, and a juster world, the world of social democracy; if, on the other hand, unmindful of its own revolutionary traditions, it allies itself with the powers of the old order, a has-been order, to avoid at any price what it calls anarchy, to subdue every revolutionary tendency; then the faith of the European people who have been oppressed by fascism, will be exhausted and all of them, Germany first, will turn toward the power of the East in whose socialism the idea of individual freedom no longer has any place.

You perceive, Ladies and Gentlemen, that I do not visualize as ideal for humanity, a socialism in which the idea of equality completely outweighs that of freedom. So I hardly can be regarded as a champion of communism. Nevertheless, I cannot help feeling that the panic fear of the Western world of the term communism, this fear by which the fascists have so long maintained themselves, is somewhat superstitious and childish and one of the greatest follies of our epoch. Communism is today the bogeyman of the bourgeoisie, exactly as social democracy was in Germany in 1880. Under Bismarck socialism was the sum of all sans-culottish destruction and dissolution, of chaotic anarchy. I can still hear our school principal shout at some naughty boys who had defaced tables and benches with their pocket knives: "You have behaved like social democrats!" Today he would say: "like communists!" for the social democrat has in the meantime become a thoroughly respectable person whom nobody fears.

Please understand me correctly. Communism is a sharply circumscribed political economic program founded upon the dictatorship of one class, the proletariat, born of the historical materialism of the nineteenth century: in this form it is the product of a particular period and subjected to the changes of time. But as a vision it is much older and contains at the same time elements that belong only to a future world. It is older because already the religious movements of the late Middle Ages had an eschatological communist character; even then the earth, water, air, wild game, fishes, and birds were to be common property, the lords were to work for their daily bread, and all burdens and taxes were to be done away with. In this sense, communism is older than Marx and the nineteenth century. But it belongs to the future in as much as the world that will be when we are gone, whose outlines are beginning to emerge and in which our children and grandchildren will live, can scarcely be imagined without certain communistic traits —that means, without the fundamental idea of common rights of ownership and enjoyment of earthly good, without a progressive equalization of class differences, without the right to work and the duty to work for all. A country of America's courageous progressivity which has never denied its origin in the pioneer spirit, gives us premonitions of this coming world in its equalitarianism and in its feeling that work disgraces nobody. The common possession of opportunities for enjoyment and education are largely achieved. The whole world smokes the same cigarettes, eats the same ice cream, sees the same movies, hears the same music on the radio; even the difference in clothing is disappearing more and more, and the college student who earns his way through college, which would have been very much beneath his class dignity in Europe, is here a commonplace.

Why do I mention this? Because I am persuaded WE MUST NOT BE AFRAID, we must not fear word spooks like "communism." For our fear is the source of courage to our enemies. Social changes are like developments in music. For the layman's ears new music is wild, lawless cacophony, the dissolution of all restraint, the end of all things. It is rejected until the ear can catch up and becomes accustomed to the new. Today it is scarcely believable that Mozart at first seemed turgid, and harmonically extravagant, that Verdi in comparison with Donizetti was terribly difficult, Beethoven unendurably bizarre, Wagner crazily futuristic, Mahler an incomprehensible noise. In every instance, the human ear caught up slowly, for people need music, and they learn to feel as music whatever the musician produces, not deliberately, not recklessly but because he MUST, because the Zeitgeist and historical developments prescribe it.

The same thing takes place in the social field. The education of the ear corresponds to the education of an organ which can be called the social conscience. What transformations and modifications, have taken place since the days when muraenae were fed the flesh of living slaves, and again since the beginning of the industrial epoch. Private property is undoubtedly something fundamentally human. But even within our own lifetime, how changed is the concept of property rights! It has become weakened and limited if not undermined through inheritance laws and taxations which in some cases approach confiscation. Individual freedom which is closely related to property rights was forced to adjust itself to the collective demand and, through the course of years, made this change almost imperceptibly. The idea of freedom, once revolution itself, realized in the sovereignty of national states, is experiencing certain modifications, that is a new equilibrium is being sought, between the two fundamental ideas of modern democracy, freedom and equality. The one is slowly modified by the other. The sovereignty of national states is being called upon to make sacrifices in favor of the common good. Common good, community—there you have the root of the frightening word by means of which Hitler made his conquests. I haven't the slightest doubt that the world and everyday life are moving, nolens volens, toward a social structure for which the epithet "communistic" is a relatively adequate term, a communal form of life, of mutual dependence and responsibility, of common rights to the enjoyment of earthly goods, as a result of the ever closer relationship of the world, its contraction, its intimacy resulting from technical progress, a world wherein each and everyone has a right to live and whose administration is everyone's concern.

Do not imagine that what I am saying means that I am in favor only of the new and the untried. By that I would become unfaithful to myself. Never is the artist only the protagonist and prophet of the new but also the heir and repository of the old. Always he brings forth the new out of tradition. Just as I am far from denying the values of the bourgeois epoch to which the largest part of my personal life belongs, just so am I aware that the demands of the times and the problems of the coming peace are not merely of a revolutionary but also of a constructive, yes, of a restorative nature. Ever and again, historical upheaval such as we are now experiencing is inevitably followed by a movement of restoration. The need to reestablish is as imperative as the demand for renewal. What needs to be reestablished more than anything else are the commandments of religion, of Christianity, which have been trod underfoot by a false revolution. From these commandments must be derived the fundamental law under which the peoples of the future will live together and to which all will have to pay reverence. No real pacification of the world, no cooperation of the people for the common good and for human progress will be possible unless such a basic law is established, which notwithstanding national diversity and liberty must be valid for all and recognized by all as a Magna Carta of human rights, guaranteeing the individual his security in justice, his inviolability, his right to work and to the enjoyment of life. For such a universal basis, may the American Bill of Rights serve as a model.

I believe, Ladies and Gentlemen, that out of the suffering and struggle of our difficult period of transition, a wholly new and more emotional interest in humanity and its fate, in its exceptional position between the realms of nature and mind, in its mystery and its destiny will emerge, a humanistic impulse which even now is alive and active in the best hearts and minds. This new humanism will have a different character, a different color and tone than the earlier related movements. This new humanism will have endured too much to be satisfied with an optimistic naïveté and the desire to see human life through rosy glasses. It will lack all bombast. It will be aware of the tragedy of all

30

human life without letting that awareness destroy its courage and will. It will not disavow its religious traits, for in the idea of human dignity, of the value of the individual soul, humanism transcends into the religious. Concepts like freedom, truth, justice, belong to a transbiological sphere, the sphere of the Absolute, to the religious sphere. Optimism and pessimism are empty words to this humanism. They cancel each other in the determination to preserve the honor of man, in the paths of sympathy and duty. It seems to me that without such a pathos as the basis of all thinking and doing, the structure of a better, happier world, the world community that we wish to achieve out of the present struggle, will be impossible. The defense of reason against blood and instinct does not imply that its creative power should be overestimated. Creative alone is feeling guided by reason, is an ever active love.

Germany and the Germans

Thomas Mann

Presented at the Library of Congress May 29, 1945

As I stand here before you, a man of seventy, contrary to all expectations, an American citizen for more than a year, speaking English or at least making an effort to do so, a guest, no, an official member of the American state institution that invited you to listen to me—as I stand here before you I feel that life is indeed of such a stuff as dreams are made of. It is all so strange, so incredible, so unexpected. In the first place, I had never anticipated that I would attain patriarchal years, although at any early age I had regarded it as theoretically desirable. I thought and said that, once having been born into the world, it was a good and honorable thing to persevere a long time, to live a full, canonical life, and, as an artist, to be characteristically fruitful in all its stages. But I had very little confidence in my own biological qualification and soundness, and the endurance that I have nevertheless demonstrated, appears to me less a proof of my own vital patience than proof of the patience of the genius of life toward me—something unmerited, an act of grace. And grace is always astonishing and unexpected. He who experiences it thinks he is dreaming.

It seems like a dream to me to be and to be here. I should have to be something other than a poet to accept it as a matter of course. It takes but little fantasy to find life fantastic. How did I get here? What dream-wave swept me from the remotest nook of Germany, where I was born and where, after all, I belong, into this auditorium, on to this platform, to stand here as an American, speaking to Americans? Not that I regard it as inappropriate. On the contrary, I fully approve,—fate has seen to that. As things stand today, my type of Germanism is most suitably at home in the hospitable Panopolis, the racial and national universe called America. Before I became an American I had been permitted to be a Czech. That was very amiable and merited my gratitude, but it had little rhyme or reason. Similarly I only need to imagine that I had happened to become a Frenchman, an Englishman, or an Italian, in order to perceive with the greatest satisfaction how much more fittingly I became an American. Everything else would have meant too narrow and too definite an estrangement of my existence. As an American I am a citizen of the world—and that is in keeping with the original nature of the German, notwithstanding his seclusiveness, his timidity in the face of the world, and it is difficult to say whether this timidity is rooted in arrogance or in an innate provincialism, an international social inferiority complex,—probably in both.

I am to speak to you today on Germany and the Germans,—a risky undertaking, not only because the topic is so complex, so inexhaustible, but also because of the violent emotions that encompass it today. To deal with it purely psychologically, *sine ira et sine studio*, would appear almost immoral in view of the unspeakable that this unfortunate nation has done to the world. Should a German avoid this subject today? But I would scarcely have known what other subject to choose for this evening, and, beyond that, it is scarcely possible to conceive of any conversation rising above the purely personal today that would not inevitably turn to the German problem, the enigma in the character and destiny of this people which undeniably has given humanity much that is great and beautiful, and yet has time and again imposed fatal burdens upon the world. Germany's horrible fate, the tremendous catastrophe in which her modern history now culminates, compels our interest, even if this interest is devoid of sympathy. Any attempt to arouse sympathy, to defend and to excuse Germany, would certainly be an inappropriate undertaking for one of German birth today. To play the part of the judge, to curse and damn his own people in compliant agreement with the incalculable hatred that they have kindled, to commend himself smugly as "the good Germany" in contrast to the wicked, guilty Germany over there with which he has nothing at all in common,—that too would hardly befit one of German origin. For anyone who was born a German *does* have something in common with German destiny and German guilt. Critical withdrawal from it should not be regarded as disloyalty. The truths that one tries to utter about one's people can only be the product of self-examination.

Already I have somehow slipped into the complex world of German psychology with the remark about the combination of expansiveness and seclusiveness, of cosmopolitanism and provincialism in the German character. I believe this observation, dating from my early youth, is correct. A trip out of the Reich, say across Lake Constance, into Switzerland, was a trip out of the provincial into the world,—no matter

33

how strange it may appear to regard the tiny country of Switzerland as "world" in comparison to the large and powerful German Reich with its gigantic cities. Still it was perfectly true: Switzerland, neutral, multilingual, under French influence, breathing western air,—notwithstanding its miniature format—was actually far more European, far more "world," than the political colossus to the north, where the word "international" had long since been considered an insult and where arrogant provincialism had tainted the atmosphere and made it stagnant.

This was the modern nationalistic form of the old German world-seclusiveness and melancholy world-unfitness, which, along with a sort of philistine universalism, cosmopolitanism in a night-cap, so to speak, had made up the German picture. This state of the mind, this unworldly, provincial, German cosmopolitanism, always had something scurrilously spooky, something hiddenly uncanny about it, a quality of secret demonism that I was particularly able to perceive on account of my personal origin. I think back of that corner of the German world that constituted the first frame of my existence, and from which the dream-wave of life swept me here: It was the ancient city of Luebeck, near the Baltic Sea, once the threshold of the Hanseatic League, founded before the middle of the twelfth century, and raised to the rank of a free imperial city by Barbarossa in the thirteenth. The exceptionally beautiful City Hall, which my father, as a senator, frequented, was completed in the very year in which Martin Luther posted his Theses on the portal of the Castle Church at Wittenberg, the beginning of the modern era. But just as Luther, the Reformer, had a good deal of the medieval man about him and wrestled with the Devil all his life, so we who lived in the Protestant city of Luebeck, even the Luebeck that had become a Republican member of Bismarck's Reich, moved in an atmosphere of the Gothic Middle Ages,—and I am thinking not only of the skyline with its pointed towers, gates, and walls, of the humorously macabre thrills that emanated from the Dance of Death frescoes in St. Mary's Church, of the crooked, haunted looking alleys that were frequently named after the old guilds, the Bellfounders, the Butchers, and of the picturesque burgher houses. No, in the atmosphere itself something had clung of the state of mind of, let's say, the final decades of the fifteenth century, the hysteria of the dying Middle Ages, something of latent spiritual epidemic. It's a strange thing to say about a sensibly sober, modern, commercial city, but it was conceivable that a Children's Crusade might suddenly erupt here, a St. Vitus Dance, an outbreak of religious fanaticism coupled with mystic processions of the people, or the like—in short, an anciently neurotic substratum was perceptible, an arcane spiritual state that was out-

34

wardly evidenced by the many "characters" to be found in such a city, eccentrics and harmless lunatics who live within its walls and who, in a sense, belong to its scene as much as the ancient buildings. There was, for example, a certain type of old woman with bleary eyes and a crutch, who was half humorously rumored to be a witch; a man, retired on a small income, with a scarlet, warty nose and some sort of nervous tic, with ludicrous habits, such as a stereotyped, involuntary bird-cry; a female with an absurd hair-do roaming through the streets in a trailing dress of obsolete style, with an air of insane superciliousness, and followed by a retinue of pug-dogs and cats. And the children, the street urchins, are a part of the picture, trailing these characters, mocking them, and running away in superstitious panic when they turn around . . . .

I really don't know why I am conjuring up these early memories here and now. Is it because I first experienced "Germany," visually and spiritually, in the form of this quaintly venerable city scene, and because I am trying to suggest a secret union of the German spirit with the Demonic, a thesis which is, indeed, part of my inner experience, but not easily defensible? The hero of our greatest literary work, Goethe's Faust, is a man who stands at the dividing line between the Middle Ages and Humanism, a man of God who, out of a presumptuous urge for knowledge, surrenders to magic, to the Devil. Wherever arrogance of the intellect mates with the spiritual obsolete and archaic, there is the Devil's domain. And the Devil, Luther's Devil, Faust's Devil, strikes me as a very German figure, and the pact with him, the Satanic covenant, to win all treasures and power on earth for a time at the cost of the soul's salvation, strikes me as something exceedingly typical of German nature. A lonely thinker and searcher, a theologian and philosopher in his cell who, in his desire for world enjoyment and world domination, barters his soul to the Devil,—isn't this the right moment to see Germany in this picture, the moment in which Germany is literally being carried off by the Devil?

It is a grave error on the part of legend and story not to connect Faust with music. He should have been musical, he should have been a musician. Music is a demonic realm; Soeren Kierkegaard, a great Christian, proved that most convincingly in his painfully enthusiastic essay on Mozart's Don Juan. Music is Christian art with a negative prefix. Music is calculated order and chaos-breeding irrationality at once, rich in conjuring, incantatory gestures, in magic of numbers, the most unrealistic and yet the most impassioned of arts, mystical and abstract. If Faust is to be the representative of the German soul, he would have to be musical, for the relation of the German to the world is abstract and mystical, that is, musical,—the relation of a professor with a touch

35

of demonism, awkward and at the same time filled with arrogant knowledge that he surpasses the world in "depth."

What constitutes this depth? Simply the musicality of the German soul, that which we call its inwardness, its subjectivity, the divorce of the speculative from the socio-political element of human energy, and the complete predominance of the former over the latter. Europe always felt it and understood its monstrous and unfortunate aspects. In 1839 Balzac wrote: "If the Germans do not know how to play the great instruments of liberty, still they know naturally how to play all instruments of music." That is a good observation, and it is not the only striking remark of this kind that the great novelist made. In *Cousin Pons* he says of the German musician Schmucke, a wonderful figure: "Schmucke, who, like all Germans, was very strong in harmony, orchestrated the scores, while Pons supplied the melody." Correct, the Germans are primarily musicians of the vertical, not of the horizontal, greater masters of harmony, with which Balzac includes counterpoint, than of melody; they are instrumentalists rather than glorifiers of the human voice, far more inclined toward the learned and the spiritual in music than toward the melodically happy-making. They have given the western world perhaps not its most beautiful, socially uniting, but certainly its deepest, most significant music, and the world has not withheld its thanks and praise. At the same time it has felt and feels more strongly than ever today that such musicality of soul is paid for dearly in another sphere,—the political, the sphere of human companionship.

Martin Luther, a gigantic incarnation of the German spirit, was exceptionally musical. I frankly confess that I do not love him. Germanism in its unalloyed state, the Separatist, Anti-Roman, Anti-European shocks me and frightens me, even when it appears in the guise of evangelical freedom and spiritual emancipation; and the specifically Lutheran, the choleric coarseness, the invective, the fuming and raging, the extravagant rudeness coupled with tender depth of feeling and with the most clumsy superstition and belief in demons, incubi, and changelings, arouses my instinctive antipathy. I should not have liked to be Luther's dinner guest; I should probably have felt as comfortable as in the cozy home of an ogre, and I am convinced that I would have gotten along much better with Leo X, Giovanni de' Medici, the amiable humanist, whom Luther called "The Devil's sow, the Pope." Moreover I do not even accept the necessity of the contrast of popular robustness and good manners, the anti-thesis of Luther and the refined pedant Erasmus. Goethe has outgrown this contrast and reconciles it. He represents well-mannered, civilized strength and popular robustness, urbane Demonism, spirit and blood at once, namely art . . . With him Germany made a tremendous stride in human culture—or

36

should have made it, for in reality she was always closer to Luther than to Goethe. And no one can deny that Luther was a tremendously great man, great in the most German manner, great and German even in his duality as a liberating and at once reactionary force, a conservative revolutionary. He not only reconstituted the Church; he actually saved Christianity. Europeans are in the habit of accusing the German nature of irreligiousness, of heathenism. That is very disputable. Germany certainly took Christianity more seriously than anyone else. In the German Luther Christianity took itself childlikely and rustically serious at a time when it did not take itself seriously at all elsewhere. Luther's revolution preserved Christianity—in about the same way in which the New Deal is intended to preserve capitalistic economics—even if capitalism refuses to understand it.

No aspersions against Luther's greatness! It was his momentous translation of the Bible that really first created the German language which Goethe and Nietzsche finally perfected; and it was also he who, through the breaking of the scholastic fetters and the renovation of the conscience, tremendously promoted the freedom of research, of criticism, and of philosophic speculation. By the establishment of the direct relationship of man to his God he advanced the cause of European democracy; for "every man his own priest," that is democracy. German idealistic philosophy, the refinement of psychology by pietistic examination of the individual conscience, finally the self-conquest of Christian morality for reasons of morality—for that was Nietzsche's deed or misdeed—all of that comes from Luther. He was a liberating hero,—but in the German style, for he knew nothing of liberty. I am not speaking now of the liberty of the Christian, but of political liberty, the liberty of the citizen—this liberty not only left him cold, but its impulses and demands were deeply repugnant to him. Four hundred years after his time the first president of the German Republic, a Social Democrat, spoke the words: "I hate revolution like sin." That was genuinely Lutheran, genuinely German. In the same way Luther hated the peasant revolt which, evangelically inspired as it was, if successful, would have given a happier turn to German history, a turn toward liberty. Luther, however, saw in it nothing but a distortion of his work of spiritual liberation and therefore he fumed and raged against it as only he could do. The peasants, he said, should be killed like mad dogs and he told the princes that they could now gain the kingdom of heaven by slaughtering the peasant beasts. Luther, the German man of the people, bears a good share of responsibility for the sad ending of this first attempt at a German revolution, for the victory of the princes, and for all its consequences.

At that time there lived in Germany a man who has my special

37

sympathy, **Tilman Riemenschneider**, a master of religious art, a sculptor and wood-carver, widely famous for the faithful and expressive excellence of his works, his profound altar painting and chaste reliefs which ornamented the places of worship all over Germany. The master had won high regard, both as a man and as a citizen, in his immediate environs, the city of Wuerzburg, where he was a member of the Council. He never expected to take a hand in politics, in world affairs—the thought lay far from his natural modesty and from his love for his free and peaceful work. There was nothing of the demagogue about him. But his heart, that beat warmly for the poor and oppressed, forced him to take the part of the peasants, whose cause he recognized as just and pleasing in the sight of God, against the lords, the bishops and princes, whose favor he could easily have retained. Moved by the great and fundamental contrasts of the time, he felt compelled to emerge from his sphere of purely spiritual and esthetic artistic life and to become a fighter for liberty and justice. He sacrificed his own liberty for the cause that he held higher than art and the dignified calm of his existence. It was his influence, chiefly, that determined the city of Wuerzburg to refuse military service to the "Burg," the Prince-Prelate, and, in general, to assume a revolutionary attitude against him. Riemenschneider paid dearly for it. For after the crushing of the peasant revolt, the victorious powers whom he had opposed took cruel revenge upon him; they subjected him to prison and torture, and he emerged from the ordeal as a broken man, incapable of awakening the beauties in wood and stone.

Such men we had in Germany too, at all times. But they are not the specifically and monumentally German type. That type is represented by Luther, the musical theologian. In the political realm he advanced only to the point of deciding that both parties, the princes and the peasants, were wrong, an attitude which soon led him to inveigh with berserk fury only against the peasants. His inwardness was in full agreement with St. Paul's admonition "Let every soul be subject unto the higher powers." But these words referred to the authority of the Roman World Empire, which was the prerequisite and the political realm for the Christian world religion, while in Luther's case it was a question of the reactionary, petty authority of German princes. His anti-political servility, the product of musical-German inwardness and unworldliness, was not only responsible for the centuries-old, obsequious attitude of the Germans toward their princes and toward the power of the state, it not only partly created and partly fostered the German dualism of boldest speculation on the one hand and political immaturity on the other. But it is also and chiefly typical in a monumental and defiant manner of the purely German sundering of the national impulse and

38

the ideal of political liberty. For the Reformation, like the later uprising against Napoleon, was a *nationalistic* movement for liberty.

Let us speak for a moment of liberty: the peculiar perversion which this concept has suffered, and suffers to this day, at the hands of a people as important as the Germans, is food for serious thought. How was it possible that even National Socialism, now ending in disgrace, could adopt the name of a "German liberation movement," when, according to universal opinion, such an abomination cannot possibly have anything to do with liberty? This appellation was the expression not only of defiant insolence, but also of a fundamental misinterpretation of the concept of liberty, that had its effects in German history again and again. Liberty, in a political sense, is primarily a matter of internal political morality. A people that is not internally free and responsible to itself does not deserve external liberty; it cannot sit in the councils of freedom, and when it uses the sonorous word, the application is wrong. The German concept of liberty was always directed outward; it meant the right to be German, only German and nothing else and nothing beyond that. It was a concept of protest, of self-centered defense against everything that tended to limit and restrict national egotism, to tame it and to direct it toward service to the world community, service to humanity. Stubborn individualism outwardly, in its relations to the world, to Europe, to civilization, this German concept of liberty behaved internally with an astonishing degree of lack of freedom, of immaturity, of dull servility. It was a militant slave mentality, and National Socialism went so far in its exaggeration of this incongruity between the external and internal desire for liberty as to think of world enslavement by a people themselves enslaved at home.

Why must the German urge for liberty always be tantamount to inner enslavement? Why did it finally have to culminate in an attack upon the liberty of all others, upon liberty itself? The reason is that Germany has never had a revolution and has never learned to combine the concept of the nation with the concept of liberty. The "nation" was born in the French Revolution; it is a revolutionary and liberal concept that includes the humanitarian, internally it meant liberty, externally it meant Europe. All the ingratiating qualities of French political spirit are based upon this fortunate unity; all the constricting and depressing qualities of German patriotic enthusiasm rest upon the fact that this unity was never achieved. It might be said that the very concept of the "nation" in its historical affinity with that of liberty is foreign to Germany. It might be regarded as a mistake to call the Germans a nation, no matter whether they or others do it. It is wrong to use the word "nationalism" for their patriotic fervor—it is a misuse of a French idea and creates misunderstandings. One should not apply the same name to two different things. The German idea of liberty is racial and anti-European; it is always very near the barbaric if it does not actually erupt into open and declared barbarism, as in our days. The esthetically repulsive and rude qualities that cling to its bearers and champions as early as the Wars of Liberation, to the student unions and to such types as Jahn and Massmann, are evidence of its unfortunate character. Goethe was certainly no stranger to popular culture; he wrote not only the classicistic *Iphigenie*, but also such ultra-German things as *Faust I, Goetz*, and the *Aphorisms in Rhymes*. Yet, to the exasperation of all patriots, his attitude toward the wars against Napoleon was one of complete coldness,—not only out of loyalty to his peer, the great Emperor, but also because he felt repelled by the barbaric-racial element in this uprising. The loneliness of this great man, who approved everything of a broad and generous nature, the supernational, world Germanism, world literature,—his painful loneliness in the patriotically, "liberally" excited Germany of his day cannot be overemphasized. The determining and dominant concepts around which everything revolved for him, were culture and barbarism,—and it was his lot to belong to a people whose idea of liberty turns into barbarism, because it is only directed outward, against Europe.

This is a misfortune, a curse, a perpetual tragedy, that finds added expression in the fact that even Goethe's disavowing attitude toward political Protestantism served only as a confirmation and a deepening of the Lutheran dualism of spiritual and political liberty throughout the nation and particularly among the intellectual leaders so that they were prevented from accepting the political element in their concept of culture. It is difficult to determine to what extent great men put their imprint upon the character of a people and mold its form,—and to what extent they themselves are its personification, its expression. This much is certain, that the German relation to politics is a negative one, a lack of qualification. Historical evidence lies in the fact that all German revolutions failed, that of 1525, of 1813, that of 1848 which was wrecked upon the rocks of the political impotency of the German bourgeois, and finally that of 1918. Further evidence also lies in the clumsy and sinister misconstruction that the Germans so easily place on the idea of politics whenever ambition drives them to engage in politics.

Politics has been called the "art of the possible," and it actually is a realm akin to art insofar as, like art, it occupies a creatively mediating position between the spirit and life, the idea and reality, the desirable and the necessary, conscience and deed, morality and power. It embraces much that is hard, necessary, amoral, much of expediency and concession to facts, much of human weakness and much of the vulgar. It

40

would be hard to find a politician, a statesman, who accomplished great things without having to ask himself afterwards whether he could still regard himself as a decent individual. And yet, just as man does not belong solely to the animal kingdom, so politics does not belong solely to the realm of evil. Without degenerating into something devilish and destructive, without being distorted into an enemy of mankind and perverting its concessive creativity into disgraceful and criminal sterility, it can never completely renounce its ideal and spiritual components, never deny the moral and humanly decent part of its nature, and reduce itself entirely to the immoral and vulgar, to lying, murder, deceit, and force. That would no longer be art and creatively mediating and actuating irony, but blind, inhuman nonsense that can never produce anything genuine, that achieves only transitory, terrifying success, and after even a brief span has a world-destroying, nihilistic, and finally self-destroying effect; for the totally immoral is by nature unfit to survive.

The peoples born and qualified for politics instinctively know how to guard the unity of conscience and action, of spirit and power, at least subjectively. They pursue politics as an art of life and of power that cannot be entirely freed from a strain of vitally useful evil, but that never quite loses sight of the higher, the idea, human decency, and morality: in this regard they feel politically, and they get along with themselves and with the world in this fashion. Such getting-along with life, founded on compromise, the German regards as hypocrisy. He was not born to get along with life and he proves his lack of qualification for politics by misunderstanding it in clumsily sincere manner. Not at all wicked by nature but with a flair for the spiritual and the ideal, he regards politics as nothing but falsehood, murder, deceit, and violence, as something completely and one-sidedly filthy, and if worldly ambition prompts him to take up politics, he pursues it in the light of this philosophy. When the German takes up politics he thinks he has to act in a fashion to dumfound humanity, that's what he regards as politics. Since he thinks it is unalloyed evil, he believes he has to be a devil to pursue it.

We have seen it. Crimes were perpetrated that no psychology can excuse, and they are least of all excusable on the ground they were superfluous. For they were superfluous; they were not essential and Nazi-Germany could have gotten along without them. She could have carried out her plans of power and conquest without their aid. In a world which knows trusts, cartels, and exploitation the idea of monopolistic spoliation of all other nations by the Goering Concern wasn't anything new and strange. The embarrassing thing about it was that it compromised the ruling system too greatly by clumsy exaggeration.

Moreover, as an idea, it came a little too late,—today when mankind is striving for economic democracy, struggling for a higher degree of social maturity. The Germans are always too late. They are late, like music which is always the last of the arts to express a world condition,—when that world condition is already in its final stages. They are abstract and mystical, too, like this, their dearest art,—both to the point of criminality. Their crimes, I repeat, were not a necessary factor of their belated embarkment upon exploitation; they were a luxury in which they indulged from a theoretical predisposition, in honor of an ideology, the fantasm of race. If it did not sound like a detestable condonation, it might be said that they committed their crimes for dreamy idealism.

At times, particularly when contemplating German history, one has the impression that the world was not the sole creation of God but a cooperative work with someone else. One would like to ascribe to God the merciful fact that good can come from evil. But that evil so often comes from good, is obviously the contribution of the other fellow. The Germans might well ask why their good, in particular, so often turns to evil, becomes evil in their hands. Take, for example, their fundamental universalism and cosmopolitanism, their inner boundlessness, which may be regarded as a spiritual accessory of their ancient supernational realm, the Holy Roman Empire of German Nation. This is a highly valuable, positive trait which, however, was transformed into evil by a sort of dialectic inversion. The Germans yielded to the temptation of basing upon their innate cosmopolitanism a claim to European hegemony, even to world domination, whereby this trait became its exact opposite, namely the most presumptive and menacing nationalism and imperialism. At the same time they noticed that they were too late again with their nationalism because it had outlived its time. Therefore they substituted something newer, more modern, for it, the racial idol, which promptly led them to monstrous crimes and plunged them into the depths of distress.

Or take that quality of the Germans which is perhaps their most notable one, designated as "inwardness," a word that is most difficult to define: tenderness, depth of feeling, unworldly reverie, love of nature, purest sincerity of thought and conscience,—in short, all the characteristics of high lyricism are mingled in it, and even today the world cannot forget what it owes the German inwardness: German metaphysics, German music, especially the miracle of the German Lied—a nationally unique and incomparable product—these are the fruits of German inwardness. The great historical deed of German inwardness was Luther's Reformation,—we called it a mighty deed of liberation and, as such, it was obviously something good. But it is evident that

42

the Devil had his hand even in that deed. The Reformation brought about the religious schism of the Occident, a definite misfortune, and for Germany it brought the Thirty Years' War, that depopulated it, fatally retarded its culture, and by means of vice and epidemics probably made German blood into something different and something worse than it had been in the Middle Ages. Erasmus of Rotterdam, who wrote the *Praise of Folly*, a skeptical humanist with very little inwardness, was well aware of the implications of the Reformation. "When you see terrible cataclysms arising in the world," he said, "then remember that Erasmus predicted it." But the venerable Lout of Wittenberg, tremendously charged with inwardness, was no pacifist; he was filled with true German acceptance of the tragic, and declared himself ready to take the blood that would flow, "on his neck."

German *Romanticism*, what is it but an expression of this finest German quality, German inwardness? Much that is longingly pensive, fantastically spectral, and deeply scurrilous, a high artistic refinement and all-pervading irony combine in the concept of Romanticism. But these are not the things I think of primarily when I speak of Romanticism. It is rather a certain dark richness and piousness—I might say: antiquarianism—of soul that feels very close to the chthonian, irrational, and demonic forces of life, that is to say, the true sources of life; and it resists the purely rationalistic approach on the ground of its deeper knowledge, its deeper alliance with the holy. The Germans are the people of the romantic counterrevolution against the philosophical intellectualism and rationalism of enlightenment—a revolt of music against literature, of mysticism against clarity. Romanticism is anything but feeble sentimentalism; it is depth, conscious of its own strength and fullness. It is pessimism of sincerity that stands on the side of everything existing, real, historical against both criticism and meliorism, in short, on the side of power against the spirit, and it thinks very little of all rhetorical virtuousness and idealistic disguising of the world. Herein lies the union of Romanticism with the Realism and Machiavellianism that celebrated its triumphs over Europe in the person of Bismarck, the only political genius that Germany ever produced. The German desire for unity and empire, directed by Bismarck into Prussian paths, was misunderstood if it was interpreted according to the usual pattern as a movement for unification of national-democratic character. It tried to be just that at one time, around the year 1848, although even the Pan-German discussions of the St. Paul's Parliament had a tinge of medieval imperialism, reminiscences of the Holy Roman Empire. But it developed that the customary European, national-democratic road to unity was not the German road. Fundamentally Bismarck's empire had nothing in common with "nation" in the democratic sense of the word. It was purely a power structure aiming toward the hegemony of Europe, and notwithstanding its modernity, the Empire of 1871 clung to memories of medieval glory, the time of the Saxon and Swabian rulers. This very thing was the characteristic and menacing factor: the mixture of robust timeliness, efficient modernness on the one hand and dreams of the past on the other,—in a word, highly technological Romanticism. Born in wars, the Unholy German Empire of Prussian Nation could never be anything but war empire. As such it lived, a thorn in the side of the world, and as such it is now destroyed.

In the history of ideas the merits of the German romantic counter-revolution are invaluable. Hegel himself has a tremendous share in them by the fact that his dialectic philosophy bridged the gulf that rationalistic enlightenment and the French Revolution had opened between reason and history. His reconciliation of the reasonable with the real gave a mighty impetus to historical thinking and actually created the science of history, which had scarcely existed before that time. Romanticism is essentially submersion, especially submersion in the past; it is longing for the past and at the same time it is realistic appreciation of everything truly past in its own right, with its local color and atmosphere. No wonder that Romanticism was particularly favorable to the writing of history and actually inaugurated history in its modern form.

The contributions of Romanticism to the realm of the beautiful, as a science, as an esthetic doctrine, are rich and fascinating. Positivism, intellectualistic enlightenment have no inkling of the nature of poetry; Romanticism alone imparted it to a world that was dying of boredom in virtuous academicism. Romanticism poetized ethics by proclaiming the right of individuality and of spontaneous passion. It raised the treasures of song and story from the depths of folk culture of the past; Romanticism was the genial patroness of the science of folklore that appears in its motley colors as a variety of exoticism. The priority over the rational which it grants to the emotional, even in its arcane forms of mystic ecstasy and Dionysiac intoxication, brings it into a peculiar and psychologically highly fruitful relationship to sickness; the late-Romanticist Nietzsche, for example, himself a spirit raised by illness to heights of fatal genius, was profuse in his praise of sickness as a medium of knowledge. In this sense even psychoanalysis, which represents a great advance toward the understanding of man from the side of illness, is a branch of Romanticism.

Goethe laconically defined the Classical as the healthy, the Romantic as the morbid. A painful definition for one who loves Romanticism down to its sins and vices. But it cannot be denied that even in its loveliest, most ethereal aspects where the popular mates with the sublime it bears in its heart the germ of morbidity, as the rose bears the worm; its innermost character is seduction, seduction to death. This is its confusing paradox: while it is the revolutionary representative of the irrational forces of life against abstract reason and dull humanitarianism, it possesses a deep affinity to death by virtue of its very surrender to the irrational and to the past. In Germany, its true home, it has most strongly preserved this iridescent dualism, as glorification of the vital in contrast to the purely moral, and likewise as kinship to death. As German spirit, as Romantic counterrevolution, it has contributed deep and vitalizing impulses to European thought; but on the other hand its life and death pride has disdained to accept any correcting instruction from Europe, from the spirit of European religion of humanity, from European democracy. In its realistic power-political guise, as Bismarckianism, as German victory over France, over civilization, and by the erection of the German power empire, apparently blooming in the most robust health, it elicited the astonishment of the world, simultaneously confusing and depressing it. And as soon as the genius himself no longer stood at the helm of this empire it kept the world in a constant state of unrest.

Besides, the united power realm was a cultural disappointment. No intellectual greatness came from Germany that had once been the teacher of the world. It was only strong. But in this strength and in all its organized efficiency, the Romantic germ of illness and death lived and worked. Historical misfortune, the suffering and humiliation of a lost war, were its nourishment. And, reduced to a miserable mass level, the level of a Hitler, German Romanticism broke out into hysterical barbarism, into a spree and a paroxysm of arrogance and crime, which now finds its horrible end in a national catastrophe, a physical and psychic collapse without parallel.

The story I told you in brief outline, Ladies and Gentlemen, is the story of German "inwardness." It is a melancholy story,—I call it that, instead of "tragic," because misfortune should not boast. This story should convince us of one thing: that there are *not* two Germanys, a good one and a bad one, but only one, whose best turned into evil through devilish cunning. Wicked Germany is merely good Germany gone astray, good Germany in misfortune, in guilt, and ruin. For that reason it is quite impossible for one born there simply to renounce the wicked, guilty Germany and to declare: "I am the good, the noble, the just Germany in the white robe; I leave it to you to exterminate the wicked one." Not a word of all that I have just told you about Germany or tried to indicate to you, came out of alien, cool, objective knowledge, it is all within me, I have been through it all.

In other words, what I have tried to give you here within the limits of time, was a piece of German self-criticism; and truly, nothing could have been more faithful to German tradition. The tendency toward self-criticism, often to the point of self-disgust and self-execration, is thoroughly German, and it is eternally incomprehensible how a people so inclined toward self-analysis could ever conceive the idea of world domination. The quality most necessary for world domination is naiveness, a happy limitation and even purposelessness, but certainly not an extreme spiritual life, like the German, in which arrogance is coupled with contrition. Nothing that a Frenchman, an Englishman, or an American ever said openly about his people can remotely be compared to the pitiless truths that great Germans, Hoelderlin, Goethe, Nietzsche, have uttered about Germany. In oral conversation, at least, Goethe went so far as to wish for a German Diaspora. "Like the Jews," he said, "the Germans must be transplanted and scattered over the world!" And he added: ". . . in order to develop the good that lies in them, fully and to the benefit of the nations."

This great good really exists, but it could not come to fruition in the traditional form of the national state. The immigration laws of the other states will probably categorically prevent that dispersion throughout the world which Goethe wished for the Germans and for which they will have a strong inclination after this war. But despite all drastic warnings against excessive expectations, that we have had from the past performance of power politics, may we not cherish the hope that after this catastrophe the first experimental steps may be taken in the direction of a world condition in which the national individualism of the nineteenth century will dissolve and finally vanish, and which will afford happier opportunities for the development of the "good" in the German character than the untenable old conditions? Should it not be possible after all that the liquidation of Nazism may pave the way for a social world reform which would offer the greatest prospect of happiness to Germany's very inclinations and needs. World economy, the minimizing of political boundaries, a certain depolitization of states in general, the awakening of mankind to a realization of their practical unity, their first thoughts about a world state,—how could all this social humanitarianism—the true object of the great struggle—which far exceeds the bounds of bourgeois democracy, be foreign and repugnant to German character? In the seclusiveness of the German there was always so much longing for companionship; indeed at the bottom of the very loneliness that made him wicked lay always the wish to love, the wish to be loved. In the end the German misfortune is only the paradigm of the tragedy of human life. And the grace that Germany so sorely needs, my friends, all of us need it.

46

Nietzsche's Philosophy
in the Light
of Contemporary Events

Thomas Mann

Presented at the Library of Congress April 29, 1947

WHEN AT THE BEGINNING of the year 1889 the news of Nietzsche's mental breakdown began to spread from Turin and Basle, many of those who, distributed throughout Europe, already possessed a measure of understanding for the fateful greatness of this man, may have repeated to themselves Ophelia's lamentation:

"O, what a noble mind is here o'erthrown!"

And of the characterizations contained in the following verses, mourning the terrible misfortune that so highminded an intellect, "blasted by ecstasy," should now disharmonize like bells out of tune, many fit Nietzsche exactly,—prominent among them the words in which the grieving heroine epitomizes her praise: "The observ'd of all observers." We would use the word "fascinating" instead, and indeed, in all the world literature and the history of the human mind, we seek in vain for a personality more fascinating than that of the hermit of Sils Maria. Yet it is a fascination closely related to the one emanating through the centuries from that great character created by Shakespeare, the melancholy prince of Denmark.

Nietzsche, the thinker and writer, "the mould of form" as Ophelia would call him, was a personality of phenomenal cultural plenitude and complexity, summing up all that is essentially European, a personality that had absorbed a lot from the past which in more or less conscious imitation and succession it reminded, repeated, in a mythical manner projected forth into the presence; and I have no doubt that the great lover of masquerade was well aware of the trait so like Hamlet in the tragic play of life he presented—I am tempted to say: he enacted. As far as I, the reader and "observer" of the next following generation immersing with deep emotion, am concerned, I sensed this relationship early and at the same time I experienced those confused sensations which especially for the young heart carry something so novel, so exciting and so engrossing: the mixture of veneration and pity. I have never ceased to experience it. It is the tragic pity for an overloaded, overcharged soul which was only called to knowledge, not really born to it and, like Hamlet, was destroyed by it; for a dainty, fine, good soul for which love was a necessity, which inclined toward noble friendship and was never meant for loneliness, and which yet was condemned to just this: the most profound, the most frigid loneliness, the aloneness of the criminal; for a spirituality at first deeply pious, entirely prone to reverence, bound to religious tradition, which was dragged by fate practically by the hair into a wild and intoxicated prophesy of barbaric resplendent force, of stifled conscience, of evil, a state devoid of all piety and raging against its very own nature.

One must take a look at the origin of this mind, investigate the influences at work on forming his personality, without his nature ever having resented them as the least bit improper,—in order to perceive the improbable adventurousness of his life's span, its complete unpredictability. Born in 1844 amidst central German rusticity, four years before the attempt of a middle-class revolution in Germany, Nietzsche on both his mother's and his father's side stems from respected ministers' families. Ironically, there is in existence a paper written by his grandfather on "The Eternal Duration of Christianity, A Reassurance during the Present Foment." His father was something like a courtier, tutor of the Prussian princesses, and owed his ministry to the benevolence of Frederic William IV. Appreciation of aristocratic form, strict morality, sense of honor, minute love of order thus were naturally a part of his home. After the early death of his father the boy lived in the religious, church-going and royalist civil service city of Naumburg. He is described as "phenomenally well-mannered," a notorious paragon of courteous solemnness and of a pious pathos that procures for him the name of "the little minister." Well-known is the characteristic anecdote, how, during a cloudburst, he stalks home from school, measured and dignified,—because school regulations impress upon the children proper conduct in the street. His senior high-school education he concludes brilliantly in the famous discipline of the monastery of Schulpforta. He inclines toward theology, and also toward music, but then decides on classical philology and studies that subject in Leipzig under a strict systematist by name of Ritschl. He succeeds so well that, no sooner has he completed his obligatory service in the artillery, he is called, practically an adolescent still, to the academic chair, and this in the serious and religious, patricianly governed city of Basle.

One receives the impression of a highly gifted noble normalcy, apparently assuring a career of correctness on an aristocratic level. Instead of that, what a drift into trackless wastes! What a getting lost in death-dealing wastelands! The expression "to get lost," which has become a moral and spiritual judgement, originated with the explorer's language and describes the situation where in the uncharted unknown, the traveler loses all sense of where he is, in which direction to seek subsistence, where he is doomed. It sounds like Philistinism to use this expression for the man who certainly was not only the greatest philosopher of the late 19th century, but also one of the most fearless heroes of all times in the realm of thought. But Jakob Burckhardt, to whom Nietzsche looked up as to a father, was no Philistine, and yet already at an early date he detected the inclination, more, the determination, to travel false trails and to become mortally confused in the mental outlook of his younger friend and wisely separated from him, dropped him with something like indifference which was really the kind of self-protection we also observe in Goethe.

What was it that drove Nietzsche into the uncharted wastes of thought, that whipped him upward into those heights in torture and made him die an agonizing death upon the cross of thought? It was his fate—and that fate was his genius. But this genius has yet another name. That name is: disease—this word not understood in the vague and generalized sense otherwise easily associated with the concept of genius, but in so specific and clinical an understanding that the observer once again braves the suspicion of being a duffer and the reproach that he would minimize with it the creative life work of a mind who changed the entire atmosphere of his time as an artist in the use of language, as a thinker and as a psychologist. That would be a misunderstanding. It has often been said before, and I say it again: disease is a purely formal phenomenon; the important point is with what it is combined, in what it fulfills itself. The point is *who* is afflicted with the disease: an average numskull in whose case the disease of course lacks any spiritual and cultural aspect, or a Nietzsche, a Dostoevski. The medicinal pathological side is *one* side of the truth, its naturalistic one so to speak, and anyone devoted to truth as a whole and determined to observe it unconditionally, will never for reasons of mental prudishness disavow any point of view from which it can be regarded. The physician Moebius has been widely criticized for writing a book in which he set forth the story of Nietzsche's development as the story of a progressive paralysis from an expert's point of view. I have never been able to join in the indignation over this. In his own manner, the man says nothing but the undeniable truth.

In the year 1865, at the age of 21, Nietzsche tells a curious tale to his friend and fellow student Paul Deussen, the later famous Sanskrit and Vedanta scholar. Alone, the young man had gone on an excursion to Cologne and there had engaged a public porter to show him the sights of the city. All afternoon they are under way and finally, toward evening, Nietzsche asks his guide to show him a recommendable restaurant. This chap however, who for me has assumed the guise of quite a sinister messenger, takes him to a bordello. The adolescent boy, pure as a maiden, all spirit, all learning, all pious diffidence, suddenly finds himself, so he relates, surrounded by half a dozen figures in flitter and gauze who look at him expectantly. Straight through their midst, the young musician, philologist and admirer of Schopenhauer walks over to a piano he espies at the rear of the fiendish salon and which he sees as (these are his words) "the only ensouled being in the group" and strikes a few chords. This breaks his fascination, his petrification, and he regains the open, he is able to flee.

The next day he was surely laughing when he told his friends of this experience. What an impression it made on him he never became conscious of. Yet it was no more and no less than what psychologists call a "trauma," a shock the ever growing after effects of which, never again relinquishing his imagination, testify to the susceptibility of the saint to sin. In the fourth part of "Zarathustra," written twenty years later, there is to be found, in the chapter "Amongst Daughters of the Desert," an orientalizing poem whose frightful jocosity with torturously bad taste betrays a repressed sensualism and its needs whilst normal inhibitions are already crumbling. In this poem of the "cute little girl-friends and girl-cats, Dudu and Suleika," a painfully humorous erotical fancy, the "flutter and flitter skirts" of those professional ladies of Cologne appear again, still preserved. The "figures in flitter and gauze" of those days evidently served as models for the delectable daughters of the desert; and from their time it is not long, it is only four years, to the Basle clinic where the patient states specifically for the record that in earlier years he had twice infected himself. For the first of these misfortunes, the medical history of Jena records the year 1866. That is to say that one year after he fled from that house in Cologne, he returns, this time without diabolic guidance, to such a place and there contracts—some say: deliberately, as a self-punishment —the malady which is to sap, but also enormously intensify his life— more, which is to stimulate, in part for good, in part for evil, an entire epoch of history.

50

The motive power which after a few years makes him yearn to leave his academic office in Basle, is a mixture of growing sickliness and a craving for liberty which fundamentally are the same thing. At an early age already the young admirer of Richard Wagner and Schopenhauer proclaimed art and philosophy as the true guiding spirits of life—in opposition to history of which philology, the subject he was teaching, was a part. He turns his back on it, gets himself pensioned off because of illness and from then on without any ties lives in international spots in Italy, Southern France, the Swiss Alps; there he writes his books, splendid of style, glittering with audacious insults against his time, psychologically ever more radical, gleaming with ever more intense, white-hot light. In a letter he calls himself "a man who desires nothing more than daily to lose some comforting faith, who seeks and finds his happiness in this everyday greater liberation of the spirit. It may be that I *want* to be a freethinker ever more than I am *able* to be one!"— That is a confession, made very early, as early as 1876; it is the anticipation of his fate, of his breakdown; the prescience of a man who will be driven to take upon himself more cruel realizations than his heart will be able to stand and who will offer to the world the spectacle of a profoundly moving self-crucifixion.

He might well have written under his life's work, as did the well-known painter, "In doloribus pinxi." With that he would have spoken the truth in more senses than one, in the spiritual as well as in the physical one. In 1880 he confesses to the physician Dr. Eiser: "My existence is a terrible burden: I should have thrown it off long ago, were it not that just in this state of suffering and of almost absolute abnegation I make the most instructive tests and experiments in the spiritual and ethical field. . . . Continuous pain, for several hours of the day a feeling closely akin to seasickness, a partial paralysis during which I have difficulties in speaking, furious attacks for a change (the last one forced me to vomit for three days and three nights, I was craving death) . . . If I could only describe to you the *continuousness* of this sensation, the constant pain and pressure in my head, on my eyes, and that feeling as though I were paralyzed from head to toe!" It is hard to understand his seemingly complete ignorance—and that of his physicians as well!—of the nature and source of these sufferings. Slowly he gains the assurance that they originate in the brain, and in this he believes himself subject to a hereditary illness: his father, he observes, perished from "softening of the brain,"—which is certainly not true; the minister Nietzsche died as a result of a mere accident, of a brain injury caused by a fall. But that total ignorance, or the dissimulation of knowledge, concerning the origin of his illness can be explained only by the fact that this illness was intertwined and connected with his genius, that the latter unfolded with it,—and that for a great psychologist *everything* can serve as an object for unmasking apperception, only not his own genius.

It is much rather a target for astounded admiration, exorbitant self-exaltation, extreme hybridity. Full of naïvety Nietzsche glorifies the enrapturing other side of his suffering, these euphoric impoundages and overcompensations which belong to the picture. He does this most magnificently in the already almost uninhibited late work "Ecce Homo," there where he praises the physically and mentally inordinately intensified state in which he created his Zarathustra poem in an incredibly short time. That particular page is a masterpiece of style, linguistically a veritable tour de force, comparable only to passages like the magnificent analysis of the Meistersinger prelude in "Beyond Good and Evil" or the Dionysiacal presentation of the cosmos at the end of the "Will to Power." "Does anybody," he asks in "Ecce Homo," "at the end of the 19th century have any idea of what the poets of powerful eras called inspiration? If not I'll describe it." And now he launches into a description of revelations, ecstasies, elevations, whisperings, divine feelings of force and power he cannot but look upon as an atavism, a demonic throw-back belonging to other "more powerful" stages of human existence closer to God and beyond the limitations imposed upon our weakly reasonable time by its psychic possibilities. And yet "in truth"—but what is truth: his experience, or medical science?—all he describes is an injurious paroxism of excitement, tauntingly preceding the paralitical collapse.

Everybody will admit that it is a hectic excess of self-esteem testifying to his slipping reason when Nietzsche calls his "Zarathustra" an achievement measured by which the entire remainder of all human activities appears poor and confined, when he claims that a Goethe, a Shakespeare, a Dante would never for a moment be able even to draw a breath in the heights of this book, and that the genius and the goodness of all great souls put together would never be capable of producing as much as one single oration of Zarathustra. Of course it must be a great delight to write down sentiments of this kind, but I find it illicit. And then again it may be that I am only stating my own limitations when I go further and confess that for me the relationship between Nietzsche and his Zarathustra creation anyway seems to be one of blind overestimation. Because of its Biblical attitude it has become the most "popular" of his books, but it is not his best by far. Nietzsche was above all a great critic and philosopher of civilization, a European proser and essayist of highest quality who came from Schopenhauer's school; his genius was at its height at the time of "Beyond Good and Evil" and of the "Genealogy of Morals." Many a poet may amount to less than such a critic, but it was this very lesser-ness, which Nietzsche lacked except in certain admirable lyrical moments, and it never sufficed for an extensive work of creative originality. This faceless and formless monster, this winged giant Zara-thustra with the rose crown of laughter on his unrecognizable head, with his "Grow hard!" and his caperer's legs is no creation, he is rhetorical, impassioned linguistic wit, tortured voice and dubious prophecy, a wraith of helpless grandeur, often touching and mostly painful to watch—an unman wavering at the borders of the ridiculous.

When I say this, I remember the desperate cruelty with which Nietzsche spoke of many, really of all things he revered: of Wagner, of music in general, of morals, of Christianity—I nearly said: also of all things German,—and how apparently even with his most furiously criti-cal attacks against these values and powers which he always respected deep within his innermost self, he never had the feeling of really impairing them, but rather seemed to feel that the most awful insults he hurled at them, were essentially a form of ovation. He said such things about Wagner that we cannot believe our eyes when suddenly in "Ecce Homo" we find mentioned the "holy hour" of Richard Wagner's death in Venice. How is it, we ask with tears in our eyes, that this hour of death all of a sudden is a "holy" one, if Wagner was the foul histrionic, the debauched debaucher, Nietzsche a hundred times described him?—To his friend the musician Peter Gast he excuses himself for his continuous controversy with Christianity: he calls it the best bit of idealistic life he had ever known. After all, he says, he is descendent from generations of christian ministers and believes that "never in his heart has he vilified Christianity." No, but with his voice at a frenetic pitch he has called it "the one immortal stain of dishonor upon humanity"—not without at the same time making fun of the con-tention that the ancient German in any way was pre-educated or pre-destined for Christianity: The lazy, but warlike and rapacious bearskin-loafer, the sensuously frigid hunting addict and beer tippler who had barely progressed as far as a halfway decent Red Indian's religion and no more than ten hundred years ago had slaughtered human beings on sacrificial stones—what affinity could he have for the highest type of moral subtlety sharpened by rabbinical intellect, for the oriental finesse of Christianity!—His assignment of values is precise and amusing. To his autobiography the "Antichrist" gives the most christian of all titles "Ecce Homo." And last scribblings of insanity he signs "The Crucified."

One can say that Nietzsche's relation to the preferred objects of his criticism was fundamentally that of passion: a passion basically neither negative nor positive, for one continually changes over into the other. Shortly before the end of his mental life he writes a page about "Tristan," vibrating with enthusiasm. On the other hand already at the time of his apparently unconditional Wagner-devotion, just before writing the festival address "Richard Wagner in Bayreuth" for the public, he made remarks about "Lohengrin" to intimate friends in Basle—remarks of such aloof perspicacity that across one and a half decenniums they presaged the "Case of Wagner." There is *no* breach in Nietzsche's relationship to Wagner, no matter what one may say. The world always wants to see a breach in the work and life of great men. It found such a breach with Tolstoi where everything is iron consistency, where all late symptoms are pre-formed in the early ones. It found such a breach with Wagner himself, in whose development reigns the same unshakable continuity and logic. It is no different with Nietzsche. No matter how much his primarily aphoristic writings gambol in a thousand colorful facets, no matter how many superficial contradictions can be shown in him—he was all there from the very beginning, was always the same; and the writings of the youthful professor, the "Thoughts Out of Season," the "Birth of Tragedy," the essay "The Philosopher of 1873, not only contain the seeds of his later doctrinary message, but this message, a *joyful* one as he believes, is already contained in them, finished and complete. The things that change are only the accentuation, growing ever more frenetical, the key of his voice, growing ever more shrill, the gesticulation, growing ever more grotesque and frightful. The thing that changes is the mode of writing which, extremely musical always, from the dignified discipline and restraint of German humanistic tradition, somewhat colored by medieval Franconian scientism, slowly degenerates into an awesomely mundane and hectically humorous super-feuilletonism, decorating itself at last with the cosmic jester's cap and bells.

But the completely unified and compact character of Nietzsche's life work cannot be sufficiently stressed. Following Schopenhauer whose disciple he remained even after he had long denied the master, throughout his life he really only variated, extended, impressed upon his readers one single omnipresent thought which, initially appearing with all soundness and undeniably justified in its contemporary criticism, in course of time falls prey to a maenadic debasement to the point where Nietzsche's story can actually be called the story of the degeneration of this thought.

What is this thought?—In order to understand it, we must take it apart down to its ingredients, to the component parts clashing within it. Listed in casual disorder, they are: Life, civilization ("Kultur"), consciousness or cognizance, art, nobleness, morals, instinct. The concept of *civilization* predominates in this complex of ideas. It is positioned almost equal to life itself: civilization, that is the nobleness of

54

life, and combined with it as its sources and premises are art and instinct, whilst as mortal enemies and destroyers of civilization or "Kultur" and life there figure consciousness and cognizance, science and finally morals—that same morality which as preserver of truth assassinates life, because life essentially bases on semblance, art, deception, perspective, illusion and because error is the father of all that lives.

From Schopenhauer he inherited the sentence that "life as a pure concept, viewed as such or reproduced by art, is a significant drama," i. e., the sentence that life may be justified only as an aesthetic phenomenon. Life is art and semblance, no more, and therefore higher than the truth (which is a matter of morals) stands wisdom (as an affair of "Kultur" and of life)—a tragic, ironical kind of wisdom, limiting science on the basis of artistic instinct, for the sake of civilization, and defending the ultimate value, life, on two sides: against the pessimism of those who slander life and propagate the hereafter or the Nirvana—and against the optimism of those who travel in rationalism and world betterment, who prattle about the earthly happiness of all, about justice, and prepare the socialist insurrection of slaves. This tragic wisdom, blessing life in all its untruthfulness, hardness and cruelty, Nietzsche baptized with the name of Dionysos.

The name of the intoxicated god first appears in his early, aesthetic mystical paper on the "Birth of Tragedy from the Spirit of Music," in which the Dionysian element as an artistic state of the soul is opposed to the artistic principle of Apolline distancy and objectivity, very similar to the way in which Schiller in his famous essay juxtaposes the "Naive" to the "Sentimentalic." Here for the first time is coined the expression "theoretical man," and the inimical position against Socrates, the archetype of this theoretical man, is taken up: against Socrates, the despiser of instinct, the glorifier of conscience, who taught that only what is conscious can be good, the enemy of Dionysos and the murderer of tragedy. According to Nietzsche, he originated a civilization of Alexandrine scientificality, pale, scholarly, alien to mythos, alien to life, a civilization in which optimism and faith in the rational reign supreme, the practical and theoretical utilitarianism which, like democracy itself, is a symptom of declining power and physiological fatigue. The human being of this Socratic, anti-tragical civilization, the theoretical man, no longer desires to have anything *entirely*, with all the natural cruelty of the world, debilitated as he is by looking at things optimistically. But, so young Nietzsche insists on convincing himself, the time of the Socratic human being is over. A new generation, heroic, temerarious, contemptuous of all weakly doctrines enters upon the stage, the Dionysian spirit is perceived as slowly awakening in our present world,

55

the world of 1870; out of the Dionysian profundities of the German spirit, of German music, of German philosophy, the tragical drama is reborn.

Later he poked a desperate kind of fun at his onetime faith in the German spirit—and at everything he read into it, i. e., himself. Indeed, his entire self is already contained in this prelude to his philosophy, as yet mildly humanitarian, as yet extravagantly and romantically intoned; and the world perspective as well, the embracing gaze upon the entire occidental civilization is already there, even though for the time being he is primarily concerned with the German civilization in whose high destiny he believes, but which he sees in gravest danger of forfeiting this destiny because of Bismarck's establishing his power state, because of politics, democratic leveling down to mediocrity and smug satiation with victory. His splendid diatribe against the senile and merry book of the theologian David Strauss, "The Old and the New Faith," is the most direct example of this criticism against a Philistinism of saturation, threatening to deprive the German spirit of all depth. And there is something deeply moving in the way the young thinker already here throws prophetic glances ahead to his own fate that seems to lie before him like an open book of tragedy. I am referring to the passage where he taunts the ethical cowardice of the vulgar illuminator Strauss who, he says, takes good care not to derive any *moral percepts for life* from his Darwinism, from the bellum omnium contra omnes and from the prerogative of the mightier, but rather only disports himself in strong sallies against preachers and miracles, for which one can always obtain the Philistine's partisanship. He himself, that he already knows deep down within him, will do the ultimate and not even shy from insanity in order to obtain the Philistine's *opposition*.

It is the second one of the "Thoughts Out of Season," entitled "On the Usefulness and the Disadvantage of Historiology for Life," in which that fundamental thought of his life which I mentioned above is preformed most perfectly, even though still draped in a special critical guise. This admirable treatise fundamentally is nothing but one great variation of the Hamlet passage on the "native hue of resolution," that "is sicklied o'er with the pale cast of thought." The title is incorrect in as far as there is hardly any mention of the usefulness of historiology—all the more however of its disadvantages for life, the dear, holy aesthetically justified life. The 19th century has been called the historical era, and indeed this century was the first to create and develop that sense of history of which former civilizations, just *because* they were civilizations, artistically unified systems of life, knew little or nothing. Nietzsche goes so far as to speak of a "historical disease," laming life and its spontaneity. Education, that today meant historical

56

education. But the Greeks had known no historical education of any
kind, and one would probably hesitate to call the Greeks uneducated.
Historiology for the sake of pure apperception, not conducted for the
purpose of advancing life and without the counterbalance of "plastic
giftedness," creative uninhibitedness, is murderous, is death. A historical
phenomenon in a state of apperception—is dead. A scientifically cog-
nized religion, e. g., is doomed, it is at an end. The historically critical
treatment of Christianity, Nietzsche says with conservative apprehension, dissolves it into pure knowledge of things christian. In examining
religion from the point of view of history, he says, "there come to light
things which necessarily destroy the reverential mood of illusion in
which alone everything desirous of living can remain alive." Only in
love, adumbrated by the illusion of love, does man *create*. Historiology
would have to be treated as a work of art in order to creatively contribute to civilization—but that would be contrary to the analytical and
inartistic trend of the time. Historiology exorcises our instincts. Educated, or miseducated, by it, man no longer is able to "drop the rains"
and to act naively, confiding in the "divine animal." Historiology
always underestimates what is growing into the future and paralyzes
action which must ever injure respectful reverences. What it teaches
and creates, is *justice*. But life is not in need of justice, it is in need of
injustice, it is essentially unjust. "A great deal of strength is required,"
Nietzsche says (and it is doubtful whether he credits himself with this
strength) "to be able to live and forget to what extent living and being
unjust are one." Yet everything depends on the ability to forget. He
wants the unhistorical: the art and strength of being able to *forget*
and to confine himself within a limited horizon—a demand more easily
made than fulfilled, we might add. For we are born within a limited
horizon; to confine ourselves within it artificially is an aesthetic masquerade and a denial of fate from which something genuine and worth
while can hardly derive. But, very beautifully and nobly, Nietzsche
wants to go *beyond* the mere historical, to divert the gaze away from
the things that are in the process of growing, toward those which give
our existence its eternal and sentient character, toward art and religion. The enemy is science, for it sees and knows only historiology and
the process of growing, nothing sentient, eternal; it despises forgetful-
ness as the death of knowledge and seeks to raise all limitations of our
horizon. But everything that lives requires a protective atmosphere, a
mysterious nebulous impassable ring and an enveloping illusion. A life
dominated by science is much less of a life than one dominated not
by knowledge, but rather by instincts and by *powerful phantasmata*.

In reading of "powerful phantasmata" today we think of Sorel and
his book "Sur la Violence," in which syndicalism and fascism are still

one and which declares the mythos of the mass to be the indispensible motor of history, entirely independent of truth or untruth. We also ask ourselves, whether it would not be better to keep the masses in respect of reason and truth and at the same time to honor their demand for justice—than to implant the mythos of the mass and to let mobs dominated by "powerful phantasmata" loose on humanity. Who is doing that today and for what purpose? Certainly not for that of promoting civilization.—But Nietzsche knows nothing of masses and wants to know nothing of them. "Let them go to the devil," he says, "and the statistics too!" He wants and proclaims an era in which people wisely refrain, against and beyond the historical way of thinking, from any constructional interpretation of the process of life or of human history as well, in which they do not regard the masses at all any more, but rather the great individuals, whose greatness makes them contemporaries regardless of time and who discourse in the spirit high above the bustling historical throng of nonentities. The goal of humanity, he says, lies not at its end, but in its highest representatives. That is his individualism: an aesthetic genius cult and hero worship which he has taken from Schopenhauer, together with the insistence that happiness is impossible and a *heroic* life is the only thing worthy and possible for the individual. Transformed by Nietzsche and together with his adoration of the powerful and beautiful life, this results in a heroical aestheticism, as whose protective diety he proclaims the god of tragedy, Dionysos. It is just this Dionysian aestheticism which makes of the later Nietzsche the greatest critic and psychologist of morals known to the history of the human mind.

He is a born psychologist, psychology is his archpassion: apperception and psychology, these are fundamentally one and the same passion, and it characterizes the entire inner contradictiousness of this great and suffering spirit that he, who values life far above apperception, is so completely and hopelessly caught in psychology. He is already a psychologist only on the basis of Schopenhauer's findings that not the intellect produces will, but vice versa, that not the intellect is the primary and dominating element, but the will, to which the intellect entertains a relationship of no more than servitude. The intellect as a servile tool of will: that is the font of all psychology, a psychology of casting suspicions and tearing off masks, and Nietzsche as attorney general of life, throws himself into the arms of moral psychology, he suspects all "good" urges of originating from bad ones and proclaims the "evil" ones as those which ennoble and exalt life. That is "The Revaluation of All Values."

What used to be called Socratism, "the theoretical man," conscious sentiency, historical disease, now is called simply "morals," particularly

58

"christian morals" which is revealed as something out and out poisonous, rancorous and inimical to life—and now we must not forget that Nietzsche's criticism of morals is in part something impersonal, something belonging quite generally to his time. It is the time about the turn of the century, the time of the first running attack of the European intellectuals against the hypocritical morals of the Victorian, the bourgeois era. Into this picture Nietzsche's furious battle against morals fits to a certain degree and often with astounding family resemblance. It is astonishing to note the close relationship between some of Nietzsche's aperçus and the attacks, by no means nothing but vain, with which approximately at the same time Oscar Wilde, the English aesthetic, shocked his public and made it laugh. When Wilde declares: "For, try as we may, we cannot get behind the appearance of things to reality. And the terrible reason may be that there is no reality in things apart from their appearances;" when he speaks of the "truth of masks" and of the "decay of lies," when he exclaims: "To me beauty is the wonder of wonders. It is only shallow people who do not judge by appearances. The true mystery of the world is the visible, not the invisible;" when he calls truth something so personal that never two spirits can do justice to the same truth, when he says: "Every impulse that we strive to strangle broods in the mind, and poisons us. . . . The only way to get rid of a temptation is to yield to it;" and: "Don't be led astray into the paths of virtue!"—then all this might very well stand in Nietzsche's writings. And when on the other hand one reads of the latter: "Seriousness, this unmistakable sign of the more laborious metabolism."—"In art the lie sanctifies itself and the will to deceive has the clear conscience on its side."—"We are basically inclined to maintain that the most incorrect judgements are the most indispensable."—"It is no more than a moral prejudice that the truth is worth more than the semblance."—then there is not one among these sentences which could not appear in one of Oscar's comedies and get a laugh in St. James's Theater. When somebody wanted to praise Wilde very highly, they compared his plays to Sheridan's "The School for Scandal." Much of Nietzsche seems to originate with this school.

Of course the juxtaposition of Nietzsche with Wilde has something almost sacrilegious, for the latter was a dandy; the German philosopher however was something like a saint of immoralism. And yet, with the more or less deliberate martyrium of his life's end, the penal institution of Reading, Wilde's dandyism assumes a touch of holiness which would have aroused Nietzsche's entire sympathy. What reconciled him with Socrates was the cup of hemlock, the end, the sacrificial death, and he believes that the impression of this on Greek youth and on Plato cannot be overestimated. And he left the personality of Jesus of

Nazareth untouched by his hatred of historical Christianity, again for the sake of the end, of the cross which he loved with all his heart and toward which he himself was striding deliberately.

His life was intoxication and suffering—a highly artistic state, mythologically speaking the union of Dionysos with the Crucified. Swinging the thyrsus he ecstatically glorified the strong and beautiful, the amorally triumphant life and defended it against any stunting by intellectualism—and at the same time he paid tribute to suffering as none other. "It determines the *order of rank,*" he says, "how deeply a man can suffer." Those are not the words of an anti-moralist. Nor is there a trace of anti-moralism in it when he writes: "As far as torture and renunciation are concerned, the life of my last years can measure up to that of any ascetic at any time." For he does not write this in search of compassion, but rather with pride: "I *want,*" he says, "to have it as hard as any man can possibly have it." He made things hard for himself, hard up to sanctity, for Schopenhauer's saint ultimately always remained the highest type for him, and the "heroic life," that is the life of the saint. What defines the saint? That he does not one of all the things he would like to do, and all the things he does not like to do. That is the way in which Nietzsche lived: "Renouncing everything I revered, renouncing reverence itself . . . Thou must become master over thyself, master also over thine own virtues." That is the act of "vaulting above the self" Novalis mentions somewhere and which, he thinks, is everywhere the supreme one. Now this "act" (an expression of showmen and acrobats) in Nietzsche's pen has not a whit of anything exuberantly able and saltatorial. Everything "choreographic" in his attitude is velleity and disagreeable in the extreme. It is much rather a bloody kind of self-mutilation, self-torment, moralism. His very concept of truth is ascetic: for to him truth is what hurts, and he would be suspicious of any truth that would cause him a pleasant sensation. "Among the forces," he says, "raised by our morals was truthfulness: the latter finally turns on morals, discovers its teleology, its *prejudiced* manner of observation." His "Immoralism" thus is the self-cancellation of morality for the sake of truthfulness. But that this in a way is exaggeration and luxuriation of morals he hints at by speaking of an inherited treasure of morality which could well afford to waste and throw out of the window a great deal without thereby becoming noticeably impoverished.

All this stands behind the atrocities and intoxicated messages of power, force, cruelty and political deception into which his thought of life as a work of art and of an unreflected civilization dominated by instinct, degenerates splendidly in his later writings. When at one time a Swiss critic, of the daily paper "Bund" in Bern, wrote that Nietzsche was entering a plea for the abolition of all decent sentiments, the philosopher was completely flabbergasted by being so utterly misunderstood. "Much obliged!" he said scornfully. For everything he had said he had intended to be very noble and humane, in the sense of a higher, more profound, prouder, *more beautiful* humanity, and he "had not really meant any harm" as it were, at any rate nothing evil, although a lot of wickedness. For everything that has depth, is wicked; life itself is profoundly wicked, it has not been thought up by morality, it knows nothing of "truth," but bases on semblance and artistic lie, it mocks virtue, for its essence is ruthlessness and exploitation,—and, Nietzsche says, there is a pessimism of power, an intellectual predilection for what is hard, horrible, wicked, problematical in our existence arising from well-being, from a fullness of existence. This "well-being," this "fullness of existence" the diseased Euphorian ascribes to himself and takes it upon himself to proclaim the sides of life so far negated, especially negated by Christianity, as those most worthy of affirmation. Life above all! Why? That he never said. He never gave the reason why life should be something worthy of being adored unconditionally and preserved above all else, but only declared that life stood higher than apperception, *for* with life apperception destroyed itself. Apperception presupposed life for its existence and therefore had in it the interest of self-preservation. It thus seems that there must be life, in order that there may be something to apperceive. But it does seem to us as though this train of logic did not suffice to motivate his enthusiastic guardianship of life. If he would see in it the creation of a god, then we should have to respect his piety, even though personally we might find little cause to fall flat on our faces before the exploded cosmos of modern physics. But instead he sees in it a massive and senseless spawn of the will to power, and it is just its senselessness and its colossal immorality which is to give us cause for ecstatic admiration. His devotee's exclamation is not "Hosiana!" but "Evoe!" and this cry sounds extremely broken and tortured. It is supposed to deny that there is something more than biological in man which does not completely expend itself in its interest in life, the possibility of backing away from this interest, a critical detachment which perhaps is what Nietzsche calls "morals" and which indeed will never seriously harm that lovable life—for that it is much too irredeemable—but which nevertheless might serve as a feeble corrective and acuation of conscience, a function only Christianity has always exercised. "There is no fixed basis outside of life," Nietzsche says, "from where one might reflect on existence, no superior authority before which life could be *ashamed*." Really not? We have the feeling that such an authority does exist, and let it not be morality, then it is simply the human spirit in an absolute sense of the word, humaneness proper as critical ability, irony and liberty, combined with the word of judgement. "There is no superior judge above life?" But somehow nature and life go beyond themselves in man, in him they lose their innocence, they take on *spirit*—and spirit is the self-criticism of life. This humane Something within us has a doubtful look of compassion for a "healthful doctrine" of life that in sober days still goes against the historical disease, but later degenerates into a maenadic rage against truth, morals, religion, human kindness, against everything that might serve to tolerably domesticate that ferocious life.

As far as I can see, there are two mistakes which warp Nietzsche's thinking and lead to his downfall. The first one is a complete, we must assume: a deliberate, misperception of the power relationship between instinct and intellect on earth, just as though the latter were the dangerously dominating element, and highest time it were to save instinct from its threat. If one considers how completely will, urge and interest dominate and hold down intellect, reason and the sense of justice in the great majority of people, the opinion becomes absurd that intellect must be overcome by instinct. This opinion can be explained only historically, on the strength of a momentary philosophical situation, as a correction of rationalistic satiety, and immediately it requires countercorrection. As though it were necessary to defend life against the spirit! As though there were the slightest danger that conditions on earth could ever become too spiritualized! The simplest generosity should constrain us to shield and protect the weak little flame of reason, of spirit, of justice, instead of taking the part of power and instinct-governed life and parading a corybantic overestimation of its "negated" side, of crime,—the moronic effect of which we living today have just experienced. Nietzsche acts—and in so doing he has caused a great deal of trouble—as though it were our moral consciousness which, like Mephistopheles, raises an icy, satanic fist against life. As far as I am concerned, I see nothing particularly satanic in the thought (a thought long known to mystics) that one day life might be eliminated by the power of the human spirit, an achievement which is still a long, an interminably long way off. The danger of life eliminating itself on this planet by perfecting the atom bomb is considerably more urgent. But that too is improbable. Life is a cat with nine lives, and so is humanity.

The second one of Nietzsche's errors is the utterly false relationship he establishes between life and morals when he treats of them as opposites. The truth is that they belong together. Ethics support life, and a man with good morals is an upright citizen of life,—perhaps a little boring, but extremely useful. The real opposites are ethics and *aesthetics*. Not morality, but beauty is linked to death, as many poets have said and sung,—and Nietzsche should not know it? "When

62

Socrates and Plato started talking about truth and justice," he says somewhere, "they were not Greeks any longer, but Jews—or I don't know what." Well, thanks to their morality the Jews have proven themselves to be good and persevering children of life. They, together with their religion, their faith in a just God, have survived thousands of years, whereas the dissolute little nation of aesthetes and artists, the Greeks, very quickly disappeared from the stage of history.

But Nietzsche, far from any racial anti-semitism, does indeed see in Jewry the cradle of Christianity and in the latter, justly but with revulsion, the germ of democracy, the French Revolution and the hateful "modern ideas" which his shattering word brands as herd animal morals. "Shopkeepers, Christians, cows, women, Englishmen and other democrats" he says, for he sees the origin of the "modern ideas" in England (the French, he claims, were only their soldiers), and what he despises and curses in these ideas is their utilitarianism and their eudaemonism, the fact that they raise peace and happiness on earth as the highest objects of desire—whereas it is just such vile and weakly values the noble, the tragic, the heroic man kicks under his feet. The latter is necessarily a warrior, hard against himself and others, ready to sacrifice himself and others. The primary reproach he throws at Christianity is the fact that it raised the individual to such importance that one could no longer *sacrifice* it. But, he says, the breed persists only through human sacrifice and Christianity is the opposing principle against natural selection. It has actually dragged down and debilitated the power, the responsibility, the high duty to sacrifice human beings and for thousands of years, until the arrival of Nietzsche, has prevented the development of that energy of greatness which "by breeding, and on the other hand by destroying millions of misfits, forms future man and does not perish from the never before existing misery he creates." Who was it that recently had the strength to take upon himself this responsibility, impudently thought himself capable of this greatness and unfalteringly fulfilled this high duty of sacrificing hecatombs of human beings? A crapule of megalomaniacal petty bourgeois, at the sight of whom Nietzsche would immediately have gone down with an extreme case of megrim and all its accompanying symptoms.

He did not live to see it. Nor did he live to see a war after the old-fashioned one of 1870 with its Chassepot and needle rifles and therefore he can, with all his hatred of the christian and democratic philanthropy of happiness, luxuriate in glorifications of war that appear to us today like the talk of an excited adolescent. That the good cause justifies war, is much too moral for him: it is the good war that justifies *any* cause. "The scale of values by which the various forms of society are judged today," he writes, "is completely identical with the one which assigns a higher value to *peace* than to war: but this judgement is antibiological, is itself a spawn of life's decadence . . . Life is a consequence of war, society itself a means for war." Never a thought that perhaps it might not be a bad idea to try and make something else of society than a means for war. Society is a product of nature which, just as life itself, bases on immoral premises; to assail these premises is equivalent to a treacherous attempt on life. "One has renounced the great life," he exclaims, "when one has renounced war." Renounced life and civilization; for in order to be refreshed, the latter requires thorough relapses into barbarism, and it is a vain whimsey to expect anything more in the nature of civilization and greatness from humanity, once it has forgotten how to make war. He is contemptuous of all nationalistic stupidity. But this contempt apparently is an esoteric prerogative of a few individuals, for he describes outbreaks of nationalistic power-lusting and sacrificial frenzy with a kind of rapture which leaves no doubt that he wants to preserve for the nations, the masses, that "powerful phantasma" of nationalism.

An insert is necessary here. We have made the experience that under certain circumstances, unconditional pacifism can be a more than questionable, a deceitful and villainous thing. During long years, throughout Europe and the world it was nothing but the mask for fascist sympathies, and true friends of peace felt the peace of Munich, which in 1938 the democracies made with fascism, ostensibly to save the nations from war, to have been the lowest point of European history. The war against Hitler, or rather the mere readiness for it that would have sufficed, was ardently desired by these friends of peace. But if we picture to ourselves—and the picture rises inexorably before our eyes!— what perdition in every sense of the word is created even by a war fought in the interest of humanity, what loss of all sense for ethics, what a release of greedily egotistical and antisocial urges; if, taught by what we have already experienced, we form an approximate conception of what the world will look like—would look like—after the next, the third world war—then Nietzsche's rodomontades on the selective function of war that preserves civilization appear to us like the phantasies of an inexperienced novice, the son of a long period of peace and safety with "gilt-edged securities," a period that begins to be bored with itself.

Besides, since with astonishing prophetic prescience he predicts a sequence of monstrous wars and explosions, even the classical period of war, "to which men of the future will look with envy and reverence," the humanitarian deterioration and castration of humanity does not yet seem to be so dangerously advanced, and one cannot see why on top of this humanity still has to be philosophically incited to the selec-

64

tive massacre. Does this philosophy want to eliminate the moral scruples standing in the way of the coming atrocities? Does it want to put humanity in training for its magnificent future? But it does this in a voluptuous manner which, far from calling forth our moral protest as intended, rather makes us sick and sorry for the noble spirit, here sensuously raging against himself. It goes painfully beyond mere education for manliness, when medieval forms of torture are enumerated, described and recommended with a titillation that has left its traces in contemporary German literature. It borders on the vile when "to console fraglings" the lesser susceptibility to physical pain of lower cases, e. g., the Negroes, is cited as a consideration. And then, when the song of the "Blond Beast" is intoned, "of the rejoicing monster," the type of man who "returns from the horrid performance of murder, arson, rape, torture,—exuberant as after a student's prank," then the picture of infantile sadism is complete and our soul squirms with pain.

It was the romantic Novalis, thus a spirit kindred to Nietzsche's, who gave the most striking criticism of this mental attitude. "The ideal of ethics," he says, "has no more dangerous competitor than the ideal of the utmost power, of the mightiest life, which has also been called (fundamentally very correctly, but very incorrectly interpreted) the ideal of aesthetic greatness. It is the maximum of the barbarian, and unfortunately in these times of degenerating civilization; it has found very many adherents precisely among the greatest weaklings. This ideal makes man into an animal-spirit, a mixture whose brutal wit is just the thing that has a brutal attraction for weaklings."

No one can say it better. Did Nietzsche know this passage? We cannot doubt that he did. But he did not let it disturb him in his intoxicated, consciously intoxicated and therefore not serious provocations of the "ideal of ethics." What Novalis calls the ideal of aesthetic greatness, the maximum of the barbarian, man as an animal spirit, is Nietzsche's superman, and he describes him as the "secretion of an excess in luxuriance of humanity, in the person of which a more powerful strain, a higher type of human being steps forth, who has different conditions of engendrure and preservation than average man." These are the future masters of the earth, this is the ornate type of tyrant, whom to engender democracy is just right and who accordingly must use it as his tool, must introduce his new kind of morals by Machiavellistically linking to the extant law of ethics, by using its very words. For this frightful utopia of greatness, power and beauty would much rather lie than speak the truth,—it takes more intelligence and will power. The superman is that man "in whom the specific qualities of life—injustice, lie, exploitation are strongest."

It would be the greatest inhumanity, to counter all these shrill and

65

tortured challenges with scorn and slight—and mere stupidity, to counter them with moral indignation. We are face to face with a Hamlet-like fate, a tragic destiny of apperception unbearably deep, one that inspires reverence and compassion. "I believe," Nietzsche says somewhere, "I have correctly guessed a few elements from the soul of highest man—*it may be that everyone* who guesses him correctly, *is destroyed.*" He was destroyed by it, and the atrocities of his teaching are too frequently pervaded by infinitely moving, lyrical sorrow, by profound glances of love, by sounds of melancholy yearning for the dew of love to quicken the arid, rainless land of his solitude, for scorn and revulsion to dare and emerge before such an Ecce Homo manifestation. But our reverence does find itself in something of a tight spot when that "socialism of the subjugated caste" which Nietzsche a hundred times scorned and branded as a poisonous hater of higher life, proves to us that his superman is nothing but the idealization of the fascist Fuehrer, and that he himself with all his philosophizing was a pacemaker, participating creator and prompter of ideas to European —to world fascism. Incidentally, I am inclined here to reverse cause and effect and not to believe that Nietzsche created fascism, but rather that fascism created him—that is to say: basically remote from politics and innocently spiritual, he functioned as an infinitely sensitive instrument of expression and registration, with his philosopheme of power he presaged the dawning imperialism and as a quivering floatstick indicated the fascist era of the West in which we are living and shall continue to live for a long time to come, despite the military victory over fascism.

As a thinker who with his entire being seceded in the very beginning from the bourgeois world, he seems to have affirmed the fascist component of the post-bourgeois time and to have negated the socialist one, because the latter was the moral one and because he confused morals in general with bourgeois morals. But in his sensitiveness he was never able to withdraw from the influence of the socialist element on the future, and it is this fact which the socialists who denounce him as a fascist pur sang, do not understand. It is not as simple as all that,— despite everything that can be said for this simplification. One thing is true: his heroic contempt of happiness which was something extremely personal and politically of little use, seduced him to see the contemptible desire for the "green-pasture happiness of the herd animals" in every aspiration to do away with the most dishonoring social and economic evils, the avoidable misery on earth. It is not without reason that his word of the "dangerous life" was translated into the Italian and became a part of fascist slang. Everything he said in ultimate surexcitation against morals, humaneness, compassion, Christianity and

66

for beautiful infamy, for war, for wickedness, was unfortunately well suited for taking its place in the trashy ideology of fascism, and aberrations like his "Morality for Physicians" with the precept of killing sick persons and castrating inferior individuals, his insistence on the necessity of slavery, added to this some of his race-hygenic precepts for selection, breeding and marriage, actually, even though perhaps without scientific reference to him, entered into the theory and the practice of National Socialism. If the word: "By the fruit of their deeds ye shall know them!" is true, then Nietzsche is in a bad way. With Spengler, his clever ape, the master-man of Nietzsche's dream has become the modern "realistic man of grand style," the rapacious and profit-greedy man who makes his way over dead bodies, the financial magnate, the war industrialist, the German industrial general manager financing fascism—in short, with Spengler, Nietzsche in one stupidly restricted sense becomes the philosophical patron of imperialism—of which in reality he understood nothing at all. How otherwise could he have at every step shown his contempt for the peddler's and shopkeeper's spirit he considers as pacifistic, and in opposition to it have glorified the heroic one, the spirit of the soldier? The alliance between industrialism and militarism, their political unity in which imperialism consists, and the fact that it is the spirit of profit-making which creates wars, these things his "aristocratic radicalism" never even saw.

We should not let ourselves be deceived: Fascism as a trick to capture the masses, as the ultimate vulgarity and the most miserably anticultural loggerheadedness that ever made history, is foreign to the very depths of that man's spirit for whom everything centered around the query: "What is noble?"; fascism lies completely beyond his power of imagination, and that the German middle-class should have confused the Nazi assault with Nietzsche's dreams of a barbarism to renew civilization, was the clumsiest of all misunderstandings. I am not speaking of his contemptuous disregard of all nationalism, of his hatred for the "Reich" and the stultifying German power politics, his qualities as a European, his mocking scorn of anti-semitism and the entire racial swindle. But I do repeat that the socialist flavor in his vision of the post-bourgeois life is just as strong as the one we might call fascist. What is it after all when Zarathustra exclaims: "I beseech you, my brethren, remain true to earth! No longer bury your heads in the sand of heavenly things, but carry it freely, a head of this earth, creating the sense of earth! . . . Guide our dissipated virtue back to earth as I do— yea, back to life and love: that it may give a sense to the earth, a human sense!"? It means the will to pervade the material element with the human one, it means materialism of the spirit, it is socialism.

Here and there his concept of civilization shows a strongly socialist, certainly no longer a bourgeois coloring. He stands against the cleavage between educated and uneducated, and his youthful discipleship of Wagner signifies this above all: the end of the Renaissance civilization, that great age of the bourgeoisie, an art for high and low, no more highest delights that would not be common to the hearts of all.

It does not testify of enmity against the workers, it testifies of the contrary, when he says: "The working men should learn to feel like soldiers: a recompensation, a salary, but not payment. They shall one day live like the middle-class does now, but *above* them, distinguishing itself by its lack of needs, the *higher* caste, i. e., poorer and simpler, but possessed of the power." And he gave odd instructions on how to make private property more moral: "Let all ways of collecting *small* fortunes by work be kept open," he says, "but prevent the effortless, the sudden enrichment, withdraw all branches of transport and commerce favorable to the amassing of *large* fortunes, thus particularly finances, from the hands of private individuals and companies—and consider those who possess too much as well as those who possess nothing as public enemies." The man who possesses nothing as a dangerous beast in the eyes of the philosophical small capitalist: that is Schopenhauer's idea. How dangerous is the man who possesses too much, is something Nietzsche learnt and added himself.

Around 1875, i. e., more than 70 years ago, he prophesied, not with much enthusiasm, but simply as a consequence of victorious democracy, a European League of Nations "in which each individual people, its frontiers drawn according to geographical suitability, has the position of a Swiss canton and its separate rights." At that time the perspective is as yet purely European. In the course of the following decennium it expands into the global and the universal. He mentions the unified economic administration of the earth as unavoidable in the future. He calls for as many international powers as possible—"to practise world perspective." His faith in Europe wavers. "Fundamentally the Europeans imagine that they now represent the higher type of human being on earth. Asiatic man is a hundred times more magnificent than European man." On the other hand he does believe it possible that in the world of the future the spiritual influence might rest in the hands of the typical European, a synthesis of the European past in the highest, most spiritual type. "The mastery over the earth—Anglo-Saxon. The German element a good ferment, it does not know how to rule." Then again he foresees the intergrowth of the German and the Slavic races and Germany as a pre-Slavic station in history, preparing the way for a Panslavic Europe. The rise of Russia as a world power is entirely clear to him: "The power shared by Slavs and Anglo-Saxons and Europe in the role of Greece under the domination of Rome."

For an excursion into world politics, made by a mind who is essentially concerned only with the cultural task to produce the philosopher, the artist and the saint, these are striking results. Across approximately a century he sees just about what we see who live today. For the world, a newly forming concept of the world, is unity, and wherever, in whatever direction so enormous a sensibility turns and gropes forward, it senses the new, the coming and registers it. Purely intuitively, Nietzsche presages results of modern physics by fighting against the mechanistical interpretation of the world, by denying the existence of a causally determined world, of the classic "natural laws," of the repetition of identical cases. "There is no second time." Nor is there any computability on the basis of which a specific cause must be followed by a specific effect. The interpretation of an occurrence according to cause and effect is false. What does occur is a struggle between two elements unequal in power, a new arrangement of forces; and the new state of fact is something fundamentally different from the old one, by no means its effect. Dynamic therefore, instead of logical and mechanic. Nietzsche's "Intuition in the field of natural science," to paraphrase Helmholtz' words about Goethe, have a spiritual tendency, they want to achieve something, they fit into his philosopheme of power, his antirationalism and serve him to raise life above the law,—because the law itself already has something "moral" in it. But whatever this tendency, in the face of natural science, for which the "law" meanwhile has been reduced to mere probability and which has lost its faith in the concept of causality to a great degree, Nietzsche was proven right.

As does every other thought he has conceived, his ideas on physics take him right out of the bourgeois world of classical rationality into a new one wherein by his provenance he is himself the most alien guest. A socialism that refuses to credit him with this fact, excites the supposition that it belongs to the bourgeoisie much more than it is itself conscious of. We must drop the evaluation of Nietzsche as an aphorist without a central core: his philosophy as well as that of Schopenhauer is a completely organized system, developed from one single fundamental, all-pervading thought. But then of course this fundamental and initial thought is of a radical aesthetic nature, by which fact alone his perception and thinking must grow into irreconcilable opposition to all socialism. In the last analysis there are only two mental and inner attitudes: the aesthetic and the moral one, and socialism is a strictly moral way of looking at the world. Nietzsche on the other hand is the most complete and irredeemable aesthete known to the history of the human mind, and his premise containing his Dionysian pessimism: i. e., that life can be justified only as an aesthetic phenomenon, is most exactly correct of him, his life, his work as a thinker and a poet—only as an aesthetic phenomenon can it be justified, understood, venerated; consciously, down to the self-mythologization of the last moments and into insanity, this life is an artistic show, not only in its wonderful expression, but also in its innermost essence—a lyrical and tragical drama of the utmost fascination.

It is strange enough, though quite comprehensible, that aestheticism was the first guise in which the European spirit rebelled against the comprehensive morals of the bourgeois era. It was not without reason that I named Nietzsche and Wilde in one breath—they belong together as rebels and specifically as rebels in the name of beauty, even though with the German breaker of law tablets the revolt may go incalculably deeper and may cost incalculably more in suffering, renunciation, self-conquest. Indeed I have read in the writings of socialist critics, especially of Russian ones, that the aesthetic aperçus and judgements of Nietzsche's often were admirably fine, but that in matters of moral politics he was a barbarian. This distinction is naive, for Nietzsche's glorification of the barbaric is nothing but an excess of his aesthetic intoxication, but it is of course true that this betrays a propinquity we have every reason to consider thoughtfully: just that propinquity of aestheticism and barbary. Toward the end of the 19th century, this sinister proximity was not yet perceived, felt, feared—otherwise Georg Brandes, a Jew and liberal writer, could not have discovered the "aristocratic radicalism" of the German philosopher as a new point of detail and have read propaganda lectures on it: a proof of the sense of security still extant at that time, the insouciance of the bourgeois era touching to its end,—a proof however also that the skilled Danish critic did not take Nietzsche's barbarism seriously, not at face value, that he understood it cum grano salis, in which he was very right.

From Nietzsche's aestheticism, which is a raging abnegation of the spirit in favor of the beautiful, strong and infamous life, i. e., the self-denial of a man who suffers deeply from life, there flows into his philosophical outpourings something unreal, irresponsible, undependable and passionately playful, an element of deepest irony that must foil the understanding of the more simple reader. Not only is it art what he offers—it is an art also to read him, and nothing clumsy and straightforward is admissible, every kind of artfulness, irony, reserve is required in reading him. Who takes Nietzsche at face value, takes him literally, who believes him, is lost. With him in truth it is the same as with Seneca whom he calls a man to whom one should lend his ear, but never "trust and faith." Is it necessary to cite examples? The reader of the "Case of Wagner," e.g., does not believe his eyes when, in a letter of the year 1888 addressed to the musician Carl Fuchs he reads: "You must not take seriously what I say about Bizet; as I am, Bizet for me is a thousand times of no account. But as an ironical antithesis against Wagner it is extremely effective." This is what remains, speaking "between you and me," of the enthralled eulogy on "Carmen" in the "Case of Wagner." This is startling, but only the least of it. In another letter to the same recipient he gives advice how best to write about himself as a psychologist, author, immoralist: not judging with Yes and No, but characterizing with spiritual neutrality. "It is *not* at all necessary, not even *desirable*, to take my part in so doing: on the contrary, a dose of curiosity, as before a strange flower, with a bit of ironical opposition, would seem to me to be an incomparably *more intelligent* approach toward me.—Excuse me! I just wrote a few naiveties—a little recipe to get adroitly out of something *impossible*."

Has any author ever *cautioned* against himself in a stranger manner? "Anti-liberal to the point of meanness" he calls himself. Anti-liberal *because of* meanness, because of an urge for provocation, would be more correct. When in 1888 the emperor of the hundred days, Frederic III, the liberal married to an English princess, dies, Nietzsche is moved and depressed like all German liberals. "He was after all a small glimmer of *free* thought, Germany's last hope. Now begins the Stoecker regime:—I draw the consequences and already *know* that now my 'Will to Power' will first be confiscated in Germany . . ." Well, nothing is confiscated. As yet the spirit of the liberal era is too strong, everything may be said in Germany. In Nietzsche's mourning for Frederic however something quite plain, simple, unparadoxical, one may say: the truth, crops up unexpectedly: the natural love of the spiritual human being, of the writer, for *freedom* which is the very breath of his life—and all of a sudden the entire aesthetical phantasmagoria of slavery, war, brute force, magnificent cruelty stands somewhere far removed in the light of irresponsible play acting and colorful theory.

All his life he maledicted the "theoretical man," but he himself is this theoretical man par excellence and in the purest form; his thinking is absolute geniality, unpragmatical in the extreme, devoid of any pedagogical responsibility, profoundly unpolitical; it is in truth *without* any relation to life, that beloved, defended life raised above every other value, and never did he worry in the least about how his teachings might look in practical, political reality. The ten thousand doctrinaires of the irrational who, under his shadow, mushroomed out of the ground all over Germany did not do this either. Small wonder! For nothing could be essentially better suited to the German nature than his aesthetic theorization. Also against the Germans, those vitiators of European history, as he calls them, he flung his sulphurate critical flashes of lightning and eventually he gave them credit for no good whatsoever. But who, in the last analysis, was more German than he,

71

who was it that once more exemplarily demonstrated to the Germans everything by which they have become a terror and a scourge for the world and have ruined themselves: the romantic passion, the urge eternally to unfold the ego into the limitless without a definite object, the will that is free because it has no aim and strays into the infinite? Drunkenness and the inclination to suicide are what he called the characteristic vices of the Germans. Their points of danger lay in everything that fetters the powers of reason and releases the passions; "for the German's emotion is directed against his own advantage and self-destructive like that of the drunkard. Enthusiasm proper is worth less in Germany than in other places, for it is arid."—What does Zarathustra call himself? "Knower of self—hangman of self."

In more than one sense Nietzsche has become historical. He has made history, frightful history, nor did he exaggerate when he called himself "a fatality." He has aesthetically exaggerated his loneliness. He belongs, in an extremely German form, it is true, to a movement general throughout the West, which counts names like Kierkegaard, Bergson, and many others among its adherents and is a rebellion in the history of the human mind against the classical rationalist faith of the 18th and 19th centuries. It has achieved its object—or has only not yet fulfilled it in as far as its necessary continuation is the reconstitution of human reason on a new basis, the conquest of a new concept of humanitarianism which has gained added depth compared to the smug, shallow one of the bourgeois time.

The defence of instinct against reason and consciousness was a temporal correction. The permanent, eternally necessary correction remains the one exercised on life by the spirit or, if one so wants, by morals. How bound in time, how theoretical too, how inexperienced does Nietzsche's romanticizing about wickedness appear to us today! We have learnt to know it in all its miserableness and are no longer aesthetic enough to fear professing our faith in good, to be ashamed of so commonplace concepts and guiding examples as truth, liberty, justice. The aestheticism under whose banner the free spirits rose against bourgeois morals, in the last analysis belongs to the bourgeois era itself, and to transcend this means stepping out of an aesthetic era into a moral and social one. An aesthetic philosophy of life is fundamentally incapable of mastering the problems we are called upon to solve—no matter how much Nietzsche's genius has contributed to the creation of the new atmosphere. At one time he presumes that in the coming world of his vision, the religious forces might still be strong enough to produce an aesthetic religion a la Buddha which would glide across the differences between the denominations—and science would have nothing against a new ideal. "But," he adds carefully, "it will not be general love of man!" And what if it would be just this?—It would not have to be the optimistic idyllic love for "humankind" to which the 18th century vowed gentle tears and to which, by the way, civilization owes enormous progress. When Nietzsche proclaims: "God is dead"—a decision which for him meant the hardest of all sacrifices—in whose honor, in whose exaltation did he do so other than of man? If he was, if he was able to be, an atheist, then he was one, no matter how pastoral and sentimental the word sounds, because of his love for humankind. He must accept being called a humanist, just as he must suffer having his criticism of morals understood as a last form of the enlightenment. The superdenominational religiousness he mentions I cannot conceive of other than tied to the idea of mankind, as a religiously based and tinted humanism which, deeply experienced, would have passed through a great deal and would accept all knowledge of what is infernal and demonic into its tribute to the human mystery.

Religion is reverence, reverence first of all for the mystery that is man. When a new order, new ties, the adaptation of human society to the requirements of a fateful moment in the history of the world are at stake, then decisions of conferences, technical measures and juridical institutions are certainly of little avail and World Government remains a rational Utopia. It is necessary first of all to change the spiritual climate, to create a new feeling for the difficulties and the nobleness of human sentiency, an all pervading, fundamental philosophy from which no one exempts himself, which everyone deep within himself acknowledges as his supreme judge. Toward its creation and stabilization the poet and artist, working imperceptibly downward into breadth from on top, can contribute to some extent. But these things are not taught and made, they are experienced in suffering.

That philosophy is no cold abstraction, but experience, suffering and sacrificial deed for humanity, was Nietzsche's knowledge and example. In the course of it, he was driven upward into the icy wastes of grotesque error, but the future was in truth the land of his love, and for posterity, as for us, whose youth is incalculably indebted to him, he will stand, a figure full of delicate and venerable tragedy and enveloped by the flashing summer lightning that heralds the dawn of a new time.

From Poe to Valéry

T. S. Eliot

Presented at the Library of Congress November 19, 1948

WHAT I ATTEMPT here is not a judicial estimate of Edgar Allan Poe; I am not trying to decide his rank as a poet or to isolate his essential originality. Poe is indeed a stumbling block for the judicial critic. If we examine his work in detail, we seem to find in it nothing but slip-shod writing, puerile thinking unsupported by wide reading or profound scholarship, haphazard experiments in various types of writing, chiefly under pressure of financial need, without perfection in any detail. This would not be just. But if, instead of regarding his work analytically, we take a distant view of it as a whole, we see a mass of unique shape and impressive size to which the eye constantly returns. Poe's influence is equally puzzling. In France the influence of his poetry and of his poetic theories has been immense. In England and America it seems almost negligible. Can we point to any poet whose style appears to have been formed by a study of Poe? The only one whose name immediately suggests itself is—Edward Lear. And yet one cannot be sure that one's own writing has *not* been influenced by Poe. I can name positively certain poets whose work has influenced me, I can name others whose work, I am sure, has not; there may be still others of whose influence I am unaware, but whose influence I might be brought to acknowledge; but about Poe I shall never be sure. He wrote a very few poems, and of those few only half a dozen have had a great success: but those few are as well known to as large a number of people, are as well remembered by everybody, as any poems ever written. And some of his tales have had an important influence upon authors, and in types of writing where such influence would hardly be expected.

I shall here make no attempt to explain the enigma. At most, this is a contribution to the study of his influence; and an elucidation, partial

74

as it may be, of one cause of Poe's importance in the light of that influence. I am trying to look at him, for a moment, as nearly as I can, through the eyes of three French poets, Baudelaire, Mallarmé and especially Paul Valéry. The sequence is itself important. These three French poets represent the beginning, the middle and the end of a particular tradition in poetry. Mallarmé once told a friend of mine that he came to Paris because he wanted to know Baudelaire; that he had once seen him at a bookstall on a quai, but had not had the courage to accost him. As for Valéry, we know from the first letter to Mallarmé, written when he was hardly more than a boy, of his discipleship of the elder poet; and we know of his devotion to Mallarmé until Mallarmé's death. Here are three literary generations, representing almost exactly a century of French poetry. Of course, these are poets very different from each other; of course, the literary progeny of Baudelaire was numerous and important, and there are other lines of descent from him. But I think we can trace the development and descent of one particular theory of the nature of poetry through these three poets and it is a theory which takes its origin in the theory, still more than in the practice, of Edgar Poe. And the impression we get of the influence of Poe is the more impressive, because of the fact that Mallarmé, and Valéry in turn, did not merely derive from Poe through Baudelaire: each of them subjected himself to that influence directly, and has left convincing evidence of the value which he attached to the theory and practice of Poe himself. Now, we all of us like to believe that we understand our own poets better than any foreigner can do; but I think we should be prepared to entertain the possibility that these Frenchmen have seen something in Poe that English-speaking readers have missed.

My subject, then, is not simply Poe but Poe's effect upon three French poets, representing three successive generations; and my purpose is also to approach an understanding of a peculiar attitude towards poetry, by the poets themselves, which is perhaps the most interesting, possibly the most characteristic, and certainly the most original development of the esthetic of verse made in that period as a whole. It is all the more worthy of examination if, as I incline to believe, this attitude towards poetry represents a phase which has come to an end with the death of Valéry. For our study of it should help towards the understanding of whatever it may be that our generation and the next will find to take its place.

Before concerning myself with Poe as he appeared in the eyes of these French poets, I think it as well to present my own impression of his status among American and English readers and critics; for, if I am wrong, you may have to criticise what I say of his influence in France with my errors in mind. It does not seem to me unfair to say that Poe has been regarded as a minor, or secondary, follower of the Romantic Movement: a successor to the so-called "Gothic" novelists in his fiction, and a follower of Byron and Shelley in his verse. This however is to place him in the English tradition; and there certainly he does not belong. English readers sometimes account for that in Poe which is outside of any English tradition, by saying that it is American; but this does not seem to me wholly true either, especially when we consider the other American writers of his own and an earlier generation. There is a certain flavour of provinciality about his work, in a sense in which Whitman is not in the least provincial: it is the provinciality of the person who is not at home where he belongs, but cannot get to anywhere else. Poe is a kind of displaced European; he is attracted to Paris, to Italy and to Spain, to places which he could endow with romantic gloom and grandeur. Although his ambit of movement hardly extended beyond the limits of Richmond and Boston longitudinally, and neither east nor west of these centres, he seems a wanderer with no fixed abode. There can be few authors of such eminence who have drawn so little from their own roots, who have been so isolated from any surroundings.

I believe the view of Poe taken by the ordinary cultivated English or American reader is something like this: Poe is the author of a few, a very few short poems which enchanted him for a time when he was a boy, and which do somehow stick in the memory. I do not think that he re-reads these poems, unless he turns to them in the pages of an anthology; his enjoyment of them is rather the memory of an enjoyment which he may for a moment recapture. They seem to him to belong to a particular period when his interest in poetry had just awakened. Certain images, and still more certain rhythms, abide with him. This reader also remembers certain of the tales—not very many— and holds the opinion that *The Gold Bug* was quite good for its time, but that detective fiction has made great strides since then. And he may sometimes contrast him with Whitman, having frequently re-read Whitman, but not Poe.

As for the prose, it is recognised that Poe's tales had great influence upon some types of popular fiction. So far as detective fiction is concerned, nearly everything can be traced to two authors: Poe and Wilkie Collins. The two influences sometimes concur, but are also responsible for two different types of detective. The efficient professional policeman originates with Collins, the brilliant and eccentric amateur with Poe. Conan Doyle owes much to Poe, and not merely to Monsieur Dupin of *The Murders in the Rue Morgue*. Sherlock Holmes was deceiving Watson when he told him that he had bought his Stradivarius violin for a few shillings at a second-hand shop in the Tottenham Court Road. He found that violin in the ruins of the house of Usher. There is a close similarity between the musical exercises of Holmes and those of Roderick Usher: those wild and irregular improvisations which, although on one occasion they sent Watson off to sleep, must have been excruciating to any ear trained to music. It seems to me probable that the romances of improbable and incredible adventure of Rider Haggard found their inspiration in Poe—and Haggard himself had imitators enough. I think it equally likely that H. G. Wells, in his early romances of scientific exploration and invention, owed much to the stimulus of some of Poe's narratives—*Gordon Pym,* or *A Descent into the Maelstrom* for example, or *The Facts in the Case of Monsieur Valdemar.* The compilation of evidence I leave to those who are interested to pursue the enquiry. But I fear that nowadays too few readers open *She* or *The War of the Worlds* or *The Time Machine:* fewer still are capable of being thrilled by their predecessors.

What strikes me first, as a general difference between the way in which the French poets whom I have cited took Poe, and the way of American and English critics of equivalent authority, is the attitude of the former towards Poe's *œuvre,* towards his work as a whole. Anglo-Saxon critics are, I think, more inclined to make separate judgements of the different parts of an author's work. We regard Poe as a man who dabbled in verse and in several kinds of prose, without settling down to make a thoroughly good job of any one *genre.* These French readers were impressed by the variety of form of expression, because they found, or thought they found, an essential unity; while admitting, if necessary, that much of the work is fragmentary or occasional, owing to circumstances of poverty, frailty and vicissitude, they nevertheless take him as an author of such seriousness that his work must be grasped as a whole. This represents partly a difference between two kinds of critical mind; but we must claim, for our own view, that it is supported by our awareness of the blemishes and imperfections of Poe's actual writing. It is worth while to illustrate these faults, as they strike an English-speaking reader.

Poe had, to an exceptional degree, the feeling for the incantatory element in poetry, of that which may, in the most nearly literal sense, be called "the magic of verse." His versification is not, like that of the greatest masters of prosody, of the kind which yields a richer melody, through study and long habituation, to the maturing sensibility of the reader returning to it at times throughout his life. Its effect is immediate and undeveloping; it is probably much the same for the sensitive schoolboy and for the ripe mind and cultivated ear. In this unchanging immediacy, it partakes perhaps more of the character of very good *verse* than of poetry—but that is to start a hare which I have no intention of following here, for it is, I am sure, "poetry" and not "verse." It has the effect of an incantation which, because of its very crudity, stirs the feelings at a deep and almost primitive level. But, in his choice of the word which has the right *sound*, Poe is by no means careful that it should have also the right *sense*. I will give one comparison of uses of the same word by Poe and by Tennyson—who, of all English poets since Milton, had probably the most accurate and fastidious appreciation of the sound of syllables. In Poe's *Ulalume*—to my mind one of his most successful, as well as typical, poems—we find the lines

> *It was night, in the lonesome October*
> *Of my most immemorial year.*

Immemorial, according to the Oxford Dictionary, means: "that is beyond memory or out of mind; ancient beyond memory or record: extremely old." None of these meanings seems applicable to this use of the word by Poe. The year was not beyond memory—the speaker remembers one incident in it very well; at the conclusion he even remembers a funeral in the same place just a year earlier. The line of Tennyson, equally well known, and justly admired because the sound of the line responds so well to the sound which the poet wishes to evoke, may already have come to mind:

> *The moan of doves in immemorial elms.*

Here *immemorial*, besides having the most felicitous sound value, is exactly the word for trees so old that no one knows just how old they are.

Poetry, of different kinds, may be said to range from that in which the attention of the reader is directed primarily to the sound, to that in which it is directed primarily to the sense. With the former kind, the sense may be apprehended almost unconsciously; with the latter kind—at these two extremes—it is the sound, of the operation of which upon us we are unconscious. But, with either type, sound and sense must cooperate; in even the most purely incantatory poem, the dictionary meaning of words cannot be disregarded with impunity.

An irresponsibility towards the meaning of words is not infrequent with Poe. *The Raven* is, I think, far from being Poe's best poem; though, partly because of the analysis which the author gives in *The Philosophy of Composition*, it is the best known.

> *In there stepped a stately Raven of the saintly days of yore,*

Since there is nothing particularly saintly about the raven, if indeed the

78

ominous bird is not wholly the reverse, there can be no point in referring his origin to a period of saintliness, even if such a period can be assumed to have existed. We have just heard the raven described as *stately*; but we are told presently that he is *ungainly*, an attribute hardly to be reconciled, without a good deal of explanation, with *stateliness*. Several words in the poem seem to be inserted either merely to fill out the line to the required measure, or for the sake of a rhyme. The bird is addressed as "no craven" quite needlessly, except for the pressing need of a rhyme to "raven"—a surrender to the exigencies of rhyme with which I am sure Malherbe would have had no patience. And there is not always even such schoolboy justification as this: to say that the lamplight "gloated o'er" the sofa cushions is a freak of fancy which, even were it relevant to have a little gloating going on somewhere, would appear forced.

Imperfections in *The Raven* such as these—and one could give others—may serve to explain why *The Philosophy of Composition*, the essay in which Poe professes to reveal his method in composing *The Raven* —has not been taken so seriously in England or America as in France. It is difficult for us to read that essay without reflecting, that if Poe plotted out his poem with such calculation, he might have taken a little more pains over it: the result hardly does credit to the method. Therefore we are likely to draw the conclusion that Poe in analysing his poem was practising either a hoax, or a piece of self-deception in setting down the way in which he wanted to think that he had written it. Hence the essay has not been taken so seriously as it deserves.

Poe's other essays in poetic esthetic deserve consideration also. No poet, when he writes his own *art poétique*, should hope to do much more than explain, rationalise, defend or prepare the way for his own practice: that is, for writing his own kind of poetry. He may think that he is establishing laws for all poetry; but what he has to say that is worth saying has its immediate relation to the way in which he himself writes or wants to write: though it may well be equally valid to his immediate juniors, and extremely helpful to them. We are only safe in finding, in his writing about poetry, principles valid for any poetry, so long as we check what he says by the kind of poetry he writes. Poe has a remarkable passage about the impossibility of writing a long poem—for a long poem, he holds, is at best a series of short poems strung together. What we have to bear in mind is that he himself was incapable of writing a long poem. He could conceive only a poem which was a single simple effect: for him, the whole of a poem had to be in one mood. Yet it is only in a poem of some length that a variety of moods can be expressed; for a variety of moods requires a number of different themes or subjects, related either in themselves or in the mind of the poet. These parts can form a whole which is more than the sum of the parts; a whole such that the pleasure we derive from the reading of any part is enhanced by our grasp of the whole. It follows also that in a long poem some parts may be deliberately planned to be less "poetic" than others: these passages may show no lustre when extracted, but may be intended to elicit, by contrast, the significance of other parts, and to unite them into a whole more significant than any of the parts. A long poem may gain by the widest possible variations of intensity. But Poe wanted a poem to be of the first intensity throughout: it is questionable whether he could have appreciated the more philosophical passages in Dante's *Purgatorio*. What Poe had said has proved in the past of great comfort to other poets equally incapable of the long poem; and we must recognize that the question of the possibility of writing a long poem is not simply that of the strength and staying power of the individual poet, but may have to do with the conditions of the age in which he finds himself. And what Poe has to say on the subject is illuminating, in helping us to understand the point of view of poets for whom the long poem is impossible.

The fact that for Poe a poem had to be the expression of a single mood—it would here be too long an excursus to try to demonstrate that *The Bells,* as a deliberate exercise in several moods, is as much a poem of one mood as any of Poe's—this fact can better be understood as a manifestation of a more fundamental weakness. Here, what I have to say I put forward only tentatively: but it is a view which I should like to launch in order to see what becomes of it. My account may go to explain, also, why the work of Poe has for many readers appealed at a particular phase of their growth, at the period of life when they were just emerging from childhood. That Poe had a powerful intellect is undeniable: but it seems to me the intellect of a highly gifted young person before puberty. The forms which his lively curiosity takes are those in which a pre-adolescent mentality delights: wonders of nature and of mechanics and of the supernatural, cryptograms and cyphers, puzzles and labyrinths, mechanical chess-players and wild flights of speculation. The variety and ardour of his curiosity delight and dazzle; yet in the end the eccentricity and lack of coherence of his interests tire. There is just that lacking which gives dignity to the mature man: a consistent view of life. An attitude can be mature and consistent, and yet be highly sceptical: but Poe was no sceptic. He appears to yield himself completely to the idea of the moment: the effect is, that all of his ideas seem to be *entertained* rather than believed. What is lacking is not brain power, but that maturity of intellect which comes only with the maturing of the man as a whole, the development and coordination of his various emotions. I am not concerned with any possible

80

psychological or pathological explanation: it is enough for my purpose to record that the work of Poe is such as I should expect of a man of very exceptional mind and sensibility, whose emotional development has been in some respect arrested at an early age. His most vivid imaginative realisations are the realisation of a dream: significantly, the ladies in his poems and tales are always ladies lost, or ladies vanishing before they can be embraced. Even in *The Haunted Palace,* where the subject appears to be his own weakness of alcoholism, the disaster has no moral significance; it is treated impersonally as an isolated phenomenon; it has not behind it the terrific force of such lines as those of François Villon when he speaks of his own fallen state.

Having said as much as this about Poe, I must proceed to enquire what it was that three great French poets found in his work to admire, which we have not found. We must first take account of the fact that none of these poets knew the English language very well. Baudelaire must have read a certain amount of English and American poetry: he certainly borrows from Gray, and apparently from Emerson. He was never familiar with England, and there is no reason to believe that he spoke the language at all well. As for Mallarmé, he taught English and there is convincing evidence of his imperfect knowledge, for he committed himself to writing a kind of guide to the use of the language. An examination of this curious treatise, and the strange phrases which he gives under the impression that they are familiar English proverbs, should dispel any rumour of Mallarmé's English scholarship. As for Valéry, I never heard him speak a word of English, even in England. I do not know what he had read in our language: Valéry's second language, the influence of which is perceptible in some of his verse, was Italian.

It is certainly possible, in reading something in a language imperfectly understood, for the reader to find what is not there; and when the reader is himself a man of genius, the foreign poem read may, by a happy accident, elicit something important from the depths of his own mind, which he attributes to what he reads. And it is true that in translating Poe's prose into French, Baudelaire effected a striking improvement: he transformed what is often a slipshod and a shoddy English prose into admirable French. Mallarmé, who translated a number of Poe's poems into French prose, effected a similar improvement: but on the other hand, the rhythms, in which we find so much of the originality of Poe, are lost. The evidence that the French overrated Poe because of their imperfect knowledge of English remains accordingly purely negative: we can venture no farther than saying that they were not disturbed by weaknesses of which we are very much aware. It does not account for their high opinion of Poe's *thought*, for the value which they attached to his philosophical and critical exercises. To understand that we must look elsewhere.

We must, at this point, avoid the error of assuming that Baudelaire, Mallarmé and Valéry all responded to Poe in exactly the same way. They are great poets, and they are each very different from the other; furthermore, they represent, as I have reminded you, three different generations. It is with Valéry that I am here chiefly concerned. I therefore say only that Baudelaire, to judge by his introduction to his translation of the tales and essays, was the most concerned with the personality of the man. With the accuracy of his portrait I am not concerned: the point is that in Poe, in his life, his isolation and his worldly failure, Baudelaire found the prototype of *le poète maudit*, the poet as the outcast of society—the type which was to realise itself, in different ways, in Verlaine and Rimbaud, the type of which Baudelaire saw himself as a distinguished example. This nineteenth-century archetype, *le poète maudit*, the rebel against society and against middle-class morality (a rebel who descends of course from the continental myth of the figure of Byron) corresponds to a particular social situation. But, in the course of an introduction which is primarily a sketch of the man Poe and his biography, Baudelaire lets fall one remark indicative of an esthetic that brings us to Valéry:

> He believed [says Baudelaire], true poet that he was, that the goal of poetry is of the same nature as its principle, and that it should have nothing in view but itself.

"A poem does not say something—it *is* something:" that doctrine has been held in more recent times.

The interest for Mallarmé is rather in the technique of verse, though Poe's is, as Mallarmé recognises, a kind of versification which does not lend itself to use in the French language. But when we come to Valéry, it is neither the man nor the poetry, but the *theory* of poetry, that engages his attention. In a very early letter to Mallarmé, written when he was a very young man, introducing himself to the elder poet, he says: "I prize the theories of Poe, so profound and so insidiously learned; I believe in the omnipotence of rhythm, and especially in the suggestive phrase." But I base my opinion, not primarily upon this credo of a very young man, but upon Valéry's subsequent theory and practice. In the same way that Valéry's poetry, and his essays on the art of poetry, are two aspects of the same interest of his mind and complement each other, so for Valéry the poetry of Poe is inseparable from Poe's poetic theories.

This brings me to the point of considering the meaning of the term "la poésie pure:" the French phrase has a connotation of discussion and argument which is not altogether rendered by the term "pure poetry."

All poetry may be said to start from the emotions experienced by human beings in their relations to themselves, to each other, to divine beings, and to the world about them; it is therefore concerned also with thought and action, which emotion brings about, and out of which emotion arises. But, at however primitive a stage of expression and appreciation, the function of poetry can never be simply to arouse these same emotions in the audience of the poet. You remember the account of Alexander's feast in the famous ode of Dryden. If the conqueror of Asia was actually transported with the violent emotions which the bard Timotheus, by skilfully varying his music, is said to have aroused in him, then the great Alexander was at the moment suffering from automatism induced by alcohol poisoning, and was in that state completely incapable of appreciating musical or poetic art. In the earliest poetry, or in the most rudimentary enjoyment of poetry, the attention of the listener is directed upon the subject matter; the effect of the poetic art is felt, without the listener being wholly conscious of this art. With the development of the consciousness of language, there is another stage, at which the auditor, who may by that time have become the reader, is aware of a double interest in a story for its own sake, and in the way in which it is told: that is to say, he becomes aware of style. Then we may take a delight in discrimination between the ways in which different poets will handle the same subject; an appreciation not merely of better or worse, but of differences between styles which are equally admired. At a third stage of development, the subject may recede to the background: instead of being the purpose of the poem, it becomes simply a necessary means for the realisation of the poem. At this stage the reader or listener may become as nearly indifferent to the subject matter as the primitive listener was to the style. A complete unconsciousness or indifference to the style at the beginning, or to the subject matter at the end, would however take us outside of poetry altogether: for a complete unconsciousness of anything but subject matter would mean that for that listener poetry had not yet appeared; a complete unconsciousness of anything but style would mean that poetry had vanished.

This process of increasing self-consciousness—or, we may say, of increasing consciousness of language—has as its theoretical goal what we may call *la poésie pure*. I believe it to be a goal that can never be reached, because I think that poetry is only poetry so long as it preserves some "impurity" in this sense: that is to say, so long as the subject matter is valued for its own sake. The Abbé Brémond, if I have understood him, maintains that while the element of *la poésie pure* is necessary to make a poem a poem, no poem can consist of *la poésie pure* solely. But what has happened in the case of Valéry is a change of attitude toward the subject matter. We must be careful to avoid saying that the subject matter becomes "less important." It has rather a different kind of importance: it is important as *means:* the *end* is the poem. The subject exists for the poem, not the poem for the subject. A poem may employ several subjects, combining them in a particular way; and it may be meaningless to ask "What is the subject of the poem?" From the union of several subjects there appears, not another subject, but the poem.

Here I should like to point out the difference between a theory of poetry propounded by a student of esthetics, and the same theory as held by a poet. It is one thing when it is simply an account of how the poet writes, without knowing it, and another thing when the poet himself writes consciously according to that theory. In affecting writing, the theory becomes a different thing from what it was merely as an explanation of how the poet writes. And Valéry was a poet who wrote very consciously and deliberately indeed: perhaps, at his best, not wholly under the guidance of theory; but his theorising certainly affected the kind of poetry that he wrote. He was the most self-conscious of all poets.

To the extreme self-consciousness of Valéry must be added another trait: his extreme scepticism. It might be thought that such a man, without belief in anything which could be the subject of poetry, would find refuge in a doctrine of "art for art's sake." But Valéry was much too sceptical to believe even in art. It is significant, the number of times that he describes something he has written as an *ébauche*—a rough draft. He had ceased to believe in *ends*, and was only interested in *processes*. It often seems as if he had continued to write poetry, simply because he was interested in the introspective observation of himself engaged in writing it: one has only to read the several essays—sometimes indeed more exciting than his verse, because one suspects that he was more excited in writing them—in which he records his observations. There is a revealing remark in *Variété V*, the last of his books of collected papers: "As for myself, who am, I confess, much more concerned with the formation or the fabrication of works [of art] than with the works themselves," and, a little later in the same volume: "In my opinion the most authentic philosophy is not in the

84

objects of reflection, so much as in the very act of thought and its manipulation."

Here we have, brought to their culmination by Valéry, two notions which can be traced back to Poe. There is first the doctrine, elicited from Poe by Baudelaire, which I have already quoted: "A poem should have nothing in view but itself;" second the notion that the composition of a poem should be as conscious and deliberate as possible, that the poet should observe himself in the act of composition—and this, in a mind as sceptical as Valéry's, leads to the conclusion, so paradoxically inconsistent with the other, that the act of composition is more interesting than the poem which results from it.

First, there is the "purity" of Poe's poetry. In the sense in which we speak of "purity of language" Poe's poetry is very far from pure, for I have commented upon Poe's carelessness and unscrupulousness in the use of words. But in the sense of *la poésie pure*, that kind of purity came easily to Poe. The subject is little, the treatment is everything. He did not have to achieve purity by a process of purification, for his material was already tenuous. Second, there is that defect in Poe to which I alluded when I said that he did not appear to believe, but rather to entertain, theories. And here again, with Poe and Valéry, extremes meet, the immature mind playing with ideas because it had not developed to the point of convictions, and the very adult mind playing with ideas because it was too sceptical to hold convictions. It is by this contrast, I think, that we can account for Valéry's admiration for *Eureka*—that cosmological fantasy which makes no deep impression upon most of us, because we are aware of Poe's lack of qualification in philosophy, theology or natural science, but which Valéry, after Baudelaire, esteemed highly as a "prose poem." Finally, there is the astonishing result of Poe's analysis of the composition of *The Raven*. It does not matter whether *The Philosophy of Composition* is a hoax, or a piece of self-deception, or a more or less accurate record of Poe's calculations in writing the poem; what matters is that it suggested to Valéry a method and an occupation—that of observing himself write. Of course, a greater than Poe had already studied the poetic process. In the *Biographia Literaria* Coleridge is concerned primarily, of course, with the poetry of Wordsworth; and he did not pursue his philosophical enquiries concurrently with the writing of his poetry; but he does anticipate the question which fascinated Valéry: "What am I doing when I write a poem?" Yet Poe's *Philosophy of Composition* is a *mise au point* of the question which gives it capital importance in relation to this process which ends with Valéry. For the penetration of the poetic by the introspective critical activity is carried to the limit by Valéry, the limit at which the latter begins to destroy the former. M. Louis

Bolle, in his admirable study of this poet, observes pertinently: "This intellectual narcissism is not alien to the poet, even though he does not explain the whole of his work: 'why not conceive as a work of art the production of a work of art?'"

Now, as I think I have already hinted, I believe that the *art poétique* of which we find the germ in Poe, and which bore fruit in the work of Valéry, has gone as far as it can go. I do not believe that this esthetic can be of any help to later poets. What will take its place I do not know. An esthetic which merely contradicted it would not do. To insist on the all-importance of subject-matter, to insist that the poet should be spontaneous and irreflective, that he should depend upon inspiration and neglect technique, would be a lapse from what is in any case a highly civilised attitude to a barbarous one. We should have to have an esthetic which somehow comprehended and transcended that of Poe and Valéry. This question does not greatly exercise my mind, since I think that the poet's theories should arise out of his practice rather than his practice out of his theories. But I recognise first that within this tradition from Poe to Valéry are some of those modern poems which I most admire and enjoy; second, I think that the tradition itself represents the most interesting development of poetic consciousness anywhere in that same hundred years; and finally I value this exploration of certain poetic possibilities for its own sake, as we believe that all possibilities should be explored. And I find that by trying to look at Poe through the eyes of Baudelaire, Mallarmé and most of all Valéry, I become more thoroughly convinced of his importance, of the importance of his *work* as a whole. And, as for the future: it is a tenable hypothesis that this advance of self-consciousness, the extreme awareness of and concern for language which we find in Valéry, is something which must ultimately break down, owing to an increasing strain against which the human mind and nerves will rebel; just as, it may be maintained, the indefinite elaboration of scientific discovery and invention, and of political and social machinery, may reach a point at which there will be an irresistible revulsion of humanity and a readiness to accept the most primitive hardships rather than carry any longer the burden of modern civilisation. Upon that I hold no fixed opinion: I leave it to your consideration.

Goethe and Democracy

Thomas Mann

Presented at the Library of Congress May 2, 1949

TWO HUNDRED YEARS after Goethe's birth, one hundred and seventeen after his death, it seems appropriate to begin a lecture about him with the sentence: I have nothing new to tell you. From the very moment of its extinction and down through the decades, this wonderful, great, and rich life has been studied, its remotest nooks have been illuminated and displayed, the magnificent work of this life has been commented upon and celebrated, it has been plowed up by philologists and discussed by rhetoricians as the life and work of scarcely any other mortal has been plowed up and discussed. The feeling that we are too late with anything that we might say about this phenomenon is therefore only too well justified. *Tout est dit*—everything has been said—by Germans and non-Germans, and the bad part about it is that I, too, have said my share and have emptied my pockets. I have done so in half a dozen essays and in a full length novel, and if I now dare to speak about Goethe once more I am not only up against the competition of the entire world but also of myself.

Frankly, I am not very proud of these contributions, neither of the critical nor even of the artistic absorption in this life and this work— an absorption which actually brought me the reputation of a certain specialization, even of an imitative discipleship. I am not proud of it because it is the absorption of a German in a German phenomenon. I am far more impressed by all that has been contributed to the understanding of this great German figure since the days of Carlyle and Emerson down to Gide and Valéry and the English Goethe-researchers —in other words, by non-Germans. Many years ago I asked a friend whom I left behind in Germany, the famous Romance scholar Carl Vossler, why he had always devoted himself so decidedly to the study of the Latinic languages and literatures,—not Hoelderlin and Hebbel, but Dante, Racine, and Calderón, who were the subjects of his brilliant publication. He replied: "It was my need for the entirely different." His answer impressed me deeply, for honorable and right as that need appeared to me, I had to confess to myself that my own development had not been decisively influenced by it, that it had drawn its nourishment chiefly from the German soil, and that even as a critical writer and as a devout interpreter I had hardly ever served the foreign subject but almost always the indigenous one. I was ashamed of it, ashamed of my Germanic scholarship—for my inner feeling told me, and will never cease to tell me, that true culture begins with the knowledge, the conquest, the penetration of "the entirely different," the foreign language, culture, and spirit, and that the German should be the last to be content with his mother tongue; he, before all others, needs expansiveness, cosmopolitanism, knowledge and admiration and acceptance and assimilation of the foreign,—and this is the very thing that he can learn from his Goethe who, at the age of seventy-eight, said to Eckermann: "If we Germans do not look outside of the narrow circle of our own environment, we fall an easy prey to pedantic conceit. For that reason I like to look around in foreign nations, and I advise everyone else to do the same. National literature is of little consequence now, the epoch of world literature is at hand and everyone must do his share to hasten the arrival of this epoch."

The imitation of Goethe, the acknowledgment of him, therefore means anything but German provincialism—moreover I can say that if I wrote much on German and little on foreign themes, yet I always looked for the world, for Europe, in the German subject, and I was always unhappy when I did not find them. It is certainly not by chance that those German figures whom I chose as my teachers and guides, Schopenhauer, Nietzsche, Wagner, and, in later years above all, Goethe, all have a decidedly supra-German, European character. What I found in them was the European in German, a European Germany, the ultimate goal of my wishes and requirements—in contrast to a "German Europe," the horrid aspiration of German nationalism which always disgusted me and finally drove me from Germany. It need scarcely be said that these two concepts form the basis for the distinction which the world makes between a "good" and a "bad" Germany: a European Germany is in the broadest sense of the word a "democratic" Germany, a country with which one can live, which does not inspire fear but sympathy throughout the world, because it shares in the democratic humanitarian religion that categorically determines the moral life of the Occident and that is meant when we use the word "Civilization."

Most unfortunately, this European democracy never attained much political power in Germany, power never entered into a union with it as it did with other peoples, but this concept was historically almost synonymous with German impotence. "Poor in deeds and rich in ideas" was Hoelderlin's characterization of the old, pious, philosophic, and impotent Germany, and the description sounds loving, it sounds like acquiescence and assent. On the other hand, the German discrepancy between spirit and power, between ideas and deeds, the paradox of cultural rank and political misery have been the cause of much suffering. Goethe, a less ethereal character than Hoelderlin, suffered manifestly from it and occasionally cursed the eremitic theoreticism of the German character. "While the Germans," he said to Eckermann in 1829, "worry about the solution of philosophical problems, the English, with their great common sense, laugh at us and win the world."

Frankly, I am none too fond of this particular remark. In the first place, England by no means laughed at the poor, philosophical, and unpractical Germany of that day. On the contrary, England was filled with respect and admiration, and the many Englishmen who made the pilgrimage to the home of the aging Goethe should have been proof of it. In the second place, it was not proper to identify England only with practical, political sense and to make it synonymous with the East India Company. After all, England gave the world its greatest dramatic writer, a long line of distinguished thinkers and authors, and sublime lyric poetry, so that the quoted comment even has a slight air of national arrogance, almost as though the Germans were the chosen people of the spirit. In the third place, however, and this is the most serious of my objections, the word contains a certain provocation for the Germans to emulate England and to apply themselves to the winning of the world,—an instigation to competitive envy, in other words, which later played a most unfortunate role in German history.

These are objections to a word that was intended pedagogically and that is not, after all, without pedagogical value. For Goethe's praise of "common sense" is equivalent to an admonition to the spirit and the intellect not to hover in the clouds but to unite with life and to assume responsibility toward it. It points in the direction of *democratic pragmatism*, which has always been lacking in Germany, even when life was dionysiacally extolled as the greatest good, and the leading German poet took its side against the arrogance of the spirit in more than one instance. In this connection I quote Maurice Barrès, who called Goethe's *Iphigenia* "a civilizing work" which "defends the rights of society against the arrogance of the spirit"—a characterization that is almost more accurately descriptive of *Tasso*, this work of self-discipline and self-chastisement, even of self-castigation, a drama which goes to

89

the verge of sacrificing poesy and poetic inspiration to the prosaic demands of the social order and of "common sense"—to the great sorrow of poets like Rilke who regard it as a betrayal, namely the betrayal of art to life. The aristocratic solitude of art and its painful segregation from life are, to them, a matter of sentimental principle, and with repugnance they see Antonio, the appalling man of the world, triumphant in the drama.

This point was recently discussed in an excellent study by Eudo C. Mason, "Rilke and Goethe," in the *Publications of the English Goethe Society*, in which the author did not neglect to draw a parallel between Rilke's resentment against *Tasso* and the Goethe-criticism of Novalis. The latter called *Wilhelm Meister* a most unpoetic work, a "*Candide*, directed against poetry." In it, he said, everything romantic was destroyed, including nature poesy, the supernatural. Nothing remained but the economic aspects of nature. He called Goethe a purely practical writer, whose works were like the commodities produced by the English: very plain, tidy, comfortable, and durable . . . There is complete unanimity of opinion between Novalis and Rilke. They speak in the same voice, vibrant with delicate bitterness, the voice of poetic-aristocratic suffering from life, and resentment against him who took the side of life and who spoke the coolly negative words: "Art, of course, has nothing to do with suffering." On the other hand, he also expressed quite different views, as, for example, his words about Raffael in the *Italian Journey:* "For we surmise the fearful conditions under which alone even the most outspoken personality can rise to the ultimate of achievement." Who can doubt that he not only surmised these "fearful conditions," but that he actually experienced them? Who can doubt that all the concepts of harmony, of auspicious inner balance and classicality, were not lightly received but were a tremendous accomplishment, the work of powers of character, by which dangerous, perhaps even destructive traits were conquered, put to use, transfigured, turned into ethical channels, forcibly directed toward goodness and greatness? His life may well appear as an uphill sword-dance, full of love of the facile, of the just-barely-possible which was genius to boot, and it may be that genius is always the just-barely possible. This life has been called a perfect work of art; it should be called a perfect stunt. He himself characterized it so in the verse that he might have chosen as his epitaph:

"Wohl kamst du durch, so ging es allenfalls.
   Mach's einer nach und breche nicht den Hals."

(You managed to get through in one way or another.
   Let someone imitate you without breaking his neck!)

I was delighted to read the following passage in Barker Fairley's splendid book, *A Study on Goethe:* "He did not foresee the coming, in the century after him, of a point of view that would have preferred to have him go to pieces at all costs like a good poet rather than make a success of things, and if he had foreseen it there was something in him, fortunately, that would have rejected it. For if the impulse to survive is more valuable to humanity than the impulse to perish, then the life and work of Goethe, as we now have it, means more than it could possibly have meant if he had crumpled under the pressure of himself or failed to do what he did."

This "to make a success of things," this will to survive for the best interest of humanity—is there not something democratic about it, compared to—and contrasted with—the aristocratic-poetic will to perish? In the epilogue to Schiller's "Glocke" Goethe uses the word "lebenswuerdig" ("worthy of life"). "He who is worthy of life," he mourns, "is to become the prey of death." As a young man who had been granted the sweeping privilege of pessimism by Schopenhauer, I was deeply impressed by this expression which, as far as I know, is a personal word-creation of Goethe's. It confused my youthful concept of spirituality, artistic calling, poesy, which had actually amounted to a genteel uselessness and unfitness for life on earth. The time was still far off when I was to regard Goethe's will and ability "to make a success of things" under the most trying conditions as the greatest and most amiable of all models. But today I am only expressing what I felt at that time when I characterize his positive attitude toward life and his rejection of poetic destruction as a democratic trait, one that can hardly be termed German, and one that may have been responsible for his inner aloofness from all things German. "The Germans love death," said Georges Clémenceau during the First World War. "Just look at their literature! Basically they love nothing but death." There is a great deal of truth in it, but the psychologizing statesman cannot have had Goethe in mind, for Goethe resisted the German-Romantic cult of death, and fundamentally—I believe—it is as a friend to life that democratic Europe claims him as its own.

At this point a brief insert may be called for. Let us remember that Goethe was neither a systematic philosopher nor a rigid adherent of dogmas and opinions but that his productiveness stemmed from his polarity, from the inexhaustible wealth of contradictions he embraced and which often led his contemporaries to accuse him of a certain demonic nihilism. Thus it has been said that each and every thing could be proved by means of his pronouncements. Nevertheless, and notwithstanding the contradictions I am about to show forth, there is in Goethe a foundation of unshakably great humanity and of a reli-

91

able goodness which reconciles all contradictions in a lofty, almost god-like fashion. And I think you will find even the political contradictions evident in his Weltanschauung to be dissolved in this unfailing humanity.

I am well aware that we have to penetrate very deeply into things and to make the definition of democracy very broad in order to include Goethe in it. For in the narrower sense and on the surface there is overwhelming evidence of his antagonism to democracy, political and moral, an antagonism, however, which, again, is rooted in his positive attitude toward life, in his natural self-reliance as a favorite of the gods and the preferred child of the creative power, a lord of the world who would consider it a misfortune to be in the opposition. He said, for instance: "If I had the misfortune to be in the opposition . . .," forgetting, it seems, that the Tories are sometimes in the opposition, too. He was quite conscious of the affinity of delicateness and tenacity which constitutes the particular vitality of the genius, he often said that unusual people, as a result of their sensitiveness, are easily exposed to chronic ailments, and he was sick a good deal himself. And yet he loved to play the part of the robust son of the soil, the oak-tree, and to boast of his durability and longevity, which Valéry admired so much: "The thing that strikes me most about Goethe is his long life, an almost patriarchal span." He himself admired it and sometimes made humorous disparaging comments about the fickle vitality of others. At the age of eighty-one he said: "I hear that Soemmering (a distinguished German anatomist) died, just a miserable seventy-five years old. People are such shrinkers that they haven't the courage to hold out any longer than that! How much more commendable is my friend Bentham (the English utilitarian economist), that radical fool! He keeps plugging right along and he is even a few weeks older than I."

I don't know how many times I have told that anecdote. I am very fond of it on account of its wealth of implications, its manifold moral and psychological content—and I am thinking chiefly of the derision of Bentham's "radicalism," which is very much a part of the thing. His partner in the conversation remarked that if His Excellency had been born in England he would probably have been a radical too and would have campaigned against abuses in the government. And Goethe, with the mien of Mephistopheles, replied: "What do you take me for? I should hunt around for abuses and expose them into the bargain—I, who would have lived on abuses in England? If I had been born in England I should have been a rich duke, or rather a bishop with an annual income of thirty thousand pounds sterling." The other one reminds him that he might have drawn a blank in the lottery of life, there are so very many blanks! And Goethe: "Not every one, my friend, is fit to draw the grand prize. Do you think I would have been fool enough to draw a blank?" This is bravado, innate boastfulness, unqualified consciousness of superiority. Incidentally it reveals that he regards his birth and existence in Germany as a misfortune, compared to what he would have been in England. But the important thing is his metaphysical certainty that he would have been well born in any circumstances, the child of Lady Luck, a great lord and a man of the world—and that indignation over the corruption of the world is a matter for the underprivileged.

He was fond of an expression that is logically untenable but sounds grandly self-evident on his lips: he speaks of "innate deserts." What does it mean? That is wooden iron. Deserts are sounds grandly self-evident on his lips: he speaks of "innate is not merited, unless the word is detached from its moral context. But that is exactly what he intends. The expression is a conscious affront to morality, to all striving, struggling, endeavoring; these are laudable, at best, but not genteel and, in the final analysis, he considers them hopeless. "One has to *be* something," he declares, "in order to bring something into being." And when someone said that thinking was difficult, he answered: "The unfortunate thing is that no amount of thinking helps one to think. *You have to be right by nature* so that all your notions and images stand before you like free children of God and call to you: Here we are!"

He undoubtedly felt himself "right by nature," a nobleman by the grace of nature, and he asserted that he had never known a more presumptuous person than himself. Such self-esteem left no room for social ambition, for any kind of snobbishness. The patent of nobility that his duke secured from the emperor for him was "nothing, nothing at all," for, he said, "We Frankfurt patricians always regarded ourselves as peers of the nobility." And he added: "Yes, I felt so well in my own skin, I felt so genteel and well-born, that, if someone had made me a prince, I would not have found it strange in the least." Incidentally, it would have been entirely up to him if he had wished to be a prince. If he had followed Napoleon's invitation, as he was at times strongly tempted to do, if he had transferred his activity to Paris and had there written the "Caesar" for which Napoleon had asked and in which he could have given free rein to his youthful hatred of the "vile" and "base" murderers, the emperor would unquestionably have raised him to the rank of prince, just as he would have done for Corneille according to his own statement. In his old age his existence actually appeared in a princely light to his contemporaries, and certain epistolary addresses give evidence of the fact. French correspondents called him "Monseigneur," a princely title. An Englishman wrote: "To His Serene

Highness, Prince Goethe in Weimar." "That," the old man explained, "might be because people are wont to call me the prince of poets."

Yet, his status as a poet was only the guise that his greatness assumed in the poor, spiritual Germany, the "land of poets and thinkers," where reality was so absent. He was more than a poet: a sage, a ruler, the last representative and spiritual captain of Europe, a great man. And now the question arises, how far greatness is compatible with democracy—perhaps an imprudent question, at least with respect to Germany, where greatness has always had a tendency toward undemocratic hypertrophy. There is in Germany an abyss between greatness and the masses, a "pathos of distance," to use Nietzsche's favorite expression, which hardly exists elsewhere, in countries where greatness does not create serfdom on the one hand and an excessive development of absolutistic egocentricity on the other. Goethe's majestic old age had much of this absolutism and personal imperialism; the pressure of this old age upon everything that was trying to live in his vicinity was tremendous, and when he died it was not only a nymphal plaint for the great god Pan that was heard but also a very distinct sigh of relief.

His alliance with life—democratic in contrast to the poetic aristocratism of death—has many facets and angles that justify all doubts whether European democracy may claim him as its own. It is no coincidence that this alliance expresses itself in the same breath and sentence as a boast of his vital durability and derision of political radicalism. His antiradicalism is deeply rooted, it is primarily connected with his idea of perfection and necessity of all existence, of a world that is void of final causes and purposes and in which evil and good have equal rights. The absence of intent in artistic as well as in natural creation is his supreme maxim, and he regards his innate poetic talent as something "completely natural," a gift of Mother Nature who embraces good and bad alike. His early enthusiasm for Shakespeare has its roots here, and in the far future Goethe's nature-estheticism and anti-moralism was to have a profound influence on Nietzsche, the amoralist, who was to go a step farther and pronounce the preeminence of evil over good, its overwhelming importance for the preservation and triumph of life.

In Goethe, of course, this conviction still rests in calm, cheerful equilibrium, it is still objective and plastic. But just as this deification of nature, this Spinozistic pantheism, is the root of his indulgence, his tolerance, his willingness to live and let live, so it is also the root of his indifference, his lack of enthusiasm and rapture, for which he was often reproached, his contempt of ideas, and his hatred of the abstract, which he regarded as destructive to life. "General ideas and great conceit," was one of his maxims, "always tend to create horrible mischief." This is

94

the motto for his well-known unfriendly attitude toward the French revolution, on which he looked as something horrid. For he was deeply convinced that "the world, divided by reason, does not come out even," and he was further convinced that "law-givers and revolutionaries who promise liberty and equality at the same time are dreamers or charlatans." Who can deny that in this word he has touched upon the fundamental difficulty of democracy, the problem that holds the world enthralled today and that threatens to lead to a fearful altercation between the revolutionary principles of equality and of liberty?

It is a fact that the Great Revolution, as a world event, tortured him more than anything else in his life and almost robbed him of his talent —although in his *Werther*, that sensational product of his youth, whose wild sentimentalism shook the foundations of the old social order, he had not only been in prophetic touch with coming events but had even helped to prepare for them. It is common knowledge that we rarely want to see as a reality the thing we wanted with our emotions, and Goethe's attitude toward the Revolution is an exact repetition of that of Erasmus toward the Reformation, for which the latter had prepared the ground and which he then rejected with humanistic disgust. Goethe himself, though in many ways obliged to Luther, coupled the names of the two great "disturbances" disapprovingly in a famous distich:

"Franztum draengt in diesen verworrenen Tagen, wie einstmals
    Luthertum es getan, ruhige Bildung zurueck."
    (In these days of confusion Gallicism repels
      Tranquil culture, as Lutheranism did in its time.)

Tranquil culture—that was not the primary concern of the patriots who were trying to educate Germany to political liberty, and just as he suffered, so also many of his highly respectable contemporaries suffered, suffered bitterly and resentfully from him: from his "tremendously obstructing power," as Boerne expressed it, from his quietism and political apathy, from the forcefulness with which his nature opposed the national-democratic idea, the passion of the time. He was opposed to freedom of the press, opposed to free speech for the masses, opposed to constitution and rule of the majority, he was convinced that "everything sensible is in the minority," and he was openly on the side of the minister who carried out his plans against the wishes of the people and the king. Picture him standing at the side of the throne in April 1816, at the inauguration of the constitution, Prime Minister of the new Grand Duchy of Saxe-Weimar by rank and title, proudly erect, the star of the "White Falcon" on his breast! He was disgusted with the entire proceeding. He had advised his ruler against attending the Congress of

Vienna which, in the end, increased the area of the little country by more than one-half and raised Karl August to the rank of Grand Duke. But the "Vienna Agreements" promised every German state a "representative constitution," and for that reason Goethe was unwilling to see his country bound by them. He can hardly be credited with statesmanlike foresight for wishing to prevent the Duke from attending the Congress. He had little of that in any case. He had firmly believed in Napoleon's eternal destiny, had assumed a most unpatriotic attitude during the Wars of the Liberation, and had said: "Rattle your chains as you will, my friends, the man is too big for you!" "The man is too big for you,"—there is truth in the words, and simply because he was too big for them he was defeated with united strength so that, in effect, Goethe was wrong and had to apologize in his *Epimenides*. He was similarly wrong with his determined opposition to early German efforts at unification, to the plan of Frederick the Great in 1784 to organize a federation of German princes, without and against Austria, that is, to create a unified Germany on a dynastic-national basis under Prussian leadership and excluding the House of Habsburg. The project, which appealed strongly to Karl August, was dropped for the time being. But it was the way that Bismarck went later, the way of history, and Goethe could not and would not see it. But no matter what the course of history may be, the essence of history is that something happens. Goethe, however, did not like history, he called the politics of this world a "medley of mistakes and violence."

It often appears as though he had little or no humanitarian faith in man, in mankind, in their revolutionary purgation, in their better future. Men cannot be taught reason and justice. There will be no end of wavering, no end of fighting and bloodshed. If he had only said these things in an access of pessimistic grief! But fundamentally he was satisfied that it had to be so, for there was little of the pacifist about him. On the contrary, he had a feeling for power, for strife, "until one proves his superiority over the other," that is strongly reminiscent of the word of Wagner's Wotan: "Where forces fearlessly stir, I frankly counsel war." Parenthetically it must be said, however, that he had no illusions about war, that he called it "in truth a disease in which the juices needed for the preservation of health are diverted to nourish something foreign, something incompatible with nature." But from a personal point of view, he remarks that it "makes him sad to be on good terms with everybody," and that he "needs anger." That can hardly be called Christian concord, although it is Lutheran and Bismarckian, too. Much evidence could be adduced of his belligerency, his eagerness "to strike in and punish," his readiness forcibly to silence adverse opinions and to "remove such people from polite society." All that, if one wishes, is only three feet or less removed from the brutal—and the same is true in general of his realism, his lack of idealistic enthusiasm, the sensuality of his nature that made him regard the pillaging of a farm as something real and worthy of sympathy but the "ruin of the fatherland" as a mere phrase.

His skepticism of liberal forms of government is deep seated. It will be found, he said, that "great kindness, leniency, and moral delicateness, applied from above, will not avail in the long run, since the ruler has to deal with a mixed and frequently wicked world and has to keep it in awe of him,"—a comment reminiscent even to its wording of his political disciple, Schopenhauer. In matters of criminal justice he was decidedly opposed to softheartedness and weakness; he was annoyed with the humanitarian tendency of the time to commute the sentences of criminals on the basis of medical opinions and certificates. He listened with satisfaction to the report of a resolute young physician on the question of the sanity of a certain woman who had killed her child, and when he stated that she was undoubtedly sane, Goethe commented: "She is not the first one." He was not in sympathy with the emancipation of Jews which was promulgated by the great Emperor whom he admired. It would not be long, he said, before they would have a Jewish chief-lady-in-waiting at the Weimar court.

He was an aristocrat in his relation to the masses and he found them respectable only in physical action, miserable in rational judgment. One of his rhymed epigrams says as much. For him, masses and culture were incompatible, for he thought of culture as a select society who converse discreetly about sublime matters with a smile. Which is why he was far from expecting his works to become popular. "Whoever thinks so and works for it," he said, "is in error. They were not written for the masses but only for a few people who want and seek something of the sort." Strangely, however, he declared at the same time that all criticism directed against his books (for example, *Werther*) had not hurt him at all, because such subjective opinions of individuals, no matter how distinguished, had been fully outweighed by the mass of readers. *But a writer who did not expect a million readers,* he concluded, *should refrain from writing a single line!*

Be that as it may: the better part of his life was devoted to his personal culture, and "to raise the pyramid of his existence as high as possible,"—and not to the improvement of the world. And he attaches immortality, finally, to the glory of personal achievement while he leaves the common herd to eternal damnation. "Whoever made no name for himself and had no noble aspirations belongs to the elements —away with him!" No one ever spoke a more aristocratic word. It expresses belief in predestination, and if that is a Christian concept then it certainly displays the most aristocratic aspect of Christianity.

And yet Christianity is democracy in the form of religion—just as it may be said that democracy is the political expression of Christianity. Goethe grasps the revolutionary spirit of Christianity in the remark: "The Christian religion is an intended political revolution, which, when it failed, became moral." That is an objective statement and it says nothing about his personal relation to Christianity. But, we must insist, what was his attitude toward it? What did he think about faith, about piety in general? I should like to quote a verse that speaks strongly to my heart, that I regard with infinite sympathy:

> "Ich habe nichts gegen die Froemmigkeit,
> Sie ist zugleich Bequemlichkeit;
> Wer ohne Froemmigkeit will leben,
> Muss grosser Muehe sich ergeben:
> Auf seine eigene Hand zu wandern,
> Sich selbst genuegen und den andern
> Und freilich auch dabei vertraun,
> Gott werde wohl auf ihn niederschaun."

(I have nothing against piety, it is a form of convenience. Whoever wants to live without piety must go to great pains: he must wander on his own, be sufficient to himself and satisfy others, and yet trust that God will graciously look down on him.)

He has faith in the good will from above even if—or especially if—he is not in the safe haven of a religion but is doing the best he can, in unprotected freedom, and on his own responsibility. The verse has a Protestant ring and it might not be too farfetched to say that a Protestant heritage and education keeps some of us today from finding a safe haven in the Communistic faith. But it is very curious that Goethe occasionally represents Protestantism as a kind of reconciliation of primitive Germanic paganism and sovereign individualism with Christianity.

> "Den deutschen Mannen gereicht's zum Ruhm,
> Dass sie gehasst das Christentum,
> Bis Herrn Karolus' leidigem Degen
> Die edlen Sachsen unterlegen,
> Und sie sich unters Joch geduckt;
> Doch haben sie immer einmal gemuckt.
> Sie lagen nur im halben Schlaf,
> Als Luther die Bibel verdeutscht so brav.

————————————————————

> Freiheit erwacht in jeder Brust,
> Wir protestieren all mit Lust."

> (It redounds to the honor of German manhood that they hated Christianity until the noble Saxons were conquered by Emperor Charles's grievous sword; and then they bowed under the yoke, yet always rebelled from time to time. They were only half asleep when Luther so valiantly Germanized the Bible. . . Liberty lives in every breast, and lustily we all protest.)

That sounds as though Protestantism were only an adaptation of Christianity to Germanic paganism—a good bit of which was alive in Goethe and for which he uttered many open and challenging attestations. We know them only too well. He called himself a "decided non-Christian," expressed his antipathy for the "Cross," vowed that humility and suffering were not for him, and declared proudly:

> "Haett' Allah mich bestimmt zum Wurm,
> So haett' er mich als Wurm erschaffen."

> (Had Allah meant me for a worm,
> In shape of worm he would have formed me.)

Very well, that is Goethe, the aristocrat. But it is a priori unthinkable that the fashioning of a spirit like his should not have been most strongly influenced by the most comprehensive revolution—or rather, mutation—that the human conscience and world consciousness has ever experienced. He must, at least, have thought of it as Lichtenberg did who, in view of the fact that a religious creation like the Christian one could never be repeated on earth, and in view of its civilizing force, decided: "We should therefore keep it." It is the civilizing force of Christianity that Goethe stressed, when, late in life, he definitely established his attitude toward religion in a conversation with Eckermann. The historical accuracy of the Gospels in every detail, he said, was not a matter of consequence. "In them there is a reflection of a sublimity that emanates from the person of Christ, of such a divine character as the divine has ever appeared on earth. . . Let intellectual culture advance as it will, let the natural sciences grow to greater and greater dimensions and depth, let the human spirit expand as it will— they will never transcend the sublimity and the moral culture of Christianity that gleams and shines in the Gospels!" It was the "moral culture" of Christianity, its humanitarianism, its civilizing, anti-barbarous tendency to which he bowed, for it was also his own tendency, and these eulogies undoubtedly spring from a feeling of alliance, an understanding of the affinity of the Christian mission in the tribal Germanic world with his own. It is a fundamentally democratic mission, for compassion with the lowly, exaltation of suffering are innate in Christianity, and nothing can be more Christian, and nothing more democratic in the finest sense than Goethe's dictum: "All suffering has something of the divine."

His Christianity, as a natural ingredient of his personality, has a Protestant tinge. He is a product of Protestant culture, and a work like *Werther* is unthinkable without long schooling in Pietistic introspection. Nietzsche was quite right when he designated Goethe's spiritual position as "halfway between Hellenism and Pietism." It is striking, however, that, in his comments on Protestantism, on Lutheranism, he stresses most strongly its democratic tendencies, and in his criticism of the Catholic Church and its hierarchy he suddenly begins to speak of the "lower masses." "The Church wants to rule," he says with a certain political acumen, "and therefore it needs an ignorant body of people who cringe and permit themselves to be ruled. The richly endowed high clergy fear nothing as much as the enlightenment of the lower masses. For that reason they have kept the Bible from them for a long time, as long a time as possible. And what would you expect a poor, Christian member of a congregation to think of the regal splendor of a richly endowed bishop when he reads in the Gospels of the poverty and neediness of Christ and his disciples! We have no idea," he exclaims, "what we owe to Luther and to the Reformation in general. We have been liberated from the bonds of spiritual ignorance. . . We have been given the means of returning to the source and to understand Christianity in its pure form. . ." What Luther brought was religious democracy, and Goethe affirms it. He is infinitely more refined, more genteel, more delicate than the man of the people, the ruffian of Wittenberg, and yet he is deeply and strongly attracted to him, he feels a genuine national-personal affinity, a recognition of himself. As a young man he incorporated the Bible translations into his *Faust* and he always had the highest esteem for Luther's linguistic work as his heir and refining continuator, adding the comment: "I might only have improved upon the tender passages, if at all."

And yet his Protestantism is not quite reliable: he is capable of admiration, not so much of the esthetic superiority as, surprisingly, of the democratically unifying forces of Catholic life. They are stronger, more satisfying, he finds, than the Protestant ones. "One should really become Catholic," he exclaimed, "to share in the existence of the people. To mingle with them as equals, to live with them in the marketplace. What miserable, lonely humans we are, in our little sovereign states!" And he lauds Venice, as a monument, not to a ruler, but to a people.

"Life among the people"—that, too, is Goethe, from the days of his early youth. Children, people, nature—the love, the *mutual* love, of the Werther-youth. We need not even think of the warm-hearted scenes among the people in *Egmont* and *Faust*, we need only think of his personal feeling of well-being at folk occasions (for example, the Rochus-Festival at Bingen) in order to realize what it meant to him to be among the people, surrounded by them at a shooting contest or at the dedication of the town-well, to understand to what extent he felt the folk atmosphere as a familiar, natural element, a nurturing valley of the subconscious and of rejuvenation. "Man cannot," he said, "abide long in the conscious realm; time and again he must take refuge in the subconscious, for that is where his roots are." Could Schiller have spoken these words—that proud invalid, the aristocrat of the spirit, the great, pathetic fool of freedom? "Schiller," Goethe remarked to Ecker-mann with a smile, "had the remarkable good fortune to be considered a particular friend of the people; just between us, however, he was much more an aristocrat than I."

That is true, without being the whole truth. For the conservative love of the popular element that Goethe knew and cherished, is something quite different from the ideal and revolutionary love of mankind that was Schiller's steep affair and that destined him for his peculiar form of popularity by making him the poet of a politically emanci-pated citizenry, a bourgeoisie fighting for economic freedom. Of this Goethe shared only the knowledge, not the enthusiasm: a neutral, factual knowledge, that prompted him to say to the military bystanders at the decisive battle of Valmy in 1792, the victory of the Revolution over the old powers of Europe: "Here and now a new epoch of world history has its beginning, and you can say you were there. The king flees, the citizen triumphs." It was to be the beginning of a utilitarian era, an age concerned with money and trade, intellect, commerce, and wealth, to all of which he had no objections, especially not since the trend toward expansiveness was something to which he felt a sympa-thetic kinship, something related to his own need for expansion. He spoke at times of "free trade of ideas and feelings," an expression that represents a characteristic transfer of liberal-economic principles to the field of the intellect. It breathes the spirit of the nineteenth cen-tury, the century of economics and technology, into which the life of this son of the eighteenth century extended for a full generation, and which he understood and prophetically proclaimed far beyond the limits of his personal life, beyond the limits of the century itself, down to the post-bourgeois period.

Goethe had a peculiar manner of equating the *knowledge* of the demands of a period with *obedience* to them, with the obligation to serve them, to promote them, and "to hasten the epoch." Therefore his knowledge of the era, his awareness of the historical hour that had struck, is tantamount to progressiveness, and he is quite right when he indignantly rejects the epithet of "Friend of the status quo," along with all that it contains of the outmoded, outworn, and worthless. "Time," he said, "constantly progresses, and human affairs have a different shape every fifty years, so that an institution which was perfection in the 1800 is perhaps an infirmity as early as 1850." Attentiveness to change in the image of truth and right, and intelligent obedience to the requirements of such change—that is, in effect, his political religion. Therefore his decree: "There is only one direction—forward!" Therefore his impatience with those who eternally live in the past, to whom he says:

> "Das ist doch nur der alte Dreck,
> Werdet doch gescheiter!
> Tretet nicht immer denselben Fleck,
> So geht doch weiter!"

(That's the same old filth, can't you ever learn? You keep treading in the same spot. Why don't you move on?)

He moved on. Thanks to his longevity he moved on much farther than Schiller who left this life at the early age of forty-six. The moral-political development of the survivor who never stood still is reflected in his great psychological novel, *Wilhelm Meister*, a life's work, begun early and completed late, which, like *Faust*, accompanied him through the decades and passed through various spiritual stages. There is a certain point, around 1795, when he was just as old as Schiller was at his death, when the transformation took place that changed a novel of the theater into a social problem novel in the grand style. When he resumed the work on the *Wanderjahre* at the age of fifty-eight, he was an entirely different person from the young enthusiast of the theater whose only intention it had been to depict the world of Dionysian gypsies, the world behind the footlights, as it had never been depicted before. The work remains autobiographical insofar as it is still a pedagogical story, an intellectual novel of adventure and experiment. But the points of view are entirely changed. The book is full of premonitory flashes of ideas that lead far afield from the esthetic cult of the personal, from everything that might be called bourgeois humanitarianism, from the classical and middle-class concept of culture which Goethe himself had preeminently helped to create and to shape. There is a vital, buoyant, curious search for the things that are "timely," those things which are imminent in the moral as well as in the external,

102

practical aspects of life, and which everyone, therefore, is in duty bound to accelerate, even at the expense of long cherished but now out-moded ideals. We have here his famed "renunciation," the favorite motif of Goethe's old age. This renunciation is the self-conquest of individualistic humanity, the resignation of the ideal of individual universalism. We find in the book the insufficiency of the individual that prevails today; the single organism becomes a function, his only importance lies in what he is able to achieve for culture as a whole, the concept of the community emerges, the "communal bond," the commonwealth. The Jesuit-militaristic spirit of the "Pedagogical Province," poetically transfigured though it may be, leaves very little of the individualistic, the "liberal," the bourgeois ideal.

Above all, the novel has an inter-continental setting; the new world, America, is brought into the picture, and the chief motif is the idea of emigration to the new continent, upon which most of the characters decide in the end. Goethe and America, Goethe as an American—an amazing combination and idea, for he is the arch-European; nothing more "continental" can be imagined than his person. Down to the very end, in the latter part of the *Wanderjahre*, he paid tribute and reiterated his devotion to European culture—this "priceless culture that, for several thousand years arose, grew, spread, was suppressed, oppressed, never quite extinguished, revivified, revitalized, continues to emerge in never ending activity." It is a veritable eulogy. And yet, at the latest from the turn of the century on, with its shocks and débacles, it becomes increasingly clear that he has ill forebodings about Europe, that his faith in Europe's future is shaken, that he feels cramped and worried on this complicated continent, and that he is occupied with thoughts of escape. Escape, flight, played a curious role in his life: he fled to Switzerland in Lili Schoenemann's time, later he fled, head over heels, to Italy, and he certainly had flight from Europe in mind when he wrote in the first canto of the *Divan:*

> "Fluechte du, im reinen Osten
> Patriarchenluft zu kosten."

(Flee, so that you may taste the air of the patriarchs in the unsullied East.)

Now America had become the goal of his inner flight, this land, far away, beyond the sea, which had just fought for and won its independence, and whose victory for justice and liberty he had celebrated in *Dichtung und Wahrheit* as "a relief for mankind." No more democratic word could be imagined! Escape to America remained a matter of thought and fancy, but he expressly blamed his old age for his failure actually to emigrate. "If we were twenty years younger," he said in 1819 to Chancellor von Mueller, "we would sail to America." It was the same year in which he dedicated his collected works to Harvard University—a little known fact—and in the accompanying letter he called the United States "a marvellous country which attracts the attention of the world through its solemnly lawful state that promotes a growth which knows no limits." And still later, in a conversation with his young friend Sulpice Boisserée, he pondered: "What might have happened if I had emigrated to America with a few friends some thirty years ago and had never heard anything about Kant, etc.!"

It reminds one of the verses in the opening canto of the *West-Eastern Divan:*

> "Dort im Reinen und im Rechten
> Will ich menschlichen Geschlechten
> In des Ursprungs Tiefe dringen.
> Wo sie noch von Gott empfingen
> Himmelslehr in Erdesprachen,
> *Und sich nicht den Kopf zerbrachen."*

(There, in purity and right, I will penetrate to the depths of the origin of mankind, where they still received divine instruction from God in earthly tongues and never racked their brains.)

And never racked their brains. That is the point. The dream-bridge to America is the desire away from the age-burdened complexity, the grievous intellectualism of the European world, overloaded with spiritual and historical tradition and finally threatened by nihilism, to a world of no preconceptions, of naturalness, of simplicity and untroubled youthful vigor. Even the flight to Italy had resulted from a thirst for the naive and natural, and that same thirst found expression in the often quoted verses:

> "Amerika, du hast es besser,
> Als unser Kontinent, der alte,
> Hast keine verfallenen Schloesser
> Und keine Basalte.
>
> Dich stoert nicht im Innern
> Zu lebendiger Zeit
> Unnuetzes Erinnern
> Und vergeblicher Streit."

(America, you are better off than is our old continent. You have no ruined castles and no basalt cliffs. In vital times you are not disturbed in your heart by useless memories and by fruitless quarrels.)

Vital times, living age—there is the crux. This conservative has his mind on new things, his old age is filled with vital curiosity, antipathy to "dead stuff," an impatient feeling of the necessity for a return to *sobriety* of a world suffering from a musty, life-hindering heritage. These feelings of his combine with a pleasurable interest in world-wide technological rational matters, an interest which is by no means entirely new, for in *Dichtung und Wahrheit* he tells us that early in life he took pleasure in the contemplation of economic and technical affairs. But this interest now becomes so engrossing that at the table of this normally stiff and solemn eighteenth-century grand seigneur the conversation revolves about steamships and the first attempts with a flying machine, about Utopian technological problems and projects, about the Panama and Suez Canals and the proposed connection of the Danube and the Rhine rather than about literature and poetry. And is it any wonder, when Faust at the end of his career experiences his instant of highest exaltation in the realization of a utilitarian dream, the draining of a swamp? "To stand on free soil with a free people"—that sounds extraordinarily American. The future belongs to the man of the day, whose mind and "common sense" are directed toward the nearest, most useful matters; it belongs to him whose energy is not tainted by the pallor of thought. Not only Germany, all of Europe is Hamlet, and Fortinbras is America.

No, it was not an illusion when Goethe's alliance with life, his gift to make a success of things, his will to survive rather than go to pieces poetically—when all this appeared to us as a democratic trait, even as the determining characteristic to prove that European democracy may claim him as its own. He is endowed with a grandiose goodwill from which our era could learn much for its betterment and salvation—an era so filled with ill-will, an era in which so much stubborn recalcitrance against the demands of life brews and broods. Another name for this goodwill, for this affinity to life is: Love. This word which, according to the word-counters, occurs more frequently than any other in his works, stands like a twin sister beside the word "life." "Let us love the living!" This command rings from his eternity to our day, and he expressed the truest moral in the most popular form in one of his rhymed maxims:

"Wer Recht will tun, immer und mit Lust
Der hege wahre Lieb in Sinn and Brust."

105

(He who wants to do right, always and with pleasure, he must cherish true love in mind and heart.)

There is nothing Mephistophelian about that, nor is there any trace of the mocking voice of opposition in the clear challenge:

> "Edel sei der Mensch,
> Hilfreich und gut!
> Denn das allein
> Unterscheidet ihn
> Von allen Wesen,
> Die wir kennen.
>
> —————————
>
> Unermuedet schaff' er
> Das Nuetzliche, Rechte,
> Sei uns ein Vorbild
> Jener geahneten Wesen!"

(Let man be noble, helpful, and good. For that alone distinguishes him from all the creatures we know. . . Let him tirelessly do the useful and the right, let him be the model of those beings whose existence we surmise.)

Am I wrong in seeing in these verses the most sublime expression of all democracy? It was always my impression that virtually everything in the dialectic of Goethe's personality that sounds and looks antidemocratic belongs to the part of Mephistopheles and is intended only to give dramatic justice to the negative. When Faust's loathsome companion derides him for wanting to rule at the imperial court in the best interests of men, for trying to use temporal power to bring about better conditions on earth, he receives the following answer:

> "So hoere denn, wenn du es niemals hoertest:
> Die Menschheit hat ein fein Gehoer,
> Ein reines Wort erreget schoene Taten.
> Der Mensch fuehlt sein Beduerfnis nur zu sehr
> Und laesst sich gern im Ernste raten."

(Hear this if you have never heard it: Mankind has good ears, and a pure word incites good deeds. Man feels his needs all too much, and he gladly accepts sincere advice.)

In the "Prologue in Heaven," the Lord Himself, the positive force, creative goodness, might give the very selfsame reply to the Devil, and our exalted friend is in complete agreement with him, he is in agree-

106

ment with the positive—it does not suit him and it does not befit him to be in the opposition.

Let us, too, agree with him, with his nobleness, with his sympathy! Then we will never have the misfortune to be in opposition to love and to life.

ACKNOWLEDGMENTS The following poems are reprinted by permission of the publishers: "A Deep-Sworn Vow," from William Butler Yeats' *Collected Poems*, copyright 1919 by The Macmillan Company, renewed 1947 by Georgie Yeats; "Leda and the Swan," from William Butler Yeats' *Collected Poems*, copyright 1928 by The Macmillan Company, renewed 1956 by Georgie Yeats; and "Medallion," from *Personae*, by Ezra Pound, copyright 1926, 1954 by Ezra Pound. Reprinted by permission of New Directions Publishing Corporation. Also reprinted by permission of Faber and Faber Ltd. from *Collected Shorter Poems*.

The Great Grasp of Unreason

R. P. Blackmur

Presented at the Library of Congress January 9, 1956

δικαίων ἀδίκους φρένας

the unjust minds of the just

IT IS ALWAYS a help to speak from a text, and it seems even necessary—in looking at 20th-century literature, so huge and amorphous a mass it is—to use two, or even three texts in order to limit our approach to the literature and to suggest a governing theme in our response to it. With our texts in mind, we can then set about further limitations—I will not say screening or testing—as to what examples of the literature we can best use to illustrate the theme. Other texts would suggest other themes and other limitations in example, and I expect our own would be much modified in their presence. I hope our own will be interesting enough to complement the order and significance of what lurks in the minds of others—or indeed in your own. This is, I think, an application in the field of literary criticism of the principle of indeterminacy, the principle of complementary variable relations; but I do not look for so much advantage from it here in criticism as it has shown in physics and mathematics. I hope only that the principle will seem vivid with possibility. Indeterminacy is life.

Here are my texts, and as it does not matter in what order they come, the most familiar shall be first. It is from *King Lear* and is an aside interjected by Edgar into a long speech by Lear to serve as dramatic punctuation—like a rest in music—while the King is gathering breath in the long late rush of his being.

> *O! Matter and impertinency mix'd;*
> *Reason in madness.*

109

It is a curious thing that we might not ourselves see any madness in Lear's words were it not for Edgar's aside. We might rather see the poetic mind at its ancient task of coping with, responding to, and acknowledging all the irrational horror and injustice and disorder of human behavior. We would see reason at work: we would see what Sophocles calls in the *Antigone* "the unjust minds of the just." Still, it is reason in madness. The scholar who edits my copy of *King Lear* (Kenneth Muir, Arden Edition, London, 1952, p. LX) complains of another scholar (Schücking) with regard to our text that he "seems to be only partly aware of the paradox that Lear when ostensibly sane cannot distinguish between Cordelia and her wicked sisters: he acquires wisdom by going mad, and his wildest speeches are a mixture of matter and impertinency—'reason in madness.' " I would complain against both my scholars only this far, and chiefly in the interest of looking at the literature of our own times—of which, of course, we want to make *King Lear* a part. Was it not by releasing himself from the bonds of both institutional and personal reason that Lear renewed in himself the task of reason? Reason is in substance all the living memory of the mind; in action (or, if you like, in essence) reason is the recognition and creation of order where disorder was. It is Edgar's aside that sees that this is what Lear was doing. Reason in madness.

Our second text is only less familiar than the first, and is like unto it because it enlightens it in terms of our own interest by setting us in our own time—or in a kind of minus version of our own time where we see where we are not as well as where we are. This is from part five of Eliot's "East Coker" Quartet:

> *So here I am, in the middle way, having had twenty years—*
> *Twenty years largely wasted, the years of l'entre deux guerres—*
> *Trying to learn to use words, and every attempt*
> *Is a wholly new start, and a different kind of failure*
> *Because one has only learnt to get the better of words*
> *For the thing one no longer has to say, or the way in which*
> *One is no longer disposed to say it. And so each venture*
> *Is a new beginning, a raid on the inarticulate*
> *With shabby equipment always deteriorating*
> *In the general mess of imprecision of feeling,*
> *Undisciplined squads of emotion. And what there is to conquer*
> *By strength and submission, has already been discovered*
> *Once or twice, or several times, by men whom one cannot hope*
> *To emulate—but there is no competition—*
> *There is only the fight to recover what has been lost*
> *And found and lost again and again: and now, under conditions*
> *That seem unpropitious. But perhaps neither gain nor loss.*
> *For us, there is only the trying. The rest is not our business.*

110

This is Eliot mixing, like Lear in Edgar's ears, matter and impertinence, and finding reason in the madness that grasps him all about. This the very last lines of the poem make plain in the way that the flushing movement of breath makes plain there is life.

* * *

Through the dark cold and the empty desolation,
The wave cry, the wind cry, the vast waters
Of the petrel and the porpoise.   In my end is my beginning.

In the long part of these quotations Eliot generalizes the pursuit of reason in madness; in the last lines—where he puts together the incarnation of reason and the beautiful and dreadful partial and always changing incarnation of behavior, the petrel and the porpoise—he exemplifies it. Matter and impertinence.

The third text has a kind of official familiarity, which we would redeem out of natural piety and because it both generalizes and exemplifies our theme; thus it needs to be quoted in two English versions. Here is a recent version of the *Antigone* 610–614: "Through the future and distant time to come, as through the past, this law will prevail, working not without calamity for the lives of men throughout this citied world." (Goheen, *The Imagery of Sophocles' Antigone*, Princeton, 1951.)   The earlier version of Jebb and Pearson gives for the sense of the last phrase: "Nothing that is vast enters the life of men without a curse" (cited *idem*, p. 143).   Jebb died in 1905 and his version reflects Victorian predilections about fate and says nothing about the *hyperbasia* or transgression, and therefore involvement by man in his fate which is present in the later version.   This is one of the differences between the age before 1914 and our own; if our age does not understand the difference, our writers have understood it very well.   Human behavior has gotten conspicuously into the second version in much the same way it had gotten into *King Lear* and *The Four Quartets*. It is the unreason of behavior that grasps reason to the quick: reason in madness.

So much for our three texts.   I should like to think that the ode from the *Antigone* sang the praises—the precious belief—of the literature of our own citied world.

The great advantage of these texts is that they come after the literature they are intended to illuminate and yet also link them to the past, and they both illuminate and link by their power as images set side by side with our literature and our lives. A later time will perhaps want different texts and will see a different literature from the point of view of a different mind—which will make a judgment more nearly right from their point of view but could not correct what we see and what we respond

111

to; we can only look at what is in front of us, with the aid of our own sense of the past and with our own lives, towards a particular future. Who knows, it may be the next age will not express itself in words (in the sense that words are poetry, that art is poetry) at all, for the next age may not be literate in any sense we understand or that the last three thousand years understood. Poetry may yet become an even more secret craft than it was during the dream of the dark ages; and indeed there is a promise of this in the very struggle towards difficulty our poetry shows, and in the very refusal it makes to come to terms with the leading features of the actual mind of the society which confronts it. This is the struggle between the old literacy and the new illiteracy, which is not ignorance but fragmented and specialized knowledge.

Toynbee has a passage of reason and madness in *A Study of History* which bears on this.

The bread of Universal Education is no sooner cast upon the waters of social life than a shoal of sharks rises from the depths and devours the children's bread under the philanthropists' eyes. In the educational history of England, for example, the dates speak for themselves. Universal compulsory gratuitous education was inaugurated in this country in A. D. 1870; the Yellow Press was invented some twenty years later—as soon as the first generation of children from the national schools had come into the labour market and acquired some purchasing power—by a stroke of irresponsible genius which had divined that the educational philanthropists' labour of love could be made to yield the newspaper king a royal profit.

The effects of free education and the Yellow Press in our field—at any rate their concomitants—were Art for Art's sake and the *Yellow Book* and the long series of increasingly intransigent declarations of independence on the part of the arts which have lasted, with diminishing intellectual force, and an increasing lack of that coherence of images which we call verisimilitude, even after the Second World War. But Toynbee has something else to say about another aspect of our society, which perhaps explains the relaxation of our educational policy, and which is also pertinent to our poetry.

Our Western scientific knowledge of which we boast, and even our Western technique for turning this knowledge to practical account—a technique upon which we depend for our wealth and strength—is perilously esoteric. The great new social forces of Democracy and Industrialism, which our Western Civilization has thrown up in the course of its growth, have been evoked from the depths by a tiny creative minority. Even this minority is wondering today whether it will be able to control and guide much longer these forces which it has let loose. . . . And the main reason why this would-be Western Salt of the Earth is in fear, today, of losing its savour is because the great mass of the Western body social

112

has remained unsalted. . . . In the latter-day perversion of our Western Press, we see the "drive" of Western Industrialism and Democracy being employed to keep the mass of Western Humanity culturally depressed at, or perhaps even below, its pre-industrial and pre-democratic spiritual level; and the same new "drive" has been put, with similar evil consequences, into the old institutions of War ànd Tribalism and Slavery and Property. [III, 241]

First, I would remind you that this passage, like the other, was written in the thirties at the safest possible distance between the two wars, and has in no wise lost its applicability. Second, so that it may apply the more closely, I would suggest that we substitute the word "poetic" for the word "scientific" in the first sentence quoted above. "Our Western *poetic* knowledge of which we boast, and even our whole Western *poetic* technique for turning this knowledge to practical account . . . is perilously esoteric." Does it not read well enough for Toynbee, and, to the present purpose, much better for ourselves? For we have not only an enormous increase in potential or required audience but also a diminution, relatively if not absolutely, in the means of reaching, let alone controlling, that audience. So put, we see at once how the new knowledges, so managed, so esoteric, have been reflected in the habit and superficial character of poetry and the poet himself. He has found himself speaking a private language and has grown proud of it.

What else could the writer do but invent a vital dogma of self-sufficiency?—and I do not say he was not right in doing so. Faced with the dissolution of thought and the isolation of the artist, faced with the new industrialization of intellect, what else could he do but declare his independence and self-sufficient supremacy both as intellectual and as artist? Let us admit the new independence came partly out of the old claims for and defenses of poetry from Aristotle through Shelley, partly from the 19th-century claims made by Ruskin and Arnold, all of which allied art deeply to society, but partly—and this is the biggest emotional part—from the blow of the First World War and what seemed the alienation of the artist from a society increasingly less aesthetically-minded—less interested in the vivid apprehension of the values of the individual. It is when you have lost, or think you are about to lose, the objective recognition of your values, that you assert them most violently and in their most extreme form—as every unrequited lover knows. You either go into the desert, kill yourself, pull your shell over your head, or set up in a new business: in any case, whether lover or artist, being as conspicuous as possible about it. To be either a dandy or dirty, and especially where out of keeping, is always a good rôle; and to be an anchorite or an oracle combines the advantages of both. You are in any case among enemies.

A Russian socialist, Georgi Plekanov, thought this sort of attitude de-

113

velops when artists feel a "hopeless contradiction between their aims and the aims of the society to which they belong. Artists must be very hostile to their society and they must see no hope of changing it." But let us put it one more way—as near neutral as possible. It has always been difficult to pay for art out of the running expenses of any form of society, and it has become unusually difficult under finance-capitalism (or any current money-based form of democracy) to find a means to go beyond the economy or find a special privy-purse. Also, it has always been difficult to find a sure or satisfactory audience for the living artist; and this has become increasingly difficult in societies like our own where education has become both universal and largely technical—at any rate less generalizably literate— and which has at the same time enormously multiplied the number of its artists. So, too, it has always been difficult for the artist to find the means of expressing his own direct apprehension of life in conventions which were, or could be made, part of the conventions of society in general; and this, also—this problem of communication—has become excessively difficult in a society which tends to reject the kind of faithful conventions under which the artist has usually worked, and a society in which, under the urban process, and under the weight of the new knowledges, so much of thought has been given over to mechanism which had formerly operated under faith. These are the conditions under which the artist has felt, in his exaggeration of them, isolated and has asserted himself under the general state of mind that runs from art for art's sake through surrealism to *Existenz*—It is no wonder. Yet it was Coleridge who, as reported in *Table Talk*, put the matter most succinctly—there were, he said, three silent revolutions in the history of England: "When the professions fell off from the Church; when literature fell off from the professions; and when the press fell off from literature." I will not say what the fourth silent revolution is: it is ours, and now going on.

But if we cannot name the fourth revolution we can discern some of its features in a sketch of some of the materials that go to make up our immediate intellectual history. We can touch on some of the conditions and forces of our minds. We can look into our fictions to see what gave them idiom. Idiom is the twist of truth, the twist, like that of the strands of a rope, which keeps its component fictions together. History is old and twisted beyond our reach in time. But the sense of moving background which we call history began to grow with Gibbon and we began to feel it imperative in the last ninety years—or since the war of 1870. We now take into account the extremes of several forms of time as part of our history which had not got much into history before that date—time outside the chronicle and the chronometer alike. We have time in anthropology, ethnology, mythology, psychology, physics, and mathematics, and as a response to these times we have changed our heroes.

114

Politics began to pretend a century and a half ago that the good society had no hero but itself, and did so on the conviction that the old heroes were malevolent. As the old Chinese believed, a great man was a national calamity. About 1870 two opposed heroic shapes were thrown up by society: the artist as hero and the heroic proletariat. Mussolini, Hitler, Stalin came to represent the hero (by dictatorship) of the scum of the earth. The scum on the pond is the reimagined primeval slime, and we are nothing if we are not primeval. In psychoanalysis we regurgitate the scum, only to discover it inexhaustible. Taboos become totems. St. Francis of Assisi becomes Vicar of our scummiest behavior. Society takes on the aspect of uniform motion. The artist is the hero who struggles against uniform motion, a struggle in marmalade.

For the artist regards uniform motion as the last torpor of life. Torpor is the spread of momentum, but we prefer to believe it is the running down of things. For three generations we have heroized the second law of thermodynamics, which is the law of the dissipation or gradual unavailability of energy within any system—which is the law of entropy or the incapacity for fresh idiom, time and perception going backwards. Entropy, from the point of view of the rational imagination, is disorder and is indeed its field. Actually, we have been as busy, as violent, and as concentrated as the ant-heap. We are torpid only because we are glutted with energy and feel it only as trouble. The strains are out of phase with each other and we have techniques only for the troubles.

If we say this sort of thing as example—and we could say so much more—are we not the first age which is self-conscious of its own fictions; and hence the first age of true pyrrhonism: doubting the value as well as the fact? We believe only in the techniques of manipulating and counting. Not in choice, not in the imperative, chiefly in opinion. Thus we believe in the analysis of conduct as a means of discounting behavior, in the drum-majorette of 14 as a means of showing sex as force without having to take account of it.

Our age is full of great hymns to the puerile, what in medicine and art are called images of fundamental frustration. If you look in the Oxford dictionary, all the early meanings of frustration were positive. You frustrated villainy, which was desirable. Now we frustrate our own good, and we lend Hamlet our own frustrations. In the history of the word there is part of the history of our psyche. When we recognize frustration as a *fundamental* condition of life, it ought no longer to be frustration, but fate, tragedy, damnation, the Cross, the other side of every infatuation. But we would not think we expressed ourselves if we said so.

Here one does not exactly ask if we are to have a deliberate resurrection of the dark ages, one only looks in the closet and under the bed and remembers how Freud said that our dreams make it possible for us to sleep.

115

If the dark ages had had a mind, it would have been both cyclical and on sale to the devil. We migrate from one to the other, from hope without longing to longing without hope, and on the whole we prefer instruments to speculation, method to madness, as if we would obliterate the *daring* part of consciousness, which looks into the glass to see. We prefer, even in our art, poetry, and religion, confused alarms on lonely shores.

It is considerations like these which make us reflect that there may actually be a new phase of culture at hand: mass culture. But it may be only that too much of our research leads us into the mass-part of man's soul: into the anonymous and communal saga in which the actions of the individual are construed as sinister and somehow less than his own. Thus the superman or hero tends to be either the mass-man or the arch-criminal or the pure heel. It is the glory of James Joyce that in the figures of Bloom and H. C. Earwicker he worked against all these in a valiant attempt to create a new kingdom of man: an independent, individual morality against the society that made it necessary. Yet he deflected the common mode of research very little. He was a proper author and redeemed the validity of experience in the theorems he called his art. Besides Joyce, there are the others, to whom we shall come if we hold out.

What holds us, what keeps us, what moves us, must be a combination of our under-momentum and our bourgeois humanism. These are the correctives as they are the aching sources, the true enliveners, of our great men. Bourgeois humanism (the treasure of residual reason in live relation to the madness of the senses) is the only conscious art of the mind designed to deal with our megalopolitan mass society: it alone knows what to *do with* momentum in its new guise; and it alone knows it must be more than itself without losing itself in order to succeed.

The decay of the prestige of bourgeois humanism was perhaps necessary, but only as an interim, a condition of interregnum, when new forces overran us. In order to restore the humanism we have to overcome the forces. We have to take stock, too, of the multiplication in the number of the artists and to remember their insistent disrelatedness. It was never to have been expected that society—especially a centralized state like our own— would be willing to pay for the cost of the artists who as a class, and often individually, raised the severest problems of that society: images of the deep anarchies out of which the order of the state must be remade if that order is to be vital. But it ought to have been expected that the incentive of the artists themselves should have remained fixed on that living relation between anarchy and order. Instead, we have the apparition of the arts asserting their authority in a combination of the spontaneous and the arbitrary, in pure poetry and pure expression and pure trouble. Instead of creation in honesty, we have assertion in desperation; we have a fanati-

116

cism of the accidental instead of a growth of will. The true anarchy of spirit should always show (or always *has* showed) a tory flavor. It is the artist above all who *realizes* that revolutions—however fresh, violent and destructive, however aspiring, or groping, or contagious—have always *already* taken place; as private murder represents a relation already at crisis or already sundered. Revolution and murder are only the gross cost, assessed too late: the usury of dead institutions.

The anarchy of our artists is in response to facts as well as in evasion of facts. The two great external facts of our time are the explosion of populations and the explosions of the new energies. The two great internal facts of our time are the recreation of the devil (or pure behavior) in a place of authority and the development of techniques for finding destructive troubles in the psyche of individuals. With neither of these pairs of facts, without a vital order in society, can the individual keep up except as corrosion may be said to keep up with the salts that cause it—to the point of incoherence in purpose and collapse of structure. The two pairs of facts are I think related. The devil and the techniques are the slow form of population and energy explosions. But if we let this relation transpire in the mind we see we have the power to cope with the facts themselves; for we then behold the nature of our troubles in what used to be called the unity of apperception. To say this is to involve bourgeois humanism once again. It may not be the right force, or the right muse, but they are the only ones we know, and the only ones which we know have within themselves the capacity to generate self-change by absorbing disorder into order. We can remember in the past it was the artists who taught society this skill.

The latter end of our time—1920–1950—is an age of critique: critique as a means of criticism and critique as a means of creation. Critique as criticism we see in the expanding omnivorous techniques for the examination of poetry. Critique as creation we see in Proust, Mann, Joyce, and Kafka. Critique is the wiggling extreme articulation of vital elements into an order of vision: especially the elements of the new powers and the new troubles.

With critique as creation we shall have much to do. Here I want a passing emphasis on criticism in its widest sense. Some of the criticism merely extends along new lines the malicious criticism of knowledge (the attack on the validity of perception) which is the net practical result of the current of philosophy beginning with Berkeley and running into the sands of the Existentialists. Epistemology was taught to prevent knowledge or at least to gravel it with doubts; so most criticism of poetry. All the apprehensive powers of the mind have been put at such a discount that they are felt to be irrational, when actually they are the fountainhead and

117

fountain reach of reason herself. It strikes me here that in result upon our general mind, modern physics and mathematics make a parallel extension of the same malicious criticism of knowledge: as refinement of critical abstraction, good for manipulation, rotten for apprehension—that is, for the sensual knowledge that is the immediate rock of physics and the thing indexed by mathematics. As compared to literary criticism, the critique supplied by physics is both more malice and more knowledge and is also more remote from the apprehending reason. The effect of these malicious critiques is profound: almost they dissolve our sense of the texture of moral experience. It is the writhing of actual knowledge under these malicious techniques that makes choice and purpose and taste so difficult, uncertain, and fractious. We tend to relapse from all human creation back into almost pure momentum (in analogy to pure sensation), with all our activity becoming mere sports on the movement of inertia. Thus it is we seem to manipulate for manipulation's sake and find the *acte gratuite* a liberation when it ought to be a warning, an explosion when it ought to be a play, a gesture, a feint. It is thus that we *become* our problem when we ought to exemplify some effort at the solution of it. We become, in Dante's language, the War of the Journey without active knowledge of the War of the Pity. It is the two Wars that need the Muses; either, taken solely, puerilizes man.

The malicious criticism of knowledge is reflected also in the unmoored diabolism that makes so many mansions in the modern sensibility, and makes them uninhabitable sink-holes of terror and dismay, full of the uncleanly and aborted approximations of the unseemly. Hysteria, which ought to be the clue to reality, becomes its creator. This we see in Freud, who began his studies with the aetiology of hysteria and proceeded with its deification: as if all the gross responses unconformable with conduct could ordain conduct. The sequence is interesting: hypnotism, psychical research, hysteria, neurosis, psychosis, psychoanalysis. The very title, *Psychopathology of Everyday Life*, in itself a lie, told that we might mistake the conditions of our struggle for its object; in short, a malicious criticism of knowledge. It is a queer thing that we should desire to make experience itself suicidal to its own impulses: queer but actual. The devil always takes the form of the actual, most conspicuously in an expressionistic age. But only the bourgeois humanist would know this.

But it must be the bourgeois humanist in his role as artist who knows—for it is he who is nearest the expressionism of our times, the artist thrown up as a heroic type and a heroic image. And indeed it has been that class which has known most, or expressed the most—especially in that explosion of talent that took place in the twenties, crystallizing between 1922 and 1925 in *Ulysses, The Waste Land, The Magic Mountain, The Tower,*

The Counterfeiters, and a great deal more. It is a version of the general *artistic* problem which gave condition to this explosion that I have been leading up to. All these books came deeply from the bourgeois humanistic tradition and come as near masterpieces as our age provides. They were a part of the great expressionistic period between the wars, not only in literature but in all the arts. Older talents crystallized and reached pinnacles and took on new dimensions; new talents were flung off like sparks from a Catharine wheel or the blobs of light from a roman candle. Expressionism—what I say is both myself in truth and creates a new world—tends to pyrotechnics; the fireworks are within us and are all around us and are their own meaning—subject to the least possible external control or common predictable forms of understanding. In expressionistic art we see what the forces are which we have to control by other means: the actual forces of human nature, of nonrational behavior, and of the industriously rational machinations of the devil—the diabolic, the daemonic, and the chthonic—the life that is in our soil. Expressionism compacts the Faustian spirit and the adventures of our conduct. This is a new claim for the arts, and perhaps the most ambitious yet in the long series since Aristotle. It is precisely the opposite from Shelley's claim that poets are the unacknowledged legislators of the world. It constitutes for itself rather the claim to undermine, to readjust, to put into fresh order the frames or forms in which we make the adventure of conduct tangible to our minds, and it therefore denies validity to pre-existent legislation on human relations.

No wonder all that we mean by the state and most of what we mean by public morals turn stony against expressionistic art. No wonder, too, that for all its talent and all its novelty, expressionistic art has never been popular with the new mass society that threw it off as a new turn—a new force—of the mind. It has been popular rather with the human fragments which the mass society also threw off—with the remainder of the old élites and with the new professional and intellectual proletariats: all those of us who, in Toynbee's phrase, are *in* but not *of* the great mass society. —All art is in a sense the daydream arrested and compacted in form. Most people like their daydreams to conform to their normal expectations and their immediate ambitions and to do so in familiar forms. Most of us like either happy endings or a lonely glory in our affairs. We dream to get rid of our reality and to charm the lights of love. Here popular art helps us out. More serious art—high-brow art—is also daydream, but it insists on responding to the pressures that make our dreams so strange and so full of prophecy: nightmare or revelation. Instead of rationalizing our experience we give our experience what form we can and set reason new and almost impossible tasks to perform. We recreate reality in rivalry with our own wishes. I think of Thomas Hardy who tried to write popular melodramatic novels for money out of ordinary melodramatic daydreams but, in what we call his better novels, found himself responding to and shaping dark forces. I think also of Henry James who wanted to write the best possible popular novels, but never knew what the deep moral troubles in his psyche were that prevented him (the very troubles which as he expressed them give him stature) until, in August 1914, he saw that *this* is what we have been leading up to all along.

We have had another war since then, and the enclosure of the two wars suggests certain things about the talent that lay between them—or at least puts certain things in a violent murky light. We lived in a time of troubles, when the very torpor of our momentum let us see what monsters and what heroes we could make of ourselves in imagination—the monsters of our behavior newly seen, and the heroes of our struggle with that conduct newly construed. Newly seen and newly construed: for not only did we live in a time of troubles, we lived also in a time when we were learning a whole set of techniques for finding—even creating—trouble: new ways of undermining personality and conviction and belief and human relation. I myself can remember when the Oedipus complex was a shattering shock and a neurosis was a ravening worm. It was not till later that we had the law of uncertainty in mathematical physics, which broke the last healthy remnants of moral determinism. But we had psychology which dissolved the personality into bad behavior, we had anthropology which dissolved religion into a competition, world- and history-wide, of monsters, and we had psychiatry which cured the disease by making a monument of it and sociology which flattened us into the average of the lonely crowd. We had thus the tools with which to construct the age of anxiety out of the older debris. Almost, the tools guided the hands and predicted the work. As if that were not enough, the same monsters, and more intolerable heroes (those who accepted the monsters) began their work in the world of managers. It was in 1922 that Mussolini made his march on Rome; and by 1939 the Faustian spirit within had come very near succumbing to the dictatorship of the scum of the earth without.

It need not have happened that way, but the risk of its happening that way was very great, and is still with us; and the arts have more than ever the job of enforcing new tasks upon reason: to show poetry as the wisdom of our violent knowledges—which is what Gianbattisto Vico said, in 1744, that poetry could do in his great work *La Nuova Scienza*, the new way of looking at knowledge. It was also, I think, how he came to say that justice was an emanation of the human conscience, and therefore changed as times and forces changed.

In the darkness and hope of these remarks something else we have long known shows the more clearly: the shifting contour and widening focus, not of one or two generations, but of three or four centuries, in the burdening and the possible scope of literature as it is a development in history. It is not the atheists and agnostics but the committed men like Reinhold Niebuhr and Arnold Toynbee who habitually say that we live in a post-Christian world; and the history of literature bears them out. In Shakespeare justice is the endless jar of right and wrong as it strikes upon the conscience. We feel in Shakespeare what troubled Joyce's Stephen Dedalus so much: the again-bite of inwit, or remorse of conscience. In Shakespeare, as in Montaigne, and not again going backwards till Dante, nor going forward till Pascal, you feel the constant explosions of violently irrational forces upon the conscience. These explosions were of their talent. From the First World War onward the explosions are commonplace, though the talent may be less or at least less acceptable. Except Dante, who I think prophesied it, we are all heirs to a realignment of the usurping and abdicating institutions which manage our relations to our irrational experience. There are many ways of putting this. Here is Marcel Raymond, who is trying to explain the apparition of nonrational French poetry from 1870 onwards: "An explosion of the irrational elements in the human personality had occurred in the era of the Counter-Reformation and Baroque art, but at that time the Church had determined the course of the mystical upsurge without much difficulty. Two centuries later, after the critique of the 'philosophers,' she was no longer in the same commanding position. It was the task of art (but not of art alone) to gratify some of the human demands that religion had thus far been able to exercise.

"From then on poetry tended to become an ethic or some sort of irregular instrument of metaphysical knowledge. Poets were obsessed by the need to 'change' life, as Rimbaud puts it, to change man and to bring him into direct contact with existence. The novelty lies less in the fact than in the intention, which gradually emerges from the realm of the unconscious, of reconquering man's irrational powers and of transcending the dualism of the self and the universe." (Raymond goes on to remark that modern civilization and Romanticism crystallized at the same moment.)

An irregular metaphysic for the control of man's irrational powers, if I may so condense M. Raymond, these words on the sequence of these remarks seem to me to enlighten the motive-power, the *moving* power, of the extraordinary outburst of creative talent in the twenties. No wonder it is sometimes called a rival creation.

Let me list a few in literature. Pirandello wrote *Six Characters in Search of an Author* in 1921, *Henry IV* in 1922: or how it is we struggle for identity. Ortega y Gasset wrote *Invertebrate Spain* in 1922, *Revolt of the Masses,* in 1930. Valéry published *Charmes* in 1922: the identity of the spirit with its senses. For that year Proust had *Sodome et Gomorrhe:* the beast which springs and is sprung of spirit. Ezra Pound had finished *Hugh Selwyn Mauberly* and some of his most characteristic *Cantos* in 1921: the artist as hero *manqué*. Wallace Stevens' *Harmonium* appeared in 1923: a dandy finding an old chaos in the sun. Mann's *Magic Mountain* came in 1924: the intellect entered literature at a new level to meet and merge with the sick and the unseemly. Two years later, 1926, Gide produced his *Counterfeiters:* the migratory black devil in Puritanism. And so on.

For our purposes, we have only to remember that Eliot's *Waste Land* and Joyce's *Ulysses* appeared in 1922, and that around that year hovers Yeats' most powerful work. Do not these works, as we lump them in one image which we cannot swallow and of which we cannot free ourselves, constitute a deep plea for the wisdom of our violent knowledge? Is not the poetry in them precisely the wisdom with which we respond to the great grasp of unreason?

The Techniques of Trouble

R. P. Blackmur

Presented at the Library of Congress January 16, 1956

One of the themes that inhabited my last lecture was that all our new knowledges—or all the new forms into which our knowledge has segregated and incriminated itself—have come out as techniques for finding trouble in ourselves and in the world. It is almost as if to make trouble had become the creative habit of the general mind. We made new violences where there had been order and as a result have been living in a combination of turbulence and apathy, of novelty and isolation, immersed in the new failures of human relationships. If Tolstoi could begin a great novel by saying that all happy marriages were the same, all unhappy ones different, we can say that every age has a new way of finding human relations difficult or impossible: the very hardship and the very joy of life we cannot and would not escape and with which we must deal. These are our techniques of trouble, and if there were no troubles we would invent them or would find new ways of looking at old troubles. In life we do what we can and what we must; in literature and the arts (and sometimes in our daydreams and what we call our thought) we make a kind of rival creation always, one way or another, in response to the actual life itself; and in our great creations we alter that actual life in the sense that we alter what we think about it, what we acknowledge about it, what we see in it, and what we do about it in our private selves where most of our time is spent. Hence our need for making desperate and preposterous cries: the form of expression in which we are best understood and where we feel most intimate with others. But hence also we cling to what we can of the cumulative memory of our past which we call reason, and of our cumulative hopes for the future which we call our aspiration or imagination; and indeed these are the substance in us which cries out: which explores and shapes and expresses the life which besets us in terms of the life which is our own. Great literature—great art of any kind—finds techniques for dealing with the trouble otherwise provided. It is with these techniques that we are now concerned as they apply to the great burst of creative talent in the twenties.

But there is nothing new about any of this. Here is Stephen Dedalus speaking of Shakespeare in the Library chapter (which may also be called Scylla and Charybdis) in *Ulysses* (p. 210): "He found in the world without as actual what was in his world within as possible. Maeterlinck says: *If Socrates leave his house today he will find the sage seated on his doorsteps. If Judas go forth tonight it is to Judas his steps will tend.* Every life is many days, day after day. We walk through ourselves, meeting robbers, ghosts, giants, old men, young men, wives, widows, brothers-in-love. But always meeting ourselves." This is Joyce's aesthetics; it is also one statement of the whole theme of *Ulysses*. But for our immediate purposes we can find in these words a motto or text for the violence of great talent in its task of meeting great trouble.

As text or motto Joyce's words given to Stephen need to be joined to others more topical to the situation at the end of the First World War. Here are some sentences from Marcel Raymond's *From Baudelaire to Surrealism* (p. 270). He is speaking of the dadaists as characteristic of "the moral crisis of the 1920's and the current of anarchistic individualism, the refusal to be useful, that upset so many slogans and age-old beliefs." Then, speaking of the contributors to the dadaists' magazine *Littérature*, he goes on: "Life itself undertook to destroy whatever illusions they might have had about the 'real' world—: the regimentation of morals, the distortion of religious feelings, a science that celebrated its greatest triumphs in the calculations of ballistics, the greatest 'trahison des clercs' (betrayal of the intellectuals) that mankind had ever seen—there was ample ground for disillusionment." In the eyes of these men "everything had already been torn down; dadaism could be only an inventory of the ruins, and a declaration of the failure, or more accurately, the death of a civilization." Later (p. 272), M. Raymond speaks of the dadaists' "sense of bitter joy, almost indistinguishable from despair—the joy of flaying a society that crushes man" and reminds us that we "must not ignore the tragic anguish they reflect. Even if all dadaist poetry were to sink into oblivion, a few sentences would still deserve to be rescued—sentences which are among the most striking ever written to express the precariousness of man's fate and the sorrow of him who is lost and cannot resign himself to his destiny." He quotes, among others, Aragon, Reverdy, and Soupault.

The sharp difference between the situation of the dadaists and that of Joyce is that where the one prevented masterpieces at all costs the other is the theme of one of the greatly ordered masterpieces of all literature. The one has forgotten its ancestry and feels itself wholly bastardised, the other springs from a full bourgeois humanism of which it has lost nothing still alive and to which it adds its own innermost life. Shakespeare, the Bible, and Aristotle are all at work here, as is also all the working of June 16, 1904, in the city of Dublin, all working together into an order of the rational imagination. Indeed, there is a sense in which we can say that *Ulysses* is the book that *made* an order out of the substance of the dadaist imagination. Perhaps we say this because Joyce's book has power to make order out of anything.

To join in our minds the sense of Joyce and the sense of dadaism, there is a little scene in Mann's *Magic Mountain* where after Settembrini the humanist and Naphtha the Jesuit have broken off one of their inconclusive debates, Hans Castorp, that young and plastic soul, turns to his friend Joachim Ziemssen. Just as always, says Hans, first an anecdote, then an abstraction; that's his humanism. Anecdote and abstraction, abstraction *and* anecdote. Otherwise, as Hans sees in his dreams of Settembrini, the humanist is only an organ-grinder, with a monkey not a man at the end of his string.

A good deal of literature is always organ-grinding, and some of it can be very good, as it reminds us or extends the sense of our common predicament, and there is perhaps no more than usual in the literature of our times; only since it is ours we see it too plainly. In Virginia Woolf human relations disappear in the very technique of sensibility in which they were supposed to be lodged and understood, and I think this is true of writers like Rebecca West, Frances Snow Compton, and most of Elizabeth Bowen (though with Miss Bowen, not at heart). In Virginia Woolf's world there is no possible society or daily life, which I suppose is its beauty; both the voices and the flesh are separated from us, and staled, by the intermission of woolen curtains through which nothing is touched; and Miss Woolf in her diary could not understand what all the bother over *Ulysses* was about. In D. H. Lawrence the hysteria of direct sensual experience destroys every structure of sensibility, and there is only as much human relation as there is possible in the swoon of the blood, which is a very powerful and very destructive relation indeed. André Malraux, as a novelist (not as an art critic, or even as a politician, and certainly not as a public figure, but as a novelist) seems to me in much the same situation; the flashes of his violence on his adventures are quite as vivid and exhibit as great a turbulence as the violence of the world itself between 1920 and 1950; and there is a part of us for which his novels cry out.

All these writers of whom I have expressed such exaggerated sentiments belong in our time not only by date but also by the nature of their talents (for Lawrence, genius besides: he is an obstacle that cannot be gotten round); but I do not think they ever overcame the techniques of trouble in our society with techniques of their own. Thus they are nearer the dadaist situation than to that of Joyce.

Of other writers, other discriminations. Let us think of Faulkner (also a man of talent and of genius) and ask of him why it is that he has deliberately surrendered the advantages of syntax without establishing any comparable control over the movements of his beautiful prose. Why has he left the harmony out at the level of notation, at the level where the reader is instructed how to read? It is precisely what the reader cannot be trusted to put in. In his books, the words if not the people fall out of relation; indeed the words heap round the people and obscure them—quite as if Faulkner used the words for which he has in fact an overwhelming gift only because on the printed page he could not do without them. As with Mallarmé deliberately, one sometimes thinks it is in the white spaces between that the thought goes on. And why, too, in Faulkner, is there a deliberate denial or abnegation or blurring of the intelligence? Why is so much of *The Sound and the Fury* told deliberately through the putative mind of the idiot Benjy? One remembers Henry James' precept, made in commenting on *The Turn of the Screw*, that what you want in fiction, at least if you want veracity, is the abnormal or evil or unusual as seen by *normal* intelligence. I am not here making a moral criticism, nor would I touch on Faulkner's metaphysics; Faulkner has a powerful moral imagination and has a kind of black Christianity of his own (a Christianity without either the gospels or the Greeks) which I do not much admire as a religious experiment but which I feel as a special revealing force in his work. I merely enquire why he blurs the operation of intelligence, and I can only suggest as an answer that he has the kind of sophistication which will accept only a low degree of order, the order of actions whether of the psyche or of the conflict of interests and loyalties before they have been understood and so have lost some intimacy.

The question about Faulkner sharpens itself if we think also about Proust. It must be a common experience, in reading the history of Proust's enormous rival creation of the world, to come with the relief of a change of weather upon those scenes where men and women burst out of analysis and the deployment of narrative into the excitement of action upon each other and into fresh voice. Many years ago Raymond Fernandez, who was a very good critic indeed, observed out of some crotchet in his mind that there was no moral progress in Proust. Fernandez was wrong, as wrong as a professional bourgeois humanist can be, which is when he regards what *ought* to be there, to the disadvantage of what is there. In Proust there is a continuous approximation of moral progress—among other places in the continuous quarrel of jealousy with the vitality and the intermittences of the heart. His whole book is morals in action, and if Fernandez did not at the moment see it, it was, I like to think, because there were so few scenes where the morals were released into actions of the whole person. Thus he is pretty much the opposite of Faulkner. His syntax is complete and is only as difficult as it needed to be, and his intelligence is used to the utmost—a kind of incalculable constant showing in approximation after approximation. Though Proust thought of himself as anti-intellectual, it was only so that he could keep himself from the fixed intellect and the formalized point of view; he maintained intelligence at the pitch where it refuses action; he preferred transmutations to action, the shifting of the phases of the heart to the phases of the reason, both somehow attached to the deep viscous memory, of which the heart and the reason are two decimations. May we not say, then, that Proust and Faulkner at bottom both suffer from absence of syntax, the power of composing or arranging things, giving them ordinance, so that their parts are in living relation to the intelligence. Faulkner runs to the syntax of analogous action; Proust runs rather to the syntax of words and intelligence and only seldom engages them in the autonomy of dramatic action.

Very similar discriminations beseech us when we think of such authors as Pirandello and Kafka. Here, in both, there is the question of human identity. In almost all Pirandello's later work the theme is that in the title of his best known play: *Six Characters in Search of An Author.* Who am I? And who can recreate me as I change? How can I *be,* both with myself and with others, and in spite of others? *Right You Are, If You Think You Are* and *As You Desire Me*—two other titles—suggest the kind of movement and the kind of withdrawal the psyche makes in its craving for that form which determines identity. It is almost a biological form and is rather like an amoeba (a figure which for this context I borrow from Francis Fergusson speaking of the psyche in Dante)—an amoeba which takes form and color and shifting contour—indeed takes its detours—from the forces which attract it or which touch it. In Pirandello the self is adaptable by contagion and by desire and by thought, and both to itself and to others. The self is dramatically creative in all the roles it assumes, but remains—whence its sufferings and its joys—through all its phases vitally itself, its own identity, something as diaphanous, as individual, and as humorous as an ever-fresh voice. This, if you like, is the *play* of modern psychology by which the personality achieves itself. To read the novels and stories, to read or to see the plays of Pirandello, leads all the amoeba in oneself to take on the successive adventures of being. In Pirandello, the principle within fasterns itself onto all the possibilities from without.

In Kafka, what happens cuts down everything but the indestructible principle of the self, and what is left alive is all that might have been become excruciating, intolerable, proud, impossible: an inner shriek of the deracinated quick of spirit: as if Pascal had become a novelist on the theme of how the monstrous world attacks the guilty self. I think of Gregor in "The Metamorphosis" who becomes a cockroach and is squashed by his family, and I think of the prisoner in the penal colony whose crime, whose identity is gradually written upon him with needles and knives; and when the writing is done he dies, or perhaps before—for it is possible that the crime of identity can only be achieved posthumously. In Kafka you find your identity in your guilt, you find it in an alien and official world, which is yet most desirable, and you find it only when you have been excluded and turn yourself in absolute isolation. In Kafka you have religious novels of rebirth where only the agony, not the birth, takes place. Kafka is a master of all that in us which craves to the point of absolute jealousy the condition of frustration: the vision of which has been one of the crimes of modern society taken from modern psychology. The jealous god excruciates the jealous soul. It is what happens when the Jewish part (some say the Calvinistic part) of Christianity forgets all practical wisdom and replaces it with the terror of logic, the nightmare from which we cannot wake up. The logic of Kafka—and no imaginative writer was ever more logical, more sharp in syntax—is like that. It is a world where to achieve identity there is a logical reduction of possibility and where, as Gide says in another context and with the opposite response, God loves us only by the calamities he imposes on us. It is no wonder Kafka never finished any of his major works; his own death had first to supervene. He had a terrible vision of all within us that is against ourselves; he did not destroy, but he inverted his bourgeois humanism; precisely as Pirandello, as all but the worst Italians do, began afresh with what made humanism worth while.

In all these writers whom we have mentioned human conduct flourishes and literature finds its life. In them all—and in so many others not mentioned—we saw fragments of the troubles that are, forms from the techniques of new troubles our age has discovered, and attempts, greater or less, to encompass and to cope with these troubles with the technical resources of the humane imagination; with whatever had survived in the gift of each author of bourgeois humanism. For another name, we could perhaps call it charity of understanding or passion of perception or the everlasting need to cry out, to cry up or to cry down, the sweetness and the torture of the human in relation to human. But to them all, I think, we had primarily to bring something which was our own and not specifically called for; we had to bring what was not there and needed. Like ourselves, the work of these writers was incomplete. Let us turn now to three writers who require us to bring a great deal, and more than our other writers, but

128

who specify in the very nature of their work what it is that we must bring; and precisely because they are writers whose work is more nearly complete and cannot easily be exhausted; work which because of its formal superiority, supplied with tact and skill by the authors, goes on if not to new life at least to new and different uses, and which as much as any of the rival creations of the mere mind has a life of its own, a life which consists precisely in having given shape and theoretic form to our troubles.

We shall speak a little of Thomas Mann, a little more of André Gide, and as much as there may be room for on James Joyce. This order and these brevities do not represent an estimate of stature or importance. I have said a good deal elsewhere on Thomas Mann and if I quoted myself at all would have to do so at great length; I myself have gotten more out of him than from any prose writer alive and working in my time, and I will say that his last book, *Felix Krull,* is in effect a marvelous and heightened version of my own autobiography, and it is with great personal regret that I remember that he died before he could carry the story beyond the hero's twentieth year. I regret that I shall never know what was in store for me in the unwritten years of my life. As for Gide, I have loved him with aversion, and have fought him with delight, for above a quarter century; he is another twist to my own Protestant New England heritage with a Mediterranean addition which is both his and mine. He looked at the world with his own need for revolt and demeaned himself with an excess of honesty, just as with an excess of economy he very often nearly threw himself away. He seems to me to have created a rival world for all those not myself, but to have used part of myself in doing so. As for Joyce, he is a part of my bloodstream since my sixteenth year, and as my blood changed so he changed within it. I knew he was a great writer, and a writer who would be great for me, before I had finished reading the Christmas dinner scene in the *Portrait of the Artist as A Young Man.* As for the rest, I give no precedence in honoring Bloomsday.

But these writers are all familiar to you; indeed they mean a great deal even to those of you who have never read them. They are a part of our conscience, and in the change of our conscience, towards the world, they are part of how we see the world. They ask for a judgment beyond the literary judgment precisely because they are masters of literature. They made great forms, and it was by their forms that they aroused antagonism and commanded assent; and they demanded attention, which they often got, beyond the habits of the amused part of the mind at this or in any other time. Let us see how this was done.

I would ask you to observe of Thomas Mann that almost all his heroes are bourgeois humanists tainted by art. Sometimes they are artists themselves like Aschenbach in "Death in Venice." Sometimes plastic imag-

129

inations like Hans Castorp in *The Magic Mountain,* sometimes poets within themselves like Joseph, and sometimes artistic scoundrels like the lamented Felix Krull. It is the taint of the artist in them that raises them to heroic proportions; for it is that which compels them to take stock of the sick and ailing, to seize on the unseemly, to expect the equivocal, and to rejoice in the problematic. These heroes are the outsiders within and participating in their society. They are all daemonic people redeemed from the diabolic by the human, but they would not have been daemonic had they not gone in for all the upsetting, all the low-grade relations we have in human nature. This, is what Mann does with the humanistic; sometimes in action as with Hans Castorp, sometimes in the refusal of action as with Joseph tearing himself loose from the clutches of the magnificently infatuated Potiphar's wife. So it is, too, with that portrait of the greatness of Goethe in *Lotte in Weimar,* where the very greatness consists in the conceit with which the hero tampers with human souls and aggrandizes his own very humanistic soul at every human expense. Almost one says that these heroes are all great, in their different ways, by reason of their infatuation. Almost, but not quite; for they all are gifted and skilled with the other lust which is the humanistic lust for knowledge, till knowledge itself seems a degradation of being or another taint in the soul, and truth becomes a kind of fiction— a kind of vital fraud practiced by the artist on his humane knowledge out of his total irresponsibility. It is by our frauds that we incriminate ourselves into the truth. "Now," says Felix Krull to himself as a boy, "Now you look plain and unpromising, but one day you will rise to the upper world magnificently adorned, to take your place at feasts, at weddings, to send your corks popping to the ceilings of private dining-rooms and evoke intoxication, irresponsibility, and desire in the hearts of men." And again, when he was living a double life as a waiter and man of the world, he says of himself: "Thus I masqueraded in both capacities, and the undisguised reality behind the two appearances, the real I, could not be identified because it actually did not exist." Thus it is that Mann does something with his bourgeois humanism; he adds the equivocalness of behavior explored.

André Gide had a lighter touch, though he, too, is aware of the heaping of knowledge, and knows how it must be made frivolous to be kept tolerable; which is a very humane sort of insight indeed, and is the way in which he knows that humility opens the gates of heaven, and humiliation those of hell. The taint in his heroes is not of the artist pure, but as the artist full of curiosity; he is aware of the sense in which even the purest artist is somehow artist *manqué,* the artist in spite at and of himself. He is the French puritan who nurses the devil within him, not as a poor relation as in Mann and Dostoevsky, but in his older and prouder role as the Prince of Darkness in whose service we must perform most of our acts, since he is our feudal self.

This I think can be illustrated in *The Counterfeiters*. You will remember that at the end of the book the young Boris kills himself for no good reason and every bad reason, the victim of the counterfeiters' plot. Just after the death Edouard, the novelist who is both a character in the book and who is writing a book of the same name, makes this entry in his journal: "I shall not make use of little Boris' suicide for my Counterfeiters . . . I accept reality coming as a proof in support of my thought, but not as preceding it . . . . Boris' suicide seems to me an indecency." The rest of the chapter explains the indecency: how the suicide was the only act not counterfeit that Gide records, how, in effect, Edouard is the greatest counterfeiter of them all. The last sentence in the book is Edouard's. He looks at his young nephew Caloub, brother to the other nephew whom he has seduced triumphantly but from whom he is now separated. "I shall be very curious to know Caloub," says Edouard, and you feel the whole thing is to do over again, and that there will be other suicides, other counterfeits. It is old La Pérouse, the dying music-teacher who makes us understand the sadness of this last sentence. La Pérouse tells us our blood makes a continual noise which drowns harmonies. ("In this world God always keeps silent. It's only the devil who speaks . . . . . No, no!" he cried confusedly, "the devil and God are one and the same; they work together. We try to believe that everything bad on earth comes from the devil, but it's because, if we didn't, we should never find strength to forgive God.") It is thus, to use La Pérouse's earlier words, that God's love for us becomes our calamity. He sacrifices his son and he gives us the devil's voice in our blood through or under which to hear the silence of his own. This is Edouard—or Gide— as the black puritan. "I feel very curious to know Caloub." As a man in the wrench of sincerity will achieve perfidy and slap our own face.

Sometimes it seems to me that Gide belongs in the tradition of Orpheus and that this work—*The Counterfeiters*—is his account of Orpheus' life between two deaths. Ovid gives it this way in the Loeb translation (*Metamorphoses*, X 79–85): "Orpheus had shunned all love of womankind, whether because of his ill success in love, or whether he had given his troth once for all. Still, many women felt a passion for the bard; many grieved for their love repulsed. He set the example for the people of Thrace of giving his love to tender boys, and enjoying the springtime and first flower of their youth (aetatis breve ver et primus)." It was a false life for Orpheus, full of true music, pure desperation, and compulsive debauchery; he had the job of finding himself, or re-creating the motive of which he had been deprived; and if Ovid is right he tried many times. I think the interest here is considerably more than anthropological. It is one of those things, this legend of Orpheus, into which the uncertain and ambivalent heroes of Gide and Proust may be made most naturally to fit, and where, once fitted, they will gain significance and an authenticated place in the order of nature. Gide could not have written this for himself; writing it himself he would I think have undermined himself—again excruciated himself as he did, it seems to me, in his *Theseus*. It is not every man who can understand *in himself* his classical matrix. I am the more sure of this when I reflect—not only on Proust and his obeisance to Mme. de Sévigné and the duc de Saint Simon—but also on George Santayana thinking he had tried twice to explain the dilemma of moral form, in *Lucifer* when he was young and in *The Last Puritan* when he was already old. The frames, not the content or the insights but the frames of the older societies were nearer to actual behavior than the Christian. But this is something to feel rather than to insist on, lest inadvertently another false frame be produced.

In any case, Gide never settled the moral question ahead of time—not the experience of morals, but the question of them. He and his books led a shady life in which the shadows exacerbated as often as they comforted, and I mean the same shadows. And this is our warrant for raising the matter substantively. It explains, I think, his need in *The Counterfeiters* for the multiple positive critique—the journals and the journals of the journals with which the book is furnished—each element of which criticizes and corrects the others constantly and with instant hind-thought. Each snaps at the tender heels of the others. But the multiple critique does not stop there, as it could not, for Gide, have arisen there. It needs as source and object the mimesis of reality, not realism, but a mimesis made out of a belief in the spontaneous, and a love of the final, and a recurrent mimetic reminiscence of society itself. Gide "knows," as in the book Profitendieu "knows" with the aid of his spies. He has the secret police of a lifetime's devoted observation of the half-instinctive, half-deep patterned secret societies of the heart. He knows the equivocal talismans that bind flesh and spirit. He knows, too, not at all equivocally but as directly as possible the shame of motives late-revealed, intermittent and shifting as the revelation may be. He knows the poverty of the body in relation to the poverty of the spirit. He knows that phase of Christian insight down to the marrow's chill and into the chill vertigo of the spirit, and how these may have joined in the swimming of blood and of silence in little Boris' head when he drew the fatal lot. He knows the devil almost better than anybody, and that as scripture says he has but a short time to live, and must needs change his form and place and latch on to a new start. Hence in his *Journal* his note that the devil is circulating incognito throughout the book. Circulating is the word; but there is a better word.

If you think the devil brings God at his heels (as he cannot help doing) and that he exists until he is recognized—just as God does not exist until

He is recognized—at least in the conscious soul—if you believe this, then you will see the advantages of saying that in Gide's novel the devil is migratory and that his migrations are desperate and rashly resolute. The devil migrates from character to character. In some he seizes the form of *dépit*—chagrin mixed with anger, rancour, and grudge as motivation: the source of what people do against their own good in relation to others. In some he floods woe and anguish, as in Laura and in La Pérouse: the source of what people do to their own ill for the good of others or the service of truth. In some he encourages instinct when thwarted or released by wealth or frustration, as in Passavant or Armand or Lillian. This devil always comes intending to stay; he is the prince of others' means. He has great strength of personality, great capacity for taking advantage of the situation, whatever turns up, or might turn up, and he cheats nobody so much as those who would woo him. Sometimes he is a mere spectre prodding energies that already exist, or precipitating a fall that was already in nature, as in Olivier the nephew whom Edouard seduces. Sometimes he is the flesh itself, as in Lillian and Vincent. Again he is *every thing but* the soul, as in Pauline who will sell her children to the devil for the sake of affection. In Boris, the boy who killed himself, this cannot be done: the disease was part of his soul. Boris is the little God who comes at the heels of the devil and the devil can only contaminate his *understanding* of God. The same thing may possibly be true of old La Pérouse: it is his understanding rather than his soul that was degraded: the mere depths of his nature. Possibly the mysterious artifact of Strouvilhou (who runs the counterfeit gang) is by *tour-de-force* one whom the devil actually makes the soul. We do not know him: in him the devil exists.

The devil, then, is what we do in our poverty to our poverty. Poverty, chastity, obedience. When the monk vows these he vows himself to accept three temptations of the devil and to meet him on his own ground, as if he could thereby be nearer to God: or to the understanding of God.

With such a bias, however described, how could Gide have been otherwise than, as a novelist, anti-mechanical, anti-James too, at every surface level. It was for him, in his obstinate black protestant puritanism, at the mechanical level that the devil could most creep in unseen; in consistencies of surface and consistencies of character . . . Like the monk, Gide wanted his novel to meet the devil face to face; wanted to find him whenever he took a fresh start. "I feel very curious to know Caloub." God too seemed possessed of a migratory habit, permanent only in transit and metamorphosis.

Gide was the most naked of all our novelists. If that is so then Joyce was the most protected. No book of our time exhibits so many deliberate and varied and compacted structures as *Ulysses,* unless it is perhaps *Finnegan's Wake;* and for something comparable we have to look back to

Dante. Think of Dante who read the soul of man, his double history pagan and Christian, through every mode of understanding from an *apex mentis,* a peak of thought, of the Christian world, just after it had begun to lose its balance. In order to read Dante we have to read his reading of the world as he himself read scripture: with *longo studio* and *grande amore* and so as not to offend the spirit of truth. It seems to me that we have to read Joyce much as we read Dante—only a little less so—with certain reservations and certain characterizations inappropriate to Dante. Our real interest is in what is there instead. It is what is underneath: the bubbling up, from under: what comes into creation, the cause and destruction of what is already created: the image of Molly-Penelope, the idea of Vico, the image of the circular cycle, the Homeric pattern, and all the various psychological and physiological and rhetorical patterns. This is the "characteristic" (not virtue, not defect) feature of the mind benefiting and suffering under the romantic impulse. To Dante there was experience which we must explore and understand. To Joyce there is unlimited experience which we must master and create, but which, in the end, reaches not into the heaven of truth but back into its sources. Nevertheless, Joyce went at his work as Dante did and tried to read his experience through every form or mode of knowledge available to him. The interesting thing is that he did so against the general will and custom of his time and without the aid of recognized modes for the creation and interpretation of such a reading. He had no four-fold pattern. He had to revolt against himself as well as his time and he had to use both himself and his time. He was compelled to create, as if single-handed, symbolic modes in which he could dramatize the city of man he knew. Whatever success he had came from his fundamental mastery of actual experience and his equally fundamental mastery of actual language, where each mastery was a foil and counterpart to the other. His failures, I suggest, came about insofar as he had hallucinations about either mastery: that omniscience is equal to total record, or that neologism is creation. But here I have no intention of judging either success or failure, only to indicate what it means to try to read Joyce as we read Dante—which is of course not at all the same as saying you would get the effect of Dante out of Joyce.

Among so many possible choices, we can perhaps do as well as not with a simple schematic comparison of the two heroes of *Ulysses:* of Stephen who moves under the sign of the Ashplant or Augur's rod, and Bloom who walks with a potato in his back pocket, the moly which is the black root with the white flower of safety in identity and conscience. Stephen is the image of Lucifer, an outcast by his own will, and intransigent to the last bite on the nail. Bloom is Christ (or, as the book says, "another"), is an alien by definition, and is supremely transigent in response to every twist of experience.   Stephen is the son Telemachus, Bloom the father Odysseus, and in either image are both Christian and Greek.   In Stephen there is the spirit of pride and warfare, in Bloom humility and persecution.   Stephen is the artist, Bloom is No-man.   Stephen mocks, Bloom accepts.   Stephen would destroy, Bloom would discover what is there.   Stephen is in isolation, Bloom is lonely.   Stephen scars himself with hatred, Bloom has falling qualms of fear.   Stephen would woo lust, Bloom love.   In Stephen there is a sequence of attributes which confront breakdown and lead to extinction; in Bloom there is a sequence which confronts the momentum of things and leads to revelation.   In Stephen there is the kingdom of the son, which is gone; in Bloom there are intimations of the Third Kingdom, which is to come.   Stephen is stricken by the agenbite of inwit; Bloom brims with full conscience.   Stephen blasphemes what inhabits him and is lacerated with the farce of things.   Bloom grasps what he does not understand and is in full accommodation to it.   Thus Stephen represents what lives but must be transformed.   Thus Bloom represents what has been transformed and what must be reformed.   Between the two is criticism and prophecy.   Here is the trouble of the two exiles, the exile of him who cannot inherit and the exile of him who cannot transmit his inheritance.   Joyce has made a rival creation in which we can become lost and can find ourselves, but which we cannot imitate except in him.

Irregular Metaphysics

R. P. Blackmur

Presented at the Library of Congress January 23, 1956

For the purpose of this lecture it is almost enough to begin by saying that where the great novelists of our times have dealt with the troubles caused by the new knowledges (and the erosion of some of the old ones) in a kind of broad and irregular psychology, so the poets have been led to deal with them (or to repel them, or rival them) in a kind of irregular and spasmodic, but vitalized metaphysics. Both have done so in terms of the charge of maintaining the health and the possibilities of language under the conditions of our knowledge. One of those conditions is the relative disappearance of generally accepted (if only for argument) systematic metaphysics that bears on daily life, the life of our own adventure, in which we have by no means lost our interest. Thus the poent and the literary man generally find themselves in the very irregular task of doing what they can by literary means to adjust the new and old relations of our knowledges to life. This is, I think, why Eliot began his early critical work by remarking on the dissociation of ideas which marks our times almost with stigmata. Thus it is that Paul Valéry could ask: "Whenever you think do you not feel you are disarranging something?" And thus, in writing about Valéry, Elizabeth Sewell could observe that "Words are the only defense of the mind against being possessed by thought or dream." Surely Housman had this in mind here:

> But men at whiles are sober
> And think by fits and starts,
> And if they think, they fasten
> Their hands upon their hearts.

Only poets have the incentive of the anti-poetic and anti-verbal. It is their material. This is an ancient condition seen in a contemporary form, and we have only to look back a little to Shakespeare to see how different our own form is, and would have seemed to him. If we think of the sonnets we see that they are instances of as near as possible straight statement, garnished with the version he used of the sonnet form; and we notice that there is the echo running through them of almost logical thought, gained from verbal syntax and retained from the medieval syllogism and the theory of destructive argument. Besides this there was at work the long history of gallant love that sprang from Toulouse and Bologna. All these surround, and feed, and it may even create, by reasonable means, the intuition and the attitude—the procession of things attended to *in form*— which, in their procession, in *that* order, constitute the poem. In the sonnets, as elsewhere in Shakespeare, reason is often queried—as the adventure of the unreasonable is often seized—but the query is always made from the point of view of Reason herself.

This is almost the opposite to Rimbaud's famous declaration in *Une Saison en Enfer,* the section called Alchemy of the Word: "I invented the color of vowels:—A black, E white, I red, O blue, U green.—I regulated the form and the movement of every consonant, and with instinctive rhythms I prided myself on inventing a poetic language accessible some day to all the senses. I reserved all rights of translation. At first it was an experiment. I wrote silences. I wrote the night. I recorded the inexpressible. I fixed frenzies in their flight."

Here, and it has been the ambition of many great writers since, the policy is taken up from *inside* the experience and outside the point of view of reason. Rimbaud would conquer fate by making one of his own. He is the permanent adolescent in us all—what lasts of adolescence—turned into, and fixed, as an eternal essence; hence his enormous and continuing appeal. He uses the trappings not the substance of his tradition—and is in his very freedom from it the more victim of its manipulations. One must be (in all prudence) as intimate with one's order as with one's disorder; else they become confused, and in a sense lose the power of existence—the experience of the love of men the Greeks called *philia.* There is no patience in Rimbaud; it is everywhere in Shakespeare.

If you do not like to think of Rimbaud in line with Shakespeare, it may be more agreeable to think of Shelley in one of those sentences struck off late at night, which yet last in the day by their own light. I have nothing to do here with the unacknowledged legislators of mankind, which was mere special pleading, but with one of those passionate insights into the nature of one's own work at its best—one's work if it really worked. It is like a Rimbaud who was not *only* adolescent. "All the authors of revolutions of opinion are not only necessarily poets as they are inventors, nor even as their words unveil the permanent analogy of things by images which participate in the life of truth; but as their periods are harmonious and rhythmical, and contain in themselves the elements of verse; being the echo of the eternal music." Here is the whole program of modern poetry and the gist of half its achievement. One would repeat, as text for everything wanted here to be said: The poets' words "unveil the permanent analogy of things by images which participate in the life of truth." The rest would be important if we were talking about prosody, but we are talking only about irregular metaphysics. The permanent analogy of things in images which participate in the life of truth, will do us very well. Shelley was only saying ahead of time, and abstractly, what Rimbaud was saying in the *élan* of ambition. Possibly this is what Maritain is saying, in the course of an examination of just the metaphysics of all modern poetry, as an afterthought about a process still going on. "Art bitten by poetry longs to be freed from reason." *This* is the disassociation of ideas, it is the fusion of senses and the exercise of their interchangeability in words and thereby thoughts and ideas, and it *is* the representative notion behind the enormous stride of sensuality in the last century of poetry—for however metaphysical or symbolical we may have become in our poetry we have also acquired for it a sensuality no modern language has hitherto known. If Rilke had his angels, Lorca had his gypsies. It is these we have put side by side, and in them seen our permanent analogies.

Analogy is exactly the putting of things side by side. In poetry they are bound together by rhythm, sped by metre, united by vision, experienced by music, said in voice. In analogy we get the relation of attributes, not substances; we get the *form* of reality as if form were itself a kind of action. If we think of the Greeks, we would say that the Oedipus of Sophocles is the more nearly logical, and that the Heracles of Euripides is the more nearly analogical; and it is for this reason that we have only lately begun to grasp the form of Euripides. Analogy is also the deep form of reminding that there is always something *else* going on: the identity which is usually a mystery apprehended in analogy; what is lost in "mere" logic, but is carried along in the story.

Analogy is like the old notion of under-plot, or second plot in Elizabethan drama. Sometimes these under-plots were only two logics, sometimes one and sometimes another; but sometimes they were a multiplying process. One times one equals one, but a one which is also a third thing, which is fused in the mind, in the looking of one working on the other. Emotions can be like plot and underplot. If we put two emotions of the established sorts in association (like love and hate) we get an artistic emotion differing from either but with attributes common to both. In association, emotions are fruitful, and we get a sense of living action where there had been sets of abstraction: as in the Mass. Feelings are even more fruitful than emotions.

138

When Robert Frost comes to the end of his poem "Stopping by Woods on a
Snowy Evening"—

> *The woods are lovely, dark and deep,*
> *But I have promises to keep,*
> *And miles to go before I sleep,*
> *And miles to go before I sleep.*

When he has got to the end, he has made a revelation in feelings; what you
cannot otherwise touch; only *so;* and the analogies multiply and deepen
into surds of feeling.

Analogy is indeed the very name for our characteristic poetic logics. No
doubt the attraction of analogy for us is in the fragmentation of faith and
the diversity of logics and the divisiveness of our minds generally. These
fragments, says Eliot, I have shored against my ruins. For two gross of
broken statues, says Pound, for a few thousand battered books. What shall
I do for pretty girls, says Yeats, now my old bawd is dead? And so on.
One should remember that the attraction of analogy for the medieval mind
(to which we so much and so diversely resort) was just the opposite. To
the medieval mind the unity of things was insistently present, and had to be
interpreted; to us unity is what we only seek by all the machineries of
desperation and longing, sometimes longing without hope; and the means
of our search is by analogy or collateral form.

The reason why "Prufrock" is *now* a popular poem (though it was a very
difficult poem for most people for its first twenty years of life) is that the
analogies with which it is composed have had time to sink in. This, too,
is how poems change and grow and even sometimes disappear: in relation
to our apprehension of what is in analogy, where the elements go on working. The obscurity is like that of the womb. Collateral or analogical form
is as near as we are likely to come to the organic. Dialectic (in the modern
sense) only excites the passion for analogy in the creative sense. We can
say for poetry that only in analogy are the opposites identical; and it was
a similar perception that led St. Augustine to say that in every poem there
is some of the substance of God.

My point had perhaps better be pushed a little further and by an analogy
taken from mathematics and physics thought of besides poetry and morals.
In mathematics it is not necessary to know what one is talking about; in
physics it is, since the test is in knowledge. Yet the mathematics (creating
out of the rigor of formal relations) generates the physics, and often does
so without being itself understood. Mathematics is theoretic form for the
feeling of the relation of things.

Poetry is like mathematics, morals like physics; and it is sometimes "true" that poetry creates the morals in the sense that poetry creates the felt relations of things which unite the substance and the problems of morals. Poetry is the rebelliousness and the pang of what is alive; poetry gives, as Dante says, the war of the journey and of the pity: creates the story of them. Poetry takes action in morals as mathematics does in physics.

There is a sense in which knowledge, when we have given it form, is creation—all knowledge, including revelation. Mathematics created the physics of the modern world, created the terms and released the powers of all our troubles. It is only an exaggeration, then, to say that poetry created the morals of the modern world, and sets in action the modes of human love and all the other heroic or rebellious modes of human behavior.

In this analogy, mathematics confronted the old physics; poetry confronted the old morals. Out of each confrontation comes the response either of a rival creation or an increment to creation, and in each case the relations between the two are likely to be irregular. The old physics and the old morals still tyrannize those parts of us and of the universe which do not conform—and because of truth or vitality—to the new powers and pangs. A firm rational view is possible in either field, but the poetic impulse is rather towards creation just as our behavior springs from the "enormous lap of the actual," and just because we believe in most, and find most precious, what of the actual we ourselves create. I do not say that this is what modern poetry "really" does, but that this is sometimes its operative ambition and its saving illusion. It is a course in which we have not—and cannot—reach the extreme. Even as our minds create new knowledge, we are still God's spies. Every new form of knowledge, or of the human, is monstrous until it is made a part of the acknowledgment of reason. Reason likes the finished job; poetry *likes* the new job—the living process rather than the vital purpose.

It is not surprising that an enterprise of this order—combining as it does, in intention, all the reach of the senses and all the norms of the mind—should have produced the first learned poetry in England since Milton, with the singular difference that it is also and deliberately irrational in its processes—is indeed an effort to erode the rational for metaphysical purposes. This is because the metaphysics was itself expressionistic, arising out of personal warrant and with a distrust of existing forms, whether intellectual or aesthetic. Many of these metaphysical poets rejected much of their traditional craft and syntax and quivered with horror at all statements not drawn from dreams. Expressionistic metaphysics has often paraded in a masquerade of painful unlearning, and a special kind of illiteracy goes with the learnedness where it remains. It knows its own fragmentariness and must reject every system as a deceit, and must therefore erect systems known to be inadequate.

Of all that has been said so far of the contours of this ambitious form of the poetic mind, there is no livelier illustration than *The Waste Land*. I say nothing here of what I hope to exemplify at the end of these remarks: the dramatic sensuality of the thought in the poem. Here I am concerned with the structures of the poem as they can be easily separated, the structures with which Eliot protects his poem from the ravages of its subject. Like the *Ulysses* of James Joyce, only less so, *The Waste Land* affords and requires a maximum of structures, and requires it in the effort to do the job of reason in the absence of effective predictive form. Reason had above all to do the labour of making the form all over again, for it had the labour of associating the elements of a sensibility believed to be dissociated empirically. This, if you like, was reason in madness, operating and drawing from madness; it was reason controlling madness. Let us list a few of the elements of this structure, and let us begin with the epigraph about the Cumean Sibyl hanging forever in a cage because she had forgotten the need for regeneration in the mere lust to endure. When, when, *when*, WHEN will the sands run out? She is perhaps the heroine of the poem, and the boys, acolytes, choirboys, scamps can only help her by jeering at her, and she can answer them only in Greek: I wish to die. She is the heroine of all that is stupid and clutching in life, if you like of all that survives, and is a little outside the poem, suspended over it in a cage. Against her, within the poem, is Tiresias, the hero of all that is numinous and comes from the godhead, but in the poem bored as well as tragic; he is the perspective and fate, of all that was created and made. He is the blind foreseer, the man who was woman. He is the hero of all our meanings that are beyond safety, the very peril of vision. Between the Sibyl and Tiresias—between the two forms of prophecy and their enactments—comes the up and down and all around the town of the poem; everything that goes with the actions of this poem and its frames, all that has to do with the Tarot pack of cards, with Christ, the Holy Grail, and Buddha. Through all these, in the walls and ceilings and floors as stringers and uprights, run various other structural elements. There is the liberating force of "literary" religion and the liberating force of "literary" anthropology (what comes from Jessie Weston and Frazer), and the preserving force of "allegorical" understanding. I do not know which of these has been more misinterpreted, and I would for myself only suggest that we accept them as part of Eliot's means of giving the weight of various intellectual orders of his poem, much as we have done with the merely "literary" references in the details of the text—all the better when we have not recognized them.

Here are two sentences that bear, taken from Basil Willy's *The Seventeenth Century Background* (Anchor edition, p. 72). "It is hard to say which is the more misleading—the 'fundamentalist' reading which mistakes mythology for history, or the Alexandrian, which sees allegory where none was intended. In both there is a lack of capacity to distinguish between what is 'statement' and what is emotive speech, a deficiency which not only effected scriptural interpretation, but rendered impossible any satisfactory theory of poetry for very many centuries." So with the interpretation of Eliot and Yeats. In these various orders which Eliot has used there is no recognizable principle of composition. Even the Sibyl and Tiresias are not enough. The reason would not have been able to take up her task of poetic thought had not the psyche (one's private share of the Numen) brought in the compulsive force of images, of the obsessions of dreams, and of the force of dramatic mimesis to set up and reveal the hidden analogies of things. Thus it was that those of us who knew the least in the intellectual sense, in the first instance understood the poem best.

To reveal the hidden analogies of things; Shelley's insight was Eliot's task as poet; he has in his images to remind reason of its material, to remind order of its disorder, in order to create a sane art almost insane in its predicament. He had to make a confrontation of the rational with the irrational: a deliberate reversal of roles.

Here is part IV of *The Waste Land*, "Death by Water":

> *Phlebas the Phoenician, a fortnight dead,*
> *Forgot the cry of gulls, and the deep sea swell*
> *And the profit and loss.*
> $\qquad\qquad$ *A current under sea*
> *Picked his bones in whispers. As he rose and fell*
> *He passed the stages of his age and youth*
> *Entering the whirlpool.*
> $\qquad\qquad$ *Gentile or Jew*
> *O you who turn the wheel and look to windward,*
> *Consider Phlebas, who was once handsome and tall as you.*

This, as you will remember, is all there is to this section of the poem; it is a lyric interlude put in to remind you what the rest of the poem is about. Here the Reason and the Psyche together make a *poetic* rival creation, and make it in analogous symbolism, not logical allegory. The analogy moves wherever you wish it and wherever it wishes to move you. Here again are Valéry's question and Miss Sewell's comment. "Whenever you think do you not feel you are disarranging something?"—"Words are the only defense of the mind against being possessed by thought or dream." It is the words working on each other that make the life and the identity in the analogy.

We could as well speak only of Eliot and Yeats, letting all others go, and still have a good image of the poetry that crystallized in the middle twenties; but that would be to regularize that poetry too much, when what we want is the sense of the rich irregularity of the time. The ripe fruit is still falling all about us in various tang, if all fed from the same soil yet variable in exposure to the weather. So let us try a handful, but returning to Eliot and Yeats at the end, with a better sense of their variety and their irregularity and, I should hope, our own practicing metaphysics, regular and irregular.

There is Hart Crane and Wallace Stevens, from whom I must beg off except to say that their stature is incontestable. The one represents every ignorance possible to talent when it has genius, every wilfulness tolerable because of expressive intention; Crane, of all American poets, could deprive words of almost all their meaning but yet could so wall them about with his poetry that they had the effect of actually inexhaustible meaning. Stevens could play with every nuance of thought and yet, because he had no generalizing or organizing power, give the effect of wayward impromptu music possible to a Harmonium. Crane you understand best if you try for nothing beyond the senses, Stevens is for relishing as the longest repetition of sweet things in the world. Crane had no manner, but a kind of fused style that strikes you. Stevens was a mannerist in thought as well as style. Crane was the vice of our time, and the strength of it never left him. Stevens was more the excess of our time, part of it only because deliberate, and the weakness of that was never quite made up for. Both men are saved by their sensuality, by "the dry sound of bees stretching across lucid space" in Crane, or, in Stevens, "the dark encroachment of that old catastrophe, as a calm darkens among water-lights."

But this is to say nothing. And there are others, like Marianne Moore, of whom there is no doubt as to stature but of whom nothing at all can be said here. It seems simpler therefore to skip over men like Allen Tate with his passionate grasp after insight, and John Ransom who makes lyric incantations in light forms of all that can be made durable through the close caressing observation of the fleeting. (Besides, I speak of friends.)

Let us look rather at the obstinate figure of Ezra Pound, and to force the point of our irregular metaphysics, let us look at him together with Whitman. Each is a barbarian, and neither ever found a subject that compelled him to composition; each remained spontaneous all his life. In Whitman you find the sprawl of repetition, in Pound the heap of ideographs; in either case we ourselves make the thought emerge. In Whitman there is the catalogue which is not catalogued. In Pound there is the catalogue, these jewels of conversation. In both you have to know your way around and who the people are.

Nobody ever learned anything but attitude or incentive from Whitman. His example liberates the vatic weakness in others—that easiest of all reservoirs, spontaneity. Everybody has learned from Pound how to go about his own work; he liberates the compulsion to knowledge of his craft—at least in those who do not look merely to express themselves for themselves. So far as influence on aspects other than craft, Whitman is a better influence than Pound because of the great general blobs in which he uses the language. Whitman could have been an influence on Melville; but Melville must have been a threatening example to Whitman. Whitman wrote *Leaves of Grass,* Melville *Moby Dick; or The Whale.* One is the rush, the other the mighty effort to organize the rush. Pound's *Cantos* are less than a rush.

The barbarians are those outside us whom we are tempted to follow when we would escape ourselves. We imitate Whitman to get emotion; we imitate Pound to strike an attitude which might destroy the emotion we already have, or at least render it harmless. There is never, except in fragments, any shape given to the emotion itself, nor any organization of the feelings into an emotion. Both are good poets when we ourselves wish to be fragmentary. This is the sort of judgment we reach if we apply Coleridge's notion that poetry should show a state of more than usual emotion in more than usual order.

Pound is a crackerbarrel Mencken proceeding by crotchets and *idées fixes;* but he is also *Il miglior fabbro* and at that level knows everything, and knows besides all that his ears and eyes could tell. Here is "Medallion":

> *Luini in porcelain.*
> *The grand piano*
> *Utters a profane*
> *Protest with her clear soprano.*
>
> *The sleek head emerges*
> *From the gold-yellow frock*
> *As Anadyomene in the opening*
> *Pages of Reinach.*
>
> *Honey-red, closing the face-oval,*
> *A basket-work of braids which seem as if they were*
> *Spun in King Minos' hall*
> *From metal, or intractable amber;*

144

> *The face-oval beneath the glaze,*
> *Bright in its suave bounding-line, as,*
> *Beneath half-watt rays,*
> *The eyes turn topaz.*

Whitman is a crackerbarrel *Song of Solomon* proceeding by seizures. But he is also the Bard of everything in us that wants to be let alone so that we can be together, and he knows how to get rid of all the futility of mere meaning and the horror of mere society. When we read him in another language, as French, all our riches are there. When we read Pound in another language, as Italian, all our poverty is there. In neither is our *miseria* or our passion.

If when we think of Pound we think of Whitman, then in thinking of E. E. Cummings let us think of Dryden. In Dryden there is the effort to find the harmony of things, in spite of any obstacle, and with echoes from everywhere present. There is the tension of the classical and the Christian, the allegory of the will of God clothed in good sense, but spangled with another will, that of poetic harmony. But there is never a serious question of what is the will of God. The created world reflects the harmony, and the will is the light shining in the darkness. There was never a serious trouble in the head or in the heart—though the heart might have occasionally to change its beat. Dryden was one of those men who could always make up his mind—and, at an easier level, could always change his mind as one changes clothes with the weather—to maintain a durable state within. But there was little balance of perilous things, no heart of silence, in his great syntax.

Cummings has no syntax, and I do not mean merely the syntax of grammar; he lays out his fragments typographically, almost topographically. His reason is in his point of view—from which he sees, argues, arranges the simplest of all conformities, that of the salutation and the insult, of assent and rejection. He marshals nothing, but wants things his own way. This is why he deprives many of his words of as much as possible of *their own* meaning: so that they may take on *his* meaning. This is also why he rids himself of the pointing power of punctuation: so that the current of *his* meaning will not aim at, or flow, against his will. I suspect that he is afraid of the music of poetry (of which his early poems show that he is a master, and of which his later poems show that he never lost the memory) for similar reasons; he is afraid that the music would communicate another enthusiasm than his. It is not so much that Cummings is a poet of the anti-intelligence; he wants rather to transform intelligence into a kind of instinct: as if instinct could be one's own creation. Hence his simplicity and his sentimentality. Hence too his use of connectives as substances, pronouns as nouns, prepositions as verbs. His unity is in the substantial unity of emotion in experience.   Dryden's unity is in the achieved unity of intellect taken as conviction.

For another sort of adventure, let us think of W. H. Auden along with Tennyson.   In Tennyson the verse and the sensibility have contour (as different from fingering or phrasing) and plastic competence (as different from substance of thought).   The wild within him is held in.   By comparison, we have in Auden the roughness which has the coherence of schist, the adherence of the particles of contrary elements.   The wild within holds itself together by force of mind.   Destruction is his pose, without composure. In Tennyson there is the role of the poet, in Auden the role of the poem: two forms of heroism.   In Tennyson, there is the maker of things beyond the reach of their tension, under another music, which belongs to the words. In Auden there is the expressiveness *of* the tension, in rough music that compacts as you hear it over, within its form of words.   In Tennyson the poems at best unite with, lead to, or are graced by *their* images.   In Auden the images habitually participate in, are functional parts, of the action of the poems, and are themselves the grace.   Of both we might say, There is the beauty in his daily life, that makes mine ugly.   In Auden it is the rugged mass that just escapes the habit of form.   In Tennyson, the habit of verse keeps warm the inner form.   Tennyson perpetuates clichés, or what must become cliché, by the very nature of the process by which he leaves things out.   Auden constantly re-expands cliché by what he puts in. Tennyson tells anecdotes of myth, Auden sees anecdote become myth. Tennyson must find room in this turmoil for his culture, he must find convenient form.   Auden must present or express or enact the internecine warfare of behavior (the turmoil) out of which culture might be *made*. Tennyson lived in an age of balance with new weights to be distributed. Auden inaugurates the second phase of the age of the techniques of trouble, the age of anxiety, as one of his books reminds us, taken not as melancholy but as ferocity or gall—something more forcible than mere "spleen."

It is along the lines of these comparisons that Tennyson and Auden acquired their characteristic moods.   The mood of a poem is as much a part of its thought as its conventions or its predilections or its ideas.   The mood is the mixture of the elements of the experience and the approach, the perception and the sensibility.   Mood is the mystique of poetic thought: the medium of participation.   Tennyson ached for finish, which made his mood. If Ezra Pound roughened the expressive surface of a mind already, and badly made up, Auden roughened the mind itself, raw for adventure; and that is *his* mood.   But all three submit, accept, assent to the force of words and all take advantage of and succumb to the prosody of their language.

Partly for the sheer pleasure of the contrast let us think together of Lord Byron and William Carlos Williams.   Neither of these two men ever reached

146

mastery of the medium of verse, towards which their attitudes were vulgar. There was the vulgarity of aristocratic carelessness and there was the vulgarity of the baby-doctor in a run-down North Jersey urban-rural community. In each the felicities are of raw perception (or unappeased sophistication). In Byron a raw (jocular) formality; in Williams a raw (gusty) magic. In neither case was there any intervention (or assistance) by unity of apperception. Byron saw no need, Williams was, and is, against it. Each had plenty of the violence of talent (the aura of genius): quite enough to require the control of style; but neither saw the requirement as worth taking up. Therefore their "thought" runs towards what with a view to poetry we call prose. In Byron, the ideas are other peoples', the attitude a pose, but the rhymes are superbly his. He rhymes his attitudes and his "thoughts." In Williams, nothing is his except the magic of his direct perception. We could not come much nearer bottom, except in the absence of talent.

That is to say that both poets depend on the rhetorical forces in language at a low state of cultivation and under a minimum state of control. Byron had a sterile state of control over a very ordinary state of emotion. Williams had a vigorous and unusual state of emotion with control vested in the fallacy of expressive form. Byron has the sneer of position, Williams the cry of sincerity. Byron is the snobbism of conventionality, Williams its primitivism. But each has his powers to an unusual degree of competence, and each in his own way to an unusual degree of freshness, to an unusual kind of immediate persuasiveness, with, in addition for Williams, the occasional *pang*.

Byron is a kind of sensorium of attitude, Williams a kind of omnibus of sensation. Remember, though, as Eliot said of D. H. Lawrence, both were careful about what interested them: Byron the rhymes, Williams the sensation. Both were prolix as only the little gift can be; neither ever found a subject to command his own powers of attention; both were spontaneous, though each from opposite ends of the rhetorical spectrum—Byron ultra-violet, Williams infra-red. These were their interests, and these the ways they worked. One wishes that both had taken deeper forms.

In the poetry of Eros—the force from below, the impulse that satisfies itself only in the instance—we see emphatic cases of the experience of thought where, if you like, the experience comes very near becoming thought— as near as symbolic action can come. This is one of the great examples of tautology: where things become their own meaning: which is the condition of poetry—however great or narrow the selection of experience may be. It is how many-modedness becomes one, how we reduce the many to the one—sometimes to one Sphinx, sometimes to one Grand Inquisitor. We think of Eros, and we think of John Donne and of Garcia Lorca as specific examples of this kind of thought in poetry.

We say of Donne that he thinks with his feelings and then go on to say that he feels his thought. The famous figure of the compasses we take as the feeling of thought. Yet we should remember that Donne needed his "platonic" thought and his scholasticism to make a structure for his feelings, but he could not trust his thought unless he could feel it. His true thought lay in the area where the jointure was made. He could not trust either his senses alone or his figures alone.

When we come to Lorca something has happened to the western mind. It has come to insist on the authority—in words, in thought—of the senses, and particularly the authority of sexual sensuality. Poetry became sensual in this fashion with the French symbolists, but hardly reached its present level till after the first world war. It was only that in this respect words had come to resemble the mediums of the other arts. Sensual experience became in poetry what it had often been in painting, sculpture, music, one of the great substances of thought; and Lorca is an example. Where the older eroticism mainly merely pointed, Lorca must present, as in these lines: "Her thighs escaped me like startled fishes, half filled with fire, half filled with frost." The feelings *are* thought, in a new way: they affect directly some of the other types of thought as another kind of the same thing. The revolution here is merely letting something in at an operative level which had previously been there at a kind of *known remove* from the words.

To think of Rilke let us also think of Robert Herrick and Emily Dickinson.[1] All three are nuptial poets. Herrick marries the created world, Dickinson marries herself, Rilke creates within himself something to marry which will—which does—marry and thereby rival the real world. In Herrick the direct experience was always for the sake of something else to be found in the plenitude of God's creation of nature. Thus it is that this clergyman played at wearing great costumes in which we must acknowledge the union of God and Nature. His order is the world's order of his time, his poetry what he did with it.

In Dickinson, one spends all one's life finding a role apart from life, in which one creates one's own role in despite of the world. Born in unity, one cuts oneself off, and cuts one's losses in the role of one's own immortality. What was sensuality in Herrick becomes in her the blow of deprived sensation on the quick. The direct experience was for her always for something else which would replace the habit and the destructive gusto of experience itself. This is the best that could be done with the puerile marriage of the self with the self: a sensorium for the most part without

---

[1] This and the next paragraph have appeared in a slightly different version in the course of my review of Johnson's edition of Emily Dickinson.

the senses, it is sometimes the vision of sense itself. In Rilke, one spends all one's life in a constant succession (almost simultaneous in experience) of withdrawal and return; withdrawal from the actual world and return to the same world, with no loss of response to it, but with something added through the figures which inhabit his poems. I think of the Angel who makes his peremptory apparitions in so many of the poems with the frightfulness of the absolute, which if one is to survive into death, must be accepted. Put the other way round, Rilke transformed, not himself, but his life into an approach to death. His books built his own death all the way from a noise in the valley to the crashing permanence of the world. This he had to do because life—God's creation alone—had lost its plenitude, its habit of continuing creation. It is the chain of being that is our own, the plenitude is for us to *find*. This is the pull in Rilke that makes him a great poet and draws us after. His order is his own: what he has done with the world in adoring it; and we use it, in those moments where we resemble him and where he creates our thoughts, as *our* own.

Yeats and together with him Coleridge (who will help us draw the picture in one more comparison) is of the same great school as Rilke, but with differences which are enlightening. Yeats is nearer the ordinary world than either. In Coleridge the dream is numinous and its cultivation is meant to discover that reality. In Yeats there is another reality made up out of the chosen rituals of soldiers, hunters, poets, wicked ladies and wenches (as earlier there had been the "false" Ireland and the "false" Joachim of Flora) and also made up out of the *poète maudit*, and the dandy. In 1900, says Yeats, we stopped drinking absinthe with our coffee. Compared to Coleridge, there is nothing numinous in Yeats, there are rather fetishes, obsessions, infatuations such as engage us all most days and hours. The matters of curiosity in *The Ancient Mariner* and *Xanadu* are mere masking fancies, here secondary creations, which fall off to reveal the reality of what is sometimes called the sacramental vision of life, and the whole is indeed a means of discovering what that reality is. In Yeats we create reality in terms of our fancies. This is what is meant by the celebrated phrase, "In dreams begin responsibilities;" and it is best commented in the late cry, "What shall I do for pretty girls now my old bawd is dead?"; or again, in "I was blessèd, and could bless."

One concludes that the power in Yeats depends very little on the machinery of his Vision (we keep it only for purposes of scaffolding, for hints on how to ad lib, and how to run the frame of the dramatization of an idea) and does depend very much on the fancies of flesh and piety on which he seized. Yeats was an erotic poet with regard to his objects, not a sacramental poet. Homer is my example, he says, and his unchristened heart; but he also needed shenanigans. Thus he had the image of a beautiful woman predominant, and the image of Dante's face, with the hollows of our own soul sunk in it, as our christendom and politics and religion; and had also the phases of the moon and the great year and *anima mundi* and larky séances; thus he had fairies; and thus he had Swift and Goldsmith, Berkeley and Burke. Yet his vision is what he saw, the actual world to which he added, but which he did not wish to rival.

One concludes that the power in Coleridge's poetry depends very little on the sensations of the actual world and very greatly, in the end exclusively, on the substance of vision—which was not his own, but with which he united through a communication of spirit. He saw what his vision compelled him to. His fascinating personal life has almost nothing to do with the power of his poetry—which may be why he wrote so little where Yeats wrote so much of worth—or only so far as he found himself revealed in his vision. There is nothing erotic in his poetry; his work is *agapé*, without either *eros* or *philia*. So in the end, we see in Yeats, character moving in the flesh, emotion trespassing on and conquering spirit, and intuition seizing hold on the whole life, including the nameless life within us; and in Coleridge we see what moves character from within, including the nameless power.

I know no sharper contrast than this to bring us to direct contemplation of the sensuality of the irregular metaphysics of the poetry of our time, or what was once our time. We have had too many comparisons and perhaps most of them were of qualities of poets which ought not to be compared. Let me hope only that there was some creative virtue (which I would prefer to the critical in any case) in the analogies the comparisons may have suggested. To close let us drop comparisons and quote three examples of what I mean by sensual metaphysics, one from Eliot and two from Yeats.

From part V of *The Waste Land*, I take these lines:

> *A woman drew her long black hair out tight*
> *And fiddled whisper music on those strings*
> *And bats with baby faces in the violet light*
> *Whistled, and beat their wings*
> *And crawled head downward down a blackened wall*
> *And upside down in air were towers*
> *Tolling reminiscent bells, that kept the hours*
> *And voices singing out of empty cisterns and exhausted wells.*

The exegetes tell us, and it is true, that we are in the Chapel Perilous and the Perilous Cemetery is no doubt near at hand, and it may be as one of the exegetes says that we hear something like the voice of John the Baptist in the last line. But for myself, I muse and merge and ache and find myself feeling with the very senses of my thought greetings and cries from all the senses there are.

150

Here is the sonnet called "Leda and the Swan":

A sudden blow: the great wings beating still
Above the staggering girl, her thighs caressed
By the dark webs, her nape caught in his bill,
He holds her helpless breast upon his breast.
How can those terrified vague fingers push
The feathered glory from her loosening thighs?
And how can body, laid in that white rush,
But feel the strange heart beating where it lies?
A shudder in the loins engenders there
The broken wall, the burning roof and tower
And Agamemnon dead. Being so caught up,
So mastered\by the brute blood of the air,
Did she put on his knowledge with his power
Before the indifferent beak could let her drop?

No doubt we have here the annunciation of Greek civilization and the turning of the Great Year, but it was not this that disturbed the churchmen of Dublin when the poem first appeared; the metaphysics was deeper than that of any existing church. It was the staggering, vague blow of the knowledge and power of the central, spreading, sexual quick: the loosening of thought into life and into itself, with a gained life.

Here, to end, is a small poem of Yeats called "A Deep-Sworn Vow":

Others because you did not keep
That deep-sworn vow have been friends of mine;
Yet always when I look death in the face,
When I clamber to the heights of sleep,
Or when I grow excited with wine,
Suddenly I meet your face.

Here the senses have given a new order to thought of all time and all eternity. It is not from wine to sleep to death, as thought without the senses might say; it is from death to sleep to wine, which the senses create the thought to say.   In these poems we have what Milton wanted poetry to be: the simple, the sensuous, the passionate. We have made the potential, within its own limits so endless, real; it is the thought which was *first* in the senses.

Contemplation

R. P. Blackmur

Presented at the Library of Congress January 29, 1956

At this point I should like to carp at myself a little. What we have been talking about as the literature of the twenties, with its grasp of the irrational, its techniques of trouble, and its irregular metaphysics—with its fear of syntax, its resort to arbitrary orders, and its infinite sensuality—may very well turn out to have been an aberration, a mere intermittence in the great heart of literature. The true current of literature may have flowed purer through other names which we have hardly mentioned. Robert Frost rather than Eliot, Robinson rather than Yeats, De La Mare rather than Rilke might be the objects of poetic study. The line of Galsworthy and Maugham, of Jules Romains' *Men of Good Will* rather than Proust's *Remembrance of Things Past,* of E. M. Forster's *Passage to India* rather than Joyce's *Ulysses,* perhaps Heinrich Mann rather than his brother Thomas may turn out to have carried the true Cross. I would not wish to presume on the judgment of another generation, but I would insist that if E. M. Forster comes to top Joyce in aesthetic estimation, it will be because another aspect of imagination than that with which I am familiar has taken over. I know some names will go up and others go down, but not that far; and as for myself, I expect the unity of literature will include them all, for unity in literature is what we feel together—as any bookshelf will show us, whether it be the books of one man or of fifty. I speak here by my bias in the presence of other biases which have shaped mine, or repelled me, or to which I have been indifferent; and I hope that they too will unite into one historical bias at an appropriate time.

At the moment I should not care to define my bias, and rest on Aristotle's ground that any occasion requires only its optimum degree of definition, usually rather less than other people think; but I will make a suggestion or so. When Eliot published *The Sacred Wood* he prefixed to the first essay— "The Perfect Critic"—this sentence written by Remy de Gourmont: *Eriger en lois ses impressions personnelles, c'est le grand effort d'un homme s'il est sincère.* I do not recollect having seen this epigraph commented in relation to Eliot's criticism, and I rather expect that most comment might refer to its irony. Yet the sentence was placed there before the age of irony and paradox had begun and now that the age of irony has passed I must insist that I do not see any irony there at all; I see rather a relation between ambition and honesty when confronted with the critical task. But I would put against it a sentence drawn from Erich Heller's admirable book, *The Hazard of Modern Poetry:* "That which is systematic in a system is merely the trivial aspect of true order." And from that I would turn back to another passage in the same book which illustrates the particular effort I have been up to in these papers. "Poetry," says Heller, "heightens and cultivates the creative element that is in experience itself. For experience is not in the impressions we receive; it is in *making* sense. And poetry is the foremost sense-maker of experience. It renders *actual* ever new sectors of the apparently inexhaustible field of *potential* experience. This is why the poet is . . . an easier prey to doubt and despair than people content to live with the sense made by others." We deal with *potential* experience in poetry, or as Ortega y Gasset says of the novel, we deal with potential psychologies; observations which have critical implications to which we shall return. Here I want only the sentiment, the possibility.

The structure of *Ulysses* seems more fully identical with its words every time it is read and at the same time (by means both of words and structure) far more fully expressive. It will bear even the falsifications of structure we put upon it and our mounting ignorance of what the words mean cognitively. In fact it is through these that the expression is made. This then is not pure expressionism, or incomplete or impure expressionism; it is a rational and traditional art. To exaggerate only a little by way of repetition, *Ulysses* is the most structured book in English since at least Milton and it does as much to maintain and develop the full language as anybody since Shakespeare. These may not be desirable features in a masterpiece when the audience cannot *apprehend* the structures, or some of them, and cannot *recognize* the words, or many of them, and when the audience is unwilling or unable to perform the enormous labor to do either—unless it be done as a parlor-game with all the counters provided and labeled. Joyce knew this very well; he expected people to work, and was arrogant in requiring maximum work—as much as he had done himself; but he had a means of commanding attention which carries the reader well on his way to the work.

The means is triple. His basic patterns are universal and are known without their names. His chief characters are interesting and alive and parallel and completing to each other. And he had a story that is gradually told in immense bursts of vivid detail good whether or not there was a story at all; the detail makes the sense of the story. What unified these means is his always availing power to raise the language to the condition of glory or beauty. Beauty is the condition of things when in apprehension they are reduced to one; so Pythagoras says. I should rather than "reduced" say, "carried away or along": given the *élan* of one, but an *élan* which sweeps in more than one direction, though one cannot say how many directions. Stephen Dedalus and Leopold Bloom are swept together, are merged or confused, and are then swept past each other, forever, in their directions, like winds at different levels in the sky, or waters of different temperatures in flooding tides. Molly Bloom's direction is different from either of theirs, but somehow both theirs rest upon hers. Each partakes of the other. Again it is something like this in the movement of tidal currents with respect to the major tidal flow.

It is our business as readers to bring as much of the structure into performance as the story will bear and at the same time to illuminate the structure with the story. It is unlikely that we shall end with a uniform action; but it will only be because we have the sense of such a uniform action that we shall be able to proceed at all. We must have a sense that what happens in Telemachus, Nestor, and Proteus and what happens in Calypso and the Lotus Eaters (these are the first three sections on Stephen and the first two on Bloom), will have, when read, a created mutually illuminating correspondence. There are weights which answer each other. The balance tilts, teeters, veers, slides, trembles and recovers; then begins all over again. It is a balancing of weights which are alive, like bodies hefted, and shift the sense and the sentiment within themselves. They correspond, at a series of given instants, and as a function of being in motion. Correspondence is the flash of vision or the pulse of feeling; never permanent, and, once had, never quite lost. There is the mockery of the Mass in the very first two pages of the book, and there is Bloom's wrongly articulated grasp of the mystery of the Mass in the Lotus Eaters. Stephen is fascinated by heresies because he knows them; Bloom has heretical notions (as all experience has) almost without knowing it—though he wishes he knew more about it. So Stephen dreams of a creative sea, Bloom of an erotic bath. Again how deep is and is *not* the correspondence between Bloom watching the cat's eyes in the dark (dark eyeslits narrowing with greed till her eyes are green stones), and Stephen's darkness shining in brightness which brightness could not comprehend. Again, Stephen devours himself with *amor matris* and Bloom rescues himself with *amor patris*. Still again, Stephen combines in one image the poet Swift and the Saint Joachim of Flora; Bloom combines the idea of metempsychosis and his lost son. Can you balance these without running one into the other?

Stephen opens on all that goes by *tradition* of mind and flesh. Bloom opens on all that comes by the *qualm* of emotion and flesh. Joyce, being

154

both, opens on all that is maintained by form and symbol. Stephen does Hamlet by algebra, Bloom wonders whether Hamlet was a woman. Each is full of the language of Hamlet: Stephen wincing, Bloom unaware of it: a part of hope and a part of speech: each with a frustrate obligation. Stephen, so to speak, knows that he has a prophetic soul—which will abort or obliterate his prophecy; his friends will walk on the track of his ashplant by night. Bloom is unaware that he is an enacted prophecy. Neither has remembered the key home when setting out on the long day. Both remember, and exchange, the ashplant and the potato, which are their symbols. Stephen calls his the augur's rod, Bloom does not know his potato is the moly Hermes gave Odysseus to protect him from Circe. Pride is consciousness, humility beyond it. Yet I think Bloom is a deeper mimesis of Hamlet than Stephen, for Bloom's form of the role existed before Hamlet did. Bloom represents, is the very taste of, the orthodoxy that we plumb; Stephen is the rising gall of that orthodoxy the mind erects. Stephen Dedalus marks what is martyrized and fashioned new in words; Leopold Bloom what grows and what things grow into. I suspect that Stephen got to be a good poet after Bloom caught hold of his ashplant and made it bud like Aaron's rod. But if that is the case, it must also be true—a true potential of psychology— that Stephen got the benefit—safety of conscience, certainty of identity— that went with the possession of the potato. Bloom had these all along, without knowing it.

Joyce has somewhere the remark that great art is concerned with the Constant and the Grave; and of these qualities Stephen and Bloom are constant analogies. Bloom adverts constantly and gravely to Molly and Rudy, his lost son. Stephen adverts constantly and gravely to his mother's death and the missing role of the father. It is the rhythms, in their constancy and their gravity, that prove the identity. This is the substance upon which the structure is reared, and which warrants its many-mindedness. I mean of course those occasions when more than words are given to their thoughts, more than gesture to their actions; so that words and images seem themselves to be moving actions. With Bloom it is more in images; with Stephen it is nearer to words; but it is the music of action moves us. All this is clear tone.

But Joyce also knows that the constant and the grave may be ambiguous and minatory, and it is for this reason that he introduces the apparition of the Man in the Brown Macintosh: he who is the incubus of death, the visitor by night, the other fellow, round the corner, up the stairs, on the slates, he whom you will momently become; the stranger that is indeed yourself, engulfing yourself. He is no doubt related to the vampire mouth in the poem Stephen wrote on the beach. For each the figure comes in day-sleep, the creative aspect of thought. Stephen asks, Why did I write it? Bloom wonders where he came from. The vampire mouth is a poem made; the man in the brown macintosh is an image thrown up out of the *nous poetikos* (the talent things have to assume meaning).

The man in the brown macintosh turns up first at the funeral, where he has the number thirteen at the grave, and his name is put down as present. He is seen eating dry bread and passing unscathed across the path of the viceroy's cavalcade. Bloom wonders who he was. He loves a lady that is dead. He is called the Walking Macintosh of lonely canyon, and we are told that we will see him today at runefall. He is the Nameless One on a jury. He springs through a trap door and identifies Bloom as himself, and a little later Bloom is seen wearing the brown macintosh. He is Mac Somebody, Unmack, I have it. He is What do you call him, Strangeface, Fellow that's like, Saw him before, Chap with. He is said to have been at the funeral by name. Lastly, for these citations are in their order of appearance, Bloom apprehends him not comprehending, but comprehends where Moses was when the candle went out.

Are not these two, the vampire mouth and the man in the brown macintosh, precisely our closest familiars, always there or at hand, not constant and not grave but rousing in each of us the yearning for the constant and the qualm of the grave?

But let us see the constant and the grave where they make action in the very music of the psyche. To introduce that action, I have a sentence from a letter of Kafka cited by Heller in his *The Disinherited Mind:* "No people sing with such pure voices as those who live in deepest hell; what we take for the song of angels is their song." Here are two forms of the action, both in the second chapter of the book, called Nestor, rather like Polonius and no more easily to be distrusted, in the guise of Mr. Deasy the headmaster. Stephen Telemachus is collecting his pay, resigning his job, and preparing to do Mr. Deasy a favor. Mr. Deasy is of good sense and of dangerous platitudes, of another persuasion, requiring a scapegoat, with conventional prejudices and good will and public spirit: he keeps the world going: he is the brightness which cannot comprehend the darkness that shines. He is one of the conditions of life that must be accepted. In his office he has a tray of Stuart coins, apostles preaching to the gentiles, world without end; he has also a stone mortar full of shells, especially a scallop or pilgrim's shell, and a savings box for small coins. He has much to say to Stephen. He speaks of Iago's "Put money in thy purse," and says that it was England's creed: I paid my way. I owe nothing. He says that the Jewish merchants were the death of England; they sinned against the light and are wanderers of the earth till this day. He speaks of the hoof and mouth disease and of backstairs intrigues, and of the women who brought sin and downfall to the world of man. To him Stephen answers

156

aloud. I fear these big words which make us so unhappy. . . . Who has not sinned against the light? . . . A merchant is one who buys cheap and sells dear, Jew or gentile, is he not? . . . History is a nightmare from which I am trying to awake . . . . God is a shout in the street. And to himself Stephen says that he can break the bond of bargain and money; that it is the Harlot's cry from street to street, not the Jews, that destroyed England. And as for the Jews, *he* sees images of goldskinned men on the Paris Bourse, with their unoffending gestures. He asks himself: What if that nightmare gave you a back kick? And when he has agreed to get a letter put in the paper about the hoof and mouth disease, he says that Mulligan will call him a new name, the bullock-befriending bard. These are Stephen's correspondences. Against them Mr. Deasy is money and sunlight and humor. "I have always struggled for the right," he says seriously, and at the end of the chapter runs after Stephen with his story as to why the Irish never persecuted the Jews: because they never let them in. "On his wise shoulders through the checkerwork of leaves the sun flung spangles, dancing coins."

Here is the other form of the action of the psyche. When school broke up one boy, Cyril Sargent, stayed behind in Stephen's class with a copybook, the word "Sums" written on the head line, and it is sums he has been copying at Mr. Deasy's orders.

"'Can you do them yourself?' Stephen asked.
"No, sir.

"Ugly and futile: lean neck and tangled hair and a stain of ink, a snail's bed. Yet someone had loved him, borne him in her arms and in her heart. But for her the race would have trampled him under foot, a squashed boneless snail. She had loved his weak watery blood drained from her own. Was that then real? The only true thing in life? His mother's prostrate body the fiery Columbanus in holy zeal bestrode. She was no more; the trembling skeleton of a twig burnt in the fire, an odour of rosewood and wetted ashes. She had saved him from being trampled under foot and had gone, scarcely having been. A poor soul gone to heaven: and on a heath beneath winking stars a fox, red reek of rapine in his fur, with merciless bright eyes scraped in the earth, listened, scraped up the earth, listened, scraped and scraped."

Notice how the rhythm of the sentence containing Columbanus rises off the page; rhythm is the music of the soul's action. Stephen watches the boy. "In long shady strokes Sargent copied the data. Waiting always for a word of help his hand moved faithfully the unsteady symbols, a faint hue of shame flickering behind his dull skin. *Amor matris*: the subjective and objective genitive. With her weak blood and wheysour milk she had fed him and hid from sight of others his swaddling bands.

"Like him was I, these sloping shoulders, this gracelessness. My childhood bends beside me. Too far for me to lay a hand there once or lightly. Mine is far and his secret as our eyes. Secrets, silent, stony, sit in the dark palaces of both our hearts: secrets weary of their tyranny: tyrants willing to be dethroned."

This is Stephen at his most tender, he transcends his intransigence, and comes on the conditions of life—which is where Bloom is all the time. If we put the two together, side by side in their fertile and permanent analogy, we have an example of the great potential psychology of which Joyce was the master craftsman. We have also one more place for the application of the words we quoted for epigraph two weeks ago. "Every life is many days, day after day. We walk through ourselves, meeting robbers, ghosts, giants, old men, young men, wives, widows, brothers in love. But always meeting ourselves." We have, I think, an irregular metaphysics of heart and head in sensual action.

Here we should come to an end, and if we pretend that we have done so we can regard all that follows as a kind of appendix. Our bourgeois humanism requires of us some account of what sort of criticism it was that surrounded its creations. What we value in the bulk of it, and in the bulk sifted out and generalized, has very much the same sources as the literature itself. Our critics became for the most part hardly at all men of letters; they became researchers, psychologists, psychiatrists, amateur mythologists, students of words in themselves, and above all technical masters of the difficulties in reading. That is, the critics used the new knowledges to apply to literature as if it were some kind of autonomous and amorphous aspect of the new mass society; but of course they did not do so purely, any more than the literature did, and there was not much more criticastry than there was poetastry. There was a renewed attention to the details of prosody and a vast new attention to the novel as a well-made object with almost mechanical rules. And side by side, and gradually, there was a renewal of a kind of neo-medieval interpretation almost fourfold in its scope. If there was no syntax in this modern literature, there was at least to be an allegorical form; and perhaps allegory goes with analogy and correspondences and symbolism generally, rather better than the logic and the syntax which the middle age also depended on as aspects of form. One risks it that in an expressionistic art and in any sympathetic criticism of it there will be a dread of any external control over the order of the elements in which the expression emerges, and at the same time a rush towards all sorts of internal, but equally arbitrary, controls. The arbitrary external controls, such as those of syntax, are likely to predict a good deal of the meaning of the work, where the arbitrary

158

internal controls, such as allegory in its modern anthropological guises, seem to liberate meaning on its own. In this area the critics, having easily the more mechanical techniques which were for all they knew everywhere relevant, got far ahead of the artists. The early exegetes of *Finnegans Wake,* which was then called *Work in Progress,* went far beyond anything that Joyce actually did, and touched very little of the flesh of his work. Similarly, those who have been overconcerned with the Rose Garden in Eliot seem never to have come across the thorns.

In another aspect, particularly with regard to the poetry, there is a remarkable and reassuring resemblance between the criticism in English between 1922 and 1940 and the criticism of the Elizabethan age. Elizabethan criticism is an example of the contest between medieval rhetoric, logic and grammar, and the techniques which went with what we call the Renaissance and the revival of learning. The literature and the theory tried to operate on both models simultaneously. Thus there was a complex struggle between the native independence and inner necessity of practice on the one hand, and the two kinds of authority on the other hand. There is a nice subject for speculation here, whether the very complex terms of the struggle, and the permanent inability of the English to reach any single conclusion, may not be responsible for the depth-structure of English literature in its great writers and the relatively shallow quality of its secondary great writers. Perhaps it is an idle speculation; but still, it is situations like this struggle which create deep contentions in the spirit and consequent many-moded expression. There is *more* to answer for, not *less.* I am suggesting of course that the confusion of the struggle of independence and necessity against the two kinds of authority, themselves deeply opposed, helped Shakespeare express his riches. Shakespearean tragedy and 17th-century pastoral as major modes in English get their forms, styles, words— it seems to me—precisely out of this confusion and this struggle. Put another way, where Dante made a generalization which released poetic power from the bonds of a learned tongue and the worse bonds of oratory, the English extended the struggle and got swept along by the momentum which underlay it. So it seems to me to be with Eliot and Yeats and Joyce.

To remind you of the details of the comparison, let me run over some of the topics that inhabited the manifestos and little magazines of our period. There was the argument for the sequence of the musical phrase as against the patter of the metronome. There was, and still is among those who bother with such things, an attempt to "restore" the sense of "quantity" in English verse. There was an Italianate idea of balance; and there were such things as neo-Websterian blank verse, the reassertion of the secret tongue, and the intense declaration of the absolute power of the word as a thing having life of its own and apart from its meaning. There was, and is, the leaning towards structure by the logic of conceit, along with structure-texture of ambiguity, structure by irony and paradox, and even the quarrel over rhyme and free verse. All these have their close counterparts in the Elizabethan age. It was all a struggle, couched in rhetoric as newly understood, for a decent condition of language governed by a decent prosody, and the struggle is not over.

The moral struggle, too, has its parallels in the same period. Some of the humanists of the Renaissance took a very high tone indeed towards the arts, and were only the predecessors of the puritans. So it was with the neo-humanists in our period, and it is worth taking a look at their rejection and denigration of modern literature if only because of the offchance that they may be followed by a neo-puritanism appropriate to the new sociological conception of the virtues and vices; for if so, we must be sure to have a Milton in the midst, and a Milton warmed by the remnants of the bourgeois tradition.

Our bourgeois neo-humanists were neither so bourgeois nor so humanistic as they thought when they came to tackle literature; for they by and large only succeeded in misusing it. It is silly to quarrel with misuses of the arts beyond the point where the misuse is established. Our particular misuse was primarily American at its center, though it had many sympathizers in England and France. In the early twenties and thirties the neo-humanist movement set itself the task of making literature conform to a particular moral and philosophical view in which alone human health could be found. It was a movement of dissident professors (the new conservatives of their time) in this country. It was representative in an extreme way of the natural prejudice the moral and intellectual half of us has: either to find our own morals and ideas in literature or to condemn it when they are not there. It is a sign of the vitality of literature, and of our own minds, and of the whole enterprise of which both are part, that this prejudice should exist and should want to take action: and there is nothing to diminish this vitality in the reflection that in history what we call living literature has never met the requirements of this prejudice. It was usually some older literature, rather remote, that filled the bill. For the American neo-humanists, it was Greek tragedy—not particular tragedies by particular poets, just the lump sum of Greek tragedy—that seemed pretty nearly right in the general ideas by which it interpreted human nature. It is precisely in the light of this last phrase that this type of mind insists on criticizing literature: the general ideas by which it interprets human nature. So far, so good. If there is a misuse of literature, it is universal. But it is wrong and does a vast amount of harm to literature, to insist on finding a particular set of ideas there, and it is even worse to reprehend literature or to accuse it of having no ideas at all or only bad ones, if literature has *done something* to

160

those ideas; if it has, for example, brought the ideas back into the realm of experience and criticized them in an imaginative way. This is the sort of thing the neo-humanists did; and the amount of literature they were able to condemn is astounding. They could never understand that the idea of murder or adultery was one thing, the experience of it another, and that a story about either was something very different: a kind of criticism, a psychological projection, of the relation between the idea and the experience. The neo-humanist wanted the police to step in where the story-teller could not properly step at all. The neo-humanist condemned what he could not correct.

This was an expected reaction of moral natures to romanticism, realism, art-for-art's sake, and all the chain leading to our own expressionism which flourished in an age without adequate thought-police, and it ought to strike you as something similar to all the activities of the neo-classicists and the puritans. They are the same type under a different cultural situation; and the sameness lies in the habitual exercise of personal authority, where the habit creates the delusion that personal authority is absolute authority— and where the penalty is the fear of any other authority whatever. The neo-classicists and the neo-humanists were alike driven to tyranny and suffered from the tyrant's characteristic privation—the lack of direct knowledge of the actual state of affairs, whether in life or in letters.

But let us pursue the comparison in more nearly literary terms. The difference between the neo-humanists and the humanists is like that between the neo-classicists and the classicists. The neo's show a lack of sensibility where the original types worked under a rush of sensibility, the pressure of experience that needed to be formed and expressed. To make up for the lack of sensibility there is a general air of witch-hunting and exorcism; a violence of language on essentially formalistic matters; and a violence of idea employed to put down or minimize the violence that exists. Thus Irving Babbitt could pursue Rousseau as the father of all modern evil, political, social, and artistic, all his life long, and never realize that he was slaying a dead horse. Thus Paul Elmer More could exclude *Antony and Cleopatra* from the canon of Shakespeare because of the lust and adultery in that play. Thus each of them could borrow phrases from the other such as "an explosion in a cesspool," for Dos Passos' *Manhattan Transfer;* or, for general abuse: "he thinks he is emancipated where he is only unbuttoned." Or again, one humanist could get rid of Shakespeare as high art on the ground that there was no transcendence or unity in him—to which Eliot's answer was that a good mirror is worth any amount of transcendence.

In ideal these men were against the absolute. In ideal they saw the hope for grace, clear conscience, individual riches, balanced diversity of needs and satisfactions. In practice they carried a whip; for nothing in literature since Rousseau approximated the ideal unless it might be that half-hero Arnold. These men could handle nothing but the *ideas* of their own time; and an idea without its medium in life, without the shapeliness it gets in action or experience is hard to see as hero, desperately easy to see as villain.

We may think that they did not see what literature *is,* through lack of sensibility. Why did they ask of literature what it has never done? I think it is partly because they looked at the mass of contemporary literature, much of it still *our* contemporary literature, and the *mass* of literature in a given time always gives much less of what literature can do than its masters, when they have been seen, will turn out to have done. This is why the *New York Times Book Review* runs leaders on the current novel, from time to time—on the average twice a year. The writer will complain that the run of our novelists do not represent us, and will list a good number, I remember once as many as thirty. When did thirty novelists represent a time; or five; or one? When did Shakespeare or Dante or Virgil represent their times in this sense? Yet it is a real question because it points to a real need in a part of all our minds, and a dominant part in those minds which seem to canalize their emotions according to an intellectual drive.

The neo-humanists, and the leader writers for the *New York Times,* perhaps ask of literature critically what it has never done, out of a deep instinctive wish that literature would give us heroic models. It was because Plato saw that this was unlikely that he excluded the poets from the *Republic.* The affair points itself when we remember that Paul Elmer More dismissed Joyce's *Ulysses* as moral and artistic chaos. Yet it was Joyce's lifelong labor to create conscience, to create, after the fashion of literature, the kind of hero More wanted. More did not understand the fashion of literature, and I do not think very much the fashion of heroes either, in or out of literature. Prudent men and practical moralists seldom do; they want their heroes to purge them without themselves having anything to lose.

This literature will not do. The cost of a hero in literature as in life is practically everything; and commonly literature has provided us with heroes whom it would be fatal to any society to take as general models. Literature and life give us heroes whom we desperately need so that we may see what we are not and cannot be in height and depth; and even in literature we can afford them only exceptionally. It is a lucky economy of the genius that creates heroes that it is so scarce. So in religion: we could not afford very many saints; and since the Reformation the Roman Church has looked long and suspiciously into the credentials of candidates. It was Eliot who remarked that as morals are only a *primary* consideration for saints, so they are only a *secondary* consideration for artists. And in politics or history we cannot afford so many great men as we have; we are always half-mired in the bloodshed which they caused by being bad great men (Napoleon; who had all the greatness possible without virtue) or in the worse bloodshed caused by our inability to keep equal to their greatness. England was lucky to have only one Cromwell, ourselves to have only one Lincoln, India only one Gandhi. All were magnanimous men: "By the bowels of Christ I beseech ye, Gentlemen, consider lest ye be mistaken"; "With malice toward none; with charity for all"; and Gandhi's spinning wheel and passive resistance. It would have paid the humanists to have looked less into Arnold and more into Arnold's contemporary, Lord Acton; Acton was a better humanist than any of them, and made a lifelong study of great men in concert and conflict with great ideas. No;—by and large we can afford the gesture of greatness better in literature and the other arts than we can in life. Half at least of our soul insists on creating images of the greatness that destroys us, so near it is to our hearts' desire. We would create experience no matter how fatal it might be for us to live what we have created, but if we could not create such images we would not live at all.

But I should not have spent so much time on the neo-humanists, as such, if we bourgeois humanists did not understand them so well, and if they did not represent perfectly, or as perfectly as any criticism can, what society thinks of its arts and what it is likely to do with its artists, whenever it takes them with mistaken seriousness in the merely intellectual sense. We do not live *in* the intellect, but *with* the intellect—and this is what our arts and letters do most severely show us. Mere intellect is the mere manners of the mind, and the man who makes himself all intellect or all opinion, is all manners and no man. The intellect should hospitably make room for what it might overlook. Hospitality is imaginative, plastic, responsive, and to practice it enriches one's manners and gives them being. Here again we may make a repetition of the remark in Mann's *Magic Mountain,* that vast account of what happens to bourgeois humanism when it turns to art. When the two young heroes of sensibility have gotten to know Settembrini, the professed humanist, quite well, and just after they have heard him discourse, Hans remarks to Joachim of him: "Just as always, first an anecdote, then an abstraction; that's his humanism." Anecdote and an abstraction, abstraction *and* anecdote. Otherwise, as Hans sees in his dreams, the humanist is only an organ-grinder, with a monkey, not a man, at the end of his string.

Questions of this sort do not arise when we look at the professional or trade criticism of the twenties which stemmed partly, as in Eliot or Wilson or Trilling or Leavis, from the old traditions of the man of letters, and partly from the special needs of the new literature to make itself available to any appreciable audience outside the general company of actual and disappointed writers. It seems that the man of letters is at present disappearing, though he is much wanted, and there is nothing that has turned up to replace him. Instead we have the rising tide of the professional, the expert, the man with the technical knowledge who is expected to save us from the need of any knowledge of our own, except as we are ourselves experts, and who makes us largely the children of other peoples' research. In the very heart of our period, A. N. Whitehead took a more optimistic view than I can in speaking of our professionalized society in general. "Professionals are not new to the world. But in the past professionals have formed unprogressive castes. The point is that professionalism has now been mated with progress. The world is now faced with a self-evolving system, which it cannot stop . . . . The problem is not how to produce great men, but how to produce great societies. The great man will put up the men for the occasions." This is from *Science and the Modern World*. A little earlier in the same chapter, he declares that "the habit of art is the habit of enjoying vivid values,"—a statement to which I would adhere. But I do not think this is precisely a description of how the most of the professional criticism of our time has worked, or wanted to work, or been permitted to work either by the audience or the art. The techniques which have become natural to us tend towards the discovery of difficulties and their exegesis or explication for its own sake and largely because it would be done. Reading these critics it would seem that all our old unconscious skills of apprehension and gradual intimacy had disappeared or become useless under the far more incomplete skills of conscious analysis. One of the conspicuous losses, which points to others in other fields of society, has been the increasing inability to appreciate the older poetry except when it masquerades as new poetry.

Let I. A. Richards, whom I admire greatly—a warm and passionate man and a lover of poetry—let Richards stand for the rest, if only for the reason that he led a great many other critics and even invented some who might not otherwise have appeared, such as William Empson. Three little passages from *Science and Poetry* (1926) may serve as texts for departure. "The necessity for independence [from beliefs] is increasing. This is not to say that traditional poetry, into which beliefs readily enter, is becoming obsolete; it is merely becoming more and more difficult to approach without confusion; it demands a greater imaginative effort, a greater purity in the reader." That is one; here is another: "A poet today, whose integrity is equal to that of the greater poets of the past, is inevitably plagued by the problem of thought and feeling as poets have never been plagued before." Here is a third. Poetry, he says, is the science of our knowledge of our experience. Poetry is "a means of ordering, controlling, and consolidating the whole experience." Thus the command of words is the command of life; or at any rate the command of all that kind of life of which the experience is its own justification.

This is quite an extraordinary claim. Richards, loving poetry, made it in this way because he was a direct product of a scientific education at Cambridge: he was full of biology, anthropology, and psychology: those great *underminers* of belief, those great *analyzers* of experience. Right or wrong, these notions with their developments, are a preparatory school for the greater part, quantitatively, of what literary criticism must consist in a society like our own, and I think this is so even when we discount by half every major statement of difficulty he has made. No schooling is ever adequate to the purposes of that schooling, and the schooling afforded by Richards in his *Practical Criticism* (1929) is no exception; but that book is still a useful guide to normal failures to master what have become the difficulties of reading poetry which was to give us command of life.

Practical Criticism was the result of sending thirteen poems, without date or authorship attached, to a number of cultivated readers, and the results were stupefying. The protocols turned in showed gross failures to understand, to appreciate, or to judge the poems at anywhere near the level they required or deserved. Yet these poems had been submitted to far more than the average scrutiny poetry gets from its regular readers: which was perhaps the trouble. The scrutiny was necessary, but it got in the way.— I think it fair to add that Richards has since made other experiments which show that the cultivated experience of poetry is no worse than that of other uses of language central to our tradition.

What is most striking about all this is, as I said above, that it represents a decay in unconscious skills confronted by an inadequacy in conscious skills of reading. The forms which excess consciousness takes are—at least when analyzed—unsatisfactory for the purposes of consciousness. Our culture has always been carried in words, and especially for purposes of action; here was the use of words breaking down.

Yet clearly—from the examples in literature we have touched on in these papers, and also in our daily lives, the breakdown is only superficial and it took place when confronted with an extraordinary burst of imaginative talent, in expression if not always in communication; and I think that as we are readers—as we are critics—we had better work from that example primarily, no matter what other techniques and metaphysics we call in to grasp our unreason. In this we are saying that criticism resembles art; and how it does so seems so important that I wish it could be said clearly, self-evidently, and irrefutably. But only revelation can do all that. I think it has something to do with radical imperfection. I risk it that in literary criticism you get the radical imperfection of the intellect striking on the radical imperfection of the imagination. Just as the imagination is never able to get all of itself into the arbitrary forms of art and has to depend on aids from the intellect, from conventions, and from the general assumptions of the time, so the intellect dealing with the imagination is itself imperfect and has to depend on conventions of its own, some of them imaginative some quite formalistic. Each of these modes of the mind avows its imperfection by making assertions about its intentions which it neither expresses nor communicates except by convention. It is of the first importance that we use pretty much the same conventions; it is of only secondary importance that we agree closely as to what the conventions mean, *e. g.:* in arts, the tragic fault: in criticism, verisimilitude. If we use whatever it is that is meant by these conventions, it does not matter too much if we define them differently: indeed we should use definition in the end in order to surround the indefinable. If you "define" the novel or the sonnet you will not be able to read the next one that alters the limits.

These remarks are in no way meant to be a confession of impotence on the part of the mind, but rather an assertion of its strength; and so far as literary criticism is concerned it is meant only as a precaution against substituting intellectual formulae for experience; or put the other way round, it is meant as an insistence that intellectual formulation is the great convenience for ordering the experience of the mind and, because of the imperfection of the mind, an even greater convenience for stepping in, in the guise of generalization or hypothesis, when there is not enough experience to go round. —Again: If either art or criticism—if either imagination or intellect—were relatively perfect, we should have no trouble and no problem, and the staring inadequacies of either with respect to the other would long since have disappeared. The contrary is so much the case that in practice we tend to get in literature immature intellect tampering with imagination, and in criticism immature imagination tampering with intellect. Hence the "claims" made for poetry, and hence the authoritarian aspect of much criticism. When you get maturity of imagination and of intellect (I do not say perfection, only maturity: balance without loss of passion or vitality), you get great literature and great criticism—or, let us say, criticism that has become a part of literature or literature that has become a part of criticism. That you get considerably more great literature than great criticism may very well be due to the fact that the imaginative mode of the mind requires so much of its skill to be developed to the point of second nature, whereas the intellectual mode of the mind rather likes to be self-conscious in its work as well as its role. But it is more likely that the paucity of great criticism may be explained by saying that by and large only second-order minds took it up, or the second-order parts of first-order minds. Of course, I should *like* to say that it was not till pretty nearly our own time—about the time you reach Coleridge or even Arnold—that we had any need of great criticism. Perhaps this is meant in praise of past times. Perhaps it is meant as reference to the enormously increased number of persons who either try to write literature or try to tamper with literature. I do not know. But it may possibly be that those of us are right who believe that both the nature of literature and the nature of the audience have changed from previous times. The literature has become more inaccessible and the audience more illiterate; I mean, of course, that Shakespeare has become more inaccessible than previously to the audience presumed to want to use him. I mean also that Shakespeare is now open to uses to which he would not previously have been put. Shakespeare has changed: anyway our consciousness of him has changed, it matters nothing which way this is put. We now look to Shakespeare to see what has happened to us; and that is naturally a hard job to find out. The change is only superficial; it is only that we are able to take less for granted than our ancestors were; it is only that we do not have nearly so adequate a set of conventions as they. We have invented so many ways of formularizing consciously what we know that it sometimes seems we know, by nature, nothing at all. We are as bad off as Socrates complaining about the specialization of knowledge at Athens in his time; by which I do not mean to be frivolous but only to suggest that the availability of our knowledge depends deeply on the attitude we take towards it.

George Bernard Shaw:
Man of the Century

Archibald Henderson

Presented at the Library of Congress November 19, 1956

On February 24, 1903, I descended to breakfast at The Harcourt, 57th Street, University of Chicago, unaware that I was on the threshold of one of the great adventures of my life: becoming the biographer of one of the greatest geniuses of the age.

"I want you to be my guest at the Studebaker Theatre tonight," said Miss Maude Miner, a teacher of the art of expression.

"What company?" I asked.

"The Hart Conway School of Dramatic Expression."

"And the play?"

" 'You Never Can Tell.' "

"No, I suppose you can't, nowadays.   And the author?"

"An Irishman, named George Bernard Shaw."

"My dear Miss Miner," I explained, "I am working night and day on one of the most difficult and complicated problems in the entire range of higher mathematics: The 27 Lines on the Cubic Surface; and you ask me to go to see a ridiculously named play by a man I never heard of and produced by amateurs.   No, Miss Miner, you really must excuse me this time." [1]

But she finally wore me down with her two complimentary tickets; and I reluctantly accepted the invitation.   In Shaw, that night, I encountered a human explosion of cosmic energy; and came out of the theater resolved to write his life.   After reading everything I could find by and about him, I wrote him a letter in the late Spring of 1904, proposing myself as his biographer.   Of course, I really kissed the letter good-bye, never expecting

---

[1] Due to exigencies of space, the original conversation is here abbreviated.   See Archibald Henderson, *George Bernard Shaw: Man of the Century* (Appleton-Century-Crofts, Inc., New York, 1956), pp. xiii–xiv.

to have a reply. To my great astonishment, exultation, and exaltation, Shaw wrote me: "If this business is to come off, we may as well do it thoroughly. Have you a spare photograph of yourself? I should very much like to see you. Failing that, your picture would be a help."

My heart sank at the thought, as my wife had often told me that all my pictures revealed the features of the congenital criminal type described by Nordau and Lombroso. In desperation, I appealed to my friend, Waller Holliday, Chapel Hill's only professional photographer. "Waller," I naively inquired, "this is a very delicate situation. I need your help. Do you think that by any possibility you could take a photograph of me which would resemble the potential biographer of a great undiscovered literary genius?" "Good God, no! I'm a photographer, not a magician," he replied. "But I have just received a new lot of film and I'll shoot you as often as you wish, and require!"

When the proofs came, my wife rejected them all and refused to have anything further to do with the enterprise. She described the portraits as "unspeakable"; but on my urgent insistence, finally chose one which she euphemistically described as the "least forbidding" of the lot. With despair in my heart, I sent it off, never expecting to hear from Shaw again; but when his reply came he said, among many other things: "Thanks for your own portrait. You seem to be the man for the job." My wife was dumbfounded, and I was elated. But I had a haunting suspicion that there was a catch in it somewhere.

More than two years later, I arrived in London with a large batch of manuscript. I found Shaw on the platform surrounded by reporters as the boat train from Southampton rolled into St. Pancras Station. Shaw casually explained that he had given out an interview about me for the last forty minutes. "Good gracious!" I exclaimed. "You know nothing about me!" "That's just where you're wrong!" suavely replied Shaw. "See tomorrow morning's newspapers." The next day all the leading London newspapers carried Shaw's interview, more than a column long. The title was as follows:

SHAW MEETS BIOGRAPHER AT ST. PANCRAS STATION.
DECLARES BIOGRAPHY A TERRIFIC TASK.
SAYS ONLY A DESPERATE CHARACTER COULD WRITE HIS LIFE.

I understood at last what Shaw had meant when he wrote me that I seemed to be the man for the job. *My wife was right!*

Another amusing incident occurred when I received a cable from Shaw asking me to meet him in New York on April 11, 1933. When I arrived, he asked me, in the best style of an American crime king, to act as his bodyguard. During his stay in New York for three days, living on the *Empress of Britain,* he was closely attended by me (I need not add that I was unarmed!). I protected him from the insistent journalists, the irrepressible photographers, the film-reel artists who were fiercely importunate, and the fanatical sensation-seekers whom I held back by sheer physical force. One woman, a representative of some woman's magazine, would not go away and tried to push past me and enter the Shaws' stateroom. I pulled her back and said to her sternly: "What is it you want?" She came close to me, stood on tiptoe, and whispered in my ear: "I just want to *touch* him!"

In his address on the evening of April 12, 1933, to a crowded audience of 4,000 at the Metropolitan Opera House, Shaw mentioned only two Americans to whom he was indebted: Henry George, who had converted him to Socialism (although Henry George was not a Socialist); and his biographer, who had made him, as he said, one of the diversions of a mathematician and thereby rendered him a great service. The next morning a very self-contained lady, with an aggressive manner, came up to me, then guarding the door of the Shaws' stateroom, and said: "I have here a copy of Henry George's *Progress and Poverty*, which I want Mr. Shaw to autograph for me." I politely inquired: "And what is your name, Madam?" She replied with a sort of proud defiance: "I am Anna George DeMille, Henry George's daughter." I took the book to Mr. Shaw and said: "You will want to receive this lady, as she is Henry George's daughter." Shaw immediately autographed the copy of *Progress and Poverty*, and said, "Bring her straight in." Then the following conversation took place:

"You mentioned Henry George in your speech last night. I am his daughter."

"You're better looking than he is," replied Shaw with Irish blarney.

"I have more hair." (I should mention that Henry George was almost totally bald.)

"Have you his beautiful hands?"

"Alas, no," replied Mrs. DeMille sadly.

"Have you inherited his great gift of oratory, or his wonderful power of persuasion?"

To everyone's surprise, Mrs. DeMille replied with great earnestness, her face transfigured with pride and love:

"All I have inherited from my father is a passionate love of ice cream."

This made a tremendous hit: Shaw, Mrs. Shaw, Arthur Brentano and I all burst out into roars of laughter. We thought she was going to say that she had inherited her father's undying faith in a single-tax on land alone, and his passion for social justice.

In May, 1937, I extended a cordial invitation to the Great Vegetarian, G. B. S., and his non-vegetarian wife, Charlotte, to attend a Birthday

170

Barbecue to which all my friends received a blanket invitation. Some six hundred attended. I described it to the Shaws as a "typical and barbaric American affair." Colored people, clad in white duck, I explained, will be busy all night long roasting the pigs over open fires in deep pits dug in the ground. The barbecue, made of pork and lamb, with many garnishes, will take several hours to prepare. There will be Brunswick stew, name reminiscent of a royal house in Britain and in Deutschland, along with Vienna sausage (Wiener Schnitzel), served very hot in a Parker House roll, with mustard, cole-slaw, and chopped-up onions, and hot corn bread made of maize or Indian corn, with a variety of delicious iced "soft" drinks on the side. Shaw's reply to the invitation, from No. 4, Whitehall Court, London, June 20, 1937, just three days after my sixtieth birthday, reads as follows:

I almost fainted when I read your barbecue menu. This is how the U. of N. C. teaches young America to celebrate great men!

> And you are sixty.
> You don't deserve it.
> How are you? Ill ever
> since, I should think.
> Serves you right!
> Don't do it again.
> [Signed] G. B. S.

During a period when Shaw's unpopularity had reached an all-time high in England and people were complaining in letters to the press of Shaw's tiresome loquacity, two English debaters, one representing the University of London, the other the London School of Economics, visited Chapel Hill. They told me the latest Shaw story, almost too ingenious not to be invented.

It seems that one day Shaw received a letter addressed to "George Bernard Shawm, Esq." He roared for his wife to come into his study, and exclaimed in high dudgeon:

"Look at that letter! Here am I, the most famous man in the world, more famous than Stalin or Gandhi or Roosevelt. And here is an idiot who addresses me as 'Shawm.' Preposterous! Besides, there's no such word as Shawm."

"Oh, yes, there is," replied Charlotte demurely. "Look in The Book of Common Prayer, ninety-eighth psalm, and you will find the sixth verse to read: 'With trumpets and with shawms make a joyful noise before the Lord the King.' "

"Confound it!" exclaimed Shaw. "What is a shawm?" Turning to the proper page in the dictionary, he read: "Shawm: definition—an old-fashioned wind instrument long since passed out of common use."

The sister of a young instructor in English at Chapel Hill kindly made a number of excellent silhouettes of me. Some time afterwards, she asked me for a letter of introduction to Shaw. When she reached London, she mailed my letter to him, requesting an appointment to make some silhouettes of him. The request came at an inexpressibly busy time for him, and he wrote her as follows: "Far too many silhouettes of me have already been cut. I must therefore firmly decline your request. I have been silhouetted so much that I am now actually black in the face."

Shaw, a teetotaler, always said that he hated to make after-dinner speeches because he was talking to people trying to be convivial who were already half-drunk. He was violently opposed to the filthy habit of smoking—because of the expense. Whenever he went to any social or business gathering, his clothes became so thoroughly impregnated with tobacco from the smoke, that he had to send them out to be fumigated before he could wear them again.

Lee Simonson writes me: "I was abroad in 1921 and being at the time a director of the [New York] Theatre Guild, my colleagues asked me, when I got to London, to sound out G. B. S. as to producing *The Devil's Disciple*. His answer is a good-natured spoofing of me and also a red-herring. And you know, perhaps better than anyone, G. B. S.'s knack of producing a red-herring and then inflating it to the proportions of a Leviathan."

November 11, 1921

My dear Simonson

The Devil's Disciple is of no great importance: what really matters is that you must give up smoking. My wife and I were perfectly horrified: we have been able to think of nothing ever since: you smoked 117 cigarettes in two hours, and you would have smoked 118 if I had not stopped you once. Where do you expect to go when you die—how do you expect to spend the brief and stupefying remnant of your days—if you give way to such reckless self-indulgence? You are worse than anyone I ever met, except my late Swedish translator, and he, alas, is dead. What you need is not The Devil's Disciple but repentance, reform, prayer, fasting, and total abstinence from tobacco. . . .

And so *bon voyage;* and, mind, no smoking on the Atlantic.

My first suggestion of a title for the centennial biography, *George Bernard Shaw: Man of the Century,* was instantly accepted by my publisher but not at all because The Century Company was one of the constituents of the amalgamated firm, Appleton-Century-Crofts, Inc. In the first place, the time interval traversed, from Shaw's birth in 1856 until now, is precisely a century. But "Man of the Century" as a title carries far more than temporal interpretation. Those who think of Shaw primarily as wit, jester, wisecracker, harlequin and clown, know only a figment of Shaw's own fancy, the fearsome and crotchety G. B. S. Shaw is the most representative figure of our era, because he embodies, as has none of his contemporaries, the challenging spirit of free and untrammeled inquiry in all realms of thought. With such specialists as Stalin, Lenin, Churchill, Wilson, and the Roosevelts in the field of international statesmanship; Gandhi, Freud, Nietzsche, Bergson, James, and Schweitzer in the fields of ethics, psychiatry, and philosophy; Marx, Mill, and Keynes in economics; Darwin, Einstein, Bohr, and Gibbs in science; and Tolstoy, Ibsen, Strindberg, and Yeats in literature, Shaw cannot compete since he is not a specialist. Shaw is truly protean in his accomplishments, a universal genius: unforgettable as personality, conversationalist, letter-writer, speaker, essayist, critic, pamphleteer, stylist, novelist, dramatist, social reformer, intellectual awakener, philosophic thinker, world-betterer. He has, more than any other man, set the tone and temper of the age in which he lived. It may well go down in literary history as "The Shavian Age." And so I give you George Bernard Shaw: Man of the Century!

Shaw is supremely representative of his era because, paradoxically enough, he was always ahead of it. He was a leader of the *avant garde,* challenging the old Victorian conventions and advocating the new outlooks. He identified himself with Fabian Socialism, but he was far in advance of his Fabian colleagues. Regardless of the labels of Socialist and later Communist which he pinned upon the lapel of his coat, I maintain that Shaw was temperamentally a democrat—a social democrat—who stood for human equality in all forms—and not merely the equality of opportunity, citizenship, and education identified with American democracy. Following in the footsteps of Baboeuf who in the midst of the French Revolution put forward his doctrine of universal financial equality, and of the American, Edward Bellamy, who advocated the same policy in his books, *Looking Backward* and *Equality,* Shaw deviated from his Fabian colleagues in advocating an equal share in the income of the Socialist state for every individual from birth until death. He outdistanced his Fabian colleagues in advocating the abolition of social classes. He thought intermarriageability should be universal, irrespective of caste, race, or color. He believed that not America alone but the entire world should be the melting-pot of all peoples, advocating the marriage of the navvy with the duchess, of the cabby with the millionairess. In his address, "The Case for Equality," before The National Liberal Club, London, May 1, 1913, Shaw gaily sketches a natural contretemps in a Fabian Utopia:

I walk down Oxford Street, let me say, as a young man. I see a woman who takes my fancy, I fall in love with her. It would seem very sensible, in an intelligent community, that I should take off my hat and say to this lady: "Will you excuse me, but you attract me strongly, and if you are not already engaged, would you mind taking my name and address and considering whether you would care to marry me?"

Shaw allied himself with the irresistible trend of the century and the spirit of the future, in proclaiming, and personally standing for, individual liberty and the untrammeled cultivation of all creative powers. Although he proclaimed himself a Communist, he was never a member of the Communist party, the arch-foe of individualism, and since the death of Stalin, of the "cult of personality." In the incredible spectacle of Shaw, the supreme individualist, as a self-proclaimed Communist, is found the perfect antinomy. On his seventy-fifth birthday, speaking in Moscow, he declared that he would like to remove to Russia and spend happily there his declining years. But I am sure he would not have enjoyed himself in Russia. I am confident that had he, as a "comrade" living in the U. S. S. R., published a pamphlet on the invasion of Hungary by twenty Russian Divisions, comparable in blistering frankness to *Common Sense About the War,* he would have been arrested, forced to read a confession of his guilt supplied him by his captors, and then mercilessly "liquidated," the genial Russian slang for "executed."

At the four schools, one later to become a college, which he attended as a lad, Shaw proudly proclaimed that he learned nothing. He was self-educated at home, with an unusually wide range of reading and study: Shakespeare, Bunyan, Scott, Dumas *aîné,* Dickens, Trollope, Thackeray, Lever, Byron, Shelley, and Mark Twain; and in a family every one of whom sang or played some sort of musical instrument, he learned by the age of fifteen to whistle and sing by ear (in Italian, and Irish Italian at that) at least one important work of Handel, Mozart, Beethoven, Mendelssohn, Rossini, Bellini, Donizetti, Verdi, and Gounod. As expert clerk and accountant for some four years in a real estate office in Dublin, he acquired a beautiful copper-plate hand and habits of industry, efficiency, and economy which eventually enabled him to become the wealthiest of British writers of his day, with Somerset Maugham as his only rival.

Although he never attended college or university, he doggedly forced himself to become probably the most acquisitive seeker of knowledge and the most widely informed English-speaking person of his day. He knew little or nothing of mathematics, physics, astronomy, biology, botany, chemistry, and the sciences generally; but by assiduous study he cultivated himself to the point of being the most devastating journalistic critic of British medical science and practice, of Listerism, and popular Darwinism. As soon as he reached London, shortly before his twenty-first birthday, he became an habitual visitor to the Reading Room of the British Museum; and, in speaking here in this presence, in perhaps the greatest and most widely useful library in the world, I can do no better than quote Shaw on his educational indebtedness to another such great institution of Western culture:

From Plato and Pythagoras to Descartes and Einstein there have been single men who would have justified all that the British Museum costs by spending two weeks of their lives in it. . . .

I myself worked in its Reading Room daily for about eight years at the beginning of my literary career; and oh (if I may quote Wordsworth), the difference to me.[2]

Shaw told me that in the British Museum he had read the entire *Encyclopaedia Britannica* straight through, with the exception of the scientific articles; and voraciously devoured hundreds of books on every conceivable subject, particularly art, music, literature, sociology and economics. Literally poverty-stricken, living on the pittance daily doled out to him by his mother, who had legal control of the Shaw children's inheritance of four thousand pounds, he was always shabbily dressed and affected clothes of a hideous mustard color. William Archer amusingly records his first view of Shaw in the British Museum—a tawny young man of tawny beard, and tawny attire, reading alternately if not simultaneously the first volume of Karl Marx's *Das Kapital* and an orchestral score of Wagner's *Tristan und Isolde!* Like O. Henry, Shaw must have made a practice of daily reading of the dictionary; for he acquired an exhaustive vocabulary and once told me, and I am sure it was true, that he was never at a loss for a word, save an occasional synonym. He used to sit in silence with William Morris while the latter was writing his famous narrative poems; and could always supply the requisite word when Morris found himself at a loss.

Although he lacked a university education, Shaw now flung himself with enthusiastic ardor into the work of many literary, discussion, and debating societies; and by the time he had completed this *uncurriculated* series of popular cultural courses, he had achieved an amazingly rich, if spotty, education far more catholic and comprehensive than that achieved by the average classics-ridden graduates of Oxford, Cambridge, London, Edinburgh, or Dublin. Over a period of a decade, Shaw took an active and highly controversial part in the meetings of the New Shakespeare, Shelley and Browning Societies, and his provocative papers and discussions always set his auditors into an uproar. In 1879 he joined a discussion club, known as the Zetetical Society (Zetetical means truth-seeking), and a little later, the famous Dialectical Society, which had been organized not long after the American Civil War for the purpose of studying the writings of John Stuart Mill. Among the other societies to which he belonged were: the South Place Institute, conducted by the Rev. Stopford Brooke; various study groups, one of which, a Marxist reading circle, developed into the Hamp-

[2] G. B. Shaw, "Neglected Aspects of Public Libraries," *Readers' Bulletin* of the Coventry Library, May, 1925.

stead Historic Society; and a private circle of economists, many of them later distinguished, which eventually developed into the Royal Economic Society. Beginning as the most nervous and hesitant of novices on the platform, Shaw eventually became through dogged persistence the most brilliant and effective public speaker in Great Britain, incomparable for lucidity, wit and ready repartee.

In his search for some group dedicated to the reorganization of Society, he attended many meetings of the Democratic Federation headed by H. M. Hyndman, Oxford graduate, man of wealth, and a close associate of Karl Marx, then living in poverty at 41 Maitland Park Road, London. The Social Democratic Federation, as it was later called, was committed to Marxian Communism; and Hyndman wished to build it up into an influential political party. I went to see him at Queen's Gate, London, in 1907; and he talked at length with me about his social and political plans. He had consulted with Disraeli, then a very old and broken man. Disraeli said to him: "England will soon be ready for a social upheaval. But the English are a very conservative people and will be very hard to move in the direction of social revolution."

Shaw attended many meetings of the Land Reform Union; and was greatly interested in the agrarian uprising in Ireland over the ruinous "rackrent" imposition. By chance, on September 5, 1882, he attended a lecture by Henry George, the great American "single-taxer," who had been speaking to tremendous crowds throughout England and Ireland. Shaw was converted to Socialism that night, and bought a copy of *Progress and Poverty* for sixpence from one of the stewards at the meeting, and later devoured it with the intensest interest. As the Social Democratic Federation was dedicated to Marxian Communism, Shaw next studied at the British Museum *Das Kapital* in Deville's French translation, as he did not read German, and there was then no English translation. Shaw was thereby converted to Communism; and remained a self-proclaimed Communist to the day of his death. After reading *Das Kapital,* volume one, he clearly saw that Henry George had not gone far enough, being convinced by Marx that social and political revolution, to be a success, must adopt Marx's principle of the nationalization of all forms of capital, including land. In the Fabian Society he found exactly the sort of organization he wished to join: a miniature people's university devoted to the study of economics and sociology, composed of energetic and dedicated members of the upper middle class. Of his little group—the Three Musketeers and D'Artagnan, as he terms them—Sidney Webb, Graham Wallas, Sydney Olivier, and himself— he was the first to join the Fabian Society; and he influenced the others to follow suit.

Shaw's association with the Fabian Society, to which he regularly con-

176

tributed financially, lasted throughout his life; and his strenuous activities as public speaker, pamphleteer, agitator, author, and politician covered a period of sixty years, as he joined the Fabian Society in 1884 and published his *Everybody's Political What's What* in 1944. During the period of some four decades, when he was the Fabian Society's most effective mob orator and platform star, Shaw told me that he had delivered upwards of two thousand speeches, from the street corner with William Morris to the City Temple, from a soap box in Hyde Park to the Albert Hall. He wrote dozens of tracts, hundreds of articles in newspapers and magazines, edited and contributed two chapters to the famous *Fabian Essays in Socialism* (1889), which is still selling briskly. Of his writings on Socialism, the most important and comprehensive are *The Intelligent Woman's Guide to Capitalism and Socialism* (1928) and *Everybody's Political What's What* (1944). The former was written at the request of his wife's sister, who had to address a woman's club and asked Shaw to write a brief answer to the question: "What is Socialism?" This enormous book, which was Shaw's answer, has been rapturously described by Ramsay MacDonald, twice Socialist Prime Minister, as "after the Bible . . . humanity's most important book."

Shaw is a man who has ploughed many furrows, some mere scratches on the surface, others deep and fertile. In his exaggeratedly egoistic way, he claims that he has fifteen different reputations; and he has actually enumerated them: a critic of art, a critic of music, a critic of literature, a critic of the drama, a novelist, a dramatist, an economist, a funny man, a street-corner agitator, a Shelleyan atheist, a Fabian Socialist, a vegetarian, a humanitarian, a preacher, and a philosopher. Each of these "reputations," as Shaw calls them, was in an air-tight compartment; and no one seemed to realize that these fifteen characters were all the same man. My purpose in attempting the formidable task of writing Shaw's *Life* was to knock down the bulkheads which isolated the separate reputations; and to reveal the single protean personality in which they were all merged. This is the meaning of *George Bernard Shaw: Man of the Century*. To pass from macrocosm to microcosm, from a biography of a thousand pages to a summary of a thousand words, is manifestly unthinkable. To narrate the story of his life of ninety-four years and to elucidate his philosophy of the Life Force, is impossible here in the time at my disposal. I shall, however, endeavor to take a cursory glance at Shaw's chief qualities and major accomplishments which bid fair to assure him the immortality of individual gratitude and public remembrance for an indefinite and unpredictable period.

A number of Shaw's "reputations" are merely characteristics of his nature, qualities of his temperament, or even, as the French put it, *les défauts de ses qualités*. These I shall discard altogether from consideration, as they add nothing to his fame, merely imparting piquancy to the portrait.

177

I shall begin with a consideration of Shaw as a novelist, as he wrote five novels in rapid succession, one a year, from 1879 to 1883. In one of the earliest interviews with Shaw, he is quoted as follows: "My destiny was to educate London, and yet I had neither studied my pupil nor related my ideas properly to the common stock of human knowledge." Late in life, he publicly acknowledged that his claim of being destined to educate London was sheer nonsense; and admitted that, at the age of twenty-three to twenty-eight, he had no "clear comprehension of life in the light of an intelligent theory" of its meaning. His novels were critical and episodic, and his knowledge of English society, its manners and customs, which he attacked relentlessly, was derived, not from first-hand knowledge, but exclusively from reading the novels of Dickens, Thackeray, Trollope, Meredith, and Lever. He proudly claimed that *The Irrational Knot,* as a study of marriage, anticipated Ibsen's *A Doll's House;* but chronologically Ibsen's play, although Shaw had not read it, for he knew no Norwegian, preceded Shaw's novel. He was proud, also, of *An Unsocial Socialist,* claiming that in this, the first English novel dealing with Socialism, he had drawn in "Smilash" a lifelike portrait of Lenin, before he had ever heard of the coldly ruthless Russian Communist leader. Shaw's novels were refused by some sixty publishers, although they ultimately found their way into print. Over a period of nine years, 1876 to 1885, Shaw's income from his novels and periodical writings was an average of one cent a day! Only Shaw's confidence in his creative powers and his conviction, wholly unsupported by his literary experience, that he belonged in the company of the immortals, enabled him to rise above one of the most devastating failures in literary history. With pawky humor, he once wrote in one of my copies of *Love Among the Artists* (January 8, 1946): "The best excuse for these old novels is that Dickens could not have written them, nor Trollope."

After his failure as a novelist, Shaw wrote voluminously for English newspapers and magazines, particularly *The Pall Mall Gazette, The World,* and *The Saturday Review,* for about ten years, ending in the Spring of 1898, and desultorily in many magazines and newspapers for the remainder of his life. He was a critic of art, literature, music, and drama; and always wrote acutely, with singular and original reactions which were both individual and racial. As a critic of art, he was mediocre, as he knew little of art save what he had derived from standard works on the subject. As a critic of literature, he achieved no eminence, for his critiques were "slanted" by his Socialist views and colored by his social and economic prejudices and predilections. But he achieved astounding popularity as a music critic, because his *feuilletons* were filled with discussions of affairs of the day commingled with music; and he once boasted that, by his lucidity and passionate love of music, he could make music interesting to the deaf. He surpassed in popularity critics far more learned in musicology than himself; yet he came to be regarded by not a few musical authorities as the most readable, entertaining, and acute of all English critics of music. One volume of selections from *The Star* and two volumes from *The World* constitute his musical monument—the former diaphanous, playful, and shamelessly, nonsensically egoistic; the latter, able, percipient, and more enthralling than most novels.

When Frank Harris became editor of *The Saturday Review* in 1895, he gathered about him a truly remarkable staff of contributors; and chose Shaw as drama critic for his wit, cleverness, and unfailing power of entertainment, although he had never before written drama criticism and had achieved no solid footing as a dramatist. With Shaw, Harris made a ten-strike. Shaw set the English reading public in a dither by three crusades simultaneously conducted: assault upon the greatest living English actor and his policy at the Lyceum, the temple of British theatric art; onslaught upon Shakespeare as an absurdly overrated dramatist, although he conceded Shakespeare to be a great poet and a supreme artist in "word-music"; and the glorification of Ibsen as a psychological dramatist and philosophic thinker far above Shakespeare. Readers by the score wrote to Harris, denouncing Shaw as a "damned Socialist" who knew nothing about Shakespeare, a mere sensation-seeker for his scarifying criticism of one of the gods in the British Pantheon, and a pernicious crank for championing the foul, obscene, and horrifying plays of the grim Norwegian. Entirely unmoved by this clamor for his head, Shaw became, if anything, more frenetic than ever in his berserker-like attacks; and particularly outraged his intimate friend, William Archer, by his merciless exposés of the shallowness and conventionality of the plays of Arthur Wing Pinero, whom Archer lauded to the skies as a great dramatist. Shaw's knowledge of acting, the stage, and dramatic literature was both comprehensive and minute; and all of his reviews were exhilarating, shocking, and acute. The most memorable were the comparison of the histrionic merits of Bernhardt and Duse, the ruthless demolition of Pinero's *The Notorious Mrs. Ebbsmith,* the destructive analysis of *Cymbeline* as Shakespeare at his worst, and the eloquent praise of Forbes-Robertson as far superior to Irving, both as classic actor and as interpreter of *Hamlet*. Shaw made no pretensions of justice, fairness, or affability. His drama critiques were assaults upon the bastions of convention, custom, and tradition; and he ruthlessly slew the defenders and threw their bodies in the moat. He knew Shakespeare from cover to cover; and he compelled a revaluation of Shakespeare, who was then worshipped in England as an impeccable dramatist and a great philosopher. Despite the "slanting" of his criticism in behalf of Ibsen, Shaw, and the New Drama, and the ferocity of his expressions, Shaw is at present rated by reputable judges as the greatest English-speaking drama critic of all time, superior to Hazlitt, Lamb, and Leigh Hunt.

Shaw's career as a dramatist, properly speaking, began in 1892 and ended in 1950, the year of his death at the age of ninety-four. Thirteen years passed before he achieved indisputable success with his coruscating comedy, *Man and Superman*. Down to this point, the critics refused to admit that his plays were dramas at all, calling them indiscriminately tracts, debates, and discussions. Shaw undoubtedly wrote some dramatic masterpieces, which challenge comparison with those of all British predecessors: *Candida, Caesar and Cleopatra, Man and Superman, Major Barbara, Androcles and the Lion, Back to Methuselah, Heartbreak House,* and *Saint Joan.* The last mentioned, a genuine chronicle play, in beauty, majesty, and universality rivals some of Shakespeare's plays. In the second rank falls a number of plays which, by reason of vivacity, quality of entertainment, and perennial interest are sure to hold the boards for an indefinite period in the foreseeable future: *Arms and the Man, The Devil's Disciple, You Never Can Tell, John Bull's Other Island, The Man of Destiny, The Doctor's Dilemma, Fanny's First Play, Pygmalion, The Apple Cart, In Good King Charles's Golden Days, The Dark Lady of the Sonnets,* and *Captain Brassbound's Conversion.* Shaw expressed the belief that his greatest contribution was a rich and extensive group of plays which were sure to be included in the repertory of a future national British theater.

Shaw's plays are conspicuous for originality and novelty of treatment; and he once remarked to me that each of his plays was *sui generis.* Although he mastered the technic of his predecessors from Aristophanes and Euripides to Molière and Ibsen, he evolved a technic peculiarly his own, writing dramas which may be classified as dialectic, disquisitory, discursive, and even digressive—his characters in a delightfully entertaining way voicing many of the most advanced and progressive ideas of our time.

At a luncheon given by the Royal Society of Literature in London in honor of Maurice Donnay, January 18, 1922, Shaw ranked Molière as the world's greatest dramatist. There can be no doubt, I think, that Shaw modeled the technic of a number of his plays on the "conversation pieces" of Molière. Shaw might have written such conversation pieces, for example, as *Le Bourgeois Gentilhomme, L'École des Femmes,* and *Critique de l'École des Femmes,* save that Molière writes with more humorous suavity and social aplomb, whereas Shaw writes with sharp irony and caustic wit. Indeed we may safely say that Shaw picked up the torch of Molière and carried it triumphantly into the future. In the great French master, as a rule, some exceptional, even abnormal character is made to suffer through public ridicule. With Shaw, the range is vastly widened; for his satire is directed, not at an individual, but at ideologies embodied in individual characters:

designs for living, codes of conduct, philosophies of life. The clash of these ideologies with each other constitutes the Shaw drama.

As a humorist, Shaw was profoundly influenced by Dickens, whom he regarded as supremely great in fiction; and by Mark Twain whom he acknowledged to have left a deep impression upon his writings (I heard him say this, as I introduced them to each other). He regarded Poe, Whitman, and Twain, he told me afterwards, as America's greatest writers. He reveled in the gargantuan humor and colossal exaggeration of both Dickens and Twain; and unhesitatingly asserted that Dickens "combined a mirrorlike exactness of character-drawing with the wildest extravagances of humorous expression and grotesque situation." He saw in both Dickens and Twain great literary "primitives" who painted society to the life, and would have been powerful social reformers and world-betterers had they not been primarily fictive artists.

Although Shaw vigorously denied any indebtedness to Ibsen, the denial is preposterous. As Molière taught Shaw how to write "conversation pieces," so Ibsen gave him the clue which enabled him to create the "debated drama," one of his most important contributions to dramatic technic. The obligatory scene in the tense debate between Nora and Helmer in the fourth act of *A Doll's House* furnished the clue. Shaw saw no reason why discussion or even debate should not run throughout the whole play; and some of his own best plays are dramas of discussion. *Candida* was Shaw's *A Doll's House;* but in Shaw's play the doll is the husband, not the wife. The auction scene is derived directly from a similar scene in Ibsen's *The Lady from the Sea,* although Shaw assured me that any imitation was entirely unconscious on his part. *Mrs. Warren's Profession* employs Ibsen's original "retrospective method"; and other similarities between Ibsen and Shaw might be cited. In his *The Quintessence of Ibsenism,* Shaw depicts Ibsen with such a close resemblance to himself, in both art and philosophy, that some mischievous German critic suggested that the title, *The Quintessence of Ibsenism,* should have been *Die Quintessenz des Shawismus.*

Shaw, I believe, owes his greatest debt as a dramatist to the man he terms his "famous rival," William Shakespeare. He has confessed that he takes the utmost pains to discover the right thing to say, and then to say it with the utmost levity. This takes care of the comedic impact of his plays. The deeper problem was to draft conversation which is not a carbon copy of the conversation of so-called "real" life, which, as you all know, is insincere, false, deceptive, and disingenuous because of the barriers and inhibitions of good taste, propriety, decency, and courtesy. Shaw's primary aim was to transcend the façade of politeness and to speak the uninhibited truth. Only in the great soliloquies of Shakespeare, Hamlet, Macbeth, and the rest, did he find this aim attained. Only in soul-communing is a man truly sincere. As the soliloquy was banished by Ibsen from the realistic modern drama, the only alternative was to lift the veristic self-communing from the Subconscious to the Conscious plane, to make the inarticulate vocal, the unspoken audible.

It is this remarkable feat which Shaw has accomplished in his plays and which I can justly term supra-natural. Shaw's characters are almost unbelievably frank, since they do not speak the inhibited language of what we euphemistically call "real" life. Shaw once said to me: "You must remember that if the characters in my plays were suddenly to come alive and step straight from the stage into 'real life,' society would be disrupted, civilization upset, and there would be the very devil to pay generally. You cannot carry out moral sanitation any more than physical sanitation without indecent exposure."

Music, more than literature, influenced Shaw in the writing of certain of his plays which may be termed operatic plays of ideologies. His supreme model was Mozart, who was both a great musician and a great dramatist. A number of Shaw's plays are "composed" like operas of Mozart, Wagner, and Gilbert and Sullivan. Plays by Shaw which naturally lend themselves as librettos for operas, grand, bouffe, and light, and musical comedies, are *Back to Methuselah, Arms and the Man* (which supplied the libretto for *The Chocolate Soldier*), *The Man of Destiny, Captain Brassbound's Conversion, Caesar and Cleopatra,* and *Pygmalion,* which gave rise to the musical comedy, *My Fair Lady,* the current colossal New York success. Tickets to this musical on the black market now sell as high as 15 times those sold at the box office.

Shaw was a profound student of the old mystery and morality plays, and had an unbounded admiration for Bunyan. *The Pilgrim's Progress,* which he regarded as a supreme fictive morality, influenced him in the writing of a number of his plays. While Bunyan personalized individual virtues, vices, and dominant characteristics, Shaw filled the stage with characters embodying class ideologies and social philosophies. It is for this reason that certain of his plays remind us of puppet plays in which the marionettes are ventriloquial mouthpieces for the Master's voice. It is significant that three of Shaw's greatest dramas, *Man and Superman, Back to Methuselah,* and *Heartbreak House,* are morality plays in the modern manner.

Shaw is the greatest pamphleteer of the contemporary era, and probably the most influential free-lance publicist since Voltaire. In satire he rivals Swift without the Dean's ferocity; in invective he was the full equal of Cobbett, Carlyle and Ruskin. Shaw is an evangelist who chose the world for his congregation. He dispensed with sweetness and light in favor of the shock-tactics of epigram, half-truth, exaggeration, and anticlimax. There is something of Barnum and Billy Sunday in Shaw. "It is not only good for people to be shocked occasionally," Shaw impishly avers, "but it is absolutely necessary to the progress of society that they should be shocked pretty often." As a philosophic thinker, he restored *mind* to the British drama; and his artistic integrity entitles him with no little justice to claim the title of artist-philosopher. He achieved the most pellucid style of any writer of his generation. He was never without his Bible, but whether he studied the incomparable King James' version for religious inspiration or as a model of literary style I am not prepared to determine. For all his startling irreverence and scarifying criticism of most of the religious creeds, he was activated by deep religious impulses and animated by a spirit of almost saintly magnanimity. It was his friend and admirer, the late Dean Inge of St. Paul's, who publicly stated that Bernard Shaw, although a convert to no religious faith, was "near to the Kingdom of God."

From the outset, I have accepted Shaw as a towering genius, a literary immortal, and one of the world's great masters of the drama. This was done in deliberate defiance of the convention that contemporary appraisal of genius and greatness lacks the perspective of time and history; and that fame, in the enduring sense, must abide the verdict of posterity. The bold assertion that enduring fame is the predestined lot of Shaw is supported and confirmed by three convincing testimonies: the character of his achievements, the quality of his writings, and the global triumphs of his dramas.

As to personality, Shaw was the most charming of companions. Having known him intimately for almost half a century, I make bold to affirm that, while he had many enemies, provoked the undying hostility of London's West End playwrights and theater managers, and had to win all his great battles against the powerful and entrenched forces of conservatism, conventional mores, cant, hypocrisy, and the serried ranks of respectability, he had countless admirers and not a few devoted friends who basked in the sunshine of his humor, reveled in the quickening spirit of his dazzling wit, and found in him a paragon of humanitarian concern, an ascetic of something not far from saintly virtue, the friend of aspiring artists, and the most courteous, considerate, and generous of men. In his later years, for his dominance of the British literary scene, he came to be regarded as the contemporary avatar of Dr. Johnson. As Johnson said of Garrick, so may it far more appropriately be said of Shaw: "His death eclipsed the gaiety of nations and impoverished the public stock of harmless pleasure." I have never known any man who entertained so deep-rooted and acute a sense of obligation to the common weal.

The germ of Shaw's philosophy of life I find in these stirring words from an address delivered at the Municipal Technical College and School of Art at Brighton, England, March 6, 1907:

I am of the opinion that my life belongs to the whole community, and as long as I live it is my privilege to do for it whatsoever I can.

I want to be thoroughly used up when I die; for the harder I work the more I live. I rejoice in life for its own sake. Life is no "brief candle" for me. It is a sort of splendid torch, which I have got hold of for the moment; and I want to make it burn as brightly as possible before handing it on to future generations.

The Biographical Novel

Irving Stone

Presented at the Library of Congress January 7, 1957

THE BIOGRAPHICAL NOVEL is a true and documented story of one human being's journey across the face of the years, transmuted from the raw material of life into the delight and purity of an authentic art form.

The biographical novel is based on the conviction that the best of all plots lie in human character; and that human character is endlessly colorful and revealing. It starts with the assumption that those stories which have actually happened can be at least as interesting and true as those which have been imagined. Alexander Pope said that the proper study of mankind is man; the biographical novel accepts that challenge and sets out to document its truth, for character is plot; character development is action; and character fulfillment is resolution.

The biographical novel attempts to fuse not only its parent sources of biography and the novel, but that of its grandparent, history, as well. It must tell the story of its main character, not in the bulk of millionfold detail, but in essence; it must recreate the individual against the background of his times, with all of its authentic historical flavor; and it must live up to the exacting demands of the novel structure.

Let me joyfully proclaim that basically the biographical novelist is a yarn-spinner, and the biographical novel a vigorous medium that has been created in order to tell the fine stories that have been lived. The form is fortunate in its opportunity to utilize the single greatest virtue of the novel: growth of character. This growth may be into good or evil, into creativity or destruction; it cannot be static. There are few joys for the reader to surpass that of watching an interesting story unfold through growth of character; and in this field no form surpasses the biographical novel, which by the very definition of its nature is always about people rather than impersonal forces.

The biographical novelist has a greater freedom to interpret than has the biographer, and the reader has a greater chance of coming away with a more personal understanding of human motivation. If there is a tendency to oversimplify, it is in the same fashion that man's memory does as he looks back on his span of time, forgetting nine-tenths of the bulk, remembering only the distillation which has meaning. For the biographical novel is based not merely on fact, but on feeling, the legitimate emotion arising from indigenous drama. Facts can get lost with almost too great a facility, but an emotional experience, once lived, can never be forgotten. Nor can this emotion be artificially induced for the sake of raising the reader's temperature. While a biography can be written purely out of a life's worthiness, with details of important names, places and dates, the biographical novel must emerge naturally and organically from the conflicts of man against himself, man against man, or man against fate. Since an experience shared will remain with one forever, it is the aim of the biographical novel to bring the reader into the very heart of the emotion being engendered so that he will make that emotion his own. For the feelings have a memory and a wisdom of which the mind could well be covetous.

In the fields of straight biography and history, the reader stands on the sidelines. What is transpiring on the page is something that happened long ago, and to other people. When reading the biographical novel he is no longer a spectator, but a participant. He starts to live the story as though its first incident had its inception at the instant he opened the book. Perhaps the biographical novel has become so popular because the reader is allowed to participate intimately in history, to become one of its prime actors and motivators. Thus all history becomes contemporary, as in truth it is. The old joke about the man who thought he was Napoleon can come true.

In the biographical novel therefore, the reading and the doing, through identification, become synonymous; the reader can live a thousand different lives during a relatively brief span of years. Therein lies the genius of the form, therein lies its enchantment and its hope for a permanent place in the literary heavens.

With the exception of Merejkowsky's *Romance of Leonardo da Vinci* and Gertrude Atherton's novel of Alexander Hamilton, *The Conqueror,* the biographical novel was unknown and unaccepted in the United States thirty years ago. Yet today it can be found in the catalogue of every major publisher. Now that the biographical novel has come of age, a few ground rules can perhaps be laid down for its practitioners.

The first of these must surely be that history is not the servant of the biographical novelist, but his master. No biographical novel can be better than its research. If the research is deep and honest, the novel will be deep and honest; if the research is sleazy, shallow, evasive or sensation-seeking, the novel will be sleazy, shallow, evasive, sensation-mongering.

186

Not every life will fit into the form of the biographical novel. There are specific dramatic elements that must be present, recurrent themes of conflict and accomplishment woven through its entirety, an overall, perceivable pattern into which the parts can be fitted to make an organic whole. There are many lives, important and significant in their end results, which are nonetheless diffuse, their content and design antithetical to the nature of the novel; others seem to have been lived as though the subject himself were constantly aware that he was creating a dramatic structure.

While the biographical novelist is assuredly licensed to search out and select those lives which make good copy, the basic demonstrable truth cannot be pushed around to serve a plot purpose. The writer who must twist or pervert the historic truth to come out with what he thinks is an acceptable or saleable story is a tragically misplaced person in his field. The biographical novelist, on the other hand, who becomes moralistic or political, turns into a pamphleteer. We have had experiences of American biographical novelists twisting history out of shape and proportion in order to make it conform to a preconceived line. What has emerged has been neither legitimate biography nor authentic novel, but propaganda. Biography is rich in materials which can be used to serve a purpose; and the biographical novel, young as it is, has not been free from those who would use the form unscrupulously. But this is a danger incident to all of the arts, particularly in a time of war for man's mind; our nostrils must become aware of the rancid smell of such books. In the biographical novel, as in all art forms, personal and professional integrity lie at the base of lasting accomplishment.

An integrated, successful, first-rate biographical novel can emerge only from a union of the material chosen and the author of the choice; from a free, mutually respectful and frequently self-sacrificing partnership in which the story that has been lived and the author who is recreating that story in print, must be equal, and the final product remain more important than either of the contributing partners. If either one assumes an ascendancy the novel will lack for balance: the material will dominate the author, take directions in defiance of the structure; or the author will dominate the material, make it a creature of his own will and desiring. Few authors are qualified to write equally well or profoundly on all subjects. The wise author waits, or searches, for that meaningful story which he can understand, which moves him, and which he senses he can bring vividly to life. If the author chooses unwisely, perhaps because he does not know his material well enough before he starts, or does not know himself well enough, the result can only be false and fragmentary or at best a dismal regurgitation.

The author has a right to ask, as he looks at the outline of a human life, "Can this story serve my purposes?"—but only after he has demanded of himself, "Can I serve the purposes of this story?"

Because of the principle of selection, the biographical novel will inevitably end up as much a portrait of the author as of the subject, for the biographical novelist is a distiller, deriving his spirits not from rye, and we hope not from corn; but from the boiling-pot of human experience. It follows that the biographical novel, even though it leans so heavily on biography and history, can be no better than the mind of its author. If the author is dull, the novel will be dull, and neither biography nor history can save him. If the author is cold, the novel will be cold, no matter how flaming the material being handled. If the author is humorless, the novel will be humorless; if the author is narrow in his interests, his novel will be narrow in its interests, no matter how wide a slice of life it may be reflecting. And if the author is dishonest, what emerges from the pages must be a dishonest novel, regardless of the integrity of the character being portrayed.

How is a reader unacquainted with the field to distinguish between the honest and dishonest biographical novel, the complete and the fractional? How can the question, "How much of this is true?" be answered? Only by insisting that the biographical novel must be as complete in its documentation as the most scholarly history and biography, and as honest in its interpretation.

If it takes four years to train a schoolteacher or engineer, five years to train a pharmacist, six a dentist, seven a lawyer, and eight a doctor, is there any reason to believe that it can take less time to develop a qualified and professional biographical novelist?

He must become experienced in the writing of imaginative novels, wrestling with this form in order that he may come up against the challenging complexities of structure, mood, master scenes, dialogue, with its accompanying lyricism of language, the mounting involvement and suspense of the fictional tale. He would be well advised to write a half-dozen plays to absorb the superb economy of the form, and learn how to stage his tale under a proscenium instead of in the wings: for what the reader does not see with his eyes he never really knows.

He must be trained as a biographer, working at the assembling of materials about one man or group of men, mastering the technic of close-knit organization of these materials, the perceiving and the weaving back and forth of the life theme, evolving a style, personality, and manner of writing by means of which one man's story can be brought to life all over again by black hieroglyphs on white paper: the eternal miracle of literature: for each life has a distinctive face and figure; and this must be captured in order to differentiate this one special story from the hundreds of millions that have been lived.

The biographical novelist must become as scientific a researcher as was

188

Dr. Jonas Salk in his medical laboratories. During the six years that I attended the University of California there were no courses in the fascinating science of research. I had to stumble my way toward a modus operandi. Today most colleges give courses in research which make the tools of this exciting trade as available and usable as those in accounting or electronics. The biographical novelist must be as dedicated to his digging as the archaeologist who uncovers ancient cities after years of pick and shovel work; and he must be grimly resolved that there is absolutely nothing in the historic record which cannot be found if one will search for it long enough, arduously enough and adroitly enough. Fresh and daring ideas about where and how to look are as important to successful research as are the extracting of fresh and daring drawings by painters from their own minds. Parenthetically the biographical novelist must be as stout of heart as the most ardent lover, for important new materials are frequently buried deep, yielding their charms and protected virtues only to importunate courtship.

Though research is as fascinating as the resolution of a crossword puzzle or a murder mystery, it is also hard work, thoroughly exhausting and unending in its demands. The researcher sometimes gets lost in his forest of facts. To change the metaphor, the biographical novel must be built like an iceberg, about one ninth of solid substance showing above the literary water line, and the other eight-ninths submerged, but giving a solid base to that which is permitted to appear. If the biographical novelist does not know nine times as much as he reveals, the substance of the print he spreads over the page will be painfully thin: for the eight-ninths which he does not reveal permeates the whole, giving to the pages a discernible bouquet, a subtle emanation which enables the reader to feel comfortable and secure.

For every printed page has a feel and a smell to it, just as surely as does a piece of fruit; it is the research which gives the page of the biographical novel its consistency, which enables the reader to feel that this particular piece of literary fruit is sound at its core, and will not soon decay if allowed to sit on the library table. In the biographical novel, research is the hard firm flesh under the surface skin of the printed page.

The biographical novelist must also be uncrushable in his faith that the truth will out, for when he finds three differing versions of the same happening, accompanied by three different sets of dates and circumstances, he must not become disheartened, but must believe that if he will continue to dig he will find a fourth, authentic version based on irrefutable documents. As Charles A. Beard, one of America's most brilliant historical researchers, told me in his library in New Canaan while helping me with an elusive problem, "Every day I find new source material which controverts something I have believed for thirty years."

To the biographical novelist history is not a mountain, but a river. Even when there are no new facts to be found, there are fresh insights, modern interpretations which can give an old story new focus and meaning; for the biographical novelist, like the archaeologist, is not just a pick and shovel man. The sweat on the forehead and the callouses on the palm are the merest preparation for the real work to come: interpretation of the uncovered materials which will throw light on a story long since lived.

The biographical novelist must also be a perennial skeptic and challenger of the printed word. My confrere, Robert Graves, recently told me in his workshop in Majorca that his biographical novel *I, Claudius* was born at the moment when, reading Tacitus, he cried out, "That's a lie!"

The number of lies and part-truths still resting comfortably and respectably in history is a constant source of astonishment to me; as I am equally amazed at the whole areas of history, even American history as late as the Civil War, or the turn of the twentieth century, that are inadequately researched, or simply not researched at all. It is here that the biographical novelist has his magnificent opportunity: for the vigor and enthusiasm, and a fresh point of view, he can change "That is a lie!" into "That is the truth!" just as he can throw beams of light into areas of history which have remained dark and damp through sheer neglect and want of a champion to rescue them from oblivion.

It also follows that the biographical novelist must be a fighter. Frequently the best stories, and the most meaningful, are those of the underdog, of the man or woman who has been vilified and traduced. From the body of my own work may I suggest as examples the stories of Eugene V. Debs, Rachel Jackson and Mary Todd Lincoln. All efforts to cut through the jungle of prejudiced print, to find the balanced, sympathetic yet judicious truth will be met not only with opposition but frequently with ridicule: for man is as unwilling to give up his vested interest in his prejudices as he is any other of his possessions.

Lastly, the biographical novelist must believe that first there came the Book; he must love books with an unflagging ardency, for he will spend the greater part of life with his nose inside one volume or another: and some of them will be mighty tough customers. He must be able to survive the eyestrain engendered by tiny type, the headaches brought on by handling crumbling yellow pages, the fading ink of aged diaries and letters; and worse, the bottomless depths of Dead Sea writing which would break the teeth of any man imprudent enough to read it aloud.

I would like to outline some specifics.

Having determined that he is going to write a biographical novel about the life of Leonardo da Vinci or Alexander Hamilton, the biographical novelist must put out of his mind for six months or a year any illusion that he is a writer, and become a library mole. He must read all the books and articles written by his subject, study the works created by him, be they art or engineering, read every findable word that has been written about the man or work. He must read all the letters that have passed between the hero and his contemporaries, as well as his private notes, journals and memoirs; or, in the case of a heroine, those wonderfully confiding diaries that are kept locked in the middle drawer of a desk. If the subject is of recent times, there will be a need to interview or correspond with everyone who has been involved in the drama, no matter how slightly.

Having grasped more fully the outlines of his story, the biographical novelist then takes to the road, seeing with his own eyes the places his hero has lived, the quality of the sunlight, the native earth beneath his feet, the personality of the cities and the feel of the countryside: for only then can he write with the intimacy and knowledgability of tactile experience.

This is the first and direct line of attack. The second is equally important: the biographical novelist must now begin the study of his hero's times, its fads and fancies, its majority and minority ideas as well as the prevailing conflicts in religion, philosophy, science, politics, economics and the arts; in short, the overall social, mental, spiritual, esthetic, scientific and international climate in which his characters lived and evolved their codes of conduct. He must read the source books of the period in order to absorb its background, the old newspapers, pamphlets, magazines, the novels, plays and poetry of the times, in order to learn the uncountable thousands of illuminating details which he must have at his fingertips in order to recreate the period: what people wear, the architecture of their houses as well as the fabric on their furniture, how they heat their homes, cook the foods they eat at the various hours of the day; what they are buying in the shops and why, how much it costs as well as how it tastes and smells and feels; what ailments they are suffering and how they are treating them; what colloquialisms they are using to enrich their conversation; what their preachers are preaching on Sunday morning and their teachers teaching on Monday morning.

If the biographical novelist has any feeling for his job he will eventually find emerging out of this seemingly vast and inchoate mass of material certain recurrent patterns, strains of character and action that provide a dominant motif and rhythm for the story he will tell, even as the dominant strains of a symphony are enunciated early. Above all, the biographical novelist is looking for those interwoven designs which are perceivable in every human life: for nearly every life works out its own tightly-woven plot structure. Any action forced upon the participants which does not arise indigenously, which arises instead from the author confusing motion with direction, tears the fabric of the story.

Yet by the same token the biographical novelist must be the master of

191

his material; the craftsman who is not in control of his tools will have his story run away with him. For after his research labors, the biographical novelist must then expend as much time and energy as the writer of fiction to create a novel structure which will best project his material, and be unique to the particular story to be told.

And all this new knowledge must never come between the reader and the narration. In the biographical novel a basic tenet is that the author must stage his story as though it were happening right now; he may not emerge at intervals to inform the reader of what will happen two or twenty or two hundred years later. The reader may never be in possession of information which is not available to those who are acting out the day-by-day passion of their lives. The story must unfold for the reader even as the pageant of events unfolds for the participants. There are few sooth-sayers; the biographical novelist may not turn himself into an a posteriori prophet. Whatever the reader may divine about what lies ahead must arise from his own perception, and not from the biographical novelist fudging on time sequence. If there be wisdom in the author (and God grant that there may sometimes be!) it will emerge from the nature of the story he wants to tell, from his selection of materials within the framework of that particular story, from his understanding of what motivates his people, and from the skill with which he shapes the unassimilated raw action of human life.

Perhaps a glimpse of my own approaches and technics from *Lust For Life* through *Immortal Wife* and *Love is Eternal* may shed further light on this still nascent form. I first stumbled across the paintings of Vincent Van Gogh when taken to an exhibition by insistent Parisian friends. Seeing a whole room of Vincent's blazing Arlesian canvases was an emotional experience that I can liken only to my first reading of *The Brothers Kara-mazov*. I left the exhibition hall determined to find out who this man was who could move me to such depths. I read all the fragments I could find about him in English, French and German; when I returned to New York and to the writing of my plays, I would spend my evenings at the public library at Forty-second Street and Fifth Avenue, reading the three volumes of Vincent's letters to his brother Theo. I had no intention of writing about Vincent; I was only trying to understand him. But slowly over the months the Van Gogh story took possession of me; I found myself waking at three in the morning, writing dialogue passages between Vincent and Theo, or describing Vincent's death scene at Auvers sur Oise. Vincent's ordeal be-came for me one of the world's most meaningful stories. At the end of a year, when I found myself unable to think of anything else, I decided that I would have to write Vincent's story if for no other reason than to clear it from my mind.

192

My background for writing such a story was inadequate, for I had grown up in San Francisco where art was a portrait of two dead rabbits hanging by their feet. My first task then, was to read all the books I could find about art and modern painters, and then to search out the canvases that were available. I returned to Europe with a rucksack on my back and followed the trail of Vincent, going down into the mines of the Borinage where he had descended, living in his bedroom at Madam Dennis's bakery, writing notes in the parsonages where he had lived with his family in Holland, and going to the south of France to work in the Yellow House, to live in the asylum at St. Remy where he had been incarcerated, and finally to sleep in the same room and bed in the little hotel in Auvers on the fortieth anniversary of his death.

Since I did not know how much I did not know about the writing of a biographical novel, I sat down to my first morning's work with a little calling card in front of me on which I scribbled four strictures: 1. Dramatize. 2. Plenty of dialogue. 3. Bring all characters to life. 4. Use anecdotes and humor.

It is somewhat chastening to me, these many years later, when I write myself fifty pages of notes on precisely how the new book must be written and, collaterally, how it must not be written, to find that I emerge with a product which a lot of people feel is no better than *Lust for Life*. I sometimes wonder if I have spent the past twenty-five years enunciating intellectually the things I knew intuitively at the beginning.

It is also a source of considerable astonishment to me that I waited through three biographies to get back to the form in which I had achieved such a happy result; and that only a fortuitous accident pushed me back into the field.

Through my chapter on John C. Frémont in *They Also Ran,* the story of the men who were defeated for the presidency, I once again came across the woman with whom I had fallen in love in college, and in whose image I married: Jessie Benton Frémont. Jessie's story came to possess me, even as Vincent's had.

In the spring of 1943 I wrote myself a list of sixty-two specifics for *Immortal Wife.* I should like to read a few of them as samples of how one biographical novelist sets the boundaries and dimensions of his task.

I quote directly from my notes:

The story must flow swiftly, smoothly, lyrically. It is a story of people, not history. People come first, history follows. It must be at least half dialogue. Jessie's interior monologue and thinking must be quietly done, understated. Everything must be seen through her eyes. All characters must be brought sharply and vividly to life. Every scene, every word, must be contemporary. Every reader must identify himself with Jessie. Pano-

193

rama of a changing world: 1840, 1900 through one woman's eyes. Nothing described for description's sake, only as seen by Jessie and as important in her life. No fact for fact's sake, everything human. Material constantly new, refreshing, yet fitting into life pattern. Humor as constant leaven. Patience in developing and revealing major themes. Must be primarily a love story. Constantly changing nature of their love, yet fundamentally same. Always the third dimension of failure, error, human failing. The fourth dimensions of mysticism: faith in each other and the world, undying hope as wellspring of human life. Thorough and penetrating job on love and marriage. Keep language universal. Never the whole story; always the essence. No skimping of material; no overblown presentation. Vivid imagery of detail of times, rich contrast of changing scene: Washington, St. Louis, Mariposa. Use interesting mechanisms for history, not just plumped down. Should embrace the whole of a life, one life, as symbolic of all.

Seven years later, when I came to the formulating of *The President's Lady*, I wrote myself advice under the heading of "What devices can be used to get inside Rachel?" some of which may prove germane at this point:

We must react to situations with her mind. We must see people through her eyes, our sense of values must be her sense of values. We must suffer from the things that disturb her, and want (at least for her) the things that she wants. We must share her love for Andrew, endure with her the long terrifying loneliness. The form of our anxieties must be identical with the form of her anxieties; we must evaluate all events through the focus of her needs. We must cling to, and love, the friends and relatives she does. We must want fame and greatness for Andrew, and yet fear them terribly too. We must turn religious, need and justify that religion when she does. She must be the stage upon which history is acted out. We must tremble, then rejoice in her few social triumphs, and die when she dies, acknowledging the lethal blow. We must like Rachel, care about her, understand, sympathize with her. We must enjoy her life from inside her mind and heart.

This can be achieved by warmth of approach; by the author liking her, himself. By a simple, honest directness of storytelling, by understatement, so that the reader builds up his own emotions. By keeping her clear; by moving her swiftly through events, almost too swiftly for her. By finding and portraying the illuminating detail about her. By finding in her the universal elements of suffering in love and marriage. By discerning the basic structure of her life, and sticking to that; by particularizing her, distinguishing her from all other women. By making her a tool and victim of fate; as we all are. Yet proving that her story has never been lived before; or since.

At the end of eighteen months of work, just before beginning the penultimate chapter, I also wrote a five-page note asking "What is the cement that holds this book together?," reviewing the whole meaning and purpose of the book to make sure that nothing that had been enunciated at the beginning had gotten lost in transit, and saying to myself, "This book doesn't have to prove anything but doesn't it have to illuminate a great deal?"

I had been interested in the Lincoln story for many years, and had read rather widely in the field, but had never been able to achieve a point of departure, for I had always said to myself, "Poor Abraham Lincoln, married to Mary Todd." After some ten years of incubation (most biographical novels come out well only if they have been incubating at least five years) while I was doing a magazine article about the Lincoln marriage, I came across some obscure source material which threw the marriage and its daily workings into high relief, particularly in relation to Mr. Lincoln in his role as a husband. I found myself exclaiming, "Poor Mary Todd, married to Abraham Lincoln." From that moment of understanding of the truly equal nature of the marriage I was able to begin work on the thesis which Abraham Lincoln inscribed inside the wedding ring he purchased in the square on the Sunday morning of his wedding, "Love Is Eternal." A little of the detail I sought before starting Chapter IV, just after the Lincoln marriage, may give an idea of the tens of thousands of questions a biographical novelist must ask: for his curiosity must be insatiable:

What changes have taken place in Mary, in Abraham Lincoln? How much time does Abraham spend with her? Where is Mary's room located in hotel? Front, back, side, corner? Does it get some sun? Is it warm or cold? Does she rearrange the room, or leave it as it was? (Rearrange to make it her own?) What are the dimensions? What does it look out over? Is it painted, or wallpapered? How much time does she spend in her room, in the parlors? Does she ask for special things, i. e., reading table; buy a few little things, i. e., lamps? How does she occupy her time in the mornings? Reading, sewing, writing letters? What kind of service is available? How does she arrange her money affairs? Does A give her money for incidentals: drugs, materials, etc. Does she have any money of her own? Does she pay at stores, or do they have credit accounts? Since Abraham wants to live economically, does she spend, or follow his wishes? Does she have visitors at hotel? Family, friends to dinner and supper? Is it expensive? She is later accused of being stingy, but if so, does she learn economy from A? Where is dining-room of Globe? How big is it? How decorated? Does Lincoln suggest they eat with others at big tables, or do they have the same table for two? Who was next to, or across from the Lincolns? We know of Bledsoes—what kind of piano, and what pieces, would Mrs. Bledsoe be playing? Would she invite Mary to play?

As I was preparing the last two chapters, I wrote myself a long, stern directive, of which the following lines are typical:

Let's get simple, and stay simple. Do only symptomatic scenes; step up pacing and speed; in perspective distant scenes are always foreshortened. Don't fight the entire Civil War, only those elements that come into the White House. Avoid name-calling, side-taking, prejudice, bitterness. Awaken no hatred, only pity and compassion. Underwrite the grief, underplay the emotion. Don't stack cards, either for or against Mary. Keep the author out, let the story tell itself.

But beyond the specifications for any one particular book, I found the following obiter dicta to be essential to all biographical novels:

No use of names because they later become important elsewhere. No asides, or smart whisperings. No fixations, or prejudices carried over from past feelings or readings. No harpings, or preconceived "theories, into which all history and happenings must fit." No name-calling, let the reader call the proper names. No fiery passions, for or against; they cloud judgment. No assumptions as to the reader's tastes, opinions, ideas, education. No writing for any one class, age or geographic group. No condemnations of people or events; give them their rightful place in the story, and let God judge them. No seeking the sensational for its own sake; and no philosophizing. No concealing of important evidence, no lies, cheating or defrauding the reader. No dullness; throw out the slow, meaningless passages. No striving for effects, no manifest anger or hatred, no browbeating. Watch comparative materials and balance them; no disproportions about materials where I happen to know more. No inheriting of other people's prejudices, hatreds, blindness. No details that illuminate little but themselves. No posturing, no exhibitionism: "See what I know!" No striving for novelty for its own sake. No doctrinairism, or fitting material into one school or pattern. No destructivism, nor defeatism. No pugilism or blind spots. No lethargy. No weasel phrases; all space is needed for direct lines. No meandering down pleasant paths. No use of material that does not tie into focal core of book.

Because of the tender youth of the biographical novel there has as yet been little discussion of its particular character, of its strengths as well as its limitations. Is it a history, a biography, or a novel? Is it none of these? Or perhaps all three? If in this paper I presume to provide a beginning critique, standards of judgment against which the biographical novel may be viewed, it is done with the happy reassurance that all such strictures will be altered, expanded and materially improved by later practitioners of the craft.

Professor Carl Bode of the University of Maryland recently wrote in the magazine *College English,* in the first serious study of the biographical novel to be published, "In the last ten years several prominent people have been doing their best to make an honest woman of the biographical novel. Con-

196

siderable progress has been made, but not quite enough. The biographical novel still goes its bosomy way, its flimsy clothing tattered and torn in exactly the wrong places." "Sometimes powerful and often picturesque, it deserves much more attention than it has received from the critics."

When Professor Bode speaks of the biographical novels going their bosomy way, their flimsy clothing tattered and torn in exactly the wrong places, I am afraid he is concerned with such books as *Forever Amber* or *Kitty*, whose writers took the license of combining sensational material from a hundred different sources, letting their fictional fancies run wild, a privilege not accorded to the biographical novelist, who must remain inside the confines of the life he is writing about. They are certainly not biographical novels, and I doubt very much that W. R. Guthrie or Robert Penn Warren would consider them historical novels.

If anything, the biographical novel has suffered from an excess of good taste and respectability, perhaps because the biographical novelist has been awed by the fact that his characters once actually lived, and hence were endowed with certain inalienable rights, not of concealment, but of privacy and decorum. Bedroom scenes of which critics complain in the lurid, so-called historical novels are not to be found in the biographical novel, a sometime limitation to the sale of the genre, but one which calls forth the subtlety of the biographical novelist if he is to convey to the reader the all-important love and sex life of his subject.

I am going to take the liberty of quoting Professor Bode's analysis of my own work because I believe he has drawn an architectural blueprint for me, and for other biographical novelists, to follow in the future. Speaking of my own five biographical novels that followed the story of Vincent Van Gogh, he writes:

Each volume showed the advances in novelistic technique. The scholarship deepened too, though less steadily. The peak for the present day biographical novel was approached with the publication of Stone's book on Mary Todd Lincoln and her marriage. The scholarship is just as sound, according to a leading Lincoln specialist, as it is in the recent and respectfully reviewed biography of Mrs. Lincoln by a trained historian. It deserves to be called meticulous. Many an example can be found of Stone's deep scholarly concern with the life he was writing. He painstakingly prepared a floor-plan of the White House of Lincoln's day—one has never been reconstructed before—as a piece of independent research, and he created most of his dialogue out of skilled paraphrases of historically accurate source material. Furthermore, the handling of the data is judicious. Mrs. Lincoln is always a controversial figure, and Stone could be excused if he slanted his information one way or the other. But he does not. Rising above his declared intention to vindicate her, he portrays her bedeviled neurotic character with fairness.   She and Abe emerge as memorable human beings, one great and the other not, but human beings both.   The minor characters are carefully differentiated, very seldom are they mere historical names. The scenes are well handled, with pace and suspense to some of them in spite of the fact that historians already know how they come out . . . The descriptions give rich color to the picture Stone creates . . .

The aim behind the best writing of this kind is a noble one.   It is to see beneath the surface reality of facts and to reveal the true reality to others.   It is to use historical data more daringly but more penetratingly than the professional historian can.

Samuel E. Morison, professor of history at Harvard University, writes in an essay called *History As A Literary Art*: "The historian can learn much from the novelist.   The best writers of fiction are superior to all but the best historians in characterization and description.   When John Citizen feels the urge to read history he goes to the novels of Kenneth Roberts or Margaret Mitchell, not to the histories of Professor this or Doctor that. Why?   American historians have forgotten that there is an art of writing history.   In this flight of history from literature the public got left behind. American history became a bore to the reader and a drug on the market."

It is to this mournful state of affairs that the biographical novel addresses itself.

It is important, too, to set down the discernible differences between the biographical novel, the fictional novel, the historical novel, and the straight biography.

A few years ago when I was visiting with Ernest Hemingway in Key West, we discussed the approaches to our two novels in progress.   Hemingway said, "There is no such thing as fiction.   Everything we write is based on the lives we have lived, and other lives we have observed."   Yet the fictional novelist has the opportunity to regroup and rechannel experience, to combine portions of a dozen different lives, to imagine a better world, or a more evil one, if that suits his temperament, and of conjuring up varying resolutions to the human situations he has evoked.

The biographical novelist is a bondsman to the factual truth; yet he will succeed very little if he remains a mere reporter.   As Robert Graves said to me, "The biographical novelist who does not have strong intuitions about his subject, and later finds from the documents that his intuition has been substantiated, is not likely to get far in understanding his subject."

Inside the skeletal outline imposed on him, the biographical novelist is free to soar to any heights which his own inner poetry and perception will allow him.   There are few if any differences of structure between the two types of novel; with the biographical novel the reader asks, "Did this happen?" and with the fictional novel, "Could this happen?"   Therein lies

198

the major distinction between them. Credibility lies at the base of both. A chance reader, unacquainted with the material, setting and character of the two stories, should not be able to tell them apart; he should be able to think that the fictional novel actually happened somewhere, or that the biographical novel was invented by the author. I remember with considerable satisfaction the day in September 1934 when Mrs. Stone asked the telephone operator in her office how she had liked *Lust for Life,* and the girl replied, "Fine, but why did Irving have to kill off the poor man?"

The historical novel is the closest to the biographical novel in its nature and scope; again the difference is not of form but of approach. In the biographical novel all of the characters have lived; in the best historical novels, such as *War and Peace,* only the history has actually happened, while the characters are invented, or built up by accretion, and then set in the authentic framework of the period and the action being written about. The main characters of the historical novel become the apotheoses of their times; they are true in that such characters did live in this particular period, and this dramatic series of events did take place, but to other people, perhaps half a hundred of them, in modified form and sequence. Sometimes the historical novel will be so close to the biographical novel, such as with *All the King's Men,* the story of Huey Long, that little is changed except the names of the characters and a few incidental pieces of personal action. In H. G. Wells' *The World of William Clissold,* Clissold and his various loves were imaginary, but the protagonists were called by their right names, and once again put through their roles in history. In still another type, roughly half of the characters are real people who act out their own historicity, while the other half, more often than not the "heroes" of the tale, are invented.

I would like at this moment to interject, with less bitterness than puzzlement, I hope, the question of why the historical novel, with its accurate background but fictional characters, should have been more acceptable to the academicians than the biographical novel, which is accurate not only in background but in the people involved? The answer to this riddle has remained a mystery to me.

The differences between the straight biography and the biographical novel are considerable, not in substance, since both draw their nourishment from the same source, but in structure, manner, attitude, and relationship between the author and the reader.

The biography has traditionally been in indirect discourse, a chronicle told by a second party, the writer, to a third party, the reader. The biographer, for example, relates what his principals have said; the biographical novelist enables the reader to listen to the conversations as they develop.

199

The biographical novelist, in order to recreate a character, must not only understand his every motivation, but must write of it from behind the eyes of his protagonist. Only then can the reader feel everything that he feels, know everything that he knows, suffer his defeats and enjoy his victories. The biography has been expected to be objective; too often it has been written in cool blood. The biographical novel must be written in hot blood.

Even so, the form of biography is changing, and perhaps the wide public acceptance of the biographical novel has had something to do with this change. The biographies I read in school contained as many footnotes as lines of text, while the quotations were indented in small type in the center of the page, presenting a pedagogical, dull and fatiguing sight to the eye as well as to the emotional interest of the reader. When in 1937 I wrote *Sailor on Horseback*, I put my quotations from Jack London on a continuing line with the main text, separated only by a comma and a quotation mark, so that there would be no break in the reading mood and the typographical page would remain unified and interesting. When I received the first half of the galleys from my then publisher in Boston, all the quotations had been centered in tiny typeknots in the middle of the page. In answer to my anguished telephone call, the proofreader said that he had set my manuscript according to the standard form, since I obviously had not known how to do so. At that point the editor broke into the conversation and ordered the manuscript reset as I had written it. By now the practice has become almost universal.

Up to recent times it was not permitted in biographies to stage dialogue sequences, even when such dialogue was completely documented, evidently on the grounds that recreated dialogue might be less true, or might lead the reader to think he was reading a novel instead of a biography, and hence not believe that what he was reading was factually accurate. This never appeared to me to be a tenable point of view, and, in 1940, when I wrote *Clarence Darrow For the Defense*, I staged, as though they were being acted under a proscenium, all of the conversations that seemed interesting and important; at the back of the book I listed my documentation for every spoken word. I feel sure they had considerably more emotional impact than if I had related at second hand what the conversations had been about.

When I was growing up, few except scholars read biographies. It is my opinion that the biographical novel arose, and has become popular, because of this failure of the biography to reach a reading public that was hungry for authentic human stories. It is also my opinion that the biography will continue to learn from the biographical novel, and lean on its technics. A book is written for purposes of communication; it does an author no service whatever to have his book unreadable and hence unread. It must also be said that the biographical novel will be eternally indebted to the straight biography, for it has learned from it the science of research and the organization of materials.

The biographical novel, like all living creatures, was born in pain. It was called a bastard form, the result of an unfortunate indiscretion on the part of its otherwise eminently respectable parents, biography and the novel.

What are the criticisms that have been and still are, in some unconvinced corners, levied against the biographical novel? It is said to debase the biography and the novel, discrediting both and adding to the stature of neither. Allegedly it mines biography without regard for the verities, strains history through the author's personality, reshapes that history to fit the novel form, oversimplifies, prevents the reader from separating fact from fiction, chooses only those subjects which allow for a lively sale, violates the privacy of people long dead, and makes character the victim of plot.

All of these criticisms have sometimes been true, and probably a good many more of which the critics happily have not yet thought. But to decide that any art form is untenable because of its weakest example or its potenial for error is similar to saying that the human race should be obliterated because of the shortcomings of its least admirable percentage. I find that in the course of my twenty-three years in the field most major critics have become reconciled to the fact that the biographical novel is here to stay. The more courageous and perceptive of them now welcome it to the literary boards; by the same token they insist that each volume achieve standards of literary and historical excellence. Instead of categorically damning the form without bothering to read the book, they are judging each succeeding biographical novel on the basis of its writing, research, storytelling, perception.

One of the assets of the human race is said to be that it can learn from experience; history and biography constitute the greatest mine of lived experience; and it is the fond dream of the biographical novelist to bring the wisdom of that experience to the problems and complexities of the modern world.

My own biographical novels have had two motivations: I have hoped to feel deeply about simple things; and I have wanted to tell the story of man, against obstacles, for man.

Remarks on the Novel

John O'Hara

Presented at the Library of Congress January 14, 1957

IN VIEW OF THE FACT that there has been no announcement of the subject of my discourse this evening,[1] you will forgive me if I am immodest enough to suspect that you came here out of curiosity, curiosity about me, and about what shocking, or provocative, or entertaining, or stimulating, or instructive things I might have to say. To some extent that curiosity has already been satisfied, in a matter of seconds. You see before you an American author, six feet tall, 195 pounds, grey at the temples, two weeks short of fifty-two years of age, obviously unaccustomed to public speaking, afflicted with an Eastern Pennsylvania twang, writer of several best-sellers, writer also of an equal number of non-sellers, occasionally banned in Detroit, Michigan, Akron, Ohio, and East Germany; and almost completely ill at ease on the platform.

For those whose curiosity can be so easily satisfied I now suggest a quick and quiet departure, and I make that suggestion with no bitterness, without prejudice—and indeed, with some envy. After all, this is "I Love Lucy" night, and I am also under the impression that it is the night when the quiz program called "21" appears at a new time and on a different network. I make mention of the latter because it will give those who leave us the opportunity to see Carl Van Doren's nephew being just as nervous as I am—at, I may say, considerably greater profit. I wonder if those of you who have watched that program have given any thought to the comments Benjamin Franklin is making to Uncle Van Doren. Carl Van Doren has been in heaven long enough to have made the acquaintance of Mr. Franklin and

---

[1] Mr. O'Hara was mistaken. As agreed upon in correspondence when Mr. O'Hara accepted the Library's invitation to lecture, his subject was announced prior to the lecture as "The Novel as a Social Document." While this title may not seem entirely inappropriate for the lecture as written and delivered, the title "Remarks on the Novel" has been retained as given on Mr. O'Hara's manuscript.

to have straightened out the differences that inevitably would come up when biographer finally meets biographee; and if heaven is everything they say it is, they must be enjoying unlimited television, and I would give a lot to hear Franklin's remarks on thrift when the younger and live Van Doren is torturing himself with his decisions as to whether or not to go on. But notwithstanding the enlightenment I offer this evening, I am obviously unable to reproduce for you the Franklin epigrams, so I shall ask those of you who are remaining to put aside the scene I have created and return with me to Washington, D. C., and these hallowed precincts.

For I have just as much curiosity about you as you have about me. I am most certainly not going to ask you to turn to your neighbor on your right and introduce yourself. This is an informal talk, but let's not get carried away with the spirit of informality. Let's keep the informality to this side of the lectern. I would not think of asking you to join me in "Old McDonald Had a Farm," or "Down By the Old Mill Stream," and I think we'll all be happier in the long run if we limit ourselves to an occasional chuckle or a burst of applause when I have sent home a point. If we get through the evening *without* the occasional chuckle, and *without* the burst of applause, *I* can always blame it on the acoustics—and *you* can blame it on the people at the Library, who didn't have sense enough to hold Irving Stone over for a second week. Parenthetically, I have been a little troubled by Mr. Stone's appearance here. I like Irving. I have been to his house and he has been to mine when we both lived in California. But what do you suppose was in the minds of the committee when they scheduled the author of *Lust for Life* to precede the author of *A Rage to Live?* Coincidence? Well, maybe. And close parentheses. I was saying that I have as much curiosity about you as you have about me.

You have no idea how strongly tempted I am to ask that lady, that gentleman, that lady, that gentleman, what their names are, what they do for a living, where you live, what you did this afternoon, what you're going to do tomorrow, and so on. There is hardly anyone I know in this room this evening. And yet for all I know, there are two people in this room now, who don't know each other, who will leave here without meeting each other, but if *I* were to meet them separately, it could easily come to pass that I would put them together in a novel or a play. It could come to pass, although not so easily, that in among you tonight there are a man and a woman whom I could put together much more permanently than a man and a woman are joined together in actual life. By which, of course, I mean no more and no less than that I might create two characters who would outlive us all. And the ultimate, of course, would be if I got really good and put together a man and a woman who would go down in literary history with Tristan and Isolde, or Romeo and Juliet—or Frankie and Johnny.

Then, too, there are quite possibly two people in this room who, I hope, will not meet, whom a competent novelist could put together to create a classic murder story. I am not opposed to classic murder stories, but sometimes life does mirror Art, and I don't want to leave here with blood on my hands.

I now have given you a glimpse of the novelist at work, and, rather sneakily, I have eased myself into my topic for the evening, which, somewhat to the surprise of no one, is: The Novel.

At the beginning I should admit, or confess, or simply state that there is probably no one in this room who is more than thirty years old, who has not read more novels than I have. Among my friends, among the people I see the most, there is a constantly surprising number—surprising *by* their number—of men who earn their living in Wall Street, or Broad Street, or Devonshire Street, who are therefore businessmen, and glad of it, who are at the same time so much more cultured than I that it is I who am more likely to be on the defensive in cultural matters than they. Now here let me quickly say that, in spite of Sinclair Lewis and my good friend the late Philip Barry, I do not believe that there is a very large number of frustrated authors and artists among our commercial men. When a foremost intellect like Thornton Wilder comes to my house I am honored and delighted to be in his company, but when inevitably he speaks the name of Sören Aabye Kierkegaard or the somewhat easier to pronounce name of Franz Kafka, I want to send out a hurry call for any of a half-dozen guys who never have written so much as a bad parody for the *Bawl Street Journal*. The incidence of cultural interest among businessmen has not yet reached proportions that should alarm any of us, but my mention of those who do read, and read a lot, and read what are acceptably called the best things, serves the double purpose of publicly refuting the intellectual snobbishness about the whole race of businessmen—and of publicly stating that if I am to be judged by my reading, I cannot be called an intellectual.

That is not to say that I don't read. I have passed a great deal of time in poolrooms and saloons, it is true, but not lately. And all my life I have managed to pay a great deal of attention to the printed word. But my reading habits are such that I am surprised that I have been able to read as many books as I have, considering the amount of reading I do and have done in the newspapers and magazines. By the look of things the newspapers and magazines are fast relinquishing their hold on me, what with the total disappearances and mergers that continue to occur. But while there are magazines and newspapers, they will have first claim on my reading interest.

Now when I make that admission, which, by the way I don't always make so freely, since I have found it not at all difficult to fake culture at a dinner party—indeed, it can be fun to see how well you can fake knowledge of a book, a play, a painting, or a symphony without getting yourself into trouble—when I make that admission, forthrightly as I am doing now, the layman, that is to say, the non-writer, is usually astounded. "You mean to say you haven't read *The Nun's Story* or *Bridey Murphy,* or whatever is under discussion? I should think you'd have to read everything." Well, one of the most obvious answers to that is that if I read half of everything, or an even smaller fraction, my own contribution to American letters would be considerably curtailed—a notion, by the way, that has occurred to more than one critic, not excluding some in this very town. My real excuse though, and no matter how lame it sounds, is that I haven't got the time. I read the newspapers and fact-pieces in the magazines very quickly. My experience on newspapers and magazines is vast. I've never been a copyboy, and I've never been a publisher, but I have done everything else on the editorial side, from covering girls' field hockey to a Congressional investigation, and I'm afraid that neither our girls nor our Congressmen are at their best in those circumstances. If you have done as much writing in journalism as I have done, you can run through, without skipping, a long piece because in many instances it is almost as though you had done it yourself. A straight, really compact, news story—let's say a disaster of some kind—does not and should not allow for elegant literary exercises. The restrictions on magazine articles are looser and fewer, but even in them I read at a pretty rapid pace, because regardless of the style that the byline encourages, I am not reading for aesthetic reasons. I am reading for information first, and style—oh, how many Rebecca Wests are there?

But when I read a novel I read it almost as though I were looking at it through a jeweler's loupe. I hope I don't move my lips when I am reading a novel, but anyone who stood behind me and watched how slowly I turn the pages would expect to see my jaw going up and down as I carefully pushed my gnarled finger from one word to the next. One time in the country I watched a fellow, who was not a great reader, try to entertain himself with a best-seller while the rain was keeping him off the golf course. Someone—I'm afraid the someone was me—said: "Look at Jack fighting a book." It was hell for the poor guy. He would look down at it as if he were in a geology class and had been given a hunk of rock to study. Then he would remember that it was a book and his eyes would focus on the print. The eyes and the head would go back and forth as though he were a spectator at a very *tiny* tennis match. Then he would sigh, look out to see what the damned rain was doing, and finally lay the book on his knee and yield to the sandman. It was a northeaster, three days, and poor miserable Jack had done just two pages—I counted—by the time the sun came out.

I am a little faster than that, but not much. I distrust all similes and metaphors, but when I read a novel by the *good* men I am at work. Mind you, I get pleasure out of work. I work hard and constantly, but whatever pleasure I get out of it, it is serious, serious work. My hard-playing, ten-goal days are over, and I'm not a bit sorry. In this respect, if in very few others, I am like my father. My father was a surgeon in a small town in Pennsylvania. He didn't drink, he didn't even smoke. But every week, every Wednesday, he took the train to Philadelphia, a hundred miles away, and spent the hours from eleven a. m. to four p. m. watching John B. Deaver perform surgical operations. I don't know enough about surgery to be able to tell the difference between brilliance and clumsiness, but I never have any trouble recognizing the skill of a Hemingway or a Steinbeck or a Faulkner. I am not like you who don't write, or most of you who write literary criticism. You can be satisfied with the emotional experience and the intellectual stimulation, and that is quite enough if you are not a critic. If you have bought or been given a novel by Ernest Hemingway you are going to read it for pleasure, and when you have finished reading it, you have had that pleasure, regardless of how much you did or did not like the book. But when *I* read a novel by Ernest Hemingway, I have had that pleasure and something more. I know, because I am a man, that I have had a pleasurable experience; I know, because I am an author, what Hemingway did and did not do that caused me to have that experience. I can see where an extra speech would have loused up a scene told in dialog, and where one extra noun of description would have been one noun too much. Sure, that extra speech and that extra noun do get in sometimes, and I want to say, "Now, Ernest, you shouldn't have." Or, "I wish you had put *that* in," when I have found something lacking. But when I criticize one of the good ones unfavorably I try not to criticize him on a basis of what *I* would do but of what *he* should have done or not done. I am not Ernest Hemingway, a vital statistic for which we both thank God. I am not Steinbeck or Faulkner. I am me, content to be me. As the Frenchmen say in a quite different context, "Vive la différence!" But I want and expect them to be at their best always, and I am heartily pleased when they are successful because I am on their side, because they care about words. And words are like all the other things that are available to you, that can help you or hurt you. When the good men are successful I am encouraged too.

A moment ago you heard me say, "regardless of how much you did or did not like the book." I would like to use that as a sort of text, but first I also would like to say that at this stage of my remarks I am using Hemingway only because he is the obvious symbol for author, as a few years ago I might have used Joe Di Maggio as a symbol for baseball player, even in this highly partisan American League town. In the past in interviews

206

I have said, and not been misquoted, that a man or a woman who buys one of my books has a perfect right to put the knock on it, just as a man who had bought a Pierce-Arrow was fully entitled to say he bought a lemon. He even had the right to say he preferred the Peerless or the Marmon or the Winton. (I hope you notice how carefully I am placing this analogy in the remote past.) I still say he has that right. If he has bought my book, he has done business with me and he becomes either a satisfied or a dissatisfied customer. I am less tolerant of the people who deal with lending libraries: they pay a few pennies, of which I get nothing, and knock the book; or they like the book but won't buy it. There is now just about nobody who can't afford to buy a book he likes. Be that as it may, while I uphold the buyer's right to pass unfavorable criticism of a purchased novel, I do not thereby yield up my own right to criticize the criticism, and I mean the layman's criticism. The paid book critic is another matter. At the moment I want to discuss the unpaid, unpublished critic, the reader.

The purchase of a novel is also in effect the purchase of the right to criticize, but it is far from being a transaction that qualifies the purchaser to speak with any authority. If you don't mind my returning to the earlier analogy, when a man bought a Pierce-Arrow a driver's license didn't come with it. The stupidest criticism that can be made of any novel, or short story, or play, or poem, is when the reader declares he didn't like the subject matter or didn't like the characters, the people. Instead of quoting examples out of other authors' experience I am perfectly willing to give you one from my own. At the end of the year 1949 Miss Dorothy Kilgallen, like many other columnists at the end of the year, made up a list of superlatives. Among her personal nominations was: "Least Worthwhile Woman in Fiction: Grace Tate in *A Rage to Live*." I have a pretty good memory, but that one would have stayed with me anyway, not only because it inevitably conjured up a sort of documentary of Dorothy going through the many, many books she sounds as though she reads every year, but going through them for *not very* worthwhile women of fiction until she found the *least* worthwhile. Assuming that she was conscientious, it must have meant an awful lot of dreary re-reading. But aside from the lady's literary chore, as I imagined it, it was noteworthy as an example of a kind of criticism that I can only deplore. I wish there were something else I could do, but deplore is the most I can do. We who write novels are fortunate that in our time there is likely to be a friendlier and wider reception for our best and truest efforts than was the case when as good a man as William Dean Howells was writing. And even later than Howells, much later. I am a new member of the Counsel of the Authors Guild, and I am going to suggest—knowing full well that I'll be wasting my time—that among all the memorials and plaques and awards and trophies, there might be one in memory of Jim Walker, yes, the former New York Mayor James J. Walker, who in the New York State Assembly once killed a so-called Clean Books Bill by remarking that no girl was ever ruined by a book. That immediately brings up the subject of censorship, but let's table that for the moment. I want to register an author's objection to the layman's objection to the author's choice of subject matter and people.

A man, or more likely, a woman who is fresh from the reading of a modern novel will say—and often say it to me—"But those awful people!" In that single comment, whether it's directed at me or at Faulkner or Steinbeck or whoever, the woman brushes off not only the immediate cause of her objection; she also thereby obliterates almost the entire literature of the world since man began to write. I know, because I have tried, that it would be a waste of breath to try to get her to consider the murderers and adulterers and liars and perverts and traitors in what is called classical literature. It would be frivolous to say that the blank verse form has obscured for her the meanings of what she has read, but would it be a form of counter-snobbism to charge her with believing that anything is all right if it was written long enough ago? Not too long ago, in the *Life* before Luce, which sometimes seems almost as charming as life after death—I once read a bit of criticism that went something like this: I don't want to see a play that is about people I wouldn't have to my house for dinner. The only legitimate reason for the layman's criticism of characters in a novel is the failure of the author to make the characters credible. It is not now, it never has been the serious author's job to make his characters nice. The author who does make his characters nice is a hack and a liar. He is a hack in the sense that he is writing nice people for those moments when we only feel like reading about nice people. If he is reporting, as a novelist, on characters he has fully understood, but reports incompletely for the sake of niceness or for fear of that awful-people criticism, he is professionally a liar. And if you care to search your mental library for authors who fit those descriptions, you have my freely granted permission to do so, although the slander and libel laws prohibit my more hearty cooperation.

It would be easy for me to stand here and say that the reader has a duty to the author, and so forth. The reader has no duty to the author whatever. Not even the duty, which someone more pompous or duty-defining than I might claim, of finishing a book. Heywood Broun used to say that he would give any book thirty pages, and I consider that a fair trial, especially since I am such a slow reader of fiction and by the time I have read thirty pages I have pretty well determined for myself how well the author can write. In the relationship between author and reader the matter of duty is all on one side. The author has the duty, which is not really so high-sounding as all that but is really only the job, of writing it the best he knows how; as honestly and as carefully and vigorously and as warmly as he can write with whatever he's got. It then becomes not the duty but the enjoyable task of the reader to get out of the book all that *he* can, with whatever *he's* got. If, as we must assume for the moment, he is reading a book that was written by a man who is out of the hack class, and does finish the book, he has my permission to criticize it on many grounds: he can quarrel with, let us say, decisions that the characters have been forced by the author to make; he can find fault with the accuracy of description and topical matters; he can doubt the trueness of the dialog; he may even have the special knowledge that gives him the privilege of criticizing such technical factors as construction. But if the people have been honestly and credibly made, the reader cannot judge the book or the author for their morals or manners. The reader who does so criticize can more profitably, and really more pleasurably, turn on the television and laugh himself silly. I'm not at all sure, though, that he and I would laugh at the same things, or for the same reasons.

I am not even going to go so far as to say that what this country needs is intelligent readers. I have written four novels that have been what you might call, or I might call, best-sellers of the first class, by which I only mean books that have been Number 1 or 2 nationally and for a fair length of time. I also have had three or four other books that got on the best-seller lists just long enough to make their quick disappearances seem like acts of vandalism. This bit of bragging, for which I have asked nobody's permission, serves the useful purpose of backing up my claim to some experience with the novel-reading public. Not all of it has been milk and honey, and I am now not only referring to the problem of taxation, which remains a problem after all the jokes have been made about it. When a novel has reached a sale of 100,000 I can be sure of several results: Bennett Cerf, my wealthy publisher, is going to give me a silver cigarette-box commemorating the event. I have two of those boxes, very handsome, and some day they may be all my eleven-year-old daughter will have to show her children as proof of what a big wheel Grandpa was. I can also be sure that there is no serious danger that I shall establish a racing stable with the money I cling to. And I am equally certain that I am going to spend a lot of time wondering about a country that I happen to love deeply, but that has 170,000,000 people, 38,000,000 television sets, and best-selling novels that get to be best-sellers on less than 50,000 sales.

Actually it takes an even smaller sale than 50,000 to get a book on the best-seller lists. Perhaps you might like to hear a small trade secret: an author, his agent, or his publisher, who wants to get a book on a national best-seller list for the purpose of stimulating a movie sale can get his book on the list by buying a few hundred books at certain carefully selected bookstores. He avoids the big stores in the largest cities, but a sale of ten books in one week at a smaller store makes his book a best-seller in that store. So he chooses half-a-dozen such stores, and those stores report his book as a best-seller. So, as I say, it isn't even necessary to sell 50,000 to have the layman believe that your author friend is now in the market for a cabin cruiser and a Picasso. There is no S. E. C. in the book trade, and the best-seller lists are somewhat less accurate than the quotation listings of the stock exchange. There are, then, best-sellers, and there are books on the best-seller lists. I have had both, although I hasten to add that I've never bought my own book to make it look big.

But suppose a novel does get to the 100,000 mark. It's a big figure in the book trade, but in relation to the population of the country, in relation to the number of owners of television sets, or even in relation to the number of Americans who buy Benson Ford's Continental, a $10,000 car, it's dismayingly small. It's less than the circulation of a daily newspaper in a medium-sized city, it's less than a quarter of the circulation of the *New Yorker* magazine, which I pick because *New Yorker* readers are supposed to be the class of the mass. (*Harper's Bazaar, Town & Country,* and *Vogue* don't even run book reviews.) It is less than the population of Waterloo, Iowa, or Durham, North Carolina, and, I am told, about one-tenth the population of this very town. But what is most dismaying is that a 100,000-sale novel has been sold, or must be presumed to have been sold, to *all, all* of the most intelligent readers of novels. With a smaller-sale novel, say, 25,000—which is a successful book, by the way—it may be that some of the most intelligent readers haven't read the book. But with a 100,000 novel you have saturated the potential market, as the merchandising boys would say. And that, my friends, is in a time of prosperity. With a sale of 100,000 books you have reached the limit of sales to the most intelligent readers, and you have begun to sell to the others. It is no use to say that the most intelligent readers don't necessarily read the best-sellers. They do. Remember now I am discussing novels, and using the terms novel and book interchangeably. I am not talking about the technical, political, economic, soul-searching books of non-fiction. I am only talking about novels, and when you hear a man, or woman, loftily say that he doesn't read best-sellers, he probably is not much of a reader of non-best-sellers either. He is, in fact, a bit of a phony, since our outstanding authors, even Faulkner, always make the best-seller lists, and the man who declares he refuses to read a best-selling novel is admitting that he isn't reading our outstanding authors. So the hell with him. Or her. But when you consider that you have reached all the most intelligent readers inside a sale of 100,000 you begin to wonder. You do if you're an author.

First of all, it is, or should be a great deterrent to the temptation to let the head swell. A prominent author is more likely to get a good table at

"21" than a good actor or a government official below cabinet rank, but that's because the people who own "21" have always had an affinity for writers, and vice versa. But this is not an author-conscious country. The lower-middle-class Frenchman who has opinions on André Gide has no opposite number in the United States. But neither has the middle-middle-class Englishman who has opinions on Graham Greene. It is my glum guess that we now have reached the highest rating we are ever likely to reach in this country, and by "we," of course, I mean the authors of novels. And when you recall a few of the simple statistics I have given you, our highest rating turns out to be dismally low.

Quickly you ask, do you mean the novel is through? Just as quickly I answer, no. Not yet, and not in the lifetime of the children of the youngest person in this room. But I do believe that when the sale of the novel, which after all is a reflection of public interest in it, begins to fall off again as it did in the early thirties and again about five years ago—when that happens again, the novel will not come back.

Why do I make this pessimistic guess? Well, the novel has been in a precarious position all along. The sale of pianos in Grandfather's day didn't help it; the phonograph in my youth and the radio as I grew older didn't do it any good. The tendency among the optimists is to say that the novel has survived the piano and the phonograph and the radio. And it has. But while surviving it was also losing out to the piano, the phonograph, and the radio. Without those various boxes there would have been more readers of novels, and the novel has remained because the population has increased. But there's never been anything like this newest box. It is standard equipment in the American home, and because of it the novel's present top level is the highest it will ever be again. With the best intentions in the world, you still do not curl up with a good book, or a bad book. And most of your children, who are being brought up in the presence of the box, are never going to be readers of novels.

I said the novel has been in a precarious position all along. The proof of how precarious is oddly enough to be found in the best, that is to say, the most cheerful figures on the novel. Taking a legitimate 100,000 sale, you come down to the maximum number of persons who really care about the novel and you discover that in the United States there are not enough of them to fill Griffith Stadium. I am neither impressed nor encouraged by figures that show how many millions of copies of novels were sold last year. I think we are all too easily influenced by, if I may coin a word, millionship. Millionship didn't do *Collier's* any good, millionship is what the television shows are after—but when they get it the shows don't always stay on the air. I *am* impressed by the dollarship of book sales, but with a big reservation. I would like to know how many of those dollars were

211

spent by people in their late teens and twenties, the people who are going to, or are not going to buy novels ten years from now. I live in a university town, have lived in it for eight years, or two full four-year cycles. I don't see or hear much at Princeton that gives me reason for a rosy view of the future of the novel. And I defy any Yale man to prove there is more culture at New Haven.

I should be able to follow up sour observations with some hopeful suggestions to make for a sweet future. But there are not even enough would-be authors to take the axe to those 38,000,000 TV sets. The Authors Guild has no trained men to sabotage the broadcasting apparatus. And even being in Washington does not make me feel that I am any closer to getting an anti-TV law passed. I'm afraid the best we can do is hold our own, and discourage our children from the novelist's career. By the time that we are able to go around the globe at its fattest in ten hours there may occur a slight national pause for the pleasures of nostalgia or the novel of protest. And there may be enough novelty value in the holding and reading of a book to make one sell like a Presley record, but the present of the novel is more within my sphere and more to my liking than its future. I therefore leave the future and return to the present.

So far I have alienated that section of the novel-reading public that has the impertinence to be critical of the novelist for his choice of material. Then I have gone on to announce that the novel is on the way out. If there is anyone who has a bus to catch, please don't miss it in the hope that in the time remaining to me I am going to turn into Jolly John, dispenser of sweetness and light. This is the part that could be sub-headed, "O'Hara Lashes out at Critics."

I am frightfully aware that it is almost impossible for an author to attempt to reply to his critics without seeming like a sorehead or becoming a bore. I confess that when one of my contemporaries, even among those I admire the most, writes a piece or tells the reporters or says in a lecture like this that he doesn't like what the critics say about him—my impulse is so say, "Come on, boy, you've had it pretty good. What are you beefing about?" I know that most of the time the author is justified, and that the critics are wrong. But it just works out that way. When a man has written a novel or a play, the reception committee consists of the critics, the professional ones. If they don't like what the author has done, they say so, and for the public that ends it. The public is not really interested in the author's problem, and therefore is impatient with his reply. The non-writer does not really care how much or how long the author has worked on his book or his drama, and the public consequently is not even interested in the merits of the dispute. The public's attitude is that the author has had his chance, and if he hasn't been able to win the critics' approval, that's too bad, but too bad only for about five minutes, if that. The public in effect tells the author to shut up and go hide, and go back to work on something else. If the author persists, he does seem like a sorehead, and he does become a bore. And I'm very much afraid that almost always I react as the public does.

Now I was not required to take a Consistency Oath before mounting this platform, so I am going to utter a few syllables on the subject of criticism. (The sibilance of the last sentence is accidental, by the way; I am not subtly hissing the critics.) If I end up seeming like a sorehead, it may be that I am a sorehead. A critic—a critic, mind you—recently called me the happy warrior of American letters, and I can't tell you how pleased I was by that, and I don't *want* to be known as a sorehead. But if I am one, it may be because I have been clouted on the skull so many times. If I am also a bore, I can't even beg your forgiveness, and that's the greater risk I run by saying anything at all about critics.

But instead of the more or less routine complaints against critics with which we are all familiar—that they can't write, that they are frustrated authors, that they are jealous, and, in several cases, parasites—I would like to get through this lecture with a minimum of reference to their personal failings and keep the discussion on a higher plane. Not too high, mind you, but on the impersonal plateau. Actually my two last novels have fared better critically than some of my earlier ones, possibly because there isn't very much left to say about me in a hostile way, and also possibly because some critics have finally realized that I am going to go right on writing in spite of their stern refusal to grant permission. After all, that works two ways, too, as I shall illustrate with one personal observation: Twenty-two years ago I was enjoying the success of my first novel, which got good, although not universally good, reviews, and sold well. One day I was reading O. O. McIntyre's column and I came upon a most complimentary mention of me. Do you think I was pleased? I was not. I was embarrassed, and I hoped that no one whose opinion I valued would also see the item. I wanted praise, but I didn't want it from O. O. McIntyre. However, two novels later he made me feel better about the whole thing when he said, and I quote from memory: "Some of the literati say John O'Hara's *Butterfield 8* is swell. I say it's swill." The score was exactly evened so far as McIntyre was concerned, but in my own opinion I gained the advantage. So praise is not all we want. We want it from acceptable sources.

But I know of a quick way to bore you and that is to tell you some of the nice things that have been said about me. I want to get on to the other stuff. The first thing an author is entitled to in a review by a professional critic is accuracy. Some of you who are keen students of the American novel must recall that I got some pretty bad reviews on *A Rage to Live*. Almost all of the unfavorable criticism was directed against (a) the social system of a small American city, and (b) the morals of the principal female character, Grace Caldwell Tate. Now I have often been accused of an overwhelming preoccupation with the American social system, and I intend to say something about that later. But the men and women who criticized that part of my novel almost invariably stated that I had returned to the Pennsylvania of *Appointment in Samarra, The Doctor's Son,* and *The Farmer's Hotel. A Rage to Live* was about a different city in a different location, with any number of subtle and obvious differences. But a disturbingly large number of the reviews even went so far as to say that *A Rage to Live* took place in Gibbsville, in spite of the fact that there is a fairly long sequence in the novel devoted to a *visit* to Gibbsville, during which the heroine finds herself in the company of people who are strangers to her. *The Farmer's Hotel* was read by many, many fewer people, but again there was a remarkable number of reviewers who whizzed through that short novel without noticing that it took place in the Pennsylvania Dutch farming country, with no connection with the anthracite coal industry that is so important a part of Gibbsville. Pennsylvania is a large as well as a glorious state, but some of the reviewers, the lazy ones, would have it about the size of Rhode Island. To them I recommend a nice stroll from Chester to Erie, just about this time of year. In the matter of the morals of the leading lady of *A Rage to Live* I suppose I had better choose my words with great delicacy. Especially since there may be listening to me some people who made the same mistake some of the reviewers made. It was frequently reported in reviews that Grace Tate was one of the most promiscuous women in literature. That may be all right as an opinion, but not very good as a statistic. The truth is that in her husband's lifetime Grace Tate was unfaithful with one man. Marital fidelity is praiseworthy and desirable, and one extra-marital love affair constitutes infidelity. But to call Grace Tate promiscuous and to throw stones at her as a chronic adulteress was shockingly bad reporting. In life, in non-literary living, you would have a hard time making the charge stick even if you included her love affairs after the death of her husband. Please take my word for it that inaccuracies of the kind I have mentioned are far from rare.

I have no doubt that what has been called the explicitness of detail in my novels is partly responsible for the mistakes that some reviewers have made in writing about the emotional life of my characters. Here I am not referring so much to the number of affairs that Grace Tate may or may not have had, but to the attacks on her as a loose woman. An Edith Wharton woman or a Willa Cather woman, or for that matter a Fran Dodsworth, does not get such harsh treatment from the reviewers, but it seems to me that the

214

difference is only in the author's treatment, and *only* in the author's treatment. The significant detail that makes for full character development is not only to be found in the kind of flowers and china and fabrics a woman shows to her friends. The novelist's privilege, and in my opinion his duty, is to tell all he has to, even when it means dispensing with the pretty reticences that his characters may affect or that he himself may have. If a man's entire work is to be judged every time he publishes a book, then judge him by his entire work. Or, if only the immediate book is to be judged, then judge that work. But not many critics are willing to settle for one or the other. They wanted to put Hemingway out of business on account of *Across the River and Into the Trees,* forgetting that *To Have and Have Not* was his least successful novel, while remembering that he had written *For Whom the Bell Tolls.* In other words, practicing an eclecticism that was unfair to the author. Either way has its good points: to review all of an author when his newest novel comes out, or to pretend that his whole career rests on this one new novel and as though he had written no other. But by the same token it is ignorant criticism to base an attack on a whole novel on what is really the reviewer's public distaste for sexual detail. There is no responsible author who gratuitously introduces sex. The author who does so is irresponsible and foolish, since it somehow becomes apparent even to the layman that it has been gratuitous and that the author hasn't much else to offer. The author who writes a novel without introducing sex has automatically limited the extent of his responsibility and is thus not entitled to full artistic consideration. And that's aside from whatever he may be inadvertently revealing about himself.

I am often asked, too often asked, what I think about censorship, and usually by people in and out of the press who don't really care what I have to say about it, just so long as I am against it and offer a quick and easy solution to a problem that has no quick or easy solution. I fancy myself as a liberal, a vanishing phenomenon, and I therefore concede to the Roman Catholic and other churches, the Anti-Defamation League, the Navy League and almost any other organization the right to invoke its own kind of censorship if that censorship is some form of the boycott. I do not recognize the right of any organization to practice censorship at the source, which is, first of all, the author, and secondly, the publisher. I have no idea—and apparently neither has anyone else—how to construct federal or state legislation that will permit freedom of political and artistic expression and at the same time restrict the publication and sale of the smut magazines at the candy store. I think we are overlegislated as it is, and not only in the book world, and I think it is also time for me to say thank you and let you go home. Thank you, and goodnight.

The Historical Novel

MacKinlay Kantor

Presented at the Library of Congress January 28, 1957

I DON'T LIKE TO MAKE SPEECHES. I told my publishers last year that I wouldn't make any, and I didn't find a bit of difficulty in turning down the various schools and universities and women's clubs. But then came the hometown of my publisher, Mr. Ben Zevin, president of The World Publishing Company of Cleveland, Ohio. Then came the United States Air Force Academy—I have a longtime spiritual identification with the Air Force and a great love for that service—so that was number two. And then came this request from the Library of Congress.

It was just about 25 years ago that I first walked through those doors under the steps out there to become one of the untold, uncounted millions of people who have profited directly or indirectly from the wealth contained within these walls. It is a lot more than the British Museum, to the American heart. The fiddle songs may play here and be heard; and we witness herein the catamount's cry, the war whoop, the scratching of pens, the quiver of campfire flames, the rifle sound, and the long intoned prayer. It is our past, kept within a strong and fruitful box. The apples and butternuts are given us by generous hands directed by wise brains, and to those brains and those hands—the instruments of the Library of Congress—I now wish to give thanks. I am glad to speak here, and I am proud that I was asked to come.

The term "historical novel" has a dignity of its own, and should be applied only to those works wherein a deliberate attempt has been made to recreate the past.

Excluded from consideration at this time are certain works which, while extremely important when the bulk of American fiction is reviewed, should not be regarded as important in the treasury of American *historical* fiction.

I want to observe first the book which is undoubtedly the favorite American novel of this speaker, and assuredly the favorite of many of those in the audience. In many other countries it is held to be the most perfect

216

flower upon our stalk, despite the decades which have elapsed since its planting and blooming. I refer of course to the rich, pungent, indigenous *Huckleberry Finn*—conceived as a boys' story, but realized as a masterly projection of the middle and lower Mississippi River, when the States through which that river flows were still raw and fresh.

In its way it is a record of the past; yet of what past? Only the past of the author's memory, of a vigorous middle-aged man's reminiscence. Clemens wrote it in the eighteen-eighties. Yet he was writing about his own childhood, and his own childhood had begun nearly fifty years before; and his own *childhood* did not include a first-hand knowlege of the regions whereof he wrote, save at the story's very inception.

Clemens had, as we know, little self-critical ability, and there is much to indicate that he believed *Tom Sawyer* to be a vastly better book. There is evidence to suggest that frequently he thought that in *Huckleberry Finn* he was writing a sequel to a previous success, and, in his opinion, a grander one.

But Huck Finn is a ragged and whimsical cartooned cousin of Tom Sawyer; and Tom Sawyer and Huck Finn were both figments of the author's boyhood—escapees therefrom, happy flotsam on the Hannibal waterfront. If we are to believe, as seems apparent, that their boyhood was the author's boyhood, then it was the Hannibal riverfront of the 1840's.

But what of the land that lay below, the wilderness of towheads and cuts, the landings in pine wilderness, the double-log houses, the Shepherdsons and Grangerfords with their loaded rifles, the thieving itinerant who was half an actor and half a printer and wholly a rogue, the rafting toughs with their Bowie knives and their black bottles of hell-fire, the State of Arkansas and State of Mississippi shorelines, where a lynching seemed the proper solution to any difficulty in the minds of the one-gallused inhabitants? This was not the Mississippi River of Mark Twain's boyhood. It was the Mississippi River of Mark Twain's young manhood. He saw it first through the eyes of a cub pilot; he learned it sublimely.

We read it now . . . it tastes like the good meat and bread of other days. It is as Stephen Vincent Benét said of the horse-chestnuts at Gettysburg: "Good to hold in the hand." Its grain and its flavor have served long and well, and they will serve longer.

But it is neither history nor any patch thereon. It is not 1838, it is not 1848, nor 1858. It is an appetizing stew of the whole, and the juice still runs from the bones. But what bones are they? Squirrel, possum, turkey? We do not know, we are never told.

Hound-dogs of Missouri, Kentucky, Tennessee, Arkansas and Mississippi blend their voices in a confused chorus, never readily identifiable; yet haunting through the primitive eternity in which they run. The judge is the judge, the constable the constable, the Black Betsy the Black Betsy in the kitchen—in whatever State and in whatever decade. They troop in a spindle-shanked horde through a mural as unrelated to historic necessity and demand as are the paintings of another and equally lovable and un-disciplined native Missourian—Thomas Hart Benton.

History of the future is a mere imagining. History of the present is purely speculative; but the *fact* of the past cannot be altered. It is calcified like a crinoid in rock.

Thus on the one hand we may not regard Herman Melville as an historical novelist. He was almost strictly contemporaneous. And contemporaneous also were the wordy romances strung together by James Fenimore Cooper, so impishly attacked by Mark Twain himself. Cooper's Indians spoke with the tongue of the Longfellow who was yet to speak in that tongue. But deerslayers were still stalking the forests of America, and in the same garb of his heroes, at the very time when he decorated his foolscap with ink. . . . Contemporaneous romances? . . . Move his Delawares and his Hurons into woods a little farther to the West, and you have a result as childishly current and of the moment as the Gene Stratton-Porter of Limberlost days, the Edna Ferber of Emma McChesney days, the *New Yorker* fiction of this day and age.

The work by R. E. Spiller, published in 1931, refers to him aptly as *Fenimore Cooper, Critic Of His Times*. Obviously the implication of criticism was inherent in consideration of *Homeward Bound* and *Home as Found;* but ironically the essential contemporaneous quality of Cooper's *Leatherstocking Tales* might also be suggested. Put a different kind of paint on the faces of Cooper's Indians, and promptly you have an extended romance of the time, if not of the place. The corn was still being parched; the eagle still saw his feathers fastened in a man's hair; the black powder was still being measured.

Now, at the risk of being accused as an impetuous and unappreciative Philistine, I am going to take my bow and arrow and go out and try to shoot a sacred cow. That sacred cow is *The Red Badge of Courage* by Stephen Crane.

It is not my wish to detract from its essential literary qualities. In re-appraising this book I had before me the Modern Library edition, issued by Random House, containing an introduction by Robert Wooster Stallman, Associate Professor of English at the University of Connecticut. In his introduction Dr. Stallman quotes from Vincent Starrett, in speaking of Crane: "His reading was miscellaneous, desultory, and unguided. In general he disliked the writers of his time whom it was the fashion to like."

That might have been a description of myself. My reading has been miscellaneous, sometimes desultory, and always unguided in any way save by the exigencies of the task before me. Your average gas-station owner has as much formal education as ever I attained. Therefore I would not feel myself capable of attempting to discuss Crane from any other point of vulnerability excepting that which I choose to attack.

I wonder if Stephen Crane was not put upon earth chiefly for the purpose of providing a field day for recondite or pedantic minds, in that they might roll his life and soul and works about the playing fields of their erudition, as they would so many medicine balls?

The extent to which Crane influenced American literature may be argued by those with the necessary qualifications for such argument; and so will be argued as long as the conceded importance of Crane lasts; and I am not at all sure how long that will be. But on the question of his influence on American *historical* literature, and his attainment in that field, I care not whether brands of Ignorance or Prejudice be burned into me. I challenge the Crane glorifiers to point out where in any way *The Red Badge of Courage* is intrinsically a novel of Chancellorsville, or even a novel of the American Civil War, or even necessarily a novel of America.

It is all wartime, every place. It is a collection of miscellaneous, colorful, poetical fragments; nor does the breath and smoke of Chancellorsville or any other definite battle blow here.

> *The trees began softly to sing a hymn of twilight. The sun sank until slanted bronze rays struck the forest. There was a lull in the noises of insects as if they had bowed their beaks and were making a devotional pause. There was silence save for the chanted chorus of the trees.*
>
> *Then, upon this stillness, there suddenly broke a tremendous clangor of sounds. A crimson roar came from the distance.*
>
> *The youth stopped. He was transfixed by this terrific medley of all noises. It was as if worlds were being rended. There was the ripping sound of musketry and the breaking crash of artillery.*
>
> *His mind flew in all directions. He conceived the two armies to be at each other panther fashion. He listened for a time. Then he began to run in the direction of the battle.*

If this were but an isolated fragment, then it would be a gross distortion of justice in literary criticism (if indeed there *is* any justice in literary criticism) to quote it. But that is not the case. It is typical of the book. That was one page, page 95 of the Modern Library edition. The average page of this book contains no more Civil War, no more Chancellorsville than was shown in those paragraphs which I just read.

There is nothing about the Civil War in this book which could not have been learned by a moderately intelligent and historically minded high school junior, in a few brief sessions with *Battles and Leaders* or whatever general secondary historical source the student chose. Dr. Stallman goes on at great length in his introduction, speaking of how Crane drew his material from "contemporary accounts of the Civil War, and very considerably, I think, from Mathew Brady's remarkable photographs."

Where is the resemblance to Brady photographs, where the actuality? Crane's people scarcely wear uniforms; you don't know what weapons they're shooting; you don't know how many rounds they've got in their pouches. It could be the Revolutionary War, it could be a Napoleonic war. There were practically no battle scenes, as such, photographed by Brady, except perhaps of artillery firing; because of the infancy of the process of photography, it would have been impossible to get troops moving in action. Brady photographs consist chiefly of a group of people posed in kitchen chairs around a farmhouse which is General So-and-So's headquarters; or a group of railroad men posed beside an engine; or a group of swollen corpses after a battle has passed.

> *Over the field went the scurrying mass. It was a handful of men splattered into the faces of the enemy. Toward it instantly sprang the yellow tongues. A vast quantity of blue smoke hung before them. A mighty banging made ears valueless.*

Well, couldn't that have been the Battle of Bennington, or the Battle of Blenheim—or Normandy, 1944? Name it.

Read this book if you will for its poetry—for its psychology—and for the disordered imaginative portrayal of a battle which the author never saw completely, even with the eye of an addicted mind. Read it for its verbe and philosophy. But pray do not regard it as a re-creation of 1863. I hold it to be no more 1863 than it is 1918 or 1814 or 1777. Let the scholars gather round for their abstruse discussions, and let the literary editors attempt to formulate a prose as descriptive and unique as Crane's prose, in their *discussion* of his prose. (The eternal habit of critics.) But show me the history. You can't; you can't show the history to anyone, because it is not there. It does not exist in this book. I declare it to be worthy of no consideration as an American *historical* novel. It is a novel *allegedly placed in an American historical background.*

No wonder that it was widely read and translated abroad. The story is the story of any nation, any war, any soldier.

Dr. Stallman says: "Zola bored him. He disliked Zola's statistical realism, and he disliked Tolstoy's panoramic method, finding 'Peace and War' (as he called it) tiresome."

Well, I can understand this perfectly. I think he disliked statistical realism and panoramas because they were too damn much work. Crane

220

was not at all interested in achieving the realism essential to bringing the past to life. Therefore I affirm that he was no historical novelist.

In wholesale fashion we should except from any claim on critical attention those stories wherein no effort has been expended to present history, even in the guise of fiction.

In the same manner we ignore the comic books of the present day newsstand when we are considering the modern novel.

Indeed, as for a segment of those same comic books, they are but the modern extension of the old-fashioned historical juvenile. Historical juveniles comprised the bulk of the historical fiction which was written in America until a long generation ago; Britain also had its share. I am thinking of the voluminous works of G. A. Henty and Harry Castlemon, and the many writers who followed them—imitators not so much in style or content as in tradition.

Certainly some of these books were not without their value as projections of the past. But since they were aimed directly at a juvenile audience, they were necessarily reduced in scope. So, too, were the romantic novels of the past designed for popular appeal to an audience more adult in years— written by people like Charles King, shall we say; or Thomas Nelson Page, or Robert W. Chambers.

Again, there were books written even by these romancers who sought inevitably the popularity which may be awarded by teen-age brains dwelling in man- and woman-grown bodies—books which bear rereading today solely for the history projected therein, however fragmentary and elusive, and because of the skill of the authors displayed in the telling.

I mean books like *Janice Meredith*. Superficially it is the story of a beautiful girl scarcely past the moppet stage, whose immediate life is caught up in and twisted by the events of the American Revolution. A narrator of rare talent such as the author of this book, Paul Leicester Ford, could erect certain murals within the limit of his novel which bear the unmistakable color of authenticity. He knew his physical, geographical locale; his research was intent and prodigious. Yet that word *limit* is the nub of the whole thing.

There was a limitation of basic conception—a limitation in the reflected social attitude of his own time, the late Nineteenth Century—that limitation wrapped like swaddling bands around any writer of America in the late Nineteenth Century who had neither the audacity nor the genius to become a Whitman.

Ruling custom and current social taste—often more or less the same thing, in this field—decreed that the beauties, glories and even dangers of the past could be painted; but that vice (as much a part of the pattern of human behavior as godliness, and, we fear, far more prevalent) must be ruled out. Vice was winked at or ignored except by a few bold reformers, according to the attitude then current. Thus historical novels such as *Janice Meredith* offer too fair and childish a face, no matter how much hard historical digging has gone into them.

The bodies were by turns pretty or ugly to look upon; often they were muscular; but they never were guilty of defecation. . . . It matters little if we present the soul and the dream, the far-reaching complexities of the human brain, and ignore the animal harbored in that same body. Any reader of ordinary intelligence must recognize the fact that a great many puzzles of our existence are born in the flesh, not in the mind.

How much human agony *and* delight have stemmed directly from the sexual compulsion? How many statesmen have made decisions influenced primarily by gout or toothache? How many delinquencies have come about merely from the need for food, shelter, clothing? How many marriages have swayed in the balance or gone tottering merely because of some deviation in the woman's menstrual cycle?

Yet the Grundies who ruled the late Nineteenth Century, and extended their sway up into the Twentieth Century, decreed that few if any of these things could be mentioned, let alone explored. Tolstoy might write of the beaming face and delighted voice which greeted the fact that the baby's napkin was spotted with a good bright yellow stain, instead of the green which had shown there when the child was sick. Tolstoy did do this, and many similar things. But if they were done in American historical fiction of that age, I have yet to hear of them.

We can assume, then, that in America for a long time the terms "romance" and "historical novel" were practically synonmous. If you attempted to present the past without its hurt and evil and shock, then simply you did not present the past. You could not, with any enduring value, project the reader into a never-never land peopled solely by curly-haired heroines in antique stomachers, immaculate in person as they were in their thoughts; or captives who embodied every noble masculine virtue; and captors whose worst oath was a *Damme!* or an *'Od's Blood!* . . . The cannon always seemed somehow a little too polished. If a cap misfired, it was only to save the life of the hero. If Washington prayed on the twenty-second of the month, his prayer could be recounted in its entirety; but if he was suffering from diarrhea, that might never be mentioned.

The life of the camp-follower was as much a part of army life as the story of the gunnery sergeant; but it could not be told. At the ultimate extreme it might be suggested that an appalling stench came from the prison ships. But had a novelist dared to recount in detail the conditions prevailing below decks on one of those Revolutionary prison ships, he could not have found

222

print, much less an audience. And, in turn, he would likely have found himself incarcerated in one of the calabooses of his own period!

Some of the legions of decency may have been sincere, but all of them were stifling. The hard flat board of prudishness was strapped across the brow of our infant literature, and thus the cranium was distorted and misshapen, as surely as were the skulls of unfortunate papooses in the Columbia Valley long ago.

But let it not be assumed for one moment that the vast bulk of printed so-called historical fiction which has come tumbling from the presses during the past twenty-odd years has *per se* an historical or even literary value comparable to the best of those restricted works of the past. The mere existence of the screen itself, and possible emoluments accruing therefrom, were sufficient in many instances to disrupt effectually the long time which should have been spent and should be spent by the writer in the absorption of what is commonly termed his background.

I feel a certain guilt in this matter, because, according to printed opinion, I had a share in designating what was then termed the modern approach to historical fiction. I am referring to my fourth published novel and my first historical novel, *Long Remember*, the story of the Battle of Gettysburg, which was a Literary Guild selection for May 1934.

At the time I was young, and thus an experimentalist (I hope that I never become too old to be one, when peculiar ambition seems to demand it). It was my great desire to make the Gettysburg battle as contemporaneous, as much a part of the reader's life, as if the wounded were still having their bandages renewed in the hospitals—as if the wheel-ruts of the Whitworth rifles were still creased across the nasturtium beds. Besides being spurred by the ordinary ambitions and considerations which impel the novelist, I was imbued deeply with the notion that I must make the lesson and tragedy of Gettysburg a part of the lives of all readers.

In the beginning I held to the notion that history—factual history—is accepted more completely if presented through the roundabout approach of a story, than on the pages of a scholarly tome intended primarily for the intelligence of fellow historians. I have not changed my mind.

It was a happy year of my young life when I saw these desires gratified, if not wholly satisfied, in the reception of the book by critics and public and historians. I was glad when I learned that *Long Remember* was to be a book club selection; but also I was glad when I found that it was to be used as a supplementary textbook at the United States Military Academy at West Point.

The historical value of previous works by Mary Johnston and James Boyd and certain other authors must not be discounted by any discerning reader; still perhaps they did not have what we might call, for lack of a better term, a modernity, a white-hot reality of the telling. I mention these writers not in the light of comparison, but as part of a chronological study of the progression of the American historical novel.

In a review of *Long Remember* which appeared in the pages of the New York *Herald Tribune Books*, Mr. Allen Tate spoke to the following effect: "It would be a distinct addition to American fiction if a school of historical novelists should pattern themselves upon this model." Possibly that school is in existence today, and has been for some time. If so, assuredly it had its retrograde dunces as well as its Rhodes scholars.

Following *Long Remember* appeared such works as *So Red the Rose, Gone With the Wind,* and a host of others—whether to the enrichment or confusion of American historical literature, I leave for skillful critics to decide. I do believe this: that today, in 1957, twenty-three years later, the average American reader knows more about the facts and the feeling of the Civil War time than the average American reader did twenty-three years ago. That might be extended to cover a number of other periods in our history as well. I am thinking particularly of novelists like A. B. Guthrie and Conrad Richter—splendid novelists who wrote of other periods. Still, the Civil War, our greatest national disgrace *and* heroism, is top dog.

Fortunate are we who were released from the constriction of prudery at a time when our family conflict was so recent in recollection that many of us could know, as living individuals, people who participated therein.

But on the heads of those of us who broke this trail a generation since must be pressed the blame as well as the wreaths. We opened up suddenly a new Miracle Mile whereon the unscrupulous could set up shop and manufacture and market their wares. The anachronisms of Hollywood are a byword; but they can be matched, page for scene, by lurid chronicles which have in part sustained the lending libraries and doped the minds of the populace for at least two decades.

People who had been flooding the market with sex novels about flappers who were lured to roadhouses found that they could write those same sex novels about the American historical scene: they had only to dress their flappers in crinolines. Many of these authors were adroit story-tellers, although wholly unequipped for such a task through any emotional addiction to the past, through any spiritual identification of themselves in that past, or through any previous condition of scholarly servitude. But, as I say, many of them *were* adroit story tellers; and have been able to buy Cadillacs and double martinis—to say nothing of an occasional mink stole!

These people piled sin upon sin, whether through the media of novel, radio, screen, or—later—television. The slipshod intellect approaches these matters with a debonair gesture. It is nearly twenty-three years since I first went to work in Hollywood; I was greeted, then as later, with the shrug and the casual annoyed reaction: "Oh, what possible difference does it make? Who will know the difference? You and six other people." To me it is worse than a crime against Nature to have extant motion pictures, dramatic projections, *or* the printed word, manhandling carelessly the sacred facts of the past.

I think that a young doctor has to study for seven years before he obtains his degree. How long does a missionary or a minister have to study—or a priest? Is it asking too much that demand or restriction be imposed (could they be imposed?—impossible, of course) on those careless hands which come fumbling into our old trunks and saddlebags?

The lack of time and attention languished by some people in their efforts to familiarize themselves with the progress of events and manner of living of another time passeth all understanding. I recall how a publisher of the late 1930's requested me to read a manuscript: a single-volume history of the Civil War. This was presented in a flighty, chatty, slangy version—designed, I assume, to catch the eye and appeal to the mind of that same portion of the reading public which depends for its formed opinion on contemporary affairs on the capsulized projection thereof presented in *Life, Time* and the *New Yorker*. (Incidentally, the author achieved later a certain stature by dealing with the naval, not the general, pageant of our past).

On reading this manuscript I was appalled by the loose flimsiness of his approach, and said so. The publisher stared at me. "Why," he said, "Do you realize that this man spent *one whole year* studying the Civil War?" I was filled with thoughts too acid, if not too full, for utterance.

There was another case, that of a young first-and-last novelist—a term on which I hold the copyright—a term which describes those persons who find that winds which blow through that dark between-the-worlds space in which novelists must wander are too cold to be endured. He came my way, sent by a dear friend, Steve Benét, whose great heart and generosity were often matched by his unrestrained enthusiasm for fledgling authors.

This man had written a book about the Iroquois, and while I knew nothing in this world about the Iroquois, the young man spun a very good yarn. I was deluded into thinking that his story represented an earnest exploration of the field.

I said to the author, in a manner of respect, "You must have spent an incalculable amount of time studying the Iroquois."

"Indeed I did," he responded feelingly. "I had to read three books."

I fumbled around for a moment. I couldn't believe my ears. I thought somehow or other that he must have said three hundred books, that my ears were tricking me. "Did I understand you correctly? Did you say three—one, two, *three* books?"

"Yes," he said. "What a job that was!"

As to whether or not his novel was ever read by anyone at all expert in the field of the Iroquois, I have no knowledge. But I believe that if anyone with a more than casual familiarity with the tribe and the time had read his book, they could have shot it full of holes.

I have no blood feud with that pouting, passionate, bare-bosomed hussy of the 1860's who comes raiding across the Ohio with Morgan, wrecks trains with Mosby, or goes loping with streaming hair through the Shenandoah Valley on the heels of George Armstrong Custer. She is by Rhett Butler out of Scarlet O'Hara, and was born under a jookbox. Her hair-do is by Antoine and her gowns by Adrian, if she *can* slug faster than Rocky Marciano and shoot straighter than Sergeant York. She is a fragrant puppet, constructed to delight those credulous souls who believe that a few "you-alls" can resurrect the Virginia past, and that the Vermont Green Mountains are made of maple sugar. She is a honey-chile, if she is a wild cat, and I think that even Bruce Catton would be willing to leer at her. But let her speak of John Hall Morgan, instead of John Hunt Morgan—let her gaze soulfully into Mosby's brown eyes instead of his gray ones—let her garb her beloved Custer in a jacket of silk instead of the jacket of velvet which actually he designed for himself—then am I ready to strip to the waist and fight her with knives!

I do not think it is being captious to demand that Fort Sumter be fired on in April instead of October; to insist that Abraham Lincoln speak in his native nasal treble, instead of a deep sonorous voice; to demand that George Pickett be placed in command, not of the fifteen thousand troops involved in the assault on the third day at Gettysburg, but in command of the five or six thousand whom actually he did command. I do not think it is being captious; I think it is exhibiting good sense. If the people are not taught to recoil from falsehood, they will never be able to award honesty the warm welcome which it deserves.

So-called historical novelists of the group I have been castigating have had a more horrific field day in the backyard of American tradition than Hollywood ever had. Last year an American publisher sent me some bound proofs while I was in Spain. These represented a novel which was soon to be published—another novel about the Civil War. (When hard at work, I don't read any books sent to me like this; I don't see how anybody could, and still get his work done. However, we were just recuperating from the flu at that time, lying around in our rooms in Madrid; so I started to read.)

Soon I was screaming. Not content with having his Civil War soldiers use G. I. slang which was not invented until World War II or the Korean War, the author had given Jeb Stuart a black beard instead of a reddish one.

He had indited also a thrilling scene in which a Union cavalryman, in disguise, finds himself confronted by a party of Confederates, and is stricken suddenly with the thought that he is wearing the belt-plate which should have accompanied his uniform. Hastily he puts his hand over the belt-plate, which, we are told, is inscribed *U. S. A.*

There was no reason in the world why he should have done this. Most of the belt-plates extant in the Confederacy, and worn by the soldiers there-of, were Northern belt-plates—Federal Government belt-plates which had been stolen from arsenals in the South, or later perhaps captured from the Yankees. This soldier should have been very proud indeed of his belt-plate. It was a museum piece, and would command a high price today. Because, inscribed *U. S. A.*, it was undoubtedly the only belt-buckle worn by a soldier of the North which bore those letters. All the rest said simply *U. S.*

However, the real payoff came on a springtime day in 1863, as recounted by the author. A soldier and his sergeant were discussing the raid on which they were about to embark. "Don't think too lightly of it," said the sergeant, or something like that. "How would you like to wake up and find yourself in Andersonville?"

Why not indeed? Andersonville, in the spring of 1863, was a very nice place: lovely pine woods, green grass, plenty of birds and bees. They didn't even start to build the stockade until the following December. The first prisoners didn't come in until the next February.

Now, I recited these details and a number of others to my friend the publisher, and the general editorial reaction seemed to suggest that I was being captious. Captious indeed! Let the historical novelist create all the fictitious characters he cares to create. Fictitious scenes, fictitious utterances . . . let him erect and polish and garb the illusion that is his . . . *so long* as he stays within the limits of his own creation But let him *not* select the fact from where it lies, a dusty sapphire in the jewel-box of Time, and take it out, recut it, reset it, and declare that he has an emerald.

There can be as many opinions about the failure of General Lee to press home his advantage on that first night at Gettysburg as there are scholars who consider the episode. These elucidations and divinations will not be history; they will be opinion *about* history, and much of it unconfirmed. History is there, in the *fact* that the subordinate in active command of the troops designated for this possible assault was Dick Ewell. It wasn't Longstreet or A. P. Hill. That is a fact.

The historical novelist himself must be the historical expert, the technical director which every Hollywood producer advertises that he has engaged.

To what avail these technical directors serve in the films, I do not quite know. I have been acquainted with some of them, and I know their frustration. I remember that once Dwight Franklin was serving in such capacity on a picture being made by Cecil B. DeMille. Dwight had his

227

pirate horde armed appropriately with cutlasses of the period; he came back from lunch to find a full-fledged boarding attack going on on the set, with pirates scrambling merrily over the bulwarks, all waving Chicopee sabres—the curved cavalry sabre commonly used in the Civil War.

When Dwight Franklin protested, DeMille made a gesture of contempt. It was the old story: who'll know the difference—you and six other guys? "Yes," said C. B., God bless his ancient soul. "You had the pirates armed with cutlasses but they didn't flash enough. I want to see a lot of *flash* in this scene."

His attitude is reflected and protracted in a great many of those authors who would nowadays engage in pursuit of that partridge so native to our mountains and our plains: the wild American historical novel.

I never had them do that to my cutlasses; but I had them do that to my Belle Isle. I spent considerable effort and many pages in *Arouse and Beware* describing the Belle Isle prison, and how it was walled merely with a ditch and low earthen parapet. But what greeted us when the film was first projected before the eyes of American audiences? A stockade a mile high. Metro-Goldwyn-Mayer *knew!*

What must the historical novelist be, as well as technical director? He must be an antiquarian of the first water. He must be at times botanist and zoölogist, entomologist and ichthyologist. He must don in turn the frilled apron of the housemaid and the leather apron of the farrier. He must wear the spectacles of the schoolmaster, the opera cape of the actor, the shabby gilt slippers of the prostitute.

The demand put upon any creative novelist, to begin with, if he would excel, is enormous: patience, penetration, sympathy . . . as much slavish devotion to humanity as was manifested by the entire throng of Apostles . . . the malevolence of a council of inquisitors: these must be his virtues and his practice.

But he who would bring the past quivering to life, cannot buy his paints at the nearest shop and spread them quickly upon his palette. He must bruise the petals of rare flowers found in unfrequented spots, and mix them with the gum that oozes from equally lonely trees. He must climb distant and dangerous cliffs in order to scrape up his ochre. He must go far into the Sahara of libraries, to shoot the lonely camel whose hair, and only whose hair, will be fit to make his brush.

All patriotism and all pride demand that he shall make a molten sacrifice of his eyes and his fingers. The past lies buried deep and cannot be torn from its immurement without pain.

Go and live in that other time, before you would tell of it. This has been done, it can be done, it will be done again.

New Poets and Old Muses

John Crowe Ransom

Presented at the Library of Congress January 13, 1958

I HAVE RISKED MAKING a disorderly beginning to this paper, which must be an unpardonable self-indulgence—if it was mistaken on my part to imagine that there is a certain public interest in the strange motions of the mind when it is working in the mode of poetry. There was a particular ghost which had to be laid before I seemed able to begin. No sooner had I adopted my high-flown title with its figure of the Old Muses, and made myself ready to let it work its way with me, than it seemed I had opened the door too wide, to figuration unlimited. Many of this audience will know from experience how the figures of some famous and unusually tuneful poem will begin suddenly to ring in one's head, and to force themselves into one's most oppressive problems as if they belonged there. So suggestible are we as we look for answers to the problems; such free and detachable and obliging busybodies are the poetic figures that form and float in the world of the imagination—as if they would come and serve us on whatever occasion if we would let them.

The poem which came to haunt me was E. A. Robinson's "Eros Turannos." I had known it and liked it a long time, but apparently had not fully realized it before. It came all the way from its New England seaboard town, where it had to do with two lovers and their doom, and was so admirably suited to its own occasion that I have been aware of a certain absurdity in trying to adapt it to my very different uses. But did not Mr. Eliot introduce to the modern audience a way of composing a poem by juxtaposing poetic fragments without showing their logical relations; and did he not accustom us to a new use of the epigraph—that placement of a bit of another poet's verse (which might be divergent in style and theme from his verse) just under the title and over the text of his poem, as an item which might throw its light upon what would follow? The Robinson poem is my epigraph, and seems to be a sort of large metaphor or parable to give advance notice of what is coming. The part of the poem which kept sounding in my ears was especially the fourth stanza and the sixth or last stanza. The fourth stanza is climactic and goes like this:

> The falling leaf inaugurates
>   The reign of her confusion;
> The pounding wave reverberates
>   The crash of her illusion;
> And home, where passion lived and died,
> Becomes a place where she can hide—
> While all the town and harbor-side
>   Vibrate with her seclusion.

The able students of Eliot have told us to "study the epigraph"; and even more than that, to study the context of the epigraph, the whole passage in which it was embedded; and then, though we may have to repair to the library, the play or book or even the theological system in which it figured. So I will offer a few notes about my epigraph. Earlier in the poem we were given the situation, where the aggressive new man comes to the town, and offers his hand to a lady who is accustomed to the town's old and ceremonious way of life. In spite of herself she has fallen in love with the new man. He imagines he will like the fashion of life as she will have it conducted; she reads his character and knows he is not suitable. Nevertheless she accepts him, and the sequel is ruinous; it is the one told in the stanza I have just read. This is a peculiar poet. He declines to tell the factual detail of his story. He does not employ a narrative style, nor yet a proper dramatic style, either of which would have required him to report the commonplace of the event. One of his unique characteristics is to evade the telling of the story at many crucial points by employing a sort of algebraic *x* which the reader must solve for himself: "We knew—what we knew." Even the opening stanza of "Eros Turannos" contains some *x*'s, which I will emphasize as I read it:

> She fears him, and will always ask
>   *What fated her* to choose him;
> She meets in his engaging mask
>   *All reasons* to refuse him;
> But *what she meets* and *what she fears*
> Are less than are the downward years
> Drawn slowly from the foamless weirs
>   Of age, were she to lose him.

What he reports in our fourth stanza is the *affect* of the event, as it registers in the woman's feelings, and these we identify sympathetically by the tremendous urgency of the natural metaphors. The language is sharply stylized. It is intended for an accomplished reader, using latinate words to make a mighty rhetorical clang (as latinate words will do if they are sparse, and cunningly placed), and altogether it is in the diction of the universities. Yet it is assimilated successfully to a stanza made of the folk line. I think there may be in our reception of the poem a slightly humorous but still delicious satisfaction over what an extraordinary thing has been attempted in that way, and pretty well carried off. Metrically the stanza is too elaborate for ballad, or even for Mother Goose, but I think we are likely to find it set to full music on certain pages of the hymnbook, if we are churchgoers.

The sixth and final stanza is the poet's epilogue upon the whole unhappy affair and his part in it:

> Meanwhile, we do no harm; for they
>   Who with a god have striven,
> Not hearing much of what we say,
>   Take what the god has given;
> Though like waves breaking it may be,
> Or like a changed familiar tree,
> Or like a stairway to the sea
>   Where down the blind are driven.*

Its author, the poet, is an anonymous citizen of the town, one of its "vibrators" whose sensibility is ravaged by the event; he is a good judge of such matters, and records his observations both in wise maxims like a Greek chorus, and in the heroic natural images. He has a right to his judgment, because the event is of public importance. And he does no harm, whether by advising against it in the first place, or by talking about it afterwards, because it was always the god who would determine it.

And now I must try to show why this poem came into my mind as if it had a bearing upon my own argument. I think I can do it. The new man stands for the new poet, and he addresses his suit of course not to the lady of the old town but to the Old Muses of my title. When they do not reject him they, like himself, are destroyed. But this is awkward for immortal Muses; and what is a Muse anyway? In prose we want to deal with such reality as we can feel sure of, and therefore we must break out of the whole clutter of the Greek mythology, which itself provides us only with figures and parables. The Muses, it will occur to us at once, might trans-

---

* The 24 foregoing lines from the *Collected Poems* of Edwin Arlington Robinson. Copyright 1916 by Edwin Arlington Robinson, renewed 1944 by Ruth Nivison. Reprinted by permission of The Macmillan Company.

late into the Spirit of Poetry; but that is not much better. Let them stand for whatever public authority there really is who accepts or rejects the new poet; the wise public censor if there could be such an officer; and failing that, the town and harbor-side, the corporate community of poetry-lovers who are anonymous citizens; perhaps including occasional professional critics, and editors. It is they whom the new poet solicits, and against their accepting him too easily comes the warning of my epigraph against a too-aggressive kind of new man. If the poetic community accepts him hastily and then he proves unworthy, both they and he are brought to public shame.

But most of all, surely, I felt the power of the god, the *deus ex machina* of the poem, as necessary to my argument. In the poem he is Eros Turannos, the god who decrees that the man and the woman shall fall in love. For my argument he is a mode of Necessity imposing itself at the right time upon the human experience; he is one of those Universals which bind the intricately constituted mind of man. In the terms offered by Immanuel Kant, which are the best for me though I choose to understand them rather too simply and to recite them too rapidly to suit a strict Kantian, the god is the Subjective Universal of Poetry; or, better as I think, the Poetic Category of the Mind, imposing the poetic mode of experience upon us when we have come into the need of it, and the capacity for it. Poetry is an advanced pattern of public behavior in the series or hierarchy of patterns. I should imagine that this is quite acording to the understanding of the anthropologist. The anthropologist is the analyst and historian who identifies the essential cultural forms of a society on the assumption that man is the measure of all things. That is a very modern sort of assumption, we are apt to think; and evidently Kant is a modern philosopher with an anthropological habit of mind, provided we may attribute to anthropology the fullest and most elevated humanism. The essential cultural forms would be those which represent the different powers of the mind engaging in common experience; and a form remains essential or categorical even though, as the anthropologist becomes comparative and goes from race to race and from age to age, its embodiments will not all turn out to be just alike. As an *a priori* mode of the mind, poetry, along with the other fine arts, is one of the categories or grand divisions of ultimate experience. The categories which are its peers would be morality and theology. Perhaps morality and theology precede it in development, in that order. Logically prior to these categories, of course, are the mathematical categories of time and space which order the data of the senses, and then the twelve so-called categories of the understanding which make up the grammar or logic of language; it is these which permit consecutive or rational discourse about the sense data, and achieve finally the great structure of natural science itself. These categories do not fail to enter into the discourse of morality and religion and art, and to keep them rational and economical, as they must be if they would be practicable behaviors and not morbid or crazy behaviors. By these (the fundamental and prior categories) we maintain physical life and material welfare; by those (the later and more metaphysical categories) we advance to the good society and to religion and beauty. Indeed, the latter ones might be said, as indeed in Germany and Italy they are said, to be the categories of the spirit, by comparison with the earlier ones which would be the categories of the animal man. But the comparison of course would not be quite accurate; for though the later ones do not condition the earlier ones (a healthy physical man is not necessarily a lover of poetry), yet the earlier ones do condition the later ones (a lover of poetry is still obligated not to sacrifice his animal necessities nor his discreet prevision for them).

The florid recital of the categories which I have just offered may have had a certain air of making fanfare. That was very nearly the intention. I hope you will take my anthropologist seriously, as he would take himself, and as he would take the object of which he treats. Poetry as an art by itself, or at any rate poetry as augmented by the sister arts, makes up a massive and distinct though fluid area of the human culture, and the anthropologist as I conceive him will admit it readily. He will honor it in the matter-of-fact respect which he is prepared to offer to its masterpieces; and perhaps he will respect at least equally the sheer bulk of its production, and the steady essential character it maintains at all levels and grades in a mixed society. It seems to me advisable to record our conviction that the bulk of our working poetry at any time is much larger than that authorized by the scholars of the universities or by the editors of *avant-garde* reviews. The anthropologist will scarcely confine his survey to the culture of an élite class. Yet it is good if he is torn between his respect for the idea of poetry as a functional pattern of the total culture and his own love for the showpieces which it achieves in its highest development. If we are lovers of poetry we are familiar with this conflict in ourselves. It is not more painful than it is comfortable to live with. The anthropologist, if he exists as I have described him, or we ourselves if we are amateur statesmen as well as addicts to poetry, obtains at least as much sense of dignity from its universality as from its choice and almost miraculous exhibits. Poetry is not a narrow accomplishment, nor a private one. We may well venture occasionally to apprise the new poets of the dignity of their calling as public functionaries.

Matthew Arnold was confident about the immensity of the future of poetry. But surely crises arise in its history. At this particular time it is not easy to say what the new poets are worth. But at least it can be said that there is immensity in their numbers; which only makes it harder to assess their quality. They number many thousands; they cannot be counted. There is a sense in which it may be properly said, as we hear it said, that there are more writers of verse than there are readers. In this sense: there are more new poets whose intentions are serious, and have to do with the creation of masterpieces, than there are readers who care to look seriously into their work. And this would be true even with respect to their published work, and aside from their mere manuscripts. The late Christopher Morley, author of many pleasantries, once remarked how, leaning over the brink of the Grand Canyon, he let fall a rose-leaf and listened for the reverberation of its landing; and before this terrific event found time to liken himself to the new poet waiting for the applause to greet his first book of poems.

The editors of *Poetry,* at Chicago, the most official organ of contemporary poetry in this country, have stated in print that they receive annually 50,000 manuscripts of verse. Other editors see less verse than those editors, though they are scarcely greater perfectionists or more exacting in their requirements. If they do not make 50,000 judgments a year, the number is still in the thousands, and I believe they have a harrowing time of it. The new poets are often aggressive in the claims with which they offer their poems, or the objections they make to the editor's judgment when it is given. This is not a consideration to hold against them. They are in their duty, and they mean business. The editor is perhaps as close as anybody to actually arriving at the status of literary anthropologist; he has to idealize this scientist, who seems as yet to have scarcely appeared in the eminent profession of anthropology as we observe it; the editor has to enact him, though remotely. Editors regard poetry as an official public function, or an estate, or perhaps a cult, which needs its neophytes or apprentices. Many offer for this cult, where few are chosen. But it is honorable to offer, and what is more, it is compulsive to offer, when the imperative of the behavior called poetry calls to the imaginative young man (or woman) who thinks his talent is verbal, and sufficient. Of course the anthropologist is by the way an ecologist, and as ecologist he is used to the consideration that Nature, as if to insure the survival of a species, creates its members with wasteful profusion; as for example the fertile seeds which more likely than not will fall in the wrong places and never take root, or take root but never find nourishment enough to survive; or the young of the animal kingdom who, because the species is already numerous beyond the prospects of subsistence, are exposed to death as soon as they have come to birth. Happily the ecologist takes the long view which immunizes him from being too much harrowed. And after all he remembers that poets who fail do not thereby lose their lives, nor are they therefore put to death. To an editor it does not seem likely that new poets who once have set themselves to be poets on the high sophisticated level—the level at which they approach the editor—will ever be good poets at the popular levels. But they may enter other vocations, even advanced and honored public vocations; as for example the teaching profession, where they may instruct the readers of poetry, perhaps adverting sometimes to the failures as well as the successes of this art.

Between the editor and the new poet correspondence is apt to arise; the editor has returned the manuscript, with some mention of the seeming flaws in the poem, and presently he finds himself reciting certain homely rules or maxims for the insistent poet's attention. He is asking the poet to observe that "this is the way it is done by experienced poets." And, for example, he says that the meters are ragged; or that the argument is not clear. Or there are places where the language is "not figurative enough," or the figures are not striking enough, and he may remind the poet of Doctor Johnson's observation that a simile, or metaphor, to be successful must not only "illustrate" but "ennoble." On the contrary, the figures may be too extravagant and far-fetched. Maxims are rules of procedure, as they have developed and become standard in the history of poetry. The content of the *Ars Poetica* is largely maxims, and the content of the *Essay on Criticism* is largely maxims. Many a good critic, like George Saintsbury, has managed very well with maxims for the staple of his critical apparatus. Many of the best poets, though surely not very many, have composed with them.

Coleridge at his best had piercing philosophical insights, but a good half of the time he is not at his best, by a defect of temperament, or perhaps of physical constitution. The revival of Coleridge in our time has been concerned principally, I think, with what I take to be a rule of practice, a maxim; but perhaps the largest and most compound maxim that could be recommended to the attention of new poets. This is his famous rule that the imagination of the poet must still be under the control or censorship of right reason. The two powers must work together in harmony, and for reasons so obvious, at the maxim level, as not to need to be recited; because without rational purpose and order the unfettered imagination will not be consecutive, and people will not care to follow it; and because the poem of reason from which imagination is absent becomes a plain morality, or a theological dogma, and is not art at all. This is not good enough for my anthropologist, but it goes a long way, and has been useful. (It is the maxim in which the young poets are particularly instructed at college, but it does not necessarily persuade the aggressive new poet who thinks it is time for a new poetry and a new maxim.)

The word for imagination at the universities nowadays is sensibility.

An editor comes upon many new poets of fine sensibility, and verbal power quite equal to reporting it handsomely, perhaps just as nicely as the eminent poets of our time do it. We read the new poet with technical admiration, from line to line, and image to image. But presently the poem seems to be getting nowhere, and we cannot continue. Sensibility is doing beautifully here, we say, but what a dangling or undirected sensibility! If only the well-turned phrases could touch and move the massive affective economy! Mr. Eliot would have put it this way: If only the little feelings which respond to the details could be incidental to the registration of some grand emotion or passion! But to keep within my own frame of reference: If only sensibility had attached itself somehow to a moral situation; or even to a systematic theology. We can surely say now that in our time there has been so much experiment with the educated yet aimless sensibility that we have found its limit by going beyond it to the point of no return. Your speaker is himself an editor, as you will have suspected, and his impression of talented sensibility working without direction is a frequent one. There are times when he wonders if he might not have waked up the new poet by saying severely: You are lacking in character, for you register no causes, passions, prejudices, nor obsessions; very possibly the failure in your development is past remedy now, because to take the remedy you would have to change your life. But that might not necessarily be quite true, and any exaggeration in the charge would not be decent. If we were editing a popular journal of poetry, I have no doubt the charge would be, as a rule, quite the obverse of this one. We might want to say: Your verse indicates a very sound morality, but what you need is a sensibility; you are a moralist rather than a poet.

Before leaving the topic of the undirected sensibility, I have one quick digression to make, because I think its pertinence will have occurred surely to some members of my audience. There is the famous case of the Symbolists, in France. My remark cannot be that of a master at the reading of the French language. But surely the Symbolists were provided with an astonishing proficiency in what we may call the pure poetic sensibility, of the kind which notes in the physical setting of the action, as for example in the landscape of the physical world, and the fauna and the flora, those configurations and motions which are dramatic in the human sense of drama. For its implement they cultivated probably the most elevated poetic language in Western history; provided we mean by poetic the language which refuses always to lapse into a rhetorical resonance with a vague meaning, but keeps the edge of its detail very sharp. There are poems by Mallarmé, Rimbaud, and Valéry, where the sensibility works beautifully in every turn of phrase, in every achieved image; yet

236

to our infinite regret seems at the end to have gone nowhere and to have no consequence. These are poets' poets, who show the extreme refinements of sensibility. But it would be rather beyond the reach of dull moralizing poets to ponder them; and their best service would be to just those new poets of considerable sensibility who are bent on perfecting it, but yet are well instructed in the maxim about the presidency of reason.

It might be said that the occasion of a poem is a *moral* situation. But immediately it must be added as a correction that the occasion of a poem is a moral *situation*. The moral is never to be emphasized as if the poem existed just for its sake, but must stay implicit in the situation. And that is rather curious. We may recite our maxim to that effect without having the faintest conscious idea of the advantage of making the moral and the situation go their way together. It sounds like a primitive wisdom, and primitive wisdom does not explain itself; or like Oriental wisdom, and we fancy that Oriental means oblique and occult. Mr. Eliot told us that about the time of the English Restoration there was a dissociation of sensibility from thinking, so that later poets have had to feel and think by turns, when they should have been combining both in one unified experience. But we still ask: Why is it better to have them together, in a single experience; and finally we ask: What is the intention of poetry anyway, that it should not covet a perfect logical clarity as prose does, but clutter its discourse incessantly with figures? So we must leave the area of the maxims, if we would find an answer to those questions. We must return to the idea of the literary anthropologist, who not only regards the distinctive forms of experience as functional, but can tell what their functions are, and how they are carried out. Again, however, we must improvise this literary anthropologist, who may not yet actually exist; but who if he did exist might be the top economist among the senior economists in the public service.

We are not entirely helpless. For there is the philosopher Kant, to whom I have attributed an anthropological cast of mind, and who was capable of probing very deeply into the economy of the spirit. And there is William Wordsworth, who is not nearly so articulate, nor so consistent, but who had a passion for exploring the depths of his poetic consciousness.

If I read Kant correctly, he has suffered a strange neglect so far as concerns that third of the famous *critiques,* the *Critique of Judgment;* I think I have never seen mention of the answer he provides for our question. But of course it is the fact that Kant was so much the pioneer in this field that his account, though repetitive, is not elaborated with much illustration, and his very technical language is exasperating.

Let us make a fresh start, at a place remote from this discussion up to here, but familiar to the anthropologist. Suppose the purpose of the

237

poem is to heal the appalling loneliness than human creatures suffer, especially when they are good creatures who act with scrupulous justice toward their fellow creatures, and even with love and charity. (Ordinarily the moral of the situation is commonplace, and the poet is a man of complete moral sense, addressing himself to his peers.)   They are isolated, and not only from men and women who do not share their moral sentiments, but even more irreparably from the physical and non-human world in which all things seem to move relentlessly on their mechanical or vegetative or animal ways.   In such a world they do not feel at home. But now, in the poem, this world figures as the setting or stage within which the human characters are placed.   The action of the human agents is in intimate association with the stage properties, so to speak; such as a view, or birds and beasts, or inanimate objects like winds, waters, stones, trees, lights and shadows.   And what happens is, simply, that the stage properties soon begin to figure in the poem as if they were moral agents too. They are not moral strictly, or at least we cannot know that they are, as Kant was careful to say; but they seem wonderfully understanding; they seem "expressive," and what they express seems to be their sympathy with the moral actions and speeches of the principals.   John Ruskin is the observer who has made the fullest report on the expressiveness of natural objects, though he would not allow it to seem immoderate past the bounds of credulity, and had a stern eye for the gross representations of it by poets whom he charges with a "pathetic" (or sympathetic) fallacy.   Shakespeare is perhaps still the poet who used it most easily and spontaneously in his verse.   The consequence is that the poet and his readers receive suddenly a wonderful epiphany, the vision of a "society" in which nature seems to associate herself with the lonely moralists, and no longer to be hostile or indifferent.   It is as if the moral order embraced and governed the whole world; at least for the time being.   I should think that is a kind of cosmic or religious experience, though not the dogmatic or theological one in which persons see marvelous prospects opening to them as the result of a sustained and difficult act of faith.   Both experiences would suffer from being identified with each other.   We do not ordinarily name the experience as either a religious experience, or a moral experience, but as a poetic or artistic experience, and the form of its happiness is the entrancing and massive satisfaction called beauty.

We may well believe that Wordsworth will always rate as having been the most determined Nature-poet in the history of literature.   For some five or six years he attached himself to a mystical dogma which accounted miraculously for the claim Nature made upon his affections.   He declared that the deity by special providence entered into the particular natural scene, and the impression the poet took of it was that of a Presence, or

238

a Voice, which manifested itself to him for his instruction, or his comfort; it calmed his spirits or aroused them, according to his need. Nature taught him more than books by human hands. But Wordsworth could not maintain this rapturous belief; it made Nature too aggressive to be quite natural; so that finally Nature with its Voices and Presences became simply—common nature, to which after a period of disillusionment he resorted as habitually as ever, not as to a God but as to a kind foster-mother or nurse. The animation of nature in these homely terms is as absolute as in the others, but these are not so grim and authoritarian. In the earlier period the poetry about Nature was better, as if by an overflow of the poet's high spirits. But the nature which figures in the later period is the one which is common, or orthodox, among the poets. This would be according to the sophistication which we attribute professionally to the poets. As children we came into the power of make-believe early, and learned presently to distinguish what we pretended to be from what we really were. Not without saying to ourselves, even in our cooler moments, that we *meant* somehow and some time to be what we had played at being; the playing idealized our total economy. Then we were given fairy tales, where miracles occurred when the beasts, or it might be the trees, came to the aid of the good child in his horrid straits. Our parents and teachers were very sure that these would not seriously impair our sense of reality. The fairy tales were just right to serve for our literature at that stage. Then we grew up, and fictions for grown-ups replaced the fairy tales, with characters which were stronger than ourselves, and better, and endings which were righter than we could easily find in life. But best of all came the poems, if we managed to find our initiation into that kind of make-believe. If Nature did not necessarily figure in the fictions, it was a primary consideration in the poems. But the wonders in the poems, where we entered into the society of Nature, were far more discreet than they had been in the fairy tales, as they must be to be reputable for our intelligence, and effective. We have found ourselves moved as deeply by the poems as we once were moved by the fairy tales. Indeed, since we are bigger than we were then, and more complex, there is *more* commotion in us made by the poems, more displacement. Wordsworth employed for his special ode the title, "Intimations of Immortality." The first word there is a very discreet one. What the poets give us is an incessant stream of miraculous intimations about nature, and "Intimations of Goodness in the Body of This World" might have been the title which Wordsworth would have employed if he had been following Kant's conception of the office of poetry. The intimations are tonic for us. They lend us morale; it is an excellent effect in an Age of Anxiety; and so far as we know every age is an age of anxiety. The poets are responsible public functionaries for doing this service; or so I think our anthropologist would say.

There is a special device to which poets have always been habituated, contributing to the dominant intention. It is the linguistic invention which we know as metaphor; the figure which towers over all the others in the poetic handbook. As if for fear the natural properties of the setting cannot be animated by direct methods in poems as in the fairy tales, as if they cannot be suddenly and heroically transformed for adult readers out of their prose or common functions, metaphor breaks into the poetic argument at any moment to endow the natural object with a human sentience. Metaphor is the equation of the human action to that of some natural object; the object really is extraneous to the human action, but it is made to involve itself in that action anyway, which in effect is to be humanized. In the Robinson poem, for example, there are such metaphors, where nature answers to human passion with like passion; at the climax of the action when all is lost, "the falling leaf inaugurates," and "the pounding wave reverberates"; at the dismal conclusion there is the "changed familiar tree" and the "stairway to the sea/ Where down the blind are driven." Metaphors are metamorphoses, though they are never so grossly miraculous as the effects described in the cruder medium of the poet Ovid.

The difference between fiction and poetry perhaps becomes clearer at this point. Many fictions are inextricably mixed with poetry; the natural setting of the great scenes being chosen to "suit the action," so to speak; the narrator speaking a language that is stylized and imaginative, perhaps luminous sometimes with modest metaphors. But there are plain fictions where the art seems most specialized and distinct. They deal with moral situations—as all arts in some sense have to do—but their emphasis is on the moral. They may work at great length and with much subtlety. Mr. Trilling has said that the proper subject for fiction is manners, which always profess moral attitudes, but sometimes hypocritically. So there may be opposition between the good manners of a set of people and the evil which they actually do; and always there will be open opposition between our own good people and those other people who are obviously bad. But now and then, and it is especially happy if this comes at the end, there is the fine scene where the good people triumph conclusively, and the evil people are removed or converted to goodness; and so massive has been the progress and the preparation toward the event that it seems to us like a vision of goodness prevailing everywhere. It is as if the whole family of mankind had turned to goodness, or might someday turn to goodness. The "intimation" is of the good society established and regnant on earth. But the earth is not involved. We have a great happiness, but it is a social or family happiness, and that is not the same as the lyrical happiness we received in poetry from the participation of nature. I think the two happinesses do not feel the same. But I hope the lovers of fiction will not mind the haste and simplicity with which I have put this distinction.

The new poet today looks back upon a half-century which may have been more eventful for new poetry than any other in the history of our language, with the exception of the second half of the 16th century, and possibly its successor the first half of the 17th century. The exhibition must be rather bewildering to review. Mr. Ezra Pound advised the poets early to "Make It New," and there was never a better time for this advice than the impoverished period from which they had to start. They founded many innovations, and engineered many revolutions. Before long an *avant-garde* was galloping off in almost every direction, and it was difficult in the confusion to tell which one the main troops were going to follow. That was a magnificent confusion. All possible poetries were being tried, and nothing could have been better for the times.

A great deal was gained in the understanding of what the capability of a poem is, and what its limits are. That is coming to light steadily, if my own impression is correct, in the utterances of critics. But the farther we stand from the peak of all that confusion, the more possible it seems that there is still going to be a continuity between the old poetry and the poetry of the future. And perhaps the reason would be that the genius of the art will refuse to go very far from the genius of the language, which is its medium; and that the possibilities of the medium were rather thoroughly explored by the able pioneers of 1550 to 1650, and other companies of pioneers who came after them and found new discoveries always harder to make. The chances are not so bright now for poetries which are radically new. But in saying this I do not mean anything which might be taken as disputing our conviction that every age must present to the anthology a poetry of its own, which must be at least new enough to distinguish it. We cannot use a tradition which is not adaptable to our own society. But at least it has appeared in recent years that the newest poets are not particularly revolutionary.

I have even noticed that the newest poets appear much more often than not to be picking up again the meters, which many poets in the century had thought they must dispense with; and by way of conclusion it seems imperative to say something about the meters, in order not to neglect altogether the half of the poetic effects made possible by the medium, which is the spoken language. This language has its meaning, as we know very well; and necessarily it makes oral sounds, which have no value at all in themselves when we are attending strictly to the meaning, but do have value in themselves if the poet makes them fit into a kind of music having fixed units like bars and measures, line-lengths and stanzas. The metered language is a double medium, with two systems of effects, which at first sight seem to have very little to do with one another. The effects which I have been remarking up to this point are almost entirely on the meaningful side of the medium, and might very well have been realized in free verse, which has no fixed system of sounds at all. Indeed, such effects have been realized in the free verse of our own century, and by admirable poets. And my feeling would be, like yours, that the meaningful effects represent the better half of poetry when it doubles its medium and has two halves. But now the question of the anthropologist must be: What is the good of the meters as the old poets regularly, and the new poets increasingly, have elected to employ them? What do they mean?

I hope everybody in the audience knows how the meters go, so that I need only to offer my guess as to what they are for.

Though we might prefer to attend only to the meaning of the poetic language, the meters would have us attending also to their music. It is not an advanced kind of music, but it is a steady music, and its simple rhythmic unit is infinitely repetitive. At long last, and against our will perhaps, we are compelled to hear it; always after that we have to be listening for it in advance. If we were provided as the ancients were with the actual oral delivery of poetry by a public rhapsode with a musical sense, we would be extremely sensitive to the meters, and never miss hearing them. But even if we are our own readers and have some slight musical sense, we will still find ourselves attending more or less to the meters, though we read in armchairs, and silently. What do they signify to us?

I think meters confer upon the delivery of poetry the sense of a ritualistic occasion. When a ritual develops it consists in the enactment, or the recital over and over again, of some experience which is obsessive for us, yet intangible and hard to express. The nearest analogue to the reading of poetry according to the meters, as I think, is the reading of an ecclesiastical service by the congregation. Both the genius of poetry and the genius of the religious establishment work against the same difficulty, which is the registration of what is inexpressible, or metaphysical. The religious occasion is a very formal one, with its appointed place in the visible temple, and the community of worshippers congregated visibly; it defines itself sharply and publicly for the anthropologist. The reading of poetry is not, since the invention of printing, so communal, so formal, so formidable. But the anthropologist will have to pay his respects to it anyhow, and give it what dignities he can. (All this is being said much too briefly.)

242

Mr. Eliot has referred to his verse as being "free verse." But that is not quite accurate, as he would know very well. He never has sustained his free verse, because, as I am obliged to think, free verse is not good enough for his purpose. Mr. Blackmur, writing about Eliot as a leading poet (and he was the master whom the new poets most followed), did not fail to remark upon the beauty of his music, and one might have thought the reference was to some sort of prose music in the free verse; for prose may have itself an irregular beauty, a free beauty which is different from the formal beauty of a measured language. But Mr. Blackmur protected himself by making two quotations from the poems, each of which was a perfect or metered unit of oral language. One was from *The Waste Land:*

> A woman drew her long black hair out tight
> And fiddled whisper music on those strings;

and the other was from one of the *Four Quartets:*

> The salt is on the briar rose.
> The fog is on the fir-tree.

We cannot doubt that Mr. Blackmur was aware that the first is from the great metrical family of blank verse, an intellectual and university-bred family; and the second is from the other great family, the folk line. He could not have displayed more briefly or more sharply Mr. Eliot's exceeding command of the meters. These metered bits, and the others in his verse, are telling, and final, when we come to take our sense of him as a poet. Incidentally, as I understand it, they go along precisely with Mr. Eliot's concern with religion and ritual, as we know it from his public deliveries other than the poems. If he turned largely to free verse, we may suppose he had decided that his age wanted and needed new and informal kinds of verse, and that this was the quickest road to loosening their language and bringing vitality back into it. As for the next age, I can imagine that he might not have in mind for it the same strategy now.

The Present State of Poetry

Delmore Schwartz

Presented at the Library of Congress January 20, 1958

ON A NUMBER OF OTHER OCCASIONS, some of them fairly recent, some of them very long ago, I have written or spoken, or I have heard what others have written and spoken about the subject of tonight's lecture, the condition of poetry in America at present. I intend to describe some of these occasions in a while, but right now, as a starting point, it is important to say that the present occasion is quite different from every past occasion, although the subject is the same; and all those past occasions seem quite different now than at the time that they occurred.

In the past, there has been little or no reason to feel as I felt when, in preparing to speak tonight, I reviewed the subject in my mind. For as I thought of the present state of poetry in America, in the middle of the twentieth century, I had two very unlike and wholly conflicting impressions. One impression was that of bewilderment and reminded me of a film I once saw in which a minor but complicated character, whenever anyone said to him, "How are you?", invariably replied, "I don't know!" So far as I can remember, this answer displeased everyone else: some were irritated, others were infuriated, no one was satisfied, and yet there was more to the answer than a simple statement of ignorance or a simple unwillingness to make a clear and unequivocal statement about one's state of being, and this was made evident when one irritated questioner said: "What do you mean, you don't know how you are?" When one says, "I don't know," whether one is speaking of one's state of being or one is speaking of the state of poetry, the answer possesses a genuine accuracy. It would be inaccurate to say that poetry at present is in a state of perfect health; at the same time, it would be still more inaccurate to say that it was in a state of severe illness or decline, as it has been, from time to time, during the latter half of the nineteenth century and the first fourteen years of the twentieth century. Perhaps to say that the condition of poetry at present is one of complicated transition is the closest one can come to a positive statement. But one must immediately add that it is in a state of transition of a special and new kind, a state of groping and uncertainty. It should be almost needless to say that this attitude toward the present is not limited to poets and the condition of poetry, nor is it confined to the United States. The second strong feeling which tonight's subject repeatedly suggested to me was not in the least a sense of doubt and perplexity, but on the contrary it was very much of an embarrassment of riches: I felt as I think Baudelaire must have felt when he wrote, in one of his best poems, "I have more memories than if I had lived for a thousand years!" There are various reasons for this abundance and excess of memory, which is common, I feel almost certain, to all the poets of my own generation, and particularly true of those who like myself have been critics, teachers, and editors as well as poets. So many changes have occurred since the time when we were adolescents: this was the time when it seemed the most wonderful thing in the world to be a poet, when any older person who had appeared in print seemed to have a God-like aura, a supernatural radiance, and when the experience of reading the work of older poets was the cause of overwhelming excitement, and at times, indeed, of an intense exaltation comparable to no other kind of experience, however pleasant or joyous.

For the poets of my own generation as for myself, some twenty, twenty-five, or thirty years of chronological time have passed since the time of adolescence or the time when we first began to appear in print. Most of us thought when we first appeared in print that all our problems were over and we were entirely unaware that on the contrary, all our problems had just begun. But even if we had possessed the knowledge of our elders, we would not have been prepared for the changes which have continually occurred during the past twenty years, changes which make the time of adolescence and of first youth appear to belong to another century and to the experience of some human being other than oneself. The apocalyptic events which have occurred since 1938 throughout the world, and in particular the five years of the second World War, would be sufficient to make the past of twenty years ago seem far more distant from us than twenty years of chronological time. But the changes which have occurred in the state of poetry, changes which could hardly have been anticipated or indeed imagined very often, can best be summarized by citing a series of examples: these examples should indicate, in one or another way, that the changes have sometimes been profound, sometimes superficial, and sometimes misleading, and it is their rapid succession during the past twenty years which makes the state of poetry very different and more difficult to define now than in 1938, or indeed at any time, in America, since the Civil War.

My first example, which may be an illustration of the most important change of all, is the visit of T. S. Eliot to America during 1932 and 1933 when, in addition to teaching and lecturing at various schools, he read his own poetry in public. My own direct experience is limited to a lecture on Milton which Mr. Eliot gave at Columbia and another lecture in New York City in which he quoted verse quite often, but I am sure that I am not mistaken in supposing that Mr. Eliot's public appearances were very different from what occurred when Dylan Thomas read his poetry in public on his visits to America between 1949 and 1953. Eliot was already famous then: his authority as a critic was already that of a literary dictator, and hence his appearances inspired a sense of awe which went beyond the admiration one would have felt in the presence of other creative writers of the same rank, such as William Butler Yeats, James Joyce and Thomas Mann. His manner of lecturing as well as the way in which he read poetry, his own or another poet's, were extremely impressive. But Eliot's public appearances only served to confirm what his audience already felt: namely, that he was a very great poet indeed and the greatest living literary critic. The experience of attending one of his lectures or readings was like that of reading his poems or his criticism; it did not create a new impression of his work. In contrast, this is exactly what Dylan Thomas' readings in public accomplished when they took place many years after. Until these readings Thomas was known in America merely as one of a number of fairly well-known poets. His readings in public made him as famous, in a short period of time, as T. S. Eliot, Robert Frost, and William Butler Yeats had become only after a good many years. And indeed if not for these readings, it is likely that he would have remained comparatively unknown to the general public. Many of the people who were excited to intense admiration by hearing his poems aloud were people who had found his poetry, when it appeared in print, opaque, impenetrable, difficult, obscure, and in a word, unreadable. Thus what Thomas accomplished by his public readings is meaningful in ways which extend far beyond the unquestionable importance of his work. He demonstrated by direct, eloquent, and vivid example a truth about the nature of poetry which no amount of critical elucidation could have communicated—the truth that the actuality of a poem is not merely a matter of the explicit meanings contained in each successive line. For many years the majority of readers had been puzzled and irritated by modern poetry's obscurity and difficulty, its esoteric allusions, sudden transitions, or the appearance of a lack of transition, connection and logical order. The irritation of many readers almost always developed into the conviction that the obscurity and difficulty of modern poetry was too great for the uninstructed reader to overcome. Yet when the same

246

readers heard Thomas' poetry aloud, they immediately forgot about their previous impressions. The aural experience of a poem, when read as well as Thomas could read his own poetry and the poetry of others also, communicated to his listeners an experience of the truth that the total being of a poem is far more than its explicit meanings, and this made the poem very different from what it had seemed to be when it was encountered upon the page and seemed very much like an inferior crossword puzzle, an unrewarding exercise in discovering concealed meanings. The living voice communicated to Thomas' readers the intensely felt attitudes and emotions which were the actual poem in its complete and concrete reality.

There would be a good deal more to say if tonight's subject were restricted to the public's skill or lack of skill in reading poetry as it appears upon the page. Here I must limit my comments to the bearing which Thomas' public readings have had upon the present state of poetry. Thomas' readings initiated what may very well be an immense change in the public's whole conception of the nature of modern poetry. The enthusiasm he awakened suggests that for the majority of readers a poem as it appears in print has the same relationship to the total reality and being of a poem as a musical score of a symphony has to the orchestral performance of that symphony. I must immediately add that it would be very easy to overestimate—or to underestimate—the advance, and to overlook the very real dangers inherent in the aural experience of poetry. Thus, those who hear a poem aloud do not invariably feel moved to seek out the poem in print. This might very well lead to the neglect of the kind of poetry in which there is a richness of style and language that requires the eye as well as the ear, and conversely it might encourage the writing of that kind of poetry which lends itself best to being read aloud. It might also encourage one or another kind of histrionic elocutionism and the vulgarity of most forms of oratory and declamation. A great and powerful voice can be extremely hynoptic and deceptive, and it can disregard the inferiority of the text: thus Sarah Bernhardt is said to have been able to reduce an audience to tears by reciting the multiplication table.

These and other dangers are all the more difficult to avoid because few poets read poetry aloud very well or indeed with any degree of the eloquence and power which Thomas possessed. The fact that many of the good poets of our time read poetry poorly may be temporary and due to a lack of training and experience. But it is also true that few human beings know how to read poetry aloud: few actors possess this skill, however good they may be as actors. This is evident in the way in which Shakespearean blank verse is spoken in most productions of Shakespeare;

it is spoken as if there were no difference between speeches in blank verse and speeches in prose. Hence it must be said that for the time being one must guard against any unqualified optimism about the effectiveness of public readings, and the need of being critical will continue until there exists for poetry as there already exists for music and the drama an independent class of performers trained in the aural realization of poetry. Those who are devoted to music do not expect a great virtuoso to be a great composer, or the reverse: there is just as little justification for expecting the situation to be otherwise in poetry.

The purpose of my second example is to illustrate another very important change which has occurred in recent years and which makes the present state of poetry very different from what it was in the past, some twenty years ago, or for that matter forty and fifty years ago. In 1936 I heard Wallace Stevens, one of the best of all American poets, read his poetry at Harvard: it was the first time Stevens had ever read his poetry in public, and this first reading was at once an indescribable ordeal and a precious event to Stevens: it was precious because he had been an undergraduate at Harvard some thirty-seven years before, at the turn of the century, and he had not returned since that time in his own person, although he had often gone to the Yale-Harvard football games incognito. Before and after reading each poem, Stevens spoke of the nature of poetry, a theme which naturally concerned him very much, and he said, among other things, that the least sound counts, the least sound and the least syllable. He illustrated this observation by telling of how he had awakened after midnight the week before and heard the sounds made by a cat walking delicately and carefully on the crusted snow outside his house. After each comment, Stevens returned to his own poems: but at one point an old Cambridge lady, holding an ear trumpet aloft and dressed in a style which must have been *chic* at the inauguration of Rutherford Hayes, shouted out, hoarse and peremptory as crows, that she must ask Mr. Stevens to speak loudly and clearly, loudly and clearly, if you please. She might just as well have been shouting at President Hayes. Stevens continued to read his poems in a very low voice, although a good many of them were written in a style as high-flown and passionate as that of any Elizabethan playwright. And throughout his reading Stevens was extremely nervous and constrained, although since this state of mind showed itself only as a rigid impassivity, his overwhelming nervousness must have been invisible to most of his audience. When the reading ended, Stevens said to the teacher who had introduced him: "I wonder what the boys at the office would think about this?" The office was the Hartford Accident and Indemnity Co., the boys were those who knew Stevens as the vice-president and legal counsel of the company and thus the most solid of citizens.

248

A good deal more might be said about the significance of this remark and how much it helps to illuminate Stevens' poetic career and the very quality of his poetry. But right now the point which must be emphasized as much as possible is this: no poet of my own or the rising generation of poets would feel as Stevens did when he made the remark, for, among other things, if one said: "I wonder what the boys at the office would think about this," it is a matter of overwhelming probability that one would be referring to the office of the English department at a university.

This is the change which has affected the condition of poetry more than any other during the past generation. The fact that in 1958 so many poets are teachers of literature and that in 1938, 1928 and 1908, this was very seldom true, constitutes a radical change which involves not only the poet and the poetry which he writes, but the readers of poetry and their concept of the poet and of poetry. Primary and important as this change is, it cannot, however, be regarded in isolation from changes of other kinds which have also taken place and which are rooted in the changing character of American life: for example, the college-educated population of the entire country has more than doubled in two generations, and since this increase is likely to continue, more and more poets may be welcomed as teachers of literature in the colleges.

The effect upon the poet of being a teacher of literature is a complicated and independent topic; what I want to point out now is the effect upon the poet's conception of himself as a poet and indeed as a human being. In the past, the poet had a sense of what he seemed to most other human beings which was identical, in one or another way, with the feelings of Wallace Stevens not only when he read his poetry for the first time in public but throughout his entire life.

Today, since so many poets are teachers, it is no longer true that the poet is regarded by most other human beings as a strange and exotic being. Moreover, as a teacher the poet makes direct use of the entire past of American and English poetry and he is in direct communication several times a week with what is known in advertising circles as a trapped audience: he has as an audience human beings at the most impressionable and receptive stage of existence, and he soon discovers that in the classroom it is possible to persuade almost all students that poetry is extremely interesting and that it is never too difficult or too obscure to be understood. This is true to such an extent that at times the problem becomes one of persuading the student that a poem is not good merely because it is difficult, or bad because it is simple and lucid. Indeed, this experience may encourage the most sanguine illusions in the poet himself. He may very well forget that the conditions which exist in the classroom do not exist outside of the classroom and hence he may suppose that the intense love of poetry which he has awakened with ease in his students will continue permanently. He may also suppose that the teaching of literature is sufficient in itself, granted the proper support, to create and sustain a genuinely literate reading public immune to all the corruptions of mass culture. Whether or not he suffers from these illusions, one thing is incontestable and makes an immense difference. The poet as a teacher has a status within the confines of the academic community which gives him a very different sense of himself and a very different sense of how he is regarded by other human beings: he is a useful and accepted member of society and not a peculiar and strange being, since the writing of poetry is clearly a natural pursuit for the teacher of literature. The fact that he is a poet is not something which in itself isolates him from most other human beings, an isolation which the poet and indeed the artist in every medium felt profoundly during every generation in the past.

My examples thus far have illustrated the extent to which the state of poetry as a whole is superior at present to what it has been for the most part during the past. Now I want to go on to a series of examples which are of a mixed character and which indicate that the present superiority is incomplete and may very well be misleading. For the advantages involve disadvantages. It is possible to overestimate or misunderstand both what is positive and what is negative.

I have just described the positive advantages of the tendency of poets to be teachers of literature. The best way I can deal with the disadvantages, which are inseparable from the advantages, is to speak directly of my own experience as a poet who has been a teacher. I feel no doubt whatever that the paradoxical character of my own experience is typical in every way of most if not all the poets of my own generation, and typical also of the experience, during the past twenty years, of poets older and younger than myself.

During the past twenty years I have been employed as a teacher of English composition, English literature, American literature, and creative writing at eight universities. I have also been a lecturer, the editor of a literary review, the poetry editor and film critic of a weekly periodical, the literary consultant for a philanthropic foundation, and in general I have been provided with a good deal of work which not only enabled me to earn a modest livelihood, but also enabled me to acquire interesting and useful skills, so many, in fact, that there was a period of fifteen months during which I had five jobs, only two of which, however, were full-time. The important and paradoxical point is that I would seldom if ever have been employed in these capacities if I had not been a poet, and my first teaching appointment certainly would not have been offered to me if I had not published my first book of poems some time before. I was asked to do many things because I was a poet: the one thing I was not asked to do very often was to write poetry. I will speak of the two occasions, seventeen years apart from each other, which are exceptions to this statement in a moment. Right now I want to try to be as concrete as possible about what I mean. When a poet is asked to teach, or to act as an editor, or to write book reviews and critical essays, the basis of his employment is such as to enable him to earn a living. When, however, he writes a poem, this is not true in the same way: for the most likely result of the writing of a poem and its publication is that he will have one or another opportunity to earn a living in some way other than that of writing poetry.

It must be said immediately that during the past twenty years the number of prizes, awards, grants, and honors given to poets has increased a great deal, and it would be ungrateful as well as untrue to say that they have not helped matters a good deal, and made the lot of the poet fortunate in ways which hardly existed at all twenty and thirty years ago. At the same time it would be wrong to suppose that the generosity with which poetry is supported does more than reduce the problem of economic necessity, which is more difficult for the poet than for other human beings precisely because he is a poet. During two of the past seventeen years, in 1940 and in 1957, I have been given sums of money sufficient to enable me to devote myself entirely to the writing of poetry: but these grants, which I was delighted, I need hardly say, to get, are based precisely on the fact that it is impossible to earn even the most modest livelihood unless, in addition to writing poetry, one does a good many other things.

The attitude of the public toward poetry and the poet is, as much that I have said should indicate, very important too. And here again it is only after one has taken account of positive and negative complications that one avoids over-simplification and arrives at an adequate conclusion.

Here is a negative piece of evidence: "A recent survey showed that sixty percent of the adult population of America did not read a book other than the Bible in 1954." And here is an even more negative piece of evidence: "If the American Festival Academy can help it, the Bard of Avon will not be the formidable bore that he is to so many students across the land." I need not mention the measures which are going to be taken to make Shakespeare something other than a formidable bore, but it is worth remarking, in passing, that if to many millions of Americans Shakespeare is a formidable bore, there is no justification for attributing the public's indifference to or dislike of modern poetry to its difficulty and obscurity. It can also be maintained that Shakespeare has stopped being a formidable bore, since the Broadway stage has discovered that Shakespeare really wrote musical comedies, a truth which remained unknown for centuries.

251

In any case, the negative evidence in both instances is misleading if either instance is regarded in isolation or if, with Whitman, one believes that "To have great poets one must have great audiences," a statement which can certainly be understood in a numerical sense. To assume, however, that mere quantity or the mere largeness of an audience is of absolute and decisive importance is just as false as to assume that the indifference of the public toward poetry and the poet makes no difference at all. To have great poetry, it is necessary to have great poets: during the past hundred years and more, there have been great poets who had little or no audience at all during their lifetime, and if the mere numerical quantity of the audience were as crucial a matter as it is often supposed to be, the best sellers of each year would be far more important than they are. One has only to ask more readers of fiction: "What were the best-sellers of five years ago and ten years ago?" to discover that their very names have been forgotten and thus that as best-sellers they have really made no lasting impression at all on the reading public.

The fact that sixty percent of the adult population does not read any book other than the Bible during the year is regrettable; and it is equally regrettable that Shakespeare is regarded as a bore by millions of human beings. But the attitude of those who do not read books at all is far less important than the attitude of those who do read books. The comments of John O'Hara when he lectured here last December, and his comments at other times, will illustrate what I mean in several ways. Mr. O'Hara is of course a very gifted novelist and he is also, it is clear, an avid reader. The dissatisfaction he expressed because some of his novels had sold no more than one hundred thousand copies should show that the possibilities of dissatisfaction are unlimited. Mr. O'Hara has made other comments of a critical kind which illustrate that fact that even a very gifted novelist and a devoted reader may not be a desirable addition to the reading public. Thus Mr. O'Hara spoke of how delighted and honored he was to have the company of "a foremost intellectual like Thornton Wilder" and yet how distraught he became when Mr. Wilder mentioned the names of Søren Kierkegaard and Franz Kafka. In a like way, Mr. O'Hara, reviewing a novel by Ernest Hemingway several years ago, declared that Hemingway was the greatest writer since Shakespeare, a statement which immediately made one wonder: what makes Shakespeare better? It also suggests that Mr. O'Hara's disgust with Kierkegaard and Kafka may extend to Shakespeare too, or at any rate to those modern poets who have been influenced by Kierkegaard, Kafka, and Shakespeare.

Mr. O'Hara's impressions as a reader are a negative illustration of what may be most defective in the reading public's attitude toward poetry at present. In the past, when a reader found that a poem or a novel did not interest him, he usually said, with humility, "I don't understand it, it's over my head."

During recent years and at present, more and more readers have adopted an attitude of extreme arrogance, declaring that a poem or novel which they were unable to understand was clearly worthless precisely because they were unable to understand it.

The number of readers of poetry is far less important than the quality of their attitude toward poetry. One hundred thousand readers who felt as passionate and devoted and sustained an interest in the work of living poets as they feel towards a good many games, sports, and avocations, would be far more desirable than a reading public of several millions who felt that their attitude as readers was an unquestionable criterion of the intrinsic value of any work of poetry or fiction.

At present, it is clear that the reading public as a whole regards the anthology as the best of all books of poetry. And the increasing popularity of anthologies during the past twenty years has certainly been the cause of more anthologies and better anthologies. It remains true that the anthology is very often a substitute for the reading of the books of any poet in particular. But again, it is also true that many readers of anthologies would not read contemporary poetry at all, if anthologies were not available to them and they had to choose among the books of individual poets.

The attitude of the American public as a whole toward poetry and the poet can be further defined by describing how *Life* magazine noted the death of Dylan Thomas in the autumn of 1953, and then, a few months after, the death of Maxwell Bodenheim. Thomas' death was mentioned in a brief paragraph of tribute which made one of the millions of readers or beholders of *Life* curious enough to write to the editors and ask: "Who is Dylan Thomas?" The letter was printed along with a small photograph of Thomas. Bodenheim's death, on the other hand, was the subject of two full pages of photographs and captions, reviewing thirty years of Bodenheim's life. Clearly poetic merit and public fame had nothing to do with the extreme contrast, since Thomas not only was a far more important poet than Bodenheim but a far more famous one. The extreme contrast in coverage, which of course would have been reversed if poetic merit had been the criterion, has only one explanation: Bodenheim was murdered; Thomas' death was the result, on the surface at least, of what are sometimes called natural causes and thus hardly sensational enough to excite and gratify the curiosity of the vast number of human beings who view *Life* weekly. This instance is grotesque and special; nevertheless it certainly suggests that a poet can succeed in attracting national attention by being murdered or by being involved in some other activity of a spectacular, scandalous or extraordinary character: the intrinsic poetic value of his work is certainly not going to win him the same attention of the entire public at present or at any time in the foreseeable future.

Two further and final examples should complete the picture and demonstrate why any positive statement about the state of poetry at present requires a negative qualification and any negative formulation the converse, so that an adequate generalization is possible only if one can say without emotional contradiction: The present state of poetry in America is superior to what it has ever been in the past; yet at the same time, the present state of poetry is not in an unquestionably flourishing state in any full sense.

Thus, when one poet of my own generation sent a copy of his first book of poems to his brother, he received a letter of acknowledgment from which I quote only the first paragraph:

Dear Brother,

I received your book and really liked it very much except that I don't like poetry as I don't understand it.   I showed your book to a few people and they were very much impressed and except for the fact that they didn't have a spare $2.50 they would have bought a copy....

This letter was written nineteen years ago; since then, it must be said again, there have continually been changes which make the present very different from the past.   The far greater number of prizes, awards, grants, fellowships, public readings and recordings, and teaching appointments are the result of a public interest and solicitude which hardly existed a generation ago.   Thus there are now five major prizes for poetry each year, and there was only one, the Pulitzer Prize, twenty years ago.   And this is very important, since it does a great deal to encourage publishers to publish new books of poetry, despite the likelihood of financial loss.   But on the whole the greatly increased interest of the public is an interest in the poet, far more than an interest in poetry itself.   The purchase of a new book of poems of most poets represents but a small fraction of the number of human beings who attend poetry readings.   And this is but one indication that it is the poet, in person, as an interesting human being, rather than his poetry, which attracts the majority of those at any poetry reading, although it is certainly true that the poet is regarded as an interesting human being only because he writes poems.   So too, time again, other poets have spoken of the experience of being invited to dinner or for a week-end and being the object of the most generous hospitality solely because they were poets.   They would otherwise have been unknown and thus out of the reach of the kindness of those who entertained them. Yet at the same time their hosts seldom showed any sign of a serious and passionate interest in their own poetry or the poetry of other writers. Nevertheless, I doubt very much that any poet does not prefer this split in interest to the total indifference which characterized every other period in the past.

Thus far I have said nothing about the kind of poetry which is being written at present, although the subject of the present state of poetry in America might be understood as requiring first of all an attempt to describe and evaluate the work of particular poets and of leading poetic tendencies and movements. The fact that the changing status of the poet and poetry, the changing attitude of the public, and the changing set of conditions under which the poet writes seemed to have a prior importance is significant in itself. It indicates how profound these changes are or may be in the future. It is also significant of the fact that there are no new poetic movements and schools as clearly defined and as strong as Imagism and the free verse movement of some forty years ago or the powerful emergence of social consciousness during the years of the depression. Indeed the very poets who first became famous as advocates of political and social revolution—for example, Auden, Spender, and C. Day Lewis— have for the past decade and more written poetry which seems so unrelated to the subject matter of their early work that no reader who knew only their later work would suspect that in their early work they called for the death of the old gang, and for the working class revolution, attacked capitalism, fascism, and war, and dismissed all other themes as unimportant. The theme of political revolution has vanished as if it had never been a preoccupation excluding all other themes. But another revolution which began before the social and economic crisis of the depression, has continued all the while: I mean the poetic revolution, the revolution in poetic taste which was inspired by the criticism of T. S. Eliot. This revolution has established itself in power so completely that it is taken for granted not only in poetry and the criticism of poetry, but in the teaching of literature.

Once a literary and poetic revolution has established itself, it is no longer revolutionary, but something very different from what it was when it had to struggle for recognition and assert itself against the opposition of established literary authority. Thus the most striking trait of the poetry of the rising generation of poets is the assumption as self-evident and incontestable that conception of the nature of poetry which was, at its inception and for years after, a radical and much disputed transformation of poetic taste and sensibility. What was once a battlefield has become a peaceful public park on a pleasant summer Sunday afternoon, so that if the majority of new poets write in a style and idiom which takes as its starting point the poetic idiom and literary taste of the generation of Pound and Eliot, the motives and attitudes at the heart of the writing possess an assurance which sometimes makes their work seem tame and sedate.

Before saying something more detailed about the character of the poetry of the majority of new poets, some attention must be given to the only recent new movement and counter-tendency, that of the San Francisco circle of poets who, under the leadership of Kenneth Rexroth, have recently proclaimed themselves super-Bohemians and leaders of a new poetic revolution. According to Mr. Rexroth, the new rebels are rebelling against "the highly organized academic and literary movement employment agency of the Neoantireconstructionists," the established poets and critics who are installed in the universities, and who form, he says, "a dense crust of custom over American cultural life." Since these poets recite their poems in bars and with jazz accompanists, and since one poet aptly calls his book of poems, "Howl," it is appropriate to refer to them as the Howlers of San Francisco as a way of labelling their leading theme, the conviction that they must scream against the conformism which prevails in society and in literary circles. The San Francisco Howlers are, however, imaginary rebels since the substance of their work is a violent advocacy of a nonconformism which they already possess and which requires no insurrection whatever, since nonconformism of almost every variety had become acceptable and respectable and available to everyone. Unlike the Bohemianism of the past, which had to attack the dominant Puritanism and Victorianism of respectable society in a variety of forms, including the censorship of books, Prohibition, and a prudery enforced by the police, the new nonconformism has no genuine enemy: it is unopposed and permitted to exist in freedom, hence the new rebel bears a great deal of resemblance to a prize fighter trying to knock out an antagonist who is not in the ring with him. The essential conviction of the San Francisco Howlers is that they are fighting the conformism of the organization man, the advertising executive, the man in the grey flannel suit, or the man in the Brooks Bros. suit. The rebellion is a form of shadow boxing because the Man in the Brooks Bros. suit is himself, in his own home, very often what Russell Lynes has called an upper Bohemian. His conformism is limited to the office day and business hours: in private life—and at heart —he is as Bohemian as anyone else. And it is often true indeed that the purpose of the job which requires conformism is solely to support his personal idiosyncrasies, tastes and inclinations. Even if this were not true, the fact remains that the nonconformism proclaimed by the new rebels is not prohibited, proscribed, regarded as immoral and anti-social by the community as a whole, and no social pressure exists to compel the nonconformist to wear a grey flannel suit instead of a turtleneck sweater, slacks, and a sport jacket. The new rebel is fighting for what he has already won and fighting against a threat which does not exist, since he does not want a grey flannel suit, he is not forced to wear one, he need not compromise or conceal his Bohemianism in any respect, he is free to dress as he pleases and behave as he feels like behaving without being guilty of disorderly conduct, vagrancy, or even eccentricity.

The extent to which the San Francisco Howlers are engaged in an imaginary rebellion becomes entirely clear when Mr. Rexroth's statements take on a political and global character, attempting to connect literary tendencies in America with Russian totalitarianism in Europe. Outside of San Francisco, Mr. Rexroth declares, there is only fear and despair: "Poets are coming to San Francisco," he adds, "for the same reasons that so many Hungarians have been going to Austria recently." This is enough to make one feel that Mr. Rexroth does not recognize the difference between the Red Army and the *Kenyon Review* critics, between Nikita Khrushchev and John Crowe Ransom, or between the political commissars of a police state and the tyrants who write advertising copy on Madison Avenue.

Ludicrous as this attitude is, it does nevertheless point to one significant way in which the international state of affairs has had a serious and adverse effect upon creative writing in America. The leading motive of classical American literature and of twentieth-century writing has been a criticism of American life. Sometimes the criticism has had a native basis: the actuality of American life has been criticized from the exalted point of view of the American Dream. And sometimes, in expatriate writers like Henry James and T. S. Eliot, the actuality of American life has been criticized by being compared with the culture of the Old World. But since the Second World War and the beginning of the atomic age, the consciousness of the creative writer, however detached, has been confronted with the spectre of the totalitarian state, the growing poverty and helplessness of Western Europe, and the threat of an inconceivably destructive war which may annihilate civilization and mankind itself. Clearly when the future of civilization is no longer assured, a criticism of American life in terms of a contrast between avowed ideals and present actuality cannot be a primary preoccupation and source of inspiration. For America, not Europe, is now the sanctuary of culture; civilization's very existence depends upon America, upon the actuality of American life, and not the ideals of the American Dream. To criticize the actuality upon which all hope depends thus becomes a criticism of hope itself. No matter what may be wrong with American life, it is nothing compared to the police state, barbarism, and annihilation.

This may be the most important cause of the tameness and the constrained calm which shows itself very often in the writing of the new generation of poets. An anthology of the work of new poets which has recently appeared and which is called the *New Poets of England and America* represents the character of their work as a whole very well. The editors say in their introduction: "What characteristics are to be discovered in the poetry of this generation, we leave the reader to discover." This statement is very revealing precisely because it is so different from the positive assertions, unquestioned convictions and intense rejections which have, in the past, marked the emergence of a strong poetic movement, school, or tendency.

The editors of this new anthology have restricted their selections to the work of poets under forty, who receive the blessing, in the form of an introduction, of Robert Frost, a very great poet indeed, and one who is now over eighty. Mr. Frost, unlike the editors, finds some positive generalization possible about the present state of poetry. The selections are gratifying evidence, Mr. Frost says, that "school and poetry come near to being the same thing." And he concludes by saying that as a result of the number of poets who have become teachers, "in a thousand, two thousand colleges," we now have "the best audiences poetry ever had in this world."

The characteristics which these new poets tend to have in common are matters of both style and subject matter. Most of these new poets have mastered poetic form and technique to a degree superior, on the whole, to that of any past generation. Until the generation of Pound and Eliot, American poets were for the most part inspired amateurs, and when deserted by inspiration, the habits of versification which they had acquired intuitively or through reading were too erratic to prevent them from writing verse which was painfully slipshod and uneven. The new generation of poets possesses a trained and conscious skill, a sophisticated mastery of the craft of versification. And this professional competence may be strengthened by the disciplined knowledge of literary form which the teacher of literature must have.

The subject matter of these new poets is also revealing. One poem is about a toothache; and one poem is about a vacuum cleaner; and in general, the objects and experiences of daily life, which in previous generations were either supposed to be outside the realm of poetry or were introduced into poetry with a conscious daring and defiance, now appear in poem after poem in the most matter-of-fact way, as if their poetic quality had never been denied, questioned, or regarded as outrageous. In a like way, there is an explicitness about sexual experience without the self-consciousness or the assertive Bohemianism which characterized the poetry written during the first postwar period.

258

The perspectives which the generation of Pound and Eliot had to discover are now taken for granted: there is a clear and explicit consciousness of the international span of experience, and a pan-historical sense of culture, art, and literature which did not and indeed could not exist in the past. The subject matter of a good many poems is based upon travel in Europe, but these poets view Europe in a very different light than that of the poets of the past. Writers like Henry James and T. S. Eliot went to Europe with a Baedeker. Writers of the generation of Ernest Hemingway and E. E. Cummings went to Europe to drive an ambulance. The new poets often consult a Baedeker, but at the same time their awareness of the international scene is such as to make them ready to drop their Baedekers at any moment and seek out an ambulance, or at least transatlantic plane reservations to bring them back to America. Thus their point of view, in general, is that of the international tourist who, as an American, regards himself as an innocent bystander in a world in which an innocent bystander is continually faced by overwhelming and inexhaustible threat: in fact, there is often a feeling that to be an innocent bystander is in itself one form of guilt. The consciousness that experience is international, pan-historical, and multi-lingual is explicit and intense to a greater degree than ever before. Hence it can be said that for the poet today, English literature no longer exists as an independent entity. Whether the poet is reading, writing or teaching, the text is a text in comparative literature. This is a very great change indeed.

I can best summarize all that I have said so far about the present state of poetry by quoting two very different poems. One is one of Robert Frost's best and best-known lyrics; the other is by W. D. Snodgrass, a poet whose work I know only through the selections in *New Poets of England and America*. The two poems are hardly comparable in poetic value, but they are worth reading for the sake of the contrast between them, a contrast which epitomizes the changes which have occurred to make the state of poetry in the middle of the twentieth century very different from what it was during the first decade of the twentieth century.

Stopping by Woods on a Snowy Evening*

Whose woods these are I think I know.
His house is in the village though;
He will not see me stopping here
To watch his woods fill up with snow.

---

* From THE POETRY OF ROBERT FROST edited by Edward Connery Lathem. Copyright 1923, © 1969 by Holt, Rinehart and Winston, Inc. Copyright 1951 by Robert Frost. Reprinted by permission of Holt, Rinehart and Winston, Inc.

My little horse must think it queer
To stop without a farmhouse near
Between the woods and frozen lake
The darkest evening of the year.

He gives his harness bells a shake
To ask if there is some mistake.
The only other sound's the sweep
Of easy wind and downy flake.

The woods are lovely, dark, and deep,
But I have promises to keep,
And miles to go before I sleep,
And miles to go before I sleep.

April Inventory‡

The green catalpa tree has turned
All white; the cherry blooms once more.
In one whole year I haven't learned
A blessed thing they pay you for.

* * *

The trees have more than I to spare.
The sleek expensive girls I teach
Younger and pinker every year,
Bloom gradually out of reach.
The pear-tree lets its petals drop
Like dandruff on a tabletop.

* * *

The tenth time, just a year ago,
I made myself a little list
Of all the things I ought to know;
Then told my parents, analyst,
And everyone who's trusted me
I'd be substantial, presently.
I haven't read one book about
A book or memorized a plot.
Or found a date I didn't doubt.
I learned one date and then forgot.

And one by one the solid scholars
Get the degrees, the jobs, the dollars.
And smile above their starchy collars.
I taught my classes Whitehead's notions;
One lovely girl, a song of Mahler's,
Lacking a source-book or promotions,
I showed one child the colors of
The lunar moth and how to love.

* * *

Though trees turn bare and girls turn wives,
We shall afford our costly seasons;
There is a gentleness survives
That will outspeak and has its reasons.
There is a loveliness exists,
Preserves us.   Not for specialists.

The Two Knowledges:
An Essay on a Certain Resistance

John Hall Wheelock*

Presented at the Library of Congress January 27, 1958

THIS PAPER has been titled "The Two Knowledges: An Essay on a Certain Resistance." It is concerned, chiefly, with lyric poetry. What it has to say is not new; it is, in fact, elementary, but perhaps it may yield us a fresh interpretation of old truths about the poetry of our time, or even about poetry in general, by the application to them of a new formula, a new metaphor, much after the method of science and of poetry itself.

The distinction between the function of the scientist and the function of the poet has always been difficult to define and never more so than today when the concepts arrived at by the inspired suppositions of science, and proved valid by later painstaking investigation, rival in beauty and imaginative insight the creations of poetry. The difference in the nature of the two disciplines or modes of knowledge is so obvious to common sense as to make discussion of it seem absurd. To put this very obvious difference into words, however, is another matter.

The poet, you may say, is concerned with the concrete. In the particular he uncovers the universal. True—yet here his activity parallels that of the scientist, who from specific events deduces his general laws. The poet, you may then counter, has always been aware of the things that lie beyond sense-perception, and is concerned with them. True again—but "in the past fifty years, under the impulse given by Einstein and Rutherford, science has increasingly turned towards phenomena that lie beyond sense-percep-

---

*The author takes pleasure in acknowledging a debt of gratitude to Mr. Charles Scribner, Jr., for extremely helpful suggestions and encouragement in connection with the writing of this paper.

tion."† Well, you reply, somewhat more confidently now perhaps, how about the early stages of poetic composition? Are not "the initial intuition, the period of careful spade-work, of testing and rejection, the state of 'watchful passivity', and the imaginative leap that may come when least expected," * are not these the stages of an experience peculiar to the poet? No—the scientist grappling with his problem is familiar with all of them.

It was Coleridge, you will remember, who defined beauty as "unity in variety." We have the word of a scientist* for it that "science is nothing else than the search to discover unity in the wild variety of nature." "All science," he says, "is the search for unity in hidden likenesses. . . . The scientist looks for order in the appearances of nature by exploring such likenesses. For order does not display itself of itself; if it can be said to be there at all, it is not there for the mere looking . . . order must be discovered and, in a deep sense, it must be created. What we see, as we see it, is mere disorder." Might not this be the voice of a poet describing his own quest? Are we, then, obliged to agree with the conclusions of our authority, when he says: "The discoveries of science, the works of art are explorations—more, they are explosions of a hidden likeness. . . . This is the act of creation, in which an original thought is born, and it is the same act in original science and original art. . . . We re-make nature by the act of discovery, in the poem or in the theorem."?

We haven't got very far, it seems, in our effort to define the distinction between the function of the poet and the function of the scientist! Both appear to be bent on the same errand; to arrive at their goals by much the same road; as poet and as scientist, to explore the same universe. Or do they? In the answer to this question we shall find, perhaps, the solution to our problem.

The universe may be conceived as divided into two parts. There is the outer, objective universe of so-called reality, the quantitative, measurable complex of mass-energy in space-time; and there is the equally real inner, subjective universe, the qualitative, undimensional complex of spirit, of feeling, of experience, which is an image of the objective universe as it is reflected in every consciousness. The inner universe is a part of, and is contained within, the outer structural universe, which, so to speak, over-arches and is mirrored in it, as the sky, with its stars, is mirrored in a lake. But here the analogy ends. Mirrored in consciousness, in the world of spirit, the objective universe is, as by a creative fusion, transfigured. It

---

†The quotations in this paragraph are from *The Times Literary Supplement,* April 12, 1957.
 * J. Bronowski: SCIENCE AND HUMAN VALUES. Reprinted by permission of Julian Messner, A Division of Simon & Schuster, Inc. © 1956, 1965 by J. Bronowski.

263

becomes other than it was. A qualitative dimension is added. What was matter revolving through space and time becomes a star. Beauty and meaning have been added. In a deeper sense, then, the inner universe includes and completes the outer structure within which, paradoxically, it is contained.

It is this inner, subjective universe which the poet and every other artist explores. The objective structural order is the field in which the scientist conducts his explorations. As a man, he shares with the poet the world of feeling, the world of experience, but in his explorations as a scientist he is obliged to exile himself from that world and to become, for the time being, at least, a citizen of the objective universe. He must divest himself of feeling. He must try to get at reality as it is before it is mirrored in consciousness; before the world of the senses and of emotion has transfigured it; before refraction, as it were, has altered perspective. The knowledge which he wrings from that objective universe, by means of imaginative suppositions and rational disciplines, can then be brought back into the subjective order and, there transvalued, find expression in that other kind of knowledge we call poetry.

In this way the two disciplines will be mutually fructifying, the one yielding data and a special form of knowledge to the other, which, in turn, may imbue those data and that knowledge with the qualitative values inherent in feeling and the subjective process. The poem, the work of art, is also a way of knowing, but it is another way and has reference to another world, the inner world of experience, as opposed to the purely objective universe, though it can assimilate, and mould to its own purposes, the knowledge brought over from that other realm.

There are, of course, peripheral areas in which poetry and science merge—in which the two worlds explored respectively by each are merged. When we step outside the physical sciences we shall find examples of these. Psychology, for instance, is a science which definitely has reference to the inner world of experience. The psychology of Freud, of Jung, of Rank, is, in its basis, a kind of poetry. Here, though the method and aim are those of science, the world explored is the world to which poetry, and every other art, has reference. But in trying to establish a clearcut general distinction it is not possible to cover these special cases.

The difference between the two worlds explored, the one by the poet, the other by the scientist, can best be illustrated by examples of the findings reported by each. Let us take a poem by Thomas Hardy called "Waiting Both": *

---

* From Collected Poems by Thomas Hardy. Copyright 1925 by The Macmillan Company, renewed 1953 by Lloyds Bank, Ltd. Reprinted by courtesy of The Macmillan Company.

264

A star looks down at me,
And says: "Here I and you
Stand, each in our degree.
What do you mean to do,—
    Mean to do?"

I say: "For all I know,
Wait, and let Time go by,
Till my change come."—"Just so,"
The star says: "So mean I—
    So mean I."

Here, in ten brief lines containing only one word of more than a syllable, we are given a glimpse of the universal order. That order is inexorable. As Whitehead has said, "The laws of physics are the decrees of fate."* The introduction, into the poem, of a subjective element, of a human consciousness, as one of the items involved in this inflexible order, and its juxtaposition to an object as vast, as far away and as different as a star, dramatizes the universality of the law. The dialogue between subject and object, between man and star, is admirably adapted to rendering concrete what is abstract, while the reiteration in the last line of each stanza conveys, with its echolalia, a tragic sense of distance, of impersonality, of passive, helpless acceptance. Even the inversion of the usual order, in "I and you," which might be thought to have been forced by the rhyme-scheme, seems, in the context, intentional and right. The inversion gives emphasis to each pronoun, where the normal order would have been banal. In this short poem, we do not merely comprehend, we experience vicariously, through the medium of feeling, rhythm, cadence, rhyme, and all the devices of art, a knowledge, a flash of a universal truth.

Now let us take the statement of a scientist. Newton's first law of motion reads: "Every body continues in its state of rest, or of uniform motion in a straight line, except so far as it may be compelled by force to change that state." Here the substance of the knowledge or truth experienced in Hardy's poem is conveyed in factual terms and thereby made available to the intellect as a practical working formula. In these terms it *is* not, and for these purposes it *need* not, be experienced, as is the case in the poem. Hardy, in his lyric, and Newton, in his law, are dealing with the same truth. The two examples quoted represent two different disciplines, two different kinds of knowledge, acquired by the exploration of two different aspects of the universe.

---

*Alfred North Whitehead, *Science and the Modern World*, the Macmillan Company, 1925.

It is not necessary to labor the point.   Other examples, from the expressions of poets and scientists, illustrating the distinction between the kind of knowledge that the poet and the kind of knowledge that the scientist brings over, will occur to all of you:

> . . . thou canst not stir a flower
> Without troubling of a star†

for instance, makes concrete, gives us in terms of feeling, the human sense of two of the basic tenets of science, the laws of the conservation of matter and of the conservation of energy.   Every act, every event, no matter how trivial, affects the entire cosmos.   These tenets have, since, been incorporated into, and reaffirmed by, a broader and more basic concept, the potential equivalence of matter and energy.   In this connection, note how deliberately purified of those elements which have the qualitative, emotional connotations capable of arousing in us a sense of vicarious experience is Einstein's famous expression, $E=mc^2$, deduced in 1905 as one of the first fruits of his amazingly heuristic Relativity Theory.   In that expression an equation takes the place of language, to announce that measurements of inertia and energy can be calculated from one another by a simple conversion of the units involved, and to suggest, as has since been abundantly demonstrated, that what we call matter and energy are mutually transformable physical states.   Matter is energy, energy is matter—one is inevitably reminded of Keats' "Beauty is truth, truth beauty," an assertion certainly less verifiable and which has had fewer consequences for the world.

The knowledge of the objective universe that the scientist claims to have brought back with him from his explorations—whether as the result of a hypothesis, or of deduction from known facts, or of a new combination of such facts—can be tested empirically and, if proven valid, becomes a truth until such time as further knowledge calls for further adjustment and modification.   What the poet feels he has discovered and made available in the process of his poem must stand the test of another kind of verification.   The knowledge he claims to have revealed is a knowledge of the subjective universe of emotion and experience, and the touchstone here is the human spirit inhabiting that universe.   To meet the test, to find acceptance as true knowledge, a poem must win the acquiescence in it of another mind.   This is no easy matter.   Reality so far transcends anything we can say about it as to make silence, for the most part, preferable. Silence says it better. Words too often violate the innocent nobility of things. Where our deepest feelings are concerned, only the spokesman supremely qualified will be tolerated. The statements of science, once checked with observable phenomena and

---

†From "The Mistress of Vision," by Francis Thompson.

266

found to embody true knowledge, are accepted as such and soon taken for granted. They are, moreover, as already remarked, subject to constant change as fresh findings make it necessary to amend or revise them. Not so the discoveries of the poet. These reach to the permanent heart of experience. They represent, always, a fresh revelation of an old, perhaps a forgotten, knowledge. We are not, ordinarily, receptive to having such a knowledge revived in us.

This brings us to our main theme, a certain deep, instinctive, natural resistance to poetry. This resistance may manifest itself in one of several reactions: indifference, embarrassment, ridicule, or acute aversion. Marianne Moore indicates that she sympathizes with the last of these when she says, in her poem entitled "Poetry", "I, too, dislike it: there are things that are important beyond all this fiddle," and Nietzsche, himself a poet in the larger sense of the word, registers that same natural resistance, in the form of combined ridicule and contempt, when he is moved to cry out, "The poets? The poets lie too much." Plato, who held that they should be banished altogether from his ideal republic, might, perhaps, have agreed with him. And how many a schoolboy would agree with Plato! How many a grown man or woman has experienced, in the presence of poetry, sensations ranging from a mild embarrassment to an acute distaste!

The kind of knowledge a poem offers us is a renewed awareness, a vicarious re-experience of the world in all its sensory and emotional impact. This awareness is lost to us, for the greater part of the time, in the act of living. In a sense, this lack of awareness may be a safeguard or even an unconscious self-protection. As Mr. Eliot has told us, "human kind/ Cannot bear much reality." Feeling, coiled in us like the spring of a watch, may find release only through the gradual, controlled unwinding of the years. To be fully conscious, except very occasionally, of the beauty, sadness, horror and mystery of the human condition would be more than the human spirit could endure.

Over our potential responses, our deeply buried emotions, a normal resistance stands guard. A native wariness, an instinctive reticence, bulwark us against the onslaughts of the poet. But these defenses are like the sonic barrier: the poet whose energy and craft enable him to break through them will meet with no further obstruction. Renewed awareness, the re-experience of carefully forgotten reality, that a poem awakens is, after all, once it has been achieved for us, a great good. A heightening and widening of consciousness then takes place, affording insights and exaltations which do not persist and cannot, perhaps, even be recalled during the lower, more comfortable moments of life. Wasn't it Aldous Huxley who said of one of his characters that he believed in God, but only while the violins were playing, and who is there who hasn't suffered diminishment on leaving the concert hall and finding himself once more in the noisy city street? He has been breathing another air, and is now "rejected into the world again." The point is that, as animals, we are anchored to this world by innumerable necessities, and our mistrust of that other realm of intensified feeling, insight, and realization, which, at best, we can inhabit only momentarily, is instinctive and perhaps wholesome. It can be overcome by those few only who command the appropriate skills and strategies.

What, then, are some of the more obvious strategies a poet must use if he is to overcome our natural resistance to the knowledge he has rediscovered and desires to share? How is he to induce in another consciousness "that willing suspension of disbelief" which Coleridge felt it was the first task of the poet to bring about in his reader? Certainly the so-called "inspired," unselfcritical poet, like the exuberant, unselfcritical acquaintance who hails you in the street and wants to tell you all about it, is merely a bore. In the making of a poem the creative impulse and the critical faculty must contend with each other. If the impulse is not strong enough and resourceful enough to prevail, there will be no poem; if the critical faculty is lacking or not sufficiently active, the poem that may result will be fatuous. Its claim on us as knowledge will be false, it will not tally with experience, it will not be able to disarm our resistance to it.

He who would win our suffrage must be self-critical. The normal human reticences, the normal resistance to the kind of knowledge recovered by poetry, the kind of awareness it arouses, will first be encountered, and dealt with, by a true poet, in himself. In him, of all men, that resistance will be strongest. Indeed, his place in the hierarchy might almost be determined by the strength of that resistance and, therefore, the corresponding strength of the impulse and the resourcefulness of the skills required to overcome it—first, in the poet himself, and, later, in others. For by overcoming it in himself, he has, in advance, as it were, overcome it in others also.

The strategies whereby the poet is enabled to outwit our natural resistance to poetry are many and various. Some of them are directed towards arousing us from an inborn, self-protective apathy, others towards lulling our active aversion, registered in embarrassment or ridicule, to anything which tries to shock us out of the sleep of action, the sleep of daily living, into a painful, if exalted, realization of the act of living and of life itself. The strategies in the first category might be subsumed under the general heading of the oblique approach.

Our natural, and probably wholesome, apathy is a deep and stubborn thing. The almost intentional lack of response we so often exhibit finds sardonic voice in a stanza from a bit of light verse by Franklin P. Adams:*

---

*From "Poetry and Thoughts on Same" in *So There!* by Franklin P. Adams, copyright 1923 by Doubleday and Company, Inc. Reprinted by permission.

> I see the business office
> And I see the floor above it.
> I see and hear a lot of things.
> Suppose I do.   What of it?

This normal, self-protective indifference is not easily overcome.   To try to overwhelm us by frontal attack, by putting things down "in so many words," as we say, will not avail.   If we are to have our eyes opened to a knowledge, if we are to be forced into renewed experience, we shall have to be tricked and startled out of our apathy.   The trope or metaphor, the simplest and commonest strategic device in the arsenal of poetry, does just this.   By discovering hidden likenesses or analogies in things, the poem surprises us, wrenches us, if you will, into renewed awareness of them.

All words are, of course, symbols.   Many of them, and particularly compound words, were originally metaphors.   But they have become worn with use.   Fresh metaphors, compounded of a number of words in new relationships, are needed.   The word "whitecaps", for instance, denoting the foam scuffed up by wind in its passage over water, has lost, because of familiarity, its original metaphoric force, but when Swinburne describes whitecaps as ". . . where the wind's feet shine along the sea," they are not merely identified, they are experienced once more.   Such lines or phrases as "Time is a harper who plays until you fall asleep," "Among the guests star-scattered on the grass," ". . . not even the rain has such small hands," ". . . hung like those top jewels of the night" achieve this immediacy by use of the same device.

Sometimes a metaphor or simile will occur in the midst of, or toward the close of, a poem so casually and unobtrusively as to seem almost accidental and yet will instantly cause everything that has gone before and that comes after it to fall into place.   The knowledge rediscovered by the poem is, in that instant, by that simile, as blindingly revealed as a familiar landscape by a flash of lightning.   This can be observed in a poem by Léonie Adams called "Song from a Country Fair."   The poem describes a country dance, attended by the village folk, both old and young.   We hear the fiddles and watch the older couples step out gaily and half-humorously to the music. The young people, whose eagerness and intensity of feeling cause them to hang back in shyness, do not participate.   Then, in the last two lines, we have the simile which suddenly illumines all:

> The heart is not so light at first
> But heavy like a bough in spring.

An old knowledge, a familiar but probably forgotten knowledge, that it is those who are most concerned and who care most—in this instance, the young—who can least participate and who will appear to care least, while

269

those who are less involved and who care less—in this instance, the old—can take part more fully and with an apparent easy abandon, this is the knowledge we re-experience in the poem, and the flash of illumination afforded by the simile is what has made that re-experience possible. No amount of exposition or direct statement could so completely have achieved it.

Again, under the general heading of the oblique approach, we might include the single miraculously right word in its divinely appointed place. Ezra Pound's "Envoi" concludes, as you will recall, with the lines:

> When our two dusts with Waller's shall be laid,
> Siftings on siftings in oblivion,
> Till change has broken down
> All things save beauty alone.

It is not difficult to put one's finger on the word which here does the work of ten. "Siftings" turns the bare statement of the line above it into full realization. Santayana, in almost the last poem he wrote, "The Poet's Testament," performs a similar miracle. The use of the word "furrow," in the context of the following lines, would mark any writer as a poet:

> I give back to the earth what the earth gave,
> All to the furrow, nothing to the grave.

An example equally outstanding is Yeats' phrase, ". . . meagre girlhood's putting on/ Burdensome beauty . . ." where the word "burdensome," in one stroke, not only brings the whole picture alive and sums up, for all time, the transition from girlhood to young womanhood, but comments on it as well. "Burdensome," here, is ambiguous; it conveys by connotation and implication meanings some of which it would be awkward to express directly.

Another device which falls within the category of the oblique approach is the use of narrative or drama, complete in itself on one level but employed to symbolize something not explicit which is, nevertheless, on another level, the poem's true concern. The entire poem, then, might be said to be a single complex metaphor. By means of this, the poet is enabled to slip over, unbeknownst as it were, on the wary reader, the knowledge he has rediscovered. If, as Mr. Eliot has written, "the chief use of the meaning of a poem, in the ordinary sense, [and here he is careful to state that he is speaking of some kinds of poetry and not all] may be to satisfy one habit of the reader, to keep his mind diverted and quiet, while the poem does its work upon him: much as the imaginary burglar is always provided with a bit of nice meat for the house-dog," then we may compare the device we have been discussing to the ladder which makes it possible for that burglar,

270

if he is a second-story man, to gain entrance to the house while its owner is busy, in his downstairs study, paying the monthly bills.

The poetry of all periods offers notable instances of the use of this device. The dialogue between poet and raven, in Poe's perhaps rather too well-known poem; the ancient mariner and his account of his voyage, in Coleridge's famous ballad; the Brooklyn Bridge, in Hart Crane's lyrical epic of America: these give us this method at work. The true concern of each of these poems, the knowledge they represent and indirectly bring through, is something other than their surfaces indicate. At the same time that these surfaces are engaging our attention, their underlying power as metaphors, as symbols, is communicating, almost unconsciously, to those capable of receiving it, the actual substance of the poem.

A well-known example of fairly recent origin, "The Listeners," by Walter de la Mare, illustrates the functioning of this device, but, in this case, there is added an element of ambiguity, which enhances its effect. The narrative episode that constitutes the symbolism of the poem is, you will recall, as simple as it is subtle and strange. A horseman, who is referred to as "the Traveler," knocks on the moonlit door of a house somewhere in a forest. There is no sound from within and the door is not opened. He knocks again, harder this time, and shouts, "Is there anybody there?". There is no answer, but in the silence that follows, the Traveler senses, in the house, the presence of listeners—their stillness is the only response they make to his question. Suddenly, he knocks on the door a third time, even harder than before, and cries out, "Tell them I came, and no one answered, that I kept my word." Again, there is no reply. No sound, until the silence is interrupted, for a moment, by the beat of plunging hoofs, growing fainter and fainter, as horse and rider gallop away. This, we are given to understand, and every word the Traveler had said, was heard by the listeners in the moonlit house:

> Aye, they heard his foot upon the stirrup,
>   And the sound of iron on stone,
> And how the silence surged softly backward,
>   When the plunging hoofs were gone.

The narrative suspense of the above brief episode, self-sufficient and fully achieved as an account of an action and its dénouement, holds us so completely that the poem, in the meantime, is able to arouse in us a consciousness of the deeper thing it was intended to convey. That thing is a knowledge of, an awareness of, mystery. It is peculiarly fitting, therefore, that what the narrative symbolizes should itself remain a riddle, a mystery. Is the Traveler who knocks on the door a symbol of perplexed humanity, with its stubborn questioning, its probing of the atom and the cell, its knocking on every gate and every door, sensing, behind the façade of appearance, presences, powers there, which could give us the answer if they but would? Does not the cry, before departure, "Tell them I came, and no one answered, that I kept my word," sum up that human quest and its frustration? Or is the confrontation of the Traveler with the listeners the old confrontation of the living with the dead, the bafflement before the inscrutable division that has been made of us into two societies no longer on speaking terms with one another? Many interpretations can be put upon the story that the poem tells, and all of them are somehow merged and blended in the awareness it awakens in us. Like the mystery of which the poem gives us an inkling, the ambiguity of its symbolization—an ambiguity that will not fit into any one of Mr. Empson's categories—teases us out of thought.

A similar use of narrative employed to communicate obliquely the true essence of a poem will be found in Vachel Lindsay's "The Chinese Nightingale." We have here, ostensibly, a story about a Chinese laundryman, Chang by name, who is discovered, late one night, at his work. The background could not well be more drab or the central figure more commonplace. As the night wears on, the barrier between the reality of the workaday world and the reality of an ancient, now only to be imagined, world of the greatest charm and distinction falls away. The tiny laundry widens into the kingdom of pre-Confucian China. The joss in the corner comes alive, and a small gray bird, a nightingale, perches on his wrist and begins to sing. The Chinese princess now appears who, in some previous incarnation, had been the belovèd of Chang, in those days a king, and there is dialogue in which the joss, the nightingale, and the princess take part. Chang, the laundryman, alone is silent, ironing away. The contrast between Chang's former glory, as related by the princess, and his present fallen state, and between the image of a long since vanished civilization, perhaps the noblest and wisest the world has known, and the tawdry interior of a Chinese laundry on a San Francisco street, brings into juxtaposition two worlds and gives one a sense of the equal evanescence of both. The nightingale serves as chorus to the drama. So much for the device used. What it actually brings over, so subtly and insinuatingly as to take the reader quite off his guard, is the poem's essence. By use of this device the poet reawakens in us, while we are absorbed in the drama and the story, an old knowledge: the perpetual recurrence of feeling, of love and sorrow, of glory and heartbreak; the persistent continuation of life, for better, for worse, amid the tragic flux:

> "One thing I remember:
> Spring came on forever,

Spring came on forever,"
Said the Chinese nightingale.

All these are ways of suggesting things without saying them in so many words—examples of the strategy of the oblique approach, whereby the poet surprises us into attention, beguiles us out of our natural apathy. There are strategies, also, for circumventing our active resistance to poetry. As this resistance differs between individual and individual, so it differs between race and race. There has been less resistance to poetry among the Latins than among the Anglo-Saxons, among certain Eastern peoples than among those of the West. The character of this resistance, too, varies, from period to period. Every age reveals the resistances peculiar to it, but all of them are, fundamentally, symptoms of the same thing, different expressions of the one deep instinctive resistance which is the theme of this paper.

It is difficult for those living in one period to think or feel themselves into the state of mind of another time. States of mind are, very largely, dependent upon conditions in the world in which we live. These are constantly changing and, with them, the values we assign them. The associational values of words, the auras surrounding them, undergo change. For the youth of today, the primary associative values of many words are quite different from what they were for the youth of fifty years ago. There is point to the account—and it describes an actual recent episode—of the boy whose Sunday school teacher had asked him to bring in, at their next meeting, a drawing that should illustrate one of the Bible stories they had been studying. The drawing the boy produced the following Sunday was a picture of a Packard limousine, with a tall man at the wheel and a small couple sitting in the back seat. "Jimmy, what Bible story does this illustrate?" his teacher asked him, and Jimmy replied, "Why, that's the Lord God driving Adam and Eve out of the Garden of Eden." The primary association that the word "drive" and the phrase "drive out" have for the rising generation is obvious.

Changes in the world we live in and, consequently, in our states of mind, have proceeded at a faster rate during the past fifty years than, perhaps, in any other half century. This has been reflected in poetry. It is a far cry from the poetry of Swinburne—words seemed fairly to boil out of him—to the spare, precise, somewhat dry and unemotional use of words as practiced by the Imagist school of poets who flourished, here and in England, some forty years ago. The state of mind their work embodies has since been superseded but, on the whole, until quite recently, the character of the resistance to poetry, as revealed in the work of the past fifty years, has remained fairly constant.

The particular elements or qualities in a poem which have aroused, in the mind of our time, the natural resistance we have been talking about might be listed as: emotion directly expressed and the romantic in general, the explicitly personal note, elevation of tone or style, effects whose purpose is aural delight—as richness of verbal texture, intricacy of form, incantatory magic—and what, for lack of a better term, might be called synthesis, the subduing of parts to a whole.   Resistance to emotion directly expressed and to the romantic is often circumvented by wit and by devices of tone: irony, indifference, self-mockery, toughness, and so on.   Personal themes and lyricism in the first person singular are usually avoided.   The language employed is the language of every-day speech, colloquial, even conversational. Resistance to the element of aural delight makes itself felt in the use of dissonance, bare statement, deliberately awkward run-overs, deliberately imperfect form and flawed meter, flat cadence, false rhyme, etc.   The poem is likely to confine itself to accurate minute observation of particulars without the coördination that would give the whole thing meaning beyond that of any of its parts.

These generalizations, like most generalizations, state the case very loosely and clumsily.   The instant they are made, exceptions leap to mind: the sonorous incantations of Dylan Thomas, a poet whose work, by its very nature, does not answer to any of the descriptions just given; the "Kubla Khan"-like magic of Wallace Stevens' "Sunday Afternoon," with its Renoir-esque mis-en-scène and richly colorful verbal texture; the aural beauty of T. S. Eliot's austere cadences and haunting repetitions and returns in such poems as "Ash Wednesday" and "Four Quartets."   This poet, in whom the resistances characteristic of the period must have been very strong, was able, by virtue of a poetic impulse still stronger, to devise a poetry which outwitted these resistances and thus fulfilled the requirements of thousands of readers in whom, since they were his contemporaries, the same resistances were to be found.

Mr. Eliot introduced into English poetry a new way of doing things and, from the first, his manner has remained substantially the same.   Yeats, on the other hand, offers us the example of a poet whose work, begun in an earlier period and expressive of that period but carried on through a time of transition and into our own day, responded to the changes that came about in the nature of our resistances to poetry as rapidly as these changes, quite unconsciously, took place in himself.   The poet of the Celtic twilight, the poet of the early romantic, rhetorical poems of love and of Celtic mythology, is barely recognizable in the robust, sometimes savage, realist of the superb later work, the author of such poems as "In Memory of Major Robert Gregory" and "Sailing to Byzantium".*   The latter may serve to

*From the *Collected Poems* of William Butler Yeats copyright, 1903, 1904, 1906, 1907, 1908, 1912, 1916, 1918, 1919, 1924, 1925, 1928, 1931, and 1933, by the Macmillan Company. Reprinted by courtesy of the Macmillan Company.

illustrate some of the strategies used by a great poet in dealing with certain contemporary resistances.

The symbolism of "Sailing to Byzantium" is defined in the title—a voyage of escape from the temporal world, the world of nature, to the eternal world of art and of the intellect. This symbolism, and the ritualistic formality and ceremony of the poem's organization, are an ingenious device for circumventing our natural resistance to the unabashed revelation which is the poem's truth: an old man's rage and dismay at the process of physical deterioration, the longing of age, and specifically of the aging artist, to escape from a temporal, disintegrating form into an eternal, unchanging one—into an art form, as Beethoven could be said to have escaped from his body into the symphonies.

Note the conversational tone of the opening lines of the first stanza, with its deliberately colloquial, slightly awkward, first line:

> That is no country for old men.   The young
> In one another's arms, birds in the trees,
> —Those dying generations—at their song,
> The salmon falls, the mackerel-crowded seas,
> Fish, flesh, or fowl, commend all summer long
> Whatever is begotten, born, and dies.
> Caught in that sensual music, all neglect
> Monuments of unageing intellect.

The last two lines, whose studied formality verges on the grandiloquent, have, in the context, an intentionally humorous effect.   But here emotion wears, for the most part, the mask of indifference.

In the second stanza, that mask is laid aside, and, in the first four lines, strong feeling, in order to elude our resistance to it, comes over in the guise of a kind of grotesque, self-deprecating mockery.   It is as if the poet said, "Look, I'm not being sorry for myself.   It's all rather absurd and amusing, really."   The effect is twofold: strong feeling is enabled to come through, in disguise; and is heightened, because of the gallantry implicit in the character of the disguise adopted.   The tone again, in the first four lines, at least, is conversational:

> An aged man is but a paltry thing,
> A tattered coat upon a stick, unless
> Soul clap its hands and sing, and louder sing
> For every tatter in its mortal dress,
> Nor is there singing school but studying
> Monuments of its own magnificence;
> And therefore I have sailed the seas and come
> To the holy city of Byzantium.

The last four lines of the stanza are, of course, a simple statement of fact, taking up again, and carrying forward, the narrative symbolism of the poem.

In the third stanza, after the restrained appeal of the first four lines, feeling threatens to get out of hand, but manages to by-pass our defenses by expressing itself, in the sixth line, in the harshest, coarsest, least romantic terms possible:

> O sages standing in God's holy fire
> As in the gold mosaic of a wall,
> Come from the holy fire, perne in a gyre,
> And be the singing-masters of my soul.
> Consume my heart away; sick with desire
> And fastened to a dying animal
> It knows not what it is; and gather me
> Into the artifice of eternity.

The phrase that refers to the self in old age as "fastened to a dying animal" is, to modern sensibility, one of the great moments in the poem. Its harshness, its brutality, like a slap in the face, takes us off our guard, thus permitting direct, personal emotion to assert itself without arousing the resistance to it so strong in contemporary readers. This phrase, "fastened to a dying animal", would not have been acceptable in Shelley's time, or in Tennyson's, or even in Swinburne's, when resistance to other elements in poetry—specifically to the unromantic, the "unpoetic"—was equally strong. It would have found ready acceptance in the time of Donne or of Swift. The last part of the concluding sentence, "and gather me/ Into the artifice of eternity," reiterates the emotion so vehemently conveyed before, but, this time, in a statement as cold as ice.

In the final stanza, where the symbolism of the poem is further extended and elaborated, the emotion that is the poem's truth is again disguised and, again, is given greater force by that disguise. The mechanical, not to say metallic, character of the metaphor employed to distinguish the world of art from the world of nature contrasts poignantly with the suppressed feeling it embodies. Here emotion wears once more a ceremonial mask:

> Once out of nature I shall never take
> My bodily form from any natural thing,
> But such a form as Grecian goldsmiths make
> Of hammered gold and gold enamelling
> To keep a drowsy emperor awake;
> Or set upon a golden bough to sing
> To lords and ladies of Byzantium
> Of what is passed, or passing, or to come.

In this magnificent poem most of the resistances to poetry encountered in contemporary sensibility are faced and dealt with by the strategies of a poet whose poetic character was formed during a period when resistances to quite other elements in poetry prevailed. Emotion here outwits resistance to it by the use of disguise and the device of an intricate symbolism; the directly personal note is ritualized; profound awarenesses are evoked in a poem that employs, for the most part, the language of everyday speech. The contemporary resistances to aural delight and to what we have called synthesis are alone ignored.

There has seldom been a time when so much was written about poetry and about literature in general. Every year brings a fresh flood of books about books, literary criticism and books about literary criticism. The quarterlies bristle with learned articles on poetry. With some notable exceptions these critics, it must be confessed, write and think very much alike, but they appear to want to quarrel. Mark Twain says somewhere that when a cat gets to pulling fur with another cat on a shed at night, it isn't the noise they make that is so aggravating, it's the bad grammar they use. Substitute "bad manners" for "bad grammar" and he might have been speaking of certain contemporary critics.

The place is full of theorists and of theory—this paper presents a theory. Sometimes one wonders whether there isn't too much of it about. There is the story of the three mountain-climbers who lost their way on a high slope in the Carpathians. One of the three was the map-man, the theorist of the group. The other two turned to him for help: "Tom, get out your chart, and tell us where we are." Tom studied his chart for some time. Then he looked up and pointed. "We're right over there on that peak on the other side of the valley," he said.

Where is American poetry today, and what direction does it seem likely to take in the immediate future? Just as the revolutionary movement begun by Mr. Pound and Mr. Eliot, under the influence of the French Symbolists, was an inevitable reaction from the rococo virtuosity of a Swinburne, so, after forty years, during which, thanks largely to Mr. Eliot, the influence of the Metaphysicals, and more especially of Donne, has supplanted that of the great Romantics, there are signs of an opposite reaction. It may be that we are witnessing the beginning of a new movement which will incorporate, to advantage, the disciplines and techniques evolved in a period of experiment and innovation. Throughout that period, Mr. Eliot's work as a critic, as much as his example as a creator, has been a dominating influence. As critic, his twofold activity, "the elucidation of works of art" and "the correction of taste" has been the prime cause of a fresh appreciation of the poetry of the seventeenth century and of a drastic reappraisal of poetic standards and values in general.

Donne, nevertheless, despite the pitch of perfection to which he brought a highly individual and accomplished style, is, as a model for our time, perhaps somewhat limited and special. As has been pointed out, in a recent issue of *The Times Literary Supplement,** the work of the Metaphysicals lends itself "to that most typical kind of modern criticism, the close examination of the texture of a poet's language," far better than does the poetry of a Shelley or a Wordsworth and this has, undoubtedly, helped to keep these Metaphysical poets alive in the critical mind of our day.

It is easy to characterize so-called "modern" poetry as a departure from the Romantic Tradition. Certainly there has been, in the poetry of the past forty years or so, a strong resistance to the kind of emotional idealism we associate with what is Romantic in the narrow sense of the word. Yet, in a broader sense, the word "Romantic", as a literary term, is hard to define. One thinks of it as representing the opposite of the Classic. Yeats, even in his later poems, where he transcends the Romantic in tone and style, belongs to the great Romantic Tradition. So, for that matter, does Mr. Eliot himself, whose Romantic irony and complicated self-mockery, at least in the earlier poems, often remind us of a similar irony and self-mockery, though of different tone, in the work of a Tieck, a Brentano, or a Heine. Mr. Eliot, clearly, is not, by any standard, a classicist, any more than are the Metaphysicals, whom he admires so much for the fusion of thought and feeling he finds lacking in the nineteenth century Romantics, with their alleged "dissociation of sensibility". But all this ground has been covered by Mr. Frank Kermode, in his recently published *Romantic Image*. There Mr. Kermode concludes that the revolution in poetry begun by T. E. Hulme, Mr. Eliot and Mr. Pound "is not a reversal of the Romantic Tradition but, like that French Symbolist tradition of which Valéry was the last great ornament, the logical continuer of it."

As far as American poetry of the past forty years is concerned, the dominant influences appear to have been Yeats, Eliot, Auden, and Frost, in that order. A waning of the influence of Auden and of Frost, however, is discernible among the younger generation. Very real today is the influence of Wallace Stevens, of Dylan Thomas and, to a lesser degree, that of Marianne Moore. The main resistances to be found in the poetry of the period, the resistance to overt feeling and to aural delight, are lacking in a good many poets who must, nevertheless, be counted a part of the movement.

The resistance to feeling directly expressed in the first-person-singular lyric, and with a fine Sapphic disregard for "the objective correlative," has, in our day, been so strong as virtually to eliminate from serious critical consideration the work of such poets as Edna Millay and Sara Teasdale. The beautiful and tragically austere later work of Sara Teasdale, in particular,

---

*"What is Romantic Poetry?," in *The Times Literary Supplement*, April 5, 1957.

appears to be unknown to contemporary critics. That later work, in its force, integrity of form, intensity and profundity of feeling, and absence of rhetoric, will, surely, more and more, reveal her as one of the purest and finest lyric poets we have. The fact that both women wrote love-poems, a genre which runs counter to the taste of the age and has been little practiced by poets of the period, may partly account for the decline in their reputations among the literati.

Further symptomatic of the strong resistance to direct personal emotion in poetry during the past three or four decades is the cult of toughness as exemplified in the comment of a contemporary critic. This comment was evoked by the statement of a writer who had expressed the hope that tenderness was coming back into poetry. In *The English Journal* for May 1957, Professor R. W. Stallman responded as follows: "As for tenderness coming back into modern poetry, such a trend (if it exists at all) would return us to the sentimental idealism of the poetry prevailing during the decades preceding the revolutionary T. S. Eliot. They were decades of wastelands-of-tenderness, . . . Our kinship is with Henry James [who said]: . . . 'I have the imagination of disaster—and see life indeed as ferocious and sinister'. . . . Tenderness must couple with toughness, in the same bed. 'Art should be hard as nails,' was James' phrase; even lyrical poetry should consist of 'stony-hearted triumphs of objective form'."

Nevertheless, the last few years have seen a definite change. "Lord, give me the strength and courage to contemplate my heart and my body without disgust," prayed Baudelaire, "and," he might have added, "to contemplate with compassion all who pass through this ferocious and sinister world." The feeling, the tenderness, the compassion that is in the poetry of such men as Blake, as Shelley, as Hardy, as Hopkins, are beginning to come back. You will find traces of them in the recent work of some of the younger American poets. Two of the elements in poetry on which our natural resistance to it has been concentrated during the greater part of the past half century, emotion directly expressed, and delight in aural beauty and in intricate form, no longer meet with the same resistance. Perhaps a new Romantic movement is in the making. One thing is certain: however the character of our natural resistance to poetry may vary from period to period, that deep, instinctive, self-protective resistance itself will remain throughout whatever forms it may take.

There have been occasions when the knowledge brought over by science has clashed with the dogmas of the church. At times, this threat has met with the sternest disapproval and opposition. And, entirely apart from its menace to doctrine, such a theory as that of Copernicus, for instance, must have seemed, to the vanity of men, far less flattering than the earlier Ptolemaic theory of the universe had been. Ordinarily, however, the statements of science do not arouse in us the kind of natural resistance we have to the revelations of poetry. Clearly, whatever their practical implications, these statements do not concern us so deeply. They are peripheral and impersonal, they do not touch that inner self which sits at the center of the web of experience.

The statements of science are hearsay, reports from a world outside the world we know. What the poet tells us has long been known to us all, and forgotten. His knowledge is of our world, the world we are both doomed and privileged to live in, and it is a knowledge of ourselves, of the human condition, the human predicament. The measure of our resistance to what the poet would remind us of is the measure of the intensity of our feelings with regard to it. There is, in all of us, a profound longing for the release of these deeply suppressed, inarticulate feelings. For that very reason, perhaps, where they are involved we find ourselves on the defensive. It is not everyone who is permitted to re-awaken in us these fiercely guarded awarenesses. But for him who, because of his skills, the labors he has undergone, the self-discipline he has endured, is equipped to pierce those defenses, to reach us and give us, despite ourselves, the release we long for— that moment of realization and reconcilement beyond the chaos of things— for him we have reserved a name that has blesséd associations, the name of poet.

Robert Burns

Robert Hillyer

Presented at the Library of Congress January 25, 1959

ROBERT BURNS was born two hundred years ago today at Alloway, in Ayrshire, Scotland.

For a general view of the countryside, let me turn to another poet, John Keats, who some twenty years after Burns's death wrote to J. H. Reynolds, "I am approaching Burns's Cottage very fast—We have made continual enquiries from the time we saw his Tomb at Dumfries—his name of course is known all about—his great reputation among the plodding people is 'that he wrote a good mony sensible things'. . . . I had no Conception that the native place of Burns was so beautiful—the Idea I had was more desolate . . . I endeavour'd to drink in the Prospect, that I might spin it out to you . . Besides all the Beauty, there were the Mountains of Annan [i.e. Arran] Isle, black and huge over the Sea—We came down upon every thing suddenly—there were in our way, the 'bonny Doon' with the Brig that Tam O'Shanter cross'ed—Kirk Alloway, Burns's Cottage and then the Brigs of Ayr—First we stood upon the Bridge across the Doon; surrounded by every Phantasy of Green in tree, Meadow, and Hill,—the Stream of the Doon, as a Farmer told us, is covered with trees from head to foot—you know those beautiful heaths so fresh against the weather of a summers evening—there was one stretching along behind the trees."

It was a pastoral countryside, with rolling hills and a verdant, cultivated plain sloping to the Firth of Clyde. The climate, however, was harsh; winter did not let go of the fields until May and the frosts started in September.

Burns was the first-born of his parents, William and Agnes, whose maiden name had been Brown. William Burns was a nurseryman and gardener, who unluckily had gone into farming. He was a noble peasant, wise, devout, and—within his limitations—well read. He looked on with approval when his son Robert ate his meals with a book in one hand and a spoon in the other. His own collection of books was meager but cherished. It was, perhaps, somewhat weighted with theology, for at that time Scotland was still in the grip of religious rivalries and passions, such as had shaken England the century before and were beginning to cool off there under the sweet reasonableness of the eighteenth century. In Scotland the nation was rent between the Old Light, that is, old-fashioned Presbyterianism based on strict Calvinism and literal interpretation of the Bible, and the New Light, which represented the milder, more liberal way of thinking. William Burns belonged to the New Light, and his son, Robert, grew up under the more tolerant theology and later on, as a relaxed Deist, was to poke fun at the hypocrisy of the Old. So interested was William Burns in these churchly matters that he compiled *A Manual of Religious Belief,* that was transcribed and corrected by the schoolmaster, John Murdoch, and there is no doubt that William Burns was interested in the history of his own times. Thus it is clear that Burns's genius as poet was early shaped not only by homely human nature and its emotions and all the traits that make his poetry companionable, but also by the sudden awakening to the quest of liberty, which was sweeping the Europe of his time, that desire

> *To raise a man aboon the brute*
> *and mak him ken himsel.*

The Burns cottage was not an outpost in the wilderness but a focus of eager discussion and exchange of ideas.

The family increased as time went on, until Robert found himself the eldest of seven children. Gilbert, his immediate junior, was his constant companion and later his partner in the family farming.

It is beyond question that the two boys had to work too hard, not because the father was a slave-driver, but because there was nothing else to do but for everybody to exert himself up to and beyond his limit. "Our lands," Burns wrote after some years, "are mountainous and barren, and our Landholders make no allowance for the odds of the qualities of the land, and consequently stretch much beyond what we are able to pay. We are also at a loss for want of proper methods . . . and few of us have opportunities of being well informed in new ones."

During Robert Burns's boyhood and youth, the family moved repeatedly from one rented farm to another, from Alloway to Mount Oliphant to Lochlie. In Lochlie, in 1783, William Burns finally went bankrupt and everything was sold from under them. William Burns himself escaped being taken off to debtors' prison only because he had already worked himself to death and survived his ruin by not more than a few weeks.

The foundation of the poet's health was thus shaken from the beginning. Before he was sixteen, when the family was under the heel of a particularly harsh landlord, at Mount Oliphant, when his decrepit father, his brother, and he had to wring subsistence for nine people out of that ungenerous soil, Robert Burns had a serious physical and nervous breakdown. When he was twenty-two he had another, followed by a period of depression and what he called "violent anguish." Later on, he seems to have had a series of heart attacks and bouts with rheumatic fever. Modern medical opinion agrees that it was the rheumatic infection of his heart that finally killed him at the early age of thirty-seven. The unavoidable hardships of his youth account for this. The fact should be emphasized, for he was not the victim of his own excesses as popular fancy and even much formal biography have insisted.

Nor was he the victim, as Wordsworth romantically imagined, of poetry and love:

> "There!" said a Stripling, pointing with meet pride
> Towards a low roof with green trees half concealed,
> "Is Mosgiel Farm; and that's the very field
> Where Burns ploughed up the Daisy." Far and wide
> A plain below stretched seaward, while, descried
> Above sea-clouds, the peaks of Arran rose;
> And, by that simple notice, the repose
> Of earth, sea, sky, and air was vivified.
> Beneath "the random bield of clod or stone,"
> Myriads of daisies have shown forth in flower
> Near the lark's nest, and in their natural hour
> Have passed away; less happy than the One
> That, by the unwilling ploughshare, died to prove
> The tender charm of poetry and love.

Wordsworth's sonnet deserves to be remembered less as a biographical footnote than as a description of Mossgiel, whither Gilbert and Robert Burns moved the family after their father's death. At Mossgiel, Robert Burns began definitely to think of himself as a poet. He was still primarily the farmer, preoccupied with seeds and methods of agriculture, working from dawn till dusk in the fields, but his collection of verses grew, their reputation spread among the neighbors, and in 1786 appeared the Kilmarnock edition of Burns's first published work, *Poems Chiefly in the Scottish Dialect*.

Burns had influential friends, in the countryside, in the market town of Mauchline and other communities nearby; and the book was well subscribed for. Among his patrons were such important people as Gavin

Hamilton, Burns's friend and landlord, to whom he dedicated the book; John Richmond, Hamilton's clerk, who was the poet's most intimate friend, and the distinguished lawyer, Robert Aiken, who subscribed to 145 copies and shortly after set in motion the machinery that was to result in Burns's appointment as Exciseman.

The reviews in Edinburgh were more than favorable—they were enthusiastic. "Though I am very far from meaning to compare our rustic bard to Shakespeare," said one, "yet whoever will read his lighter and more humorous poems . . . will perceive with what uncommon penetration and sagacity this Heaven-taught ploughman, from his humble and unlettered station, has looked upon men and manners."

Robert Aiken was overjoyed with the success of his friend's book and arranged with two of his acquaintances in the capital for a second edition of *Poems Chiefly in the Scottish Dialect,* which was published in Edinburgh in 1787.

Meanwhile Burns had written to his friend Mrs. Dunlop that he had decided to try his own luck in Edinburgh. There he stayed until the publication of his book. Edinburgh was the home of a large number of cultivated people of literary tastes who felt themselves cut off from the great world they were interested in. Their last distinguished visitor had been Dr. Samuel Johnson, fourteen years before Burns entered the scene. Burns's reputation as a "Heaven-taught ploughman" had preceded him. He had good introductions from the gentry at home, and in Edinburgh, all classes, the nobility, the professional people, and the artisans, took him to their heart. The young girls did, too, of course, and at least two of them had good reason to remember him later when they looked at their bairns.

There was the Earl of Glencairn, of whom Burns wrote that he had chosen him as his "Titular Protector." Through the Earl, Burns met a number of people in good society among whom he moved in perfect ease and dignity. Even more important than the Earl were the Duke and Duchess of Gordon. These amiable people loved Burns sincerely, kept in touch with him after his departure from Edinburgh, and, a year later, during his tour of the Highlands, welcomed him to their castle. Writers, scholars, and critics opened their doors to him. At the same time he began his correspondence with Dr. John Moore, a well-known Scottish writer and traveler of the period, author of the once-famed novel, *Zeluco,* which later influenced Byron's *Childe Harold.* Moore was a curious creature; he had a high reputation, which Burns deeply respected, and sometimes he would say things that astonish us with their insight. Burns was so impressed by him that he continued in lively correspondence, and it was to Moore that Burns addressed what has been called his "autobiographical letter," giving all the details of his life up to that point. But Moore sometimes made notable blunders. Moore was certain that Burns would do best to abandon the Scottish dialect and write his poems in standard English. The fact seems to have escaped him that Burns often did write in standard English and that the results were almost invariably the weakest of his poems. Even the famous "Cotter's Saturday Night," although partly in Scottish dialect, suffers from the imposition of the formal Spenserian stanza, so far from his natural idiom and from the shape in which his emotions generally flowed. It may be said at once that, in spite of the reverence in which he held Dr. Moore, Burns disregarded his advice, very much as Emily Dickinson, a century later, ignored Thomas Wentworth Higginson's plea to polish her rhymes.

It was during Burns's first visit to Edinburgh that Sir Walter Scott saw him. Scott was a boy of sixteen at the time. Forty years later he wrote to Lockhart, "I saw him one day at the late venerable Professor Ferguson's, where there were several gentlemen of literary reputation. The only thing I remember which was remarkable in Burns's manner was the effect produced upon him by a print . . . representing a soldier lying dead in the snow . . . Burns seemed much affected by the print, or rather, the ideas which it suggested to his mind. He actually shed tears . . . His person was strong and robust, not clownish; a sort of dignified plainness and simplicity . . . The eye alone, I think, indicated the poetical character and temperament. It was large and of a dark cast and glowed (I say literally *glowed*) when he spoke with feeling and interest. I never saw such another eye in a human head, though I have seen the most distinguished men in my time."

Burns charmed everybody who met him. He was never spoiled and never played a consciously rustic part, but bore himself with modesty and ease. Between two visits to the capital, he went on a holiday tour through the Highlands of Scotland. By this time he was a national figure and found himself received everywhere with honor and warmth. No poems have come down to us from these travels, for he was, as Professor F. B. Snyder has pointed out in his excellent biography, "interested in human nature, not in scenery."

In April 1788 Burns was at last and officially married to Jean Armour, by whom he had already had two sets of twins. They were destined to have five more children born to them during their marriage, the last one after Burns's death; indeed, while his funeral services were being conducted. For three years the family lived on a farm near Dumfries, then, after Burns's appointment as Exciseman, they moved into the town itself. The last five years of his life were marked by his excise work—he sometimes had to ride 200 miles a week in connection with his official duties—the composition of scores of songs, and an occasional drunken evening at the tavern.

Burns was not, however, an habitual drunkard, as he is usually pictured, nor was his death the result of carousing. It was his misfortune to have as his first biographer Dr. James Currie, a Liverpool physician who admired Burns but had seen him only once in his life. Currie was a rabid fanatic on the subject of alcohol. It was his best intention to conceal Burn's faults, but in trying to do so and at the same time remain truthful, he deprecated a constant indulgence that never took place. He pictured Burns as always under the stimulation of drink, a state of affairs that had no ground in fact whatsoever.

Nearly all the biographers of the nineteenth century followed and even improved on Currie's version, sometimes adding as pretext the grinding poverty that drove Burns to such excesses, although, in matter of fact, Burns passed his last decade in comparative comfort and left not a debt behind him. His income of £70 a year was the same as Dr. Johnson's. The major work after Currie's was the biography by John G. Lockhart, published in 1828, in which all the mistakes of the earlier life are incorporated and many others added. Throughout the century Lockhart's biographical work was standard; it was as a review of that, for example, that Thomas Carlyle's great essay on Burns was written, and this popular work was required reading in every school in the English-speaking world and did more than any other to shape the image of Burns in the public mind.

I recently received an amusing letter from my friend the poet Witter Bynner, in which he recounts an incident that we may take as typical of the conception of Burns held by all classes: "Speaking of Burns," Mr. Bynner writes, "I engaged a carpenter one morning and expected him to put up some bookshelves by five o'clock. When I returned home the carpenter was stretched out on a Morris chair, an empty bottle of rye in one hand and a book of Burns's poems in the other. He grinned and said, "Bobby Burns was a bit of a bum, too.' " So it would seem that Burns was lovable and dissolute—perhaps lovable because he was dissolute. This impression is not altogether wrong, but it is far enough from the truth to need modification.

We have already seen that in the first reviews of his book Burns was referred to as a "Heaven-taught ploughman." The general notion seems to be that he was uneducated almost to the point of illiteracy. On the contrary, as he matured, Burns became a highly educated man—much better educated, for instance, than the majority of our college graduates. With him education was not something detached from life that one succumbed to for a few years until the age of twenty-two and then abandoned as something done with and alien to one's career. With Burns, education, the reading and contemplation of books, and discussion of them with fellow students, was a process that was part of his natural life and continued as long as he drew breath. He himself was either too modest or too careless to correct the conception of the "Heaven-taught ploughman." At one point in his life, Mrs. Dunlop, who knew him well through many years, attempted to obtain for him the professorship of agriculture of the University of Edinburgh, a position that would have demanded academic decorum as well as a knowledge of farming. It is just as well that this fantastic scheme did not go through; Burns as a university professor carries our rehabilitation of him a little too far, but it does show how keenly aware of his intellectual powers and his personal bearing were those who knew his mind intimately.

In Burns's case, education had little to do with formal schooling. Of this he had less than three years, beginning when he was six and ending when he was nine. In considering these ages we must allow for the precocity of the children of the eighteenth century, who would have found our children somewhat retarded by our so-called progressive methods. Robert and his brother Gilbert had great good fortune in the community teacher, John Murdoch, then a youth of eighteen, who had studied in Edinburgh and combined with a love of good reading a natural zeal for teaching. He was engaged by the poet's father and four of the neighbors. According to his account, Robert and Gilbert were grounded in English and at once made a rapid progress in reading and a tolerable progress in writing. Murdoch noted that "Robert and Gilbert were generally at the upper end of the class, even when ranged with boys far their seniors. The books most commonly used in the school were *The Spelling Book*, the *New Testament*, the *Bible*, Mason's *Collection of Prose and Verse*, and Fisher's *English Grammar*." Among the first books that Burns read was *The History of William Wallace*, of which he later wrote, "The story of Wallace poured a Scottish prejudice into my veins, which will boil there till the floodgates of life shut in eternal rest"—a rhetorical flourish, by the way, that is all too typical of the embellished English of Burns's correspondence.

When Burns was fourteen, he spent three weeks in Murdoch's lodgings in Ayr in order to qualify himself for teaching his brothers and sisters at home. At the same time he made what must have been the most intensive study of the French language in the history of education. "Now there was little else to be heard," Murdoch wrote, "but the declension of nouns, the conjugation of verbs, etc. . . . He took such pleasure in learning and I in teaching that it was difficult to say which of the two was the most zealous in the business; and about the end of our second week of our study of the French, we began to read a little of the *Adventures of Telemachus* in Fénelon's own words." Burns went on with his French studies and became fairly proficient in the language. He also attempted the rudiments of

287

Latin, but later candor led him to declare that "all I know of Latin is contained in three words—*omnia vincit Amor.*"

Schooling was only the beginning of Burns's education. He and Gilbert founded a debating society to take up the issues of the day, and there followed a succession of reading and discussion groups in which he was active to the end of his life, sometimes acting as purchaser for the society and thus leaving lists of the books he had bought. Even as a young man he was well acquainted with Shakespeare, Milton, Dryden, Gray, Pope, Addison, and other standard authors, and was versed in history, theology, and philosophy. He was more deeply involved in the revolutionary trends in France and America than was always good for his emotional serenity or discreet in view of the government office he subsequently held. His knowledge of Scottish song was, of course, prodigious. As it should be, education was with Burns a continuous flowering of the mind, stimulated by constant reading, correspondence with learned friends, and a more thoughtful outlook on life, especially human society, than would be ordinarily possible for a man of so many pursuits and responsibilities.

His political views are somewhat difficult to fix and have been the object of a good deal of free interpretation. There is no doubt that Burns was moved to impulsive wrath, sometimes in his verse, by general injustices or private thwarting. It is hard to reconstruct the temper of the times even with the aid of history. Some fourteen years before Burns's birth, the Jacobite invasion under Prince Charles Edward Stuart had penetrated the lethargic northern counties of Hanoverian England before being thrown back and decisively beaten at Culloden. The destruction of the Young Pretender's hopes and the fearful vengeance taken on his Scottish followers by the Duke of Cumberland helped to break down the feudal system still flourishing in the Highlands and bring Highlanders and Lowlanders closer together in patriotic union as one Scottish nation. Yet even as late as 1776 we find Dr. Johnson, partly to tease his Scottish friend Boswell, saying to John Wilkes that "the Clannish slavery of the Highlands of Scotland was the single exception to Milton's remark of 'the Mountain Nymph, sweet Liberty' being worshipped in hilly countries."

Burns himself was born a Lowlander, but his grandfather on his father's side had been involved in early Jacobite uprisings under the Old Pretender. "My forefathers," he wrote to Dr. Moore, "rented land of the famous, noble Keiths of Marshal and had the honor to share their fate." And to a Jacobite friend, Lady Maxwell Constable, "Though my fathers had not illustrious Honors and vast properties to hazard in the contest; though they left their humble cottages only to add so many units more to the unnoted crowd that followed their Leaders; yet what they could they did, and what they had they lost."

288

Romantic regret for the lost cause of the Stuarts always colored Burns's imagination, though it was totally inconsistent with everything else he believed in and every liberal impulse of eighteenth-century Europe. He went back even farther and more fantastically in his sympathies, and wrote a "Lament of Mary Queen of Scots," whom he frequently invoked in his letters, thus becoming the first romantic poet to attempt to transfigure that six-foot hussy, "the daughter of debate" as Queen Elizabeth called her, into a symbol of beauty and martyrdom. Neither history nor common sense seems to have been able to offer any cure for this illusion.

Burns's devotion to the Stuarts was at variance not only with his political ideas but his religious leanings as well. Both Mary of Scots and Charles Edward represented Roman Catholicism at its most reactionary and monarchy at its most absolute. His verses on these personages are far from the spontaneous thrust of such a stanza as

> *A prince can mak a belted knight,*
> *A marquis, duke, an' a' that!*
> *But an honest man's aboon his might—*
> *Guid faith, he mauna fa' that!*
> *For a' that, an' a' that,*
> *Their dignities, an' a' that,*
> *The pith o' sense an' pride o' worth*
> *Are higher rank than a' that.*

When Burns was in his twenties, the American Revolution broke out. At that time he was overwhelmed with work on the farm; there was scarcely any period in which he was more involved with the mere struggle to survive and help the family survive than those years when our Revolution was being fought. Later on, when the outbreak of the French Revolution gave such ideas fresh impetus, he wrote to Mrs. Dunlop, "I am just going to trouble your critical patience with the first sketch I have been framing as I passed along the road. The subject is Liberty; you know, my honored friend, how dear the theme is to me. I design it as an irregular Ode for General Washington's birthday." He had already written, in a letter to the *Edinburgh Evening Courant*, that "I dare say the American Congress in 1776, will be allowed to have been as able and enlightened as the English convention in 1688, and that the fourth of July will be as sacred to their posterity as the fifth of November is to us."

The French Revolution shook Burns to his inmost fibre. He wrote to Mrs. Dunlop that his feelings were so violent that he should confine his real sentiments regarding that "gallant people" to his letters to her— a decision which, unfortunately, he did not hold to. The more extreme become one's expressed views, so much more sweeping must be one's recantation—especially if one holds a government job. So it was with Burns. In England, Wordsworth and Coleridge, who had at first rejoiced at the outbreak of the French Revolution, recoiled as it took its bloody course to the Reign of Terror and hastily moved their politics back to more conservative ground. A sympathy for the revolutionists had become, by 1793, a sign of sympathy for revolution at home. The Hanoverian monarchy was badly shaken; discontent was widespread. People were extremely touchy about any statements or sentiments that might be interpreted as hostile to the Crown.

Burns, according to Professor Snyder, "had always been inclined to recklessness in conversation, and must have said many things which it was easy for malice or ignorance to distort. He had written verses showing a questionable sympathy with the American Revolution; he had been an enthusiastic votary of France in 1789; he had written Jacobite songs aplenty, . . . and even a poetical espousal of the Stuarts was ill calculated to please a Hanoverian administration . . . Beyond a doubt he had composed other pieces of liberal verse that have not been preserved. All in all, then, Burns the Exciseman had been playing with fire ever since he had gone on active duty in the fall of 1789. That he was merely advised, in a friendly way, to be more reticent in the future, was due to the fact that his superiors knew him to be a good officer, despite his political heterodoxy, and were glad to shield him from official disapproval."

At least, Burns thought, his old friend Mrs. Dunlop could serve as a sort of safety valve for his pent-up revolutionary emotions. Mrs. Dunlop, an elderly gentlewoman, had been charmed by the Kilmarnock volume, and she and Burns had corresponded eagerly ever since its publication. After the execution of Louis XVI and Marie Antoinette, two events that shocked all Europe, Burns impulsively wrote to her that he could not see any reason to whine over the fate of a perjured blockhead and an unprincipled prostitute. The bad taste of the remark strikes us even at this late date. It horrified Mrs. Dunlop. Burns seemed to have forgotten that his old friend was at heart a conservative and, furthermore, that two of her daughters had married two members of the French nobility who had fled to Scotland. It was all a grave mistake. Mrs. Dunlop never answered his letter and brought their correspondence to a close. When he was on his deathbed he sent her a feverish plea for a reconciliation and she wrote to him then, a last letter of farewell.

As a whole, Burns's politics seem to have been a combination of instinct and concession. In his verse and his letters, and doubtless in unguarded moments at the tavern, he felt free to soar on the unbridled wings of liberty or bemoan the fate of the Stuarts. But when his job as Exciseman, a job dependent on the government, was involved, he made haste to declare his

290

loyalty to monarchy in general and the house of Hanover in particular. To have done otherwise would have been to play the fanatic, and fanaticism was a disease far removed from Burns's essentially hardheaded and practical constitution. Lest he be accused of hypocrisy, we may point out that in only a few of his poetic flights did he outdistance all allegiance to the reigning family and the British Constitution, and in none of his explanations did he relinquish some hope for enlightened reform. He summed up the whole matter in his noble letter of 1793 to his patron Robert Graham of Fintry. Then, enclosing a copy of what he termed a "tippling ballad" for Graham's perusal, he went on to say, "Lest Mrs. Fame should, as she has already done, use and even abuse her old privilege of lying, you shall be the master of everything, le pour et le contre, of my political writings and conduct. This, my honored Patron, is all."

Thanks to his common sense and conscientious work, Burns continued in his position as Exciseman until his death. His duties were to make up an account of all taxable articles in shops and warehouses, collect the revenues due the government, keep watch against smugglers, and report all who failed to list their taxable articles. It was an onerous job, and involved riding out in all kinds of weather, but the steady income, small though it was, relieved Burns from farming during the last five years of his life. The Exciseman was not, of course, a popular figure in the countryside, and no one knew it better than Burns, author of the ballad "The Deil's Awa' wi' th' Exciseman."

> *The Deil cam fiddlin thro' the town,*
> *And danc'd awa wi' th' Exciseman,*
> *And ilka wife cries:—"Auld Mahoun,*
> *I wish you luck o' the prize, man!* . . .

> *"There's threesome reels, there's foursome reels,*
> *There's hornpipes and strathspeys, man,*
> *But the ae best dance e'er cam to the land*
> *Was* The Deil's Awa wi' th' Exciseman."

Everything in his life was a subject for balladry, and, as might be expected, the great majority of his songs deal with the art of love. Burns, it must be admitted, was a promiscuous lover, and here he sets a pretty problem for the professional moralists. I do not feel called on to mention extenuating circumstances, but we may acknowledge that the ladies of his acquaintance were at least as eager for his advances as he was to make them. The number of his known illegitimate children was nine, though four of these—two sets of twins—subsequently were made legitimate by his marriage to their mother, Jean Armour.

Burns first fell in love when he was fourteen. His partner in the fields, he wrote, "was a bewitching creature who just counted an autumn less . . . She was a bonnie, sweet, sonsy lass . . . In short, she altogether initiated me into a certain delicious passion, which . . . I hold to be the first of human joys, our chiefest pleasure here below . . . Among her other love-inspiring qualifications she sung sweetly . . . Thus with me began love and poetry." So it was that Burns's Muse arrived in company with the goddess Venus, and they were seldom thereafter to be parted for any great length of time. His first poem was entitled "Handsome Nell" and celebrated the nymph of the harvest field, whose name was actually Nellie Kirkpatrick.

A certain amorous liberty in the behavior of eighteenth-century peasants is not to be wondered at. Some years ago I attended a lecture by an Indian—Hindu—speaker on the situation in his country. Among his other remarks he noted that "you of the Western world blame us for our constantly increasing population, but you should not forget that the only recreation possible to the very poor is procreation." The same situation prevailed among the hard-working young farmers of Burns's time. Even the strict Scottish Kirk was cognizant of the way matters stood and made provision for it.

In 1786 Burns's affair with Jean Armour was so confused that he nearly took ship for the West Indies. It is interesting that the Armour family, not Burns, were the ones to oppose the marriage, even when Jean was within a month of giving birth to his first-born, a set of twins. It should be noted, too, that that year was marked by the appearance of Burns's first book and of his mysterious love affair with Highland Mary. In July, Jean Armour and Burns, in company with other sinners, stood up in church to receive the ministerial rebuke for their transgressions. They were then declared absolved of their sin, and Burns was restored to official bachelorhood.

James Armour, Jean's father, was not, however, satisfied. He would not consent to Jean's marriage to a young farmer with such meager prospects, but he was by no means willing for Burns to escape without providing for his offspring. He persuaded Jean to sign a civil warrant against her lover, which Burns countered by signing over all his property to his brother Gilbert as well as the copyright on his forthcoming poems. It was a desperate time. Burns went into hiding so that the warrant could not be served on him, and wrote to his friend Dr. Richmond: "My hour is now come—You and I will never meet in Britain more—I have orders within three weeks at farthest to repair aboard the *Nancy,* Capt. Smith, from Clyde to Jamaica. . . . I am wandering from one friend's house to another, and like a true son of the gospel, 'I have no where to lay my head.' I know you will pour an execration on her head, but spare the poor ill-advised girl for my sake! though may all the Furies that rend the injured enraged lover's bosom await the old harridan, her mother, until her latest hour!" Just after that letter, Burns's *Poems* appeared. Apparently the Armour family were deeply impressed by this event and the friends it raised up for the poet throughout the countryside. They let the warrant fall into inactivity, and Burns did not, after all, sail for the West Indies.

In passing, it is curious to note that Scottish customs, otherwise so severe, were realistically lenient in dealing with the sins of the flesh. The English, so much more easygoing in other ways, were much stricter in regard to deviations from the moral law. We find Robert writing to his brother William, who was on his way to England, "I need not caution you against guilty amours—they are bad anywhere, but in England they are the very devil."

The end of Burns's affair with Jean Armour was their marriage in 1788 after their second set of twins. She was in love with him from the beginning, and though it would be hopeless to attempt to bind his passion to a single object, it may be said that she was the best possible wife for him. Nor was her fate in any way tragic. After his death she was the recipient of a handsome sum of money raised by his admirers, and she survived him in the full sunlight of his fame for thirty-eight years.

Two others of Burns's love affairs deserve mention, for they do not run according to form. During his second visit to Edinburgh, Burns met an attractive married woman named Mrs. Agnes M'Lehose. With her he established a pastoral correspondence at once innocent and more than a little silly. "I must chide you for writing in your romantic style," she wrote, "Do you remember that she whom you address is a married woman?" Perhaps she should have added that her husband was far away in Jamaica. Soon she and Burns were addressing each other as Sylvander and Clarinda. Burns imagined himself in love with this incredibly sentimental woman; he told a friend that love reigned and reveled in his bosom. Clarinda, for her part, delighted in the literary flirtation, but whenever Burns's letters became too warm she took refuge in quotations from the Bible. Reviewing this correspondence, however, it seems that at their infrequent meetings the lady was more ready to yield to physical passion than was Burns himself. He could write her from a distance, "Will you open, with satisfaction and delight, a letter from a man who loves you, who has ever loved you, and who will love you to death, though dead, and for ever?" These are high words, but when Clarinda wrote Sylvander a furious letter at the news of his marriage, he remarked, "When you call over the scenes that have passed between us, you will survey the conduct of an honest man, struggling successfully with temptations the most powerful that ever beset humanity and preserving untainted honor in situations where the austerest Virtue would have forgiven a fall." These are higher words

293

yet, and written, as can be seen, by one who feels himself to be more sinned against than sinning.

They became reconciled, and shortly thereafter Burns asked her to deliver a sum of money to a servant girl in Edinburgh who had borne him a child. Three years later poor Clarinda sailed to join her husband in Jamaica and immediately fled home again when she discovered him in the arms of his Negro mistress. She settled down in Edinburgh and confided only to her journal, as late as 1831, that on December 6, 1791, she parted from Burns "never more to meet in this world. O, may we meet in Heaven!"

The Sylvander-Clarinda correspondence is artificial and absurd. These ardent lovers always address each other as "Sir" or "Madam," and have much to say about pleasures of the mind and raptures of the heart. One is at a loss to account for this pseudo-Platonic episode in Burns's life. Mrs. M'Lehose could not have been ravishingly beautiful, or the chances are that the affair would not have been Platonic at all. She certainly was no social catch to the intimate of the Duchess of Gordon or of Mrs. Francis Dunlop, who was descended from William Wallace himself. We can only believe that in some way the devoted Clarinda gave Burns a glimpse of something with which he was not familiar though it is prevalent enough—the adoration of lonely women for poets. Somehow Burns's curiosity was aroused, his heart touched, and his vanity gratified.

Highland Mary is a much livelier ghost. At the time when he was having trouble with Jean Armour's family, he spoke of another bride whom he would rather have. This young woman seems to have been Mary Campbell, the Highland Mary of the poem by that name and of the reminiscent "Thou Lingering Star," which, by later editors, was called "To Highland Mary in Heaven":

> *Thou ling'ring star, with less'ning ray,*
> *That lov'st to greet the early morn,*
> *Again thou usher'st in the day*
> *My Mary from my soul was torn.*

All we know of her is that she came from the Highlands, that Burns fell in love with her, presented her with an inscribed Bible, and asked her to marry him about the time he was considering going to the West Indies, and that she died in that same troubled year of 1786. When her grave in Greenock was opened in 1920, she was found to be buried with an infant, in another coffin at her feet. The suggestion has been made that she was on her way to meet Burns and marry him, being already with child by him, and that she got as far as Greenock, where she died in childbirth.

This may or may not be true. Whatever the circumstances, Highland Mary represented to Burns the essence of all earthly love and her death

294

the epitome of all earthly loss. Whether or not they had been actual lovers makes little difference. Her death put her beyond all possible censure, and she remained for Burns a vision of that heavenly beauty that mortals are always about to win, something that, unlike other mortal things, grows ever more beautiful with the passage of time.

Love, freedom, and humor were the three main impulses in Burns's poetry. In most of his work he anticipated the great English romantic poets. He was the near-contemporary of William Blake, who was also a romantic forerunner and bore several striking resemblances to Burns. Blake's tenderness toward all living things, as in the "Auguries of Innocence," finds its counterpart in Burns's "On Scaring the Water Fowl," "On Seeing a Wounded Hare," and many other pieces on animals and birds. Blake and Burns shared the same philosophy of sexual freedom, although with Blake the doctrine remained merely theoretical; they both wrote outrageously amusing epigrams on people and things they did not like; they were both moved with indignation against tyranny in government and the conventions of society. The basic difference between them was that Blake was a visionary, a mystic, whereas Burns was as realistic as Chaucer, and his poetry came straight from the soil and those closest to it.

Some fifteen years earlier than Wordsworth, Burns accomplished without definite programme what Wordsworth consciously aimed at; that is, the expression of high poetic moments in simple, everyday diction. Wordsworth strove for this but is chiefly remembered for poems in a heightened vocabulary; Burns incorporated his daily speech into his best work as naturally as a bird singing.

Burns—and perhaps this was a limitation—was less imaginative than the great English Romantics. His eyes were focused on the people and things around him and he did not look farther than the area immediately known to him. For example, he lived within sight and smell of the sea, yet he failed to write any poems about it. Harvests and harvesters were his province and he did not gaze out toward blue horizons and the sails of ships vanishing into the west. Again, in his childhood he often heard from the lips of Betty Davidson, a relative of his mother's, a wealth of stories about ghosts and goblins and other superstitions. Such fantasies would have inspired the Gothic imagination of later Romantic poets, especially Coleridge and Keats, but Burns's earthy humor pervades every presentation of them, and his masterpiece in the use of this material, "Tam o' Shanter," is a rollicking farce. The farmer's cry, "Weel done, Cutty Sark," in the midst of the witch's dance and the plucking off of his horse's tail on the bridge, dispel all the shudders dear to the heart of Gothic writers. Burns loved this story of Tam o' Shanter in its ludicrous aspects. He wrote two long prose versions of the tale to Dr. Moore as legends of "Alloway's auld haunted Kirk." After he had completed it he distributed copies of it to his friends and declared that "it had a finishing polish that I despair of ever excelling." This was a late poem, written at a time when Burns had fully realized his technique and his idiom.

I have already stated my agreement with the consensus of critics that Burns's poems in Scottish dialect are superior to those in which he employed standard English. Of course there are several exceptions, such as the scathing "Ode, Sacred to the Memory of Mrs. Oswald," and the graceful "My Heart's in the Highlands." It is a mistake to assume that the general superiority of the poems in Scottish can be accounted for by the supposition that Burns was not quite at ease in English. We have much evidence to the contrary, including Professor Dugald Stewart's testimony. Writing of his conversations with Burns in Edinburgh he said that "nothing, perhaps, was more remarkable among his various attainments than the fluency, precision, and originality of his language when he spoke in company; more particularly as he . . . avoided more successfully than most Scotchmen the peculiarities of Scottish phraseology." The fact is that when Burns wrote in English—and this applies to his prose as well as his verse— he did not write naturally, because for him English, as a written language, was a literary medium heavily influenced by the books he had read in that tongue. In English his humor strained toward the epigram in the manner of Pope, his romantic scenery and pastoral sentiment unfolded in the diction of Gray or Thomson, his odes, also influenced by Gray, took on rhetorical flourishes that did not quite ring true to his own genius. In other words, he had too many predecessors in English.

In Scottish he had no predecessors except for Allan Ramsay and, more important, Robert Fergusson. Fergusson, who was born nine years before Burns and lived to be only twenty-four, was already famous by 1771. He was a city man, a poorly paid lawyer's clerk, who escaped from routine into rural districts, largely imaginary, and the milder dissipations of city life. His consistent use of the Scottish dialect gave Burns the courage to devote himself to that form of expression. "I strung anew my wildly-sounding rustic lyre," he wrote, "with simulating vigor." When Burns was in Edinburgh in 1787, he discovered that Fergusson's grave was unmarked. He wrote an epitaph and got permission to have a headstone erected. Four years later he paid for it, explaining that the designer had taken two years to set it up so he had delayed two years in sending the money for it. He wrote that "considering that the money was due by one Poet for putting a tomb-stone over another, he [the designer] may, with grateful surprise, thank Heaven that he ever saw a farthing of it."

Combined with the Scottish dialect, Burns's satires gain a strength and point otherwise unobtainable. There are a score of masterpieces in this vein in which fantasy and realism are mingled. One of the best of these, "The Holy Fair," is a burlesque of hypocrisy. Each year, when the Kirk celebrated its yearly sacrament, tents were set up for preaching in the fields and tables for drinkers, and the crowds who gathered from the surrounding countryside turned what was intended to be a religious revival into an orgy. There are twenty-seven stanzas in Burns's wild ballad. As the crowd is collecting, three women appear, two of them clad in black, the third in "shining fashion." The poet asks the cheerful one of the trio what her name is, and she answers

> *"My name is Fun—your cronie dear,*
> *The nearest friend ye hae;*
> *An' this is Superstition here,*
> *An' that's Hypocrisy.*
> *I'm gaun to Mauchline Holy Fair,*
> *To spend an hour in daffin:*
> *Gin ye'll go there, yon runkl'd pair,*
> *We will get famous laughin . . ."*

Then follows an account of the preaching, the visions of Hell fire, and the drunkenness of the mob until

> *Wi' faith an' hope, an' love an' drink,*
> *They're a' in famous tune*

and

> *How monie hearts this day converts*
> *O' sinners and o' lasses!*
> *Their hearts o' stane, gin night, are gane*
> *As saft as onie flesh is:*
> *There's some are fou o' love divine;*
> *There's some are fou o' brandy;*
> *An' monie jobs that day begin,*
> *May end in houghmagandie . . .*

The meaning of "houghmagandie" I leave to your imagination.

The "Address to the Unco Guid or the Rigidly Righteous" is the well-known satire on conventionally virtuous people. "Holy Willie's Prayer" deals with the doctrine of predestination and the self-righteous hypocrisy of Holy Willie, who believes himself to be among those chosen by God. In another poem, "The Poet's Welcome to His Love-Begotten Daughter," Burns defies the scandalmongers and hypocrites and ends on a note of paternal tenderness. Sometimes, as in some of the epigrams, he blends his love for dumb creatures with his hatred of the ministers of the Kirk:

> *Peg Nicholson was a guid bay mare,*
> *An' the priest he rode her sair;*
> *And much oppress'd, and bruis'd she was,*
> *As priest-rid cattle are.*

As has been noted, Burns always felt a kinship with animals and all the small creatures of the world, a feeling like that of Marius, in Walter Pater's book, who had "a sympathy for all creatures, for the almost human troubles and sickness of the flocks—a feeling of veneration for life as such." There is something deeply touching in Burns's two poems about his ewe named Mailie. Incidentally, Molly seems to have been a generic name for ewes through many centuries: we call to mind the farm wife in Chaucer's "Nun's Priest's Tale" who had "eke a sheep that highte Malle." In "The Death and Dying Words of Poor Mailie, the Author's Only Pet Yowe," Burns tells of the sheep's last word to her lambs, of the need for being kind to one another, and of the cruelty of binding animals up in tethers. This poem may be interpreted symbolically. Its sequel, "Poor Mailie's Elegy," is a lament for a dead pet that will find an echoing chord in most of us.

In the famous "To a Mouse on Turning Her Up in her Nest with a Plough" the poet makes himself one with the "wee, sleekit, cowrin, tim'rous beastie," who was spending the winter cozy and snug in her "wee bit heap o' leaves an' stibble," only to be turned out to suffer in the wintry sleet. Then the poem expands, and, again symbolically, the lot of the human race is drawn into the picture with the proverbial

> *The best-laid schemes o' mice an' men*
> *Gang aft agley,*
> *An' lea'e us nought but grief an' pain,*
> *For promis'd joy!*
>
> *Still art thou blest, compared wi' me.*
> *The present only toucheth thee:*
> *But och! I backward cast my e'e,*
> *On prospects drear!*
> *An' forward, tho' I canna see,*
> *I guess an' fear!*

In this translation of the woes of small things into the fate of human beings, Burns sometimes reminds us not only of Blake but also of Robert Herrick. "The Mountain Daisy" is a more extensive poem than Herrick's "To Daffodils" or "To Blossoms," but again the sorrow of the ephemeral world is invoked in the contemplation of the flowers that, like men, are withered by passing time or crushed beneath "stern Ruin's ploughshare." In a lighter poem, "To a Louse on Seeing One on a Lady's Bonnet at Church,"

298

the insect is warned off such a fashionable prominence and commanded to go elsewhere "and seek your dinner on some poor body." But there the louse remains, on the proud lady, who is unaware that "winks an' finger-ends . . . are notice takin!" Then follows the familiar stanza:

> O wad some Power the giftie gie us
> To see oursels as ithers see us!
> It wad frae monie a blunder free us,
>   An' foolish notion:
> What airs in dress an' gait wad lea'e us,
>   An' ev'n devotion!

"The Jolly Beggars" is, on the surface, a drunken hurly-burly of lowlife characters who are chirping over their cups and singing at Poosie Nansie's tavern, frolicking away the night in defiance of the world outside. Underneath it has the grim humor of a Hogarth drawing; these are people who, having lost everything, sing away their despair. They are the outcasts of reality, who find happiness only in delusions. Burns's friend, John Richmond, wrote how he and Burns and another friend dropped into Poosie Nansie's one night and "after witnessing much jollity amongst a company who by day appeared as miserable beggars, the three young men came away, Burns professing to have been greatly amused by the scene—but particularly with the gleesome behavior of an old maimed soldier." In the poem, this old fellow leads off the series of songs, sung also by a tinker, a highwayman's doxy, a drab of the regiment whose lovers included not only all the dragoons but the chaplain as well, and various other characters who had sunk to the bottom of the heap and had nothing further to lose. There is a wild gaiety, a desperate gusto, about the entire medley. The power and inventiveness of the versification show the height of artistry. And there are shrewd darts of satire:

> Poor Andrew that tumbles for sport
> Let naebody name wi' a jeer:
> There's even, I'm tauld, i' the Court
> A tumbler ca'd the Premier.

The swirling, changing stanzas come to a climax with a chorus that includes the key passage:

> Life is all a variorum,
>   We regard not how it goes;
> Let them prate about decorum
>   Who have character to lose.

The luxuriant variety of Burns's work defies the commentator, but no choice of his poems would exclude the "Address to the Deil" and the many epistles in verse to his friends, which reveal clearly his fundamental beliefs and his transient moods.

The best-known of his works and nearest to the heart of the world are his songs. Burns turned these out in amazing quantity and quality, first for James Johnson's *The Scots Musical Museum* and, after 1793, for George Thomson's *Select Airs,* for which he wrote some sixty songs, including many of his finest such as "Highland Mary," "Duncan Gray," "Bonnie Leslie," "Scots Wha Hae wi' Wallace Bled," "Auld Lang Syne," and "A Man's a Man for A' That." For these songs he refused any payment, regarding them as a tribute to the land of which he was the foremost patriot. We note, too, as proof against the legend that Burns ended his days in miserable drunkenness, that up to seven days before his death he was still engaged in composition and in correspondence with Thomson about their project.

It is strange that as a boy Burns was supposed to be deficient in music, even tone-deaf. There was some mistake somewhere, for an ear as sensitive as his cannot be acquired. It is probable that the boy, like so many others, felt shy about performing before his elders. In any case, the pure singing quality of his lyrics had not been heard since Elizabethan times. It is, like the Elizabethan airs, a combination of simple folk melodies and variations in more intricate form. In one aspect, Burns stands out as an unusual master. The common procedure is to have a poem set by a musician. This arrangement leaves the poet all the metrical freedom he needs. It is uncommon for a poet to write words to a tune, for then he is already bound to a set form before he puts a word on paper. Yet Burns very often performed this feat, composing his lyrics to some old tune already in circulation. The freshness and spontaneity of the words under these circumstances are hardly less than miraculous.

Most of his texts are concerned with love, patriotism, humor, and rural life. Occasionally the old note of social protest is heard, as in

> *Then let us pray that come it may*
> *(As come it will for a' that)*
> *That Sense and Worth o'er a' the earth*
> *Shall bear the gree, an' a' that!*
> *For a' that, an' a' that,*
> *It's coming yet for a' that,*
> *That man to man the world o'er*
> *Shall brithers be for a' that.*

When this mood rose to the heights of patriotism, the result was a national war-cry, "Scots Wha Hae wi' Wallace Bled."

The underlying harmony of most of these songs, however, is tenderness, a sweet melancholy, a constant observance of the passing of youth and beauty, and regret at the artificial barriers set up against their love in its brief season. The key is minor, the echo of farewell:

> *And fare thee weel, my only luve*
> *And fare thee weel awhile!*
> *And I will come again, my luve,*
> *Though it were ten thousand mile!*

But we know that the lover will not come again, that inconstancy, or time, or even death itself lies in wait for him even as silence swallows up the last vibration of the song. Only memory is left, and, after memory, sleep.

> *Flow gently, sweet Afton, among thy green braes!*
> *Flow gently, sweet river, the theme of my lays!*
> *My Mary's asleep by thy murmuring stream—*
> *Flow gently, sweet Afton, disturb not her dream!*

With such lines Robert Burns touched not only the heart of Scotland but of the entire world.

Lines of Force in French Poetry

Pierre Emmanuel

Presented at the Library of Congress March 2, 1959

ALL MODERN French poetry bears first of all the stamp of the intellect. Sensibility takes only second place, when it is allowed to function at all. The masters, the doctors, of this poetry are still Rimbaud and Mallarmé: the "seer" and the ascetic. Rimbaud gives himself over in complete lucidity to the imaginary. His "disorder of the senses" is the opposite of vertigo or self-forgetfulness. Ever watchful, constantly on the lookout, the poet reproduces, by means of the most accurate word, motions of the greatest spontaneity and deliriums of the greatest incoherence. It is Mallarmé who scrutinizes "the act of writing . . . back to the very origin of it." That is to say, to the point which he describes as that of: "Knowing whether there is any real place for writing." Verse, the word itself, can have only rare and evanescent successes. From a deep base of "impartial silence" the voice lifts itself up and immediately falls back again, that a revelation may sparkle, an ideal object of the mind, lasting only long enough to bring to life at rare intervals these highly infrequent surprises . . . .

Goodbye, then, to the elegiacal tradition, to the personal *me* and its communicative sensibility. The *I* will be cosmic, in the manner of Rimbaud: it will be the integral of all the possibles, confined in their very inordinacy within the impassable barriers of reason. One understands why Paul Claudel was a disciple of Rimbaud if one accepts for a fact that madness is an extreme action of the intelligence, and immeasurability a way of taking final measure. Rimbaud never surrendered himself to his monsters; he always endeavored to bring them under the submission of his will. In all of his entire self, he is ever present and exerts his own will. His *I* is the principle of sovereign identity; so is the *I* of Claudel. Claudel admires in Rimbaud a tenacity in obliterating one's confines; the nothingness in which this effort ends is the emptiness in which the Absolute reverberates. But Claudel, "Catholic soul," is filled with the presence of an *Other* which lays the foundation for his own presence and establishes it in right proportion to the All. Thus Prometheus, stealer of fire, begets his apparent opposite: the adorer of God, sun of spirits.

From Mallarmé to Valéry, the filiation is from mystic to intellectualist. Valéry is too intelligent not to call in question the very operation of the mind. As to the vital silence out of which the Mallarméan Word surges up, Valéry does not believe in it and has no nostalgia for it: everything is a matter of the art of speaking well, not of suggesting the ineffable. His Word is only a game, and the work simply the fruit of the pleasure which the mind gives itself in exercising itself according to certain laws which it has laid down for itself. Mallarmé believes in the enigmatical hazard suspended as it were from a word which calls it forth into being; everything in his poetry and in his prose suggests the need of recovering or of inventing an oracular magic. Valéry holds only with the supreme competency of the intelligence: the singular word is the result of a combinative power which disposes words at will; thence the formula, the striking image, which only long and patient exercise can release. (Simply to follow the process of creation in the rough drafts of *La Jeune Parque* is enough to be convinced of it). *Homo faber:* the poet is just like any artisan; but his material is language, not iron or wood. In a world without reason for being, which is none the less ordered by the mind, the poet creates this "beautiful lie" of art, which diverts us from our emptiness and furnishes us with the illusion of a beyondness, of a fullness, of a fulfillment of the mind in its creature. What does it matter if this illusion is limited to the pleasure which the arrangement of certain rebuses brings about—since a poem is hardly anything more than that. "Paul Valéry," writes Claudel, "was all his life bent upon denying inspiration." It is true that Claudel adds, "And yet his own work sufficed to give him the lie pointblank." Of that I am less sure. I do not know of anyone who, as much as Valéry, labored so exteriorly at what he produced. One may be permitted to think that rarely has labor been so much in vain.

Claudel and Valéry, who dominated half a century, are dead; surrealism, which came after them, was dead before them, without glory it seems. The aim of the school was very clearly defined in the *Manifestoes* of its principal, André Breton: it was all a question of being attentive to the marvelous hazard or chance that surrounds us, and which the order we imposed upon the world destroys. It became especially necessary, then, to protect oneself from such order—particularly in language—since order prevents the marvel from appearing, from making itself known to us. Surrealism hoped to attain to a language that was "without reserve," the home of a sacred disorder of the spirit where there would be produced, more and more frequently with the development of the method, the unforeseeable encounters and the "miraculous compensations" of fantasy. To liberate oneself from logical constraints meant not only to abandon oneself to the solidarity of vocables lacking any logical succession; it also meant to abolish within oneself the principle of contradiction. It meant losing sight of one's identity and that of the world, and simply being the premises within which the impossible becomes real. This metamorphosis was accomplished by Rimbaud—at least by Rimbaud as the surrealists saw him. Like him, they changed themselves, and their world at the same time, into a fabulous opera in which these artful vigilants, intoxicated with intelligence, observed all the mechanisms as though through a false and superbly lucid bewilderment. What remains to us of the enterprise? A great many modes, an infinity of familiar forms, vulgarized, the cream of contemporary "taste." Nothing, in short, except the daily atmosphere that washes over us, and of whose origin we are unaware. But the Promethean ambition of our betters has not left us any body of work: only a vivid nostalgia, the passion of an instant which the epoch pushed to the point of paroxysm, and perhaps the powerlessness to grow old. Poets will still speak: an inexhaustible reservoir of images. But when all is said and done, the surrealists have had their day; they have believed less in literature than in their faculty of metamorphosis. The greatest poet of the group, Eluard, belongs, it may be, only by virtue of having known how to limit himself to one unique theme: the eternal commonplace of love. But by this same token he renounced the "permanent revolution" which only Breton and a few of the faithful tried to prolong beyond their youth.

Modern French poetry has known other experimenters besides the surrealists, but isolated, not grouped together in a school. Jean Cocteau is one of them. His exercises in white magic never give us metaphysical shivers, though sometimes they arouse a sense of the bizarre or of a slightly conventional fairyland. Henri Michaux aims at something very different: his preoccupation with himself, fortified by the act of writing, is an adventure into unexplored territory, a way of breaking through the very frontiers of being. "Think? Act, rather, upon my machine; both to be and to think, in order to find myself in the situation of having the power to think in a new way . . . . In this sense, I'd like to have done some experimental thinking." If this experimenter takes drugs, ". . . this too is an exploration. Of words, signs, patterns. Mescaline is the explored." And he writes his *Misérable miracle*. Of course poetry for him is only one of the systems of possible forms for making rise up into view, in its endless and redoubtable novelty, the sempiternal enigma of being. "One must have being," is the cry of a Shade in *Face aux verrous*. But being is found only in confines; he is beyond being. In particular, beyond language. There is in the poetry of Michaux the paradox of all experimental poetry since Rimbaud: being

304

constrained to have recourse to language in order to pass beyond it results in being resolved in multiform intelligence which soon espouses the very matter of dreams and, with microscopic discrimination, concentrates its sharpest attention upon a vital point.

The "experimentations" or "explorations" just referred to are distinguished in this way: their guide is that faculty of seeing clearly which we call intelligence and which, even in its maddest adventures, never forgets it is reason. If the unconscious is studied by these adventurers of the mind, it is in the hope of a final explanation, a transfiguring elucidation of man. With the surrealists, this illumination must result from a Promethean action. In the case of Michaux, it is the mysterious grace, perhaps vainly awaited, of a certainty and peace which are recompense for the rendering useless the great effort of the mind within its confines. Another poet, Pierre Jean Jouve, has not pressed forward to the frontiers of being, but instead has penetrated his own central and visceral obscurity, where the *act of incarnation* is accomplished: in other words, he has entered into the fullness of the unconscious life. In starting out from a "thought influenced as much as possible by the unconscious," he sets himself the task of extricating the elemental figures and symbols which dominate our affective life. In order to understand the poetry of Jouve, it is first necessary to admit that the darkness which forms a part of the psychical depth cannot be dispelled by any intellectual enlightenment; the poet tries to cling as it were to these confused and profound motions, to symbolize them by certain unwieldy and clouded forms, sacred and sacrilegious, letting them stand for our most secret fears in that place where man acts out his own peculiar *Mystery*—the theatre of the instincts.

Jouve and Michaux plunge into the interior space of dream, a place preexistent to their attention to it. For Jules Supervielle, the dream is a latent form of life: when the poet wishes to, he creates his dream by interiorizing everything into his "own mental world." There comes to mind at once a word to characterize this attitude: it is reverie. But it runs the risk of not recognizing the exactness of the "dream" for Supervielle. When the poet is in the *action of the dream,* he is aware of all his powers, and he is entirely attentive to himself. Someone has compared Supervielle's poetry to the act of a cardiac patient listening and waiting for each beat of his heart: and suspended, consequently, between being and non-being; a borderland, but a fruitful soil for the spirit. Thanks to the danger that keeps him on the lookout for all signs that attest life, Supervielle has no equal in expressing wonder, the astonishing freshness of the instant: and in counterpoint to— or as counterpart of—his "amazement before the world," there is the revelation of nothingness, of the cracked interior, with each thrust of the battering ram launched by the inmost enemy. "It was necessary for me to have strong enough nerves to face the vertigoes, the traps of the interior cosmos, to which my feelings have always been very much alive and as it were coenesthesic." These coenesthesic feelings of being are so concrete that one may be deceived as to the depths in Supervielle. The reader is seized by what seems a very simple sensation, almost banal by dint of its simplicity, and only discovers after reflection, and with a certain maturity of mind, that the poet has him suspended over an abyss. Life for Supervielle is vertigo and wonder.

There are few theoretical texts of Saint-John Perse to help us form an idea of his poetics outside of his poetry. And it is true also that his poetry is simultaneously a poetics and the action which translates it into a work. Different as his work may seem, in its apparent aspirations, from the rest of the poetry of his time, Saint-John Perse does not appear to consider it a stranger in the family tree whose roots are Rimbaud and Mallarmé. "Modern French poetry," he writes to Mr. George Huppert, "believes itself to be poetry only in so far as it integrates itself, a living thing, with its living object, by embodying itself fully within it, confounding itself with it, substantially, up to the point of a perfect identity and unity of subject and object, of poet and poem." To be sure: but the poetic action of Saint-John Perse is the opposite of what we have observed in the others. He puts his trust in the unity of man and the world. He chooses to remain oblivious to that spiritual torture which is the calling of being into question before it can be; he is among those who prove movement in moving, and follow the course of the vast common history, mingling with the crowd which mingles with them, never distinguishing themselves from it, except by this law which they lay down for themselves: "I shall live in my name." When Saint-John Perse speaks to us of *Man,* his purpose is not to render empty the concept, as does almost all art today and a large part of modern letters; his purpose is to affirm man's presence in the world as proceeding from himself, and to justify the world by this presence which creates it. The petty personal abysses, the obsessions which the megalomania of weak individuals presumes to enlarge to cosmic dimensions, the false depths of visceral bogs, leave indifferent this man of the here-below who believes in the grandeur of human action in history and knows the just proportion between the individual and the universe. Few poets would dare to write what he has artlessly and superbly written of the thematics of *Amers,* after having extolled the unity of the action and of the contemplation which surpasses it: "The recapture of the grand human phrase, at its highest sea-motion, for a total reintegration of man, on his two complementary planes—that for me would be the answer to this human fragmentation, to this wholly passive nihilism, to this actual abdication which some would make the stream bed of our materialistic epoch."

306

I like this profession of faith because it is both proud and modest. Others have recaptured in their own manner, isolated within the general tendency to consider poetry as a more and more mysterious spiritual activity, rare, and quintessential. This tendency, already conspicuous between the two wars, found its theoretic expression in a number of the review *Fontaine,* published under the German occupation, and entitled *La Poésie comme exercice spirituel.* A title which lends itself to worse confusion by proposing itself as an implicit definition which some poets were very eager to adopt in order to justify their dubious alchemies. Why is there, with poets, this need to assign an excessive value to their language and the experience from which it derives, true or pretended? Is it not enough to know that poetry, when it attains certain summits, is one of the highest forms of thought? Why want it to be something more—a gnosis, an initiating Word? Does this post-symbolist mania bear witness to the feeling of inferiority which poets experience in a world in which poetry no longer has any place—but is a genuine philosophy any better treated? If our contemporaries are for the moment indifferent to poetry, it is because they are oriented and impelled toward the future, in the sense of a running away, and are consequently cut off from the third dimension of language which is silence, height, and depth. People no longer read poetry because people no longer know how to read. To read today is only to take flight; to be distracted instead of concentrated. All creation of any amplitude becomes difficult in such an atmosphere; the faith of the few in language is impaired by the indifference and disorder of the great masses who have no idiom of their own and apparently desire none. The contemporary neo-language, the residual expression of a reality which has lost all substance, is at the antipodes of the willed poverty of a certain poetry: to seek out the simple, and the naked, and the essential, is to struggle with the misery of a language in which the meaning of the most concrete vocables has been frittered away. But this effort is just what it is, and no more; one could hardly apply the term "mystical" to it, simply out of respect for the etymology of the word.

But this abuse of terms is met with again and again among poets and critics of poetry. A large part of modern French poetry, from the time of its two great ancestors, was resolutely atheistic, although it tended surreptitiously to deify a mind already raised to the rank of a demiurge. Today the Promethean pride is appeased; the pyrotechnics of the atomic era have made the marvels of poetic flame-stealers grow pale. Either the poets have altogether deserted actuality, or they have become Cassandras prophesying fire from heaven. In jealous crispation, they have retired into their innermost being, into the tabernacle of their narcissistic singularity. All the magical associations of which they hold the secret—their manner of becoming intoxicated with space, with memory, or with nostalgia, by the ability of putting two words together—their spiritual sensuality which the touch or savor of a single vocable satiates—finally their art, composed of intervals of silence, separated by a brief word or two, their long patience in producing a single line, an apt epithet, a rhythmic element in the right place: all of this gives them the air they affect of guarding secrets jealously. Many are sad, engulfed as they are in this life in the melancholy which is born of the certainty there is no other; for them and those who admire them, their poetry is the substitute for an illusory paradise. We are bidden to entertain the emptiest of false mysticisms, to savor the charms of a dead life, the unspeakable distress of the absurd man who adores himself in the midst of his wailing.

Such is the latest avatar of idealism in a society whose values lie buried under the rubbish of a history which these perhaps have brought to ruin instead of controlling and directing it: a belated, defeated poetry which calls mankind to witness its folly, instead of trying to fathom the importance of man. Are we weak creatures who seek in word games and rarefied irisations of memory an antidote to our inanity, the assurance of being the little band, the chosen few, of those who know, happy or unhappy? Who know what? If the latest effort of poetry, the end of its post-Mallarméan ascesis, must bring us to chiseled enigmas like secret jewels—if truly the ideal of modern poetry, in extreme opposition to the world in which it lives, is this highly conventional baroque stylization of a taste of which the true masters are not so much Mallarmé and Valéry as Giambattista Marino or Vion Dalibray, it is not from such objects, pleasing as ornamentally they may be, that we shall extract that simple knowledge of being, that immediate rapport with a common and unfathomable reality, that experience of unity which poetry sometimes gives us.

But I must stop talking this way. The great danger which threatens us, poets tempted by philosophy, is that we should be drawn into explaining our aims instead of writing our work. Criticism judges us on our aphorisms, and not on our poems. We have been contaminated by German philosophy, saturated with commentaries on Hölderlin, and I need not so much as mention our familiarity with the pre-Socratics. All of this constitutes our Canaanitish patois. Shall I give two examples of it? The first is by one of the most firmly established of our recent poets, Yves Bonnefoy, in his preface to *Les Fleurs du Mal:* "I ask myself why the truth of the word appeared in *Les Fleurs du Mal.* If one can define the work otherwise than by noting its perfect strangeness and its nature of pressing to extremity a theological negative, I should call it an *acquiescence.* Another voice than his own, a voice far remote from his own, is accorded him who speaks. Purer than words, it yet delights in words. And what is, and what should be, cease for an instant to be two opposable worlds. There is an abatement of the eternal fever." This assertion of Bonnefoy's about Baudelaire is actually a definition of the personal aesthetics of Bonnefoy; when he becomes the critic of any other work than his own, every poet looks for himself in the mirror.

And now the second text: it is by the author of these remarks and is taken from the introduction to his latest book, *Versant de l'Age:* "The World is an offering to Being of the first fruits of being: we are presented to It, and Being accepts us in presenting Itself to us, within us. The human condition is that of being in sight of Being: my proper vocation is to be called by Being in the very call which I launch forth toward Being. He who responds to the call utters the call; he becomes the oblate of Being." Who wants to read these two texts, so like and unlike each other? They point out a temptation that Bonnefoy defines—and to which he succumbs—in the final words of his preface: "Baudelaire restored to life the great sacrificial idea inscribed in poetry. He discovered, when for many God had ceased to be, that death could be efficacious. That it alone will form anew the unity of lost man. And indeed through the work of Mallarmé and of Proust, and of Artaud and of Jouve—heirs of the spirit of *Les Fleurs du Mal*—one can imagine it servant of souls, in a world finally free and pure. For it would fulfill the destiny of the Word. It would open up to religious feeling, at the end of its long wandering, the abode of poetry."

I resist this temptation. This "purity" in pursuit of which poets hurl themselves into the view that this world here and now is the contrary of a free and pure world, "the verdant paradise of infantine loves," the world of memory transfigured by narcissistic regret—or orphic, if you will, for Narcissus and Orpheus are twins, it is a Catharian purity in which poetry would play the role of *consolamentum* of the perfect. Whether it is nostalgia, or the mystique of being, or madness pure and simple, this activity which goes against the grain throws into discredit our presence in this world. Certainly it abolishes the hereafter: but it is in an *imaginary elsewhere* that true life is made to exist. The deadly malady of poets, their powerlessness to "possess the truth in a mind and a body" (when Rimbaud arrives at it, he stops writing), is evidently at the source of all idealism in poetry. Alas! Almost all poetry is ideal, an embellishing mirror of the soul. "If, in the future, in France, there is ever a revival of religion," writes Mallarmé, "it will take the form of a thousand-fold amplification of the joys of the instinct of the sky in each person." In other words, poetry is a play of looking-glasses whose false depths and complicated perspectives give the illusion—of what, great God? Why change nothingness into a *Palace of Mirages?* This spiritualist and "religious" atheism is not the equal of the other, which simply clings to the earth and does not interrupt its singing.

Whatever one thinks of the ideal line of French poetry—from Mallarmé

309

to Bonnefoy—one has to recognize in it a continuity of thought conferred upon it by the calm effrontery with which it identifies itself with the very idea of poetry. To shatter this stronghold of peremptory assertions to which all of us have carried our building-stones for nearly a hundred years, a race of giants would be necessary—or a catastrophe of thought. Nevertheless the poets entrenched in their fortress merit more and more the name of artists of hunger—or the end. This anemic poetry which macerates in memory, regret, and the unhappiness of being, is *Sehnsucht* and not living spirit. It is a matter of reducing it—it has already reduced itself—to absolute famine, in order that it become what it is: a rare and perfect thing, the object of that strange joy, instantaneous and immediately vanishing, which is born of suddenly discovering that one is infinitely more than oneself: the fetish, in sum, of an intermittent auto-idolatry.

But what of the poetry that only wants to be a form of language, the poetry that restores song to men in order that they may praise and prophesy, celebrate and judge man integral to all the heights of reality and throughout the entire hierarchy of being? That poetry transcends all definitions and all limits, since it comprises the most diverse and violently opposed aesthetics; and that is what we find, despite the theories which claim to purify it of this diversity of which its very substance is composed, right down to the most ascetic of contemporary French poets. The true poetic successes have little to do with the abstract reflections of their authors: it would be utter vanity to range the disciples of Plato against the students of Aristotle. The French poem has as much horror of angelism as it has of excessive expressionism; it is mind within body, spiritual form "enlivened from within," as Saint-John Perse has so well said. It is only the critics who deceive themselves, preferring to read the prose of the poets instead of their poetry. One may well deplore taste in French criticism for the abstractions which it uses as a pretext for its own creative divagations: abstractions of an aesthetics which is almost always formulated outside its object, and which has nothing at all to do with the act of *making* in general, but only with the singular fashion *"in which it is made in this case."* The identity of being and doing is poetic creation. It is the unity the poet seeks in work and that sustains the "inspiration" of his presence. Only Claudel has known how to express it perfectly in his *Art Poétique:* he has the intuition, in this identity, of the figure of a still higher identity, truly cosmic, which language would have the function of releasing. This presence of man in the world is called universe.

Alfred Edward Housman[1]

Cleanth Brooks

Presented at the Library of Congress March 26, 1959

It is tempting to regard A. E. Housman's poetry as classical—in its lucidity, its symmetry, its formal patterning, its laconic bite and edged intensity. Our disposition to do so is encouraged by the fact that Housman was a professor of Latin at Cambridge University and an eminent scholar of the classics. But, as has been frequently observed, Housman is actually the most romantic of poets, and he himself pointed to thoroughly "romantic" sources for his own poetry in naming "Shakespeare's songs, the Scottish border ballads, and Heine." The essentially romantic nature of his conception of poetry was confirmed in Housman's famous lecture, *The Name and Nature of Poetry*. To a Cambridge that had largely shifted its allegiance and worshipped new gods, Housman proclaimed the old gospel: his summary of the history of English poetry still saw the Romantic revolt as the one far-off, divine event to which, from its first beginnings, the whole creation of English poetry had moved. But Housman's poetry is not only generally and fundamentally romantic: it reflects its particular era, the romanticism of the late nineteenth century. As the late John Peale Bishop once put it: "He is the poet of the end of an age. . . ."

But, of course, this again is not the whole story. Here, on the centenary of the poet's birth, we are concerned with what in his poetry transcends his own time and speaks to us now in the mid-twentieth century. Beyond even that, of course, we are interested in what is truly timeless in Housman's poetry. Perhaps a useful means for realizing this timeless quality is to see what he has in common with some of the writers of our own day.

---

[1] Quoted poems from THE COLLECTED POEMS OF A. E. HOUSMAN. Copyright 1922, 1939, 1940, © 1965 by Holt, Rinehart and Winston, Inc. Copyright 1950 by Barclays Bank Ltd. Copyright © 1967, 1968 by Robert E. Symons. Reprinted by permission of Holt, Rinehart and Winston, Inc.

311

Two of Housman's constant themes are courage and stoic endurance, and these are themes which are almost obsessive for several of our best contemporary writers. To name only two, there are William Faulkner and Ernest Hemingway. The gap between Housman's Shropshire lads and Hemingway's bullfighters or boxers or big-game hunters may seem shockingly wide, but it is actually less wide than we think. The gap narrows when we place beside Housman's doomed young soldiers the typical Hemingway hero as man-at-arms during the first World War. The idioms used, I grant you, are sharply dissimilar. Hemingway's brilliantly realistic, acrid Midwestern American speech is a whole world away from the faintly archaic, wholly British idiom which is the staple of Housman's lyrics.

> *The street sounds to the soldiers' tread,*
> *And out we troop to see:*
> *A single redcoat turns his head,*
> *He turns and looks at me . . . .*
>
> *What thoughts at heart have you and I*
> *We cannot stop to tell;*
> *But dead or living, drunk or dry,*
> *Soldier, I wish you well.*

But, I repeat: beneath these surface differences, the situation, the stance taken, the attitude assumed, may not be different at all. Indeed, Hemingway, it seems to me, can throw a great deal of light upon Housman and, though I venture this more hesitantly, Housman may throw a good deal of light on Hemingway.

A good place to start is with one of Housman's finest short poems, but a poem too little known, his "Epitaph on an Army of Mercenaries":

> *These, in the day when heaven was falling,*
> *The hour when earth's foundations fled,*
> *Followed their mercenary calling*
> *And took their wages and are dead.*
>
> *Their shoulders held the sky suspended;*
> *They stood, and earth's foundations stay;*
> *What God abandoned, these defended,*
> *And saved the sum of things for pay.*

It has been said that this brilliant little poem commemorates the small British professional army which heroically took its beating in the early days of the first World War, but which, in spite of terrible losses, managed to slow down and finally to stop the German advance, and so held the Channel ports. I dare say this may be true, so far as concerns the specific occasion.

But the poem has a universal application. It does not celebrate merely the tough professional soldier who fights for his country, not because of some high-sounding ideal but because fighting is his profession—because that is the way he makes his living. The poem surely celebrates all of those hard-bitten realists who are often regarded as mere materialists and yet who frequently outdo the perfervid idealists and self-conscious defenders of the right.

If this is what the poem celebrates, then we are not so far from Hemingway's characteristic stance after all. One remembers, in *A Farewell to Arms*, Lt. Henry's disgust for the great value terms which, for him and his comrades, had become pretentious and empty and therefore lying.

> There were many words that you could not stand to hear and finally only the names of places had dignity. . . . Abstract words such as glory, honor, courage . . . were obscene beside the concrete names of villages, the numbers of roads, the names of rivers, the numbers of regiments and the dates.

But can one really be hired to die? Do Housman's "mercenaries" save the sum of things, as the poet asserts that they do, "for pay"? Isn't there a concealed idealism after all, despite the poet's refusal to allow anything more than the materialistic reason? Of course there is, and this, I suppose, is the point that the poem is making: that the courage to stand and die rather than to run away usually comes from something like *esprit de corps* or professional pride or even from a kind of instinctive manliness rather than from adherence to the conventional rubrics of patriotism and duty. But if this is what Housman's poem implies, then we are indeed in the general realm of Hemingway's fiction, for the mercenaries' gesture is completely consonant with the Hemingway ethos. The Hemingway hero, like Housman's, faces the insoluble "troubles of our proud and angry dust," and in his own way subscribes to the sentiment that

> *Bear them we can, and if we can we must.*
> *Shoulder the sky, my lad, and drink your ale.*

Of course, it must be added that the drink of the Hemingway hero is more likely to be *grappa* or brandy or seven-to-one martinis.

But Hemingway can show what is *wrong* with a Housman poem just as effectively as he can show what is right. Consider a well-known poem by Housman which I think has to be set down as a failure:

> *Could man be drunk for ever*
> *With liquor, love, or fights,*
> *Lief should I rouse at morning*
> *And lief lie down of nights.*

> *But men at whiles are sober*
> *And think by fits and starts,*
> *And if they think, they fasten*
> *Their hands upon their hearts.*

These tough lads who avoid a contemplation of the essential horror of life by keeping the senses occupied with liquor and lechery and fighting are obviously in the same plight as those that we find in *The Sun Also Rises*. Jake, the hero of that fine and sober book, is in spite of himself sober at times, and thinks by fits and starts. But in this case, Hemingway has all the advantage. We can believe in the toughness of his hero and also in his pathos, for both are presented realistically and convincingly. Jake Barnes is never made to fasten his hand upon his heart, and it is this theatrical gesture, so out of keeping with these lusty, brawling, hard-drinking young men, that lets Housman's little poem collapse. The failure does not stem from the fact that the poem falsifies the typical Hemingway situation; it fails because it is inconsistent with its own premises. It is not that the gesture is foreign to Hemingway's Nick Adams: it is a gesture which could not occur in the Shropshire pub of the 1890's. But of course in justice to Housman, Hemingway has his failures too. *Across the River and into the Trees* sentimentalizes the heroic gesture into its own kind of theatricality.

I do not mean to press unduly the Hemingway-Housman analogy. I shall be principally concerned with those qualities that make the finest of Housman's poetry perdurable. But I think that the comparison with Hemingway can be extremely useful in opening up to a contemporary audience the problems which Housman faced and the characteristic failures and characteristic successes which he achieves. In both authors, so dissimilar in so many ways, there is a fairly narrow ambit of interests. The same theme and the same kind of character occur over and over. There is the danger of monotony, the danger of repetition. It seems sometimes to a reader that Housman has only one poem to write, which he writes and rewrites tirelessly, though oftentimes with very brilliant and beautiful variations. With the general narrowness of the ambit there is, as we have seen, the possibility of sentimentality. In general there is a serious problem of tone. The poem must not seem arch or cute. It must achieve its intensity while making use of understatement or laconicism. The close-lipped courage and the stoic endurance must elicit an intense sympathetic response and yet the hero, from the very terms of the situation, is forbidden to cry out or make any direct appeal for our sympathy.

This is the general problem that besets the presentation of the Hemingway hero: he is the tough guy who because of his very toughmindedness sees into the nature of reality and indeed is more sensitive to the tears of things than are those soft and blurred sensibilities whose very fuzziness of response insulates them against the tragic aspects of reality. Yet Housman is a poet who elects to work within a tiny lyric form, barred from the factuality and massively detailed sense of the world which a writer of fiction like Hemingway rightfully has at his disposal.

Let us see how Housman manages the matter in a tiny lyric, which after years of reading remains one of my favorites, a poem entitled "Eight O'Clock."

> *He stood, and heard the steeple*
> *Sprinkle the quarters on the morning town.*
> *One, two, three, four, to market-place and people*
> *It tossed them down.*
>
> *Strapped, noosed, nighing his hour,*
> *He stood and counted them and cursed his luck;*
> *And then the clock collected in the tower*
> *Its strength, and struck.*

We learn in the poem almost nothing about the condemned man. We are never told what his crime was. The poem does no more than give us the last half minute of his life. But how brilliantly that half minute is evoked, and with it some sense of his incorrigible spirit as he waits for the clock's stroke which announces the hour of his execution. Everything in the poem cooperates to dramatize the experience. In the last moments of this man's life, time takes on a monstrously heightened quality. The clock, I take it, is one which sounds a musical phrase for each of the quarter hours and finally, at the hour, after the little tune has been completed, the number of the hour is hammered out with separate strokes. The musical phrases, then, are the "quarters" which he hears the steeple "Sprinkle . . . on the morning town." By the way, an earlier draft of the poem is preserved in one of the notebooks possessed by the Library of Congress—notebooks which the Library owns through the generous gift of Mrs. Gertrude Clarke Whittall. The notebook draft reads:

> One, two, three, four, on jail and square and people
> They dingled down.

Housman's second thoughts are a brilliant improvement. One does not need the mention of the jail. Suspense requires that the reason for the man's intent listening should not be divulged until we come to the second stanza. Contrast requires too that the "morning town," as it is called in

315

the first stanza, be simply presented as a crowded market place down to which the steeple clock almost gaily "tosses" its chiming quarters.

But with the second stanza, now that we know that the listener is strapped and noosed, the clock, though it continues to dominate the scene, changes character and collects itself to strike the prisoner himself. True, the eighth stroke will not be launched vindictively at the prisoner. It will only signal to the hangman the moment to pull the trap. But by a brilliant telescoping, the clock, the recorder and instrument of time, becomes itself the destroyer:

> *And then the clock collected in the tower*
> *Its strength, and struck.*

Time is, with Housman, always the enemy. Housman's Shropshire lad characteristically views the window pane, "blind with showers" and grudgingly checks off one day of his brief springtime that is ruined. Or he speaks to a loved one urgently

> *Now—for a breath I tarry*
> *Nor yet disperse apart.*

One of Housman's finest poems turns not upon reference to a clock but to a calendar. The speaker faces the advent of the first winter month and faces it with a heavy heart.

> *The night is freezing fast,*
> *To-morrow comes December;*
> *And winterfalls of old*
> *Are with me from the past;*
> *And chiefly I remember*
> *How Dick would hate the cold.*

Dick, the friend who is mentioned almost casually in the last line, is of course the occasion for the poem, and as we shall see in the next stanza, it is the first fall of snow upon Dick's grave that becomes the matter of the poem. But Dick, his friend observes with a kind of wry humor, has outwitted winter.

> *Fall, winter, fall; for he,*
> *Prompt hand and headpiece clever,*
> *Has woven a winter robe,*
> *And made of earth and sea*
> *His overcoat for ever,*
> *And wears the turning globe.*

316

Housman has been very daring here. The metaphor with which the poem ends is as bizarre and witty as one of John Donne's. For the speaker insists that the earth has not swallowed up Dick but that the dead man has wrapped the earth about himself "And wears the turning globe." For a poet so Victorian in his tastes as Housman was, and a poet generally so inimical to witty conceits—in his famous lecture on poetry Housman will hardly allow the seventeenth-century metaphysicals the name of poets—his conceit of Dick's wearing the globe is very curious indeed. But the bold figure works. The suggestion of schoolboy slang, "prompt hand and head-piece clever," help to prepare for it, and something of extravagance is needed if the poem is not to dissolve into a kind of too pure and direct pathos. But what makes the last lines work is Housman's audacity in using the commonplace and matter-of-fact word "overcoat." He has already called it a "winter robe," and now if he were to name it a "cloak" or a "toga" or even a "garment," the poem would close on a kind of strained embarrassment. But *overcoat* here is triumphantly right. It represents the brilliant handling of tone which is to be found in nearly all of Housman's successful poems. Dick, with his "headpiece clever," the man never at a loss, has finally outwitted the cold, which he always used to hate. This at least is the way in which one might imagine Dick's accounting for the situation: it is a gay piece of schoolboy extravagance and the jest, because it is characteristic of the dead youth, actually renders the sense of grief not less but more intense. There is not a trace of sentimentality.

Sentimentality is a failure of tone. The emotion becomes mawkish and self-regarding. We feel that the poet himself has been taken in by his own sentiment, responds excessively, and expects us to respond with him in excess of what the situation calls for. And so the writer who, like Housman, insists so uniformly upon the pathos of loss, upon the imminence of death, and upon the grim and loveless blackness to come, must be adept at handling the matter of tone.

Housman's great successes (as well as his disastrous failures) are to be accounted for in terms of tone. It does not matter that Housman never himself employs the term. *We* need it, nevertheless, in order to deal with Housman's poetry: for control of tone is the difference between the shrill and falsetto and the quiet but resonant utterance; it is the difference between the merely arch and self-consciously cute and the full-timbred irony; it is the difference between the sentimental and the responsibly mature utterance. Housman's characteristic fault is a slipping off into sentimentality. (One may observe in passing that this is also Hemingway's characteristic fault.) Conversely, Housman's triumphs nearly always involve a brilliant handling of tone—often a startling shift in tone—in which the matter of the poem is suddenly seen in a new perspective.

"The Night is Freezing Fast" exhibits the kind of tonal shift of which I am speaking. "The Immortal Part" will furnish an even clearer example. In this poem, the speaker perversely insists that the immortal part of man is his skeleton—not the spirit, not the soul—but the most earthy, the most nearly mineral part of his body. The bones will endure long after the "dust of thoughts" has at last been laid and the flesh itself has become dust.

The device on which the poem is built is the grumbling complaint of the bones. The speaker begins by telling us that he can hear his bones counting the days of their servitude and predicting the day of their deliverance in which the flesh will fall away from them and leave them free and unfettered. Housman allows to the bones a certain lugubrious eloquence.

> *"Wanderers eastward, wanderers west,*
>   *Know you why you cannot rest?*
>   *'Tis that every mother's son*
>   *Travails with a skeleton.*

The reference to "wanderers" makes one suppose that "travails" is spelled "travels," but in fact the word is "travails"; and this suggestion of the travail of childbirth is developed fully in the next two stanzas:

> *"Lie down in the bed of dust;*
>   *Bear the fruit that bear you must;*
>   *Bring the eternal seed to light,*
>   *And morn is all the same as night.*

> *"Rest you so from trouble sore,*
>   *Fear the heat o' the sun no more,*
>   *Nor the snowing winter wild,*
>   *Now you labour not with child.*

> *"Empty vessel, garment cast,*
>   *We that wore you long shall last.*
>   *—Another night, another day."*
>   *So my bones within me say.*

The colloquy of the bones is brilliant. But can the brilliance be indefinitely sustained? After nine stanzas, there is every danger of monotony. What climatic threat is there left for the bones to utter? And if there is none, how end the poem?

What Housman does is to introduce a brilliant shift in tone. The man answers back:

Therefore they shall do my will
To-day while I am master still,
And flesh and soul, now both are strong,
Shall hale the sullen slaves along,

Before this fire of sense decay,
This smoke of thought blow clean away,
And leave with ancient night alone
The stedfast and enduring bone.

But this defiance of the bones implies in fact a conviction of the truth of their ultimate triumph. Indeed, the "I" who speaks concedes the bones' eventual victory, and furthermore the last four lines of his speech of defiance simply turn into an echo of the chant of the bones. But the tone of the poem has shifted: the conscious sentient being has refused to collapse before the certain onslaught of time. The human spirit is given its due. The worst has been faced and faced down, though not denied.

Housman's use of a shift in tone is so important in his poetry generally that I should like to exhibit still another instance—one of Housman's finest, that which he employs in "Bredon Hill."

The lovers on many a Sunday morning on Bredon Hill have listened to the church bells ringing out through the valleys.

In summertime on Bredon
  The bells they sound so clear;
Round both the shires they ring them
  In steeples far and near,
    A happy noise to hear.

Here of a Sunday morning
  My love and I would lie,
And see the coloured counties,
  And hear the larks so high
    About us in the sky.

In their own happiness the lovers would put words to the sound of the bells:

  The bells would ring to call her
    In valleys miles away:
  "Come all to church, good people;
    Good people, come and pray."
    But here my love would stay.

> *And I would turn and answer*
> *Among the springing thyme,*
> *"Oh, peal upon our wedding,*
> *And we will hear the chime,*
> *And come to church in time."*

But his sweetheart comes to church before their time.

> *But when the snows at Christmas*
> *On Bredon top were strown,*
> *My love rose up so early*
> *And stole out unbeknown*
> *And went to church alone.*

> *They tolled the one bell only,*
> *Groom there was none to see,*
> *The mourners followed after,*
> *And so to church went she,*
> *And would not wait for me.*

This last stanza, as the notebooks preserved in this Library reveal, gave Housman great trouble. He made at least five attempts to get the phrasing right. I hope that it is not too irreverent of me to suggest that he never did get it precisely right. I cannot help resenting the line "The mourners followed after"—not because it is not true—presumably there were mourners—but because it is unnecessary—we do not need to be *told* in so many words that the girl died. Moreover, the direct reference to her death works against the indirect presentation of it through the poem's basic metaphor—which treats the funeral as if it were a marriage, in which the lover is betrayed by his sweetheart who jilts him and steals away to church to be wed to another.

> *And so to church went she*
> *And would not wait for me—*

not *could* not wait, but *would* not wait, as if her failure to wait for him were a matter of her own volition.

But whether or not I am right in thinking that Housman's "explaining his metaphor" is a slight blemish in the sixth stanza, how brilliantly the poem recovers in the seventh, and is brought to an ending that is beautifully right! I think that you can "hear" the shift in tone as I read this last stanza:

> *The bells they sound on Bredon,*
> *And still the steeples hum.*

> *"Come all to church, good people,"*—
>> *Oh, noisy bells, be dumb;*
>> *I hear you, I will come.*

The note of exasperation—the irritated outburst against the noise of the bells—is a powerful, if indirect way, of voicing the speaker's sense of loss. All come to death; he will come to the churchyard too; but now that his sweetheart has been stolen from him, what does it matter *when* he comes. The bells whose sound was once a happy noise to hear have become a needless and distracting noisiness.   The lover shuts them up as he might the disturbing prattle of a child:

> *Oh, noisy bells, be dumb;*
> *I hear you, I will come.*

One of Housman's surest triumphs of tone is the first poem of *A Shropshire Lad*, the poem simply entitled "1887."   The year 1887 was that of Queen Victoria's Jubilee.   The village is celebrating the fiftieth year of her accession to the throne.   The beacons have been lighted and in the village pub they are singing "God Save the Queen."

> *From Clee to heaven the beacon burns,*
>> *The shires have seen it plain,*
> *From north and south the sign returns*
>> *And beacons burn again.*
>
> *Look left, look right, the hills are bright,*
>> *The dales are light between,*
> *Because 'tis fifty years to-night*
>> *That God has saved the Queen.*

But after the light dancing measures and the flickering alliteration of the opening lines, line eight brings us down with a solid bump.   "God save the Queen" is a ritualized phrase.   One invokes God's favor. One recommends the sovereign to His mercy.   But one does not bring the prayerful imperative down into the dust and sweat of ordinary syntax by turning it into the present perfect of an ordinary work-a-day English verb:

> *Because 'tis fifty years to-night*
>> *That God has saved the Queen.*

It is as if a piece of ritual furniture were suddenly put to some common use: we get a comparable shock.

I shall have more to say of this device in a moment: suffice it to observe at this point that notice has been served that this will be no ordinary Jubilee tribute.   And it is not.   For the speaker goes on in the stanzas that

321

follow to talk about the absentees on this occasion, the boys who had been abroad on the Queen's business, who did not come home.

> *Now, when the flame they watch not towers*
> *About the soil they trod,*
> *Lads, we'll remember friends of ours*
> *Who shared the work with God.*

Again, with the last line there is a shock: God has saved the Queen, but He has required the services—or at least has chosen to make use of the services—of human helpers. And some of these have proved to be expendable. The irony is as edged as a knife—and yet it is a quiet and unforced irony; for the statement "Who shared the work with God" is perfectly consonant with the stated premises. For if the defeat of the Queen's enemies is to be attributed ultimately to God, the humbler means, the British infantrymen who have stood off her enemies, have had a share, even if only a humble share, in God's work. But many of the Shropshire lads who went into the armies of the Queen have not returned.

> *To skies that knit their heartstrings right,*
> *To fields that bred them brave,*
> *The saviours come not home to-night:*
> *Themselves they could not save.*

Here the irony achieves a sort of climax, for the last lines echo the passage in the Gospels in which Christ, hanging on the cross, is taunted with the words: "Others he saved; himself he cannot save." To apply the words associated with the Crucified to the dead soldiers is audacious, but again the words are perfectly applicable, quite simply and literally fitting the case of the absent soldiers. Indeed, a reader who failed to catch the Biblical allusion would not feel that the lines were forced or strained. For soldiers, who must necessarily risk losing their own lives in order to save others, are often to be found in such a plight: Others they saved, "Themselves they could not save."

With the fifth stanza, the poem moves away from the local scene. The speaker lets his imagination wander over the far places of the earth where the dead soldiers now lie.

> *It dawns in Asia, tombstones show*
> *And Shropshire names are read;*
> *And the Nile spills his overflow*
> *Beside the Severn's dead.*
>
> *We pledge in peace by farm and town*
> *The Queen they served in war,*

322

And fire the beacons up and down
The land they perished for.

We need this expansion of view and we need a momentary rest from the irony that has closed so powerfully stanzas two, three, and four. But after this shift of perspective and alteration of tone, we are returned once more to the Jubilee occasion. The lads of the Fifty-third Regiment—those who did come back, that is—join in the celebration.

"God save the Queen" we living sing,
From height to height 'tis heard;
And with the rest your voices ring,
Lads of the Fifty-third.

Oh, God will save her, fear you not:
Be you the men you've been,
Get you the sons your fathers got,
And God will save the Queen.

It is a powerful ending of a brilliant poem. Anyone can feel that. But it may be worth examining a little further the speaker's final attitude. Is the poem anti-royalist? Anti-religious? More specifically, is the man who speaks the poem contemptuous of the lads of the Fifty-third because they naively sing "God save the Queen" and do not realize that it is they who have had to do the dirty work themselves?

As a matter of fact, Housman's own views on the ending of his poem are on record. Frank Harris, in his *Latest Contemporary Portraits,* tells of a talk with Housman about this poem. He writes:

I recited the last verse as if it had been bitter sarcasm which in all sincerity I had taken it for and I went on: "It stirs my blood to find an Englishman so free of the insensate snobbishness that corrupts all true values here. I remember telling Kipling once that when he mixed his patriotism with snobbery it became disgusting to me; and here you have poked fun at the whole thing and made splendid mockery of it."

To my astonishment, Housman replied sharply: "I never intended to poke fun, as you call it, at patriotism, and I can find nothing in the sentiment to make mockery of: I meant it sincerely; if Englishmen breed as good men as their fathers, then God will save their Queen." His own words seemed to have excited him for he added precisely but with anger: "I can only reject and resent your—your truculent praise."

Housman's angry outburst might seem to settle the matter. But does it? It may dispose of Harris's attempt to read a "bitter sarcasm" into the last stanza. But even Housman's own word for it will hardly smooth the irony out of this poem.

Lads, we'll remember friends of ours,
Who shared the work with God.

> *The saviours come not home to-night:*
> *Themselves they could not save.*

These passages simply defy an innocently literal reading; and in view of Housman's frequently expressed scepticism about the existence of God, the last lines of the poem likewise defy a literal reading.

In angrily rejecting Frank Harris's bitter sarcasm, Housman over-corrected the error. If one reads the entire account printed by Harris, it is easy enough to see what happened. Harris and a pair of his friends had got to talking about Housman's poetry, and one of them proposed that they look the poet up at King's College, London, where he was teaching, and take him to lunch. They called, introduced themselves, and fairly swept him along to lunch with them. This was not the sort of thing that Housman, a shy and fastidious man, would take to, and Frank Harris, with his breezy confidence and his trace of vulgarity, was exactly the sort of man that Housman would abominate. Harris makes it quite plain that no rapport had been established, the conversation had been forced and difficult throughout the luncheon. Resentments of a more pervasive kind and a general antagonism burst forth in Housman's explosion over the meaning of his poem.

We are back, then, once more with the problem of tone. Is it possible to describe the tone of this poem without misrepresenting it on the one hand as a heavy sarcasm and without, on the other hand, falsifying its evident irony? I think that it is possible.

The key to the poet's attitude is to be found in a line of the poem upon which we have already commented:

> *Because 'tis fifty years tonight*
> *That God has saved the Queen.*

There, as we remarked, a ritualistic phrase, a pious sentiment, a patriotic cliché is suddenly taken seriously and is made to work in a normal English sentence. It is as shocking as if a bishop suddenly used his crozier like a shepherd's crook to lay hold upon a live sheep.

But to consider soberly the implications of the phrase that is bandied about so thoughtlessly on this jubilant occasion—to reflect upon what is involved in the prayer "God save the Queen"—does not necessarily involve mockery of the Queen or of the young men who have helped save her. Housman's protest here is well taken. His consideration of the cliché, however, does involve a realistic appraisal of the issues and a penetration beneath patriotic shows and appearances. The speaker clearly admires the lads of the Fifty-third but his angle of vision is different from theirs. What they accept naively and uncritically, he sees in its full complexity and ambiguity. But his attitude is not cynical and it is consonant with genuine

324

patriotism. The irony that it contains is a mature and responsible irony whose focus is never blurred. The closing stanza, with its quiet insistence that God will save the Queen but with its conjoined insistence on the all important proviso that they shall get them the sons their fathers got dramatizes the speaker's attitude to a nicety.

A little while ago, I called Housman a romantic poet, a late romantic. If I have emphasized Housman the ironist, it is because I think his irony is important and that its presence does not make him the less a romanticist. But a more obvious aspect of his romanticism may be his treatment of nature.

Many of the poems—and not only those of *A Shropshire Lad*—are given a pastoral setting. The English countryside is everywhere in Housman's poetry. A typical appearance is revealed in the charming lyric which is printed on the back of your programs. To see the cherry in blossom is one of the delights of the year, and how few years there are vouchsafed us in which to see it. Time is the enemy of delight and yet the cherry tree is the product of time. The very description of the springtime beauty is ominous: if "hung with snow" is a way of stressing the unbelievable whiteness of the blossoms, the phrase also hints of winter and the death to come.

But Housman's view of nature looks forward to our time rather than back to that of Wordsworth. If nature is lovely and offers man delight, she does not offer him solace or sustain him as Wordsworth was solaced and sustained. For between Wordsworth and Housman there interpose themselves Darwin and Huxley and Tindall—the whole achievement of Victorian science. The effect of this impact of science is not, of course, to make Housman love nature less: one could argue that it has rendered nature for him more poignantly beautiful. But his attitude toward nature is not that of the early Romantics and we must take into account this altered attitude if we are to understand his poems.

In this general connection allow me to remark, by the way, that we have had in our day the revival—though it has gone largely unnoticed—of a very fine nature poetry. This nature poetry reveals the somewhat altered perspective of the twentieth century—as is natural and inevitable. But the delight in the rich qualities of the natural scene is extraordinary. Let me extend the term *poetry* to include some of our finest prose fiction. Look at the rendering of nature—to be found, say, in Hemingway and Faulkner. There is a loving attention to detail and faithful evocation of the quality of a scene. The natural world is reflected with beautiful delicacy and even radiance in the fishing episode in Hemingway's *The Sun Also Rises,* or in the hunting scenes of Faulkner's "The Bear." This latter story concludes with what can only be described as a great hymn to nature. If keeping in mind such nature poetry as this, we remember also the characteristic depiction of nature by poets like Thomas Hardy or Robert Frost, we may begin to realize that the twentieth century, in spite of industrialization and the growth of world cities, has indeed produced a rich nature poetry.

Our immensely increased knowledge of nature has not destroyed her charm. Even the so-called scientific neutralization of nature has not done that—not at least for many of our poets. But it has altered their attitudes toward her and it has tended to stress man's sense of his alienation from nature. (Of course, even this sense of alienation is not strictly "modern"— I find it, for example, in Keats' "Ode to a Nightingale.") But the fact of alienation tends to be determinative for the modern nature poet. The poems of Robert Frost testify again and again to the elemental attraction of nature of which man is a part, but Frost never yields to the delusion that man can slip through the invisible barrier to merge himself into nature. The speaker of the poem in every case remembers his manhood and ruefully or with a half-serious jest or with a stoic brusqueness puts down the temptation. When the falling leaves of autumn beckon to Frost's "leaf-treader" to come with them in their descent to death, the man acknowledges the "fugitive in his heart" that wants to respond to the leaves' "invitation to grief," but finally, with a small boy's impudence, he shrugs off the impulse:

> But it was no reason I had to go because they had to go
> So up my foot to keep on top of another year of snow.

Again, the traveler in "Stopping by Woods on a Snowy Evening" pauses and as he enjoys the beauty of the lovely scene, feels the attraction of nature:

> The woods are lovely, dark and deep . . .

But he has promises to keep and it is significant that he drives on. Or again, the man who comes upon the site of the burned farmhouse and abandoned barn is struck by the melancholy of the scene. The very birds who haunt the scene seem to be mourning. But the observer knows better, though

> One had to be versed in country things
> Not to believe the phoebes wept.

But he is versed in country things, and in spite of the temptation to feel that nature sympathizes with man, he knows that she does not. However melancholy the birds may sound to him, they are simply singing out of the fullness of their own activity; they know nothing and care nothing for man's sorrow.

Frost's treatment of nature can help us to understand Housman's, particularly that revealed in what is in some respects Housman's finest poem, with a comment on which I mean to close this lecture. But I am not, of course, so absurd as to suggest that the attitudes of Frost and Housman are identical; and in any case, the poetic strategies of these two fine poets differ in a dozen ways. They speak in different idioms, different intonations. But the resemblance is worth pointing out in order to stress an element of the modern in Housman that we may easily overlook.

Housman expressed his characteristic attitude toward nature in the beautiful poem numbered XL in *Last Poems,* his farewell to nature. The matter of the poem is the speaker's resignation of his mistress Nature to another. The resignation is forced; he does not willingly relinquish her. He has possessed her too completely to feel that she is less than a part of himself and his appetite for her is not cloyed. At this moment of conscious relinquishment, nature has never been more compellingly the enchantress.

> *Tell me not here, it needs not saying,*
>   *What tune the enchantress plays*
> *In aftermaths of soft September*
>   *Or under blanching mays,*
> *For she and I were long acquainted*
>   *And I knew all her ways.*

How thorough is his knowledge of her ways is quietly but convincingly made good in the second and third stanzas.

> *On russet floors, by waters idle,*
>   *The pine lets fall its cone;*
> *The cuckoo shouts all day at nothing*
>   *In leafy dells alone;*
> *And traveller's joy beguiles in autumn*
>   *Hearts that have lost their own.*

> *On acres of the seeded grasses*
>   *The changing burnish heaves;*
> *Or marshalled under moons of harvest*
>   *Stand still all night the sheaves;*
> *Or beeches strip in storms for winter*
>   *And stain the wind with leaves.*

These beautiful stanzas do more than create a series of scenes from nature. They insinuate the speaker's claim to his possession of nature through an intimate knowledge of her ways. Each of the vignettes suggests the secret life of nature revealed to a rapt and solitary observer: the tap of the falling pine cone, audible only because the scene is hushed and breathless; the shouts of the solitary cuckoo, who seems to be calling to no other bird and not even to a human listener but with cheerful idiocy shouting "at nothing"; the flower called "traveller's joy" in the autumn sunshine silently extending to the joyless wayfarer its grace of self, the namesake of joy.

The "changing burnish" on the "acres of seeded grasses," I take to be the shimmer of light that one sees play upon a hayfield in late summer when the wind heaves and ripples the long grass stems to catch the light. You who have seen it will know that "burnish" is not too extravagant a term, for the grass sometimes shimmers as if it were metallic. The wind that heaves the grass is a fitful wind of late summer. That which strips the beech trees of their leaves is a late autumn gale. But the third scene portrayed in this stanza—

> *Or marshalled under moons of harvest*
> *Stand still all night the sheaves—*

is windless: that is the point, I take it, of the statement that under the harvest moon the sheaves "Stand *still* all night." The secret life of nature is thus depicted through all weathers and throughout the round of the seasons. All of it has been observed by the speaker, all of it has been made his own possession through knowledge and is held now in memory. But the various scenes of the changing year are but the magic spells woven by the one enchantress.

The fourth stanza stresses his claim to possession. The first line rings the changes upon the word "possess" and the very last word of the stanza, the emphatic closing rime word, is "mine." But the action of the stanza is a relinquishment of his claims. The speaker conjures the companion to whom he speaks the poem to

> *Possess, as I possessed a season,*
> *The countries I resign,*
> *Where over elmy plains the highway*
> *Would mount the hills and shine,*
> *And full of shade the pillared forest*
> *Would murmur and be mine.*

His claim to possession is based upon a shared experience, a secret knowledge, the kind of bond that unites two lovers who feel that they belong to each other. But in this instance, the beloved is nature; and nature is not one to recognize any lover's claim to possession.

> *For nature, heartless, witless nature—*

328

Nature is not only the fickle mistress, she is the idiot mistress, having no more mind than heart.

> For nature, heartless, witless nature
>   Will neither care nor know
> What stranger's feet may find the meadow
>   And trespass there and go,
> Nor ask amid the dews of morning
>   If they be mine or no.

Nature, for all her attractiveness to man, is supremely indifferent to him. This is the bedrock fact upon which the poem comes to rest, but if the fact constitutes a primal irony, it is accepted in this poem without rancor or any fierce bitterness. The very charm of nature is the way in which she can give herself freely to all of us who will strenuously try to claim her. And moreover, if nature, in this last stanza, is heartless and witless, she is still as freshly beautiful as the morning. Notice how concretely Housman says this in the closing lines. Nature spreads her dewy meadow as virginally fresh for the imprint of the feet of the trespasser as for those of the old lover who would like to believe that he alone possessed her.

The attitude toward nature here is not Wordsworth's confident trust that "Nature never did betray / The heart that loved her." Yet the poem may be said to illustrate the Wordsworthian formula

> How exquisitely the individual Mind . . .
> . . . to the external World
> Is fitted: —and how exquisitely, too— . . .
> The external World is fitted to the Mind.

True, it is Housman's mind, not Wordsworth's, that is fitted to the landscape here described; but the exquisite fitting is there just the same—so much so that the nature that Housman depicts seems to answer at every point the sensitive and melancholy mind that perceives it, and in its turn implies in its aloof and beautifully closed order the loneliness and austerity of the mind of its observer.

Housman's feet no longer print the dew of his favorite English meadow. What he predicted in the poem has obviously come to pass. The ageless enchantress nature spreads her blandishments now for other men—for us, if we care to respond. But it ought to be noted that Housman has himself responded with an enchantment of his own: I mean the poem itself. The poem matches the immortality of nature with its own kind of immortality—the immortality of art. For, if nature, changeless through all the vicissitudes of change, is unweariedly the same, so also the experience that Housman has dramatized for us here may be endlessly repeated and is eternally recapturable. *Ars longa, vita brevis.* *We* may trespass into the poet's ancient dominion, see and possess as the poet himself "possessed a season" the woods and fields of Shropshire or of Cambridgeshire. But in participating in his *poem* we will possess more: we will possess his hard-won knowledge of the meaning of possession. Through the poem we shall come to know more deeply what our relation to nature is and what we as men are. Our feet, then, that "trespass" on the poet's ancient dominion, in the magical world of his poem, commit no trespass. His footprints become our own; we stand in his shoes; we share in his experience, which has been treasured up and given a life beyond life. That is what art can do. That is why we must always feel a deep gratitude to the poet. That is why we celebrate Alfred Edward Housman's one hundredth birthday this evening.

The House of Poe

Richard Wilbur

Presented at the Library of Congress May 4, 1959

A FEW WEEKS AGO, in the *New York Times Book Review,* Mr. Saul Bellow expressed impatience with the current critical habit of finding symbols in everything.   No self-respecting modern professor, Mr. Bellow observed, would dare to explain Achilles' dragging of Hector around the walls of Troy by the mere assertion that Achilles was in a bad temper.   That would be too drearily obvious.   No, the professor must say that the circular path of Achilles and Hector relates to the theme of circularity which pervades *The Iliad.*

In the following week's *Book Review,* a pedantic correspondent corrected Mr. Bellow, pointing out that Achilles did not, in Homer's *Iliad,* drag Hector's body around the walls of Troy; this perhaps invalidates the Homeric example, but Mr. Bellow's complaint remains, nevertheless, a very sensible one.   We are all getting a bit tired, I think, of that laboriously clever criticism which discovers mandalas in Mark Twain, rebirth archetypes in Edwin Arlington Robinson, and fertility myths in everybody.

Still, we must not be carried away by our impatience, to the point of demanding that no more symbols be reported.   The business of the critic, after all, is to divine the intention of the work, and to interpret the work in the light of that intention; and since some writers are intentionally symbolic, there is nothing for it but to talk about their symbols.   If we speak of Melville, we must speak of symbols.   If we speak of Hawthorne, we must speak of symbols.   And as for Edgar Allan Poe, whose sesquicentennial year we are met to observe, I think we can make no sense about him until we consider his work—and in particular his prose fiction—as deliberate and often brilliant allegory.

Not everyone will agree with me that Poe's work has an accessible allegorical meaning.   Some critics, in fact, have refused to see any substance, allegorical or otherwise, in Poe's fiction, and have regarded his tales

331

as nothing more than complicated machines for saying "boo." Others have intuited undiscoverable meanings in Poe, generally of an unpleasant kind: I recall one Freudian critic declaring that if we find Poe unintelligible we should congratulate ourselves, since if we *could* understand him it would be proof of our abnormality.

It is not really surprising that some critics should think Poe meaningless, or that others should suppose his meaning intelligible only to monsters. Poe was not a wide-open and perspicuous writer; indeed, he was a secretive writer both by temperament and by conviction. He sprinkled his stories with sly references to himself and to his personal history. He gave his own birthday of January 19 to his character William Wilson; he bestowed his own height and color of eye on the captain of the phantom ship in *Ms. Found in a Bottle;* and the name of one of his heroes, Arthur Gordon Pym, is patently a version of his own. He was a maker and solver of puzzles, fascinated by codes, ciphers, anagrams, acrostics, hieroglyphics, and the Kabbala. He invented the detective story. He was fond of aliases; he delighted in accounts of swindles; he perpetrated the famous Balloon Hoax of 1844; and one of his most characteristic stories is entitled *Mystification.* A man so devoted to concealment and deception and unraveling and detection might be expected to have in his work what Poe himself called "undercurrents of meaning."

And that is where Poe, as a critic, said that meaning belongs: not on the surface of the poem or tale, but below the surface as a dark undercurrent. If the meaning of a work is made overly clear—as Poe said in his *Philosophy of Composition*—if the meaning is brought to the surface and made the upper current of the poem or tale, then the work becomes bald and prosaic and ceases to be art. Poe conceived of art, you see, not as a means of giving imaginative order to earthly experience, but as a stimulus to unearthly visions. The work of literary art does not, in Poe's view, present the reader with a provisional arrangement of reality; instead, it seeks to disengage the reader's mind from reality and propel it toward the ideal. Now, since Poe thought the function of art was to set the mind soaring upward in what he called "a wild effort to reach the Beauty above," it was important to him that the poem or tale should not have such definiteness and completeness of meaning as might contain the reader's mind within the work. Therefore Poe's criticism places a positive value on the obscuration of meaning, on a dark suggestiveness, on a deliberate vagueness by means of which the reader's mind may be set adrift toward the beyond.

Poe's criticism, then, assures us that his work does have meaning. And Poe also assures us that this meaning is not on the surface but in the depths. If we accept Poe's invitation to play detective, and commence to read him with an eye for submerged meaning, it is not long before we sense that there *are* meanings to be found, and that in fact many of Poe's stories, though superficially dissimilar, tell the same tale. We begin to have this sense as we notice Poe's repeated use of certain narrative patterns; his repetition of certain words and phrases; his use, in story after story, of certain scenes and properties. We notice, for instance, the recurrence of the *spiral* or *vortex*. In *Ms. Found in a Bottle*, the story ends with a plunge into a whirlpool; the *Descent into the Maelstrom* also concludes in a watery vortex; the house of Usher, just before it plunges into the tarn, is swaddled in a whirlwind; the hero of *Metzengerstein*, Poe's first published story, perishes in "a whirlwind of chaotic fire"; and at the close of *King Pest*, Hugh Tarpaulin is cast into a puncheon of ale and disappears "amid a whirlpool of foam." That Poe offers us so many spirals or vortices in his fiction, and that they should always appear at the same terminal point in their respective narratives, is a strong indication that the spiral had some symbolic value for Poe. And it did: What the spiral invariably represents in any tale of Poe's is the loss of consciousness, and the descent of the mind into sleep.

I hope you will grant, before I am through, that to find spirals in Poe is not so silly as finding circles in Homer. The professor who finds circles in Homer does so to the neglect of more important and more provable meanings. But the spiral or vortex is a part of that symbolic language in which Poe said his say, and unless we understand it we cannot understand Poe.

But now I have gotten ahead of myself, and before I proceed with my project of exploring one area of Poe's symbolism, I think I had better say something about Poe's conception of poetry and the poet.

Poe conceived of God as a poet. The universe, therefore, was an artistic creation, a poem composed by God. Now, if the universe is a poem, it follows that the one proper response to it is aesthetic, and that God's creatures are attuned to Him in proportion as their imaginations are ravished by the beauty and harmony of his creation. Not to worship beauty, not to regard poetic knowledge as divine, would be to turn one's back on God and fall from grace.

The planet Earth, according to Poe's myth of the cosmos, has done just this. It has fallen away from God by exalting the scientific reason above poetic intuition, and by putting its trust in material fact rather than in visionary knowledge. The Earth's inhabitants are thus corrupted by rationalism and materialism; their souls are diseased; and Poe sees this disease of the human spirit as having contaminated physical nature. The woods and fields and waters of Earth have thereby lost their first beauty, and no longer clearly express God's imagination; the landscape has lost its original perfection of composition, in proportion as men have lost their power to perceive the beautiful.

Since Earth is a fallen planet, life upon Earth is necessarily a torment for the poet: neither in the human sphere nor in the realm of nature can he find fit objects for contemplation, and indeed his soul is oppressed by everything around him. The rationalist mocks at him; the dull, prosaic spirit of the age damps his imaginative spark; the gross materiality of the world crowds in upon him. His only recourse is to abandon all concern for Earthly things, and to devote himself as purely as possible to unearthly visions, in hopes of glimpsing that heavenly beauty which is the thought of God.

Poe, then, sees the poetic soul as at war with the mundane physical world; and that warfare is Poe's fundamental subject. But the war between soul and world is not the only war. There is also warfare within the poet's very nature. To be sure, the poet's nature was not always in conflict with itself. Prior to his earthly incarnation, and during his dreamy childhood, Poe's poet enjoyed a serene unity of being; his consciousness was purely imaginative, and he knew the universe for the divine poem that it is. But with his entrance into adult life, the poet became involved with a fallen world in which the physical, the factual, the rational, the prosaic are not escapable. Thus, compromised, he lost his perfect spirituality, and is now cursed with a divided nature. Though his imagination still yearns toward ideal beauty, his mortal body chains him to the physical and temporal and local; the hungers and passions of his body draw him toward external objects, and the conflict of conscience and desire degrades and distracts his soul; his mortal senses try to convince him of the reality of a material world which his soul struggles to escape; his reason urges him to acknowledge everyday fact, and to confine his thought within the prison of logic. For all these reasons it is not easy for the poet to detach his soul from earthly things, and regain his lost imaginative power—his power to commune with that supernal beauty which is symbolized, in Poe, by the shadowy and angelic figures of Ligeia, and Helen, and Lenore.

These, then, are Poe's great subjects: first, the war between the poetic soul and the external world; second, the war between the poetic soul and the earthly self to which it is bound. All of Poe's major stories are allegorical presentations of these conflicts, and everything he wrote bore somehow upon them.

How does one wage war against the external world? And how does one release one's visionary soul from the body, and from the constraint of the reason? These may sound like difficult tasks; and yet we all accomplish them every night. In a subjective sense—and Poe's thought is wholly subjective—we destroy the world every time we close our eyes. If *esse est percipi*, as Bishop Berkeley said—if to be is to be perceived—then when we withdraw our attention from the world in somnolence or sleep, the world ceases to be. As our minds move toward sleep, by way of drowsiness and reverie and the hypnagogic state, we escape from consciousness of the world, we escape from awareness of our bodies, and we enter a realm in which reason no longer hampers the play of the imagination: we enter the realm of dream.

Like many romantic poets, Poe identified imagination with dream. Where Poe differed from other romantic poets was in the literalness and absoluteness of the identification, and in the clinical precision with which he observed the phenomena of dream, carefully distinguishing the various states through which the mind passes on its way to sleep. A large number of Poe's stories derive their very structure from this sequence of mental states: *Ms. Found in a Bottle,* to give but one example, is an allegory of the mind's voyage from the waking world into the world of dreams, with each main step of the narrative symbolizing the passage of the mind from one state to another—from wakefulness to reverie, from reverie to the hypnagogic state, from the hypnagogic state to the deep dream. The departure of the narrator's ship from Batavia represents the mind's withdrawal from the waking world; the drowning of the captain and all but one of the crew represents the growing solitude of reverie; when the narrator is transferred by collision from a real ship to a phantom ship, we are to understand that he has passed from reverie, a state in which reality and dream exist in a kind of equilibrium, into the free fantasy of the hypnagogic state. And when the phantom ship makes its final plunge into the whirlpool, we are to understand that the narrator's mind has gone over the brink of sleep and descended into dreams.

What I am saying by means of this example is that the scenes and situations of Poe's tales are always concrete representations of states of mind. If we bear in mind Poe's fundamental plot—the effort of the poetic soul to escape all consciousness of the world in dream—we soon recognize the significance of certain scenic or situational motifs which turn up in story after story. The most important of these recurrent motifs is that of *enclosure* or *circumscription;* perhaps the latter term is preferable, because it is Poe's own word, and because Poe's enclosures are so often more or less circular in form. The heroes of Poe's tales and poems are violently circumscribed by whirlpools, or peacefully circumscribed by cloud-capped Paradisal valleys; they float upon circular pools ringed in by steep flowering hillsides; they dwell on islands, or voyage to them; we find Poe's heroes also in coffins, in the cabs of balloons, or hidden away in the holds of ships; and above all we find them sitting alone in the claustral and richly-furnished rooms of remote and mouldering mansions.

Almost never, if you think about it, is one of Poe's heroes to be seen standing in the light of common day; almost never does the Poe hero breathe

the air that others breathe; he requires some kind of envelope in order to be what he is; he is always either enclosed or on his way to an enclosure. The narrative of William Wilson conducts the hero from Stoke Newington to Eton, from Eton to Oxford, and then to Rome by way of Paris, Vienna, Berlin, Moscow, Naples, and Egypt: and yet, for all his travels, Wilson seems never to set foot out-of-doors. The story takes place in a series of rooms, the last one locked from the inside.

Sometimes Poe emphasizes the circumscription of his heroes by multiple enclosures. Roderick Usher dwells in a great and crumbling mansion from which, as Poe tells us, he has not ventured forth in many years. This mansion stands islanded in a stagnant lake, which serves it as a defensive moat. And beyond the moat lies the Usher estate, a vast barren tract having its own peculiar and forbidding weather and atmosphere. You might say that Roderick Usher is defended in depth; and yet at the close of the story Poe compounds Roderick's inaccessibility by having the mansion and its occupant swallowed up by the waters of the tarn.

What does it mean that Poe's heroes are invariably enclosed or circumscribed? The answer is simple: circumscription, in Poe's tales, means the exclusion from consciousness of the so-called real world, the world of time and reason and physical fact; it means the isolation of the poetic soul in visionary reverie or trance. When we find one of Poe's characters in a remote valley, or a claustral room, we know that he is in the process of dreaming his way out of the world.

Now, I want to devote the time remaining to the consideration of one kind of enclosure in Poe's tales: the mouldering mansion and its richly-furnished rooms. I want to concentrate on Poe's architecture and decor for two reasons: first, because Poe's use of architecture is so frankly and provably allegorical that I *should* be able to be convincing about it; second, because by concentrating on one area of Poe's symbolism we shall be able to see that his stories are allegorical not only in their broad patterns, but also in their smallest details.

Let us begin with a familiar poem, *The Haunted Palace*. The opening stanzas of this poem, as a number of critics have noted, make a point-by-point comparison between a building and the head of a man. The exterior of the palace represents the man's physical features; the interior represents the man's mind engaged in harmonious imaginative thought.

> *In the greenest of our valleys,*
> *By good angels tenanted,*
> *Once a fair and stately palace—*
> *Radiant palace—reared its head.*
> *In the monarch Thought's dominion,*

> It stood there!
> Never seraph spread a pinion
>   Over fabric half so fair!
>
> Banners yellow, glorious, golden,
>   On its roof did float and flow
> (This—all this—was in the olden
>   Time long ago),
> And every gentle air that dallied,
>   In that sweet day,
> Along the ramparts plumed and pallid,
>   A wingéd odor went away.
>
> Wanderers in that happy valley,
>   Through two luminous windows, saw
> Spirits moving musically
>   To a lute's well-tunéd law,
> Round about a throne where, sitting,
>   Porphyrogene,
> In state his glory well befitting,
>   The ruler of the realm was seen.
>
> And all in pearl and ruby glowing
>   Was the fair palace door,
> Through which came flowing, flowing, flowing,
>   And sparkling evermore,
> A troop of Echoes, whose sweet duty
>   Was but to sing,
> In voices of surpassing beauty,
>   The wit and wisdom of their king.

I expect you observed that the two luminous windows of the palace are the eyes of a man, and that the yellow banners on the roof are his luxuriant blond hair. The "pearl and ruby" door is the man's mouth—ruby representing red lips, and pearl representing pearly white teeth. The beautiful Echoes which issue from the pearl and ruby door are the poetic utterances of the man's harmonious imagination, here symbolized as an orderly dance. The angel-guarded valley in which the palace stands, and which Poe describes as "the monarch Thought's dominion," is a symbol of the man's exclusive awareness of exalted and spiritual things. The valley is what Poe elsewhere called "that evergreen and radiant paradise which the true poet knows . . . as the limited realm of his authority, as the circumscribed Eden of his dreams."

As you all remember, the last two stanzas of the poem describe the physical and spiritual corruption of the palace and its domain, and it was to this part of the poem that Poe was referring when he told a correspondent, "By the 'Haunted Palace' I mean to imply a mind haunted by phantoms— a disordered brain." Let me read you the closing lines:

> *But evil things, in robes of sorrow,*
> *Assailed the monarch's high estate.*
> *(Ah, let us mourn!—for never morrow*
> *Shall dawn upon him, desolate!)*
> *And round about his home the glory*
> *That blushed and bloomed,*
> *Is but a dim-remembered story*
> *Of the old time entombed.*
>
> *And travellers, now, within that valley,*
> *Through the red-litten windows see*
> *Vast forms that move fantastically*
> *To a discordant melody,*
> *While, like a ghastly rapid river,*
> *Through the pale door*
> *A hideous throng rush out forever,*
> *And laugh—but smile no more.*

The domain of the monarch Thought, in these final stanzas, is disrupted by civil war, and in consequence everything alters for the worse. The valley becomes barren, like the domain of Roderick Usher; the eye-like windows of the palace are no longer "luminous," but have become "red-litten"—they are like the bloodshot eyes of a madman or a drunkard. As for the mouth of our allegorized man, it is now "pale" rather than "pearl and ruby," and through it come no sweet Echoes, as before, but the wild laughter of a jangling and discordant mind.

The two states of the palace—before and after—are, as we can see, two states of mind. Poe does not make it altogether clear *why* one state of mind has given way to the other, but by recourse to similar tales and poems we can readily find the answer. The palace in its original condition expresses the imaginative harmony which the poet's soul enjoys in early childhood, when all things are viewed with a tyrannical and unchallenged subjectivity. But as the soul passes from childhood into adult life, its consciousness is more and more invaded by the corrupt and corrupting external world: it succumbs to passion, it develops a conscience, it makes concessions to reason and to objective fact. Consequently, there is civil war in the palace of the mind. The imagination must now struggle against the intellect and the moral sense; finding itself no longer able to possess the world through a serene solipsism, it strives to annihilate the outer world by

338

turning in upon itself; it flees into irrationality and dream; and all its dreams are efforts both to recall and to simulate its primal, unfallen state.

The Haunted Palace presents us with a possible key to the general meaning of Poe's architecture; and this key proves, if one tries it, to open every building in Poe's fiction. Roderick Usher, as you will remember, declaims *The Haunted Palace* to the visitor who tells his story, accompanying the poem with wild improvisations on the guitar. We are encouraged, therefore, to compare the palace of the poem with the house of the story; and it is no surprise to find that the Usher mansion has "vacant eye-like windows," and that there are mysterious physical sympathies between Roderick Usher and the house in which he dwells. The House of Usher *is*, in allegorical fact, the physical body of Roderick Usher, and its dim interior *is*, in fact, Roderick Usher's visionary mind.

The House of Usher, like many edifices in Poe, is in a state of extreme decay. The stonework of its facade has so crumbled and decomposed that it reminds the narrator, as he puts it, "of the specious totality of old wood-work which has rotted for long years in some neglected vault." The Usher mansion is so eaten away, so fragile, that it seems a breeze would push it over; it remains standing only because the atmosphere of Usher's domain is perfectly motionless and dead. Such is the case also with the "time-eaten towers that tremble not" in Poe's poem *The City in the Sea;* and likewise the magnificent architecture of *The Domain of Arnheim* is said to "sustain itself by a miracle in mid-air." Even the detective Dupin lives in a perilously decayed structure: the narrator of *The Murders in the Rue Morgue* tells how he and Dupin dwelt in a "time-eaten and grotesque mansion, long deserted through superstitions into which we did not enquire, and tottering to its fall in a retired and desolate portion of the Faubourg St. Germain." (Notice how, even when Poe's buildings are situated in cities, he manages to circumscribe them with a protective desolation.)

We must now ask what Poe means by the extreme and tottering decay of so many of his structures. The answer is best given by reference to *The Fall of the House of Usher,* and in giving the answer we shall arrive, I think, at an understanding of the pattern of that story.

The Fall of the House of Usher is a journey into the depths of the self. I have said that all journeys in Poe are allegories of the process of dreaming, and we must understand *The Fall of the House of Usher* as a dream of the narrator's, in which he leaves behind him the waking, physical world and journeys inward toward his *moi intérieur,* toward his inner and spiritual self. That inner and spiritual self is Roderick Usher.

Roderick Usher, then, is a part of the narrator's self, which the narrator reaches by way of reverie. We may think of Usher, if we like, as the narrator's imagination, or as his visionary soul. Or we may think of him as a *state of mind* which the narrator enters at a certain stage of his progress into dreams. Considered as a state of mind, Roderick Usher is an allegorical figure representing the hypnagogic state.

The hypnagogic state, about which there is strangely little said in the literature of psychology, is a condition of semi-consciousness in which the closed eye beholds a continuous procession of vivid and constantly changing forms. These forms sometimes have color, and are often abstract in character. Poe regarded the hypnagogic state as the visionary condition *par excellence,* and he considered its rapidly shifting abstract images to be— as he put it—"glimpses of the spirit's outer world." These visionary glimpses, Poe says in one of his *Marginalia,* "arise in the soul . . . only . . . at those mere points of time where the confines of the waking world blend with those of the world of dreams." And Poe goes on to say: "I am aware of these 'fancies' only when I am upon the very brink of sleep, with the consciousness that I am so."

Roderick Usher enacts the hypnagogic state in a number of ways. For one thing, the narrator describes Roderick's behavior as inconsistent, and characterized by constant alternation: he is alternately vivacious and sullen; he is alternately communicative and rapt; he speaks at one moment with "tremulous indecision," and at the next with the "energetic concision" of an excited opium-eater. His conduct resembles, in other words, that wavering between consciousness and sub-consciousness which characterizes the hypnagogic state. The trembling of Roderick's body, and the floating of his silken hair, also bring to mind the instability and underwater quality of hypnagogic images. His improvisations on the guitar suggest hypnagogic experience in their rapidity, changeableness, and wild novelty. And as for Usher's paintings, which the narrator describes as "pure abstractions," they quite simply *are* hypnagogic images. The narrator says of Roderick, "From the paintings over which his elaborate fancy brooded, and which grew, touch by touch, into vaguenesses at which I shuddered the more thrillingly because I shuddered without knowing why—from these paintings (vivid as their images now are before me) I would in vain endeavor to educe more than a small portion which should lie within the compass of merely written words." That the narrator finds Roderick's paintings indescribable is interesting, because in that one of the *Marginalia* from which I have quoted, Poe asserts that the only things in human experience which lie "beyond the compass of words" are the visions of the hypnagogic state.

Roderick Usher stands for the hypnagogic state, which as Poe said is a teetering condition of mind occurring "upon the very brink of sleep." Since Roderick is the embodiment of a state of mind in which *falling*— falling asleep—is imminent, it is appropriate that the building which symbolizes his mind should promise at every moment to fall. The House of

Usher stares down broodingly at its reflection in the tarn below, as in the hypnagogic state the conscious mind may stare into the sub-conscious; the house threatens continually to collapse because it is extremely easy for the mind to slip from the hypnagogic state into the depths of sleep; and when the House of Usher *does* fall, the story ends, as it must, because the mind, at the end of its inward journey, has plunged into the darkness of sleep.

We have found one allegorical meaning in the tottering decay of Poe's buildings; there is another meaning, equally important, which may be stated very briefly. I have said that Poe saw the poet as at war with the material world, and with the material or physical aspects of himself; and I have said that Poe identified poetic imagination with the power to escape from the material and the materialistic, to exclude them from consciousness and so subjectively destroy them. Now, if we recall these things, and recall also that the exteriors of Poe's houses or palaces, with their eye-like windows and mouth-like doors, represent the physical features of Poe's dreaming heroes, then the characteristic dilapidation of Poe's architecture takes on sudden significance. The extreme decay of the House of Usher— a decay so extreme as to approach the atmospheric—is quite simply a sign that the narrator, in reaching that state of mind which he calls Roderick Usher, has very nearly dreamt himself free of his physical body, and of the material world with which that body connects him.

This is what decay or decomposition mean everywhere in Poe; and we find them almost everywhere. Poe's preoccupation with decay is not, as some critics have thought, an indication of necrophilia; decay in Poe is a symbol of visionary remoteness from the physical, a sign that the state of mind represented is one of almost pure spirituality. When the House of Usher disintegrates or dematerializes at the close of the story, it does so because Roderick Usher has become all soul. *The Fall of the House of Usher,* then, is not really a horror story; it is a triumphant report by the narrator that it *is* possible for the poetic soul to shake off this temporal, rational, physical world and escape, if only for a moment, to a realm of unfettered vision.

We have now arrived at three notions about Poe's typical building. It is set apart in a valley or a sea or a waste place, and this remoteness is intended to express the retreat of the poet's mind from worldly consciousness into dream. It is a tottery structure, and this indicates that the dreamer within is in that unstable threshold condition called the hypnagogic state. Finally, Poe's typical building is crumbling or decomposing, and this means that the dreamer's mind is moving toward a perfect freedom from his material self and the material world. Let us now open the door—or mouth—of Poe's building and visit the mind inside.

As we enter the palace of the visionary hero of the *Assignation,* or the house of Roderick Usher, we find ourselves approaching the master's private chamber by way of dim and winding passages, or a winding staircase. There is no end to dim windings in Poe's fiction: there are dim and winding woods paths, dim and winding streets, dim and winding watercourses— and, whenever the symbolism is architectural, there are likely to be dim and winding passages or staircases. It is not at all hard to guess what Poe means by this symbol. If we think of waking life as dominated by reason, and if we think of the reason as a daylight faculty which operates in straight lines, then it is proper that reverie should be represented as an obscure and wandering movement of the mind. There are other, and equally obvious meanings in Poe's symbol of dim and winding passages: to grope through such passages is to become confused as to place and direction, just as in reverie we begin to lose any sense of locality, and to have an infinite freedom in regard to space. In his description of the huge old mansion in which William Wilson went to school, Poe makes this meaning of winding passages very plain:

> But the house!—how quaint an old building was this!—to me how veritable a palace of enchantment! There was no end to its windings—to its incomprehensible subdivisions. It was difficult, at any given time, to say with certainty upon which of its two stories one happened to be. From each room to every other there were sure to be found three or four steps either in ascent or descent. Then the lateral branches were innumerable—inconceivable—and so returning in upon themselves, that our most exact ideas in regard to the whole mansion were not very far different from those with which we pondered on infinity.

Dim windings indicate the state of reverie; they point toward that infinite freedom in and from space which the mind achieves in dreams; also, in their curvature and in their occasional doubling-back, they anticipate the mind's final spiralling plunge into unconsciousness. But the immediate goal of reverie's winding passages is that magnificent chamber in which we find the visionary hero slumped in a chair or lolling on an ottoman, occupied in purging his consciousness of everything that is earthly.

Since I have been speaking of geometry—of straight lines and curves and spirals—perhaps the first thing to notice about Poe's dream-rooms is their shape. It has already been said that the enclosures of Poe's tales incline to a curving or circular form. And Poe himself, in certain of his essays and dialogues, explains this inclination by denouncing what he calls "the harsh mathematical reason of the schools," and complaining that practical science has covered the face of the earth with "rectangular obscenities." Poe quite explicitly identifies regular angular forms with everyday reason, and the circle, oval, or fluid arabesque with the otherworldly imagination. Therefore, if we discover that the dream-chambers of Poe's fiction are free of angular regularity, we may be sure that we are noticing a pointed and purposeful consistency in his architecture and décor.

The ball-room of the story *Hop-Frog* is circular. The Devil's apartment in *The Duc de l'Omelette* has its corners "rounded into niches," and we find rounded corners also in Poe's essay *The Philosophy of Furniture*. In *Ligeia*, the bridal chamber is a pentagonal turret-room; however, the angles are concealed by sarcophagi, so that the effect is circular. The corners of Roderick Usher's chamber are likewise concealed, being lost in deep shadow. Other dream-rooms are either irregular or indeterminate in form. For example, there are the seven rooms of Prince Prospero's imperial suite in *The Masque of the Red Death*. As Poe observes, "in many palaces . . . such suites form a long and straight vista"; but in Prince Prospero's palace, as he describes it, "the apartments were so irregularly disposed that the vision embraced but little more than one at a time. There was a sharp turn at every twenty or thirty yards, and at each turn a novel effect." The turret-room of *The Oval Portrait* is not defined as to shape; we are told, however, that it is architecturally "bizarre," and complicated by a quantity of unexpected nooks and niches. Similarly, the visionary's apartment in *The Assignation* is described only as dazzling, astounding and original in its architecture; we are not told in what way its dimensions are peculiar, but it seems safe to assume that it would be a difficult room to measure for wall-to-wall carpeting. The room of *The Assignation*, by the way—like that of *Ligeia*—has its walls enshrouded in rich figured draperies which are continually agitated by some mysterious agency. The fluid shifting of the figures suggests, of course, the behavior of hypnagogic images; but the agitation of the draperies would also produce a perpetual ambiguity of architectural form, and the effect would resemble that which Pevsner ascribes to the interior of San Vitale in Ravenna: "a sensation of uncertainty [and] of a dreamlike floating."

Poe, as you see, is at great pains to avoid depicting the usual squarish sort of room in which we spend much of our waking lives. His chambers of dream either approximate the circle—an infinite form which is, as Poe somewhere observes, "the emblem of Eternity"—or they so lack any apprehensible regularity of shape as to suggest the changeableness and spatial freedom of the dreaming mind. The exceptions to this rule are few and entirely explainable. I will grant, for instance, that the iron-walled torture-chamber of *The Pit and the Pendulum* portrays the very reverse of spatial freedom, and that it is painfully angular in character, the angles growing more acute as the torture intensifies. But there is very good allegorical reason for these things. The rooms of *Ligeia* or *The Assignation* symbolize a triumphantly imaginative state of mind in which the dreamer is all but free of the so-called "real" world. In *The Pit and the Pendulum*, the dream is of quite another kind; it is a nightmare state, in which the dreamer is imaginatively impotent, and can find no refuge from reality, even in dream. Though he lies on the brink of the pit, on the very verge of the plunge into unconsciousness, he is still unable to disengage himself from the physical and temporal world. The physical oppresses him in the shape of lurid graveyard visions; the temporal oppresses him in the form of an enormous and deadly pendulum. It is altogether appropriate, then, that this particular chamber should be constricting and cruelly angular.

But let us return to Poe's typical room, and look now at its furnishings. They are generally weird, magnificent, and suggestive of great wealth. The narrator of *The Assignation,* entering the hero's apartment, feels "blind and dizzy with luxuriousness," and looking about him he confesses, "I could not bring myself to believe that the wealth of any subject in Europe could have supplied the princely magnificence which burned and blazed around." Poe's visionaries are, as a general thing, extremely rich; the hero of *Ligeia* confides that, as for wealth, he possesses "far more, very far more, than ordinarily falls to the lot of mortals"; and Ellison, in *The Domain of Arnheim,* is the fortunate inheritor of 450 million dollars. Legrand, in *The Gold Bug,* with his treasure of 450 *thousand,* is only a poor relation of Mr. Ellison; still, by ordinary standards, he seems sublimely solvent.

Now, we must be careful to take all these riches in an allegorical sense. As we contemplate the splendor of any of Poe's rooms, we must remember that the room is a state of mind, and that everything in it is therefore a thought, a mental image. The allegorical meaning of the costliness of Poe's decor is simply this: that his heroes are richly imaginative. And since imagination is a gift rather than an acquisition, it is appropriate that riches in Poe should be inherited or found, but never earned.

Another thing we notice about Poe's furnishings is that they are eclectic in the extreme. Their richness is not the richness of Tiffany's and Sloan's, but of all periods and all cultures. Here is a partial inventory of the fantastic bridal-chamber in *Ligeia:* Egyptian carvings and sarcophagi; Venetian glass; fretwork of a semi-Gothic, semi-Druidical character; a Saracenic chandelier; Oriental ottomans and candelabra; an Indian couch; and figured draperies with Norman motifs. The same defiance of what interior decorators once called "keeping" is found in the apartment of the visionary hero of *The Assignation,* and one of that hero's speeches hints at the allegorical meaning of his jumbled decor:

To dream [says the hero of *The Assignation*]—to dream has been the business of my life. I have therefore framed for myself, as you see, a bower of dreams. In the heart of Venice could I have erected a better? You behold around you, it is true, a medley of architectural embellishments. The chastity of Ionia is offended by antediluvian devices, and the sphynxes of Egypt are outstretched upon carpets of gold. Yet the effect is incongruous to the timid alone. Proprieties of place, and especially of time, are the bugbears which terrify mankind from the contemplation of the magnificent.

That last sentence, with its scornful reference to "proprieties of place, and . . . time," should put us in mind of the first stanza of Poe's poem *Dream-Land:*

> *By a route obscure and lonely,*
> *Haunted by ill angels only,*
> *Where an Eidolon, named NIGHT,*
> *On a black throne reigns upright,*
> *I have reached these lands but newly*
> *From an ultimate dim Thule—*
> *From a wild weird clime that lieth, sublime,*
> *Out of SPACE—out of TIME.*

In dream-land, we are "out of SPACE—out of TIME," and the same is true of such apartments or "bowers of dreams" as the hero of *The Assignation* inhabits. His eclectic furnishings, with their wild juxtapositions of Venetian and Indian, Egyptian and Norman, are symbolic of the visionary soul's transcendence of spatial and temporal limitations. When one of Poe's dream-rooms is *not* furnished in the fashion I have been describing, the idea of spatial and temporal freedom is often conveyed in some other manner: Roderick Usher's library, for instance, with its rare and precious volumes belonging to all times and tongues, is another concrete symbol of the timelessness and placelessness of the dreaming mind.

We have spoken of the winding approaches to Poe's dream-chambers, of their curvilinear or indeterminate shape, and of the rich eclecticism of their furnishings. Let us now glance over such matters as lighting, sound-proofing, and ventilation. As regards lighting, the rooms of Poe's tales are never exposed to the naked rays of the sun, because the sun belongs to the waking world and waking consciousness. The narrator of *The Murders in the Rue Morgue* tells how he and his friend Dupin conducted their lives in such a way as to avoid all exposure to sunlight. "At the first dawn of the morning," he writes, "we closed all the massy shutters of our old building; lighting a couple of tapers which, strongly perfumed, threw out only the ghastliest and feeblest of rays. By the aid of these we then busied our souls in dreams . . ."

In some of Poe's rooms, there simply are no windows. In other cases, the windows are blocked up or shuttered. When the windows are not blocked or shuttered, their panes are tinted with a crimson or leaden hue, so as to transform the light of day into a lurid or ghastly glow. This kind of lighting, in which the sun's rays are admitted but transformed, belongs to the portrayal of those half-states of mind in which dream and reality are blended. Filtered through tinted panes, the sunlight enters certain of Poe's rooms as it might enter the half-closed eyes of a day-dreamer, or the dream-dimmed eyes of someone awakening from sleep. But when Poe wishes to represent that deeper phase of dreaming in which visionary consciousness has all but annihilated any sense of the external world, the lighting is always artificial and the time is always night.

Flickering candles, wavering torches, and censers full of writhing vari-colored flames furnish much of the illumination of Poe's rooms, and one can see the appropriateness of such lighting to the vague and shifting perceptions of the hypnagogic state. But undoubtedly the most important lighting-fixture in Poe's rooms—and one which appears in a good half of them—is the chandelier. It hangs from the lofty ceiling by a long chain, generally of gold, and it consists sometimes of a censer, sometimes of a lamp, sometimes of candles, sometimes of a glowing jewel (a ruby or a diamond), and once, in the macabre tale *King Pest,* of a skull containing ignited charcoal. What we must understand about this chandelier, as Poe explains in his poem *Al Aaraaf,* is that its chain does not stop at the ceiling: it goes right on through the ceiling, through the roof, and up to heaven. What comes down the chain from heaven is the divine power of imagination, and it is imagination's purifying fire which flashes or flickers from the chandelier. That is why the immaterial and angelic Ligeia makes her reappearance directly beneath the chandelier; and that is why Hop-Frog makes his departure for dream-land by climbing the chandelier-chain and vanishing through the sky-light.

The dreaming soul, then, has its own light—a light more spiritual, more divine, than that of the sun. And Poe's chamber of dream is autonomous in every other respect. No breath of air enters it from the outside world: either its atmosphere is dead, or its draperies are stirred by magical and intramural air-currents. No earthly sound invades the chamber: either it is deadly still, or it echoes with a sourceless and unearthly music. Nor does any odor of flower or field intrude: instead, as Poe tells in *The Assignation,* the sense of smell is "oppressed by mingled and conflicting perfumes, reeking up from strange convolute censers."

The point of all this is that the dreaming psyche separates itself wholly from the bodily senses—the "rudimental senses," as Poe called them. The bodily senses are dependent on objective stimuli—on the lights and sounds and odors of the physical world. But the sensual life of dream is self-sufficient and immaterial, and consists in the imagination's Godlike enjoyment of its own creations.

I am reminded, at this point, of a paragraph of Santayana's, in which he describes the human soul as it was conceived by the philosopher Leibniz. Leibniz, says Santayana, assigned

346

a mental seat to all sensible objects. The soul, he said, had no windows and, he might have added, no doors; no light could come to it from without; and it could not exert any transitive force or make any difference beyond its own insulated chamber. It was a *camera obscura,* with a universe painted on its impenetrable walls. The changes which went on in it were like those in a dream, due to the discharge of pent-up energies and fecundities within it . . .

Leibniz' chamber of the soul is identical with Poe's chamber of dream: but the solipsism which Leibniz saw as the normal human condition was for Poe an ideal state, a blessed state, which we may enjoy as children or as preexistent souls, but can reclaim in adult life only by a flight from everyday consciousness into hypnagogic trance.

The one thing which remains to be said about Poe's buildings is that cellars or catacombs, whenever they appear, stand for the irrational part of the mind; and that is so conventional an equation in symbolic literature that I think I need not be persuasive or illustrative about it. I had hoped, at this point, to discuss in a leisurely way some of the stories in which Poe makes use of his architectural properties, treating those stories as narrative wholes. But I have spoken too long about other things; and so, if you will allow me a few minutes more, I shall close by commenting briskly on two or three stories only.

The typical Poe story occurs *within* the mind of a poet; and its characters are not independent personalities, but allegorical figures representing the warring principles of the poet's divided nature. The lady Ligeia, for example, stands for that heavenly beauty which the poet's soul desires; while Rowena stands for that earthly, physical beauty which tempts the poet's passions. The action of the story is the dreaming soul's gradual emancipation from earthly attachments—which is allegorically expressed in the slow dissolution of Rowena. The result of this process is the soul's final, momentary vision of the heavenly Ligeia. Poe's typical story presents some such struggle between the visionary and the mundane; and the duration of Poe's typical story is the duration of a dream.

There are two tales in which Poe makes an especially clear and simple use of his architectural symbolism. The first is an unfamiliar tale called *The System of Dr. Tarr and Prof. Fether,* and the edifice of that tale is a remote and dilapidated madhouse in southern France. What happens, in brief, is that the inmates of the madhouse escape from their cells in the basement of the building, overpower their keepers, and lock them up in their own cells. Having done this, the lunatics take possession of the upper reaches of the house. They shutter all the windows, put on odd costumes, and proceed to hold an uproarious and discordant feast, during which there is much eating and drinking of a disgusting kind, and a degraded version of Ligeia or Helen does a strip-tease. At the height of these festivities, the keepers escape from their cells, break in through the barred and shuttered windows of the dining-room, and restore order.

Well: the madhouse, like all of Poe's houses, is a mind. The keepers are the rational part of that mind, and the inmates are its irrational part. As you noticed, the irrational is suitably assigned to the cellar. The uprising of the inmates, and the suppression of the keepers, symbolizes the beginning of a dream, and the mad banquet which follows is perhaps Poe's least spiritual portrayal of the dream-state: *this* dream, far from being an escape from the physical, consists exclusively of the release of animal appetites—as dreams sometimes do. When the keepers break in the windows, and subdue the revellers, they bring with them reason and the light of day, and the wild dream is over.

The Masque of the Red Death is a better-known and even more obvious example of architectural allegory. You will recall how Prince Prospero, when his dominions are being ravaged by the plague, withdraws with a thousand of his knights and ladies into a secluded, impregnable and windowless abbey, where after a time he entertains his friends with a costume ball. The weird decor of the seven ballrooms expresses the Prince's own taste, and in strange costumes of the Prince's own design the company dances far into the night, looking, as Poe says, like "a multitude of dreams." The festivities are interrupted only by the hourly striking of a gigantic ebony clock which stands in the westernmost room; and the striking of this clock has invariably a sobering effect on the revellers. Upon the last stroke of twelve, as you will remember, there appears amid the throng a figure attired in the blood-dabbled grave-clothes of a plague-victim. The dancers shrink from him in terror. But the Prince, infuriated at what he takes to be an insolent practical joke, draws his dagger and pursues the figure through all of the seven rooms. In the last and westernmost room, the figure suddenly turns and confronts Prince Prospero, who gives a cry of despair and falls upon his own dagger. The Prince's friends rush forward to seize the intruder, who stands now within the shadow of the ebony clock; but they find nothing there. And then, one after the other, the thousand revellers fall dead of the Red Death, and the lights flicker out, and Prince Prospero's ball is at an end.

In spite of its cast of one thousand and two, *The Masque of the Red Death* has only one character. Prince Prospero is one-half of that character, the visionary half; the nameless figure in grave-clothes is the other, as we shall see in a moment.

More than once, in his dialogues or critical writings, Poe describes the earth-bound, time-bound rationalism of his age as a *disease*. And that is what the Red Death signifies. Prince Prospero's flight from the Red Death is the poetic imagination's flight from temporal and worldly consciousness into dream. The thousand dancers of Prince Prospero's costume ball are just what Poe says they are—"dreams" or "phantasms," veiled and vivid creatures of Prince Prospero's rapt imagination. Whenever there is a feast, or carnival, or costume ball in Poe, we may be sure that a dream is in progress.

But what is the gigantic ebony clock? For the answer to that, one need only consult a dictionary of slang: we call the human heart a *ticker,* meaning that it is the clock of the body; and that is what Poe means here. In sleep, our minds may roam beyond the temporal world, but our hearts tick on, binding us to time and mortality. Whenever the ebony clock strikes, the dancers of Prince Prospero's dream grow momentarily pale and still, in half-awareness that they and their revel must have an end; it is as if a sleeper should half-awaken, and know that he has been dreaming, and then sink back into dreams again.

The figure in blood-dabbled grave-clothes, who stalks through the terrified company and vanishes in the shadow of the clock, is waking, temporal consciousness, and his coming means the death of dreams. He breaks up Prince Prospero's ball as the keepers in *Dr. Tarr and Prof. Fether* break up the revels of the lunatics. The final confrontation between Prince Prospero and the shrouded figure is like the terrible final meeting between William Wilson and his double. Recognizing his adversary as his own worldly and mortal self, Prince Prospero gives a cry of despair which is also Poe's cry of despair: despair at the realization that only by self-destruction could the poet fully free his soul from the trammels of this world.

Poe's aesthetic, Poe's theory of the nature of art, seems to me insane. To say that art should repudiate everything human and earthly, and find its subject-matter at the flickering end of dreams, is hopelessly to narrow the scope and function of art. Poe's aesthetic points toward such impoverishments as *poésie pure* and the abstract expressionist movement in painting. And yet, despite his aesthetic, Poe is a great artist, and I would rest my case for him on his prose allegories of psychic conflict. In them, Poe broke wholly new ground, and they remain the best things of their kind in our literature. Poe's mind may have been a strange one; yet all minds are alike in their general structure; therefore we can understand him, and I think that he will have something to say to us as long as there is civil war in the palaces of men's minds.

Willa Cather

Leon Edel

Presented at the Library of Congress October 12, 1959

IT IS A GREAT PLEASURE to commemorate the name and the work of Willa Cather in this city and in this Library under the auspices of the Gertrude Clarke Whittall Poetry and Literature Fund. I do not have to remark upon the appropriateness of the place. Concerning Willa Cather and this city, however, a few words might be said. She was of two minds about the capital. I suppose many Americans are. About the city as symbol of American life she had many eloquent things to say: its stateliness, its power, its art, could hardly be lost upon her. But there were certain misgivings which I suppose the most patriotic Washingtonian is likely to experience at one time or another. The sense of a capital's largeness, its labyrinthine character, its impersonality—these were matters upon which she seems to have brooded with an intensity that is reflected in *The Professor's House*, in Tom Outland's account of his stay in Washington. It is one of the most moving sections in the novel: Tom's feeling that he spent all his days in the capital in outer offices, in which persons like himself, imbued with some ideal, wait and wait, and find themselves the object of a sharp indifference; the overwhelming helplessness sometimes of the individual before what we speak of as the *machinery* of government. All this oppressed Willa Cather's young hero.

Willa Cather mistrusted machinery, whether of the farm or of the Government. Some of you may have read one of her lesser novels, *One of Ours*—considered good enough in the 1920's, however, to have been given the Pulitzer prize—and you may recall her account, often humorous, of the second generation on the Nebraska farmlands, purchasing all kinds of machinery to do the work of the pioneers; and how, after a while, the machines piled up in cellar and yard, a rusty wilderness of gadgets and implements. If we look at Miss Cather from our angle of vision, from the electronic age, we might say that she doubtless made too much of a virtue

350

out of the farmer's sweat of his brow; but the deeper meaning of her protest must not be allowed to escape us. It has been reiterated by William Faulkner in one of his rare letters to the press, in which he expressed a fear that fliers who fly by instruments alone are abdicating their human role. This is what Willa Cather was trying to say. She expressed it on one occasion in a newspaper interview when she said: "Restlessness such as ours, success such as ours, do not make for beauty. Other things must come first: good cookery, cottages that are homes, not playthings; gardens, repose. These are first-rate things, and out of first-rate stuff art is made. It is possible that machinery has finished us as far as this is concerned. Nobody stays at home any more; nobody makes anything beautiful any more."

One expects such utterances from old persons, set in their ways, and quite content to do things as they did them in their youth. But Miss Cather gave this interview in her prime. To understand her refusal to move with her era—and her refusal was adamant—we must recognize that Willa Cather was not a child of the 20th century. She had been a child of the frontier; and long after the frontiers were gone she yearned—with an ache that had all the poetry of youth and adolescence in it—for the old, the cherished things she had known. This she expressed in one form and another in 12 novels; it is the best aspect of her talent and the one that gives her a claim upon us on this occasion. It also reflects the limitations of her talent. Our task will be to try to understand this, in order that we may the better define that essence in her work which has had—and still has—so strong an appeal to her public.

I

I must confess to a certain constraint in speaking to you of Willa Cather now, on the periphery of the 1960's—constraint because we have moved so far away from her world. It is gone, gone as if it had never existed, save for the fact that it does exist in some of the best pages of her writing. To use an exaggerated image, I would say that to talk of Miss Cather's world is a little like trying to extol the Stone Age to a Renaissance man. We must remind ourselves, as we survey the big-finned automobiles, conquering more space than any human being is entitled to on the highway, that Miss Cather belonged to the age when there were still horses hitched to hitching posts in the Western towns; when one walked a good deal more and wrote letters instead of telegraphing or telephoning; when life in the small remote community and on the farm was more isolated and lonely than it is today—and offered more time for reading and reflection; and it was a life that was hard indeed by our cushioned standards, hard with the work of the hands, and not of the same hands running machines. This was before the broad and smiling countenance of our country was offered the sonorities of the jet in the sky, or the cacophony of the dishwashing machine in the kitchen, or the vibrations of Hi-Fi and television within the walls of our dwellings. It is indeed of an ancient world that I must speak tonight if I am to do justice to Miss Cather—and to Miss Cather's problem of reconciling herself to a time in which life altered so radically that even those of us who have bridged some part of this period still rub our eyes in amazement. We wonder, sometimes, whether we have awakened from the realities of our childhood into the fantastic world of science fiction. I am just old enough, and was just young enough, to have lived in a semi-frontier town and to have seen the old farmcarts hitched to hitching-posts and the horses knee-deep in mud; and I watched the last of the peasants, immigrants from the old world, being transformed from Europeans into North Americans. I sometimes wonder, when I fly in a plane, or read about our spacemen, whether I am the same person who used to walk to school in terrible blizzards without benefit of the school bus and knew the joys of the horse-drawn sleigh on frosty winter nights.

The questions Willa Cather raised about the changes in her time are extremely important in this second half of our century, for they relate to the whole problem of art in an age of science, to the role of the artist when he is faced by a self-assured technology, supremely aware of the comforts it brings to man. C. P. Snow, the English novelist, has written much about this. He was a scientist before he recognized that art could express for him something that lies beyond the boundaries of science; and he has sought, with high seriousness and great imagination, to establish a bridge over the gulf that exists between the specialists of science, who converse in their own particular language, and the creative artists who deal in words, and who use them to express the quick impulses, the ready feelings by which men discover their kinship with one another. In his Rede lecture, delivered at Cambridge earlier this year, Sir Charles was forthright about this chasm, and quite right, I think, in suggesting that there is a great deal of ignorance on both sides. Those of us who are concerned with imaginative literature must recognize that this *is* the age of science, and that we live in a time of great scientific wonder and adventure. But we know what Willa Cather would say if C. P. Snow pointed out to her that man's new discoveries necessitate new ways of seeing the world. She would say, as she made the Indian say in *Death Comes for the Archbishop:* "Men travel faster now, but I do not know if they go to better things."

Sir Charles Snow is certain that men are going on to better things, thanks to technology; and he feels that the answer to the alienation of the two cultures, those of the scientists and the nonscientists, lies in educating the world to understand that technology is an irreversible process: for machines, at their best, and in spite of new problems which they have created, have made life better and often much less arduous. There can be no turning back from the bulldozer and the dishwashing machine even though these create, I'm afraid, more noise than man or animal was intended to hear. There can be no turning back from social progress save through violence and war; as Sir Charles remarked, man is no longer resigned to wait for periods longer than a person's lifetime. But if this is the optimistic side of the Machine Age, I am reminded of the words I heard Alberto Moravia address to a congress of writers last July. He spoke, in a sense, like Miss Cather, not of the achievements of technology, but of the relationship of the human being to them. Novelists, after all, write about men, not machines. Signor Moravia was justifiably querulous about humans who are asked to do something, or feed something, into the maw of a machine on some eternal and irreversible assembly line. He wanted to know what could be done to keep such men from becoming a part of the mechanical continuum into which they are drawn, and the effect it has upon their lives. It was understandable that Moravia, with his quick sense of human values, should point to the heart of the problem, as Willa Cather had done before him. The novelist wants to know, when he is confronted with a machine, whether it will confer new benefits or new slaveries upon man. The discussion is not new; it has been going on since the dawn of the Industrial Revolution, ever since those primitive days when the machine-breakers hoped to wipe out sudden unemployment by destruction of the metal Frankensteins. Their lives had been disrupted overnight; they protested in the only way they knew at that time. The novelist protests out of a concern with man's spirit, and out of his quick insight into the new feudalism: that of a science which now bids man to obey and be mastered and offers him, instead of the old iniquities, the narcotics of cushion comfort. The ambiguity of this was not lost upon Willa Cather. She was caught, in the end, in a revolt against the very achievements she had praised, the very successes—that of the pioneers of our land—of which she made herself the fictional historian. But this only partly expresses what I meant when I proposed to speak to you tonight of the "paradox" of success in the literary career of Willa Cather.

II

The story of Willa Cather's literary career is an American success story of the most charming kind. She spent her childhood in Virginia, member of a then-increasing and ultimately large Southern family. She was taken, before adolescence, to Nebraska, in that movement westward of the American population in which the Southerners encountered westward-drifting New Englanders on the common ground of the prairie—there to encounter new pioneers from Europe. This episode in Miss Cather's life, her uprooting from old familiar things at an early age, has been well told both in E. K. Brown's critical biography (which I completed after his death) and in the memoir written by Edith Lewis, who knew Miss Cather during the greater part of her writing years. Willa was nine when she was transferred from a South still filled, in the early decades after the Civil War, with a sense of an old aristocratic way of life, to the life of the prairie, with its new dynamism, that of creating everything from scratch. To have lived in a stately rambling house in Virginia and then to discover the sod houses of the settlers on the Divide, was revelation enough for a pre-adolescent girl. Willa Cather's experience was common to most of the members of her migratory generation in Nebraska: they had been uprooted out of older places, many out of centuries of civilization in the Old World. The difference between her and her contemporaries is that she was an observer from the start: an observer in the little town of Red Cloud, Nebraska, who came to know the countryside intimately. She played with the children of the pioneers; they lived their lives on the prairie; and Willa was to write about the lives they lived. Somewhere she quotes the words of Virgil: *Primus ego in patriam mecum . . . deducam Musas.* She was indeed the first to woo the muse in her wild land. The early and late settlers were essentially non-literary: they could hardly have been otherwise. They were concerned with doing, on the plane of struggle and conquest. To take hold of the land, to tame it, to build on it, to make it yield life; the goals were simple, and they were among the most difficult of all of man's goals. Schools, culture, wise words, all this had to come in good time. The Bible had wisdom enough for them as they did their rude tasks; and those who came from other lands brought their memories of song and dance and tale out of the old cultures with which to relax after their toil.

Willa Cather at first does not seem to have dreamed of being a writer. She would be a scientist, or a doctor; there was a phase during which she sought for truth by dissection, like Turgenev's young men and their frogs; and looked at the stars and had a vision of new worlds. In this period of her girlhood the only hint of her later aesthetic idealism might have been found in her addiction to reading. What we discover in Miss Cather's personal life, which the literary biographer must explore if he is to understand the later public life of the writer, is that in Nebraska, amid the pioneers, she was caught up in the very heart of the "American dream": opportunity, equality, competition for achievement, above all the idea of "success." One *had* to succeed. One could not be a failure. And if one's individuality and courage were not appreciated in the home town, then success was the way to conquest. The sculptor who left the Nebraska town to become famous, and whose funeral we attend in one of Willa Cather's early stories, is eulogized in these words: "There was only one boy ever raised on this borderland between ruffianism and civilization who didn't come to grief, and you hated Harvey Merrick more for winning out than you hated all the other boys who got under the wheels."

She was determined to "win out," and from her first days in Lincoln when she went to the city to prepare for college, she addressed herself to this end. Her early essays won the admiration of her teachers and they published them in the local paper as examples of a literary gift on the frontier. Willa obtained thereby a precocious local fame. The story of her striving years is a record of a persistent and highly determined young woman possessed of an assertive ideal of achievement: the dawn could not come soon enough for Willa Cather during those years when she rose at five and built a fire in her coal stove with coal she had herself carried up a flight of stairs, and sat down in her small room in snow-piled Lincoln to study her Greek and her Latin. Happy day indeed when our youth rose as early as this—and to study the old languages! Miss Cather, we might add, passed first in a class of 53. Throughout her works we come upon such phrases as "the passionate struggle of a tenacious will," and the "loyalty of young hearts to some exalted ideal and the passion with which they strive." The passion was in the striving. Ultimately she was to say that "success is never so interesting as struggle—not even to the successful."

We will have to come back to this statement, made years later, when she herself had tasted the fruits of success and yet found the world to be out-of-joint, and longed nostalgically for the older time when there were still frontiers to conquer. Her own frontiers had been conquered by the process of doing things for herself, knowing what she wanted to do, and taking every step of life as a challenge: what we speak of as "rugged individualism." From Lincoln, after she graduated, she went to Pittsburgh, and, after a decade of journalism and teaching, published her first volumes—her verses and a book of her tales. After that there came the further temptation of a high position on a national magazine, *McClure's*, and to this she gave several of her best years. Only then did she find her true path and, turning her back on journalism and administration forever, she settled down to be a novelist. But 10 or 15 years were to elapse before her work would become widely read and receive the recognition every novelist desires. Willa Cather was almost 50 by the time she reached the end of her strivings and became famous. No wonder that she looked back and murmured the third *Georgic* of Virgil: *optima dies . . . prima fugit,* "the best days are the first to flee."

III

It has become fashionable among certain of our critics to talk of literature as if it were a created object, an ingenious contrivance, a vase, a mechanical butterfly—and to insist upon the impersonality of art. Literary art, it seems to me, is the most personal creation of man: it is the use of words to express feeling and experience in story and poem, in metaphor and simile. Far from ignoring the life of an artist, as these critics would have us do, we must encounter that life in the artist's work. We can hardly avoid it, for the work is a kind of supreme biography of the artist: it is by his work that the artist asserts himself, and writes his name, his voice, his style—his and no one else's—into the memory of men. These may be truisms but we have listened to so much talk about the function of criticism that I find myself pressed to reassert them on an occasion such as this one, in the interest of the things I want to say.

What I want particularly to say is that if we examine the work of any novelist in the sequence in which it was written we can always discover an inner core of narrative, and an inner pattern—due caution being taken, as it must, to read the pattern *out of* and not *into* the work. I speak inevitably of the writer of genius, and not of the hack, the artist who creates out of personal necessity, not out of the expediencies of journalism. Creative writers do their work out of profound inner dictates, they write in compliance to an imperious self-demand for expression. With all the world to choose from, they almost invariably select subjects closest to their hearts, even though the story they write may seem on the surface remote and unrelated. This can be stated as a literary axiom; and the subject selected more often than not reveals some emotion the writer had to express, some particular state of feeling, some view of life which demanded articulation. In this sense it might be said that writers—and writers of fiction in particular—are engaged in creating parables about themselves.

Thus, if we listen carefully to Tolstoy as he tells us the story of Anna Karenina, we discover that he is not merely writing a novel about his overt subject: the consequences of blind passion. His novel is a novel about two persons, both in a state of despair, and we are shown the different solutions each finds to his dilemma. I speak of Anna and of Levin. And if we turn to Tolstoy's life, we have very little difficulty in discovering that the despair projected into this work was his own: indeed there were days when he thought of taking Anna's solution, and others in which he reasoned himself into the states of mind of Levin. So, if we try to listen to what Willa Cather is really saying in her sequence of novels, we can discover a pattern ineluctably woven through her work; and an analysis in sequence enables us to discover the meaning of the particular parables Miss Cather was impelled to write.

Let us take her short stories first of all, since they reflect her earliest moods. These deal largely with artists and what they must do in a world that tends to be hostile to art and in which artistic success can be obtained only by bitter toil and often at a forbidding price. These stories represent largely the phase of Willa Cather's revolt against Nebraska and her strong

356

conviction that the prairies would have confined her talent. They express the artist's need to overcome the tyranny of family and the pressures of environment, the need to move out into a receptive world in order to conquer. Professor Howard Mumford Jones, some years ago, used Miss Cather's image of Youth and the Bright Medusa (the title of her best-known collection of tales) as the subject for a vivid series of lectures on artists, poets, and radicals. The tension in Miss Cather's tales, he observed, arises from the "conflict between the desire of the artist to pursue beauty and the necessity of the craftsman, if he is to live, to make some practical adjustment to the workaday world." The Bright Medusa, she who could lure but who also turned those lured into stone, represents, said Professor Jones, "the fascination of art, or at least of aesthetic experience, as this works its havoc or its charm." And in a happy contrast between Miss Cather's tales of artists and the stories on the same subject written by Henry James, Professor Jones remarked that for James the problem was one of culture, whereas for Miss Cather the problem was one of energy. This strikes me as profoundly true. On rereading the stories recently, I was inclined to add that this fascination for art, and the art world, on the part of Miss Cather's heroes and heroines, was a fascination essentially with success; the energy represented is not aesthetic, it is that of conquest; of overcoming nature and competition and standing firm and free among the Philistines and resisting their inevitable demands that talent become as mediocre as themselves.

Miss Cather's central theme is that of people who pull themselves up by their bootstraps. What is interesting for us in a novel such as *The Song of the Lark* is that once the would-be opera star, Thea, arrives at her goal, the story has nowhere to go. The love affair Miss Cather created in the novel is artificial; it has had little meaning beside the main impulse, which was Thea's, to be a great singer and a great star. And when the characters meet sometime afterwards, I think in Denver, on a crisp starry night, all they can do is to be very smug about all that they have accomplished. They discover, perhaps, what Henry James meant when he remarked that success was like having a good dinner. All that you can say is that you have had it.

The inner voice of the early novels of Willa Cather suggests this fascination with, and need to describe, various forms of success—but also certain forms of failure. The drive to power in these books is overriding, with the result that the novels contain no complicated plots, no complexity of human relationships, no love affairs that we can take seriously. Her heroines, those women with feminized masculine names, Alexandra, Ántonia—and the name Alexandra itself reminds us of one of history's greatest conquerors—have tenacious wills and an extraordinary capacity for struggle. Miss Cather's first four novels seem to say that a great engineer may build his bridges, but bridges sometimes collapse; that the pioneer must do what he is ordained to do as Alexandra is ordained to conquer the land and finish the task her pioneer father had but half completed—and in the process impose her will on her brothers; and that the children of the pioneers who remained within the tradition of struggle had hard lives, but in the end achieved a rugged kind of happiness. Already in *O Pioneers!*, and in the finest of the prairie novels, *My Ántonia*, the younger rebel in Willa Cather is making her peace with the Nebraska she had fled and is discovering a deep love for the place and the people she had known.

When a writer turns to things as they were, and conveys them with an ache as powerful and poignant as Willa Cather's, we can wonder whether this may not express a profound uneasiness with things as they are. There is always a certain ache, inevitably, for old days and bygone experiences which we cherished; the question is the degree to which that ache prevails in the midst of the here and the now. Miss Cather's novels, those she wrote in her second phase, leave no doubt that for her the here and the now was deeply depressing. This is what the inner voice says in the four novels Miss Cather wrote during the early 1920's. In *One of Ours*, to which I have already alluded, the hero makes an unhappy marriage and escapes from it and the prairie by going overseas during the First World War; he escapes also from the new machines and the new men who are betraying the promise of the pioneers. Death in battle comes to him as a happy release. The title of the next volume expresses a further stage in this mood of despair, decay, death. *A Lost Lady* expresses the nostalgia for a lost aristocratic order on the frontier. This short novel, which achieved extraordinary popularity during the 1920's, paints with vividness and economy a heroine who cannot yield the old for the new, but who in her love of pleasure is prepared to accept shallow compromises. The story conveys to us a kind of lonely ache for the swagger of the railroad pioneers and the early tycoons. *The Professor's House*, which followed, tells us much more. If the lost lady is lost indeed, the professor has everything to live for: he is a prize-winning historian, his work is recognized, he is about to become a grandfather. There is a forward movement in the life around him, but also within it a decline in old high values; and his reaction to this decline is to decline himself into apathy and bitter premature old age. Indeed, he all but commits suicide. *My Mortal Enemy*, the last novel in this group, ends in the death of the heroine, and in it Willa Cather seems to offer herself a kind of ambiguous resignation and the possible solace of religion. But the novel is of a piece with its immediate predecessors and the view of life in it is dark and ominous.

IV

What, then, emerges from these eight novels, representing two stages in Willa Cather's artistic progress? If we seek their essence—and I am not concerned for the moment with their beauty as narrative and their lyrical quality—we discover in them two subjects: conquest and death. The triumph and achievement of the pioneer yields to disillusion, and disillusion harbors in it a wish for extinction. A whole world has been lost and seems irretrievable save in memory. It was Miss Cather who spoke of "the precious, the incommunicable past." The present, we take it, had ceased to be precious to her. "Some memories," she said, "are realities, and are better than anything that can ever happen to one again." There is a deep pessimism in this statement. Let me digress for just a moment to underline that I am not suggesting that Willa Cather should have been other than she was; nor am I of the opinion that writers should be optimists. The critic and the literary biographer are concerned only with things as they are, or as they have been; a critic is presumptuous indeed when he tells a writer how he should have written his work; a biographer is worse than presumptuous if he tells his subject how he should have lived his life. The task in each case is one of trying to perceive, to understand, to place in context, to evaluate—but not to sit in judgment. For Miss Cather, the American past was heroic, and it had been her privilege to witness one phase of it. The present seemed drab. Her picture of soldiers returning from the First World War and finding life an anticlimax after the excitement and danger of the field of battle is consonant with her feelings about the conquest of the frontier. The past was splendid; the present was dull and she seems to have arrested her experience of the old splendor at its moment of triumph; nothing that came after could equal it. The process of growing older, the calm of quieter years, the dropping away of early intensities for later insights, could offer little satisfaction. The only thing that had possessed fundamental meaning for Willa Cather were her striving years. And this brings me to what I have spoken of as the "paradox of success" in the work and in the life of Willa Cather.

There is, in *A Lost Lady*, a highly significant passage. Miss Cather, speaking in the voice of the omniscient author, expresses contempt for the new generation which succeeded the pioneers on the frontier, the young men who were diluting the achievements of their parents and destroying the values of the earlier world. (The new men are Bayliss Wheeler of *One of Ours*, Wick Cutter of *My Ántonia*, Ivy Peters of *A Lost Lady*, and the smooth-talking Louie Marsellus of *The Professor's House*.) This type of man, would, Willa Cather wrote, "drink up the mirage, dispel the morning freshness, root out the great brooding spirit of freedom, the generous, easy life of the great landholders. The space, the colour, the princely carelessness of the pioneer, they would destroy and cut up into profitable bits, as the match factory splinters the primeval forest. All the way from the Missouri to the mountains this generation of shrewd young men, trained to petty economies by hard times, would do exactly what Ivy Peters had done when he drained the Forrester marsh."

We can respect the feeling in this passage, but we must recognize the curious fallacies it contains. It is written on the assumption that a shimmering mirage can last, that early morning freshness can continue throughout the day, that "princely carelessness" can be possible to all generations. It is precisely the "princely carelessness" of the first-comers, to whom the riches of nature seemed endless, that brought on the duststorms of later years, and created a need, doubtless unprincely and parsimonious, to start conservation of our resources lest our entire heritage be swept away. But with an emotion such as Miss Cather's one cannot be logical: and the beauty of her statement is its high romanticism and the firmness with which she clung to the fine old things. To such a person, who cannot tolerate change, it is useless to say that change is simply one of the hard facts of life. Moreover, it is difficult to say this, since change is not always for the better, and certainly some of the sterling pioneer qualities did decline. Miss Cather remained unreconciled. The drama of the frontier had been too vivid; it came to seem miraculous. She could not believe, she did not like to believe, that the curtain had come down. She became involved in one of those anomalies of human existence in which, when the struggle ceases, there seems to go with it all reason for pursuing anything new. The land was tamed and productive; it was being re-worked and re-parceled by a new generation. And like her pioneers Willa Cather had conquered too. She had made herself powerful as a writer; her books were read; she had financial ease. She, too, had been a pioneer and now she had her success. She could live and work for her art, but apparently this was not enough, as it might have been in other circumstances and to other artists. If it had been, she would have been capable, in the large way of the great novelists, of being forever immersed in the world around her; she would have found it constantly interesting and curious and filled with abiding truths of human character and an ever-continuing battle between good and evil. Balzac died with dozens of novels unwritten. Dostoyevsky dropped his pen only when his physical strength failed him. Henry James' notebooks are crammed with tales he never had time to write, and he wrote ceaselessly. Miss Cather, coming of a different race of novelists and driven by a single vision, does not seem to have possessed such resources. As she looked back at her heroine in *The Song of the Lark* many years after the book was written, she remarked: "The life of a successful artist in the full tide of achievement is not so interesting as the life of a talented young girl 'fighting her way' as we say. Success is never so interesting as struggle—not even to the successful, not even to the most mercenary form of ambition." And when we open this particular novel which tells of the singer's career, step-by-step, a prairie girl's rise to the operatic stage, we find that as epigraph Willa Cather placed the following words from Lenau's *Don Juan* on her title page: "It was a wondrous lovely storm that drove me."

V

It was a wondrous lovely storm that drove Willa Cather, and what she cared for above all was the storm. With success achieved, she was like her professor in *The Professor's House*. She felt depressed. She didn't know what to do with success; or rather, she seems to have experienced a despair altogether out of proportion to the actual circumstances of her achievement. She blamed it on the changed times: on the bothersome little men who seemed to clog a foreground formerly filled with giants; on machines; on new and less simple values; on complexities which had not existed in the early flush of the American dawn. She had, in her personal triumph, outdistanced competition—had surpassed her classmates, her father, her brothers—and yet she could not give herself up to the enjoyment of the fruits of her success. This was the paradox, and it is more common in American life than one might think. I do not propose here to generalize on it, save to remark that I suppose it is a part of our endless consuming energy and our need to go on endlessly doing, endlessly creating the bigger and sometimes the better, without pausing to grasp fully what we have. It must be a part of our belief, like Willa Cather's, that the dew of morning will not go away, even after the sun is already high on the horizon, if only we can maintain a life of consuming action. Success, by the very testimony of the tales she wrote, created for Willa Cather a deep despair and even a wish for death, as with the pioneer farmer in her story "Neighbour Rosicky," who wanted to go on pitching hay, after the doctor told him he had a bad heart and reminded him that he had strong sons to pitch the hay for him. When the frontiers have been conquered, the alternatives would seem to be simple: one accepts this fact and goes on to new problems or one mourns for their disappearance as if they could have existed forever.

I suspect that the more Miss Cather succeeded in her career, the more despair she experienced without quite understanding why. We get evidence of this not only in the turn she gave to her tales, but in the ways in which, for instance, she chose to put together her essays. The essays in themselves were a series of reminiscences about old and valued things: her days in the Charles Street house of Mrs. Fields in Boston, where all the

361

Brahmins used to visit and where Dickens and Thackeray had once stayed; her friendship with Sarah Orne Jewett; her meeting with Flaubert's niece. To these essays, in their book form, she gave the provocative title, *Not Under Forty*. She herself was past 50 then, and the preface which she wrote was a belligerent explanation of the title. The essays, she said, were for those who were not under 40, because anyone younger could not understand or appreciate what they meant. And in this preface she said that "the world broke in two in 1922 or thereabouts," choosing the year in which she stood on the threshold of her 50th birthday. We need not go here into the other circumstances which may have contributed to this belligerency. I have dealt with them in a long chapter in my book on literary biography. I am concerned tonight principally with the aspect of success in Miss Cather's career.

Many are the consequences of success. Some persons understandably thrive on it and even revel in it. Others seem to do their utmost to turn it into failure. And some are even killed by it. We have read of persons so driven by their pursuit of their life goals that they collapse utterly when these goals are reached. Overnight their lives acquire an emptiness that can be overwhelming. There has been such a tremendous expenditure of energy in the struggle that there is still too much left to accept a halt. Much more might be said about this wondrous lovely storm which drives such persons. But alas, storms blow themselves out and calm follows. Youth does not last. The best days are doubtless the first to flee, and for Miss Cather the rest seemed to be defeat. Yet her career did not end here as well it might have. She saved herself from defeat in two ways: one was by the instinct to write about her feelings and thereby ease herself of inner burden. The other resided in the intensity with which she clung to her embeddedness in her personal past. Out of that intensity she had already created the powerful nostalgia which illuminates *My Ántonia*. And now she found another way of defeating this static element within herself. It was a happy and resourceful solution. But it had an uncomfortable circumstance in it. It made her more successful than ever.

VI

To understand the burden of my theme tonight, it is necessary once more to underline the process of my reasoning. In seeking the inner voice of Willa Cather's novels, I started with the axiom that the individuality of a novel resides particularly in its being a reflection of the novelist himself. It is a truism to say that a poem is the poet's, and the novel, no less than the poem, is the novelist's. "Poetry," said Thoreau, "is a piece of very private history, which unostentatiously lets us into the secret of a man's life." No one but Willa Cather has written anything quite like her novels for the simple reason that they are tissued out of *her* memories, memories of experience as well as of reading, stories lived and stories told, the materials of her life gathered and re-experienced in words. We can say this of any novelist whose writings lay claim to a personality and to a style. And in saying this, I reject the old belief that a story just "flies" into a novelist's mind, that creation is a fortuitous circumstance, a happy inspiration. It is nothing of the kind. Inspiration there may be, but the flight of the story is, if anything, outward from within; it comes from the mind and the heart and the whole consciousness of the artist. I predicate a series of choices open to the artist. Of all the frontier stories available to Willa Cather, why, we can ask, did she particularly cling to this one rather than that; why did a night of talk with a blue-eyed girl at some party in the 1890's, a girl whose name was Gayhardt, end in a novel almost half a century later titled *Lucy Gayheart;* why had it long been dreamed of as a story to be called "Blue Eyes on the Platte?" Some buried intensity of experience, some deep core of meaning had existed for Miss Cather in the blue eyes and the bright talk of the Gayhardt girl, and in the fullness of time this became the novel we can read. But this novel contained in it other materials also tissued out of old experience; it was again the story of an active young woman setting out on a career; she is again a musician; she has a love affair with an older man; and of importance also in the story is Lucy's relationship with her father; and significant too is Lucy's early death. The novel dissolves itself in the break of a bright promise; and Lucy's death is as arbitrary as death can be. The novelist had the choice of giving the heroine life and adventure, but she chose a skating accident as a way of ending her novel.

I have used this novel as I might any other of Miss Cather's, to show that a work of fiction, like a poem, is a reflection of a state of feeling in the writer. As I say, Willa Cather might have chosen some other girl in Nebraska, when she came to write this novel; another Alexandra or Ántonia or Thea, but she chose Lucy instead, and she might have given her victory and success as she does her earlier heroines, but she *chose* to give her an early death. These were choices made by the writer for reasons she could doubtless have explained rationally, and for deeper reasons of which she was unaware and about which we speculate now by examining the choices made in her other works, and noting similarities and dissimilarities. Since the novels all issued out of the single consciousness, we are likely to discover more similarities than dissimilarities in the fundamental treatment of the material, in the predicaments pictured, the solutions reached.

If we had had the opportunity to ask Miss Cather why, when she reached the impasse of near-death with the professor in *The Professor's House* and the death of Myra in *My Mortal Enemy*, she then turned to a distant past and wrote *Death Comes for the Archbishop*, she might have answered that she had for long been interested in the work of the early French missionaries in the American Southwest; that she had read such-and-such books about them; that she had conceived the idea of writing a novel about them. What I would like to submit to you is that the inner story of *Death Comes for the Archbishop* is something quite other than the overt material shows: it illustrates the marvelous way in which the creative consciousness operates in an artist as determined as Willa Cather, as tenacious in keeping her personal world intact and allowing neither time nor world upheaval to alter it. Indeed we might observe that Miss Cather instinctively found a solution, a triumphant solution, in terms of her personal as well as her artistic needs. Up to this time she had lived over her Nebraska past and the past of her Southwest in her novels, as well as her memories of Pittsburgh and her life in New York. Then her world broke in two, as she said, and she wrote out her despair in *A Lost Lady, The Professor's House,* and *My Mortal Enemy.* Where her theme had been power and conquest, it had become frustration and death. And now she wrote a novel of an older pioneering time which had required the same courage as that of her Nebraska pioneers, and even greater hardihood. If the Western frontiers of her own time had disappeared, Miss Cather's inner voice seemed to say to her, there were still older frontiers available—those which existed before her time and which she could relive in the history books, in anecdote, in memories other than her own, and then retell them. Stated in other terms, Miss Cather's greatest fictional success, her chronicle of two missionaries in the Southwest carrying out their great religious and civilizing tasks, was a discovery that she could still—and indeed better than ever— do what she had always done. But see how insistent inner claims can be! The word Death is the first word in the title, even though the novel is once again a novel of conquest, conquest alike of a new land and of the souls of men. Indeed, for all the insistence of the title, the book is in reality not about death; it is about Archbishop Latour's courage and steadfastness, his gentleness and his worldly wisdom. His death at the end is simply the death that comes to all men—but in giving it significance, Miss Cather may have betrayed her deepest awareness that she was herself engaged in this novel in an act of exhuming the dead past.

Miss Cather had embodied all her major themes in the *Archbishop.* Yet she dealt with them on a different footing; they could touch her less in a personal way, being remote in time. She could write this book without the anxieties betrayed in the novels which preceded it. Her friend Miss Lewis testifies to this when she tells us that the writing of the *Archbishop* gave Miss Cather such an intense joy that she promptly tried to recapture it by writing another historical fiction. She went, for the material of *Shadows on the Rock,* into an even more remote time—17th-century Quebec. Miss Lewis writes: "I think Willa Cather never got so much happiness from the writing of any book as from the *Archbishop;* and although *Shadows on the Rock* is of course altogether different in conception, in treatment and in artistic purpose, it may have been in part a reluctance to leave the world of Catholic feeling and tradition in which she had lived so happily for so long that led her to embark on this new novel." There is doubtless a fund of truth in this; but a curious critic might still ask why Miss Cather experienced a pleasure so intense, even allowing for the intellectual and emotional interest she (herself an Episcopalian) found in the history of Catholicism in America. I would be inclined to the view that Miss Cather experienced great joy in writing the *Archbishop* because for the moment she had laid aside all the frustrations which had engendered the despair reflected in the books of her middle period. *Death Comes for the Archbishop* could be written in a kind of easy freedom, a joy of identifying herself with the old things, the great wide American out-of-doors of her childhood which touched all that was deepest in Willa Cather and in which she could roam while remaining firmly embedded in her own past.

Shadows on the Rock sold even more copies than the *Archbishop* and was an even greater material success. But it was not as good a book. For in it old problems began to intrude again: and, as E. K. Brown has shown, in writing about the apothecary in Quebec and his 12-year-old daughter, Miss Cather was returning to her own early adolescence and reliving some of the memories of her father, who had recently died. She had found in the pages of history what her own time could no longer furnish her and she could do again what she had done before. These two books were the sum of her escape from her fundamental dilemma; and their overwhelming success revived a sense of frustration again. Then illness and late middle age closed in upon her. Two more novels were written, both retrospective, but Miss Cather's best work was done. Unlike some other writers, she could create only from what had happened to her, or what had happened in a history to which she was personally attuned.

One more word about *Shadows on the Rock:* in choosing the rock of Quebec for her story, and that part of society on this continent which has undergone the least change since the old time, Miss Cather was once again testifying to her own reluctance to accept change. She spoke of the rock, indeed, as "the utmost expression of human need." A strange statement, for rocks are hard and singularly unfertile; they symbolize stratification and rigidity. Miss Cather's formulation suggests that for her the symbol of the rock means none of these things. Rather, it symbolized for her something that expressed durability, steadfastness, something to which one could cling. Well, this *is* the use it had for her, and we must recognize that Willa Cather needed something to hold on to; her life had assumed, given its particular circumstances, an inescapable bitterness. A last story upon which she was working and which she ordered destroyed (but the content of which Miss Lewis has revealed to us) would have taken her even farther into the past, the past of the Avignon of the Popes.

VII

You will say to me that I have given you a strange account of Willa Cather; that I came here to commemorate her and that instead I have drawn boundaries about her and shown how, for her, life seemed to become static and despairing once she achieved her goals. My account is not strange, however, for it is in some such searching light that we in the second half of our century must place the writers of the first half. Moreover, I have taken Miss Cather at her own word. She wrote of Sarah Orne Jewett, who deeply influenced her, and to whom she was devoted: "To note an artist's limitations is but to define his talent." This cuts through to a valuable critical truth and it is indeed by seeing Miss Cather's limitations that we can see her whole. I have told you what her struggles were, with what deep and bitter problems she had to contend, problems of life and of the inner spirit. In doing so I am proclaiming the triumph, not the defeat, of her talent. It is the triumph of any artist to be able, in the teeth of difficulties, to achieve artistic utterance. I have said that Miss Cather's life and work constitute a success story of the most characteristic kind. Her books, her best books, are, in their simple and direct appeal, success stories, uncomplicated by subtleties of analysis or complexities of plot. She is a writer of people in action; and their action is characteristically American. She was one of those whose energies in a pioneering world were boundless; Tennyson's words, wafted over the seas during the Victorian century, to strive, to seek, to find—and he added also *but not to yield*—meant much to the pioneers who were striving and seeking and finding and seldom yielding. And Willa Cather had experienced her early life with such extraordinary intensity that she refused ever to let it go. It is this life, when it flows into her novels, that gives them their warm glow and reveals what Justice Holmes called her "gift of the transfiguring touch." Those novels of hers which are suffused with all the ache and nostalgia of youth, those elegiac pages which speak for the joy and sorrow of things gone by—these are the lyrical pages of her novels which touched the heart of her generation and will probably touch those who read her in the future. It is something for a writer—a writer with Miss Cather's distinct limitations—to have so warmly encountered her own time and to have done so with dignity and devotion to her art and with an unfaltering belief in her world that amounted to dogma, an unshakable faith in the old true things. If this belief made life hard for her in a civilization as addicted to shaking up the old things as our own, it was also often a solace to her and to many of her readers.

Willa Cather clung to her rock no matter what tide swept in and swept by. She would certainly have been happier, I think, if she could have been a little more yielding. That which is new is not always a destruction of the old; it can also be a phenomenon of re-birth, of things rising from the ashes of older things to new life and new achievement. Nevertheless, I admire the consistency, the stubbornness, the pride, and the hard and rugged individualism with which Willa Cather lived and wrought. That which diminished her work also proved its strength; the very collapse of her world gave her that radiance of spirit by which Archbishop Latour and Father Vaillant traveled on in the strange land, remote from familiar things, and carried their faith with them. As I say, to have wrought this with distinction and feeling is achievement enough in our time, and indeed in any time.

Latest Trends in French Prose

Alain Bosquet

Presented at the Library of Congress January 11, 1960

THE REASON WHY this lecture has been entitled "Latest Trends in French Prose," is that fiction and memoirs, aphorisms and essays, in the last 15 years, have been classical, on the one hand, and experimental on the other. My purpose is to determine which forms these two endeavors have taken; whereas if I were to consider the complete picture of French literature, I would conclude that poetry is experimental only, and theatre is a compromise between pure literature and the necessities of the stage. The other reason why we shall examine prose only is that the writer accepts a notion of distance between himself, as a human being, and the result of his writing, at the very moment he decides to convey something through a work of prose. This necessity of acknowledging a definite distance does not exist in French poetry, for the simple reason that, ever since Rimbaud, it wants to dive as deeply as possible into the field of subconscious feelings; the poet only knows what his intentions were at the time he rereads his poem. In other words, he feels an imperative urge to express something he cannot define, but, after having expressed it, he is perhaps capable of defining it. This is what might be called the *knowledge of oneself* through the exercise of poetry and poetic imagery. The rational and conscious distance I just mentioned becomes a concern for several other people than the author, such as the creator of settings, director of theatre, etc., if the author wants to write a play and have it produced. Many people other than the author are involved in the creation of a play; whatever happens, the play is, in the end, a compromise between what the author wanted to write, has written, has agreed to alter, and has changed according to the wishes of half-a-dozen people.

This notion of distance being accepted, let us try to grasp the philosophy of a few trends in French prose. I would like to be permitted to propose three main fields: one will be what Englishmen and Americans call fiction, the second will be aphorisms and essays, and the third what I might call

368

absolute or *total* prose. What are the main characteristics of a work of fiction? We assume that the writer consciously and willingly uses the language, vocabulary, and expressions of a certain kind in order to convey feelings, facts, and figures about either himself, considered as an object, or other people, considered as characters he invents, or even things that are known to others. I might say that this sort of fiction always deals with human beings that are not monsters or, if they are, monsters who can be analyzed; it also deals in truths that are not secret and too particular to the author, but can be expressed and therefore translated, into anyone's language. My second category, aphorisms and essays, does not deal, of course, with events nor characters, nor the projection of the author's desires into some sort of external embodiment. It simply deals with the pursuit of eternal truths in a new form or, shall we say, the pursuit of new truths that might be accepted by anyone as soon as they fit into a more or less abstract and short formula. My third category is, to a certain extent, a more exciting and difficult one to define. *Absolute* or *total* prose is, to be true, the only experimental form of prose which is possible today, although the two previous forms may contain some novelty that is accepted rather easily. Total or absolute prose is a genuine laboratory of ideas, feelings, contradictions. One is, to a certain extent, in a field very close to that of poetry, a poetry that is not allergic to antipoetic words such as adverbs; nor does absolute prose care for any musical quality, so important in poetry. Total or absolute prose requires its author to reduce the distance mentioned hitherto. He projects himself into writing, not exactly for his own sake, not exactly for other people, but for a conglomerate where he, himself, is the center and where he still hopes that other people will understand what he writes, although he may not be able to guarantee that his language is immediately understandable. In short, this category of prose leads to the discovery of new truths which are posterior to the act of writing.

It would be impossible to give a complete picture of all the trends now acknowledgeable in French prose. Nor would it be fair for me to put on the same level writers whom I personally consider important and others who, for one reason or another, might be more famous than those. I will thus beg to be both harsh and partial in my choice of what I consider to be the highlights of French prose literature in the last 15 years. Fiction, with its array of stories that can be summed up and characters whose names are known, has followed several paths, the origin of which is remote and could be traced back for one or even two centuries. There is such a thing as classical prose which, because of the age of its authors, might be called neoclassical. This type of fiction can also be termed as naturalistic, realistic, or, if you prefer, postnaturalistic or neorealistic. The term really matters little. It is to be recognized by the avowed aim of the author to write something which is clear, understandable, and of immediate use to the masses.

369

As such, this classical prose does not require a great amount of intellectual effort. It is either willingly social or antisocial. It comes in the form of a protest or in the form of a fairly impartial report on social conditions. At all times, however, it wants to convey the true picture of a given social milieu, be it a milieu of outcasts. In its external form, it follows the recipe of such great writers as Flaubert or Maupassant. In its impact it follows the democratic virulence of a man like Zola. It may also be termed as being rather carefully written prose, that is to say, without any excess of flourishes. It is not written as it would be spoken in the streets, but represents a compromise between the way one should write to the President of the Republic and the way one speaks to the grocer. In this respect, writers like Armand Lanoux, Henri Troyat, or Robert Sabatier have written fiction that has a particular taste of twentieth-century Parisian or provincial landscapes. Other writers closer to the Pigalle and Ménilmontant type of gangster would rather use the very colorful "argot" that changes so often and makes the reader wonder what they meant after the vocabulary has changed, five years later. It is colorful, undoubtedly exciting, and pretends to be as true as possible to the inventiveness of the sidewalk lingo. Novelists like René Fallet and Louis Calaferte have been most effective in serving this order of frog-legs and snails. Whatever the merits of this type of writing, it is nothing more than an obvious report on what goes on between la rue Lepic and la Place Blanche. None of these writers wish to invent anything new nor do they seem to be able to reconsider the relations between the writer and the written word. This relation inevitably remains one of common usage and of relative mastery on the part of the writer towards the word. At no time does the word become a challenging being nor the equal of those who use it.

As we know, the other tradition of French classical prose may be traced back to Voltaire. It is what I would call prose of a résumé: in other words, the account of adventures, events, happenings, feelings, dreams, and so forth, is told without the full weight of naturalistic descriptions. Transitions are skipped, and one has the impression that the writer wants to keep the essential, and doesn't care to describe photographically the pimple of each one of his characters; nor does he want to necessarily tell of the gardener who planted the tree of which the wood has been used to manufacture the door that his hero is about to open. Things move quickly. They do not have to be too specific; one witnesses an aristocratic game where all the trivialities are mercilessly avoided in order to arrive at some sort of moral or indeed very immoral conclusion. The sarcastic smile of Voltaire thus has had many admirers and has attracted the talent of writers who want to be elegant, clever, intelligent, but do not pretend to be truthful to any active phase of French life today. Needless to say, the special wit of the eighteenth century has been slightly altered and has now acquired a flavor of its own, which I would call *tender cynicism*.

The tender cynics of French letters today are novelists like Antoine Blondin, Roger Nimier, and, to a lesser extent, those shameless ladies by the name of Christiane Rochefort and Françoise Sagan. What is the nature of this tender cynicism? In a manner close to that of Voltaire and Diderot some 20 years before the French Revolution, a certain casualness of manners and thought became noticeable after all literary aspects of the Résistance, the war, and the Liberation had exhausted themselves around 1949 and 1950. By that time existentialism, as it became known through the special brand of Jean-Paul Sartre, had again a certain Germanic and English flavor: Germanic because the young writers of France thought that no clear purpose was necessary in order to live a normal life, and English because of the French way of interpreting a certain snobbish attitude whereby one does not reveal one's true feelings. Thus, five years after victory, young writers such as Antoine Blondin and Roger Nimier were engaged in disengaging themselves from all the nationalistic literature that had been so popular in the dark years. The first true reaction was to be a really cynical one for the simple and deep reason, although unconscious at times, that France had no role to speak of in the Second World War, and further because one lived in a state of peace without peace treaty and a postwar period without anyone having officially declared that the war was really over. Normal values were again at stake and one took great pleasure in juggling with them, if not merely discarding them as obsolete. As years went by, these cynics also became convinced that no real revolt was necessary against anyone, that nihilism, avant-garde, or simply a show of bad temper were completely out of date as well. This cynicism, completely inactive, simmered and nurtured on one's own Buddhist-like contemplation until such time as it developed to be a simple and superficial game, soon open to feelings of candor and kindness. Without any noticeable transition, the cynics then became romanticists. If there is a certain dandy-like attitude among most of them, some, on the contrary, are passive to the extent that they really are unaware of the peculiar philosophy of life they actually convey through their works. Françoise Sagan may be considered as a sort of tender cynic, although undoubtedly she has never thought of putting a label on her most inarticulate feelings and thoughts. Rather than a writer or an artist, she is a very typical example of a middle-bracket bourgeois young woman for whom practically everything in life is too difficult and uproariously indifferent. Why this deep indifference in perhaps the world's most intelligent nation? Why this manner of shunning any deep concern about what goes on in such melting-pots as the United States, Russia, or, during the last few years, around the earth and the moon? It seems to me that the reason can be sought in the feeling that French youth has had no part in any of the tremendous changes that have occurred throughout the globe and that, therefore, such momentous problems as that of the atom bomb, or the

371

survival of humanity, or the struggle between capitalism and communism, will and even should be solved without their having anything to say nor to offer. They would rather remain with their very shallow feelings and lack of stamina. They are what I would call the second generation of existential-ists, and if one would permit me to dwell upon the etymology of the word itself, I would venture to say that they *exist,* but that they are not. Not to be or to be hardly, that is their question.

Some in this Voltairian tradition are amorphous, amoral, careless about their own writing, and very little concerned by what goes on inside of them or outside. Others have a very typical Gallic way of elegantly dismissing important matters. Among the latter a late-comer, Jacques Bureau, the author of a charming and boisterously hilarious novel published in 1959 and called *Trois pierres chaudes en Espagne (Three Hot Stones in Spain),* is perhaps the quintessence of wit that stands for depth or ideas. The artistic form of his prose and the manner in which he cuts short through the magma of modern feelings is, moreover, both most refreshing and new. He, too, is a post-existentialist, a pupil of Voltaire and Giraudoux, but because he doesn't strive to lead his novel into a moralistic mood and does not aim at leaving any tangible message, he is in a way a modern version of a type unknown to France since the early years of this century and which was embodied so well in writers like Oscar Wilde. The novel ends with the needless and joyous death of the hero. Here is his outcry to the world, an outcry that will remain without echo and is only aimed at laughing at himself:

Between two worlds some hesitation is needed that will last either a second or a century; its time is today. Soldiers stop running, light a cigarette and look at me. An ambulance stops on the road. Clouds are motionless, for the winds rest while battles are fought. A little higher, three planets used to turning together come to a halt facing our own; the smallest handful of stones launched into the darkness of time wonders what we are about to do: the universe checks with its own anxiety the changes of man. Surely from far away the earth seems quite motionless: from Mars, for example, it looks covered with straight channels, or the road to Chicago or the flight of a swallow. From the Moon one sees small, round craters, the tent of a Barnum circus, the arena of Nimes. I myself am dying without a gesture, and I have chosen a posture kept in marble taken by forgotten gods from the hearts of the deserts. But I am a victor: tomorrow everything shall start anew. Tomorrow everything shall begin. Farewell! Be intelligent!

Most certainly the widest field of today's experimental prose in France is that of ideas about writing expressed in the body itself of the novel. In other words, the whole novel has become a sort of laboratory for writers to try out new forms of rhythm, new forms of ideas, and a way to ascertain that they are not only writing a story, but that they are indeed completely renewing a field which in their mind has been weakened by the classical character as it was known throughout the nineteenth century. This classical character, be it that of Stendhal or Flaubert or Zola or even Proust, was an alive person with a name, an age, an identity, and especially a psychology different from that of the author. What we are witnessing now is an amalgamation of the character and the ego of the author. This fusion leads to a definite confusion; the distance I spoke of is now reduced to the bare minimum. The author may know what he wants to write but, in the process of writing, he is bound to ascribe to his characters the ideas he fishes out of his own subconsciousness. Whenever the author's mind is solid enough, we are confronted with a most rational, dry, and sometimes elaborately difficult demonstration of what future fiction prose ought to be. On the other hand, when the writer possesses a certain stamina and does not care about explaining how he arrives at new formulas, we may be plunged into an utter confusion of purpose and temperament. Among those who do know what they want but lack a certain natural gift for creation, one should single out a writer like Alain Robbe-Grillet. His fame is now well established throughout the world, and at the age of 37 he already has several imitators. His philosophy is a rather simple one, but one can say that his way of implementing each detail thereof is stubborn and effective, if we accept that a novel might be just that: a theorem. Robbe-Grillet is an enemy of subjective writing and subjectivity in the act of writing. He wants prose to be a most accurate objective account of what can be seen. The author himself should not intervene and never be the judge of what his character does, nor of what the landscape he describes seems to be, from a completely neutral and cold viewpoint. The novel moves at the speed of a slow-motion camera. It is a photographic process. The vocabulary itself is one of weights and measures. Constantly, such words as "angle," "perpendicular," "lateral," "interval," "centimeter," etc. are used to convey an impression of keen and stern precision. Each door, each window, each movement, each feeling are submitted to this cold geometrical analysis. The author remains impassive. Are we, if this process is to be repeated and generalized, going back to the good old formulas of realism and naturalism? Although Robbe-Grillet is by no means explicit in this respect, his philosophy may be an answer to the danger of atomization of the language such as is pictured in other contemporary works; a scientific usage of the French language may be a way to react against the possible explosion of grammar and vocabulary, so characteristic of writers in other countries. If this be true, Robbe-Grillet's attempt is a narrow reactionary return to a steadfast and outmoded notion of literature. Should language learn from the conquests of science? Robbe-Grillet's answer is that science has no power to change the nature of language. His latest novel appeared in October 1959 and is called *Dans le labyrinthe* (*Inside the Labyrinth*). Here is a first excerpt:

On the polished floor the soft felt shoes have drawn shiny patterns, from the bed to the cupboard, from the hearth to the table, and, on the table, displaced objects have disturbed the continuity of the dust; the latter, more or less thick, according to the age of the surfaces, is missing in spots: thus a square of varnished wood occupies the left corner as if it were drawn by means of a rule; it does not have the same angle as the table but is parallel to its edges and distant from them by approximately 10 centimeters. The square itself, 15 centimeters long on each side, is brownish red, and shines there almost devoid of any deposit of dust.

Here is a second excerpt:

Further, there is a lamp on the right corner of the table: a square base 15 centimeters on each side, a circle of the same diameter, a fluted column bearing a dark shade very slightly conical. On the upper circle of the shade a fly moves slowly in a continuous movement. It projects on the ceiling a deformed shadow where no element of the initial insect can be recognized: neither wings nor body nor legs; all of them have become one single threadlike stroke, a regular broken line, which is not continuous as if it were a hexagon without one of its sides: it is the image of the incandescent filament of the electric bulb. This little open polygon touches, through one of its angles, the interior rim of a vast, luminous circle produced by the lamp. It moves slowly but with a continuous movement all along the circumference. When it reaches the vertical side, it disappears inside of the heavy red drape.

Alain Robbe-Grillet is only a characteristic prose writer devoted to the exploration of new relationships between man and object, subject and object, and, in a deeper sense, creature considered as a creator and writing considered as a sub-creature. From an existentialist viewpoint, creature and sub-creature are on the same level, and the possibility above them of any sort of creator is nullified by the fact that no such notion as God or inspiration is admitted. If therefore no real scale of values prevails throughout a world of things and beings that simply are but do not signify anything, it is possible to create any amount of new relations between them, provided one has a certain amount of imagination. To search for an absolute truth becomes unnecessary, and if neo-rationalists such as Alain Robbe-Grillet do aim at defining a new truth or at least a new mode of expressing relations, they obviously err, since they must know that any other angle is as purposeful or as purposeless as the one they have chosen. This perpetual relativity is also the deep concern of writers such as Nathalie Sarraute or Michel Butor. In the case of Nathalie Sarraute, who is of Russian origin, the Cartesian demonstration is replaced by a sort of pleasure in sinking into a magma, a morass, and a marsh of half-finished images and truly swarming vocabulary. Instead of looking at things and beings from a calculated angle, one is drowned among them. With Michel Butor, the problem is a more artistic one, since instead of seeking a new formula he prefers to choose an original viewpoint, but, without exploiting it, he stops at some halfway acceptable demonstration, because he knows that a normal reader is attracted by feelings or sensations, and not by intelligent rules. The success of Michel Butor is that of a fairly new idea that one has shrunk from exploiting as it might have deserved. On the other hand, it has a charm and a flavor that make up for its apparent poverty as a venture into the field of new monstrosities.

Now that we have glanced at prose writers who follow set rules or would rather smile at their own works with a traditional mixture of boldness and artificial sarcasm, writers who are both the victims and defenders of France's general mood since the second World War, be it a mood of rather grey subconsciousness or, on the contrary, of self-defense in form of a dictatorial advance-guard aimed at imposing upon the reader a new set of esthetical rules, we should have a glance at those who shun fiction and prefer giving their prose the shortest possible form, that of an aphorism or a portrait-like essay. Why does a part of the public prefer this type of prose and seem to distrust any of the forms of fiction previously analyzed? Here again we must consider the notion of distance, and realize that an aphorism or a page of essay is a clear admission that such a distance *ought* to exist, and, moreover, it ought to be a long distance. The personality of the writer disappears almost completely, as far as his ego is concerned, in an aphorism or essay. He does not want to intervene personally in the partial or explosive truth he is about to express. He seems to write out of any context and outside of any notion of time and space. We can assume that in this sort of writing what Lao-Tse or Plato have expressed is not far from the form used by more modern writers such as Proust, Valéry, or Henry James. In such flashes of truth, questions of style are secondary, circumstances disappear in the background, characters vanish, dates, places, names, events are of little importance, and, to a certain extent, the author places himself in the absolute. Most of his sentences seem to begin, whether they actually carry these words or not, by something close to: man is, or man should, or God said, and so on . . . . When he uses the pronoun "I," it is a most universal way of speaking of oneself, and we are never interested actually in the incident that is responsible for the little spark of truth we are about to discover. Of course, if the author is a powerful and original one, we may define his own wit and replace him within the spiritual framework of his time as soon as we discover what his inner culture is. He cannot only deal in generalities, nor in images. It may be said that the author of aphorisms is perhaps the only one who is easily translated into any language and who, through the depth and concision of his formulas, follows a humanistic tradition that goes back to the 5th century B.C. Needless to say, there are very few such writers in France today, as there are few in other countries. The only one who has achieved both depth and a mastery of form is a still rather unknown writer, internationally speaking, of Rumanian origin, E. M. Cioran. He has published three books since 1949: *Précis de Décomposition* (*Epitome of Decomposition*), *Syllogismes de l'Amertume* (*Syllogisms of Bitterness*), and *La Tenta-*

tion d'Exister (*The Temptation of Being*).   Since hardly any of his works have been translated, we have attempted to put into English some of his shortest and most striking aphorisms:

> *Each word hurts me.   How sweet it would be, however, to hear flowers speak of death.*

> *There is no salvation except in the imitation of silence.*

> *Before being a fundamental error, life is lack of taste that neither death nor even poetry succeed in correcting.*

> *I dream of a world where one would die for a comma.*

> *If we believe with such candor in ideas, it is because we forget that they have been conceived by mammals.*

> *How sad to see great nations beg for a supplement of future.*

> *A thousand years of war have strengthened the West; one century of psychology has made it disappear.*

> *The West?   A possibility without future.*

> *I only live because I have the power to die whenever I wish: without the idea of suicide, I would have killed myself long ago.*

> *Why do away with God and come back to oneself?   Why replace one corpse by another?*

> *To hope is to deny the future.*

> *Argument against suicide: isn't it unfair to abandon a world which has so kindly put itself at the disposal of our sadness?*

> *I have strolled around God like an informer; incapable of praying, I spied on him.*

> *For two thousand years Jesus has been punishing us because he didn't die on a sofa.*

> *Without Johann Sebastian Bach theology would be senseless, creation would be fictive, nothingness would be preposterous.   If there is anyone who owes everything to Bach, it is God.*

> *I love those nations of astronomers: Assyrians, Aztecs, etc., who, because of their taste for the skies, went bankrupt on earth.*

> *How have I come to terms with life?   I have changed despairs as one changes shirts.*

At the beginning of his career each thinker chooses either dialectics or weeping willows.

We are phonies: we all survive our problems.

Philosophy is a medicine against sadness. There are still people who believe philosophy is profound.

Objection against science: this world does not deserve being known.

Reality gives me asthma.

In a world without sorrow, nightingales would burp.

Every day I have private conversations with my skeleton, and this is what my flesh shall never forgive.

I walk through my own daze as a whore in a world without sidewalks.

We stop being young when we stop choosing our enemies and are satisfied with those that are handy.

Don't ask for my intentions: isn't to breathe a sufficient one?

Each action flatters the hyena in us.

No one should try to live if he has not completed his education as a victim.

What a pity that to reach God one has to go through faith.

Only optimists commit suicide, optimists who have ceased being optimists. The others, having no reason to live, have no reason to die.

Creation was the first act of sabotage.

The main virtue of a writer like Cioran is in his concision and deep knowledge, translated into a sharp and, in a way, neutral look at man and events. This mastery allows each one of his findings to be the possible jumping-board for any novel or lyrical development. In this respect, a work like his is perhaps more valuable in the long run than philosophical essays hidden in the form of fiction by such contemporaries as Jean-Paul Sartre and Albert Camus.

At the other extreme, no visible mastery, no immediate control, either of oneself or of the act of writing, no balance seems to be necessary in the case of a writer who chooses to express himself in what we have called total or absolute prose. Whenever such a temperament is led to writing, it seems to us that a long and painful incubation is necessary. The writer is unaware of what really goes on in his consciousness and subconsciousness. He does not plan a novel. He does not want to create a character that would more or less reflect his own general ideas, nor does he care about the manner in which he conveys his emotions. He waits, he accumulates strength and contradictory images; he is in a way the very victim of every single syllable, idea, or sensation that might strike his spirit and his senses. And then, one day, he decides he finally has to come out with an irresistible stream of indigestible but magnificent clouds of thought and imagery. He enters a sort of trance, does not really know what he writes, and merely translates himself into correctly but subconsciously built phrases that are a true reflection upon everything he had thought and has been for weeks, and possibly months. The distance we spoke of in the beginning of this lecture disappears entirely, and in a way he transforms himself into words, of which he is not entirely aware. The only thing he does know is that his own complete self reappears on the page he is writing and cannot help filling to the utmost. Once he is completely exhausted, he may then, if he has a sense of artistic necessity, change a comma here and there, but he will not care to organize what remains and should remain a magma, whether it can or cannot be analyzed by his own brain. In a way, he gives himself to the act of writing and has no clear idea of where he is going nor why. So he is very close to the lyrical poet, with perhaps something which is purer and, at the same time, more remote from purity: it is purer because the fantastic necessities are natural and because he does not force himself to really choose nor decide that such-or-such element is or is not acceptable; it is less pure inasmuch as this very choice is at all times absent. Ethically speaking, this procedure has one advantage. It does give a true picture of what a man thinks without knowing it and without any self-control. If this is true, we can learn from a global experiment of this sort to approach the deepest nature of man better than if too many corrections and too many interventions of one's own self-control were to sift the very mass of impetuous imagery or vocabulary. At this stage, literature looks like a scientific process, where the notions of beauty and ugliness, usefulness or uselessness are replaced by a general dynamic picture of an intricate personality. Esthetically speaking, we may or may not follow the writer, and we are probably led into regretting that such-or-such detail has been left in or that such-or-such phrase contradicts what was written two lines before. We thus have mixed feelings. We are fascinated by the depth and the riches of the experiment, and we are, to a certain extent, sorry that this experiment does not find the possibility of becoming an object of beauty, a perfect medal, something that we can live with in perfect agreement and harmony. But then again, do we have to consider prose as an object of beauty and comfort, or do we have to consider it as a major challenge? It would possibly be pretentious and presumptuous to try to solve this question. The answer is in a medium that has not been found yet, a medium that would satisfy our internal upheavals, the falls and flights of our own hidden ego, and, at the same time, our centuries-old need for comfort at first glance. Very few writers are capable of burying us under such a fantastic mass of wriggling contradictions. We must, although our means of measuring this magma are never accurate, feel that the temperament we are confronted with can transmit its own enthusiasm or gloom; otherwise, we would only face a mountain of ugly debris. The only recent writer who has been able to exasperate us to such an extent is Samuel Beckett. As one knows, he has been writing both in English and in French for the last 23 years. The reason why his major works have been written in French is, according to the author himself, that French syntactic rules are more elaborate and stern than the English ones, and therefore his suspicion toward them is more visible and more enervating; in English, grammatical rules are easier and great audacities more palatable. Aside from his known novels and plays, his most important works are, we believe, contained in *Nouvelles et textes pour rien* (*Stories and Texts for Nothing*). Here is a typical excerpt from an unpublished piece of prose which was given to me two months ago. It has not been translated into English by Samuel Beckett, who usually hates to go through the pangs of putting himself into the other language.

Here thus at last the second part where I must say how it was with Pim so that I would not have to say how it has been since, I have said and it is true that I don't see the meaning of before and it is true but imagination isn't dead, not yet, it is lucky, I would rather be revived than talk of memories but I have some perhaps too bad it's unimportant, the voice as well but little waves assail me from everywhere reaches me this is better pictures him some time or else the voices I am speaking of Pim, with all that I will be able to say how it was our common life a hatred said the poet is all the hatred it is a good formula, it was a happy period in its way good moments I mean for myself although I were Pim it seems to me I could have been very happy I will know it later perhaps, I don't say I was happy as I have just been or as I am one doesn't have to be happy always in the same way, there are less good moments as well when one is to it is natural it seems.

In this intricate example of Samuel Beckett's prose, which we termed a total or absolute prose, the full impact of language in the upheaval it causes throughout the conscious and unconscious layers of man's soul is closer than ever to the most radical disintegration of language in its normal function between human beings. Here all feelings, perceptions, and collisions are devoid of any aim, be it simply the aim of pleasing or displeasing. This prose is so compact, and so disorganized at the same time, that any philosophical explanation as to its meaning or purpose is possible. By the same token, none of these explanations could be fully satisfactory. The accumulation of meanings is immediately akin to the full disintegration of language, so that actually we are faced with the most powerful way of denouncing the so-called poetic beauty of language. No communication is possible any more, or, which means the same thing, in any attempt to communicate there are several dozens of possible and secret meanings. The end result is a fantastically vivid way of expressing something which is different from what the author might have wanted to express and, at the same time, different from what we think he has expressed. So that even in the careful analysis of each phrase, we in turn are unable to express the nature of his approximatet expressions.

A few months ago, a gifted young writer, René de Obaldia, published another example of absolute prose, in an excitingly challenging novel, *Le Centenaire* (*The Centenarian*). I wish to quote from a phrase that is four pages long:

I was walking on wings and heels, and I saluted my wings, I recognized everything, I recognized much more than I knew: everything! I recognized my sister who was passing by, my little sister under her light clothes; she wasn't even twenty, she was dancing among passersby: we had played together for hours; I remember those fabulous games in the washing room in the cellar, in the garden, behind those large barrels full of rain water—and one remained sometimes whole years without seeing each other—she turned around and recognized me, and we saluted each other, and I saluted a blade of grass and a little further another blade of grass that hardly breathed; I dug the earth under it so as to give it more room, and I have promised never to tear it as I have done so often, and I pulled its thin, green body between my thumbs and blew on it, and from its belly came a terrible cry which for a moment stopped all the animals, and I saluted a waiter who sat obnoxiously at the terrace of a café, and I ridiculously saluted a policeman, he perspired terribly under his coat, O! my salutations were not dignified, I have no back left . . . and I saluted a crowd: although it seems that I have grown I was not tall enough to see nor strong enough to get through to the front, but I imagined that in the center of the crowd there must have been a man who was being crucified once more, and inside of myself I saluted this center, and 30 yards further I saluted a street cleaner—the water was running in the gutter sparkling joyously as a male dog, its music was that of a celestial fountain, a watery exhalation that I hardly recognized and which also came from me—and I saluted a deaf leaf, and I saluted a Negro, and the Negro answered my salute with a jump, and I continued my luminous walk, and I recognized you in the belly of a woman, my little darling who always hides, your mother almost touched me, without knowing, without knowing (for a long time women ignore that they are pregnant) and you, too, I saluted you, and I saluted a piece of silence that lay on the pavement of Four Winds Street, and I saluted a car full of corpses, and I saluted a cigarette butt, a nutshell, a sewer, a reputable urinal (I tried to enter it, to learn by heart the obscene inscriptions and to recite them as if they were litanies) and I saluted two young people in love and a flea that almost got into my eye—I apologize— and a flower-vendor, and I saluted His Highness the Count who was in a puddle: a very nebulous young man, a mountain of joyous tears, an inconceivable availability . . . .

A hardly conceivable availability, this may be one of the keys to contemporary thinking and writing in France.

We don't believe a conclusion would be wise after our quick survey of the general landscape presented by the various trends of French prose. Whether it be in its classical form, in its aspect as a research for new ideas, or in its wild quest for new impossibilities as well as possibilities, French prose remains true to its own self. It is versatile. It has thousands of intellectual paths, all of which are clever, profound, elaborate, and, to a certain extent, Byzantine. New formulas are born every day! New manifestoes, although they don't bother to be explicit, are implicit in practically every writer's "ars poetica" of prose. Little truths are superseding little truths of yesteryear, only to be hidden by little truths of tomorrow. The mind and the senses are excited at all times. The fields of spiritual perversion are trespassed, and the reader is at all times confronted with seducing oddities. The simple human qualities are by no means lacking, but they are taken for granted to the extent that they sometimes disappear in the background. One may wonder if a certain freshness, a certain candor are not absent from this prose. The sort of great and irresponsible foray into human strength which is so frequent in the works of American novelists is being shunned by French writers. To be alive to them is less important than to be intelligent. To be clever is more important than to be powerful. This has been the lot of French literature ever since the beginning. Titanic greatness has never felt at home in France, and France still remains the country where Shakespeare and Cervantes are misunderstood. We can rely on French prose, as we have so far, for showing new ideas, new means, new subtleties, and for paving the way to be followed by titanic geniuses from other countries.

Crossing the Zero Point: German Literature Since World War II

Hans Egon Holthusen

Presented at the Library of Congress January 25, 1960

OUR POINT OF DEPARTURE, and at the same time the very focus of our whole enquiry, must needs be the German catastrophe of 1945. In all languages the word "apocalypse" crops up nowadays with probably too high a degree of smoothness and even lightheartedness. Yet there was, believe me, no suggestion of literary metaphor in the manner in which a great many of my fellow-citizens experienced what happened in that year: for those who had preserved their capacity for feeling anything at all, it was, literally, the apocalypse; that is to say, a revelation of *truth* through the very stuff of which reality was made, a total conquest of reality by truth. It became clear then that for 12 years Germany had been the prisoner of untruth. Now at last this untruth had died at its own hands: morally, politically, militarily, and with a physical and personal directness unknown in modern history. For one moment it seemed as if the meaning of history had emerged with terrifying concreteness, and as if this meaning were, simply, the final reconciliation of justice and power, truth and reality. It was a moment when everything appeared to be at stake and nothing as yet decided: it was the zero point of our history.

It was as if German history had come to an end, as if it had been reduced to absurdity by Hitler. And strangely enough, it was precisely some of the most typical, some of the nationally most cherished political and cultural traditions—those connected with the names of, for instance, Luther, Hegel, Bismarck, Nietzsche—that now could be seen in an extremely dubious if not diabolical illumination. The State lay in ruins, society was an amor-

382

phous mass of lost men, women, and children. Total anarchy had taken the place of total tyranny. The codes of law had become invalid; every individual had become his own lawgiver. The complicated system of an economy entirely harnessed to the needs of warfare, and the whole organization of providing sustenance for a totally embattled people, had collapsed; and still, miraculously, one was alive; somewhere, somehow, it was possible to find something to eat and drink; somehow one got along by swapping goods as men did in primitive times. There were no means of communication, and nonetheless the whole nation seemed to be on the move. The ironically radiant sun of this early summer fell upon a scene of unimaginable wretchedness, and yet the nation as a whole had survived; and in the boundless poverty of this survival there was, at the same time, an unheard-of sensation of freedom, the feeling that now any hopeful potentiality of humankind might be translated into actuality. It was, despite everything, a little like that bliss of a very early morning, when nothing is as yet realized, of that hour which Paul Valéry was so fond of describing in his letters. But he who knows human nature also knows how soon the day that follows will be dimmed by disenchantment.

Only a mind of exceptional naïveté could expect that this rare experience of having reached zero point in every conceivable concern of the body politic would find its expression in literary achievements equal to the novel and revolutionary character of this situation. It would indeed be due to a misreading of literary history if anyone complained about the absence from the German literary scene of a new Thomas Mann, a new Rilke, or a new Kafka. The great events of *literary* history have hardly ever coincided with the turning-points of *political* history: thus it is by no means surprising that no new literary epoch can be said to begin in 1945: for when we—with some justification—speak of "modern poetry" or "modern art," we are guided by a concept of "epoch" big enough to comprehend at least the last 50 years. The idiom of modern literature has emerged from a revolution that occurred roughly between 1910 and 1925. It was then that the great decisive breakthroughs were made, in Germany as well as in England, France, America, Italy and Russia. It was then that the new territories of expression, within which we still have our literary homes, were conquered; and so far-reaching a revolution in significant themes and forms can neither be completed nor outlived in a few decades. It naturally must be followed by a lengthy period of assimilation in which language becomes acclimatized to new experiences, by a phase of cultivation and cautious expansion of the newly won fields. If today we find nothing absolutely new in any national literature of the West, this is because we have been living in a post-revolutionary situation for at least 30 years.

Therefore it may be paradoxical but, in fact, not surprising that after 1945 it was the older generation of writers who knew how to express the new experience with authority. Even then, however, we have to be careful to distinguish between two strands of tradition: one which was conservative in the spirit of German classicism and German burgherdom, and another which had its roots in the Expressionist era. The latter, of course, enjoyed the additional prestige of having been violently suppressed by the petit-bourgeois, obstinately narrow-minded *Kulturpolitik* of the Nazis; its half-forgotten treasures waited to be unearthed from beneath the debris of the Third Reich. Concerning the older tradition, many of its representatives, poets and novelists of celebrated names and big careers, are still with us and have had, even after the war, considerable success with old and new books, and are able to count on a numerous public. Unfortunately it is impossible for me today to devote much of my time to them, although their achievement must not be underrated, and is indispensable in the economy of intellectual energies. I'd rather concentrate on the assets of the newer tradition and talk about a number of authors who have contributed to the formation and expression of a specifically modern sensibility. For it is these who have, in a new language, raised the problem of man living under the conditions of the twentieth century, and answered it in their own personal way. All of these had been known and had been successful as early as the 20's and had been compelled to accept the fate of emigration, either literally abroad or even at home, in their own country, before recapturing once more public attention in Germany. Their names are Gottfried Benn, Bertolt Brecht, Thomas Mann, and Ernst Jünger.

The Berlin dermatologist, essayist, and poet Gottfried Benn (1886–1956) had reached the age of 60 by the end of the war. He was the only important survivor of the generation of revolutionary poets who, between 1910 and 1920, had led to victory the German Expressionist movement. The extraordinary success which he enjoyed during the last 10 years of his life bears witness not only to the enduring and irrevocable effect of the Expressionist achievement upon the history of poetic language, but also to the prevailing mood of the German intellectual public after the catastrophe.

The young Gottfried Benn, who as early as 1912 had caused a literary sensation and shocked the bourgeois by virtue of the boldness of a new lyric diction, may perhaps be compared with T. S. Eliot in his early Bostonian period. The radical disenchantment with the world of the bourgeois, the fearless disregard of all social, sexual, and aesthetic taboos, and an all but clinically-minded obsession with the symptoms of physical and emotional corruption—all this is used by him for the purpose of pushing through to a new image of human existence. The most impressive feature of his poetry, however, is the surprising combination of disillusionment and ecstasy. What comes together in these poems, indeed is excitingly fused in them, is an assortment of seemingly most contradictory moods: the grim cynicism of a surgeon and a nostalgic dream of Southern seas, the desire to be released from the painful self-consciousness of a latecomer within the European tradition and an impassioned mysticism of the dawn of mankind, a mysticism which strives to enlarge the traditional horizon of history by ten-thousands of years. The classical chronology of the Occident is replaced by an anthropological vision which attempts to come to grips with the Age of Man as such, that is, man of the quaternary, as Benn puts it, who now approaches the end of his history. The prophet of this final phase is Nietzsche; and one of Nietzsche's themes sounds for Benn the note of inescapable destiny: it is the theme of nihilism which Benn was to follow up in innumerable variations throughout his work. Yet in Benn's version of it nihilism acquires a curiously positive meaning: "Nihilism is a sensation of bliss." Benn believes that this *nihil*, this Nothingness, is an irresistible challenge to man's creative powers. Once all traditional truths have been given the lie by history, and once it has become impossible even to acknowledge the very idea of Truth, there still remains something which is beyond all change and decay; and this imperishable something is the forms and shapes created by art, the absoluteness of a piece of art which, scarab-like, outlives the cataracts of time.

After 1933 Benn identified himself for a brief period with the ideology of National-Socialism because he saw in it a variation upon his own intellectual biologism. Yet soon he was a deeply disappointed man. Attacked by the German press of the time as a "Kulturbolschewik," he sought the relative anonymity of a doctor in the German Army, which at that time had still preserved a good deal of its political detachment. In 1949, after having been banned for many years, first by the Nazis and later by the authorities of the Allies, Benn had his literary comeback. Although it sounded somewhat forced when he proclaimed Phase II of Expressionism, he yet almost immediately drew applause from the critics as well as from a large section of the younger generation. A message, known for more than 30 years, was only now truly felt to be the legitimate expression of a generally acknowledged situation. Nobody, it seemed, was on such intimate terms with the pessimism of German intellectuals, with their outraged scepticism vis-a-vis every conceivable form of ideological construction, as this old man who was to become so astonishingly productive during the last decade of his life. Nobody else seemed to lend so powerful support to the natural desire to escape from history—that very history which he was so exceedingly fond of describing as a chaos of rapacious nonsense, good for nothing except, perhaps, for provoking a creative genius to ever greater feats of the imagination. Nobody showed himself as adept as he at coining brilliant cynicisms concerning the tragic meaninglessness of the political world and the rummage sale of all spiritual traditions. At the same time it is true to say that nobody else had at his disposal the persuasive expressiveness and the haunting mellowness of Benn's verse; nobody else came so close to tuning in with the most enchanting melodies of our classical and Romantic poetry (as are associated with the names of Goethe, Novalis, and Eichendorff) and even, surprising though this may sound, with the dedicated inwardness of seventeenth-century ecclesiastical hymns.

Bertolt Brecht (1898–1956), known as the most outstanding talent of Communist literature, returned to Germany in 1948 from his American exile. Political considerations persuaded the Allied authorities that it was inadvisable for him to live in the Western half of Germany; thus he entered East Berlin with a Czechoslovakian passport and founded there the celebrated Berlin Ensemble, which is held by many experts to be the best theatrical group of Germany, if not of Europe. Here he directed in quick succession all the works of his mature years, above all *Mother Courage and Her Children, Galileo Galilei, The Good Woman of Setzuan,* and *The Caucasian Chalk Circle.* He succeeded in making this group of actors into an all but perfect instrument of his revolutionary theatrical style. There is ample justification for regarding him as the most important German dramatist of our time, but we shall have to be more guarded in accepting the claim that he is also *the* poet of Marxism.

The name of Brecht is usually recited together with that of Benn—perhaps for reason of alliteration; yet it would be difficult to think of a more radical contrast than that between these two men. Benn's language is sophisticated, "artistic," the soliloquy of a solitary self, entranced by its own lyrical intoxicants; Brecht's language is the opposite of all this: it is ingeniously simple, sensuous, down-to-earth, straightforward, outspoken, schooled in the school of Luther's Bible and dedicated to what its writer believes to be the cause of the common people. Like Benn, he has foresworn every brand of metaphysics or religion, but, different from Benn, he is a believer in the meaning of history as a history of class struggles, a history which is bound to lead to the victory of socialism. Where for Benn all historical meaning is submerged in a whirlpool of nihilistic meaninglessness, Brecht sees before himself the possibility of radically changing the human world by taking reasonable action. For him the zero point of 1945 does not mark the disappearance of the last trace of any reason in history, but, on the contrary, the beginning of a new era—at least in the Eastern part of Germany.

Benn's aestheticism—and indeed anything that has any kinship with it— appears to Brecht as a mere attempt to obscure what he believes to be the real world. Art must not, according to Brecht, escape from history into some sort of narcissistic detachment, but must be tested every day and every hour with regard to its social usefulness. He has explained in numerous essays the principles of his "epic theatre": theatrical illusion, the *sine qua non* of classical drama, must be overcome; the spectator has to be educated in his political and social consciousness by means of what Brecht used to call the "alienation effect," of announcements breaking the flow of the action, of explanatory interruptions, songs, and self-interpretations of the actors, and of masks meant to destroy theatrical illusion.

There is little doubt that Brecht, from a certain moment of his development, did believe in the truth of dialectical materialism. Yet this does not answer the question to what extent this belief dominated his consciousness, and, above all, how much it meant, or could possibly mean, for his imaginative vision of man and his world. It is certainly true to say that in none of his major plays has he managed to create a class-conscious proletarian, and none of these plays can profitably be interpreted in terms of Communist ideology. Georg Lukács, the oracle of Socialist Realism, has never acknowledged Brecht as a genius of Socialism. Certainly, there was no scarcity of friction between Brecht and the regime of East Germany. There was a whole series of humiliating compromises, and I think it may be taken for granted that he died as a doubting if not a desperate man. Whatever he has published in his later years in praise of Stalin and the Communist State is so platitudinous as to lend credence to the assumption that we must look for the springs of his creative power in a region deeper than politics. The prototype of all his heroes is a certain Baal, the unheroic hero of one of his early plays. It is no mere chance that he bears the name of the Syrian god of the earth and of fertility. He is the god of vitality, of the insatiable will to live at any price—the god who gloatingly feeds on all the pastures of this world. He is the anticipated allegory of Brecht's later idea of "the people," that anonymous and vital entity, "irrepressible and indestructible" despite all the murderous frolics into which it is led by the directors of history. "I shall fight to the last drop of blood," says Baal; "I shall live on even without my skin, I shall withdraw into my own toes. I shall sink down like a bull: into the grass where it is at its softest. I shall swallow my own death and know of nothing." It is this Baal whom we easily recognize in many of the protagonists of Brecht's later dramas: for instance in the voluminous frame of the learned Galileo as well as in the skinny indestructibility of Mother Courage, the tough, sly, greedy, and wretched canteen woman of the Thirty Years' War, the most impressive creation of his mature years. The tin spoon, which Brecht's wife, Helene Weigel, always carries in the button hole of her Mongolian quilt-jacket when playing the part of Mother Courage, is the simple but eloquent symbol of Baal, the hungry, voracious, indomitable god.

Compared with this primitive but expressive symbol, the later works of Thomas Mann have the appeal of an infinitely complex epilogue to the splendour, irretrievably lost, of the burgher's cultural achievement. When, soon after the war, Thomas Mann returned to Europe and settled, if not in Germany herself, at least at Germany's doorstep, in Zurich, his name was weighty with the whole weight that the literary world had accorded to his work, as it had to no other German writer of the century with the exception, of course, of Rilke and Kafka. He had remained inescapably loyal to his people even in his most violent denunciations of its apostasy. He had felt and thought most deeply about the meaning of the word "German," about the greatness as well as the utter precariousness of German history. Thus he was justified in making the German catastrophe itself the subject of a vast symphonic narrative. His *Doctor Faustus,* published in 1947, is without the slightest doubt the most direct, and in all probability the most important, attempt at coming to literary terms with the German apocalypse. The book is conceived as a tragic parody, if you will allow me to use the word "parody" as Thomas Mann himself used it, of the greatest achievement of our classical literature. But it also goes back, in its almost inexhaustible range of literary allusions, to the original figure of Faust, hero of the most famous morality of the late Middle Ages; and it does so through the central motifs of unforgivable guilt and eternal damnation. Thus it is, at the same time, a kind of diabolically ironic refutation of the post-Goethean idea of "Faustian Man" and his ruthless optimism. It tells the tragic story of the life of a modern German composer who sells his soul to the Devil for the otherwise unobtainable gifts of genius, originality, and creation, and who finally goes to Hell, a Hell not of mythic but psychological reality. In this strangest of his novels Thomas Mann retells the ancient tale which, in his handling, becomes a vast essay, by means of innumerable allusions, overtones, and undertones, on the whole spiritual history of the German people from Luther to Nietzsche; and he even tries to synchronize this fable in the most ingenious manner with the Third Reich's descent to Hell. Again, as he had done in *The Magic Mountain,* Thomas Mann sketches the intellectual scene of an epoch, this time in the key of an apocalyptic *furioso* and with the desperate consistency of a man who will not allow for even the slightest doubt that Germany had reached its end, that by its fruits it had been reduced to absurdity.

Clearly it would be impossible to accept all this except as a parable, a metaphor. It must needs remain problematical, sharing as it does in the extreme problem of literary language: to be driven into saying the unsayable, in this case to make articulate something that is so elusive, so transcendent, and at the same time so concrete, as the meaning of a nation's history. The truly terrible effort of writing this, his most unruly and most agonized book, led to illness, even to the verge of death. But he *did* survive the crisis, he *did* write books after *Doctor Faustus,* books that were easier to write and easier to read, and thus proved in his own person that German intellectual and literary history had, in fact, the audacity to continue. In 1954 he published his last masterpiece, *The Confessions of Felix Krull, the Confidence Man.* Cast in the form of a modern picaresque tale, it is a summing-up, blessed by the comic muse, of all the *leitmotifs* of his mind and imagination; it is, once again, a splendid accomplishment of the genius of his irony and of his style, ceremoniously involved and designed to provide higher amusement for a world deserted by the Muses.

And finally Ernst Jünger (born in 1895), the fourth of the established authorities of the older generation. He is, second to Benn, the most important writer of the kind of prose writings which are bound to come into their own where it seems no longer possible or desirable to employ the imagination in the business of inventing the plot of a novel; where indeed the principle of invention is replaced by the principle of transformation, the transforming power of an imaginative style which distills poetic patterns from the given data of the real world. Like Benn, he too has his roots in the literary sensibility of Expressionism and, like Benn, has moved, with varying degrees of steadiness, in the orbit of Nietzsche's thought. But what, above all, he shares with Benn is the readiness to reflect upon his own historical situation. Their common theme lies in the persistent exploration of the conditions imposed upon their minds and souls by the fact that they happen to be born in this particular age and no other: it is the diagnosis of the *Lage.* The German word *Lage,* the "position," of which both are singularly fond, carries with it something of the atmosphere of the diction of military headquarters. And this is by no means accidental: in the case of both these writers it is of considerable biographical *and* thematic significance that their idea of living was partly determined by their experience as soldiers. Benn would define the *Lage*—the Nietzsche-*Lage,* as he calls it—as characterized by the fact that "every thought ever thought in Europe, every truth ever held to be true, has irrevocably lost its absolute validity and has become entirely relative." Thus he describes, with ever new and always fascinating prose conjurations, contemporary man, deeply faithless and haunted by nihilistic melancholies. The inner life of this creature of modern history is seen to consist of an irredeemable tohubohu of fragmentary thoughts and allusive fragments: "a whirl of ideas, dogmas, and trends—and no answer." Benn's own solution is a brave stoicism in the face of a horizon without God or light: "to live in the dark, to work in the dark, as well as we can."

Jünger, too, has recognized and tried to assess the nihilistic tendencies of the age. But he never knew the temptation to surrender to Benn's bliss of nothingness and to raise art to the position of the only surviving Absolute. All his life he has tried hard to extract some compelling meaning from the catastrophes of history, and to arrive at some moral values with which and by which to live. Once upon a time, about 1920, he made himself the prophet of the heroic life in the warrior, an ideal which he himself was close to attaining when, during the battles of the First World War, he performed legendary deeds of bravery. It is true that he was, in this sense, a militarist and a technocrat when in 1932 he published his famous *Der Arbeiter (The Worker)*; but when both militarism and technocracy celebrated their perverse triumphs a few years later, he radically revised all his doctrines. His diaries from the Second World War, above all the volume *Strahlungen* (1949), bear witness to his struggle for moral and intellectual self-preservation in the underworld of armed nihilism. It would be hard to think of a more complete contrast than that which exists between Thomas Mann and Ernst Jünger, between their respective careers, characters, styles, and themes; and yet we find that Jünger, in the hour of German collapse, arrives at precisely the same conclusion as the author of *Doctor Faustus*. At the same moment when Thomas Mann—he too a disciple of Nietzsche—inaugurates his Californian alliance with Roosevelt's anti-fascism, Jünger enters into secret negotiations with high-placed German Army officers in Paris, sworn enemies of Hitler; and while Thomas Mann commissions his new Faust "to take back, to cancel, the Ninth Symphony" and to compose the desperate oratorio with that uncannily high note which was to express hope beyond hopelessness, Jünger, in the uniform of a captain of the German *Wehrmacht,* immerses himself in the meditation of history's "absolute zero point." It is possible to say that he has signed, by the side of Thomas Mann, the capitulation of the German Doctor Faustus.

This, I fear, is all I have time to say about the older generation among whom, for the sake of simplicity, I count all those writers who were born before 1900. From them I should like to distinguish a middle generation, those who were born between 1900 and 1920, *and* a young generation, born after 1920. Both these more recent groups are represented by a number of remarkable and even distinguished talents, but not one of them has attained the same position on the literary scene of Germany which in France was conceded, say, to Albert Camus, and in England to Dylan Thomas. The economic prosperity of West Germany, it is true, has produced a veritable surfeit of literary and intellectual stimulants on every price level of consumers' goods, distributed throughout the nation by a ceaselessly busy cultural industry and spreading an atmosphere of hothouse luxuriance. Between 15,000 and 20,000 new books appear on the market every year and a legion of critics is feverishly at work to come to grips with this profusion, to create best-sellers and again sink them into oblivion, and to array and disarray values, merits, and accomplishments in the battles of cliques, gangs, and uncertain tastes. And yet there is widespread scepticism concerning the present life of literature, a nervous *malaise,* a sort of inferiority complex vis-a-vis, for instance, the rebellious and robust self-confidence of the "roaring '20's." I know people, whole families, who discover every three months an ever-so-fascinating new author, a ravishing new book, an alarming, unheard-of, unparalleled literary event, and who, three days later, indulge in deep mourning about the shameful worthlessness and unredeemed flatness of our literature. "Can *you* see *anything* new, *anything* interesting *anywhere?* I am bored to death." To this attitude, which is less critical than depressive, corresponds, on the part of writers, a certain modesty of their intellectual and social claims and ambitions, a wholesome unbelief in the impression literature could possible *make* on the actual life of society. The time for the great, comprehensive poetic interpretations of the universe seems to be a thing of the past. The kind of grandiose prophetic gesture or quasi-religious solemnity, which goes with George's or Rilke's poetic doctrine about life and existence, is hardly thinkable any more. Nor does there seem to be a strong desire to produce a vast summing-up of the *Lage* in the manner of Gottfried Benn, Ernst Jünger, or Thomas Mann. All that matters appears to be the poetic or literary articulation of a narrowly defined sphere of personal experience and the cultivation of a small allotment of reality.

But what is this "reality?" Many of the younger poets seek to find it in their emotional responses to the concrete manifestations of city life, to the conditions of a technological civilization; others again in Nature and her continuous offer of ever-new motifs. Both groups can boast of remarkable achievements: they have enlarged the scope of lyrical sensibility, and enriched the idiom of German poetry with modes of expression of which even the Expressionists had as yet no inkling. In my opinion, the most interesting and successful poets of the now middle-aged generation belong to the tradition of nature poetry. They provide a particularly impressive example of the fact that the life of poetry does not simply reflect, as Marxist theorists would have us believe, the social and political developments of an epoch, but follows the "laws" of its own history, which at times seem to dictate to poets thoroughly, and in a sense rebelliously, *un*historical preoccupations. Where the public powers of history terrorize man to the very roots of his physical and spiritual existence, there it may be the *historical* duty of poets to conjure up the natural powers of resistance against the destructive processes of history, and remind man of a timeless order of being. Then the poets begin to speak again of the seasons rather than the historical hour, of Nature rather than the manmade world. The grand old man of this school is Wilhelm Lehmann, born in 1882, who is to Gottfried Benn as Robert Frost is to T. S. Eliot. He stubbornly refuses to have any dealings

391

with what in the cities of modern man is taken for history. His imagination dwells in the company of the god Pan at an eternal midday hour of life, where man is stripped of his historical self and is at one with the world-soul revealed in the omnipresence of mythic constellations. To him Tristan and Isolde, Oberon and Titania, Daphne and Apollo are deathless entities, emerging again and again whenever their hour strikes. The meaning of existence is to be found in the eternal Here and Now of such pagan archetypes.

Lehmann's younger friends and followers have considerably loosened the grip of the archetypes and in various ways modified the rigid structure of his lyrical patterns. Their writing, after all, could not help being affected by their experience of war and captivity, and by the particular social and moral problems of the postwar period. The most important and most prolific poet of this group is Karl Krolow, born in 1915. Starting with the simplest designs in the idyllic or bucolic manner, Krolow, endowed with a huntsman's instinct for hidden words and a passion for adventures in the field of metaphors, has expanded, like no other poet among his contemporaries, the boundaries of poetic expression. He accepted the example of French and Spanish Surrealists, without, however, losing himself in the modishly uninhibited anarchy of automatic writing. He does not limit himself, like Lehmann, to the celebration of the eternal midday, acquainted as he is with the demons of the night, with the nocturnal aspects of Nature, reflected in the world of history as terror, war, and political catastrophe. What existentialist philosophers are in the habit of calling *Angst* has found its frighteningly literal, indeed neurotic expression in the verse of this poet. *Angst* and the magic power of poetry—these constitute the polarity of his themes: on the one hand, a total eclipse of all the luminous ideas that had lighted up the world of the West—in fact, the utter obscurity of nothingness; on the other hand, the triumphant conquests, despite everything, of the Imagination. He is fond of seeing himself as a man "with singing birds under his hat" with which to transform the world.

As to the prose writers among this generation, I should have, in order to be exact, to draw a confusing variety of patterns. Kafka's influence is still very noticeable. It was he who helped a great many talented authors to form their own handwriting. A smaller group of men of letters, mostly of the Christian-conservative observance, have learned from Ernst Jünger how to fashion a style, at once narrative and reflective, and attaining a considerable height of civilized and pugnacious elegance. Others again have chosen as their models or inspirations the masterpieces of the modern American novel, such as Hemingway's or Faulkner's; and of course, the memory of James Joyce is also not entirely absent from the scene. I shall not bore you with a long list of names, unfortunately almost as quickly forgotten as mentioned; instead, I shall confine myself to a brief discussion of only two writers who, by virtue of the steadiness of their growth as artists, the originality of their themes and conceptions, and the unmistakable identity of their language, deserve particular attention and justly have achieved a measure of international reputation: Heinrich Boell (born in 1917) and Gerd Gaiser (born in 1908).

Both have made their names with books about the war; and both books—just as do most of the other examples of the all but unmanageable welter of books about this subject—show that the *Fronterlebnis,* the front-line experience, of the First World War, again and again interpreted in either a "leftist" or "rightist" manner, either in the spirit of militarism or of pacifism, had not repeated itself in this generation. Anything that smacks of "patriotism" or "ideology" had no chance of being taken seriously any more, albeit as an object of embittered satirical derision. To bear testimony—this, these writers feel, is all that can be done: faithfully to report on a new and extreme form of the human condition which transcends everything hitherto believed to be possible. The very structure of Boell's novel *Wo warst du, Adam? (Where Were You, Adam?)* (1951) embodies the vicious circle of total senselessness. The compulsion to serve in the war is shown here to be the cowardly alibi of man, morally challenged by the question "Where were you, Adam?". The book conveys a sense of an extreme God-forsakenness, almost identical with Camus' myth of the "absurd," and yet not without more hopeful undertones: "We must pray in order to console God." Artistically more powerful, by virtue of the poetic intensity of its language, if religiously and morally less assertive, is Gerd Gaiser's prose epic about the destruction of the German *Luftwaffe* fighters in Norway. It was published in 1953 under the title *Die Sterbende Jagd (The Last Squadron).* The world of technological warfare is here illuminated by a truly poetic imagination. The soldier's slang, the grotesquely mannered lingo of the airman, have been—a unique stroke of literary luck—completely fused with the poetic suggestiveness of an epic idiom sustained by the sources of ancient traditions: the Bible, the Greeks, and the rich poetic emanations of the Swabian soil. The story which is told is of a team of men, a gang of highly trained technicians, ironical and sophisticated, and destined to die; and yet, in a sense, not to die but simply to vanish one after the other. It is a book infused with brittle melancholy eloquently suggestive about the unspeakable, rationally impenetrable, moral predicament of the German soldier: "There is no way out. You simply are not made to give up your mother or your wife because she is possessed by the devil."

Boell's later novels and short stories usually have as their scenes the world of the present-day German lower middle-class. They show that their author is endowed with a shrewd sense of the problems besetting a postwar society oscillating between material prosperity and moral depression. Boell has mastered a narrative form which has been rare in German literature: the social novel which is not overcharged with intellectual reflection and yet artistically intelligent enough to live up to the higher expectations of contemporary consciousness. His language is concrete, sensitive, and often satirical, his moral seriousness is determined on the one hand by a kind of rebellious Catholicism, and on the other hand by his sympathy with "the little man," the man in the street. Secure within the Catholic tradition of the Rhineland, his home, and nonetheless a social critic, a melancholy, grumbling non-conformist: this is a mixture of ingredients almost bound to be successful in Adenauer's Germany; for in Adenauer's Germany the universal malaise of the intellectuals is merely the logical response to the "economic miracle," the so-called *restauration* of bourgeois society. At bottom, the proverbial optimism of the Minister of Economic Affairs and the furious pessimism of financially affluent writers get on excellently with each other; indeed, one is tempted to speak of a harmonious cooperation.

Compared to Boell, Gaiser is an outsider; for this is what a man is in contemporary Germany if he does not share the general conformism of nonconformists. Gaiser is hardly interested in social criticism; he steers free of all ideological whirlpools, even where his subject matter is a sector of contemporary society, as for instance in his most recent novel *Schlussball* (*Coming Out Dance*) (1958). Here, as elsewhere, Gaiser's dominant theme is the mysterious interweaving of human destinies within the timeless order of love, death, and character, as well as within the temporal disorder of an epoch shaken by every conceivable social catastrophe. His characters, above all his men, are solitary, shy, silent, and brooding. There is about them something wild, untamed, reminiscent a little of the mystery-stricken bums and tramps of Knut Hamsun or the martial eccentrics, the *dynamiteros* of the lethal involvments in Hemingway's or Jünger's stories. This tribe of men, in whom there has survived something of the ruthless spirit of the ancient Germanic saga, knows, when it comes to it, of only one theme: its own defeat. Thus Gaiser returns again and again to the contemplation of Germany's military catastrophe during the years 1943 to 1945. For during these years he had experienced what Karl Jaspers, in his philosophy, calls "in Scheitern das Sein erfahren": to become truly aware of existence at the moment of shipwreck.

Unfortunately there is no time for doing full justice to the achievements of the youngest generation, those writers born between 1920 and 1935. A few observations will have to suffice. There is, believe me, no scarcity of new lyrical talent. Every year witnesses the emergence of at least half-a-dozen exciting newcomers. Many of them are preoccupied with artistic experiments derived from Surrealistic metaphorical anarchy; others are writing in the manner of Ezra Pound; others still are busy creating the so-called "abstract" poem which is at the same time also "concrete." "Abstract" and "concrete" are obviously the same thing, just as in electronic music or on the radical wing of contemporary painting. Most of these young authors, without realizing it, have developed a kind of collective style that makes their poetic individualities all but indistinguishable. They have founded a kind of supermodern Meistersinger cult which reminds me vividly of the frenzied activity in the American "little reviews." But this generation too has produced three or four poets who even now, in their early 30's, have discovered their own unmistakable mode of expression and have gathered about themselves a congregation of devoted, even ardent, admirers. I am genuinely sorry that I cannot name them, for were I to do so I should feel obligated to discuss them.

Of the ideas and moods with which this generation is preoccupied I shall mention but a single one, that is the socio-political passion which motivates so many of them. They are wild-eyed opponents of the Adenauer regime and its social atmosphere. Their orientation is instinctively leftist, although they do not believe in a German political left wing. They hate power as such and its institutions; they hate the Church, capitalism, the atom bomb, money, and organized society, without thereby becoming Communists. Although they despise the bouregois, they cannot take the worker seriously either. With all the means at their disposal they attempt to shatter taboos, to make scandals, to provoke cries of indignation, and in return they are regarded with benevolence by the cultural managers of the Maecenas of big industry, who crown them with literary prizes. In a word: they are the "angry young men" of the Federal Republic.

They live in precisely the same grotesque euphoria as their spiritual brothers in England. The very society which they attack with such fury is enchanted with their bad manners and is charmed above all by their talent for giving such ebulliently youthful expression to the general malaise. The most gifted lyric poet of this group is Hans Magnus Enzensberger (born in 1929) who gave his first volume of verse (1957) the ironically aggressive title *A Defense of the Wolves*. Just as in the socially critical animal fable of the Middle Ages, so here society is divided into wolves and sheep, that is, the powerful and the defenseless, the exploiters and the exploited, the executioners and the victims. The enemy is government, organized society, power as such. But, unlike the social critics of the older generation, Enzensberger no longer has a revolutionary prescription in his pocket with which the world can be altered. If he does have any idea at all to proclaim, then it is the idea of felicity; his word is *Glück*, an absurd utopian felicity that lies beyond all institutional forms in the realm of total anarchy. Friendship and love are the natural powers of resistance of a humanity threatened by gas chambers and atom bombs. Under the influence of Brecht, Benn, and W. H. Auden, he has developed a gripping, sophisticated virtuosity of style in order to depict the man of technological society, his mechanized environment, and his neurotic consciousness. And yet he is also master of simple, sincere modes of expression with which he conjures up a world of nonpolitical existence, for example a pastoral scene, a Macedonian love tryst, a poverty-stricken tramp on the road. An echo of the message of Baal sounds from his poems, of Brecht's Baal who gloatingly feeds on the pastures of this world.

Of the prose achievements of this group I would like to mention but a single novel, the highly acclaimed *Blechtrommel (The Toy Drum)*, last year's literary sensation. Its author is Günter Grass, born in 1927, an artist of extraordinarily diverse talents who had already distinguished himself as a sculptor and lyric poet, and as the author of some grotesque little plays in the manner of Beckett, Jonesco, and Adamov before he occasioned so much furor with his book and with it alone put himself at the pinnacle of his generation. His 750 pages are an irresistible whirlpool of narrative vitality and well-nigh inexhaustible imagination. In this book Oskar Mazerath, a man some 30 years old who is a patient in a mental institution, tells the story of his life and that of his ancestors and his family. He comes from Danzig, his grandparents are a Polish pyromaniac and a Kashubian peasant girl, his father a little grocer from the Rhineland, and he grows up in a petit-bourgeois atmosphere or, to be more exact, he doesn't grow up, for he decides at the age of three not to grow any more but to observe the world for the rest of his life from the point-of-view of a child. This dwarf has a passion for toy drums, of which in the course of his life he uses and destroys dozens, in fact hundreds, until he has managed to turn himself into a well-paid drum virtuoso. And he has a second talent, an unbelievable and grotesque one: he can sing glass to pieces. Church windows, streetcar and shop windows, beer bottles, and eyeglasses disintegrate whenever he raises his voice. With these two remarkable gifts he makes his way in the world and through a considerable span of contemporary history which extends from the Nazi era through the war and the conquest of Danzig by the Russians, ending with a few wretched, chaotic years in post-war Düsseldorf. This grotesque hero is the perfect outsider of society, the "isolated animal with the exaggeratedly twisted horn." His lifelong drumming is the symbol of his absolute nonconformity, his stubborn mutiny against the insanity of the times, the infinite stupidity of the living generations. He narrates from the perspective of a malicious, chilling infantilism, with icy understatements where one conventionally expects sympathy and with a rhapsodic outburst where it is his intent to arouse compassion: for example for the fate of the Jews in Danzig, for the annihilation of the "lunatic" Polish cavalry, for the death of his beautiful, adulterous mamma. A raging cynic, carrying blasphemy as far as the Black Mass, a satirist with a touch of genius, an unrestrained violator of the most precarious taboos, where there are thought to be no more taboos. Grass is the author of the most scandalous book of our day, more scandalous than half-a-dozen *Lolitas*.

A priapic hero; sexuality the ultimate directional principle in a world without a moral or ideological compass; sexuality, esprit, and a tremendous facility with narrative invention; biography as a breathtaking succession of scurrilous episodes. The book is a barbaric counterpart to Thomas Mann's *Felix Krull:* a picaresque novel on a grand scale. Numerous writers since 1945 have felt the need to renew this form of the novel, a form that, like no other, seems to be suited to express the human condition in a world of total anarchy and of all-disrupting catastrophe. A whole series of very promising attempts has been made, but no author before Günter Grass has approached so near the great immortal prototype of the German picaresque novel, Gerimmelshausen's *Simplicius Simplicissimus,* which was written shortly after the Thirty Years' War, and which is perhaps the greatest novel in the history of German literature. In *The Toy Drum,* too, there prevails the mentality of Simplicissimus, the art of mere survival, the Baalian passion to laugh history in the face where history tries to annihilate man and his world.

And so, ladies and gentlemen, we near the end of this brief stroll through the contemporary German literary scene. It is certainly not the most glorious period of our literary development. With all its shortcomings, however, its dissatisfaction with its own achievement, and its deeply troubled restlessness, it displays one very significant trait that cannot be replaced by any formal masterpiece of timeless dignity. It's the expression of our own experience, our life as we live it HERE AND NOW.

The Modern German Mind:
The Legacy of Nietzsche

Erich Heller

Presented at the Library of Congress February 8, 1960

IN 1873, two years after Bismarck's Prussia had defeated France, a young German who happened to live in Switzerland, teaching classical philology in the University of Basle, wrote a treatise concerned with "the German mind." It was an inspired diatribe against, above all, the German notion of *Kultur* and against the philistine readiness to believe that military victory proved cultural superiority. This was, he said, a disastrous superstition, symptomatic in itself of the absence of any true culture. According to him, the opposite was true: the civilization of the vanquished French was bound more and more to dominate the victorious German people that had wasted its spirit upon the chimera of political power.

This national heretic's name, rather obscure at the time, was Friedrich Nietzsche. What, almost a century ago, he wrote about the perverse relationship between military success and intellectual dominance proved true: not then, perhaps, but now; and it was precisely through him, through his intellectual vision of a world to come, that Germany appears to have invaded vast territories of the world's mind at the very moment when the German body politic was utterly prostrate. Among all the thinkers of the nineteenth century he is, with the possible exceptions of Dostoevsky and Kierkegaard, the only one who would not be too amazed by the amazing scene upon which we now move in sad, pathetic, heroic, stoic, or ludicrous bewilderment. Much, too much, would strike him as *déjà vu:* yes, he had foreseen it; and he would understand: for the Modern Mind speaks German, not always good German, but fluent German nonetheless. It was, alas, forced to learn the idiom of Karl Marx, and was delighted to be introduced to itself in the language of Sigmund Freud; taught by Ranke and, later, Max

Weber, it acquired its historical and sociological self-consciousness, moved out of its tidy Newtonian universe on the instruction of Einstein, and followed a design of Oswald Spengler's in sending from the depth of its spiritual depression most ingeniously engineered objects higher than the moon. Whether it discovers, with Heidegger, the true habitation of its *Existenz* on the frontiers of Nothing, or meditates, with Sartre and Camus, *le Néant* or the Absurd; whether—to pass to its less serious moods—it is nihilistically young and profitably angry in London or rebelliously debauched and buddhistic in San Francisco—*man spricht deutsch.* It is all part of a story told and foretold by Nietzsche.

As far as modern German literature and thought are concerned—and this is, of course, what we mean by the somewhat giddy abstraction "the modern German mind"—it is hardly an exaggeration to say that they would not be what they are if Nietzsche had never lived. Name almost any poet, man of letters, philosopher, who wrote in German during the twentieth century and attained to stature and influence; name Rilke, George, Kafka, Thomas Mann, Ernst Jünger, Musil, Benn, Heidegger, or Jaspers—and you name at the same time Friedrich Nietzsche. He is to them all—whether or not they know and acknowledge it (and most of them do)—what St. Thomas Aquinas was to Dante: the categorical interpreter of a world which they contemplate poetically or philosophically without ever radically upsetting its Nietzschean structure. Therefore, and in order to escape the embarrassment of vague generalities, I have elected to equate the modern German mind of my title with the mind of Friedrich Nietzsche.

Nietzsche died 60 years ago, after 12 years of a total eclipse of his intellect, insane—and on the threshold of this century. Thinking and writing to the very edge of insanity, and with some of his last pages even going over it, he read and interpreted the temperatures of his own mind; but by doing so, he has drawn the fever-chart of an epoch. Indeed, much of his work reads like the self-diagnosis of a desperate physician who, suffering the disease on our behalf, comes to prescribe as a cure that we should form a new idea of health, and live by it.

He was convinced that it would take at least 50 years before a few men would understand what he had accomplished; and he feared that even then his teaching would be misinterpreted and misapplied. "I am terrified," he wrote, "by the thought of the sort of people who may one day invoke my authority." But is this not, he added, the anguish of every great teacher? He knows that he may prove a disaster as much as a blessing. The conviction that he was a great teacher never left him after he had passed through that period of sustained inspiration in which he wrote the first part of *Zarathustra*. After this, all his utterances convey the disquieting self-confidence and the terror of a man who has reached the culmination of that paradox which he embodies, a paradox which we shall try to name and which ever since has cast its dangerous spell over some of the finest and some of the coarsest minds.

Are we then, at the remove of two generations, in a better position to probe Nietzsche's mind and to avoid, as he hoped some might, the misunderstanding that he was merely concerned with the religious, philosophical, or political controversies fashionable in his day? And if this be a misinterpretation, can we put anything more valid in its place? What is the knowledge which he claims to have, raising him in his own opinion far above the contemporary level of thought? What the discovery which serves him as a lever to unhinge the whole fabric of traditional values?

It is the knowledge that God is dead.

The death of God he calls the greatest event in modern history and the cause of extreme danger. Note well the paradox contained in these words. He never said that there was no God, but that the Eternal had been vanquished by Time and the Immortal suffered death at the hands of mortals: God is dead. It is like a cry mingled of despair and triumph, reducing, by comparison, the whole story of atheism and agnosticism before and after him to the level of respectable mediocrity and making it sound like a collection of announcements of bankers who regret they are unable to invest in an unsafe proposition. Nietzsche, for the nineteenth century, brings to its *perverse* conclusion a line of religious thought and experience linked with the names of St. Paul, St. Augustine, Pascal, Kierkegaard, and Dostoevsky, minds for whom God was not simply the creator of an order of nature within which man has his clearly defined place; but to whom He came rather in order to challenge their natural being, making demands which appeared absurd in the light of natural reason. These men are of the family of Jacob: having wrestled with God for His blessing, they ever after limp through life with the framework of Nature incurably out of joint. Nietzsche is just such a wrestler; except that in him the shadow of Jacob merges with the shadow of Prometheus. Like Jacob, Nietzsche too believed that he prevailed against God in that struggle, and won a new name for himself, the name of Zarathustra. But the words *he* spoke on his mountain to the angel of the Lord were: "I will not let thee go, except thou curse me." Or, in words which Nietzsche did in fact speak: "I have on purpose devoted my life to exploring the whole contrast to a truly religious nature. I know the Devil and all his visions of God."

"God is dead"—this is the very core of Nietzsche's spiritual existence, and what follows is despair, *and* hope in a new greatness of man, visions of catastrophe *and* glory, the icy brilliance of analytical reason, fathoming with affected irreverence those depths hitherto hidden by awe and fear, and,

400

side-by-side with it, the ecstatic invocations of a ritual healer. Without knowing Hölderlin's dramatic poem *Empedocles,* the young Nietzsche, who loved what he knew of Hölderlin's poetry, at the age of 20 planned to write a drama with Empedocles as its hero. His notes show that he saw the Greek philosopher as the tragic personification of his age, as a man in whom the latent conflicts of his epoch attained to consciousness, as one who suffered and died as the victim of an unresolvable tension: born with the soul of a *homo religiosus,* a seer, a prophet, and poet, he yet had the mind of a radical sceptic; and defending his soul against his mind and, in turn, his mind against his soul, he made his soul lose its spontaneity, and finally his mind its rationality. Had Nietzsche ever written the drama *Empedocles,* it might have become, in uncanny anticipation, his *own* tragedy.

It is a passage from Nietzsche's *Gaya Scientia,* his *Cheerful Science,* which conveys best the substance and quality of the mind, indeed the whole spiritual situation, from which the pronouncement of the death of God sprang. The passage is prophetically entitled "The Madman." Here is a brief extract from it:

Have you not heard of that madman who, in the broad light of the forenoon, lit a lantern and ran into the market-place, crying incessantly: "I am looking for God!" . . . As it happened, many were standing there who did not believe in God, and so he aroused great laughter . . . The madman leapt right among them . . . "Where is God?" he cried. "Well, I will tell you. *We have murdered him*—you and I . . . But how did we do this deed? . . . Who gave us the sponge with which to wipe out the whole horizon? How did we set about unchaining our earth from her sun? Whither is it moving now? Whither are we moving? . . . Are we not falling incessantly? . . . Is night not approaching, and more and more night? Must we not light lanterns in the forenoon? Behold the noise of the grave-diggers, busy to bury God . . . And we have killed him! What possible comfort is there for us? . . . Is not the greatness of this deed too great for us? To appear worthy of it, must not we ourselves become gods?"—At this point the madman fell silent and looked once more at those around him: "Oh," he said, "I am too early. My time has not yet come. The news of this tremendous event is still on its way . . . Lightning and thunder take time, the light of the stars takes time to get to us, deeds take time to be seen and heard . . . and *this* deed is still farther from them than the farthest stars—*and yet it was they themselves who did it!*"

And elsewhere, in a more prosaic mood, Nietzsche says: "People have no notion yet that from now onwards they exist on the mere pittance of inherited and decaying values"—soon to be overtaken by an enormous bankruptcy.

The story of the Madman, written two years before *Zarathustra* and containing *in nuce* the whole message of the Superman, shows the distance that divides Nietzsche from the conventional attitudes of atheism. He is the madman, breaking with his sinister news into the market-place complacency of the pharisees of unbelief. They have done away with God, and yet the report of their own deed has not yet reached them. They know not what they have done, but He who could forgive them is no more. Much of Nietzsche's work ever after is the prophecy of their fate: "The waters of religion," Nietzsche writes at the time of *Zarathustra*, "recede and leave behind morasses and shallow pools . . . Where we live, soon nobody will be able to exist." For men become enemies, and each his own enemy. From now onwards they will *hate*, Nietzsche believes, however many *comforts* they will lavish upon themselves, and hate *themselves* with a new hatred, unconsciously at work in the depths of their souls. True, there will be ever better reformers of society, ever better socialists, and ever better hospitals, and an ever increasing intolerance of pain and poverty and suffering and death, and an ever more fanatical craving for the greatest happiness of the greatest numbers. Yet the deepest impulse informing their striving will not be love and will not be compassion. Its true source will be the panic-struck determination not to have to ask the question "What is the meaning of our lives?", the question which will remind them of the death of God, the uncomfortable question inscribed on the features of those who are uncomfortable, and asked above all by pain and poverty and suffering and death. Rather than have that question asked, they will do everything to smooth it away from the face of humanity. For they cannot endure it. And yet they will despise themselves for not enduring it, and for their guilt-ridden inability to answer it: and their self-hatred will betray them behind the back of their apparent charity and humanitarian concern. For *there* they will assiduously construct the tools for the annihilation of human kind. "There will be wars," Nietzsche writes, "such as have never been waged on earth." And he says: "I foresee something terrible. Chaos everywhere. Nothing left which is of any value; nothing which commands: Thou shalt!" This would have been the inspiration of the final work which Nietzsche often said he would write and never wrote: *The Will to Power,* or, as he sometimes wanted to call it, *The Transvaluation of All Values.* It might have given his full diagnosis of what he termed nihilism, the state of human beings and societies faced with a total eclipse of all values.

It is in defining and examining the (for him *historical*) phenomenon of nihilism that Nietzsche's attack on Christianity sets in (and it has remained the only truly subtle point which, within the whole range of his more and more unrestrained argumentativeness, this Anti-Christ makes against Christianity). For it is at this point that Nietzsche asks (and asks the same question in countless variations throughout his works): What are the *specific* qualities which the Christian tradition has instilled and cultivated in the minds of men? They are, he thinks, twofold: on the one hand, a more refined sense of truth than any other civilization has known, an almost uncontrollable desire for absolute spiritual and intellectual certainties; and, on the other hand, the ever-present suspicion that life on this earth is not in itself a supreme value, but in need of a higher, a transcendental justification. This, Nietzsche believes, is a destructive, and even self-destructive alliance, which is bound finally to corrode the very Christian beliefs on which it rests. For the mind, exercised and guided in its search for knowledge by the most sophisticated and comprehensive theology the world has ever known—a theology which through St. Thomas Aquinas has assimilated into its grand system the genius of Aristotle—was at the same time fashioned and directed by the indelible Christian distrust of the ways of the world. Thus it had to follow, with the utmost logical precision and determination, a course of systematically "devaluing" the knowably real. This mind, Nietzsche predicts, will eventually, in a frenzy of intellectual honesty, unmask as humbug and "meaningless" that which it began by regarding as the finer things in life. The boundless faith in truth, the joint legacy of Christ and Greek, will in the end dislodge every possible belief in the truth of any faith. Souls, long disciplined in a school of unworldliness and humility, will insist upon knowing the worst about themselves, indeed will only be able to grasp what is humiliating. Psychology will denigrate the creations of beauty, laying bare the tangle of unworthy desires of which they are "mere" sublimations. History will undermine the accumulated reputation of the human race by exhuming from beneath the splendid monuments the dead body of the past, revealing everywhere the spuriousness of motives, the human, all-too-human. And science itself will rejoice in exposing this long-suspected world as a mechanical contraption of calculable pulls and pushes, as a self-sufficient agglomeration of senseless energy, until finally, in a surfeit of knowledge, the scientific mind will perform the somersault of self-annihilation.

"The nihilistic consequences of our natural sciences"—this is one of Nietzsche's fragmentary jottings—"from its pursuits there follows ultimately a self-decomposition, a turning against itself," which, he was convinced, would first show as the impossibility, within science itself, of comprehending the very object of its enquiry within *one* logically coherent system, and would lead to extreme scientific pessimism, to an inclination to embrace a kind of analytical, abstract mysticism in which man would shift himself and his world where, Nietzsche thinks, they were driving "ever since Copernicus: from the center towards an unknown X."

It is the tremendous paradox of Nietzsche that he himself follows, and indeed consciously wishes to hasten, this course of "devaluation"—particularly as a psychologist: and at the onset of megalomania he called himself "the first psychologist of Europe," a self-compliment which Sigmund Freud all but endorsed when, surprisingly late in his life, he came to know Nietzsche's writings. He had good reason to do so. Consider, for instance, the following passage from Nietzsche's *Beyond Good and Evil:*

> The world of historical values is dominated by forgery. These great poets, like Byron, Musset, Poe, Leopardi, Kleist, Gogol (I dare not mention greater names, but I mean them)—all endowed with souls wishing to conceal a break; often avenging themselves with their works upon some inner desecration, often seeking oblivion in their lofty flights from their all-too-faithful memories, often lost in mud and almost in love with it until they become like will-o'-the-wisps of the morasses and simulate the stars . . . oh what a torture are all these great artists and altogether these higher beings, what a torture to him who has guessed their true nature.

This does indeed anticipate many a more recent speculation on traumata and compensations, on lusts and sublimations, on wounds and bows. Yet the extraordinary Nietzsche—incomprehensible in his contradictions except as the common strategist of two opposing armies who plans for the victory of a mysterious third—a few pages later takes back the guessing, not without insulting himself in the process: "From which follows that it is the sign of a finer humanity to respect 'the mask' and not, in the wrong places, indulge in psychology and psychological curiosity." And furthermore: "He who does not *wish* to see what is great in a man, has the sharpest eye for that which is low and superficial in him, and so gives away—himself."

If Nietzsche is not the first psychologist of Europe, he is certainly a great psychologist—and perhaps really the first who comprehended what his more methodical successors, "strictly scientific" in their approach, did not see: *the psychology and the ethics of knowledge itself;* and both the psychology and the ethics of knowledge are of particular relevance when the knowledge in question purports to be knowledge of the human psyche. It was, strangely enough, Nietzsche's a-moral metaphysics, his doubtful but immensely fruitful intuition of the *Will to Power* being the ultimate reality of the world, that made him into the first *moralist of knowledge* in his century and long after. While all his scientific and scholarly contemporaries throve on the comfortable assumptions that, firstly, there was such a thing as "objective," and therefore morally neutral, knowledge, and that, secondly, everything that *can* be known "objectively" is therefore also *worth knowing,* he realized that knowledge, or at least the mode of knowledge predominant at his time and ours, is the subtlest guise of the Will to Power; and that *as a manifestation of the will it is liable to be judged morally.* For him, there can be no knowledge without a compelling urge to acquire it; and he knew that the knowledge thus acquired invariably reflects the nature of the impulse by which the mind was prompted. It is this impulse which *creatively* partakes in the making of the knowledge, and its share in it is truly immeasurable when the knowledge is about the very source of the impulse: the soul. This is why all interpretations of

404

the soul must to a high degree be self-interpretations: the sick interpret the sick, and the dreamers interpret dreams—or, as the Viennese satirist Karl Kraus—with that calculated injustice which is the prerogative of satire—once said of a certain psychological theory: "Psychoanalysis is the disease of which it pretends to be the cure."

Psychology is bad psychology if it disregards its own psychology. Nietzsche knew this. He was, as we have seen from his passage about "those great men," a most suspicious psychologist, but he was at the same time suspicious of the impulse of suspicion which was the father of his thought. Homer, to be sure, did not suspect his heroes, but Stendhal did. Does this mean that Homer knew less about the heroic than Stendhal? Does it make sense to say that Flaubert's Emma Bovary is the product of an imagination more profoundly initiated into the psychology of women than that which created Dante's Beatrice? Is Benjamin Constant, who created the dubious lover Adolphe, on more intimate terms with the nature of a young man's erotic passion than is Shakespeare, the begetter of Romeo? Certainly, Homer's Achilles and Stendhal's Julien Sorel are different heroes, Dante's Beatrice and Flaubert's Emma Bovary are different women, Shakespeare's Romeo and Constant's Adolphe are different lovers, but it would be naive to believe that they simply differ "in actual fact." Actual facts hardly exist in either art or psychology: both interpret and both claim universality for the meticulously particular. Those creatures made by creative imaginations can indeed not be compared, but they are incommensurable above all by virtue of incommensurable *wills* to know the human person, to know the hero, the woman, the lover. It is not better and more knowing minds that have created the suspect hero, the unlovable woman, the disingenuous lover, but minds possessed by different affections for a different knowledge, affections other than the wonder and pride that know Achilles, the love which knows Beatrice, the passion and compassion which know Romeo. When Hamlet comes to know the frailty of woman, he knows Ophelia not better than when he was "unknowingly" in love with her; he knows her differently and he knows her worse.

All *new* knowledge about the soul is knowledge about a *different* soul. For can it ever happen that the freely discovering mind says to the soul: "This is what you are!"? Must not the soul speak first? And worse: having revealed its secret, the soul is no longer what it was when it lived in secrecy. There are secrets which are *created* in the process of their revelation. And still worse: having been told its secrets, it may cease to be a soul. The step from modern psychology to soullessness is as imperceptible as that from modern physics to the dissolution of matter.

Tell an oyster that its pearl is the result of a pathological irritation. It will neither stop producing healthy pearls nor fall in love with pathology.

405

The human soul, on being similarly enlightened, may do both, and must in fact have subtly done so before the mind could tell. Once it is told, the price of pearls drops in the exchanges of the spirit while the demand for pathological irritations soars. They are sold now as chances for winning a pearl, a poet, an artist—still desirable things even with their value reduced. It is this disturbing state of affairs which made Nietzsche deplore "the torture" of psychologically guessing "the true nature of those higher beings" and, at the same time, recommend "respect for the mask" as a condition of "finer humanity." It is a great pity that those parts of Nietzsche's *Transvaluation of All Values* which, if we are to trust his notes, would have been concerned with the literature of the nineteenth century, never came to be written. For no literary critic of the age has had a more penetrating insight into the "nihilistic" character of that "absolute aestheticism" that, from Baudelaire onwards, is the dominant inspiration of European poetry, an aestheticism the *negative* side of which Nietzsche read in the utterly pessimistic image of reality provided by the realistic and psychological novel of that epoch, and above all in the extraordinary fusion of absolute pessimism, radical psychology, and extreme aestheticism achieved by Flaubert.

For Nietzsche, however, *all* the activities of human consciousness share the predicament of psychology. There can be, for him, no "pure" knowledge, only satisfactions, however sophisticated, of the ever-varying intellectual needs of the *will* to know. He therefore demands that man should accept *moral responsibility* for the kind of questions he asks, and that he should realize what *values* are implied in the answers he seeks. "The desire for truth," he says, "is itself in need of critique. Let this be the definition of my philosophical task. By way of experiment, I shall question for once the value of truth." And does he not! And he protests that, in an age which is as uncertain of its values as is his and ours, the search for truth will issue in either trivialities or—catastrophe. We may well wonder how he would react to the pious hopes of our day that the intelligence and moral conscience of politicians will save the world from the disastrous products of our scientific explorations and engineering skills. It is perhaps not too difficult to guess; for he knew that there was a fatal link between the moral resolution of scientists to follow the scientific search *wherever,* by its own momentum, it will take us, and the moral debility of societies not altogether disinclined to "apply" the results, however catastrophic. Believing that there was a hidden identity between *all* the expressions of the Will to Power, he saw the element of moral nihilism in the ethics of our science: its determination not to have "higher values" interfere with its highest value—Truth (as it conceives it). Thus he said of the kind of knowledge which the age pursues with furious passion that it was "the most handsome instrument of perdition."

"God is dead"—and man, in his heart of hearts, is incapable of forgiving himself for having done away with Him: he is bent upon punishing himself for this, his "greatest deed." For the time being, however, he will take refuge in many an evasive action. With the instinct of a born hunter Nietzsche pursues him into all his hiding-places, cornering him in each of them. Morality without religion? Indeed not: "All purely moral demands without their religious basis," he says, "must needs end in nihilism." What is there left? Intoxication. "Intoxication with music, with cruelty, with hero-worship, or with hatred . . . Some sort of mysticism . . . Art for Art's sake, Truth for Truth's sake, as a narcotic against self-disgust; some kind of routine, *any* silly little fanaticism . . .". But none of these drugs can have any lasting effect. The time, Nietzsche predicts, is fast approaching when secular crusaders, tools of man's collective suicide, will devastate the world with their rival claims to compensate for the lost Kingdom of Heaven by setting up on earth the ideological rules of Love and Justice which, by the very force of the spiritual derangement involved, will issue into the rules of cruelty and slavery; and he prophesies that the war for global domination will be fought on behalf of ideological doctrines.

In one of his notes written at the time of *Zarathustra* Nietzsche says: "He who no longer finds what is great in God, will find it nowhere. He must either deny or create it." These words take us to the heart of that paradox that enwraps Nietzsche's whole existence. He is, by the very texture of his soul and mind, one of the most radically religious natures that the nineteenth century brought forth, but endowed with an intellect which guards, with the aggressive jealousy of a watch-dog, all the approaches to the temple. For such a man, what, after the *denial* of God, is there left to *create?* Souls, not only strong enough to endure Hell, but to transmute its agonies into superhuman delight—in fact: the Superman. Nothing short of the transvaluation of all values can save us. Man has to be made immune from the effects of his second Fall and final separation from God: he must learn to see in his second expulsion the promise of a new paradise. For "the Devil may become envious of him who suffers so deeply, and throw him out—into Heaven."

Is there, then, any cure? Yes, says Nietzsche: a new kind of psychic health. And what is Nietzsche's conception of it? How is it to be brought about? By perfect self-knowledge *and* perfect self-transcendence. But to explain this, we should have to adopt an idiom disturbingly compounded of the language of Freudian psychology and tragic heroism. For the self-knowledge which Nietzsche means all but requires a course in depth-analysis; but the self-transcendence he means lies not in the practice of virtue as a sublimation of natural meanness; it can only be found in a kind of unconditional and almost supranatural sublimity. If there were a Christian virtue, be it goodness, innocence, chastity, saintliness, or self-sacrifice, that could not, however much he tried, be interpreted as a compensatory maneuver of the mind to "transvalue" weakness and frustration, Nietzsche might affirm it (as he is constantly tempted to praise Pascal). The trouble is that there cannot be such a virtue. For virtues are reflected upon by minds; and even the purest virtue will be suspect to a mind filled with suspicion. To think thoughts so immaculate that they must command the trust of even the most untrusting imagination, and to act from motives so pure that they are out of reach of even the most cunning psychology, this is the unattainable ideal, it would seem, of this first psychologist of Europe. "Caesar—with the heart of Christ!" he once exclaimed in the secrecy of his diary. Was this perhaps a definition of the Superman, this darling child of his imagination? It may well be; but this lofty idea meant, alas, that he had to think the meanest thought: he saw in the real Christ an illegitimate son of the Will to Power, a frustrated rabbi who set out to save himself and the underdog humanity from the intolerable strain of impotently resenting the Caesars: *not* to be Caesar was now proclaimed a spiritual distinction— a newly invented form of power, the power of the powerless.

Nietzsche had to fail, and fail tragically, in his determination to create a new man from the clay of negation. Almost with the same breath with which he gave the life of his imagination to the Superman, he blew the flame out again. For Zarathustra who preaches the Superman also teaches the doctrine of the Eternal Recurrence of All Things; and according to this doctrine nothing can ever come into being that had not existed at some time before. Thus the expectation of the Superman, this majestic new departure of life, indeed the possibility of any novel development, seems frustrated from the outset, and the world, caught forever in a cycle of gloomily repeated constellations of energy, stands condemned to a most dismal eternity.

Yet the metaphysical nonsense of these contradictory doctrines is not entirely lacking in poetic and didactic method. The Eternal Recurrence of All Things is Nietzsche's mythic formula of a meaningless world, the universe of nihilism, and the Superman stands for its transcendence, for the miraculous resurrection of meaning from its total negation. All Nietzsche's miracles are paradoxes designed to jerk man out of his false beliefs—in time before they bring about his spiritual destruction in an ecstasy of disillusionment and frustration. The Eternal Recurrence is the high school to teach strength through despair. The Superman graduates from it *summa cum laude et gloria*. He is the prototype of health, the man who has learned to

408

live without belief and without truth, and, superhumanly delighting in life "as such," actually *wills* the Eternal Recurrence: "Live in such a way that you desire nothing more than to live this very same life again and again!" The Superman, having attained to this manner of existence which is exemplary and alluring into all eternity, despises his former self for craving moral sanctions, for satisfying his will to power in neurotic sublimation, for deceiving himself about the "meaning" of life. What will he be then, this man who at last knows what life *really* is? Recalling Nietzsche's own accounts of all-too-human nature, and his analysis of the threadbare fabric of traditional values and truths, may he not be the very monster of nihilism, a barbarian, not necessarily blond, but perhaps a conqueror of the world, shrieking bad German from under his dark moustache? Yes, Nietzsche feared his approach in history: the vulgar caricature of the Superman. And because he also feared that the liberally decadent and agnostically disbelieving heirs to Christian morality would be too feeble to meet the challenge, having enfeebled the idea of civilized existence and rendered powerless the good, he sent forth from his imagination the Superman to defeat the defeat of man.

Did Nietzsche himself *believe* in the truth of his doctrines of the Superman and the Eternal Recurrence? In one of his posthumously published notes he says of the Eternal Recurrence: "We have produced the hardest possible thought—the Eternal Recurrence of All Things—now let us create the creature who will accept it lightheartedly and joyfully!" Clearly, there must have been times when he thought of the Eternal Recurrence not as a "Truth" but as a kind of spiritual Darwinian test to select for survival the spiritually fittest. There is a note of his which suggests precisely this: "I perform the great experiment: who can bear the idea of the Eternal Recurrence?" This is a measure of Nietzsche's own unhappiness: the nightmare of nightmares was to him the idea that he might have to live his identical life again and again and again; and an ever deeper insight into the anatomy of despair we gain from this note: "Let us consider this idea in its most terrifying form: existence, as it is, without meaning or goal, but inescapably recurrent, without a finale into nothingness . . . ." Indeed, Nietzsche's Superman is the creature strong enough to live forever a cursed existence and even to transmute it into the Dionysian rapture of tragic acceptance. Schopenhauer called man the *animal metaphysicum*. It is certainly true of Nietzsche, the renegade *homo religiosus*. Therefore, if God was dead, then for Nietzsche man was an eternally cheated misfit, the diseased animal, as he called him, plagued by a metaphysical hunger to feed which all the Heavens may be ransacked without result. Such a creature was doomed: he had to die out, giving way to the Superman who would miraculously feed on barren fields and finally conquer the meta-

409

physical hunger itself without any detriment to the glory of life.

Did Nietzsche himself *believe* in the Superman? In the manner in which a poet believes in the truth of his creations. Did Nietzsche believe in the truth of poetic creations? Once upon a time when, as a young man, he wrote *The Birth of Tragedy,* Nietzsche did believe in the power of art to transfigure life by creating lasting images of true beauty out of the meaningless chaos. It had seemed credible enough as long as his gaze was enraptured by the distant prospect of classical Greece and the enthusiastic vicinity of Richard Wagner's Tribschen. Soon, however, his deeply romantic belief in art turned to scepticism and scorn; and his unphilosophical anger was provoked by those "metaphysical counterfeiters," as he called them, who enthroned the trinity of beauty, goodness, and truth. "One should beat them," he said. Poetic beauty *and* truth? No, says Zarathustra, "poets lie too much"—and adds dejectedly: "But Zarathustra too is a poet . . . *We* lie too much." And he did: while Zarathustra preached the Eternal Recurrence, his author confided to his diary: "I do not wish to live *again.* How have I borne life? By creating. What has made me endure? The vision of the Superman who affirms life. I have tried to affirm life *myself*—but ah!"

Was he, having lost God, capable of truly believing in anything? "He who no longer finds what is great in God will find it nowhere—he must either deny it or create it." Only the "either-or" does not apply. All his life Nietzsche tried to do both. He had the passion for truth and no belief in it. He had the love of life and despaired of it. This is the stuff from which demons are made—perhaps the most powerful secret demon eating the heart out of the modern mind. To have written and enacted the extremest story of this mind—a German mind—is Nietzsche's true claim to greatness. "The Don Juan of the Mind" he once called, in a "fable" he wrote, a figure whose identity is hardly in doubt:

The Don Juan of the Mind: no philosopher or poet has yet discovered him. What he lacks is the love of the things he knows, what he possesses is *esprit,* the itch and delight in the chase and intrigue of knowledge—knowledge as far and high as the most distant stars. Until in the end there is nothing left for him to chase except the knowledge which hurts most, just as a drunkard in the end drinks absinthe and methylated spirits. And in the very end he craves for Hell—it is the only knowledge which can still seduce him. Perhaps it too will disappoint, as everything that he knows. And if so, he will have to stand transfixed through all eternity, nailed to disillusion, having himself become the Guest of Stone, longing for a last supper of knowledge which he will never receive. For in the whole world of things there is nothing left to feed his hunger.

It is a German Don Juan, this Don Juan of the Mind; and it is amazing that Nietzsche should not have recognized his features: the features of

Goethe's Faust at the point at which he has succeeded at last in defeating the plan of salvation.

And yet Nietzsche's work, wrapped in paradox after paradox, taking us to the limits of what is still comprehensible and often beyond, carries elements which issue from a center of sanity. No doubt, this core is in perpetual danger of being crushed, and was in fact destroyed in the end. But it is there, and is made of the stuff of which goodness is made. Nietzsche once said that he had spent all his days in philosophically *taking sides against himself*. Why? Because he was terrified by the prospect that all the better things in life, all honesty of mind, integrity of character, generosity of heart, fineness of aesthetic perception, would be corrupted and finally cast away by the new barbarians, unless the mildest and gentlest hardened themselves for the war which was about to be waged against them: "Caesar with the heart of Christ!"

Time and again we come to a point in Nietzsche's writings when the shrill tones of the rebel are hushed by the still voice of the autumn of a world waiting in calm serenity for the storms to break. Then this tormented mind relaxes in what he once called the *Rosengeruch des Unwiederbringlichen*—an untranslatably beautiful lyricism of which the closest equivalent in English is perhaps Yeats'

> *Man is in love and loves what vanishes.*
> *What more is there to say?*

In such moments the music of Bach brings tears to his eyes and he brushes aside the noise and turmoil of Wagner; or he is, having deserted Zarathustra's cave in the mountains, enchanted by the gentle grace of a Mediterranean coastline. Contemplating the quiet lucidity of Claude Lorrain, or seeking the company of Goethe in conversation with Eckermann, or comforted by the composure of Stifter's *Nachsommer*, a Nietzsche emerges, very different from that who used to inhabit the fancies of Teutonic schoolboys and, alas, schoolmasters, a Nietzsche who is a traditionalist at heart, a desperate lover who castigates what he loves because he knows it will abandon him and the world. It is the Nietzsche who can with one sentence cross out all the dissonances of his apocalyptic voices: "I once saw a storm raging over the sea, and a clear blue sky above it; it was then that I came to dislike all sunless, cloudy passions which know no light, except the lightning."

In these regions of his mind dwells the terror that he may have helped to bring about the very opposite to what he desired. Then he is much afraid of the consequences of his teaching. Perhaps the best will be driven to despair by it, the very worst accept it? And once he put into the mouth of some imaginary titanic genius what is his most terrible prophetic utterance: "Oh grant madness, you heavenly powers! Madness that at last I may believe in myself . . . I am consumed by doubts, for I have killed the Law . . . if I am not more than the Law, then I am the most abject of all."

Small wonder that few can think in Germany without thinking of Nietzsche. He is the master-mind of modern Germany—a country with open frontiers.

Russian Soviet Literature Today

Marc Slonim

Presented at the Library of Congress January 9, 1961

I AM OFTEN ASKED what is, in my opinion, the main difference between the literatures of the United States or Great Britain and that of the Soviet Union. If I happen to be in a jocular mood, my answer is that while one can speak of American short stories or the British "angry young men" without mentioning President Eisenhower or Elizabeth, Queen of England, it is out of the question to appraise Russian fiction without referring to Mr. Khrushchev; and while no English-speaking reviewer of current books feels compelled to explore the views of the Republican Party on the comparative merits of epic and lyrical narrative, or the English Laborites' theories on the use of symbolic images in modern poetry, it is simply inconceivable for any student of contemporary Russian letters to ignore the last resolution of the Central Committee of the Communist Party on the aims and style of Soviet poets, novelists, and dramatists, or not to quote the statements made by the Russian Prime Minister in his address to the Third Congress of Soviet Writers in May 1959. And this is not a superficial remark. It goes to the heart of the matter, since neither Mr. Khrushchev's speech nor the Central Committee's declarations were merely political statements; they actually have a strong bearing upon all departments of fiction and determine substantial changes in literary production.

No adequate judgment of Soviet literature is possible unless one is constantly aware of the fact that it is, like all other activities in Russia, an integral part of the whole mechanism of the State. Creative writing in the USSR is a public function and as such is controlled by the Party and the Government and is subject to pressure by their agencies. In times of crises, this pressure degenerates into disciplinary measures, such as banishment from the press and literary unions, or into such administrative forms of persuasion as arrest, exile, and concentration camps.

413

But literary conditions in the Soviet Union also have positive aspects, and whenever Soviet critics and journalists compare their native literary scene with that of the capitalist world, they point out all the advantages and privileges the Russian writers enjoy at home. It might appear odd to an outsider that the Soviet Government should discuss literary questions and the Party devote so much time and attention to the formulation of artistic policy at every turn of its turbulent and tortuous evolution, but these very facts suggest a recognition of literature as a powerful cultural factor and indicate the important place it occupies in Soviet society. Nowhere in the countries of the West is this recognition as complete and emphatic as in Russia. An historian would trace this attitude to the pre-revolutionary past and would conclude that the Communists are simply following a century-long tradition. From the introduction of Christianity to Peter the Great, literature in Russia was called upon to help the church and to fulfill a religious mission; in the eighteenth century the Empire expected the poets and writers to glorify the exploits of its sovereigns and generals, and throughout the nineteenth century and at the beginning of the twentieth, writers were regarded as the spokesmen of the nation, the leaders of public opinion, the representatives of the intelligentsia. They were honored and loved by the educated classes, who called them "the intellectual rulers of a generation." This respect for the writer and the recognition of his place in society assumed wider proportions after the revolution, when the liquidation of illiteracy and the general growth of culture among working people created millions of new readers. Today writers serve the new State as they once served the Church and the Empire and later the liberal movement. The present masters of Russia are well aware of the traditional influence of literature on the minds and moods of the people. Stalin called the writers "engineers of human souls." They are assigned a key role in the blueprint of national development. It is well known that they receive all sorts of State awards, including such eagerly coveted decorations as the Order of Lenin, the Order of the Red Banner, and the Order of the Hero of Socialist Labor, and that they are elected to the Supreme Soviet and other high councils, on the ground of their literary activity; at the same time, novelists and poets of the past are honored by numerous monuments, and squares and avenues are named after them. The Russians are so used to it that Soviet citizens who come to the United States automatically look for statues of Mark Twain or Fenimore Cooper and expect to find an Edgar Allan Poe place in Washington and a Walt Whitman park in New York. The material security of contemporary writers in the Soviet Union is firmly established on high royalties, large printings, serial rights, and State pensions, as well as on subsidiary favors such as writers' sanitariums, vacation centers, housing, etc. Russians are

414

avid readers, and the Soviet Union produces more books and in larger printings than any other country in the world; an average work of fiction easily sells from 20 to 75 thousand copies, and collections of poems also have a great appeal to popular audiences. Classics, Russian and foreign, are steadily in demand, and collected or individual works of great authors reach a circulation of hundreds of thousands and even millions of copies. There is no doubt that writers (as well as artists and scientists) are the best paid and probably the richest people in the Soviet Union, and their social status is truly elevated. As a group, they certainly have a very considerable moral and political weight. It is well known to foreign diplomats in Moscow that writers, for example, are permanent guests at all big receptions in the Kremlin.

The sum total of all these benefits is, unfortunately, counterbalanced by serious and obvious drawbacks: the writer always carries a heavy burden of social responsibility; he is not a free agent in our sense of the word; he is compelled to meet a whole list of political and social requirements as a member of a Communist collective; and, not only as a citizen but as an artist, he has to do what is expected of him for the glory of the cause. His merits are therefore assessed not from the aesthetic but from the socio-political standpoint of service. A large number of writers accept the theoretical premises and the practical consequences of such a situation—and there are many of them who not only carry a membership card but share completely the Communist ideology and sincerely try to create a litera-ture of social significance. Quite a few become so involved in administering literature that they hardly have any time left for writing. Others resent this bureaucratization of letters and grumble about the red tape in the Ministry of Culture or about the stupidity of censors, but, while they may question the value of certain practices, they do not question basic beliefs. Serious opposition to existing conditions stems from those writers who dream of a separation between literature and the State. Their discontent and demands for real freedom became vocal after Stalin's death, and par-ticularly during those four years (1953–56) of the general thaw, when a liberalization of the literary regime seemed possible. The events in Hun-gary and Poland set the clock back again, but on the whole the situation has improved greatly in the last six or seven years. Of course, there was no change in the guiding principles, but their application became much milder and elastic, and the writers felt the possibility of expressing themselves with greater courage and sincerity. The rehabilitation of those who had been taboo in the Soviet press for more than two decades also added to the feel-ing of relief. If one compares, for example, novels and plays published in 1952 and in 1960, one would notice immediately a difference in tone and diction; today there is more diversity in plot, more humanity in the treatment of emotions, more independence in the description of the bright and dark sides of Communist reality. But despite all these gains and the change of leadership in the Union of Soviet Writers (Konstantin Fedin, a venerable writer, instead of Alexey Surkov, a great bureaucrat but a small poet), the whole structure of the relationship between literature and the State remained unaltered. The road to be taken by Russian writers is still officially prescribed by the decisions of the Central Committee of the Communist Party, which never misses an opportunity to stress the education of the masses as the supreme goal of fiction. In its message to the Third Congress of Soviet Writers in May 1959, the Central Committee reiterated its old tenets: "Soviet writers must inspire people in their struggle for Communism, must educate them according to Communist principles, must develop in them high moral virtues and intransigent rejection of bourgeois ideology and morals. . . . Writers must become passionate propagandists of the seven year plan and bring cheerfulness, vigor and energy into the heart of man." Mr. Khrushchev, in his speech to the Congress, made relatively moderate remarks about writers like Dudintsev (the author of *Not By Bread Alone*, which criticized many defects of the Communist state), who commit political errors, and he even drew a line between unconscious transgressors and the deliberate opponents of the regime. This seemed like a good omen, but a couple of months later Smirnov, chief editor of *Literary Gazette*, the organ of the Writer's Union, made a rather disturbing comment: "The Party," he said, "did not want its organs to direct the work of the writers by telling them what and how to write, because Party's guidance in literature is based on the fact that Soviet writers in all their work are consciously led by the ideas of Communism." This implies a unanimity of ideology which actually is far from existing; it assumes a gladly accepted agreement between the faithful of the same church. Of course it would be false, even preposterous, to imagine that Soviet poets and novelists simply obey orders and fulfill the "social command." In fact, the vast majority of Soviet writers hail a literature "realistic in form and socialist in content," and they accept its educational task. The works usually quoted by the Communist critics as the great achievements of the revolutionary period, works such as Gladkov's *Cement*, a novel of economic reconstruction, Fadeyev's *The Rout* (or *The Nineteen* in its English version), Nicholas Ostrovsky's *Tempering of Steel*, a novel of the civil war, or, the best of all, *The Silent Don* by Sholokhov, were all written by authors who believed in the revolution and wholeheartedly agreed with Lenin and Stalin. I can make but one reservation in regard to Communist writers: since the creative act is basically an attempt at freedom and an affirmation of artistic independence, even those who wanted to support the Party one hundred percent are often worried and annoyed by the consequences of government

416

controls. The same Sholokhov, or Konstantin Simonov, another Communist, or Panferov, who died a few months ago after having written highly critical novels of Soviet life, made pointed declarations against bureaucratism and intellectual conformity, which, in their opinion, lead to artistic obtuseness. What they failed to acknowledge, however, is the reason for all the errors they deplore: the Party does tell the writers what to write and how to write. In whatever manner it is done, with velvet gloves or with an iron hand, it can only create tensions, conflicts, hidden opposition, and, in extreme cases, open revolt independently of an artist's political tendencies. It is easy to say that whoever disagrees with the Party's views on literature is an enemy of the people, but the truth is that this disagreement stems from the very nature of artistic activity.

The literary policy of the Communist Party in Russia has gone through various phases in the last 40 years, and all of these have corresponded to fluctuations of opinions and the struggle of tendencies within the Party itself, as well as to transformations throughout the whole country. Ideological and organizational shifts in literary strategy and tactics reflected therefore wider general modifications of Russian life. The future historian will study with amazement all the changes of scenery and actors in the motley panorama of Soviet letters since 1917. In the early twenties, immediately after the ascension of Lenin and Trotsky to power, and later, during the era of civil war, famine, and terror, and then in the years of respite under the NEP (or New Economic Policy) of the years 1922–28, poets and novelists were intoxicated with the tragic and magnificent sweep of events, with the grandiose unfolding of a tremendous historical drama, and they still enjoyed a certain freedom of expression and experimentation. Pre-revolutionary currents, such as symbolism, imagism, and futurism in poetry, and expressionism and neo-realism in prose, overflowed into the Soviet epoch, and the writers of the twenties combined a search for new forms with the crude but fantastically rich living matter of revolutionary upheaval. What they saw and heard and experienced was so incredible and intense that many of them made the error of believing that a simple transcript of an extraordinary reality could result in an interesting literary work. In any case, it was the most fruitful and diversified period of Soviet fiction. This was the age of Mayakovsky, Pasternak, Khlebnikov, and Esenin—the greatest and most famous Russian poets of the last 40 years—and a whole generation of talented newcomers followed in their wake: Tikhonov, Selvinsky, Bagritsky, Kirsanov, Zabolotsky, and many others. Not less outstanding were the new prose writers, most of them sponsored and often taught by Gorky, Zamiatin, and other older masters. Among the young writers were Pilniak, the symbolist Slavophile, Babel, the exquisite story-teller, Vsevolod Ivanov, the exotic chronicler of the civil war in Siberia, Fedin, the traditional realist, Leonov, the intricate psychological Romanticist in a Dostoevskian vein, Fadeyev, the disciple of Tolstoy's psychological realism, Zoshchenko the humorist, and the whole group of sophisticated young men united under the sign of "Serapion Brothers" of E. T. A. Hoffmann. And I mention only the leading ones among dozens and dozens of young writers. In fact, the best and most prominent representatives of Soviet letters came into literature during the twenties. The literature of this period was rich and diversified, it did not ignore its ties with preceding artistic trends, and it cherished connections with the Western avant-garde. But all these traits appeared politically suspect to the Communist lawgivers. They acknowledged that most of these young writers were fellow travelers, but their artistic independence and their interest in formal innovations conflicted with the aesthetics of dialectical materialism. The new regime moved toward complete control of all communications media, and literature of course was the main target. After a short-lived flirtation with the avant-garde groups, including Mayakovsky's "left front," the Party decided that experimentation was a bourgeois whim, good only for a restricted circle of snobs and connoisseurs, and that the masses needed the simple and plain fare of realistic narrative with a social message. Hence the condemnation of everything that did not fit into the scheme of mass education and adherence to the spirit of Communism. The offensive on the economic front with the five-year plan, the collectivization of agriculture, and the final eradication of vestiges of the past began around 1928, and it coincided with a tightening of the Party's grip on literature. In 1932 the picture became quite clear; the Communist leaders firmly pushed literature into pre-established channels and created a Union of Soviet Writers, which assumed the role of policeman in the battle of ideas. The Union was a professional organization through which the government could administer literary production. Officials ruled this powerful body for twenty years, and only after the death of Stalin did the pressure lessen and a breath of fresh air pass through the stuffy offices of the Union, which has recently been called the "literary Pentagon" by an American visitor.

But much more significant than the organizational structure was the official canonization, also in 1932, of the following literary dogma: "Socialist realism, being the basic method of Soviet literature and literary criticism, requires from the artist truthful, historically concrete representation of reality in its revolutionary development. Moreover, truth and historical completeness of artistic representation must be combined with the task of ideological transformation and education of the working man in the spirit of Socialism." From 1932, and until 1953, with an interval for the war years when the writers were allowed more leeway, this formula reigned supreme, and all Soviet poets and novelists had to march in the boots of Socialist realism. Under Stalin "realism in form and socialism in content" became the official standard by which literary achievements were appraised. Whoever failed to conform or showed a dangerous deviation toward symbolism, formalism, intuitivism, and other bourgeois trends, was branded a cosmopolitan, a lackey of capitalism, and an "inner emigré." The name-calling in the press was often a prelude to something worse—including administrative punishment.

Theoretically, the formula of Socialist realism was vague and contradictory, since it confused such different concepts as aesthetic method, artistic intention, requirements of a school, and political demands. But in practice it determined the character and the direction of Soviet prose and poetry. In fact, what may truly be called Soviet literature is what has been written in accordance with the formula. For two decades it was as sacred as any of the fundamentals of Communist faith. In the last seven years there were many attempts to revise it, particularly under the impact of criticisms by authors from Hungary and other satellite countries. In December 1955 the Congress of Soviet Writers decided to drop the second sentence of the resolution adopted in 1932—thus provoking bad feelings among influential members of the Communist hierarchy. But despite all the obvious defects of the socialist realism formula, it is still operating as "the most advanced, most progressive and fruitful literary method" and as "a weapon which dialectical materialism handed over to us in order to create Communist culture." And even the startling revelation that no great or even internationally significant literary works have been written according to the official recipe is not sufficient to undermine its power; it is today, as it was some three decades ago, an integral part of the Communist credo in Russia.

Socialist realism produced in Russia a staggering amount of novels, poems, dramas, comedies, and short stories—the actual number of artists, or "workers of intellectual labor" as they are categorized, is tremendous—and each beginning writer is helped by dozens of State "literary consultation bureaus." Whether written cynically or in good faith, the literature of socialist realism presents a picture of dull homogeneity. It portrays stock characters in black and white, it has the same tone of optimism (until recently suicides in novels were frowned upon by the critics), with the same exaltation of heroism in war or industrial effort, and with the same rhetorical cataloguing of Communist successes. In its structure it is similar to the long-winded Victorian novels, and it also discloses the same moral prudery, the same avoidance of embarrassing problems of sex, misery, and psychological complications.

It has often been pointed out that the themes of this literature are taken either from the civil war or from the process of Russia's industrialization.

(In the latter category we have novels on coal mining, steel plants, power stations, colonization of virgin soils, cattle-breeding in State farms, or wheat harvest in *Kolkhoze*.) This is perfectly true, but I do not agree with those who attribute the dullness of contemporary Soviet fiction to these subjects. Of course, when an author goes into the details of autogenous welding or the use of fertilizers for technical plants, he might become boring. Yet there is nothing wrong with the themes themselves. Some good Soviet novels on industrialization, such as *Time, Forward!* by Katayev, depicting a contest in the fabrication of cement during the first five-year plan, or Leonov's *Sot'* (*Soviet River* in the American edition), which elevates the construction of a dam in the far north into a mythological deed, are as exciting and absorbing as any Western thriller. I also believe that problems of technology and industrial progress can be made as attractive to modern readers as "boy-gets-girl" tales or variants of the Cinderella story. I disagree with many European and American critics who look with contempt at many Soviet novels merely because they are devoted to man's manifold material activities. Nor is it wrong to tell us how heroes behave in the office, in the factory, or in the fields—as working individuals. The dullness does not come from the themes, which are perfectly legitimate and tend to embrace most diversified areas, but from the uniform and dated literary fashion in which they are explored. Just as we possess the pattern for detective stories, so Soviet authors follow an archetypal outline in their industrial novels. The majority of the latter are composed in a style which again reminds us of the Victorian era, or of the naturalistic-minded Russian realistic writers of 1860 and 1870. They have long dialogues, a plethora of detail, all-inclusive descriptions of environment, either trivially colloquial or artificially rhetorical diction, and stock characters coming from the same mould. For instance, a favorite literary gambit of such novels, which often sound like a movie script, is the opposition of industrial conservatism to innovation. In dozens of narratives, the director of a plant, or his chief engineer, who until recently was a villain and an agent of American capitalism, does not want to recognize an invention made by a foreman or by a young specialist who seeks to increase production and save time. After a struggle in which occasional help is offered to the hero by his girl friend, the Kremlin promotes the revolutionary innovation, and virtue triumphs, often with a Hollywood-like happy ending—which includes the marital bliss of the main protagonists. Sometimes the talent of the author brings some saving grace to this dead scheme, but the fundamental structure remains the same. I open the November 1960 issue of *The Banner* (*Znamia*), an important literary monthly, and I find a novelette by Sergei Snegov entitled *Pineghin's Plan*. It depicts a vast industrial syndicate beyond the Arctic circle directed by the stubborn bear-like Pineghin, an old Communist. His explorers have found coal some 60 miles from the central mills and Pineghin gets Moscow to approve his plan of industrial expansion, by which the newly discovered mine will be exploited and will feed with coke the old smelting furnaces of the plant. But Shelepa, a young engineer, comes out with a counter-proposal: he wants to replace the existing equipment by modern electrical installations—and all the problems and difficulties connected with this daring project stir up the whole administration. The violent controversy causes Pineghin to have a heart attack, but in the calm of a hospital room he analyzes the situation, understands where the truth lies, renounces his plan, and promotes the counter-proposal of his opponent—not without the help of the local Party secretary. In another novel of 1960 by Vera Ketlinskaya, clumsily entitled *It Is Not Worthwhile Living Otherwise,* the main plot hinges on the project of turning coal into gas in the very bowels of coal mines, and so its technical realization involves scientists, industrial bosses, high Party officials, engineers, and average workmen in a maze of struggle, steps and countersteps, victories, defeats, hopes and disappointments—the whole story being heavily burdened with all sorts of sentimental and family complications. This is, by the way, a recent phenomenon: the industrial or agricultural novel has been enlivened lately by what the editors call "the human element." Seldom, however, have all these personal sub-plots been integrated into the main body of the narrative.

At times all fictional adornment is abandoned, and the novel becomes a report, a factual narrative. This genre is extremely common in Russia and forms an important segment of the national literature. Its aim is "accurate and faithful reproduction of people and conditions of labor with an emphasis on industrial, agricultural, military and other achievements of the country," and it often assumes the form of sketches and novelettes. This descriptive prose has, among the latecomers, such masters as Ovechkin and Soloukhin, who continue a long line of successful predecessors.

There are many reasons why Soviet audiences respond favorably to this kind of literary production, as well as to the industrial novels, despite the fact that most of the latter are devoid of any literary merit. First of all, there is the joy of recognition; all those novels are telling how things are done—a problem in which the population of the Soviet Union is vitally interested. We might be reluctant to read a novel about the building of the Moscow subway, but some 20 years ago the Russians found it very exciting, and there were a few popular novels on that subject. Narratives about oil wells, dams, and mining, or dairy farms, fishing, and harvesting have the appeal of fascinating documentary films. The students of Russia in the Western World also read this material as illustrative of contemporary Soviet reality. Communist critics, however, warn us that the main merit of all those books lies in their underlying idea: the praise of human effort, of resilience, stamina, and courage—which they believe to be the virtues of Soviet man, of the product of a socialist society. They insist that the writer make the portrayal of this new man his supreme goal, and most violent discussions in the contemporary Russian press revolve around the problems connected with this assignment.

In no other literature of the world do I know of so many attempts to depict a positive hero as in the fiction of the Soviet Union. This hero has undergone a long and complex evolution. The flat personification of all virtues in the image of a steel-armored, uncompromising Party secretary, which was the fashion under Stalin, has now been replaced by a more sophisticated figure. Fyodor Panferov, one of the leading novelists, provoked endless controversy by his recent *Volga, Mother River* and *Meditations,* not only because of their openly critical rendition of current life, but mainly because of his attempt to portray Morev, a Communist dignitary, as a man with all sorts of weaknesses, defects, and irrational emotions, including a premarital love affair. When Dudintsev in 1957 published his sensational *Not By Bread Alone,* which was considered a most daring exposé of Communist red tape and the new class of Party "monopolists," his hero, Lopatkin, was just an ordinary man with the mannerisms and extravagances of a technical visionary, while his adversaries, top administrators or scientists, men filled with pompous smugness and narrow-mindedness, were not very different from their capitalist counterparts. Dudintsev challenged the cliché of the positive hero to such an extent that the Party felt it necessary to answer him by another work of fiction. Vsevolod Kochetov, in his novel, *Brothers Yershov,* provided not only a refutation of Dudintsev's heresies but presented a family of one hundred percent pure Communists, whose high morality matched their inflexibility in matters of Leninism.

The need for a living positive hero, instead of a cardboard figure, is today so strong among Soviet writers that each new novel brings a new variant on the same theme. But with the exception of Sholokhov, whose protagonists are always vital men and women, no socialist realist has given a credible and lasting image of the positive Communist hero. By a strange irony of Apollo and the Muses, the best portraits of Communists in Soviet literature were drawn by writers whose work remains outside the enclosure of socialist realism. Such were in the past the creations of Babel, Fedin, Leonov, Katayev, Kaverin, Pavlenko, and Paustovsky, or, in recent times, those of Panova, Simonov, Nekrasov, Nilin, and others.

In juxtaposition to the positive hero is the figure of the villain. Here too the evolution is very remarkable. In the 1930's, and immediately after the war, the villain was similar to the shady characters in old dime novels: he was so sneaky and had such a black soul and an evil exterior that the reader could not understand why all the intelligent Communists had failed to see through him. He was a saboteur, a spy, a rapist, he was selling his country to foreign counterespionage agencies, and in his past were hidden crimes of civil war and emigration. This grim individual has been replaced in the last few years by a more subtle personage. Already in *The Russian Forest* by Leonov (1953), the villain is a decadent professor, Graziansky, who, though he still hides his infamous past and is connected with the capitalist West, does not behave as a blackguard and offers quite a few psychological problems. In Kochetov's above-mentioned novel, villains are replaced by light-minded, easily influenced people. In Dudintsev, the chief negative figure is Drosdov, who is a good Communist but has no feeling for anything outside his professional duty and can be quite unscrupulous when fighting against any opposition. It is obvious that such diversified treatment of villains (followed also by Panferov) opens a new chapter in the otherwise highly conditioned literature of socialist realism. Until the late 1950's, the sex life of Communists was exemplary in all novels, but now we find that they even commit adultery, elope with married women, or seduce young girls—things that could never have happened in the respectable works of the 1930's and 1940's, when Stalin would not permit his generals and marshals to divorce. Another feature is the appearance in fiction of children born out of wedlock and wives abandoned by Communist officials.

Socialist realism created in Russian literature a whole code of conventions. The most important of these is optimism. Its foundations are, of course, ideological; according to its promoters, Soviet poets and novelists oppose the pessimistic, suicidal, gloomy works of American and European decadent capitalist authors, bent on psychopathological madness, violence, and sexual perversions, with the life-affirming, healthy, and joyful songs and epics of a society on the move toward a dazzling future. To stress this basic difference, a dramatist, Vishnevsky, called his play, in which the Reds are killed by the Whites, *An Optimistic Tragedy,* thus challenging old definitions. Even if the events of a narrative are far from being cheerful, the reader must be left with a hopeful feeling—this is the first commandment of socialist realism. It is easy to imagine how such a categorical demand generated a series of artificially jubilant endings and plots. This official and obligatory optimism often gave a tone of mendacity to a large number of literary works in which the archetype of the wise old man was represented by the figures of great scientists who join the proletariat under the influence of Lenin, or by veteran revolutionists who give invaluable advice to bright youth bent on Communist conquest. The rhetoric of the heroic also rang false quite often, and this is truly regrettable, because the

Russian revolution certainly offered thousands of examples of courage, devotion to ideals, the spirit of sacrifice, and high civic virtue. But those whom Soviet critics themselves called the "hallelujah men" and the "lacquerers of reality" put a deceptive and often dishonest varnish on all their descriptions and portrayals. Pseudo-vigorous hosannas became a familiar feature of verse and prose. Here again the fabrication, the falsehood should be distinguished from what really forms the foundations of Russian vitality and courage. I would say that in many instances the writers did not need to be prodded from above to show the vigor and the strength of the Russian people. There are two groups of works which prove this point. The first are war novels. Their number is very large, probably larger than in any country of the world and, although many of them are not perfect technically, they are moving and sincere and do represent the grim reality of Russia's destruction by Hitler's armies, and the superhuman patriotic effort of a whole nation fighting for its very existence. This is particularly true of works which appeared during the war years: *The People Immortal* by Vassily Grossman, *Days and Nights,* the epic of Stalingrad by Simonov, *In Stalingrad Trenches* by Viktor Nekrasov, *They Fought for Their Motherland,* the unfinished novel by Sholokhov, the dramas *Invasion* and *Lenushka* by Leonov and his novelette *The Taking of Velikoshumsk,* as well as hundreds of poems, *Vassily Terkin,* a popular novel in verse by Alexander Tvardovsky, and many other quite good specimens. Unfortunately, after 1945 the conventional pattern also contaminated the war novel, with a few exceptions, such as the novelettes by Kazakevich, or *The Living and the Dead* by Simonov, which was finished in 1960. This gripping narrative tells with frankness and simplicity the reasons for Russian unpreparedness and for the reverses of 1941–42.

The second group consists of novels which might seem juvenile to sophisticated Western readers. These are also topical novels, often on industrial themes, but their action takes place in far distant, exotic regions, and their heroes have to fight against nature. Whether they depict young men and women breaking the ground of virgin soil in the Southeastern steppes (see the last novel by Mikhail Bubennov, *The Eagle's Steppe*) or building new cities in the Far East (Pavlenko's *In the Far East*), or transforming the extreme north (novels by Chakovsky), or exploring the taiga (novels by Zadornov or *The Salt of the Earth* by George Markov, a bestseller of 1960), they are all adventure stories, and their appeal is akin to that eternally exercised by *Robinson Crusoe* or Hugo's *The Toilers of the Sea*. They are tales of pioneers, of colonizers, of discoverers of new lands, of conquerors of the earth; and from their pages "the Muse of Far Distant Travels" calls on us as the poet Gumilev said half a century ago. The pathos and enthusiasm of these works is undeniable; a genuine smell of forests, the odor of fields and mountains, comes from their pages. Of course, many authors of these exciting tales want to prove a point: namely, that this struggle with nature which aims at her complete control is the essence of Communist humanism, as opposed to decadent Western mysticism or a pessimistic surrendering to nature's destructive brutality. They repeat Gorky's slogan, "Man, this sounds grand," and they represent the powerful offensive for the possession of nature's secrets and riches, which is a part of the great industrialization under Communist guidance.

One may object that such obvious "messages" and even such simple attractions as travel, adventure, and the struggle with nature can seldom be on a very high literary level. This is true, and not only of this particular kind of narrative. The majority of works inspired by Socialist realism are marred by naïveté and primitivism. Some of them are grossly exaggerated and badly put together. Even in the historical novels, a favorite genre into which writers and readers escape from present-day pressures, the desire to modernize or correct history and to find in the past parallels to contemporary events is so strong that blunders are made all the time in style, language, characterization, or mere description. This is how a military commander speaks in a chronicle of fifth-century Georgia: "let us call a meeting and put the problem of the organizational measures for the defense on the agenda."

Usually we are inclined to reproach Soviet fiction for its insistence on social significance and propaganda. But it has other more dangerous flaws. I am afraid that we are throwing around the term "propaganda" in the same indiscriminatory way that we do other clichés such as "art for art's sake," "there is no artistic creation without freedom," etc. As a matter of fact, "the art for art's sake" formula is as inept as that of socialist realism, and in a large sense, all art is propaganda, because every writer wants to infect the reader, the spectator, the listener with his own feelings and ideas, with his own vision of the world. His main wish is to communicate all this in the most convincing and impressive fashion, and great works of literature have always had this power of suggestion and persuasion, from Greek tragedy down to Dante or Tolstoy or Dostoevsky. And a great many masterpieces were produced in times of slavery and reaction, thus showing all the precariousness of making a causal connection between environment and creativity. But aside from all these extremely interesting and controversial points, we must say that the trouble with Soviet literature lies not in its desire to preach but in its incapacity to do it effectively. Chesterton said that "a bad fable HAS a moral, a good fable IS a moral." We blame the average Soviet novelist for not having realized this simple truth. Art first of all requires a special individual organization of material which the author has gathered from his observation, meditation, and

425

direct life-experiences. A month ago, a prominent Soviet writer who was visiting the United States asked me at the Pen Club cocktail party: "Why do American publishers avoid publishing translations from the Russian?" I told him they were not doing it for political reasons. They are eagerly looking for works that could interest the American reader. But although the material depicted in modern Soviet novels is often interesting as such, it is so poorly organized, so clumsily presented, or has such a local—I should say provincial—ring and is so outdated in its literary manner that it has only subsidiary or indirect value to the Russian readers, because they know what the author is talking about and can ignore his artistic inefficiency, and to a restricted group of specialists abroad, who take fiction as documentary evidence. But it has no intrinsic qualities of artistic attainment.

On the other hand, there are Soviet writers of high standards and achievements. But they do not write as socialist realists. I should like to single out for praise *The First Joys* or *Unusual Summer* by Fedin, despite a few annoying ideological blemishes, or *Harvest on the Don* by Sholokhov, which came out in 1960 as the sequel to his previous novel, *The Virgin Soil*, or the excellent autobiographical narrative by Konstantin Paustovsky, one of the most talented storytellers of the older generation, or novels and tales by Vera Panova, a younger writer, author of the delightful *Serezha,* a child's story, or *Men, Years, and Days* by Ehrenburg, who in the evening of his life began to remember its dawn and early morning—all these and quite a few works by other, lesser-known prose authors.

In poetry, we have a high level of culture and technical skill, and Aseyev, Kirsanov, Antokolsky, and Tikhonov, among the old guard, and Tvardovsky, Martynov, Yevtushenko, and many others, among the young, represent Soviet poetic effort in a worthy fashion. Lately there is a definite upward movement in poetry, and the young are eager to break away from familiar rhythms and meters. They are usually very interested in such currents as symbolism and surrealism. Moreover, many intelligent writers and critics in Russia conduct—against great odds—a relentless campaign to raise the artistic level of average production and to liberate literature from too many guardians and protectors. There is no doubt that the movement which started on the morrow of Stalin's death has already succeeded in breaking with many clichés and in ridiculing many conventions fixed by socialist realism. It has widened the subject matter of recent Soviet novels and tales, introduced a much deeper treatment of problems of love, family, growth, and inner moral struggle, and even dared to begin a frank discussion of the real state of Soviet society and morals. It made audible new and refreshing voices during the period known as the thaw, between 1954 and 1957. This was the time when Pasternak decided to publish his *Doctor*

Zhivago, and this extraordinary poetic narrative gave us a glimpse of what was hidden behind the respectable façade of Soviet law-abiding letters. It is amazing that the novel, which has been read more widely throughout the world than any work of fiction that has come from Russia since the Revolution, has not even been printed in Moscow, and, in some way, has to be considered outside the panorama of Soviet literature. There are other signs, however, that the new generation of writers, and particularly the poets, is again interested in formal experimentation, which the Government has banned from Russian literature, and that they have grown out of the strait jacket of the official but declining socialist realism.

Party theoreticians are so keenly aware of what is going on that in the last three years they have begun a counteroffensive under the general signboard of "anti-revisionism." They concede that many "obnoxious ideas" have lately infiltrated into art and literature, and that what the young poets and writers say among themselves could not even be reproduced in the columns of the censored Soviet press. They know that certain poems are circulating in manuscript, that young authors are reading to friends first works that show no connection whatsoever with socialist realism, that the interest in such condemned Western writers as Gide, Proust, Kafka, Joyce, and other moderns, dubbed by the Communist conservatives as "formalists" and "irrationalists," is steadily growing, and that the new generation is generally sick and tired of the dull conventions and false idols of the Stalin era. It is very difficult to guess what direction all of these tendencies will take, and how the national and international situation will influence the liberalization of literature. At present the Party and the Government have to shut their eyes to many things which a visitor to Moscow calls "official clandestinity." We do not know whether the clandestinity will become an open situation and whether the writers will be able to express themselves without being nursed and guided by the members of the Central Committee and bureaucratic officials in literary unions, publishing houses, and other editorial boards. But it seems to me, as it does to many other observers of the Russian scene, that this process is irreversible. Many incidents, retreats, and misfortunes are probably in store for the seasoned and embattled Soviet writers, but the phase of socialist realism has come to an end artistically and ideologically, and today Russian literature in the USSR begins to navigate to other and more attractive shores.

Chinese Letters Since
the Literary Revolution (1917)

Lin Yutang

Presented at the Library of Congress January 16, 1961

I

LITERATURE is an expression of the individual human spirit, and the study of an epoch of literature is the study of the spirit of man in that epoch—whether it is self-assured and serene, or imaginative, vital, and creative—or merely restless and confused. Furthermore, we wish to inquire whether, out of the tumult and impact of social and political changes, there have come creations that are deep and mature and lasting; whether, in the turmoil of an age, some spirits have achieved a complete maturity and self-possession and created a thing of beauty destined to last. That is the rather high goal one must set for literature, but that is what we are interested in, is it not? It is difficult to appraise one's contemporaries, but one must try.

The modern age is an age of spiritual restlessness, both in the East and in the West. Modern art is illustrative of this restlessness. There is a closer connection between the atomic age and modern art than is commonly realized. The artist is the man to sense first the disintegration of the world of old, comfortable beliefs, and when you see modern, non-representative art, or art of "internal vision," or cubism, there is made visible to you a disintegration of matter, which is indicative of the disintegration of the spirit of man. Dali's surrealism is merely a protest against logic. This goes on, and will continue to go on, until we can be sure—and the artist helps us to make sure—that in a modern painting any resemblance to objects or persons known to us is purely coincidental.

All I can say is that this type of art is experimental—very experimental. There is nothing inherently wrong in restlessness. Restlessness means vitality. We only ask whether—after all the effusions about a dissected and

428

split-up universe, and being sick with one thing after another—something remains.

Modern China, too, has been undergoing a period of intense restlessness since 1917, the year of the Literary Revolution. And my question is: after these 40-odd years of restlessness, does something of value remain?

I will only add, by way of introduction, that literature is always the creation of an individual. When we try to sum up an epoch and speak of the spirit of man in that epoch, we really mean that we seem to see in certain outstanding writers, as individuals, a spirit indicative or symptomatic of that age.

A writer is a man who reacts to his period with the whole force of his personality. A difference must be made between scholars and writers. Scholars often try to write, and writers, too, are interested in learning. Of these two, only the writer concerns us here. You can no more see the spirit of the individual in an abstruse scholar's work than in an almanac. He is interested in facts. His personal opinions? No, he is Olympian, objective, impersonal. The writer, on the other hand, is a man whose personal feelings, likes and dislikes, opinions and prejudices drip down from the point of his pen. After all is said and done, the force of literature is only the force and vitality of a group of individual spirits reacting to life and to their era.

It is easier to see the personality of William James than of Josiah Royce. William James once spoke of his "raids into philosophy," almost implying that he was an amateur, not because he was less learned than his professional colleagues, but because his spirit was always open and free, curious and inquisitive, afraid to be shut up within the "grey-plastered walls" of modern scholasticism. The idea of adventure, of a raid, a quest, is implicit in all that he wrote. It is for this reason that William James made a greater impact than Royce.

I say, in the study of the literature of an epoch, we are interested in the discovery of a few important individuals. All real thinking and all creative writing is the result of individual insights and perceptions, responsible to no one but God and the writer himself. When such individual expressions are forbidden, the garden of creative literature becomes sterile and runs to seed, and this is what has already happened in Communist China.

II

The area covered tonight dates from 1917, the year of the Literary Revolution, because that was when the restlessness of spirit began. I prefer to speak of the Literary Revolution, rather than the Literary Renaissance, as is sometimes done, because the word "Renaissance" expresses so far only a hope rather than a reality. I have the feeling of something

429

half-accomplished, neurasthenic, and not quite mature, not quite satisfying. I avoid the word "Renaissance" also because it suggests going back to the classic antiquities, whereas the literary movement starting in 1917 was a solemn pledge to break with the past of classical China and to make a leap into the broad stream of Western thought and literature. The only connection with the Italian Renaissance, as far as I can see, is the breakaway from the classical, archaic Chinese and the use of the vernacular as the medium of writing, as in the case of Dante, Petrarch, and Boccaccio.

The hotbed of the Literary Revolution was the Peking National University, and its literary organ was *La Jeunesse* or *Hsin Chingnien*. Curiously, the first shot was fired, not from Peking, but from New York, when Dr. Hu Shih, later the Chinese Ambassador to Washington during part of the war years, was a postgraduate student at Columbia. In a sober, clear, but unemotional style, he advocated the use of the modern spoken Mandarin, in place of classical Chinese, as the medium of literary expression. It was revolutionary to the point of shocking. It was shocking because the idea had never been thought of, but more particularly because the classical language was sacrosanct, because it meant a great challenge and a great liberation. The difficulty of mastering the classical language consumed a scholar's lifetime, and the result was seldom worth the trouble. Dr. Hu showed that the literary language had degenerated into a system of literary, often pedantic, allusions and dead, outworn clichés. Mastery of the literary language was often just mastery of the clichés and the learned, obscure allusions. There was hardly freedom in inventing new, graphic expressions. Writers in classical Chinese were walking in mincing steps, rather than in broad, natural strides—and I mean all of the writers, including the best. On the other hand, the modern man has a living language, rich in expressions. Dr. Hu pointed out that Chinese novels had for centuries been written in the vernacular and had much greater flexibility and greater resources in expressiveness. Several 17th-century critics, like Chin Shengtan, Li Chowu, and Yuan Chunglang, had long ago recognized the literary value of these novels. To the youth of China Dr. Hu's proposal meant an emancipation from life-consuming labors. Somewhere a sacrosanct idol had been smashed. The banner of revolt against the classics was raised. It is difficult for Westerners to imagine the impact. Intellectual China was set afire—particularly among the younger generation.

All of China's students then looked to the Peking University for leadership. The Peking University, then under Chancellor Tsai Yuan-pei, was the citadel of liberalism. It had within its walls professors of the most diverse shades of opinion; old scholars who belonged to the Manchu Dynasty, such as Tang Erh-ho and Lin Chin-nan, and moderns like Hu

Shih and Hsü Tse-mo, and such Communist firebrands as Li Ta-chao and Chen Tu-hsiu. A few diehard old scholars, like Lin Chin-nan and Ku Hung-ming, laughed with scorn at all this innovation; Lin Chin-nan called the modern spoken tongue the "language of the peddlers and pushcart rabble." How dared anyone think of displacing the classical language, in sole use for over 2,000 years?

Incidentally, I may note here that, in point of grammar and syntax and vocabulary, the classical language was the equivalent of a foreign language for the modern Chinese. Modern Chinese says "I know it," but ancient Chinese says "I it know," like French "Je le sais." And instead of saying "buying three feet of cloth," one has to write in ancient Chinese "buying cloth three feet." You see that it was, in point of difficulty, a foreign language to the student, and its mastery is as difficult as true mastery of any foreign language. We spoke of writing "ancient Chinese" (ku-wen), but there were very few people in my generation who could write pure "ancient Chinese."

However, the Literary Revolution was more than a linguistic gesture of revolt. Socially and culturally, it meant a definite break with the past. It was a state of mind, a mood, a temper of radicalism—the temper of revolt against the past. You will note this word "radicalism," for I shall show how it led directly to the leftist, Marxist tendency of today.

During the 19th century, through a series of defeats in war, foreign encroachments, and losses of territory, the Chinese people learned at first to treat the foreign gunboats with respect. The conclusion was forced upon them that foreign gunboats, telegraphs, telescopes, and cameras were better. At the turn of the century, they made the further unwilling admission that Western scientific and political ideas were better. They realized that behind the machines there was science. Yen Fu had translated Huxley's *Evolution*, Montesquieu's *Spirit of the Laws*, and Adam Smith's *The Wealth of Nations*, and Sun Yat-sen advocated the republican form of government. The Literary Revolution went a step further and spearheaded the general awakening to the fact that, perhaps, the whole Western civilization, Western ideas and philosophy and literature and social consciousness, were also better and richer. It said, "Face West, young man." It was a revolution in outlook, in ideas.

Dr. Hu Shih returned to China in 1918, at the age of twenty-six, and was received with national acclaim. He was well-grounded in classical scholarship and trained in Western academic discipline, eminently qualified to lead the revolution. But the other three editors of *La Jeunesse* were like a rickety, three-legged table. Three of the four editors did not really understand the West; one of them was clearly a psychopath. Professors Chien Hsüan-tung and Liu Pan-nung were just enthusiastic radicals. Professor

Hu Shih continued to write his sober, clear, rationalistic essays. It was the Communist professor, Chen Tu-hsiu, an ultra-radical Marxist, who furnished the ammunition and the war-cries. He was smashing right and left at Confucianism, the family system, the cult of widowhood, the planchette, etc. He had an idea of rectilinear progress; he said, "As we today are the vanguards of progress and throw over those before us, so shall the future generation step over our bodies and advance forward." His words were prophetic. The temper of radicalism went from the liberalism of the 1920's to the leftist radicalism of the 1930's.

In the generation which grew up in the 1920's, thinking was curiously lacking in ballast. The old China had been uprooted. There was no continuity with the past. Young China did not study the classics. The old had the flavor of being "feudalistic." Students who had come to Peking or Shanghai laughed at their elders in their home towns. Nor was there a deep root in or real understanding of the West. The Chinese youth fell prey to the Communist propaganda, for Communism sounded the most radical to their young ears and therefore seemed the best. Communism held out great promises and hope, and young people have always had hope. It demanded faith, and the young people have always had plenty of faith. Into this vacuum of ideas, Communism rushed like a sucking wind and found ready acceptance among the young students. Few understood Russian; almost all Communist literature came through translations from the Japanese or the French. Communists captured the minds of youth before they captured China militarily.

III

Such in brief was the Literary Revolution. What about the literary results and accomplishments? If we take stock of the creative writing in these four decades, writing done in the new medium, we may find half-a-dozen or so gifted writers, each of whom has in his own way left something worthwhile, or has advanced in some way the literary effort. On the other hand, I doubt that anything great has emerged from the literary harvest. I think I am justified in speaking of a certain halfheartedness, of a curious nervous debility, of the failure to reach great depth and power.

The causes of this phenomenon are not far to seek. They are due to factors in a transitional age, and perhaps also to the economic insecurity of the writers. In the first place, there is the question of the mastery of form, whether in verse, or the short story, or the novel, or the drama. The new literature in general takes modern Western works for its models. Some authors are clearly imitative, as in the case of the playwright Tsao Yü, who derives a great deal from Eugene O'Neill, or in the case of the novelist

432

Mao Tun, who handles the novel like Upton Sinclair. Secondly, there is the problem of fashioning and developing a new, adequate, and beautiful language from the spoken vernacular. Everyone tries to write in the Mandarin of Peking, but few have really mastered it. Instead of writing a language the common people really speak—graphic, picturesque, idiomatic, robust, taking its strength from the soil—most writers write a thin, attenuated, academic Mandarin, and some, under the leadership of Lusin, affect Europeanisms. Writers avoid the homely "jen-chia" for "people," and use an impossible innovation, "jen-men," because they wish to appear modern and indicate a plural. Instead of saying "happiness" by using the simple, homely "kuai-lo," or still better, "lo," as the common people speak, they use the atrocious "yü-kuai."

This is more important than one might think. One can always write tolerable Mandarin, but rare is the writer who writes beautiful Mandarin; just as it is not enough to write English, one must write good English, and good English is always pure, natural, concrete in imagery. In the case of exposition or essays discussing ideas, the problem is not so important; but in narrative prose, describing gestures, feelings, and dialogue, it is very important. On the other hand, on account of the affectations of Europeanization, much of the beauty and the elegance of the traditional tongue is gone. Sentences have become long, involuted, affected, and tortuous—something like Thomas Mann's German.

Assuredly, the spoken tongue is graphic and expressive. But there is so much beauty in the classical language, which must be drawn upon and forged into the fabric of the new language before the modern tongue can have both vigor and elegance. Of the characteristics in the current Chinese writing, elegance is perhaps the trait least to be found. All the established writers I shall mention have a good grounding in the classical language, which the younger generation by and large lacks.

Thirdly, there is the economic factor. Few writers have the security to devote themselves to writing. Writers, men and women, find it easier to write a short essay or a travel sketch, such as a trip to a certain temple, and call it a day. A great deal of so-called writing is journalism. A teacher will put together a dozen or two dozen sketches or essays and publish them as a book. Perhaps there is also not enough monetary incentive in a successful novel to justify a continuous, great creative effort. The most successful popular writer, Chang Hen-shui, often wrote a novel in serial installments for a daily paper.

Perhaps I am wrong. Charles Dickens wrote *The Pickwick Papers* in serial form; yet it lived. Maupassant and a host of others also wrote serially. Perhaps monetary incentive was important; perhaps it had nothing to do with it. Balzac, Sir Walter Scott, and Mark Twain in his later days wrote novels to pay debts. On the other hand, Tsao Hsüeh-chin, author of *The*

Dream of the Red Chamber, wrote the greatest novel without expectation of monetary reward. Shakespeare himself was quite busy and well-employed as an actor and shareholder in a theatre. He did not need to write plays for a living when he nevertheless wrote his great tragedies. Something has to come from the inside—an inner creative urge—the way *Uncle Tom's Cabin* was written. Perhaps external circumstances have nothing to do with it. Continuity, steady application, and concentration are required—but in the case of William Shakespeare, he didn't have time even to concentrate as he was called upon to walk in and out on the boards and to discuss business matters.

IV

I shall discuss a few names in connection with each of the categories: poetry, non-fiction, and fiction. I shall single out the more important ones.

The gatherings are most meager in poetry. This may seem strange in a land where once almost every scholar could write poems. The traditional Tang poem was thrown overboard. Dr. Hu Shih had advocated the free verse of Amy Lowell, and of course every young writer wrote free verse very freely. It was generally admitted that such attempts were sickening—not because free verse, with its subtler rhythm, could not be beautiful, but because freedom alone does not make verse. The majority of it was artless, jejune, puerile. First, because these would-be poets did not understand the technique of indirection and suggestion—an elementary mistake. Secondly, because they did not know that rhythm was essential in all poetry, as rhythm was rich, varied, and extremely pleasing in Sung lyrics. These writers had not grown up with Tang poetry, or Sung lyrics, or Yuan drama. There was no experiment in form; freedom meant no form. Free verse is more difficult to write well, having dispensed with known rhythms and the discipline being invisible. Worst of all, these writers nevertheless try, in place of varied rhythm, to use a kind of loose rhyme. So long as two lines end in something like loose rhyme, they call it a poem.

One exception is Hsü Yü. His lines, instinct with rhythm, come naturally. But perhaps the best poet was Hsü Tse-mo, who was a flambuoyant personality as well as a poet, and who died melodramatically when his plane crashed on the peak of Taishan. He studied at Clark University in this country and at Cambridge. I asked him what he did at Clark, and he answered drolly: "I attended classes." He was tremendously gifted. He alone, among my associates, had mastered, I may almost say created, a beautiful language out of the modern vernacular. Hsü Tse-mo is a case in point, proving that a modern tongue could be beautiful provided the writer knew how to draw upon the resources of the past. I recall my own vivid discovery. I had not heard of Hsü Tse-mo until after I had returned from Germany. One day I picked up a daily, the *Chenpao Fukan,* in my Peking hotel. I read a sketch of a walk in the rain by an unknown person, who signed himself Hsü Tse-mo. I was stunned. Here was the modern vernacular with all its power and beauty and glory. I had never read anything like it. Tse-mo had drawn fully, and richly, upon the Yuan dramas and Sung lyrics. The Yuan dramas, as you may know, were written in patois. I was sick of the debilitated, thin, quasi-modern Mandarin.

I give an example. The modern imported word for "idea" is "kuan-nien," but the real authentic vernacular word is "nien-tou." "Nien-tou" is a fine word; it has a certain tang; it means not only an idea, but also a secret thought, sometimes also a hankering, an itch, to do something. Nowadays, every writer has forgotten the use of this word and prefers to use the colder, academic word for "idea," "kuan-nien." Here was Hsü Tse-mo, who dared to use this word, and who gave us the vernacular with all its expressiveness and the overtones of the Yuan masterpieces and the Sung poets.

Lao Sheh, or Shu Sheh-yü, the author of *Rickshaw Boy,* is among the few who can write real Pekingese. He was born in Peking, and his style has the color and solidity of the North. However, he is not a poet, but a novelist, and while his prose is strong and vigorous, he has not the beauty and elegance of Hsü Tse-mo, drawn from the Sung and Yuan writings. Tse-mo forged the old and the new together into a thing of beauty.

V

In prose, I must speak of the Chou brothers, Chou Tso-jên and Lusin (Lu Hsün), both acknowledged masters. Like Chinese brothers and sisters, they are apt to fall into different political camps. Both the Chou brothers knew a great deal about old China—too much. Politically, Chou Tso-jên was a conservative, but his elder brother, Lusin (legal name, Chou Shu-jên), a caustic satirist, is now the hero of the Communists.

Hu Shih, writing always clearly and precisely, has gone more and more into research; his prose is in the service of historical research, distinguished by precision and clarity but not by beauty of style. It is the logical style of a rationalist.

Chou Tso-jên and a younger man, Chu Tse-ching (educated in London), stand out as examples of writers who give us pure, perfect prose in the modern vernacular. By pure prose I mean that natural flow of language, often conversational in tone and not keyed too high, such as we see in G. K. Chesterton or Hilaire Belloc, or, if you like, George Santayana. (I think Santayana's *Soliloquies in England* contains some of the most beautiful prose passages in English.) Chou Tso-jên gives eminently that sense of low-keyed natural flow of language. It is perfect in its way. It has always the tone of a familiar discourse. But his subject matter is old books and antiquities, and one must be pretty far detached from contemporary politics to enjoy reading him in serenity, with a cup of bitter tea. The familiar essay is his home ground.

However, I must hasten on to Lusin, the firebrand critic who exercised a power over the younger generation in the 1920's and 1930's, somewhat like H. L. Mencken, and who was just as caustic. (I mean the Mencken before he got married.)

Lusin wrote both short stories and witty, caustic comments on current topics, and he was quite successful in both forms. He is regarded today in Red China as Gorky is in Russia; both dead idols with their mouths shut. Stalin ostensibly highly esteemed Gorky, so long as he kept his mouth shut; and Lusin in his last-day conversation with Hu Feng sensed what was coming to freedom of thought and expression in individuals under a Communist regime. But idols are useful (provided their mouths are shut) and can be worshipped if they are dead. Lusin died at the beginning of the Japanese war. But he was a great voice crying death to the old society, and in the 1930's was influential as an instrument turning young China towards the left.

Thin, dour, small, a yellow face with a black bristly moustache and nicotine-colored teeth, he practically flayed old Chinese society alive with his wit and satire. His pen was vitriolic, rapier-like, or like barbed, poisoned arrows. He thought of himself more as a fighter than a writer. I can recall his wide grin when he knew his poisoned arrows had struck their victims. (I knew him in Peking, in Amoy, and in Shanghai, almost to the last years of his life.) Lusin's was a keen, sharp mind, reacting to a society and a political regime crying for a catastrophic change. He himself was a trained old bureaucrat; all the time he was egging the Peking students on to revolt, he was quietly drawing salary from the old tottering Peking government he was denouncing. The trouble was that he knew ancient China very well—too well—with its sophistication and its worldly-wise philosophy of living. He had studied in Japan (his brother had a Japanese wife), but he was from Shaoshing (Ningpo) and his style was based on the style of "Shaoshing shysters" ("shihyeh"), who knew how to kill a man with a single word placed in a precise position.

Of the writers destined to last as writers in this generation, I think Lusin was one. I always suspected that the man knew too much. The Communists were carrying on an intense fight to win over the minds of the students and writers in general at Shanghai in the 1930's. This fight to capture

436

and control the writers was as tightly organized as in a labor union, through cells directed from the top. It was a death struggle for the minds of youth in China. The Communists knew that those who controlled the youth of China controlled her future national destiny. It had its own vocabulary, war cries, and slogans. The so-called "Peh-hua" literature was not enough; it invented a term "mass literature" (tachung wenhsüeh). They also needed a leader and a symbol who would sway and influence the younger generation. Hu Shih was of course out of the question for the leftists. Lusin fitted into such a role perfectly. The Communists concentrated their fire on him, deriding him for his amorphous liberalism. His *Life of Ah Q* was considered an unwarranted attack on the proletariat. I was at the time living in Shanghai and saw the fight. Works by those who had joined the ranks, like Mao Tun, were invariably and disproportionately praised; those who refused to toe the line were invariably criticized and denounced. As we say in Chinese, one dog barks at a shadow, and a hundred dogs bark at barking. It was very hard for a young, aspiring writer to resist joining their ranks. I saw Lusin resist, argue, and fight for a year; then he turned tail and joined them to receive the crown which he knew was awaiting him. Overnight, his picture of Ah Q, the village idiot, instead of being a travesty on the masses, became the symbol of a class hero struggling against the oppressive bourgeoisie. If we understand his Shaoshing worldly-wisdom, we can understand why he became a convert. He knew he had a shrine guaranteed in the Communist pantheon.

However, there is a sad sequel. His widow, a very nice person, is now in Peking. I was ashamed to read the report that, when Miss Ting Ling, a veteran Communist writer was being disciplined and made to scrub floors because she had been haughty toward a local commissar, Mrs. Lusin also joined the pack of wolves and denounced her in rather unforgettable words: "Miss Ting Ling, by her haughty attitude toward our party comrade, showed that she has only contempt for the masses." This is what has happened to the widow of Lusin—a very nice person, as I knew her years ago.

VI

It is not possible to cover all the writers of fiction. I need only say that there were more successful writers of short stories than of novels. Of the writers of short stories, Lusin, Shen Tsung-wen, Feng Wen-ping (less known), and Hsü Yü are the best.

The most popular novelists today in Free China or Hong Kong are Chang Hen-shui and Nankung Po. Chang Hen-shui did some fine things in the past. Nankung Po is today writing historical novels; at least his novels have the faster pace required by the modern reader.

The other novelists now living in mainland China have quickly shut up. If you ask me what creative literature has come out of Red China in the last ten years, my answer is: Do not expect it. Of these novelists, Mao Tun has become a minister of culture. Kuo Mojo is reduced to writing paeans of praise to Chairman Mao Tse-tung and Stalin: "O thou sun in the heavens!" "O thou shining steel!" You keep repeating in this strain twenty or thirty times, and it is thought that by repeating it, it becomes poetry. Pajin, one of the most popular novelists, read by all school students, has not written anything under Communism. Miss Ting Ling, whom we have mentioned, received the Stalin prize for her novel, *The Sun Shines over the Sangkan River*, but she is now in disgrace because she personally offended a commissar. She has been a woman Communist writer from as far back as I can remember.

I think especially of Lao Sheh, the author of *Rickshaw Boy*. He also wrote a novel about a troupe of professional boxers, and he has seven or eight novels to his name. I knew him as a man of great integrity. He has a perfect command of Pekingese dialogue and a humorous style; his stories seem to spring from the soil of Peking. I remember seeing him during the war years in Chungking, and later at New Year. And I remember how he raved against the Kuomintang. He is completely silent now; he is not raving against anybody in power; nor is he prominent in the Communist hierarchy, like Mao Tun. He is completely silent. I wonder what he is thinking now.

VII

It is not that writers are unwilling to leave politics alone, but that politics will not leave the writers alone. The systematic persecutions of Hu Feng and of Yü Pingpo over the right of an individual to think his own thoughts assumed national proportions. It is almost incredible that the national campaign against Yü Pingpo on his interpretation of *The Dream of the Red Chamber* is not only ridiculous in its forcing politics upon a point of purely literary criticism, but also frightening in showing the statewide control of thinking. The articles against Yü in the papers in all the provinces, written on party orders, were published in two volumes, numbering over 600 pages. The USIS of Hong Kong has published a report on this case, extending to about 70 pages.

In conclusion, I should like to say only this: the spring of creative activity must always come from the individual spirit. Literature cannot be written to a formula. Where the individual spontaneity is suppressed, the creative spirit is choked at its source. A good land grows all kinds of flowers, all graceful and all different. In a marshy land, your eyes see for miles only a stretch of one color, the color of the reeds. In the spring of 1957, Chairman Mao Tse-tung told the writers: "Let the hundred flowers bloom, and all schools of thought contend." The writers were encouraged officially to express themselves. Presumably, we were going to see a sudden flowering of Mao Tse-tung's garden. Two months later the policy was reversed and the purge of the rightists began. Most writers who had dared to express their true feelings and opinions were sent to colonize Lanchow, Kokonor, Hainan, or some other frontier country. The beauty of a dictatorship is that a dictator does not have to explain why he condemned the free expression of opinions he so explicitly and officially invited two months before. He did not have to—that's the beauty of it—and nobody dared to ask why. I myself would like to ask Mao Tse-tung one question: "Mr. Mao, what about your garden now?"

The Progress of Realism in the Italian Novel

Giose Rimanelli

Presented at the Library of Congress January 23, 1961

ITALY IS A COUNTRY difficult to write about, and yet it calls out for writing. In Italy the novel as a literary form has no great tradition, but, paradoxically, Italian literature has a strong narrative vein.

We go in for miracles and paradoxes, or rather we delight in contradiction. For this reason, perhaps, we have a very special sense of humor, smiling but not ferocious, imaginative but never gloomy. We like to play with both the devil and holy water, to confound tragedy with farce and Shakespeare with the *commedia dell' arte*. It is through paradox that we manage to bare our souls. Without sacrificing our pride we manage to temper our paradoxes with realism.

Italian society is difficult to write about because it does not lend itself to the novel form. It is not a spiritually unified whole, whose various strata are in active relation one with the other through the common denominator of a language.

The reading public in France, England, and America has for over two hundred years found a recognizable picture, both individual and collective, in the novel. But in Italy this is not so. The historian Guicciardini said, at the time of the Renaissance, that our society had a fragmented soul, indicative on the one hand of vitality and genius, on the other of individuality pushed to the point of provincialism and jealous secretiveness, secretiveness turned upon itself and suspiciously resentful of probing.

Italian novelists—the great novelists, such as Verga and Manzoni— have had to work both upon this society and against it, like stoneworkers boring through layers of solid rock, not only from an artistic but also from a spiritual and social point of view. We have only to reflect that writers like Corrado Alvaro, Vitaliano Brancati, and Prince Tomasi di Lampedusa—

the first a Calabrian, the other two Sicilians—are considered in their native regions as slanderers and scandalmongers, to form an idea of the society which rejects them.

Corrado Alvaro is said to have disgraced Calabria by having poetically revealed the existence of deep psychological fractures in its social make-up. These fractures are bound up with the historical development of the region; the writer has uncovered them with deep and bitter understanding, as the products of an ancient and long-enduring civilization.

Prince Tomasi di Lampedusa, whose novel, *The Leopard,* is an international best-seller, was born, lived, and died in Sicily. He was a highly cultivated nobleman and, above all, a humane and melancholy observer of its people and places. He seems to be obsessed by the pervasive, congealing influence of the island's implacable sun. Under its stultifying rays there is no possible system of refrigeration or air-conditioning such as to preserve values from their inevitable decomposition. Even poverty is fossilized.

Here are a few lines from his book: "All around quivered the funereal countryside, yellow with stubble, black with burnt patches; the lament of cicadas filled the sky. It was like a death rattle of parched Sicily at the end of August vainly awaiting rain."

Elsewhere he observes that education, religion, law, and social relationships have not the same meaning as they have in other places. Pondering the decline of the Salina family, which is the protagonist of the novel, from a feudal status to a new condition brought about by Garibaldi's arrival, he notes with bitter scepticism that it is a microcosmic representation of universal misery—t' e misery of Sicily, a land sick for centuries, which has undergone numberless deaths without ever fighting against them; the prey of conquerors, who have brought with them both grandeur and destruction but have never been able to change the toneless character of the island and its people.

Geographical characteristics—the sun, the climate, the curse of the elements—have formed the singular character of the Sicilian people, which no government, no external factor, has power to change. These are the objects of Lampedusa's accusation. And the accusation takes the form of ironical self-criticism when he says: "I don't deny that a few Sicilians may succeed in breaking the spell, once off the island; but they would have to leave it very young; by twenty it's too late: the crust is formed; they will remain convinced that their country is basely calumniated, like all other countries, that the civilized norm is here, the oddities are elsewhere."

It is this analysis, distilled from the blood and tears of a dying man, a man who has known and loved his native island all too well, that has called down upon Lampedusa's head the appellation of slanderer.

It is plain, then, that the decline of neo-realism in Italian films is due not merely to the process of decay inherent in any artistic flowering but also to Italian society's inability to face the truth about itself or even to submit to a serious exploration of its character and situation. And society, of course, is equivalent to tradition.

We may, for instance, sum up the character of France by pointing to Paris, where all the provinces run naturally together. But we can never epitomize the character of Italy and Italian social life in the name of Rome, Florence, Naples, Venice, Sicily, or Lombardy. In every Italian novel we see not Italy as a whole, but only one particular aspect, because of the lack of a planned or unified society.

Naturally there is no question here of blame. For too many centuries Italy was only a geographical expression, divided into greater and lesser states, duchies and principalities, townships and villages. Although ever since the Middle Ages it produced literary and artistic masterpieces, they were the isolated accomplishments of a richly talented people rather than the expressions of an over-all Italian society.

The idea of an ethnically and spiritually united Italy was, from the 14th century on, a generous aspiration of our greatest statesmen and poets. If Dante Alighieri called upon Henry VII of Luxemburg to come rule Italy, it was not simply in order that he himself might return from exile to his native Florence, torn by the struggle for power between the two opposing factions of the Guelfs and the Ghibellines. It was because Dante saw in this emperor the only sovereign farsighted enough to achieve Italian unity, to found a civilization as durable as that of the Roman empire, a civilization which would bring a stable society in its train.

Centuries went by before this ideal of an Italian society took concrete shape at the time of the Risorgimento, with men like Mazzini and Cattaneo battling to build it. Before 1860, the year in which we won independence and Dante's dream became a reality, where was there any social and cultural background, such as that possessed by other nations for the novel as a reflection of manners or ideas? In Italy the novel came in only with the Romantic period.

Only when national unity is an achieved fact can it acquire value, consistency, and a character of its own. Until the development of Naturalism, during the last decades of the 19th century, the Italian novelist did not know to what segment of society he should address himself in order to be understood. Usually he wrote for an upper middle-class public, which was the only one that went in for reading. Most often his novels contained what this public wanted: not the honest and discriminating picture of a class-ridden society, a society of humble and downtrodden men and women, grappling with debts and the necessity of earning its daily bread at the price of daily death, but a picture of dancing legs and fancy-dress balls, of fairy

442

princes who occupied the dreams of adolescent girls, and, of course, of tears, facile, sentimental tears, devoid of sorrow or thought. For this public did not wish to think.

Uncertainty as to for whom and in what vein he should write drove the Sicilian novelist of this period, Giovanni Verga, who was born in 1863 and died in 1922, to turn inward and follow the dictates of his conscience by treating humble people. With the boldly experimental *House by the Medlar Tree,* Verga restored life to the submerged current of Realism, whose beginnings dated back to a remote past.

For there is genuine realism in the account of the damned in Dante's *Inferno,* and realism, in the sense of *realization* of the actual world and the human condition, although veiled in a conventionally theoretical form, in his *De Vulgari Eloquentia* as well. The Italian realistic tradition, which includes in its progress such a great Romantic novel as Manzoni's *I Promessi Sposi* (The Betrothed), came straight down from Boccaccio, Aretino, Lasca, and Bandello, all the way to Verga and such present-day writers as Silone, Pavese, and Moravia. Its vitality was manifest in the *dolce stil nuovo* of the 14th century with the *Chronicles* of Dino Compagni and Villani, then in the Renaissance, again in the period following the Risorgimento, and finally in our own day, after the Second World War.

As I have said before, the novel came to Italy in the Romantic period. And while the tradition of Realism was confined to the *novella,* or long short story, practiced by Boccaccio, Sacchetti, and Bandello, Verga was the first writer to bring Realism to the novel.

In between the late 19th-century naturalistic school and the neo-realist movement of today, many other kinds of novels were written. Among the most important was the historical or semi-historical novel, from the Risorgimento examples of D'Azeglio and Ippolito Nievo down to Riccardo Bacchelli's *Mill on the Po* and *The Leopard* by Lampedusa.

Although not realistic in character, many of these novels reflect the historical events of their time: war, social change, and scientific and philosophical discoveries. Others were affected either by the period of literary decadence, as in the works of Gabriele d'Annunzio (1863–1938), a past master of hedonism and an incomparable, although purely theoretical, instigator of the will to power and the glory of superman; or by the current of so-called *prosa d'arte,* dedicated to verbal dexterity and the cult of the written word drawn from the Aristotelian principle of "art as a source of pleasure and instruction"; and finally a few more by the rise of Fascism.

Fascism went in for appearances: for beautiful façades rather than the squalor which lay behind them; it had no basis of historically realistic theory. If Fascism had had anything realistic about it, it would have been aware of the absurdity and impossibility of its own existence and it would have expressed itself in a more human, less over-ebullient and damaging fashion. Fascist writers closed their eyes to reality and prated of the "Latin race" and the "Roman salute."

What, then, is the status of the realistic novel, this novel with no tradition among us, between Verga's day and our own, and who are its practitioners? Some writers now dead and some still living.

If you will allow me to make an admittedly personal choice, that is, one not yet bolstered up by any textbook, I shall venture to give you these names: Giovanni Verga, Italo Svevo, Federigo Tozzi, Corrado Alvaro, Francesco Jovine, Cesare Pavese. These are the dead. And among the living I place Alberto Moravia, Ignazio Silone, Vasco Pratolini, Giuseppe Berto, Italo Calvino, and Domenico Rea. There are also contemporaries who have made a stylistic and philological experiment in Roman dialect: Carlo Emilio Gadda and Pier Paolo Pasolini, and younger men who are trying out still other forms, such as Giovanni Arpino and Mario Pomilio, who have nevertheless not abandoned the mainstream of Realism.

Present-day Italy is full of youthful vigor. The Italian novel is gaining strength and maturity; it is attempting to defy the erosion of time. If it does not yet portray the multiple aspects of social life, it is because our society is still under construction. A new world, a new society, and a new tradition are in the making. We believe in the novel, in history, in man; and we believe, above all, in the implacability of life. Our belief has a deep-seated, almost scientific character. Our realism represents a humane, almost disconsolate vision, an attempt to take a segment of the world around us, to depict it with poetical intensity and endow it with a universal value.

Our realistic tradition, like our national life, is only a hundred years old. A hundred years seems a long time, if we stop to reflect that almost the whole of the Renaissance was encompassed by a single century. But it is a short time if we consider that the Elizabethan idiom could not have flowered as it did without the Humanism or the Renaissance that had gone before and the pictorial imagery of the French Pleiade, and that Dante's *Divine Comedy* was grounded in two centuries of Provençal literature, in the Sicilian school of Frederick II and in a hundred years of incubation in Tuscany.

A few names are sufficient to enhance the history or the literature of an entire century, and the contemporary Italian generation is one in which we may take pride. From a broader, European point of view, this century is quick-witted, dissonant, provisory, fantastic, and despairing, torn between willful mystification and obsession with truth; it is the century of Picasso, Garcia Lorca, Stravinsky, Schönberg, Valéry, Eliot, and Ungaretti. Painting, music, and poetry of the most extreme, sharp-edged kind predominate. But this age is not too propitious to fiction, except for the isolated examples

444

of the French Proust, the German Thomas Mann and Robert Musil, and the Irish James Joyce. In Italy, where the eclipse of Fascism was succeeded by a veritable rebirth, a return to the tradition of Verga caused the narrative form to come into its own.

The spiritual ancestors of contemporary Italian fiction are, then, Verga, Svevo, and Tozzi, whose talent developed in the period between the unification of Italy and 1928, but whose true significance was discovered only after the Second World War. Verga was overshadowed by the overwhelming vogue of d'Annunzio, Svevo declassed by the Fascists because he was a Jew, and Tozzi ignored on account of the fashion of *prosa d'arte*.

With his two novels, *I Malavoglia* (*The House by the Medlar Tree*) and *Mastro-Don Gesualdo,* and his short stories, Verga revolutionized Italian style. He focused his attention upon poor, humble, defeated people, depicting life not as a dream but as a reality, based upon genuine and fundamental feelings. Unlike the Naturalists of the turn of the century, who went in for realistic details but remained indifferent to them, Verga bent compassionately over the poverty of his Sicilian people, finding in them a source of distress and sorrow. Lampedusa, who was less close to Verga than to Stendhal, was so obsessed by the implacable nature of the land—a land prey to the elements and above all to a mythical, Babylonian, deified sun— that he said: "The fire could be said to snow down on us as on the accursed cities of the Bible." But Verga treated Sicily and its people in a tone of universal sadness and pity; he communicates to us the impression that all life is this way.

In several of his short stories and in the novel *Mastro-Don Gesualdo,* he lends concrete form and drama to the feelings for home and family; at the same time he uncovers another passion, the passion for land, and money, and possessions. The desire for wealth is not always inspired by solicitude for our children; it has an insatiable and unhappy existence of its own and is the cause of life-consuming grudges and quarrels. A donkey, passing from one master to another, symbolizes to Verga the weariness and futility of peasant existence, in which every ideal bows before the power of money. For the sake of land, the source of bread and death, the peasant wears his life away. After working his fingers to the bone and falling into the madness of avarice, the petty-minded peasant Mazzarò, in the short story *La Roba* (Property), is compelled to die and leave his worldly goods behind him.

Verga is not a pessimist; he is an interpreter of elemental and eternal feelings, overhung, as in Greek tragedy, by fate.

Italo Svevo was born in 1861 and died in 1928 in Trieste, a city which was under Austrian rule until the end of the First World War. His real name was Ettore Schmitz, but he adopted a pen-name, which may have

445

been meant to symbolize his mixed upbringing, half German, half Italian. Svevo was the son of a businessman, went to school in Germany, and held the job of a bank clerk. After his marriage, he became a director of his father-in-law's business and lived without financial worries until his death. Only his death was unconventional; it was caused by an automobile accident.

Even as a young man, Svevo had literary ambitions. He wrote and published three novels: *Una Vita, Senilità* (*As a Man Grows Older*) and *La Coscienza di Zeno* (*The Confessions of Zeno*), but no one paid them any attention. Two years before his death, when he was already an old man, he achieved fame, not in Italy but in France. When Italian critics learned that there was a "great" writer among them, they rushed to read his books. But, except for the poet Eugenio Montale, they said that there was a "strange" quality but nothing really worthy of note about him. Soon after this, for racial reasons, Fascism hushed up his name.

How did it happen, we may ask, that Svevo won recognition in France rather than in Italy? There is a very simple reason. One day there arrived in Trieste a wandering Irishman, who was at home nowhere in the world, neither in Dublin, nor Paris, nor Rome. This was James Joyce, the author of *Ulysses*. In order to help him out, the businessman, Ettore Schmitz, asked Joyce to give him English lessons. In the course of these lessons, Joyce read Svevo's manuscripts and sent one of them to Valéry Larbaud in Paris. Larbaud translated it and published it in an international review called *Commerce,* and Svevo emerged from obscurity to become a figure on the international scene.

The Confessions of Zeno is Svevo's masterpiece, the first important novel to reflect the discoveries of psychoanalysis. Svevo had met Freud in Germany and embraced many of his theories, although he proceeded to treat them in a half-joking manner. The theme of the novel is this: Zeno Cosini, an elderly, somewhat lethargic businessman of Trieste, is involved in sentimental complications and intoxicated by an excess of smoking. Having tried in vain to achieve a cure by conventional methods, he decides to submit himself to psychoanalysis. For six months, patiently and incredulously, he abandons himself to the free flow of his memories, which the psychiatrist has ordered him to put down on paper. This is the genesis of a succession of stories told in the first person, each one of them about some vice or unsuccessful experiment.

The novel oscillates between the two extremes of comedy and pathos. Zeno is ludicrous on account of the unpredictable vagaries of his character, pathetic in his desire to be normal. To be exact, he is neither a comic nor a tragic figure. He has a magnetic personality, which attracts both the comic and the tragic elements of life. But Zeno himself is unchanging;

446

his greatness lies in the fact that he remains a mediocre, average man. His attitude toward life is not unlike that of a Charlie Chaplin character. He has at the same time illusions of grandeur and disgust with its attainment. But whereas Chaplin's protagonists make heroic efforts to cope with life and love, the businessman Svevo is totally devoid of heroism. The moral which Svevo seems to draw is this: no man can be sure of his sanity. The world is sick, and not even psychoanalysis can cure it.

The Confessions of Zeno, published in Italy in 1923, ends with this frightening prophecy:

"Under the law of the greatest number of machines, diseases will prosper and the diseased will grow ever more numerous . . .

"When all the poison gases are exhausted, a man, made like all other men of flesh and blood, will in the quiet of his room invent an explosive of such potency that all the explosives in existence will seem like harmless toys beside it. And another man, made in his image and in the image of all the rest, but a little weaker than them, will steal that explosive and crawl to the centre of the earth with it, and place it just where he calculates it would have the maximum effect. There will be a tremendous explosion, but no one will hear it and the earth will return to its nebulous state and go wandering through the sky, free at last from parasites and disease."

Federigo Tozzi, the third great early twentieth-century writer, is quite the opposite of Svevo, inasmuch as he is concerned with an essentially religious problem. Tozzi was born in Siena in 1883 and died in Rome, at the age of 37 years, in 1920. Unlike Verga and Svevo, whose literary reputation is now fully assured, Tozzi still awaits discovery and recognition. He was neglected by his own generation, and ignored by the one that followed. Only the young people of today read him with pleasure.

Outside of Italy Tozzi is completely unknown. And yet he is the forerunner of a new type of fiction, concerned with the man whom the French call *l'étranger,* or *l'homme révolté,* and the Anglo-Saxons the "outsider." This literature is introspective and at the same time highly imaginative, based on the hallucination of living and an obsession with feeling; a literature of immobility and aimlessness, at whose center there is a man incapable of living in his own time, not because he fails to understand it but because he finds it confining; the maladjusted and unadjustable man, who moves without motivation and is driven to project himself beyond the limits of law and morality, the man who is alone in the world and knows it.

Tozzi's most important work, written in haste toward the end of his life, is composed of both novels and short stories: *Il Podere, Tre Croci, Giovani, Gli Egoisti, Ricordi di un Impiegato,* most of which were published only after his death, at a period when stylistic elaboration and cold-blooded aestheticism were in vogue. Tozzi wrote so crudely that the aesthetes saw in him nothing but bad grammar. Italian is an essentially lyrical language, just as German is energetic and Castilian formal. In one of his Italian sonnets Milton said: "Questa è lingua di cui si vanta amore" (this is the language of which love is proud). And an English translator of the Restoration period described it, somewhat exaggeratedly, as "the language of angels." Tozzi reduced this lyrical expression to everyday terms. Only in literature does a language, any language, attain rotundity and fullness. Spoken language is abrupt and contracted and capable of assuming unexpected power. To reproduce this power, which means to reproduce life itself, was Tozzi's unconscious aim; the same unconscious aim which led Emily Dickinson to write in a language wrought out of a raging earthly and yet heavenly passion.

Tozzi's novel *Il Podere* begins this way:

"In 1910 Remigio Selmi was twenty years old and assistant to the station-master of Campiglia. For some time he had been at odds with his father and he did not know that a sore on one of his feet, provoked by a shoe-nail, was rotten with gangrene. On the contrary, he thought that it had begun to heal . . . ."

The theme of loneliness, coupled with revolt, stems in Tozzi and in many of his European and American contemporaries from a feeling of physical discomfort. The fictional hero of our time, the man who is his own prison, is physically as well as spiritually disabled. We have only to open the books of Ralph Ellison, J. D. Salinger, Hortense Calisher, Samuel Beckett, and, above all, Carson McCullers, to find him "immobilized" for physical as well as psychological reasons. He is inept, out of place, a misfit, and a failure. What is the cause of this preference for the abnormal, when abnormality is not the general rule? Obviously, it is the fact that the misfit is more eloquent than the everyday man; he has a more intense and pitiless awareness of his own isolation. When his abnormality is raised to a poetic plane, it assumes the value of a symbol, of an interior predicament.

This is Tozzi's achievement. In Pirandello (a writer whom he greatly admired), the chasm between one human being and another is so deep that his heroes must don a mask in order to be their true selves. In Tozzi and his successors, an abnormal situation mirrors the spiritual isolation in which every one of us has his being. This does not mean that we have gone back to Schopenhauer, to a philosophy of total pessimism and negation. The weakling, the deformed and abnormal man has greater faith than his healthy, well-balanced brother. He has faith because nobody more than he feels the painful need of an escape into mystery. He believes because he is innocent. And innocence is both the greatest good and the greatest evil.

As I explained before, the absence in Italy of a society which lent itself to the novel prevented the continuation of Realism after Verga, Svevo, and Tozzi. But the realistic current came to the surface again in the 1930's, in such powerful writers as Corrado Alvaro (who died in 1956) and Alberto Moravia (born in 1907)—the former the author of *Gente in Aspromonte* and *Man Is Strong*, the latter of *The Time of Indifference*. It was reinforced by a group of younger writers: Elio Vittorini with *In Sicily*, Carlo Bernari with *Tre Operai*, Francesco Jovine (who died in 1950) with *Un Uomo Provvisorio*, and Ignazio Silone with *Fontamara*. But Silone lived in exile abroad, and it was only after the war that we came to know his approach to political and social problems.

In the 1930's, at the apex of Fascism, these anti-Fascist writers opened a new horizon. But it took the Second World War to create a real demand for a realistic treatment of man. Cesare Pavese, who has become the symbol of a whole generation, confessed: "We felt ourselves to be uprooted and primitive." This feeling of rootlessness characterized the earliest postwar writing. Behind us there was a blank wall, and our hearts were filled with bitterness and hate. But we took a step forward and resumed our writing. On what grounds none of us knew. We built on the smoldering ashes left by bombardment; we told stories of bloodshed and persecution, of the suffering of the whole world, and the offenses committed against the spirit of man. "Neo-realism" was born, or rather we turned back to the great Italian realistic tradition.

The postwar years constituted a veritable rebirth. Italian writers did not seek to parade their intelligence and talent; they wrote under the pressure of an internal necessity of expression, the expression of torment and sorrow. Italy's new culture brought out of the tragedy of a long-suffering world the redemption of the writer's art, restoring its original dignity, its purifying function as a collective catharsis for the human race.

The term "neo-realism" was first applied to motion pictures such as Rossellini's *Open City*, De Sica's *Bicycle Thief*, and De Santis' *Bitter Rice*, which portrayed man's desperate and defenseless existence in a world stripped of its myths and ravaged by war. Finally the term came to be applied to literature, to a literature concerned with peasants and partisans, with laborers and white-collar workers, with prostitutes and street urchins. Carlo Levi's internationally famous *Christ Stopped at Eboli* was the first documentary witness of the return to man and his tragic human condition, man at the same time Christian and pagan, poor but not despairing, resigned to the political tyranny of the centuries, and just beginning to understand how to go about overcoming it and obtaining the material and spiritual sustenance which is his due.

Years before, in *Gente in Aspromonte,* Corrado Alvaro had described the hard and lonely life of the Calabrian shepherds, from a humane point of view, which was almost mystical or mythical in nature.

"It is not easy, the life of the shepherds of Aspromonte in winter, when the swollen streams run down to the sea and the Calabrian land seems to float upon the waters. The shepherds live in huts made of reeds and mud and sleep beside the sheep. They go about in long cloaks, attached to a rectangular cape thrown over their shoulders, in the guise of a wandering and wintry Greek god."

But in the postwar years the search for reality became more detailed, more pointed, and the new writers were guided not only by a reawakened conscience but by a sense of history as well.

Both these elements are found in the work of Ignazio Silone, who came back to Italy from exile after the war and made a notable contribution to our rediscovery of ourselves and the reality around us. Silone is constantly concerned with the problem of freedom. "In the world of today," he writes, "a culture which cannot resolve the class struggle and the status of colored peoples is a dead letter." At the same time, his work gives a new dimension to the social novel; it goes beyond mere investigation or political doctrine and encompasses the color and sound and fabric of the human condition.

In Alberto Moravia, who together with Silone is perhaps the Italian writer most widely known abroad, the "human condition" seems, at first glance, to be restricted to a mixture of lethargy and vice. As one of his characters says: "You're wrong. . . . There's no purification, no expiation, no family to fall back on, only indifference, nothing but indifference." His "courtesans" habitually wallow in vice and turpitude, without believing in either sex or reason, simply because they have not enough initiative to rise above a background of unhappiness and dirty sheets.

Moravia's world, like Svevo's, is sick. But unlike Svevo, Moravia does not treat it ironically. His art is hard and metallic. He does not take refuge in pretense or escape, because he does not believe in them, or in pity either. He sees no refuge for man except in vice, and for this reason his picture of society is a deformed one. He is not negative, but he is completely pessimistic. Having his cultural roots in post-Romantic decadence, he is attracted by the violent erotic contortions of the Marquis de Sade, rather than by the healthy lustiness of the characters, such as Moll Flanders, created by Daniel Defoe. Nevertheless his work is important. *The Time of Indifference, Agostino, Two Women,* and his most recently published novel, *La Noia,* have a delicate, poetical feeling.

Vasco Pratolini, born in Florence in 1913, is another realist who nurtures the honest ambition of making a narrative reconstruction of the Italy of the past century and our own. His best-known novel, *A Tale of Poor Lovers*, does not put forward the unattainable claim of mirroring the whole of Italian society, but it does mirror a street and a period. The period is Fascist, the street Florence's Via del Corno, and the novel is their epic. In his more recent books Pratolini is trying to widen his horizon. Under the comprehensive title, *Una Storia Italiana*, he has published two volumes, *Metello* and *Lo Scialo*, of an over-all picture of Italian life. Pratolini is a writer deserving of our sympathetic attention.

Other realists are Giuseppe Berto (born in 1914), whose novel, *The Sky is Red*, written in a Texas prison camp, is a tellingly dramatic account of Italian children under bombardment; Domenico Rea (born in 1921), whose volume of short stories, *Gesù Fate Luce*, and the novel, *Una Vampata di Rossore*, give an incomparable picture of the irreverent and pitiful aspects of the lower class of Naples; and Italo Calvino (born in 1923) who has written, with artful linguistic dexterity, a series of erotic, sentimental, courtly tales, which hark back to the period of pre-Romanticism and 18th-century Enlightenment. The three short novels, *Il Visconte Dimezzato*, *Il Barone Rampante*, and *Il Cavaliere Inesistente*, are apparent satires of the courtly life of far-removed, almost legendary times, with picaresque themes reminiscent of Ariosto and Cervantes. But they are also impregnated with modern "awareness" and human feelings which go deeper than their manneristic form.

Unfortunately, for lack of time, I cannot speak at further length about these and other writers such as Ugo Moretti, Carlo Cassola, Michele Prisco, Natalia Ginzburg, Mario Soldati, and Elsa Morante. But before concluding our panoramic view of the contemporary novel I should like to talk, in greater detail, of a writer who contains within himself the creative and spiritual travail of our whole generation. This writer is Cesare Pavese.

Pavese was born in a Piedmontese village in 1908 and began his literary career—or rather acquired his early reputation—as a translator. Along with Elio Vittorini, he made American literature available to Italy. He did excellent translations of Melville's *Moby Dick*, of Sherwood Anderson, Faulkner, Gertrude Stein, and Dos Passos, and his critical essays were the first precious clues to a school of fiction and a society heretofore almost unknown to Italians. His first novel, *Paesi Tuoi*, came out during the war, but only when the war was over did he completely reveal himself. He brought out one book after another: *Feria d'Agosto*, *Il Compagno*, *Prima che il Gallo Canti*, *La Bella Estate*, and, finally, *The Moon and the Bonfires*.

On August 27, 1950, a year in which he had reached the peak of his fame, he killed himself in a Turin hotel. Something almost impossible to understand had happened to him. As he gained in objective, human

understanding, and poetic purity, he felt his own personality and psychological endurance slipping. His life was a continuous dialogue with death,
in which he saw the only possible means of escape. He was a solitary,
tormented man, who failed in love, friendship, and political coherence.
His only positive achievement was that of a writer, and this did not give
him satisfaction. Pavese left an important legacy behind him. The subject matter and style of his books have been widely imitated, and he has
attained the status of a classic. He was a faithful interpreter of the age
of anxiety; his courageous insistence upon learning and speaking the truth
was the foundation of his artistic gestation and the path which led him
to poetic expression.

Pavese's work has the dual theme of city and country. The country
was a reservoir of recollections, the hills among which he grew up, the
mythical age of childhood; the city was a symbol of crowded streets and
intellectual development. This theme is like that of Sherwood Anderson,
to whom the whole modern world lies in the contrast between country and
city, between innocence and empty vanity, between the grandeur of nature
and the pettiness of man. In the virile loneliness in which all his characters are enveloped, Pavese entered into the world of myth.

When we read Pavese we must not look for a logical story, for definite
characters, and a clear succession of events. Pavese makes use of symbols,
and these are the elements of his poetic power. His poetry consists of
rhythm, of the color of the hills, the passing of seasons, of villages, trades,
of inarticulateness and stubborn solitude, of the pain of living, and of a
melancholy hope. His protagonists are often women, city women and
country women, who pass by, leaving in their wake an odor of skin and
daily renewed life, like that of grass and earth and stars. This is true also
of the woman he loves, on whom he weaves endless variations: "You are
life and you are nothing"; "You are morning and sunlight"; "You are the
expectant earth"; "You are life and death"; "You step lightly."

In the adventure of postwar literature, Pavese was our dearest, most
trusted companion.

As of today, the novel is undergoing a process of change and fragmentation the world over. The experiments of the French writers Butor, Simon,
Robbe-Grillet, and Nathalie Sarraute are signposts. To many contemporary novelists, lost in the technique of expression, man is a "superannuated animal." To others, the novel is a literary form which is doomed to
oblivion. Are we to write novels that are no longer novels, until the novel
loses all value and there is a psychological or psychoanalytical disintegration of the whole literary form?

In music and painting this disintegration is already here. Many contemporary pictures are beyond the limits of human feeling and understand-

452

ing. They lie on a crystal bier of time; the life and heart have gone out of them, and only intellect remains as a source of emotion. D. H. Lawrence's call of nature is a fossil, relegated to pre-history. There is today an attempt to achieve something new, not a form of art such as man has practiced from his beginnings until the present day, but something that goes beyond art, in a world where only technique, working not through the spirit but through the automatized human carcass, is capable of reproducing the arabesques of a lost world, a world gone by.

There is an attempt to achieve something new, and already we have entered a state of profound crisis. We ask: Where are values? Did values ever exist? What use are they? Terrestrial, human, carnal, pathetic, miserable, useless, necessary values, as necessary as hope, as indispensable as love. Where are values, if everything is doomed to perish in the abyss prophesied by Italo Svevo?

I am a contemporary writer, a product of my time. I refuse to wear blinders. I refuse to perch on a pillar, like Saint Simon Stylite, intent upon the contemplation of the abstract. Abstraction is an escape from responsibility, a form of cowardice. I am convinced that man will never be a superannuated animal. Whether he lives in a happy or a bankrupt society, it is only when he ceases to look into his heart that art is obliterated. The more responsible Italian writers know this. They know that, whatever the future may hold, art will continue to exist, just as long as the real and tangible world in which we are living. Our only faith in life and in the art which we are striving to attain by writing is in these words: May life go on!

The Contemporary Literature of Spain

Arturo Torres-Rioseco

Presented at the Library of Congress January 30, 1961

Poetry

TO WRITE ABOUT the contemporary literature of Spain we must keep in mind two important factors: one of a literary nature, the existence of the Generation of 1898, the other of a political nature, the Civil War of 1936.

The Generation of 1898, comparable in its brilliancy and its depth to the Golden Century, will have to be restudied and redefined. After two centuries of literary mediocrity, lack of artistic sensibility, emphasis on erudition rather than on creative intelligence, verbose display of virtuosity, prosaic expression and didactic conceptions, after many years when such names as those of Larra, Bécquer, and Pérez Galdós were exceptional, the writers of 1898 played the role of vindicators, pioneers, and saviors. Never before in the literary history of Spain had there been—except in the Golden Century—such a compact, integrated group of authors. Every literary genre was represented by an outstanding figure: the novel by Baroja, Unamuno, Valle-Inclán; the essay by Unamuno, Azorín, Maeztu, and a little later by Ortega y Gasset; lyric poetry by Antonio Machado and Juan Ramón Jiménez; the drama by Jacinto Benavente. The excellence of this generation made it difficult for future writers to surpass their achievements.

The Civil War of 1936 had a tremendous impact on the intellectual life of the nation. Some of the great writers were killed (Maeztu, García-Lorca); a few died as a direct result of the tragedy (Unamuno, Machado); many went into exile and died abroad (Jiménez, Salinas, Barea); others are still living in foreign lands (Guillén, León Felipe, Alberti, Francisco Ayala, Sender). For a few years Spanish literary works were written and published in France and in Mexico, Argentina, or other Latin American

454

countries. We may, then, set the year 1936 as a dividing point between two types of literature; before the Civil War we find the traditional free expression of Spanish genius; after the war we observe an inner struggle, a disintegration of moral purposes.

For reasons better known to the sociologist than to the literary critic, the period preceding the Civil War was one of great lyrical intensity. A pleiad of great poets appeared in the 1920's under the influence of Antonio Machado and Juan Ramón Jiménez. These poets were characterized by an unusual knowledge of literary technique and by a spirit of experimentation. For this reason, the celebration of Góngora's third centenary, in 1927, gave them a pretext to graft avant-garde theories upon a traditional "culteranismo" and appear at the same time as national and universal poets.

Significantly, the pioneers of the new school in Europe were second-rate poets and have already been forgotten. The forgotten are the futurist Marinetti in Italy, the ultraist Guillermo de Torre in Spain, the creationist Vicente Huidobro, as well as the Rumanian dadaist Tristan Tzara. These earlier poets thought that the essence of poetry was a formula and that the relation between poet and life was that of the mechanic and the machine. However, their achievements were so bold that they cleared the way for the generation of 1927, a group of seven poets: Pedro Salinas, Jorge Guillén, Federico García-Lorca, Rafael Alberti, Dámaso Alonso, Vicente Aleixandre, and Luis Cernuda.

This pleiad, although compact and characterized by the highest aesthetic attitude, was formed by strong individualists. They all shared the knowledge of Spanish popular poetry, French symbolism and surrealism, the complex technique of gongorism. Their masters are Juan del Encina, Gil Vicente, Garcilaso, San Juan de la Cruz, Lope de Vega, Góngora, Bécquer, Machado, Juan Ramón Jiménez, Mallarmé, Baudelaire, Paul Valéry. All these poets are intellectual, scholarly, abstract, with a deceiving appearance of simplicity. But here the similarity ends. Temperamentally they have little in common; organically they seem to belong to different periods and geography.

Strictly intellectual and abstract is Jorge Guillén (1893), author of the book *Cántico,* in which, following Mallarmé and Valéry, he reaches the peak of artistic perfection in form and deep poetic vision. Pedro Salinas (1892–1952) is also an intellectual poet, a high exponent of the tendency of "pure poetry" and conceptual expression. His best book, *La voz a ti debida* (1949), shows perfect command of technique and genuine sentiment. Federico García-Lorca (1899–1936) is the most popular and best-known poet of the group. His tragic death gave him universal renown. *Romancero gitano* and *Bodas de sangre* are known the world over. Lorca is an intuitive, organic, spontaneous, and passionate poet, a virtuoso of form, a magician of the metaphor and of the picturesque. In his poem *Poeta en Nueva York* he fell under the spell of Walt Whitman. Lorca is also the only truly memorable dramatist of modern Spain. Rafael Alberti (1902) is the airy poet of Andalusian charm, a poet "con ángel," as they say. He goes from one formula to another with agility and grace: traditionalist in *Marinero en tierra*, gongoristic and baroque in *Cal y canto*, surrealist in *Sobre los ángeles*, proletarian in his later years. At present, like his compatriot Leon Felipe, he may be called the poet of sorrow and exile. Dámaso Alonso (1898), the most distinguished aesthetician and literary critic of his country, is also a remarkable poet. His book *Hijos de la ira* reveals the tormented mind of modern man, lost in his own liberty, facing the unknown. He is distressed by human limitations, searching in vain for the ultimate truths. Between the skillful manipulation of his verse and his agonizing search for revelation, one may find one of the most original poets of present-day Spain. Vicente Aleixandre (1900) is a vital and intense poet, who accepted early in his life the surrealist credo. Poetry for him is a serious job, dedicated to the knowledge of man and his fate. *La destrucción o el amor* shows his anguish in a chaotic world and also his hope for human salvation. Surrealism acquires a new dimension in this poet, a human intensity in the expression of his favorite themes: love and death.

The last poet of this intellectual generation is Luis Cernuda (1904). He followed first the romantic poetry of Bécquer and later that of Jiménez. Pedro Salinas initiated him into the cult of French poetry, and Cernuda became a follower of Baudelaire, Mallarmé, Laforgue, Reverdy, and the surrealists. During the Civil War, Cernuda went to Oxford and Glasgow and Cambridge (1938), and there he read T. S. Eliot and the English metaphysical poets. Cernuda is a poet who in a few years has passed through several tendencies. He began as a classical writer; then he became intoxicated with the metaphor of Góngora; in England he decided to write free verse and to establish a balance between the spoken and the written language. As in the case of Aleixandre, his simple style has changed the surrealist patterns. Cernuda is above all an Andalusian poet.

All these poets cultivate the abstract, metaphorical form of "poesía pura," but they overworked literary techniques to such an extent that their work became dehumanized. Perfection in itself is not the ultimate ideal of the poet. The present generation of poets, those born about 1910—Vivanco, Panero, Rosales, Hernández—reacted against the dehumanization in the work of their predecessors and returned to a conception of poetry in which human values were more important. As a matter of fact, the later poets of this group acquired a real social consciousness. And yet, they continued to be, above all, artists and to consider that the essence of poetry is beauty. The desire of these writers to harmonize the spoken

456

language with the written language and to respect the traditional Spanish style led them to Garcilaso instead of Góngora, to Unamuno instead of the modernists.

Luis Felipe Vivanco (1907) is a Catholic poet who follows in intensity Unamuno's religious anguish. Juan Panero (1908–37) is a neo-petrarchian poet. Through human love he reaches a mystic level of beauty and achieves a sense of immortality in solitude and death. Leopoldo Panero (1909) follows the theory of the "spoken language" and daily inspiration. One of his collections of poems, entitled *"Escrito a cada instante"* (1949), presents a basic existentialist reality. Luis Rosales (1910) returns in his poetry to the cult of the word over the image. Even the titles of his books reveal this fact: *Abril* (1935), *Retablo sacro* (1940), *La casa encendida* (1949). Rosales displays in his work the classical severity of Valéry and the technical skill of Góngora, but again he makes use of the spoken language and of the charm of everyday expression.

Miguel Hernández (1910–42) is the legendary poet of the Civil War. He was originally a goat-herder, then a poet, endowed with a rich imagination and a sensitive temperament. Hernández is potentially as great a poet as García-Lorca. He assimilated conventional formulas and poetic devices. In his youth, under the influence of Góngora, he writes *Perito en lunas* (1933), a vivid mosaic of primitive forces and of intellectual patterns. Then, when Hernández discovers love in the person of Josefina, his senses and his ideal of beauty fight an ardent battle in his next book, *El rayo que no cesa* (1936). In 1936 Hernández, now a soldier in the Civil War, writes his vigorous *Viento del pueblo* (1937), in which he anticipates his death: "I shall die singing, like the bird." Blood and Death are the subject matter of his great poem, "Es sangre, y no granizo." Finally, in his *Cancionero y romancero de Ausencias* (1938–41), Hernández laments his last years in jail, his physical and moral tortures, the separation from his wife and child. Every verse in this book is a fragment of death, a needle of agony, a tacit accusation of a callous, stony world.

Dionisio Ridruejo (1912), the last poet of this group, shows the struggle between the realistic experience, the human condition, and the deep-rooted literary influences of Garcilaso, Quevedo, and Unamuno. He returns to a more traditional approach to poetry in his *Elegías,* to become later a social poet.

Finally, Victoriano Crémer (1910) and, of the more recent poets, a few such as Carlos Bousoño (1923), Eugenio de Nora (1923), and José María Valverde (1926), all scholarly writers, believe in popular poetry. They have a traditional understanding of poetry, due to the influence of the 15th-century writers, and a certain regional coloring, Galician or Andalusian. But let us not forget that all the modern poets of Spain, from

Manuel Machado to José Hierro—including such abstract poets as Guillén and Salinas—evidence a great fondness for the popular forms.

It would be more logical to expect the popular forms in the poets of social inspiration. Among these, Victoriano Crémer believes that poetry must have a message and must communicate such a message to the "men who work, suffer and die," that its ideas should be clear, and that the poet should have a kind heart. Gabriel Celaya (1911) is of the opinion that poetry is the best instrument for transforming and improving the world. Blas de Otero, temperamentally the most dissatisfied and rebellious poet of his generation, is a true existentialist, like Miguel de Unamuno. His poem "Crecida" is the clamor of a young man walking upon the old earth of Europe with a horrible feeling of thirst, screaming in a vortex of blood, "with blood up to his waist, sometimes up to the edge of his mouth; a young man who walks with a rose of blood in his bloody hands, because there is only blood in Europe."

The Novel

By 1925 Ortega y Gasset had begun to expound his ideas about the decadence of the novel. Statistically he proved that books with an ideological content were more in demand than works of fiction. He denied that the artistic creation depended exclusively on that subjective and individual gift, inspiration and talent. To him talent is a subjective faculty acting on objective matter. This matter is independent of the individual gift and, if it is lacking, ability and genius are of no use. The first problem of the modern novelist is this: the novel as a genre has only limited possibilities. In its origins it was rich and abundant, but the earlier novelists exhausted the primary source and now there is little left. Today it is practically impossible to discover new themes.

The second problem is more serious: as the novelist discovers and uses new themes, the sensibility of the reader becomes more exacting; he demands better, more unusual, and newer themes. It becomes increasingly difficult to please the modern public, and even the classic novels lose their appeal. On the one hand, the novelist has great difficulty in finding new topics; and on the other, he has created a more sophisticated public.

For these reasons, Ortega believed that if the genre was not completely exhausted, it was in a dying stage, and that the thematic poverty was such that the novelist had to compensate for it with the exquisite quality of the other ingredients necessary to integrate the work of fiction.

These theories were not new and did not presage the death of the novel; on the contrary, they clearly showed its vitality, the modernization of the genre, for, if the story runs thin, the causality of the narrative, the plot,

458

may be more logical; the penetration into the characters deeper and their relation and the inner life of the author more intimate; the display of imagination stronger; the realm of fantasy touching on the supernatural; a new view of humanity more authentic; and, finally, the thin thread of the narrative will be strengthened by the precision and beauty of the style.

It is strange that Ortega should have written his observations on the decadence of the novel at a time of new experimentations in the world of fiction. Ramón Pérez de Ayala wrote his intellectual novels during those years: *Belarmino y Apolonio* (1921), *Tigre Juan* (1926), *El curandero de su honra* (1926). Gabriel Miró, a great stylist rather than a novelist, published *El humo dormido* (1919), *Nuestro padre San Daniel* (1921), *El obispo leproso* (1926), and *Sigüenza* (1917), in which the anecdotic story is only a pretext to show his incomparable artistic sensibility. Ramón Gómez de la Serna published *Pombo* (1918), *El doctor inverosímil* (1921), *El torero Caracho* (1926). Ramón transformed the "greguería" into a novel and became the king of the metaphor and the grotesque. Pérez de Ayala is essentially an essayist; Miró is basically a lyric poet; Ramón is a great humorist. And yet, the three are the representative novelists of Spain during a period of revolution and artistic experimentation.

Ortega y Gasset, explaining the importance of subject matter in fiction, uses this plastic metaphor: "Imagine a gifted woodman in the Sahara. His elastic muscles and his sharp ax would be useless. The woodcutter without the forest is an abstraction."

Thinking of what has happened in Spain in recent years, I feel a strong desire to reverse the metaphor and say: Imagine a woodcutter with a broken ax in the Amazonian jungle; or better still, let us imagine the forest without a woodcutter. A forest without a woodcutter becomes an abstraction.

The following affected the contemporary novel in Spain. The Civil War began in 1936 and ended in 1939; its devastating consequences are still affecting the Spanish nation. The rhythm of life has been altered so radically that a man living in 1935 could hardly understand Spain in 1961. The novel, a direct product of life, suffers a similar fate, and I do not think that the readers of today could enjoy the novel of Pérez de Ayala or Miró, and even less the works of Azorín or Valle-Inclán.

It is understandable that between 1936 and 1939 nothing of lasting value was produced in Spain. It is obvious that in the following years a sense of disappointment and defeat kept the creative genius of the Spaniard under a heavy cover of disillusion, fear, and a constant feeling of guilt; many writers died during the conflict; many others went into exile. The Spaniard who had participated in the war or witnessed it knew that his world was coming to an end, as it really did. It was up to the new generation to re-establish

459

the continuity of the intellectual and artistic life, without which the Spanish nation would have no meaning in the world today.

After six years of literary silence, the first novel of a new Spanish society appeared in 1942. It was entitled *La familia de Pascual Duarte* [1] and the author was Camilo José Cela (1916). The novel became a bestseller and more than eight editions were published in a few years. This fact in itself was a poor sign. The main character of the novel, Pascual Duarte, is, according to his father confessor, "a sweet lamb, harassed and frightened by life." The only trouble with the "sweet lamb" is that his tender hands— like the hands of Lenny in Steinbeck's *Of Mice and Men*—have the instinct to kill. First he kills innocent animals, then he kills a man, later he kills "el estirao," his wife's lover, and finally he kills his own mother. Pascual Duarte's life is then a gallery of crime, presented in a strong vernacular style and by the extraordinary boldness of the author, who challenges the reader with arbitrary and picturesque expressions of form and depictions of character.

This is one novel that should not be analyzed. One must accept it or not, as it is. Some people may take it as a tragic book, man's fate; others as an amusing book in which anything may happen. Cela himself believes that Pascual is a primitive and logical man; he seems to justify the assassination of the mother who had caused Duarte's unhappiness. The tremendous brutality of the book has given birth to a new movement in Spanish literature, the "tremendismo." Parenthetically, it is interesting to note that *Pascual Duarte's Family* was published the same year as *L'Étranger*, by Albert Camus. There are certain technical and philosophical similarities between the two books: the element of man and his circumstances, the sense of blind fate, a disdain for institutional justice, etc. But what an abysmal difference in the construction, sincerity, and sensibility of the two novels!

Encouraged by the great success of his first novel, Cela wrote in 1953: "I consider myself the most important novelist since the Generation of 1898 and I am shocked to consider how easy it has been. I apologize for being unable to avoid it." [2]

Cela's most ambitious work, *La colmena*, was published in Buenos Aires in 1951.[3] I do not know why Cela published the book outside his country, or if this edition was sold in Spain. In 1955 a second edition appeared in Barcelona.[4] In a short note to the first edition Cela offers some glimpses of his state of mind. He tells us that *La colmena* is a pale reflection

---

[1] (Madrid, Burgos, 1942). Translation: *Pascual Duarte's Family* (London, Eyre and Spottiswoode, 1946.)

[2] *Baraja de invenciones* (Valencia, Castalia, 1953.)

[3] (Buenos Aires, Emecé, 1951.)

[4] (Barcelona, Noguer, 1955.)

of harsh, deeply felt, painful reality. *La colmena* is a slice of life narrated step by step, without reticence or strange tragedies or charity, exactly as life is: "today the only way to write novels is the way I do it. It was difficult for me to write this novel; its construction is complex; the action takes place in Madrid, in 1942, among a torrent of people, sometimes happy, sometimes not; the 160 persons (somebody has counted 346) that move through its pages, have brought me during five long years along roads of bitterness. I do not know whether this novel is realistic or a novel of manners. Nor do I care." The novel is of the crudest realism. It deals with the life of Madrid seen in the café, the brothel, the dairy bar. Society is like a beehive in which every being has its role and its importance. There are no heroes and heroines; no character has more value than another. The overwhelming forces in the novel are hunger and sex; there is no emotion although sometimes a reflected tenderness. There is no construction, no plot, no development—only sketches, incidents, endless dialogue. The characters are presented as if they were things, in brief action, objectively. They remain coldly incomplete, like people in a movie. Luckily so, for had Cela developed his characters, he would have given us a novel of a hundred thousand pages.

The style of *La colmena* is rich, abundant in slang, full of popular flavor, crude, vulgar, profane, but with a masculine charm, with that typically Spanish bravado called "machismo." I believe that from the time of Cervantes nobody has surpassed Cela in the mastery of the vernacular, in the unusual capacity for the linguistically grotesque, in the use of the picaresque expression, the savory adjective, and the humor with which he adorns his baroque descriptions.

Although *La colmena* may not be a novel in the conventional sense of the word, it deserves to be considered as an outstanding fictional creation, a vigorous presentation of life with intense human pathos, buried under an apparently total cynicism and sarcasm. And beyond, perhaps, there is a deeper significance, a human message that the author had to veil. Let us remember that Cela said in the brief note of introduction to *La colmena*: "My novel is being published in Argentina for special reasons."

In other novels Cela experiments with new themes and new forms of style. In *Pabellón de reposo* (1944), he describes in a poetic form life— or rather death—in a tubercular sanitarium; in *Nuevas andanzas y desventuras de Lazarillo de Tormes* (1944), Cela is at home both in subject matter and language; in *Mrs. Caldwell habla con su hijo* (1953), Cela has proved that his confidence in his own talents, and in the reader's patience, is inexhaustible.

Lately, Cela has written several books of short stories, travels, descriptions of small towns, people, institutions, customs. Here, in this genre, he is at

461

his best. He has Cervantes' talent for observation, the distorted but deep penetration into reality of a Goya, and a unique gift of language. Perhaps the field of the sketch is his "forte," but I do not expect Cela to share this opinion.

In 1944, after a long slumber of the intellectual life of Spain, the novel *Nada* appeared in Barcelona. The author was an unknown young girl, Carmen Laforet. *Nada* was awarded the first Eugenio Nadal Prize. These three factors—the literary vacuum, the sex of the author, and the award— were all important for the destiny of a book which took Spain by storm. *Nada* became a best-seller overnight because thousands of copies were sold, differently from the case of *Pascual Duarte's Family*, about which thousands of articles were written. *Nada* was published in Spain, in Latin America, and as a textbook in the United States.

Did Miss Laforet write her novel with the hope that it might be made into a motion picture? *Nada* does have many of the features of a scenario: movement, realism, drama, pathos, superficiality, mystery, declamatory style, abnormal characters, intensity. Juan Luis Alborg reminded us that Charlotte Brontë's *Wuthering Heights* was, at the time, extremely popular in Spain as a picture, as a novel, and as a radio narrative. The two novels have elements in common, yet the subject matter is entirely different.

Nada is strictly an autobiographical novel. The narrator, Andrea, goes to Barcelona to live at her relatives' home. What happens to Andrea among her uncles and aunts is the story of the book. The house is old and the family is disintegrating after the Civil War. The first part of the novel, in which Andrea describes her conflicts with her relatives, is intense, passionate, of great human interest; the second part, which deals with Andrea's university friends, is inane. The characters of the first part are convincing in their psychoses, their abnormality, or their lack of spirit. Román, a frustrated artist, is a perverse type of Don Juan, crowned by a halo of vice and decadence. He ends his life by suicide. His brother Juan is an abnormal and brutal individual, redeemed by his love for his child. Gloria, his wife, is superficial, beautiful, lazy, but she has a good heart. Angustias, a strong woman who lives on her memories of the old grandeur, hides behind a domineering front a great hunger for tenderness. She becomes a nun. The grandmother is kind and humble like all Spanish grandmothers, and, like them, shallow and foolish. Finally, the most striking person in the book is Antonia, the servant, who is silently in love with Román. Constantly followed by her black dog, she resembles a tragic figure in a painting by Goya.

Miss Laforet describes the hatred, love, suffering, goodness, or perversity of these people. She grows in intensity with them. The effects of the Civil War take on a new dimension in this novel, as if people had lost contact with their reality and were living in some spectral and ghastly world.

But Andrea revolts. She attends the university and meets normal people, which in her life constitutes her salvation, but in the novel becomes her doom. The level of the work of fiction descends; it becomes a bit too normal. Her friends of the "new generation" call for more common adjectives. Her best friend, Erna, is "intelligent, beautiful, alert"; Erna's fiancé is "good, serious and rich"; Andrea's boy friend, who belongs to a "social generation," is soon disillusioned by her lower condition in society. *Nada* has an optimistic denouement: Andrea, now a woman of the new generation, forgets her sweetheart, abandons Juan, Gloria, and her grandmother, and leaves for Madrid. All this is mechanically and easily done with the coldness and logic of a twenty-year-old girl.

Nada is a one-dimensional novel. It is a realistic book in the sense that Miss Laforet narrates her own life experiences. She has been in contact with real people. Some critics affirm that her style is precise, simple, poetic. I find it rather weak, poor in texture, limited in vocabulary, somewhat declamatory.

Miss Laforet has written two other novels: *La isla y los demonios* (1952) and *La mujer nueva* (1955). The first one, in spite of some changes in style, is a repetition of *Nada;* the other one belongs to what is called the Catholic cycle. It treats the conversion of an adult woman to the Catholic faith and—according to the author—to good moral behaviour. In my opinion Miss Laforet's name will not remain very long in the annals of Spanish literature.

These two novelists were the pioneers of a rather important development in fiction. Many problems confront the Spanish writer now; some are of a technical nature, others of a political character, but more important yet is the great question of "man and his circumstances." Since the political climate is not propitious to the enunciation and discussion of advanced social theories, the writers observe man in his "condition humaine," in his relation to his family, in his love affairs, in his games, in his professional activities, in his economic struggles and religious problems, and, above all, in his attitude toward death.

A great feeling of solidarity, compassion, tenderness, gives a comforting warmth to novels otherwise violent, or written in a coarse, vulgar, profane style. That strange human sweetness of the Spaniard, side by side with the new discovery of "tremendismo" and the old overwhelming feeling of man's pride and importance; "machismo," the male cult; reality and evasion in one breath; escape to the religious or the moral, as in the case of Zunzunegui, Laforet, Gironella, or to the world of fantasy and imagination, as in the case of Ferlosio's *Industrias y andanzas de Alfanhui;* or the morose delectation in the grotesque and the ugly in Cela's *La colmena,* or in the appalling reverence for what is trite and photographic found in *El Jarama,* a work by Ferlosio—all these elements serve to offset the crudity of the materials utilized by the novelists.

Most of the new novelists are very serious about the subject matter of their work and they are concerned with new, original forms to convey the novelistic substance. In this attitude we discern two striking characteristics: the realistic and objective presentation of life through the novel and the experimental tendency found in the technical devices showing unavoidable influence of Joyce, Dos Passos, Faulkner, Hemingway, Sartre, Camus, Huxley.

At the head of the novelists of the present decade I would place one man and one woman. The woman is Ana María Matute (1926), the man Ignacio Aldecoa (1925). Aldecoa wrote *El fulgor y la sangre,*[5] *Con el viento solano,*[6] and *Gran sol.*[7]

Like Cela, Aldecoa returns to a traditional posture in the novel. He is a realist, even a neo-realist. Let us look at his first work, *El fulgor y la sangre.* The story unfolds a few years after the Civil War. It deals with the world of the mounted police. Six civil guards are on duty in an isolated castle. Four of them are maintaining order at some distant fair, and the other two are on duty at the castle. One of the four dies. The wives of those on duty at the fort are informed of his death and they, in turn, notify the other women. Since the dead man, the corporal, is a bachelor, there are only three wives to notify. Chapter one, Noon, describes the scenery, the castle. Chapters two to seven tell of the wedding and the former life of each woman. The last chapter, Twilight, describes the death of the corporal.

Throughout the novel Aldecoa maintains the anguish of the women, the painful tension of this situation, and a terrific suspense which lasts an afternoon. Fate plays chess with its victims and the writer with the reader. The technique seems to me impeccable, especially during the flashback accounts of the earlier life of each woman. In each reminiscence we live in many cities and towns, we witness the Civil War and what followed, we see the poverty, the vices, the misery of the people. Had it not been for this device, how could he have filled these hours? The atmosphere of the castle had already been created, and the women had nothing else to say in the hour allotted to each, and Aldecoa knew that he was writing a novel and not an elegy.

The author shows a sharp social conscience. He has sensibility and tenderness, he presents life in its many facets, but he always finds the good in

---

[5] (Barcelona, Planeta, 1954.)
[6] (Barcelona, Planeta, 1956.)
[7] (Barcelona, Noguer, 1957.)

man. He has deep compassion for the poor women who were once able to enjoy living, to dream and to laugh, and who are now prisoners in the fort, in themselves, of their implacable fate, and for their men, who are stoically fulfilling their duty, living poorly and dangerously, vaguely hoping for something better to give their wives, their children, and themselves too. This compassion compelled him to kill the only bachelor in the group. The victim was a man without attachments, without obligations, perhaps even without memories.

This novel belongs to the "tremendista" tendency because of its impending sense of tragedy, the tense climate of agony, the heavy atmosphere of foreboding. *Con el viento solano* is also "tremendista." [8] A gypsy kills a civil guard and for a few days eludes justice. He feels fear and remorse; he is persecuted by the police and rejected by his friends and relatives, but in the midst of his anguish he comes across some wonderful men and learns many things about life. Finally, he surrenders because to do so is the command of his destiny.

In *Gran sol* we find the themes of the sea—the sea in its material beauty and in the heroic life of the fishermen—and of man and his circumstances, his solitude, but, above all, in the exemplary conception of duty and of the purpose of his work.

In spite of the dramatic and the heroic, these fishermen are simple men, made of blood and bone. In them there is nothing of the grandiose psychosis of an Ahab, in *Moby Dick,* or the masculine bravado of the *Old Man and the Sea,* by Hemingway. As the "patrón" is dying in the fishing boat, the fishermen forget their differences, their quarrels, and, in order to conceal their emotions they talk, curse, and drink.

Gran sol is, like Ferlosio's *El Jarama,* an extremely realistic novel, written in the jargon of the profession, in a monotonous dialogue. The conversations are superficial, uninteresting. But once the novel has run its course, the reader realizes that he has been living in a new world, among tough, tender men, perfectly described by the pen of a writer who is also a sailor and a deep-sea fisherman.

Ana María Matute has so far published *Los Abel,*[9] *Fiesta al noroeste,*[10]

---

[8] *See* Jerónimo Mallo, "Caracterización y valor del tremendismo en la novela española contemporánea," *Hispania,* 39 (March 1956, 49–55).

[9] (Barcelona, Destino, 1948.)

[10] (Madrid, Aguado, 1953.)

Pequeño teatro,[11] *En esta tierra,*[12] *Los niños tontos,*[13] *Los hijos muertos,*[14] and *Primera memoria,*[15] the first volume of a trilogy entitled *Los mercaderes.* Miss Matute is primarily a poet; hence she is an excellent prose writer. She creates her own world of fiction with a vision of her own, a unique sensibility, and a very personal style. She excels in the penetration of child psychology, in the creation of admirable types of precocious children. Her first great novel is *Fiesta al noroeste.* The protagonist is an antihero of contemporary fiction: a puppet-show man. He travels in his cart and wishes to bypass his village. But fate interferes, for he runs down and kills a village child. He is arrested and seeks the protection of his old friend Juan Niño, the rich man of the village. At the child's funeral, the focus is shifted to Juan Niño who remembers the story of his own family. The father, violent and wild; the birth of his half-brother, Pablo, son of his father by Salomé, the servant girl; the suicide of his mother on the very day of his half-brother's birth; the life of the two brothers—Pablo, young, independent, rebellious; Juan Niño, cowardly, timid, mediocre. Juan's greatest wish had been to bring Pablo to live at the old house, and being rich and powerful he had married Pablo's fiancée. But Pablo refuses to live with them and leaves town. Juan leaves his bride and runs to Salomé's home in hopes of finding his brother there. Only Salomé is there, alone. Salomé resembles her son. Juan sees wild horses running down the sierras. Blind with love, hatred, desperation, he bites Salomé's neck, her round chin, and gasping hopelessly empty reasons, breathing like a lion, he throws her on the yellow leaves.

These are the reminiscences of Juan Niño as he looks intently at the little corpse. A description of the funeral is then given.

En esta tierra is a novel of ambitious dimensions. Its background is the city of Barcelona during the Civil War. Necessarily, it is a novel of social impact, passionate, intensely real. There is a suppressed hatred in this book, but also, as in the case of Aldecoa's novel, love for the poor, the humble people. *En esta tierra* constitutes the author's first attempt to write a novel of transcending significance, to reveal the soul of a society suffering through a period of violent change.

Of even greater proportions is the novel *Los hijos muertos.* It has to do with the disintegration of the Spanish family after the Civil War. It is divided into three sections: Time, Hunger and Thirst, and The Undertow. In the first section the protagonist, Daniel, returns to his native woods to

---

[11] (Barcelona, Planeta, 1954.)
[12] (Barcelona, Exito, 1955.)
[13] (Madrid, Arión, 1956.)
[14] (Barcelona, Planeta, 1958.)
[15] (Barcelona, Destino, 1960.)

466

die. In this solitude he recreates the time of his youth, a great love, the Civil War, his life in Barcelona, the death of his wife, and the death of his child in an air-raid. In the second part, the author introduces a new generation through an eight-year-old boy, Miguel Fernández, and his memories of the war, and his adventures, first in France and then in Barcelona, after the revolution. In the third section, she narrates the fall and death of Miguel and Daniel's loss of all hope in human destiny. This is indeed a great novel. What matters in the mind of the writer is the human conflict, the sense of tragedy in the lives of a group of beings created by her, yet perfectly real. In this world of anguish there are many ideas, feelings, passions, and events, and, carried off by the undertow of the war, many men, women, and children, living and dying in solitude, fear, insecurity, and pessimism, in shattered hopes and dreams.

María Matute's latest novel, *Primera memoria,* is the first book of a trilogy entitled *Los mercaderes.* A whimsical girl, 12 years old, relates episodes of her life on an island during the Civil War. In her frankness and innocence, she uncovers the hypocrisy, cruelty, and brutality of children and adults in a town torn by religious and political conflict. The rhetorical style of earlier novels has yielded to a simple and precise, poetic language, in perfect harmony with the subject matter and the atmosphere, in such a way that the author approaches the balance and mastery of classic execution. Ana María Matute, who has the potential of a novelist of density and broad perspective, and who is capable of writing an epic and grandiose fictional work, may give us her best work in some brief, artistic, exquisitely human novel, shining with lyricism and tenderness. This *Primera memoria* may be a foreshadowing of it.

Dissatisfied with his world, his society, and probably with his own artistic endeavours, Rafael Sánchez Ferlosio does not find the expression of his genius in the two books he has published up to the present: *Industrias y andanzas de Alfanhui* [16] and *El Jarama.* [17]

Both are extremely original and altogether unlike each other. *Alfanhui* is the book of a poet, an allegorical conception of a new picaresque novel. Persons, episodes, things, narratives are exalted by the richest imagination and fantasy. The language is lyrical and sensuous, metaphorical and direct, according to the requirements of the subject matter. At times *Alfanhui* has the natural depth of a symbolist poem, at times the simplicity of a fairy tale. It often becomes capricious, like a surrealist dream. There is realism in the novel, however—geographic reality. Perhaps one could call it a dehumanized novel. But even so, it is beautiful.

---

[16] (Madrid, Talleres, 1951.)
[17] (Barcelona, Destino, 1956.)

Why did Sánchez Ferlosio give up this artistic type of creation to write *El Jarama?* I believe it was because he is a nonconformist, dissatisfied even with his own personality. I would call *El Jarama* the most tedious book I have read, if it were not for the language, alive, real, and at times humorous. It is the language of a new low middle class, full of puns, jokes, popular expressions, slang. For nearly 300 pages the writer repeats the inane dialogues of a group of young "madrileños" on a Sunday picnic. Men and women talk as only Spaniards can talk and never say anything of any interest. The author goes among these people with a tape recorder. The tape is, of course, monotonous and commonplace. This novel is an exegesis of vulgarity and nothingness. Finally, the author decides to bring in a tragic note: one of the girls drowns in the Jarama river. Nevertheless, Sánchez Ferlosio remains impassive and restricts himself to the description of the drowning, the arrival of the police, and similar minutiae objectively reported, and yet extremely uninteresting. Fortunately, the entire action takes place in one day.

Ferlosio has locked up his imagination and his exquisite sensibility to give us the most objective picture of mediocrity and the commonplace. There is no purpose and no message, unless the haughtiness of the "guardia civil" and the spirit of conformity and official routine of a judge are being used in a symbolic manner. He has certainly vivisected a section of modern society, but who is interested in these people? In answering this question we may find the key to the problem. As human beings, they have no transcendental value, no inner radiance; but as fictional types they are perfect specimens, conceived with logic and reasonably presented. Ferlosio has created a flat world, a chessboard world on which the wooden figures move as they should to make the game exact and scientific.

Ferlosio in *El Jarama* is one case of self-mutilation not infrequent in other Spanish writers of today. Peculiarly enough, his first book reveals a process of evasion of reality. By self-mutilation I mean that he has tried to destroy certain creative elements of good taste and imagination present in his earlier book; by evasion I mean disguising his unique vision of real life by means of an elaborated style—sometimes hermetic or surrealist. Quite disconcerting!

Elena Quiroga's (*ca.* 1920) first work was a novel of regional inspiration, *Viento del Norte,*[18] which really belongs to the "costumbrista" tendency of the last century. But in 1952, in her novel *La sangre,*[19] the author abandons the picturesque descriptive element and tries to give universal perspective to her characters. However, they—men, women, children—are of the

---

[18] (Barcelona, Destino, 1951.)
[19] (Barcelona, Destino, 1952.)

468

purest Spanish extraction. A chestnut tree is the narrator of the story. It tells what it sees in the tower of a castle. Four generations of a family are presented to the reader in a naked picture of joys, sorrows, nobility, and villainy; of neurotic, generous, daring, or cowardly men; of chaste, pure, sensuous, or cruel women; of children who inherit the qualities of their parents; of great conflict caused by tormented blood in which the will of domineering men clashes with the kindness of understanding women. *La sangre* follows the old technique of the anecdotal form and the succession of dramatic episodes. The story is as important as the psychology—Miss Quiroga is a sentimental and romantic writer. She exalts the primary feelings of man; she creates heroes and heroines of great proportions. She is somewhat grandiose and nowhere shows a sense of humor, but she tries desperately to be modern. She believes that her happiest piece of mechanism is to have made a tree the narrator. But since we know that a tree cannot talk—or write—we labor under a feeling of insincerity; we feel dismay at the absence of verisimilitude in her work—a great pity, for the dramatic tension of the characters often reaches a very high aesthetic force.

There is an evident desire for originality at all costs in this novelist.

Some of the artistic shortcomings of Miss Quiroga—rhetorical outbursts, padding, conventional scenery—are overcome in her novels *Algo pasa en la calle* [20] and *La enferma*.[21] Other resources, such as the converging levels of narration, continuous use of the "flashback," change of narrators, repetition of events, economy of description, replace the old patterns. Thus, *Algo pasa en la calle* is a beautiful work of art as well as a deeply human interpretation.

In *La careta* [22] she introduces the social point of view in her work. Moisés, who as a child witnessed the assassination of his parents in the course of the Civil War, attends a family dinner. Being a lonesome, disillusioned man, he tries to destroy the sense of "reality" and security of his brothers and sisters. Using several planes of time, he remembers their youth and compares it to this compromise between pretentiousness and deceptive reality of the present, where material preoccupation, selfishness, easy success, hypocrisy replace the old moral values. Miss Quiroga gives especial attention to a neurotic, bitter, solitary man, and to a modern, independent girl. The style is impressionistic and elegant, but the construction of the novel is unnecessarily abstruse, and has a technique in which the stream of consciousness, the breaking of the time element, dis-

---

[20] (Barcelona, Destino, 1954.)
[21] (Barcelona, Planeta, 1955.)
[22] (Barcelona, Noguer, 1955.)

rupts an otherwise elementary theme. The poetic gift is present through all the pages, as is the gift for observation and imagination. If she did not try so hard to be modern, Miss Quiroga could be a great writer. In other words, the experimental method is not always the most successful.

Juan Goytisolo (1931), the youngest of this group of novelists, has published the following books: *Juegos de manos;* [23] *Duelo en el paraíso;* [24] *El circo;* [25] *La resaca;* [26] and *Fiestas.* [27] *Fiestas* is an ideal blend of realism and imagination, truth and poetry, in both the depiction of characters and the description of things and events. The author comes very close to the danger point in controversial matter, but wisely stops there. The novel begins with the celebration of a religious congress in Barcelona, which serves as a pretext to enter into the anarchical life of the city, especially among the lower classes of society. There is a positive social attitude in this book. There is the problem of the displaced people of Murcia who, having settled in the hills of Barcelona, are violently dispossessed and violently thrown out of town; there is the case of señor Ortega, a republican schoolteacher, who attacks Catholic hypocrisy, the venality of the newspapers, the abuses of the local authorities, who quarrels with everybody and finally loses his job. There is the continuous presence of the civil guards. But the strength of Goytisolo is his mastery of psychological technique. Most of his characters are extremely well conceived: El Gorila, true to his brutal vigor, his rebellious nature, his kindness; the small Pipo, the imaginative child, seeking adventure and tenderness in the slums, the boy who unwittingly betrays his best friend, Gorila, to a civil guard. Pipo gives up his bohemian friends and joins the religious procession. Does he see the light? What does the author think? The most pathetic character is that of Pira, an abandoned little girl, whose mind is full of beautiful dreams, and whose strongest desire is to visit her father in Italy and see the Pope. Carried away by her imagination, she falls into the hands of a degenerate and is murdered.

Goytisolo has a keen gift for observation, a sharp intuition, understanding, tenderness, depth. He is attracted by the merely picturesque and is given to "tremendista" effects. He is very fond of bohemians, anarchists, bums, rebellious and imaginative children. Goytisolo is one of the most promising novelists of today. He has a vigorous imagination, a tragic sense of life, a solid capacity for character delineation, a rich style, a mastery of dialogue. I am in agreement with Ramón Sender's judgment: ". . .

---

[23] (Barcelona, Destino, 1954.)

[24] (Barcelona, Planeta, 1955.)

[25] (Barcelona, Destino, 1957.)

[26] (Paris, Club del Libro Español, 1958.)

[27] (Buenos Aires, Emecé, 1958.) English translation: *Fiestas* (New York, Knopf, 1960.)

Fiestas is a model of harmony, sharpness, love of things and beings, originality of vision . . . Most of the strata of Spanish society are masterly described in this new novel by Juan Goytisolo, who is without a doubt the best of the young Spanish writers. Some day perhaps he will be the best of both the young and the old." [28]

In conclusion: the contemporary poet of Spain maintains a balanced position between the intellectual poetry of Mallarmé or Paul Valéry and the realistic poets of the Spanish tradition. Thus he speaks a modern and universal language and preserves at the same time that regional flavor that has distinguished the Spanish poet through the centuries.

It is clear that the intellectualistic or the poetic novel of the 1920's does not appeal to the fiction writers of today. The intense preoccupation of the French novelists with stylistic problems does not disturb these Spaniards; the experimentalist in words has no place here. Communication is direct, forceful, and sincere. The novelist is too serious to play with rhetorical tricks. The historical moment is dramatic. Man is again the center of interest: man in his strength or weakness; man alone, in solitude; or man in society, in the human beehive. Unfortunately, this man is geographically and psychologically limited; he is always the Spaniard. To attain greatness this man has to be lifted to a universal plane.

---

[28] *The Saturday Review,* XLIII (June 11, 1960), 35.

The Imagination as Verb

Stephen Spender

Presented at the Library of Congress February 26, 1962

THE SITUATION OF THE POET is certainly a topic much discussed at literary conferences. Often, the discussion takes the form of poets' telling a large audience that they cannot communicate with its members. Sometimes, it takes the more practical one of discussing how to give economic aid to poets by making them do other things than write poetry—teaching, for example. Anyway, it offers a picture of poets as being peculiarly helpless in the circumstances of modern life.

The question "What can poets do to save civilization from destruction?" is often asked by some member of the public at the very conference where the poet is on show in his role of helpless, hopeless anachronism. This suggests that poets, though neglected, somehow command the secret of the time in which we are living. If the Voice of the Imagination were heeded, enemies would be reconciled and the hungry fed. Two confusions are involved here. One is that there is a tendency for the poet to be more a matter of concern than the poetry. The other is the idea that if poetry and the poet were given their true place, this would really have some effect on a world distracted and tormented with fear. This second proposition is one that poets—that is, imaginative writers (whether they write poetry, fiction, or drama) sometimes share.

The belief that poets can alter and have altered the world is contained in Shelley's famous claim that poets are the unacknowledged legislators of mankind. No modern poet would regard this as anything but preposterous. Yet underneath the denials, the idea that the life and works of the imagination somehow provide an incandescent center in which human personality and even social forms can become molten and transformed certainly persists in Lawrence, in Rilke, even in Joyce.

So much preoccupation with the situation of the poet and with the function of the poetic imagination results doubtless from the feeling that, in the past, poets fitted better into the community, and their poetry was better understood. Certainly, we are right in feeling that there was a difference, but I doubt whether this was it. There were perhaps merely different expectations on the part of the poets, different misunderstandings on that of the public. What may be a modern peculiarity is that poets today expect to be understood for the qualities they regard as intrinsic to their poetry being poetry, just as painters expect their paintings to be admired not for their subjects or their beauty but for qualities called painterly, perhaps even for the texture of the surface of the pigment.

No one could say that the poets of the Victorian era—Tennyson, Browning, and Arnold—were neglected or even went unappreciated. And yet they seem rather like displaced persons who enacted to their audience the Victorian public's idea of "the poet," rather as a refugee may, in his exile, find himself having to act out the accent and behavior which his neighbors expect of someone coming from the country of his origin. "Vex not thou the poet's mind, With thy shallow wit," Tennyson growled at a public expecting the cloaked and bearded poet to growl. And if one glances back rapidly from precedent to precedent of English poets across the centuries, one finds poets who were courtiers, cavaliers, politicians, customs inspectors, ambassadors, writers of flourishing dedications to patrons, lunatics, and gangsters, but rarely a situation which could be regarded as favoring them simply because they wrote poetry. This is true even of the greatest. We feel that Milton belonged to the conscience of a puritan revolution (though he had friends who were poets and scholars), that Shakespeare belonged to a very fertile period in history and a group of players, that Chaucer was one of his own Canterbury pilgrims, that Wordsworth was the property of the Wordsworthians, that the Romantics belonged to their biographies, that Tennyson belonged to Arthur Hallam and Queen Victoria.

If we are discouraged by the thought that modern poets don't "communicate," we may find comfort in the reflection that there have been few periods when their poetry communicated *as poetry*. In the opinion of his contemporaries, Shakespeare seems to have been only one among a number of playwrights who were doubtless judged not for the poetry but for the play being the thing. He comes rather low on the list of playwrights supplied by his contemporary, Meres.

Yet I would not care to dispute the truth of the observation of someone who said that a modern poet, launching forth his slim volume of verse today, is like someone dropping a feather over the edge of the Grand Canyon and then waiting for the echo. Nevertheless, certain living poets get back a considerable reverberation. We ought to remember this. What is more important, there never was, as I have written above, a period in which the arts were more appreciated for the specific qualities that are considered peculiar to each of them. In fact, the arts run the risk of being overpurified and the artists of feeling obliged to produce some quintessential extract of the qualities of their art, so great is the pressure of critical connoisseurs on them to produce only the real, right thing.

It is really as though, in an age of specialization, poetry only has to communicate along the pure packed line which Keats, reproaching Shelley, said should be "loaded with ore." This means that we do ask ourselves "Is this poetry?"; where in the past people might have asked: "Does it tell a story?" "Does it praise the king?" "Has it a moral?" "Does it conform to the standards which we call beautiful?"

Poetry is an end, where previously it was often regarded as a means, a vehicle for carrying flattery, beauty, melodrama, religion, a moral, or just the world. And this situation seems acceptable to some poets, notably Robert Graves, who draws the logical conclusion that poets should write only for other poets and should take in one another's washing. In one of his early letters, Ezra Pound declares that a poet should not expect to find more than thirty readers who appreciate his work for its true qualities.

I do not take it for granted that poets today have a grievance. Nevertheless, we do feel—and rightly, I think—that whether poetry is admired for the wrong or the right reason, there is, as it were, a reduction of scale in its relation to a world of machines, scientific inventions, world power-politics. This diminution corresponds, perhaps, to the ratio of modern man to the almost annihilating scale of the time-space universe, of modern man even to his own inventions. There is, perhaps, not so much a breakdown of communication as a kind of shrinking of the imagining, the feeling, the flesh and sense tissues through which the poetic communicates, in relation to the great exaggeration of impersonal, inhuman forces.

Critics have offered many reasons for this state of affairs. Ever since Matthew Arnold, they have been telling us that there is a decay of the institutions which communicate values in society itself, and that therefore poetry cannot today become (using Matthew Arnold's own epithet, in his lecture on *The Function of Criticism at the Present Time*) "important."

It is symptomatic, perhaps, that in the late nineteenth century Arnold used the word "important" with regard to poetry, where we should probably write "significant." We avoid "important" because it sounds too public; "significant" can be as private as we want it to be. If you say an art is "important," you imply that there is a confluence of subject matter, interest, and values within the art, with things outside that are important by standards outside it. Our current use of the word "significant" can have no reference to anything outside the standards set up by the work itself, just as a symbol can, with the "Symbolistes," symbolize only itself. What was important to Matthew Arnold was important to Mr. Gladstone. Nothing that is significant to me is important to Mr. Harold Macmillan. So in using the word "significant" in modern criticism, we limit ourselves to that which is signified within the terms of the art, to the reader trained to receive what the poem communicates.

So, it has come to be accepted that what is significant along the channels of communication between poet and reader is not important in public thought. Poetry—and hence imaginative literature—has become "significant" when it has ceased to be "important." Poet and reader are inmates of the prison cell shared by Lear and Cordelia, when Lear has abandoned all power and most claims on life:

> *. . . Come, let's away to prison;*
> *We two alone will sing like birds i' the cage;*
> *When thou dost ask me blessing, I'll kneel down*
> *And ask of thee forgiveness. So we'll live,*
> *And pray, and sing, and tell old tales, and laugh*
> *At gilded butterflies, and hear poor rogues*
> *Talk of court news; and we'll talk with them too—*
> *Who loses and who wins; who's in, who's out . . .*

We accept the idea that there is an almost autonomous outside world of science, invention, and power, evolving and revolving according to laws of economics, etc., which has become unimaginable within the individual consciousness. This was not so for Shakespeare or Milton. Their imaginations roamed over the whole world and over the forces that controlled the history of their time. Here, surely, there is a real break between past and present.

The reasons for regretting the separation of the automatism of social forces from the shrunken inner worlds of individuated experience are not so obvious as might at first appear. The common misunderstanding started by Shelley is to regard the separation as a public catastrophe, as though poets might save civilization but are prevented from doing so by the forces of machinery and politics. It is not a catastrophe, and poetry cannot save nations, nor could it ever do so, though perhaps we should not overlook the capacity of poets in the past to create what politicians today call an "image." Virgil set out to create a pattern for Romans in *The Aeneid,* and Shakespeare (perhaps more successfully because less purposively) certainly created an "image" of England's country and soldiers, which perhaps helped to win the Battle of Britain. It certainly seemed incarnate in the few who won the cause of the many. Whitman, in *Song of Myself*, became the experiences of all America in order to provide Americans, in his self-portrayal, with a personalized image of America for which they might live.

We should all agree, though, that today poetry cannot save civilization. Nevertheless, to agree about this is not to argue that poetry cannot and should not make inner worlds of elements in the public world which are "important." There seems to be a tendency today to think that, in their poetry, poets should not reconcile outward things with inner life but should deal only with such things as are already inner, personal, private, or literary. One can sympathize with this tendency, which can become both stoic and playful in poems as excellent as those of Philip Larkin. Nor am I suggesting that there is some obligation imposed upon poets to be socially responsible, if I add that the mind which creates from imagination should be able, ideally, to imagine what seems impersonal, or even unimaginable. If none of the contemporary poets is able to compose inner worlds that include elements of the public world—the world that was felt in *The Waste Land* as in Auden's *Spain*—then contemporary poetry reflects a partial failure to imagine the disturbing modern environment. The reader or aspiring young writer (over-impressed perhaps by C. P. Snow's *The Two Cultures and the Scientific Revolution* or concerned with the Bomb) may well find himself apparently confronted by a choice between the limited, private, personal, literary-academic world of the imagined and the abstract, threatening, open world of the unimaginable. There is the suspicion today that poetry is the playground of perpetual students—or perpetual professors—who have achieved their maturity at the price of refusing to have dealings with the world. Robert Graves, in answering a questionnaire, declared in *The London Magazine* of February 1962 that "personal issues are all that interest people, not newspaper issues," a statement which can only be taken to mean that Mr. Graves thinks that nothing of public concern, which is discussed in the newspapers, can be felt by the reader to be his personal concern. Since questions involving the survival of the reader and of his loved ones are newspaper issues, this seems an ostrich-like attitude. It also seems characteristic of a habit among modern writers of setting up false dichotomies between "public" and "private," "personal" and "impersonal." The contradiction between "personal issues" and "newspaper issues" disappears when one reflects that no newspaper issue is a subject for art unless it is felt by the artist as one affecting him personally—as the bombing of Guernica affected Picasso. In the past there was major and minor poetry but no idea that it was honorable for all poetry to be minor and poetically disgraceful to attempt the major themes of the whole of life viewed as a whole. There was no idea that the world of art was somehow the opposite of the world of historic action.

476

When Matthew Arnold set himself up as the advocate of the Function of Criticism, his plea (more influential than the one on another occasion that poetry might replace religion) was that "creative power works with elements, with materials," and that if these are not present, "it must surely wait till they are ready." In the present century, critics like T. E. Hulme, I. A. Richards, and T. S. Eliot have explained that the elements which are lacking are values and beliefs, fragmented and decayed in modern scientific and materialist societies. In some quarters, the decline of institutions in society upholding values and beliefs has led not so much to the view that criticism can prepare the ground for "important" poetry as that it must take the place of major creative effort by keeping open the connections with the past organic society of living values through the selection and analytic study of those works which are truly in the Great Tradition. The Great Tradition and the analysis of the values in these works replace both poetry and religion.

The view is that poetically we live in a vicious circle which completely conditions literary creation. There are no effective institutions of faith and values because there are not the faith and values, and there are not the faith and values for poetry to draw on because there are no such institutions. This vicious circle is also held responsible for the breakdown of communication in poetry.

This depressive analysis leaves out one thing. It does not explain why, until recently, there have been poets of the stature of Yeats, Eliot, and Frost writing great poetry. Moreover, it should be pointed out that this very habit of explaining the situation of poetry in terms of the collapse in values, itself shows one of the symptoms of the situation complained about—a desperate dependence on outward circumstances, a materialist tendency to explain the inner state of the individual artist as entirely the result of outward conditioning.

I think criticism has been too preoccupied with conditioning circumstances. It is inevitable that it should be so. Critics deal, after all, with things given, what is already written, what they find going on in the life around them, the already read, not the as yet unwritten. One of the things that creative talents do is change into favoring circumstances the unfavorable conditions out of which they create. Eliot, writing as a critic, easily demonstrates the impossibility of Eliot's writing *The Waste Land*. I cannot accept altogether the view that poetry is the result of analyzed circumstances. So what I have set myself to do here is to separate, for the time being, the idea of poetic imagination from the context of conditioning history, to consider it as an activity per se, to take it, as it were, out of the context of conditioning non-values.

Shakespeare wrote comparatively little about poetry. When he describes the process of making poetry, he suggests the operation of an independent creative faculty upon things immediately apprehended:

> *The poet's eye, in a fine frenzy rolling,*
> *Doth glance from heaven to earth, from earth to heaven;*
> *And as imagination bodies forth*
> *The forms of things unknown, the poet's pen*
> *Turns them to shapes and gives to airy nothing*
> *A local habitation and a name.*

The citation is so familiar and itself so airy, so Mozartian, that it slips by almost unconsidered. But what is said is surely astonishing: that the form of things remains unknown until the poet, standing midway at the center of his universe, bodies them forth; that the imagination is a pure activity, making named forms out of nothings.

It is noteworthy that Keats and the other Romantics returned to this Shakespearean view of the imagination as an independent sovereign activity, centered in the poetic genius and owing allegiance to no superior intellectual authority. In doing this, the Romantics rejected the practice of the Augustan poets, who put their great imaginative gifts at the service of theological, aristocratic, and rationalist-philosophic views of their times. Eighteenth-century poets like Pope considered the imagination to be the servant of the intellectual rationalizations of the age, which seemed to reconcile the reasoning of God with that of scientists. To the Augustans, poetry was an intellectual synthesis which, in its transparent imagery, had the ambition of resolving discords between different spheres of contemporary reasoning.

Keats returned to the view, which he discovered in certain passages of Shakespeare, that imagination is a primary faculty of the poetic sensibility, whereas fancy and wit are secondary, illustrating already conceived ideas. Imagination can be thought of as purely inventive, conjuring shapes out of nothing, or as the center of poetic sensibility acted upon by experiences. It receives these experiences and transforms them so they can be related one to another within the harmonious unity, the world in little, which is the poem. Imagination comes before intellectual concept, whereas wit or fancy or illustration demonstrate idea.

The Romantics rebelled against their predecessors, the Augustans, against the poets of wit, because in them the imagination had become adjectival, imaginative. The imaginative was put to the service of reason. The Romantics returned to the concept of the imagination as verb, the Word made flesh, the dream which is Adam's. As Coleridge wrote: "to contemplate the ANCIENT of days with feelings as fresh, as if all had then sprung forth at the first creative fiat."

478

The great revival of interest in Shakespeare which we find in Blake, Wordsworth, Coleridge, and Keats was a return to the Shakespearean as source in English poetry of primary imagination. The Romantics bring us back to the idea of poetic imagination as dreaming yet revealing consciousness, in which the circumference of brute facts, experiences, and disparate ideas becomes self-aware and, in the moment of self-awareness, is transposed into symbols and images harmonious within the complex unity that is the poem.

Ideally, the circumference comprises the whole world of knowledge, experiences, and events, past and present, which are undigested in the sense that they can only be interpreted into the significance of inner life through the power of the imagination to relate them within the unity of the poem. The force of Shelley's *A Defence of Poetry*, which remains impressive—however many holes may be picked in his argument—is his vision that, ideally, the real world is material potentially capable of being transformed by the imagination. He realized, too, that the world—in its most ancient history as in its most recent inventions—is always contemporary consciousness, coming alive within the awareness of individuals living at a particular moment, people having the attitudes of their generation, their situation in time and place.

Shelley, in his view of poetry, was of course concerned with an ideal, not with a program that could be laid down for poets. He was writing of a desideratum, not of what was necessarily within the capabilities of his contemporaries, when he wrote in 1820:

> . . . The cultivation of poetry is never more to be desired than at periods when, from an excess of the selfish and calculating principle, the accumulation of the materials of external life exceed the quantity of the power of assimilating them to the internal laws of human nature. . . .

Here, imagination is regarded as the transforming center of poetic consciousness, a task, and perhaps a body of contemporary achievement above and beyond any individual poet "imagining that which we know" for his generation, as task and sum of scientific knowledge stand beyond the individual scientist.

In spite of the reaction today against the Romantics, modern poetry and criticism have taken over the view of the imagination as center, acted upon by experiences and inventing its own harmonious inner world; and, in spite of talk of a revival of classicism, they have not returned to the essentially classical view that imagination is the power of illustrating theology, monarchy, or philosophy, dressing up, as it were, preconceived ideas about the important values of living. Baudelaire was anti-Romantic, theologically minded—yet he regarded the imagination as standing above the experiences on which it operated:

> The whole visible universe is but an array of images and signs to which the imagination gives a place and relative value; it is a sort of fodder which the imagination must digest and transform. All the faculties of man's soul must be subordinated to the imagination, which can call upon them all at once.

Coleridge, in one of the most famous passages of *Biographia literaria,* defines imagination as "the power in which one image or feeling is made to modify many others, and by a sort of fusion to force many into one."

And, in a still more famous passage:

> The poet, described in ideal perfection, brings the whole soul of man into activity, with the subordination of its faculties to each other according to their relative worth and dignity. He diffuses a tone and spirit of unity, that blends and (as it were) *fuses,* each into each, by that synthetic and magical power, to which I would exclusively appropriate the name of Imagination. . . .

In the present century, at a later stage of modern poetry, imagination begins to be regarded as arbiter in a world of fragmented values, or, in the thought of Rilke, as the molten memory of traditions which have vanished from the world, in Yeats as mouthpiece of the "images in the Great Memory Stored." Rilke is perhaps the twentieth-century poet most seized with the idea of the poet having a task of fulfilling the past so that it redeems the present. In doing this, imagination becomes the force in which memory of traditions which once gave living significance is reinvented. In a letter to Witold von Hulewicz explaining the purpose of his *Duineser Elegien,* Rilke writes:

> The Elegies show us engaged on this work, the work of the perpetual transformation of beloved and tangible things into the invisible vibration and excitability of our nature, which introduces new "frequencies" into the the pulsing fields of the universe. . . . And this activity is sustained and accelerated by the increasingly rapid disappearance today of so much of the Visible which we cannot replace. Even for our grandfathers, a house, a fountain, a familiar tower, their very clothes, their coat, were infinitely more, infinitely more intimate. . . . The lived and living things, the things that share our thoughts, these are on the decline and can no more be replaced. *We are perhaps the last to have known such things.* . . . The earth has no alternative but to become invisible IN US. . . ."

So Rilke regards the task of poetic imagination to be that of setting up a kind of machinery which connects the reinvented past with the present. The angels in the elegies might be compared to vast transformers standing above a human landscape, converting the energy of the divine and the traditional into power which flows over and redeems the banal life of the fair in the valley below, whose values are those of money.

Rilke's purpose calls to mind Matthew Arnold's suggestion that "religion . . . will be replaced by poetry." This idea has, on the whole, received a bad press from critics, especially from those, like Eliot, who think that poetic imagination should at some point fuse with impersonal authority, and who would reinforce authority with irrefutable dogma. However, Rilke could not accept the Roman Catholicism in which he had been brought up. For him it was clear that poetry is not so much a replacing of religion as a path hewn out, leading back to that in religion which is not dogma but imagined idea. "For poetry," writes Arnold, "idea is everything," whereas "our religion has materialized itself in fact, the supposed fact." But religion is, at some point, imagination identical with idea, and the attempt of the *Duineser Elegien* might be defined as that of tracing back both poetic symbol and religious belief to the place where the Word is flesh.

In an essay, *An Anatomy of Orpheus; Rilke Among the Critics,* Michael Hamburger cites several authorities to show that Rilke did in fact attempt to make his poetry a substitute for religion. To F. R. Leavis there is no question that D. H. Lawrence's message is "religious." Yeats makes a mosaic of fragments of Oriental and Western beliefs and varieties of mysticism, a religion as eclectic as the picture of art, selected from all times and places, which André Malraux, in his *Le Musée imaginaire de la sculpture mondiale,* supposes modern men and women to carry round in their heads.

So, although Arnold's idea is in disrepute among critics, it is to some extent prophetic of the development of modern poetry. When Arnold wrote that religion had "materialized itself in fact," he was doubtless thinking of the Victorian controversy between the religious and the evolutionists of his time over the origins of man. What has happened since is that the exaltation of the act of the creative imagination as a visionary or intuitive judging of the values of life in a civilization of fragmented values has, as a first stage, separated the imagination from current orthodoxies and brought it back to the idea of religion as imagination in action, creating the world. That "art creates values" was an idea frequently expressed by writers at the beginning of the present century. And the point I want to emphasize is that, although the view of poets having become dogmatically religious seems completely opposed today to that of the heretically undogmatic, the disagreement is in fact more apparent in their critical prose views than in their poetic imagination. Michael Hamburger gives some striking quotations from Wallace Stevens to show how close his attitudes are to those of Rilke:

> The poet has 'immensely to do with giving life whatever savour it possesses. He has had to do with whatever the imagination and the senses have made of the world. . . .'
> 'The world about us would be desolate except for the world within us. . . .'
> 'The major poetic idea in the world is and always has been the idea of God. . . .'

481

'After one has abandoned a belief in God, poetry is the essence which takes its place as life's redemption.'

This expresses the loneliness of the artist with his creation. It is the attitude of Henry James and of Joseph Conrad, which greatly influenced the early Eliot, and what I am suggesting is that it remains the attitude of modern poets in the actual creation of their poetry, and if they have reintroduced the idea of dogmatic religion, it is as corrective to what is dangerous and nihilistic in such an isolated imagination; but their reintroduction of dogma into their thinking is not a return to the kind of religion for which Arnold thought poetry might become a substitute, the religion "materialized . . . in fact." Dogma is to them not the center out of which they create but as a disciplining of the imagination. Dogma is to the pure imagination that which critical sense is to technical performance.

In the same article, Michael Hamburger observes that "religious faith is one thing, poetic imagination another," and the distinction he makes is that "faith demands a concentration of the will, whereas will is the enemy of imagination." This seems a bit baldly stated, since there have been, without their suffering inner contradiction, religious imaginative poets. Perhaps, though, in ages of belief, the inner imagining of poets is corrected by the surrounding discipline of an external will to believe. Thus, when Coleridge writes of the imagination as though it were a completely self-sufficient mediator between different faculties of the soul, he takes for granted that in acting thus it has already been influenced by ideas of "worth and dignity." In a time of disbelief, there is a danger of art's resulting from altogether uncontrolled imagination, from a surrender of the poet to his perhaps destructive and diabolic fantasies. For this reason, Eliot and Auden distrust the heresies of the imagination which has become a value to itself. Nevertheless, to say that the religion of T. S. Eliot and W. H. Auden is the contrary of the irreligion of Lawrence and Rilke is to set up a false opposition. Religion in Eliot's poetry may involve insistence on dogma and traditional attitudes, but it is not a return to the religion that seemed unacceptable to Arnold. Indeed, in its imagining of mystical situations outside the temporal order, it might appear to Arnold to have some of the characteristics of poetry substituting for religion. In Eliot imagination remains the primary activity, just as it is in Yeats, or Rilke. Dogma has been introduced not at the center of the inspiration but as a principle of correction of extravagant despair or eclectic invention.

In the letter to his Polish translator already quoted, Rilke goes on:

> If one makes the mistake of applying Catholic conceptions of death, the Hereafter and Eternity to the Elegies or Sonnets, one isolates oneself completely from their conclusions and becomes involved in a fundamental misunderstanding. The angel of the Elegies is that Being in whom the

transmutation of the Visible into the Invisible, which we seek to achieve, is consummated.

For Rilke imagination was, as it were, an acted-upon instrument played upon by traditional symbols and exposed to the modern environment. His sensibility—deliberately weaned from the Catholicism of his childhood—was to him the channel whereby religious symbols could become poetic ones, and his religious attitudes evolve within his poetry.

First Eliot and, much later, Auden supported orthodox Christianity, as converts, and in their stated views. But whereas Eliot's dogmatic faith seems to distinguish him sharply in his life and intellectual attitudes from a poet like Rilke (and still more from a Christian heretic like D. H. Lawrence), in *Four Quartets* and the *Duineser Elegien*, their *poetic* attitudes are not opposed. In the long run, and despite Eliot's earlier attacks on him, even Eliot and Lawrence meet in their having religious imaginations. It would be far truer to say that in the *Four Quartets* the poet uses theology and dogma in order to release his mystical imagination, than to say that he uses his imagination to illustrate his dogma. Perhaps Auden sometimes falls into a kind of Christian classicism—but this is where he is most willed and least convincing. Rilke, the non-Catholic but with his Catholic upbringing, uses his angels, saints, and dead souls much as Eliot uses sanctified places. The central experience of the *Four Quartets* is the pure imagining of ecstatic and mystical states of awareness—timeless within time, the striving of prayer towards identification of the self with the past of ritual.

* * * *

What is common to these views—and I think to all major attempts in modern writing—is the view of imagination. The imagination has been restored in modern literature to its position of Verb. The reinstating of imagination as primary, central, the verb, was perhaps the attitude responsible for the greatest modern achievements: works like the last novels of Henry James (particularly *The Golden Bowl*), Joyce's *Finnegans Wake*, Yeats' Byzantium poems, and the *Duineser Elegien* put these writers in the God-like position of being isolated within their own creations, of having to reinvent the world and all its values within their art.

It is now possible, perhaps, to reconsider the problem of communication today in a way that is not the stereotype of sociological and analytical critics. As I remarked earlier, many of the misunderstandings which poets, and critics for them, complain about seem to have been always true of their situation, although it becomes clear that today an ancient problem takes special form. For example, I suppose it has always been true that poets and other artists are isolated. But in the past this has only been so in the sense that others also are alone. Shakespeare seems able to rely on

483

the fact that the situation of Hamlet or Lear going to his doom is, in its essential relation to the human condition, only an extremely conscious and developed example of what each member of his audience might feel. The peculiar modern nightmare is that the artist appears to be working under circumstances in which he is not only solitary in his exceptional awareness of the human condition, but he is, as it may seem, alone in being alone. He is operating on an awareness of being alive in a world where people are encouraged in every way to identify themselves, not with the other people around them, all trapped in the same human situation, but with a whole machinery of getting through life, which distracts them from the fact that they are spiritual animals. This produces the special kind of modern incommunicability. If you are a poet, often you are talking about things which are real to you and which have been real to people in the past, but to which many contemporaries appear to have deadened themselves, assisted in the deadening process by all the machinery of advertising and distraction.

At this point there appears to be a failure of nerve, and a demand on the part of writers that they should return not to their humanity but to the traditional institutions which have, as it were, knocked into people's heads the situation of living a shared awareness as it was in past times; hence the return to dogmas and establishments and critical interpretations of past literature, the insistence on the selected volumes of the Great Tradition and their accompanying exegeses as Holy Writ. I wonder, though, whether the flight from creative into critical attitudes, which has been so much a feature of the past two decades, is itself not an escape from the main reality to be faced—the common fact of the humanity of each of us isolated within his modern situation. The point I am laboring is put far better in Joseph Conrad's *Heart of Darkness,* that work which seems to go further than any other into the implications of modern materialism. When Conrad's narrator, Marlow, has gone far into the jungle of the Belgian Congo (the passage has the significance of prophecy realized today)—with his dehumanized fellow explorers, who, in their search for ivory, are driven to their own deaths and to mass-murdering natives—he hears through the jungle the great roar of the savages who, concealed from the white traders, have been watching their approach. Suddenly he sees these hordes:

> . . . They howled and leaped, and spun, and made horrid faces; but what thrilled you was just the thought of their humanity—like yours—the thought of your remote kinship with this wild and passionate uproar. Ugly. Yes, it was ugly enough; but if you were man enough you would admit to yourself that there was in you just the faintest trace of a response to the terrible frankness of that noise, a dim suspicion of there being a meaning in it which you—you so remote from the night of first ages—could comprehend. And why not? The mind of man is capable of anything—because everything is in

it, all the past as well as all the future. What was there after all? Joy, fear, sorrow, devotion, valour, rage—who can tell?—but truth—truth stripped of its cloak of time. Let the fool gape and shudder—the man knows, and can look on without a wink. But he must at least be as much of a man as these on the shore. He must meet that truth with his own true stuff—with his own inborn strength. Principles won't do. Acquisitions, clothes, pretty rags—rags that would fly off at the first good shake. No; you want a deliberate belief. An appeal to me in this fiendish row—is there? Very well; I hear; I admit, but I have a voice, too, and for good or evil mine is the speech that cannot be silenced. . . .

It seems to me that we have paid too much attention to the circumstances that condition the creating imagination. We lament the breakdown of beliefs, the decline in traditional values, the havoc wrought on civilization by the mass media—all these things—which add up to what we call the breakdown of communication. In painting ourselves as products of our social conditioning, we have not paid sufficient heed to the common and continuing human condition, the shared existing and experiencing within differing environments which is the real basis of communication.

If it is true that the poet today experiences alienation, it may also be true that there is a humanity of the nonliterary which he partly ignores. There is the poet, situated perhaps at the university; his loyalties and special interests are those of the literary group and his mental picture of the world is one of modern people whose attitudes he views as the results of the mass culture which is the worst enemy of his poetry. He regards his poetry as conditioned because he regards this public as conditioned. He only regards those who have critical consciousness, who are immersed through their reading and writing in values outside the contemporary ones, as being liberated from conditioning. But it may be that this picture of a public wholly conditioned by advertising, television, etc., is at least partly false, and that the literary intellectual's view of his isolation may be due to his having cut himself off from those equally aware of their human situation but as little able, in the circumstances created by his elite culture, to communicate with him as he is with them.

The difference between the poet with a view of catastrophe isolated in his literary consciousness, and the same view when it is an agonized state of consciousness shared with other lives, may be demonstrated by comparing two major works written out of the mood of World War I; these are *The Waste Land* and that little-known masterpiece, *In Parenthesis,* by David Jones. It does not make any difference to my argument that *In Parenthesis* is written in a style which owes something to Joyce and Eliot and that it is by a Roman Catholic. The point is that *In Parenthesis* celebrates communication of awareness, as the result of a common suffering, between the consciousness which is that of the poet, and that of the group of soldiers which it concerns. Both Eliot and David Jones see the same modern scene of the physical collapse of Western civilization. But the characters of the bank clerk, the secretary-typist, the pub-talkers in *The Waste Land* are psychological stereotypes projected by the surrounding moral chaos. In *The Waste Land,* it is only the consciousness of the poet, the sensibility realized in the poem, that expresses its awareness of a situation in a landscape in which all the other characters are unconscious, products of circumstances, lay figures. The characters of the soldiers in *In Parenthesis* become aware through that realization which is the result of having to act in the circumstances that were the Western Front: "the 'Bugger! Bugger!' of a man detailed, had often about it the 'Fiat! Fiat!' of the Saints." Thus, the soldiers are redeemed through the awareness revealed in their acceptance of duty and suffering into the writer's vision of Arthurian legend, Shakespeare's histories, and the offices of the Roman Catholic Church—just such values as are absent from the "young man carbuncular" in *The Waste Land.* But the soldiers walk in light:

> *Every one of these, stood, separate, upright, above ground,*
> *blinkt to the broad light*
> *risen dry mouthed from the chalk*
> *vivified from the Nullah without commotion*
> *and to distinctly said words,*
> *moved in open order and keeping admirable formation*
> *and at the high-port position*
> *walking in the morning on the flat roof of the world*
> *and some walked delicately*
> *sensible of their particular judgment.*

In Parenthesis celebrates the redemption of the soldiers, not the poet's awareness of them conditioned by circumstances which make redemption impossible to anyone except, perhaps, the poet.

Reading recently in *The Hudson Review* a selection of letters from German soldiers in Stalingrad, I had again the impression that where men are made aware of the extremes of the human condition in many cases the values whose loss the intellectual critics have so long deplored emerge. For those values are, at least in part, not institutional and doctrinal but potential in human individuals. What we lack more than values is awareness (when we are not by nature serious or made serious by being thrust into extreme situations) of what it means to be alive. But we can have faith that people are capable of being made conscious. I cannot believe that the decay of the "organic community" has deprived people of the potentiality to be awakened to the implications of consciousness.

486

By this I do not mean that the creative imagination must work upon that kind of chill contemporary humanism which is sometimes served up as the lowest common denominator of science and lost beliefs. What I do suspect, though, is that dogmas and orthodoxies are no way round the fact that in modern conditions all we can be sure of *knowing* is the common humanity of those who consider themselves civilized and those who howl and make faces on the shore. Beyond this, every "belief" is "deliberate" and deliberated. If it rests on institutions and dogmas, then those only divide it from the modern environment. Where it links up with others is in the common human need for affirmation from which it derives. That this is so is demonstrated, I think, not by current critical attitudes but by the greatest poetic achievements of our time which, in spite of dogma and orthodoxies, have rested on the idea of the liberated, unconditioned imagination.

I suggest that Yeats and Eliot and Lawrence and Faulkner, in spite of the fact that they themselves were traditionally-minded artists who deplored the breakdown of tradition in the life around them, clung nevertheless to the idea that the imagination must in modern circumstances reinvent values. It is the contradiction between an eighteenth-century, almost classical critical awareness and artistic self-consciousness, and this trust in the miracle-producing resources of the individual imagination, to which we owe the great achievements of modern art. There is danger today of the paradox being forgotten.

The Organic, the Orchidaceous, the Intellectualized

Stephen Spender

Presented at the Library of Congress February 27, 1962

WE CAN HEAR THROUGH POETRY and criticism of the past 150 years a note of regret already poignant in Wordsworth and Coleridge. It is in Wordsworth's *Intimations of Immortality* in lines such as:

> *What though the radiance which was once*
> > *so bright*
> *Be now forever taken from my sight,*
> > *Though nothing can bring back the hour*
> *Of splendour in the grass, of glory in the*
> > *flower. . . .*

For Wordsworth, this hour belongs to the poet's childhood. But we feel that before Wordsworth's day it belonged to a life in harmony with poetry.

The note is taken up by Coleridge in *Dejection: An Ode:*

> *But now afflictions bow me down to earth:*
> *Nor care I that they rob me of my mirth;*
> > *But oh! each visitation*
> *Suspends what nature gave me at my birth,*
> > *My shaping spirit of Imagination.*

The regret is for a period of innocence in which environment, existence, and poetic expression formed a single harmony.

This vision of childhood is celebrated, also, in Blake's *Songs of Innocence* in poetry of a spontaneous, seemingly still childlike kind. It is significant that the *Songs of Innocence's* "opposite" (to use the word in the Yeatsian sense), the *Songs of Experience,* embraces evil as the price paid in order that the poet may continue to experience life as existential:

> *'Love seeketh only Self to please,*
> *To bind another to Its delight;*
> *Joys in another's loss of ease,*
> *And builds a Hell in Heaven's despite.'*

It is as though Blake thinks that for the adult the childhood immediacy can only be retained by seeking evil in experience where the child found good. The view was expressed, with a sophistication which Blake would probably have disliked, by Baudelaire in *Les Fleurs du mal*. The world of Newtonian science and of "the dark satanic mills" which Blake saw emerging substracts the qualities that are personal and immediate from human relationships. Instead of innocent contact with good, or guilt-ridden but still personal contact with evil, there is, like the fogs of that black country of industrialist barracks which Blake saw covering the green English countryside, the screen between man and man of depersonalized values of power and materialism. Later poets have felt envy for poets preceding the industrial revolution, whom they believe to have lived in the presence of those forces of nature which are today screened from us as much by the inner processes of abstract thinking as by the outward appearances of industrial civilization.

Twentieth-century criticism is full of sophisticated attempts to explain what has been lost—the once associated forms of a sensibility now become dissociated, the pattern of living of the "organic community." But there is the possibility that the sophistication hides a nostalgia just as heavily romanticized as that of Thomas Carlyle for monastic life in the eleventh century, or William Morris for Merrie England. Eliot looks back to the Elizabethan age as "a period when the intellect was immediately at the tips of the senses. Sensation became word and word sensation."

From Carlyle, Ruskin, Morris, and Arnold to T. E. Hulme, Ezra Pound, Yeats, Eliot, Lawrence, and Leavis there is the search for a nameable boojum or snark that can be held responsible for splitting wide apart the once-fused, being-creating consciousness. The Renaissance, the puritan revolution, the French Revolution, the Industrial Revolution, have all been named as villains. There runs through modern criticism the fantasy of a Second Fall of Man. The First Fall, it will be remembered, had the result of introducing Original Sin into the world of Man, exiled from the Garden of Eden and knowing good and evil. The Second Fall seems to result from the introduction of scientific utilitarian values and modes of thinking into the world of personal choice between good and evil, with the result that values cease to be personal and become identified with the usefulness or destructiveness of social systems and material things.

489

Just as I tried before to separate the romantic concept of the power of the sovereign imagination from the picture given by critics and sociological analysts of poets writing in a society where their works are conditioned by modern circumstances, now I want to consider the idea of organic poetry as something separate from the conditions which are held to have produced the dissociation of sensibility.

I do not know whether it is possible to define organic poetry. But it should be possible to cite examples of poetry in which "sensation became word and word sensation," and to indicate the tendency of poetry to be organic in the work of poets who aim at this quality. Poetry tends to be organic when the words and form of the poem seem to grow out of the poet's experience of his environment, particularly, I should say, when that environment and experience seem "natural." There is a continuous process as from environment, through the poet's sensuous nature, into words and form. This is surely what Keats means when he says that poetry should grow as naturally as the leaves of a tree. By growing he does not mean that poets should not work, but that the work itself should resemble the process of diligently growing rather than intellectualization.

Organic poetry is, then, that in which there is identification of the poet's experience of nature (meaning by this the life around him sensuously apprehended) with the words used, without the feeling that mental activity falls like a shadow between the experience and the realized words and form. In such work, sensibility is sensuous, and if there is idea, then it also is experienced sensuously. In the poetry, the reader feels himself present with articulated life realized like leaf or flower by the words.

It is the quality in the speeches of Shakespeare's characters which caused Dryden to comment: "All the images of Nature were still present to him, and he drew them, not laboriously, but luckily; when he describes any thing, you more than see it, you feel it too."

The simplest and clearest examples of organic poetry are, perhaps, to be found in certain passages of Shakespeare's sonnets, for example, Sonnet 12 which contains the lines:

> *When lofty trees I see barren of leaves,*
> *Which erst from heat did canopy the herd,*
> *And summer's green all girded up in sheaves,*
> *Borne on the bier with white and bristly beard. . . .*

It is impossible, I think, to apprehend these lines except as the identification of the object with the feeling clothed in the language. It is as if one were standing in a harvest field with great trees very close and felt within the ripeness of the single moment the turning of all the seasons of the year, and as if at the same time this sensation was clothed in words directly springing from it. Intelligence and feeling are realized in sap and leaves.

Nineteenth-century attempts to produce a similar effect show the contrast between organic poetry and writing which, marvelous as it may be, springs not from immediacy but from the straining of memory after immediate effect. An example is the famous stanzas of Tennyson from *In Memoriam:*

> *By night we linger'd on the lawn,*
>   *For underfoot the herb was dry;*
>   *And genial warmth; and o'er the sky*
> *The silvery haze of summer drawn;*
>
> *And calm that let the tapers burn*
>   *Unwavering; not a cricket chirr'd:*
>   *The brook alone far-off was heard,*
> *And on the board the fluttering urn:*
>
> *And bats went round in fragrant skies,*
>   *And wheel'd or lit the filmy shapes*
>   *That haunt the dusk, with ermine capes*
> *And woolly breasts and beaded eyes;*
>
> *While now we sang old songs that peal'd*
>   *From knoll to knoll, where, couch'd at ease,*
>   *The white kine glimmer'd, and the trees*
> *Laid their dark arms about the field.*

This certainly paints a picture in the mind's eye. It is, indeed, a word painting; that is to say, it attempts in words what a painter does in his different medium. One art is skillfully used to suggest another. The words are chosen with conscious painterly precision and put on the paper at the brush's tip. "Underfoot the herb was dry." One savors the choice of *herb*. It is distinguished from *grass*, and at the same time contains the French word for grass. One may wonder whether in the recollected instant of regret for Hallam there is not too much observation in the "woolly breasts and beaded eyes" of the bats. The fact that the scene is dusk when one could not see "beaded eyes" suggests that the visual mind is working too hard. Too much meticulously detailed emotion seems to have been recollected in too much tranquility.

If, indeed, organic poetry was produced in nineteenth-century England, it is to be found, perhaps, not in the poets but in painters such as Samuel Palmer in his early watercolors and drawings, Constable in his sketches, and, above all, Turner.

The lines from Sonnet 12 which I have quoted might be taken as purely descriptive. It could be argued that they have something of the Words-worthian approach to nature in that they are, perhaps, recollected from childhood; in the most English of meadowy, tree-weighed, river-woven landscapes, one imagines the boy Shakespeare standing in the ripe fields. But Sonnet 26 has the same quality of potent innocence, here embodied in thought removed from immediate observation:

> *Till whatsoever star that guides my moving*
> *Points on me graciously with fair aspect,*
> *And puts apparel on my tatter'd loving,*
> *To show me worthy of thy sweet respect. . . .*

In some of his later poems, Yeats celebrates the purity, strength, and sweetness which seem inseparable from lives lived passionately, in surround-ings identified with vision handed down from the past. He praises those who have the aristocratic view, who live in the country, in great houses, in-herit ancestral properties, ride to hounds, fish, are not "intellectuals." But he does so out of an awareness of his own divided being, torn by regret, filled with remorse:

> *Through intricate motions ran*
> *Stream and gliding sun*
> *And all my heart seemed gay:*
> *Some stupid thing that I had done*
> *Made my attention stray.*
>
> *Repentance keeps my heart impure;*
> *But what am I that dare*
> *Fancy that I can*
> *Better conduct myself or have more*
> *Sense than a common man?*
>
> *What motion of the sun or stream*
> *Or eyelid shot the gleam*
> *That pierced my body through?*
> *What made me live like these that seem*
> *Self-born, born anew?*

Yeats makes a sharp distinction between the life that is a poem, and the sedentary, reflective, remorseful, and nostalgic life which is that of the poet writing poetry. The life that is a poem unreflectingly fuses environ-ment with living. It is the life of people who have not thought and who therefore, if they are privileged, can go on living as their forebears did. But this is impossible for the modern poet, who must needs be reflecting, responsible, remorseful, conscious of a fate of the world wider than the sphere of life he might sensuously apprehend. There is much regret in

492

Yeats for a time when, as he thinks, it was possible to be poet, scholar, and gentleman. So where in Shakespeare there was the unity of unconscious being with conscious creating, in Yeats there is an almost bitter admiration for the "dumb" life of uncreative full-blooded action, bitter regret that the poetic occupation has barred him from poetic existing:

> *I leave both faith and pride*
> *To young upstanding men*
> *Climbing the mountain-side,*
> *That under bursting dawn*
> *They may drop a fly;*
> *Being of that metal made*
> *Till it was broken by*
> *This sedentary trade.*

* * * *

What is called Nature poetry began with the industrial era. With the covering over of the countryside by the industrial slums, untouched nature became a spiritual value. The deeper significance of Nature poetry is surely that it was the attempt of certain poets to return to organic poetry by placing themselves within a setting from which they rejected the values of their contemporaries, those of the town, and put them back into the period of history which belonged to the countryside. The movement from London to the Lake District was not just a geographical withdrawal. It was also a retreat into a fortress of past time. It is significant that Wordsworth, in the introduction to the *Lyrical Ballads,* is not just concerned—as the Wordsworthians sometimes seem to think—with natural scenery and picturesque peasants. He was also concerned with *natural* people—those who lived in Cumberland, their behavior and view of life, and the language they used, which he felt should be the idiom of poetry, because it was the idiom of lives in contact with nature. They were not the lives of the town.

Wordsworth identified the nature of Windermere and Derwentwater with his own childhood. He sought to recover a fusion of nature and being, which he once enjoyed, by reliving those surroundings in his poetry. His greatest descriptive passages have kinetic energy. "Kinetic" is defined in the *Shorter Oxford English Dictionary* as "the power of doing work possessed by a moving body by virtue of its motion." When Wordsworth is actually walking, in motion, literally with muscles and mind going over the territory of his childhood, his memory functions intensely, and his poetry communicates re-lived physical sensation and spiritual exaltation with correspondence of word after word to footstep after footstep. *The Prelude* is the first great *A la recherche du temps perdu.* What is being recaptured is not just the poet's own past but the past relationship of English poetry to the natural environment. And if the Nature poetry of the lake poets is a reaction against industrialism—against the nineteenth century—it is also a reaction against the urban poetry of Pope—against the eighteenth century—whose poetry, in its ideas, was the instrument of a rationalist aristocratic elite.

Augustan poetry was illustrative then of attitudes toward life, theses, rationalism, social hierarchy, fashions, belonging to that age, to the mentality and intellectual life of the town. Wordsworth turned away from the town to seek out the sources of being and feeling as against those of will and reason. This choice is clear enough. The child cannot distinguish between its own body and its mother's, inner self and outer world. It is this sense of returning to an almost pre-conscious level which results in an ambiguous vagueness when Wordsworth attempts to restate his sensations as a philosophy of the unity of being and experiencing:

> . . . . . . *a sense sublime*
> *Of something far more deeply interfused,*
> *Whose dwelling is the light of setting suns,*
> *And the round ocean, and the living air,*
> *And the blue sky, and in the mind of man* . . . .

Here is the *idea* of the organic, but it is not organic in expression.

The ode on *Intimations of Immortality* is one of the great poems in the English language. Having said this, one might well add that it is both profoundly unsatisfactory as communicated innocence and profoundly unconvincing as philosophy. It opens with the poet's recollections of the time that was when the earth seemed "apparelled in celestial light," the light of a glory which has now passed away from the earth. In his childhood, the poet both saw and was one with what he saw. Today, he looks, and things are as beautiful as they were, and yet they remain outside him, they are not an inseparable part of his own being. The being-creating fusion has been split apart. He attributes this calamity to his exile from his own childhood. The view of life he offers to justify the intensity of childhood experiences seems taken for granted by Wordsworthians. It has not always aroused sufficient amazement. It is usually accepted, I think, as belief in reincarnation, and Indians are pleased to think that it provides one of those occasions when English poetry links up with Oriental philosophy. Actually, it puts forward a theory of pre-incarnation, in which we are invited to look backward to a state of existence precedent to birth but not forward to later incarnations. The title, indeed, fits strangely with this view, which suggests that impressions grow ever fainter as our days distance from the mystical state before birth. There is no indication that posthumous intimations will be stronger than the pre-natal ones, unless perhaps we are to suppose that they precede later births. But this is unlikely, since

494

the pre-natal experience is not represented as being posthumous to a previous life.   In fact, any given moment of consciousness is the faintest, because the last, in a line of impressions ever weakening as they grow further away from pre-natal bliss:

> Our birth is but a sleep and a forgetting:
> The Soul that rises with us, our life's Star,
>   Hath had elsewhere its setting,
>   And cometh from afar:
>   Not in entire forgetfulness,
>   And not in utter nakedness,
> But trailing clouds of glory, do we come
>   From God, who is our home. . . .

We are asked, here, to share the feelings of a consciousness which laments the loss of its unconsciousness but which at the same time romanticizes unconsciousness, as a peculiar and intense state of consciousness, of organic union with the mystical sources of nature.   The objection to this is obvious— that unconscious bliss only exists at the moment when it becomes conscious, and that Wordsworth never entered into the full innocence of being a child until he wrote this poetry.   All the same, this answer does not entirely cover the case.   For childhood in his poetry is also a metaphor for a world in which there is no divorce between feeling and creating.

Coleridge, in his *Dejection: An Ode,* analyzes more prosaically the split between childhood joy and adult awareness, between consciousness and unconscious nature.   He admits that it is our own consciousness which gives unconscious nature its attributes:

> O Lady! we receive but what we give,
> And in our life alone does Nature live:
> Ours is her wedding garment, ours her shroud!

What is true of nature is also true of childhood fused with its surroundings. Wordsworth "creceived"—to use Coleridge's word—his childhood because he realized it through his adult consciousness by means of the poetic gift in which that memory was more aware.   Coleridge goes on:

> And would we aught behold, of higher worth,
> Than that inanimate cold world allowed
> To the poor loveless ever-anxious crowd,
>   Ah! from the soul itself must issue forth
> A light, a glory, a fair luminous cloud
>   Enveloping the Earth—

495

Here, the accusing finger points, the boojum is named. It is the "inanimate cold world" with its "loveless ever-anxious crowd" and its material goals and debased values, the urban consciousness, which has set a barrier between the abstract aims of living and "joy," "the shaping spirit of the imagination." It is this which has thrust the poets and "the happy few" (as Stendhal named them) back upon their own resources, so that they must create out of themselves the luminous values which may still envelop the earth.

Coleridge thinks that he might—as he believes Wordsworth succeeded in doing—win back that unity of inward being with outer nature which makes it possible to write organic poetry, the line that springs directly from "the shaping spirit of imagination," which is the result of world-excluded "joy." And certainly the characteristic of the greatest passages in *The Prelude* is that the language and the thought expressed become one with the sensation experienced.

For later poets, what may seem enviable about the lake poets is that they were living in an early phase of modern history when it was still possible for them to reject industrial civilization and choose natural scenery as though it were an alternative which met the life of the town on equal terms, without too much sacrifice of significant expression. Of course, there have been poets since who have rebelled against industrial society— D. H. Lawrence did. But despite his hatred of the towns, Lawrence thought in the idiom of the Nottingham of the coal mines and the chapels in which he had grown up; and the "nature" which he invoked against the industrial urban consciousness had much more of rebellious instinctual human nature about it than of natural scenery, the moods of the weather, and the annals of the peasantry.

Historically, Wordsworth was the last poet who, making such a choice, could write great poetry. This is perhaps to put the matter too crudely; but at the stage of the industrial revolution that was Wordsworth's youth the country and the town life might still have seemed in balance, just as Blake's protests against science and rationalism still had the force behind them of a time when it might have been possible to choose a path other than the one that led to the "dark satanic mills," to reaffirm the England that was Blake's Jerusalem. But, already in the mid-nineteenth century, for a poet to have devoted himself to writing about the scenes and experiences of his childhood in the countryside would have been to write poetry about things that no longer seemed to constitute "important" experiences in the history of modern civilization.

The scene of the larger battle for writing poetry about the human condition in modern times had to be transferred to the towns and the preoccupations of people living in the world of industry and science. Yet, the lake poets defined a choice which still remains between organic, imaginative writing and that which Lawrence called "cerebral," but for which—since cerebral seems denigratory—I prefer to use the term "intellectualized."

That which to Wordsworth was nature was to Keats the poetry of Chaucer, Spenser, and Shakespeare, his deliberately sought-out environment. His was a life lived as far as possible as poetry. Everything in his letters points to his intention of living in the world as though it were palpable poetry, everything in his poetry to his determination to regard his poetry as surrounding life. "Oh, for a life of pure sensation!" he cries, meaning by this not what the editor of the *Chicago Tribune* or the London *Daily Express* might mean, but that he wished to live in a continuity of a sensuously apprehended experience which was one with the sensuous experience of the poetry he read and wrote. In his poetry there is a tendency to identify experienced sensation with sensation imagined, to think that if he could not live a life that was poetry, then he could inhabit a poetry that was life. He recounts the experience, apparently frequent with him, of being rapt from the actual world—the anatomy lesson at the medical school where he was an apprentice—to a far realer world of poetic imagining. What he expected from his friends—Reynolds, Hunt, Shelley, and the others—was that they should form a magic circle which would exclude nearly all experience except the life of the imagination. The kind of reality which makes us call certain novelists realists was to Keats a stiletto pointed at the ruby jugular vein of lived dream. His identification of beauty with truth was simply a way of stating his lived identification of imagination with a passionately sought-out reality. In the context of his poetry and letters, what he meant by "Beauty is truth, truth beauty,—that is all/ Ye know on earth and all ye need to know" is so clear that it is difficult not to suspect critics of bad faith when they pretend not to know what it means.

In his uncannily perceptive study of Keats, Middleton Murry shows the extent to which Keats identified his poetry with the Shakespeare of *Romeo and Juliet, A Midsummer Night's Dream,* and *King Lear.* What corresponds in Keats to the pre-natal Wordsworth "trailing clouds of glory," is a pre-natal Keats who was the young Shakespeare. We are often told that Keats wrote "pure poetry." This is true if we mean by it that he invented lines which, while remaining original to him, were yet a concentrated essence of Chaucer, Spenser, Shakespeare, and Milton become his own spiritual habitat. But such quintessentialized poetry is not the same thing as what I call organic poetry, which springs directly from nature and life. Murry almost convinces himself—as he convinced me when I was 17—that through identification the 23-year-old Keats *was* the young Shakespeare. Beware! Such identification results in extreme dissimilarity to the person with whom one is identified. Shakespeare, himself, was

Shakespeare and not identifying with, say, Chaucer. Keats' poetry, like the poetry of Walter de la Mare, fed off other poetry and the idea of poetry. It is exotic, parasitic, orchidaceous. However, sometimes—through the veils of his own and other men's dreams—experience poignantly personal to him, a real anguish, a real love which refuse to be fobbed off with the poetic, break through and become disturbing autobiographic poetry.

What I have been trying to show is that at the beginning of the Industrial Revolution and until our own day, two interconnected things have happened, which have had revolutionary effects on imaginative writing. One is that poets have felt threatened by a change in consciousness from organic and concrete to scientific and abstract thinking. This has cut them off from a past when poets were intimately and, as it were, immediately in touch with the sacramental, the personal, and the natural forces that were once the ritual of living. The other is that, as a result of this sense of an irremediable change, there began to be an examination and re-evaluation of the once-primary place of imagination in life as in poetry. Although there has been a reaction against the Romantics, there has been no return to the idea that the imagination could or should be put at the service of a rationalistic or politic view of life.

Nostalgia for organic poetry, in which the poetic flows, as it were, in an interrupted continuum out of living experience causes perhaps the bitterest reaction of the modern poet to life as it has been since the Industrial Revolution. It may seem curious that this is so, since organic writing makes up only a small proportion of past literature. It is rare even in Shakespeare's sonnets. Shakespeare usually uses the devices of intellectualized poetry in the way in which a modern poet would. He constructs, for example, metaphors from the machinery of the law to demonstrate his complex feelings about his relationship with a friend. The irony with which, in Sonnet 87, the friendship that is of feeling, without calculation, based on genius, nature, and generosity to the poet, is recognized as being calculated and contractual on the part of the young man, is also modern:

> *Farewell! thou art too dear for my possessing,*
> *And like enough thou know'st thy estimate.*
> *The charter of thy worth gives thee releasing;*
> *My bonds in thee are all determinate.*
> *For how do I hold thee but by thy granting?*
> *And for that riches where is my deserving?*
> *The cause of this fair gift in me is wanting,*
> *And so my patent back again is swerving.*

Organic poetry, as I have attempted to describe it, arises out of an assumed harmony not just between man and his fellow beings, not just between man and social institutions, but between man and the forces in physical nature, perhaps the nature round him, perhaps his own instinctual nature. The supposition is that the powers, deriving from the star, the sap, the soil, reaffirm the natural order of society, the naturalness of human love. The feeling of nature, moving with the forces of stars and weather and beasts magnetically through individual life and through the social hierarchy, is very strong in *King Lear*. Rereading the play recently, I noticed how it is underlined by the character of Albany, husband of Goneril. He is, militarily speaking, on the wrong side in the conflict between the forces of Edmund and those of France. But it is he who abandons the cause of his wife when he sees that her and her sister's behavior is not just wrong but against nature:

> *That nature which contemns its origin*
> *Cannot be bordered certain in itself.*
> *She that herself will sliver and disbranch*
> *From her material sap, perforce must wither*
> *And come to deadly use.*

So passionate regret is expressed by Eliot for the period before the dissociation of sensibility, and by Yeats for a life in which there is no division between the "wise and simple man," "A man who does not exist/ A man who is but a dream"—the fisherman—and the poet, with his sedentary trade, which cuts him off from that time when he himself was of those who "drop a fly" "under bursting dawn." The bitterness is the sense that he is cut off because of the poetry; and yet he feels that in differing circumstances, the poetic imagination would have been entrance to that very sensuous being from which the poet, doomed to intellectualization, is now barred. It seems impossible today to think of the poet as Marvell did when he wrote in *The Garden* of a correspondence between being and creating like intellect complementary to nature:

> *Mean while the Mind, from pleasures less,*
> *Withdraws into its happiness:*
> *The Mind, that Ocean where each kind*
> *Does streight its own resemblance find;*
> *Yet it creates, transcending these,*
> *Far other Worlds, and other Seas;*
> *Annihilating all that's made*
> *To a green Thought in a green Shade.*

What seems to have been disrupted, then, is the being-creating fusion, where in participating in the resemblances which are nature, the poet also comes into possession of his own mind, and makes a fusion which transcends both nature and intellect.

The bitterness at the splitting of the being-creating fusion is, in Yeats, peculiarly personal, a special grudge which the poet bears against his time. The reason for this grudge may be that poets not only want to make poetry, to enjoy the consciousness of a poetic kind of being, they want the experience of poetic living to be realized in the lines of their poetry, poetry and life at times to be one in the writing of the poetry. It is the sense that he has been exiled from being the fisherman who symbolizes the being-creating fusion that is the bitterness in Yeats. Poets do not want to be "Intellectuals."

The bitterness of which I am speaking takes the form, in Lawrence, of rage against what he calls "cerebral" writing, and the program he set himself for being himself in all he wrote. "I write with everything vague— plenty of fire underneath, but, like bulbs in the ground, only shadowy flowers that must be beaten and sustained, for another spring" (letter to Edward Garnett, 29 January 1914). Lawrence—if any modern writer— is organic, but that is both his strength and his weakness. There is something about his work, even at its best, which is like material splitting at the seams. And the split is caused, I think, by the separation of his view of what is life from his practice of literature. His philosophy of living through the senses and through instincts suppressed in the modern age leaves little room for art, because it is a revolt against the aesthetic consciousness, a return to a more primitive poetic activity. It is an attitude which can be preached but which cannot attain an expression in which the famous Laurentian sense of life and full artistic awareness resolved in satisfactory form are fused. Thus, in certain passages about the dark gods, phallic consciousness, sex, and the like, Lawrence gives the impression that the life expressed does not lie in the art realized but in the physical body or the instinctual life of the reader. Sometimes the printed page, as it were, sacrificially or sacramentally represents the physical or the instinctual and sexual body of Lawrence himself. He makes it clear that by phallic consciousness he means only his own particular variety of blood consciousness and sexual feeling, and that he disapproves of behavior which does not accord with the models he lays down.

Thus, although there is modern organic poetry, it is the result of a fusion which seems forced, and this is felt in a cerain jarring quality in the technique and form. In a way different from Lawrence, but which leads me to think that he would have preferred Lawrence—as he did Walt Whitman—to many of his contemporaries, Gerard Manley Hopkins is organic; his poetry seems always the result of the fusion of the external experience acting directly upon his sensibility and producing language and form. But

500

the identification with external circumstances is either the result of deliberately willed involution with nature—what Hopkins called "inscape"—or of great anguish. One may merely prefer the poetry of Hopkins to the literary flow of Tennyson—and, still more, of Swinburne—yet the willedness makes for unbearable strain, and the suffering seems at times the perverse result of Hopkins' violation of his own poetic nature. Just as the organic in Wordsworth seems the kineticism of muscular movement across a childhood scene returned to by the poet, producing a kinetic poetry, so with Hopkins there is the kineticism of willed visual concentration, grinding despair.

We have the sense, then, that modern circumstances have set up a screen between nature and man so that the harmonious relationship realized in organic poetry, in which the soul sees itself reflected in the physical environment, is prevented. The only way of return to the being-creating fusion is through spiritual or physical violence, tearing down the screen and forcing the inner sensibility into contact with the external.

Hence, it seems that intellectual awareness of the situation which has set up the barrier is necessary for poetry to develop language and forms which do not appear to be the result of a forced juxtaposition of inner and outer situations:

> *Between the conception*
> *And the creation*
> *Between the emotion*
> *And the response*
> *Falls the Shadow.*

What I call "Intellectualized" is the work in which consciousness of the task undertaken, the means employed, the necessary strategy, dominate the writing. Instead of the old being-creating thee is the poetic-critical fusion.

Imagination Means Individuation

Stephen Spender

Presented at the Library of Congress February 28, 1962

THE ATTITUDES OF MODERN POETS cannot be understood, even in the case of Eliot, simply as their being a reaction against Romanticism and a return to tradition and othodoxy. On the surface it would, of course, seem that the most obvious characteristic of the movement in poetry initiated by Hulme, Pound, and Eliot early in the present century was a revolt against Romantic standards. And it is true that the great bloc made by the Romantics (shutting out the view of everything beyond the early nineteenth century except the highest peaks of English poetry—Shakespeare, Chaucer, and Milton) has been removed. Today, students realize that Shelley, Keats, and Byron were extraordinary men with extraordinary gifts living in an extraordinary time, but they know, also, that these poets had little time in which to mature, and that the collected works of Shelley are a wild, exotic, and unweeded garden.

With the Romantic bloc removed, words concretely used, metaphors that are coherent and not vague have, as it were, surged forward, passed through the undisciplined Romantic lines, and joined hands with present poetry. Marvell, Dryden, and Pope have become accessible to us in a way that perhaps they were not to Victorian readers. *I read Othello's visage in his mind:* a generation that began by learning the calm and beauty realized in the surface of seventeenth- and eighteenth-century poetry, stayed to prefer that order to the Romantic disorder.

However, this cutting of Romantic poetry down to size did not lead to the new classicism which T. E. Hulme predicted in his *Speculations*. What it did initiate was a revolution in method, in technique, in spreading the idea that writing poetry was deliberate and conscious work and not a matter of entering into an effluvial state of self-intoxication. Yet against this picture of return to a pre-Romantic consciousness of the intellectual problems of writing poetry, we have to bear in mind that, by and large, the criticism of the Augustan poets by the Romantics has, with certain qualifications, been accepted by the anti-Romantic moderns, perhaps on the grounds of its *historic necessity* rather than its critical justice but accepted nevertheless. When Eliot retracted some of his early attack on Milton, he gave as his excuse that, as a young man, it had been necessary for him to attack Milton for the sake of the development of his own poetry, just as it had been a poetic necessity for Wordsworth to attack Pope.

So we are confronted with the paradox that, although there has been a reaction against the Romantics and back toward the poets who preceded them, nevertheless, the same poet-critics who made this revolt have taken over the subjective view of the imagination which was Romantic. Joyce, Yeats (in his later work), Eliot, and Pound combine critical consciousness in the *act* of writing with instinctive subjective consciousness in their use of material from dreams, as well as in their fragmentariness, obscurity, mysteriousness, and the like. They are objective in being extremely aware of what they want to say and how to say it; they are subjective in their realization that everything said has to be reinvented from the deepest and most isolated center of individual imagination. They are aware of the importance of contemporary idiom; but they are also aware of the greater importance of the magic of language which is "rich and strange."

There could not be a return to eighteenth-century classicism—to the idea of the unified intellectual culture of an elite, exercising reason to reconcile science, God, and the aristocracy, and sublimating the arguments in transparent poetry. The Romantics are of our modern world, and modern poetry comes out of their situation. When we uphold Pope against the Romantics we are, after all, only expressing the view that Byron also expressed—despising the works of himself and his contemporaries, and advocating Pope but having to be Byron.

There has been talk, on and off, ever since T. E. Hulme's *Speculations,* of a new classicism. Hulme thought that a movement of Cubists and Vorticists in painting and of Imagists in poetry could be founded on a synthesis between the tradition of pre-Renaissance nonindividualist Byzantine art and the cold abstract forms of the dehumanized modern age of machinery. But classical revivals cannot be based on dubious historic analogies. Interpreted into political action, Hulme's wish to put the clock back to an authoritarian age, indifferent to human values, was Fascism. His aesthetic ideas became economic theory and Fascist ideology in the *Cantos* of his admirer, Ezra Pound. The obvious objection to a classical revival is that there is no unity of outlook in our modern age, divided between science and the humanities. The only unity we can have is of a kind forced upon us by state-directed politics. A willed and forced modern parody of classicism is that branch of propagandist advertising extended into art, which is called social realism.

503

So, in a civilization split in its allegiances between scientific scepticism, specialization, and utilitarianism and the surviving religious and cultural traditions—more powerful, these, than is generally admitted—there can be no classical revival. What we have instead, is the setting up of outposts of orthodoxy and dogma in the modern waste land. Eliot, Auden, and others have established fortresses of past tradition, reimagined, reinvented in the contemporary idiom of their poetry. But just because terms like tradition, orthodoxy, and dogma are employed, we should not confuse the comparatively isolated position of the orthodox with a time when whole societies were orthodoxies. A dogma today remains sectarian in a society of sects, religious and secular. Orthodoxy today is not that of society but of the orthodox only.

I am here considering literature and not religion. For I well understand that from a religious standpoint it is not very important whether there are few believers or many. Faith may burn more intensely in the day of outcasts than in that of complacent establishments. But for literature, the question whether the religious symbolism and tradition of poets correspond to those in the minds of their readers does matter. For nonbelieving readers, I do not think that there is a great difference between the orthodox symbolism of writers like Eliot and Auden and the heterodoxy of Rilke or the eclectic religion of Yeats, as realized in their poetry. Moreover, I think this is recognized by Eliot in his poetic practice. For he does not write so much as one conforming to a doctrine already present and accepted in the mind of his reader, as like one who invents (just as much as Rilke or Yeats) his symbols and values.

There is every difference, of course, between religious faith and poetic imagination. But the modern poet may have to reinvent his faith as poetic imagination; and so to the common reader the difference between the dogma of Eliot and the private religions of Rilke or Yeats may not seem apparent or to matter to the poetry.

This brings us back to the central role of the imagination in modern as in Romantic poetry. In a world of fragmented values, the imagination cannot illustrate accepted doctrines, cannot refer to symbolic meanings already recognized by the reader, symbols of the faith he believes in and imbibed with his education. Everything has to be reinvented, as it were, from the beginning, and anew in each work. Every position has to be *imagined* in the poem. The imagining cannot be left to the social environment.

But if there are not ceremonies, symbols, sacraments, generally accepted by the community, within the ritual of living—if society offers no face but the mere machinery of receiving work and giving pay, and providing amusement and distractions; and if beyond this there lurk only the life-or-death, promising-or-threatening abstract hopes and fears of the machines—

504

then, nonetheless, the artist has to find referents of human consciousness on which to work. These referents are inevitably the elemental qualities of the individual's experience of life—his inescapable awareness, after all, that he is alive and situated in a time and place—his hopes and fears, his loves and hates. He is capable of being shown of what consciousness consists.

There is in much modern literature an evocation of compensatory depths in individual human life. Everyone carries round an infinity, if not in his head, then in his sex. If his thoughts are cupboard-size, his dreams, nevertheless, open onto prairies, constellations. Art invokes the subconscious world to counterbalance the conscious results of materialism. The most potent and awesome lesson of Joyce's *Ulysses* and *Finnegans Wake* is that an eyelid, open or shut to let in the light of consciousness, the dark of sleep, can open out in every direction into memories which, through chains of association, would traverse the whole past and future of humanity. Sometimes Lawrence seems convinced that the forces of the unconscious released by the sexual act might transform the whole world, make men and women become gods instead of being social units.

It is this appeal to forces stronger than those in conscious individuality, but which yet *are* the individual and of which he can be made conscious, that writers as opposed as Lawrence and Joyce and movements as divergent as futurism, dadaism, surrealism, and existentialism yet have in common. Freud, Jung, and other psychologists have, of course, provided a theoretical background for this literature, which could hardly have been written without them.

In times when here are no generally shared religious or societal interpretations of experience, the artist may take over the task of inventing his own referents, or of reinforcing past ones as though they were reinvented for his poetic purposes. There is the idea of a burden, a task, a pressure of disparate outer things seeking to realize themselves as inner significance, running through the history of poetry during the past hundred and more years. One may, of course, resent this burden, on the grounds that it puts responsibility of a too vast and altogether too public and impersonal kind on the artist, who can only retain his integrity by limiting his experience within the scope of that which he can personalize. The objection to Shelley's "we must imagine that which we know" is on these grounds. A history of poetry during the past hundred years and more could be written that would relate it to swings between the pole of the idea of the imagination as a task imposed, and that of it as strictly limited to the poet's most confined personal awareness.

As so often in such controversies, there is no real contradiction here—for in fact nothing is artistically significant unless it has become personalized. But there are, nonetheless, pressures and tensions from the outside life upon

505

the inner consciousness. Social conscience can easily work a destructive effect upon artistic conscience, which is not a duty toward society at all but a duty of being conscious as an individual and as an artist. And those who are aware of this danger may insist too much that consciousness can only be about things that are private.

The ideal and often evoked task for the poet in society is to personalize in his work the greatest possible amount and intensity of interest outside his private concerns. A world of external impersonal forces must be sacrificially reinvented as the poet's inner personal world, so that, for his readers, the impersonal modern world may be personalized in poetry. To avoid misunderstanding, I repeat that I do not mean that a poet has to become a public figure or that—to use Keats' phrase—the shadow of public life must fall across his work. What I am concerned with is his awareness of a contemporary situation which affects personal relations and art itself, and which is different from past situations.

The great example of an attempt to personalize the contemporary situation was, of course, Walt Whitman's, especially in *Song of Myself*. Walt Whitman took upon himself the task of imagining the America of his day and of seeking to invent in his poetry the geographical and historical concept of America which his contemporaries and future generations of Americans might themselves realize in their feelings and attitudes. In order to accomplish this, Whitman had not only to invent a kind of poetry different from European models, but he had to become America, as America had, in a sense, in his own imagination, to become Whitman. A great deal of his poetry is about this process, about how Whitman became the wounded of the Civil War, how the continent entered into and absorbed the consciousness of Whitman (just as in *Finnegans Wake* the landscape becomes the consciousness of Joyce's dreamer). Whitman summarizes himself:

> *Immense have been the preparations for me,*
> *Faithful and friendly the arms that have help'd me.*
>
> *Cycles ferried my cradle, rowing and rowing like cheerful boatmen;*
> *For room to me stars kept aside in their own rings;*
> *They sent influences to look after what was to hold me.*
> *Before I was born out of my mother, generations guided me;*
> *My embryo has never been torpid—nothing could overlay it.*
>
> *For it the nebula cohered to an orb,*
> *The long slow strata piled to rest it on,*
> *Vast vegetables gave it sustenance,*
> *Monstrous sauroids transported it in their mouths, and*
>   *deposited it with care.*

All forces have been steadily employ'd to complete and delight me;
Now on this spot I stand with my robust Soul.

Everything has to become thus personal and individuated to be imagined, because there is no such thing as a public imagination. Imagination means individuation. What is imagined may be a world as large as that of Shakespeare or Dickens; but it is imagined by one person, the writer. And it becomes part of the life of one person, the reader.

The kind of communication that is art rests on the truth that individuation is the basic pattern of all experiencing—that everyone, in his view of everything outside him, in his knowledge of past and present, in his relations with other people, and even in what he has read, makes, and is, his own world. He may be influenced by others, he may be unoriginal and be scarcely conscious of having an identity separate from that of colleagues or tribe, but the fact remains that he is irreducibly himself, filling a body and occupying a time and space that are no one's but his own and perceiving things through his sense organs that are no one else's. The "truth" of poetry is that it discourses on this just assumption that poet and reader are unique. Every poet begins again from the beginning that is himself, and outside experience meets in the center that is his unique sensibility.

Poetry is, then, not a cooperative effort leading to collective results, as is science, in which the personal contribution becomes absorbed into the body of collected impersonal knowledge and the personal quality of the scientist disappears. There is, of course, in each country, a "sum" of poetry which consists of all the poems written in that language; and they add up to more than any poem or poems. But, supposing that the total poems in a language could be signified by the figure 100, then it is a total in which each figure remains, as it were, separate, a sum of 1 and 1 and 1, each retaining its uniqueness though a fraction of, and contributing to, the whole. Through the fusion of the imagination of the writer with that of the reader, the reader is able to hear with the ears, see through the eyes, and feel with the feelings of the writer, the world which becomes that of both. This is possible because the outward forms and techniques of art imitate— as the leaf the seed—the inner mode of perception of the poet, a person, experiencing through his unique mind and body the world outside himself. The poet is writing as one person for the reader reading as one person.

A situation which holds true of poetry in all its communication is that expressed in *A Shropshire Lad* by Housman, dramatizing to the person he loves—who certainly will not understand—that ideal communication which is simply that of one life situated, speaking to another also situated:

> *From far, from eve and morning*
> *And yon twelve-winded sky,*

> *The stuff of life to knit me*
>   *Blew hither: here am I.*
>
> *Now—for a breath I tarry*
>   *Nor yet disperse apart—*
> *Take my hand quick and tell me,*
>   *What have you in your heart.*
>
> *Speak now, and I will answer;*
>   *How shall I help you, say;*
> *Ere to the wind's twelve quarters*
>   *I take my endless way.*

It is extremely important, I think, to insist that the poetic imagination is centripetal, a bringing together of experiences from a circumference which could theoretically be enlarged to include all pasts and presents, all things known and experienced, into the center of the artist's individual sensibility where they are the projected patterns which communicate that consciousness to readers.

The view has been put forward recently by C. P. Snow, in a famous and much-debated essay, that there are today two cultures, a scientific and a literary. It is clear that what Sir Charles means by "culture" in this context are, on the one hand the ideas and *mores* of scientists and those, on the other, of writers. He is concerned with what is being discovered and what is being imagined. Sir Charles reproaches scientists for their ignorance of literature and the literary figures for their ignorance of science. He wants there to be bridges between the so-called two cultures. He tries to apportion blame equally to both sides in the alleged controversy, but it is evident that his sympathies are really with the scientists. He enters into their reasons for not appreciating the poets. He does not enter into the reasons of the poets for not appreciating the scientists. For he bases his whole case on ignorance and knowledge. The scientists do not *know* literature and the men of letters do not know science. Put like this, obviously the writers are the more to blame, for science is knowledge, whereas literature is the imagining of that which can be imagined. On grounds of knowledge, the scientists are not to be blamed for not knowing works of the imagination, since from their point of view they offer little to know. The members of the literary culture have, in his view, ignored a renaissance taking place in science; all that the scientists, on their side, appear to have ignored are the medieval ideas of antiprogressive men of letters.

As a thesis, a good deal of this seems open to dispute. I happen to know that the favorite reading of one of the most eminent physicists, J. D. Bernal, is *Finnegans Wake*. In itself this may not be statistically significant. Yet

508

one can see why a physicist might be interested in Joyce, whose novels are just as much an invention of the modern mind as is a jet aircraft, whose technique has resemblances to work in the laboratory, and whose intelligence expresses a new kind of sensibility. It would be crude, surely, of scientists to think that novels to be scientific have to be about scientists or about matters of social administration, and poems, about social progress. A scientist would surely agree that if literature is scientific it is nevertheless dealing with special kinds of material and uses special techniques. An argument defending poetry, on the ground that poets employ extremely subtle and complex techniques for expressing the psychology of individuals, has been put forward by I. A. Richards, and it should have been considered by C. P. Snow if he wished to avoid the charge that what he really meant was that literature should reflect scientific progress and so earn the interest of scientists.

Sir Charles raises important points which have not, perhaps, so much to do with culture as with the education of children who later become scientists or writers, but he blurs the distinction between the world as viewed by science and the world as viewed by poetic imagination. Restricting even the difference to the level of Sir Charles' debate (that the scientists are progressives and the writers reactionaries), it remains true that science is concerned with the extension of the resources of materials and power which can be put to general use, while literature is concerned with the meaning that individual life has in the world in which these resources have been made available.

It may be true that certain modern writers—poets, especially—have shown too great antipathy to the beneficial aspects of science. Though the reason they have done so is because they are quite rightly concerned not with science but with the modern world which is so largely the result of science. It is a world in which past values have been fragmented, in which the constructive powers of science are balanced by its powers of destruction, in which the forces of human personality have broken down, and men and women have come to think of themselves as "social units." But to blame scientists, in their disinterested pursuit of knowledge, for all this would be as unwarranted as to blame writers for delivering their warnings against progress. On the whole, it would seem that for the so-called literary culture to be critical of the so-called scientific is right. As the most interesting poet of World War I, Wilfred Owen, wrote in the preface to his poems: "All a poet can do to-day is warn."

By a literary culture we should mean, I think, the poems, plays, novels— and perhaps also works in new media and forms, such as radio and television and science fiction—which, ideally, should imagine the whole experience of living, should treat the past as well as the present as a single whole within individual consciousness. The literary culture is essentially critical of the contemporary world, which is the result of the scientific. This criticism may be expressed explicitly in critical works or imaginatively in poetic ones. It keeps alive the sense of the past as living thoughts and feelings crystalized, and in this way it judges present living by the realities of past life. Thus, in America today there are traditions still vital within the work of classic American writers, which, as it were, stand in perpetual court of judgment over what is today American life. Modern American literature seems, moreover, to indicate that everyone is not happy in a civilization largely devoted to flooding consumers with consumer goods.

Sir Charles Snow attacks the representatives of the "literary culture" (he means Ezra Pound and T. S. Eliot) for their hostility to progressive ideas, and he argues that to take sides against progress today means letting large numbers of people starve. But even while he is making this attack, the moral bias of it does not come out of the methods of science, which are conducive equally to killing large numbers of people and to feeding them. "Progress" is one of those ideas with roots in primitive Christianity, humanism, and the French Revolution, which form one aspect of a long debate that is an important part of Victorian and twentieth-century literature. Scientists who support progress do not belong to a special scientific culture, but to that of Dickens, Shaw, and Wells.

Science today is concerned with research and technology; the poetic imagination is concerned with testing the values of the modern world, which is so largely the result of science as experienced good or evil, by the standard of the past tradition relived in the consciousness of the artist, realized in his work, and judged by his reader. Progress produces material benefits, but it is only through the alive intelligence of the imagination that these can be related to significant values. And although the great material needs of the world can and should be satisfied by progress, there is the great spiritual danger of judging individual lives as units in the progressive society, that is, as social units which ought to be statistically happier and to live statistically better lives because statistically they are better fed. But perhaps a parallel problem with undernourishment is that people are not automatically better or even happier as a result of social improvements. For example, it is notorious that in England the real benefits accomplished by the Welfare State have produced an unprecedented spiritual malaise. If there were danger of stopping progress as a result of T. S. Eliot's "reactionary" attitude towards it, there might be justification for the charge that the supporters of the literary culture are in favor of taking potential bread out of the mouths of the starving. But since this is not the case, they are surely right in drawing attention to the spiritual crisis which results from beneficial materialism.

510

Though I do not agree with the formula of the "two cultures," I think that within the "literary culture" itself, it may well be just to criticize poets for their ignorance of the great advances made by science. This criticism leads back to the problem of the imagination. For there are examples enough to show—the effect on Coleridge's poetry of his delvings into abstract philosophy is one—that the poetic imagination is harmed by absorbing more intellectual knowledge than it can digest. The poet can use no more knowledge than he can transform into his poetry, the novelist no more than he can make the behavior and dialogue of realized action and characters.

What writers may fruitfully know is that which they can experience with their sensibility. So it is not so important that they should know the second law of thermodynamics as that they should perceive the subtle changes effected in the rhythm of language by the environment resulting from inventions and its influence on human behavior and modes of feeling. It is not scientific knowledge but its effects which become part of the experience of modern life. Joyce, Eliot, and Lawrence certainly reflect in their works the results of science. Even in his own novels, C. P. Snow creates fiction about the results of science and bureaucracy, not about scientific theories and business management. And if one were to defend the two-dimensional characters in these novels, one would argue that these embodiments of ideas and petty ambitions are studies of the effect on human beings of working in laboratories, colleges, and government departments. It may be that without knowing it, with his imagination Snow creates a picture which is critical of progress, and that as an artist he agrees with T. S. Eliot, whom as a critic he dismisses as reactionary, that "we are the hollow men."

Shakespeare did not have to know the philosophical and scientific theorizing of his time to reflect the passionate individualism of the Renaissance. Dante, of course, was immensely learned in the theory of the universe of his age. The knowledge of his time was of a kind which interpreted the whole of existence within the unity of a single view of of life. Knowledge and imagination were then one and the same. It is possible, of course, that the present revolution in science might arrive at the point where analytic and statistical inquiry broke down, and the behavior of infinitesimally small impulses, particles of energy, appeared entirely accidental, and their interpretation was inevitably subjective to the scientist. In that event, the poetic imagination would link up with the scientific, and perhaps we would, at the end of an immensely long journey, return to a culture based on the unity of logic and imagination. Saint-John Perse pointed out in his Nobel Prize acceptance discourse at

511

Stockholm: "Le mystère est commun. Et la grande aventure de l'esprit poétique ne le cède en rien aux ouvertures dramatiques de la science moderne. Des astronomes ont pu s'affoler d'une théorie de l'univers en expansion: il n'est pas moins d'expansion dans l'infini moral de l'homme—cet univers."

But visions of modern experience of life seen as a whole seem to depend on the imaginative interpretation of the forces that are the results of science. And in the twentieth century, the standpoint from which it has been possible for poetic imaginations to envisage modern life as a whole seems to be that of life viewed as tragedy, a position made more convincing by our catastrophic modern history. The modern works in which life has been seen steadily and whole are the pessimistic poetry of Hardy, the apocalyptic *Waste Land,* and the dancing over the graves of the dead of the later Yeats.

The poetic imagination is, then, individual, and the ideal task of modern poetry, as it was envisaged by the Romantics, and as it haunts the artistic conscience still today, is to imagine the modern experience of life through the sensibility of the individual poet and as a whole. The history of modern literature is one of writers approaching and withdrawing from this challenge.

When the withdrawal occurs because the poet feels that his talents or interests or view of poetry should be limited to what he can best deal with, there is no cause for protest. The concept of a great task like a public duty should not be set threateningly over art.

So the use of the phrase "the two cultures" blurs the distinction between two different things by treating them as if each were the same kind of thing. The idea that the literary culture is opposed to, or that it should be complementary to, the scientific culture, and that intellectual life is split into these two halves, suggests one of those false dichotomies, like "personal issues" and "newspaper issues," which today bedevil intellectual debate. Adding to the confusion is the difficulty attached to defining the word "culture" itself. Sometimes Snow uses this as though he means a center of contemporary awareness, sometimes as if he means the symptomatic behavior of a group. One might say that scientific workers show certain dispositions, develop certain propensities—a liking for gadgets, for example, and an indifference to modern poetry: this makes them a culture. And from the same sociological viewpoint, writers have traits in common which make them a culture: some of them smoke pipes, wear tweeds, and pretend to be countrymen or farmers.

But if the two cultures are in competition it is because each of them has claims to interpret the significant life of the time. From this point of view the characteristic of the literary culture is the attempt of writers to create forms that express the significance of life which they have both

512

experienced and imagined. What is so expressed can be summed up in the phrase: "how it is to be alive in a given set of circumstances." Imagination is that which enables the poet to enter into situations which extend beyond himself, into other lives, other times, other places.

Thus, a Wordsworth, a Blake, or a Lawrence, while being himself—and thus representing in his work the mode by which experience is felt, through his individual sensibility—is also occupied with interpreting into artistic forms the effects on individual life of what are, in the widest sense, contemporary conditions, which he measures against the imagined past and his appreciation of the potentialities of life.

Obviously, the functions of science have been quite different from this, and are in no way competing with or parallel to it. Historically, scientists have been preoccupied with accumulating knowledge, theories, techniques, instruments, machinery. It has been the understanding of science that knowledge is pursued for its own sake, and that its discoveries and inventions are handed over to those who use them without the scientist having responsibility beyond the research which has gone into them, the validity of the experiments by which they have been proven or tested. The scientist is responsible to a kind of truth which is not human in its concern for its effect upon human beings.

The individual scientist uses the knowledge and instruments which have been put at his disposal by past and present other scientists. He does not have a vital concern with the past of science, because there is no question but that science is progressive. The most recent stage of development of any branch of science is an advance on previous ones. The new discovery absorbs into itself past discoveries—unless there is question of an error which has to be uncovered and corrected.

Literature is not in this way progressive. On the contrary, poets are dogged with the feeling that earlier poetry may be better not only than theirs but better than anything they are able to do: and since they regard poetry as in some respect the measure of the individual condition in its time, the fact they feel that conditions undermine their talents bears witness, also, against the life of this time.

Recent American Fiction

Saul Bellow

Presented at the Library of Congress January 21, 1963

GERTRUDE STEIN is supposed to have explained to Hemingway that "remarks are not literature." Tonight I am offering some remarks, and I make no claim for them whatever. A writer's views on other writers may have a certain interest, but it should be clear that he reads what they write almost always with a special attitude. If he should be a novelist, his own books are also a comment on his contemporaries and reveal that he supports certain tendencies and rejects others. In his own books he upholds what he deems necessary, and usually by the method of omission he criticizes what he understands as the errors and excesses of others.

I intend tonight to examine the view taken by recent American novelists and short-story writers of the individual and his society, and I should like to begin by telling you the title of a new book by Wylie Sypher. It is *Loss of the Self in Modern Literature and Art*. I do not propose to discuss it; I simply want to cite the title of Mr. Syphers' book, for in itself it tells us much about the common acceptance of what the Spanish critic Ortega y Gasset described some years ago as "the dehumanization of the arts." One chapter of Mr. Sypher's book is devoted to the Beats, but, for the most part, he finds, as we might have expected, that the theme of annihilation of Self, and the description of an "inauthentic" life which can never make sense, is predominantly European and particularly French. The names he most often mentions are those of André Gide, Sartre, Beckett, Sarraute, and Robbe-Grillet. These are writers whose novels and plays are derived from definite theories which make a historical reckoning of the human condition and are peculiarly responsive to new physical, psychological, and philosophical theories. American writers, when they are moved by a similar spirit to reject and despise the Self, are seldom encumbered by such intellectual baggage, and this fact pleases their European contemporaries, who find in them a natural, that is, a brutal or violent acceptance of the new universal truth by minds free from intellectual preconceptions. In the early twenties D. H. Lawrence was delighted to discover a blunt, primitive virtue in the first stories of Ernest Hemingway, and 20 years later André Gide praised Dashiell Hammett as a good barbarian.

European writers take strength from German phenomenology and from the conception of entropy in modern physics in order to attack a romantic idea of the Self, triumphant in the 19th century but intolerable in the 20th. The feeling against this idea is well-nigh universal. The First World War with its millions of corpses gave an aspect of the horrible to romantic over-valuation of the Self. The leaders of the Russian Revolution were icy in their hatred of bourgeois individualism. In the communist countries millions were sacrificed in the building of socialism, and almost certainly the Lenins and the Stalins, the leaders who made these decisions, serving the majority and the future, believed they were rejecting a soft, nerveless humanism which attempted in the face of natural and historical evidence to oppose progress. A second great assault on the separate Self sprang from Germany in 1939. Just what the reduction of millions of human beings into heaps of bone and mounds of rag and hair or clouds of smoke betokened, there is no one who can plainly tell us, but it is at least plain that something was being done to put in question the meaning of survival, the meaning of pity, the meaning of justice and of the importance of being oneself, the individ-ual's consciousness of his own existence.

It would be odd, indeed, if these historical events had made no impres-sion on American writers, even if they are not on the whole given to taking the historical or theoretical view. They characteristically depend on their own observations and appear at times obstinately empirical. But the latest work of writers like James Jones, James Baldwin, Philip Roth, John O'Hara, J. F. Powers, Joseph Bennett, Wright Morris, and others shows the indi-vidual under a great strain. Laboring to maintain himself, or perhaps an idea of himself (not always a clear idea), he feels the pressure of a vast public life, which may dwarf him as an individual while permitting him to be a giant in hatred or fantasy. In these circumstances he grieves, he com-plains, rages, or laughs. All the while he is aware of his lack of power, his inadequacy as a moralist, the nauseous pressure of the mass media and the weight of money and organization, of cold war and racial brutalities. Adapting Gresham's theorem to the literary situation one might say that public life drives private life into hiding. People begin to hoard their spiritual valuables. Public turbulence is largely coercive, not positive. It puts us into a passive position. There is not much we can do about the crises of international politics, the revolutions in Asia and Africa, the rise and transformation of masses. Technical and political decisions, invisible powers, secrets which can be shared only by a small elite, render the private will helpless and lead the individual into curious forms of behavior in the private sphere. Public life, vivid and formless turbulence, news, slogans, mysterious crises, and unreal configurations dissolve coherence in all but the most resistant minds, and even to such minds it is not always a confident certainty that resistance can ever have a positive outcome. To take narcotics has become in some circles a mark of rebellious independence, and to scorch one's personal earth is sometimes felt to be the only honorable course. Rebels have no bourgeois certainties to return to when rebellions are done. The fixed points seem to be disappearing. Even the Self is losing its firm outline.

One recent American novel deals openly and consciously with these problems. It is *The Thin Red Line* by James Jones, a book which, describing the gross and murderous conditions of jungle combat, keeps a miraculously sensitive balance and does not weary us with a mere catalog of horrors. What Mr. Jones sees very precisely is the fluctuation in the value of the life of the individual soldier. Childhood in some cases ends for the fighting man as he accepts the lesson of realism. The attitude of Storm, one of the older soldiers, towards Fife, a younger man, is described as follows: "He [Fife] was a good enough kid. He just hadn't been away from home long enough. And Storm, who had started off bumming during the Depression when he was only fourteen, couldn't find kids like that very interesting." Storm, the mess sergeant, tolerates the inexperienced Fife, but First Sergeant Welsh has no such tolerance. He cannot abide softness and the lack of realism, and he cruelly and punitively teaches the hard lesson to his undeveloped subordinates. Real knowledge as he sees it is brutal knowledge and it must be painfully and brutally learned. The heart of the lesson, as Welsh understands it, is that it matters little—it matters, therefore, not at all—whether any single man survives or falls. Welsh offers no indulgence to anyone and asks none for himself. When, under fire, a young soldier asks permission to dig his foxhole near him, Welsh curses him off savagely. When, under stress, unable to bear the groans of a dying man, Welsh leaves his shelter under fire to bring the soldier in, he wonders at himself. His heroism is useless and he returns. "Sobbing audibly for breath, he made himself a solemn unspoken promise never again to let his screwy wacked-up emotions get the better of his common sense." Sergeant Welsh has one word to which he refers all matters which press for explanation, and that magical word is Property. In Welsh's view the idea of Property alone makes the behavior of mankind intelligible. But Property is not an unassailable certainty. The word is used for purposes of incantation and has no real meaning to Welsh. His message to mankind is that you must cast the cold eye on life, on death.

Mr. Jones shrewdly understands that the philosophy of Welsh is not

516

ultimately hard. Towards himself the sergeant is not fanatically severe, and his toughness betrays a large degree of self-pity. What Jones describes here is the casting off of a childish or feminine or false virtue, despised because it cannot meet the test of survival. In apprehending what is real, Jones' combat soldiers learn a bitter and levelling truth and in their realism revenge themselves on the slothful and easy civilian conception of the Self. The new idea cruelly assails the old, exposing its conventionality and emptiness. Young Fife, after he has gone the rugged course, kills like the rest, becomes quarrelsome, drinks and brawls, and casts off his hesitant, careful, and complaining childishness.

A very different sort of novel, in a peaceful sphere far removed from the explosions and disembowellings of Guadalcanal, is J. F. Power's *Morte d'Urban*, which does not so much study as brood over the lives of priests belonging to the Order of St. Clement. Father Urban, a well-known preacher and a man of some talent, is transferred for reasons not clearly understood from Chicago, where he has worked effectively, to a new Foundation of the Order in Duesterhaus, Minnesota. To Urban, a sociable and civilized priest, this transfer can only be seen as a mysterious banishment, and he is described by Mr. Powers looking from the train windows at the empty country beyond Minneapolis. ". . . flat and treeless, Illinois without people. It didn't attract, it didn't repel. He saw more streams than he'd see in Illinois, but they weren't working. November was winter here. Too many white frame farmhouses, not new and not old, not at all what Father Urban would care to come to for Thanksgiving or Christmas. Rusty implements. Brown dirt. Grey skies. Ice. No snow. A great deal of talk about this on the train. Father Urban dropped entirely out of it after an hour or so. The Voyageur arrived in Duesterhaus a few minutes before eleven that morning, and Father Urban was the only passenger to get off."

In more ways than one, Father Urban is viewed as the only passenger. At the new Foundation he is, without complaint, in a solitary situation. In charge of the Duesterhaus Foundation is Father Wilfred ". . . who, on account of his broad nose and padded cheeks, had been called Bunny in the Novitiate. Bunny Bestudik." Father Wilfred's concerns are all of a practical nature. His interests are the interests of any Midwestern American who has to run a place efficiently; he watches the fuel bills, thinks about the pickup truck and its rubber, the cost of paint, and is anxious to have good public relations. This religious Order is described as a community of consumers. It is the American and average character of activities whose ultimate aim is religious that Mr. Powers wants to describe. His tone is dry and factual as he tells of the discussions of the Fathers who have to heat, paint, and renovate their buildings, sand the floors, tear up old linoleum, lay new tile in the bathrooms, and this light and dry comedy cannot be maintained through such a long account of the effort to fill up a great emptiness with activity which is insufficiently purposeful. The religion of Father Urban is expressed in steadiness and patience, in endurance, not in fiery strength. His resistance to the prolonged barrenness and vacant busyness of this thoroughly American Order is made in a spirit of mild and decent martyrdom. Indeed the only violent and passionate person in the book is a certain Billy Cosgrove. Billy is rich and generous. He gives lavishly to the Order but he expects also to have his way. He and Father Urban eat shish kebab and drink champagne, play golf and go fishing. With Billy one talks of cars and sailing boats. Urban gets along rather well with spoiled and boisterous Billy until Billy tries to drown a deer in the water of Bloodsucker Lake. Billy has been fishing and is in an ugly mood because his luck has been bad. Seeing a swimming deer, he decides to seize it by the antlers and hold its head under water. As hungry for trophies as the soldiers in *The Thin Red Line*, Billy wants those antlers. Father Urban, who cannot bear his cruelty, starts up the motor of the boat, and Billy falls into the water. For this outrage Billy will never forgive him.

What Father Urban had been thinking just before the appearance of the deer was that in the Church there was perhaps too great an emphasis on dying for the faith and winning the martyr's crown. "How about living for the faith? Take Lanfranc and William the Conqueror—of whom it was written (in the Catholic Encyclopedia and Father Urban's notes on a book he might write someday): 'He was mild to good men of God and stark beyond all bounds to those who withsaid his will.' " Billy Cosgrove turns out to occupy the position of the Conqueror. He is stark beyond all bounds, and Urban is never again to see his face. Nor does Urban seem destined to write his book. He goes to the Novitiate of the Order as Father Provincial, there to deal with practical matters to the best of his ability. But he appears to be succumbing to a brain injury he received while playing golf. He had been struck in the head by a golf ball in Minnesota and is now subject to fits of dizziness. A martyr's crown seems to be awaiting Urban as the book ends.

Powers does not look at the issue of the single Self and the multitude as nakedly as Jones does, and it is a pity that he chose not to do so, for he might have been able to offer us a more subtle development of the subject. He would have been examining what Mr. Sypher calls "Loss of the Self" from the point of view of a Christian, that is, from the point of view of one who believes in the existence of something more profound than the romantic or secular idea of selfhood, namely, a soul. But there is curiously little talk of souls in this book about a priest. Spiritually, its quality is very thin. That perhaps is as Mr. Powers meant it to be. Even at play Father Urban

518

is serving the Church, and, if he is hit in the head by a golf ball, we can perhaps draw our own conclusions from that about the present age viewed as a chapter in the spiritual history of mankind. Here great things will only be dimly apprehended even by the most willing servant of God. Still this seems to me unsatisfactory, and I am not sure that I can bring myself to admire such meekness. A man might well be meek in his own interests, but furious at such abuses of the soul and eager to show what is positive and powerful in his faith. The lack of such power makes faith itself shadowy, more like obscure tenacity than spiritual conviction. In this sense Mr. Powers' book is disappointing.

The individual in American fiction often comes through to us, especially among writers of "sensibility," as a colonist who has been sent to a remote place, some Alaska of the soul. What he has to bring under cultivation, however, is a barren emptiness within himself. This is, of course, what writers of sensibility have for a long time been doing and what they continue to do. The latest to demonstrate his virtuosity with exceptional success is John Updike, who begins the title story of his new collection, *Pigeon Feathers*, "When they moved to Firetown, things were upset, displaced, rearranged." The rearrangement of things in new and hostile solitude is a common theme with writers of sensibility. David, the only child of a family which has moved to the country, is assailed by terror when he reads in H. G. Wells' *The Outline of History* that Jesus was nothing more than a rather communistic Galilean, ". . . an obscure political agitator, a kind of hobo in a minor colony of the Roman Empire." The effect of this is to open the question of death and immortality. David is dissatisfied with answers given by the Reverend Dobson and by his parents. He cannot understand the pleasure his mother takes in her solitary walks along the edge of the woods. ". . . to him the brown stretches of slowly rising and falling land expressed only a huge exhaustion." " 'What do you want Heaven to be?' " asks David's mother. "He was becoming angry, sensing her surprise at him. She had assumed that Heaven had faded from his head long ago. She had imagined that he had already entered, in the secrecy of silence, the conspiracy that he now knew to be all around him." Young David in the end resolves the problem for himself aesthetically. Admiring the beauty of pigeon feathers he feels consoled by the sense of a providence. ". . . the God who had lavished such craft upon these worthless birds would not destroy His whole Creation by refusing to let David live forever." The story ends with a mild irony at the expense of the boy. Nevertheless, there is nothing to see here but the writer's reliance on beautiful work, on an aesthetic discipline and order. And sensibility, in such forms, incurs the dislike of many because it is perceptive inwardly, and otherwise blind. We suspect it of a stony heart because it functions so smoothly in its isolation.

519

The writer of sensibility assumes that only private exploration and inner development are possible and accepts the opposition of public and private as fixed and indissoluble.

Perhaps it would be useful before I continue with my examination of recent American books of fiction to recapitulate. We are dealing with modern attitudes towards the ancient idea of the individual and the many, the single Self in the midst of the mass or species. In modern times the idea of the unique Self has become associated with the name of Rousseau. Nietzsche identified the Self with the God Apollo, the god of light, harmony, music, reason and proportion, and the many, the tribe, the species, the instincts and passions, with Dionysus. Between these two principles, the individual and the generic, men and civilizations supposedly work out their destinies. It is to Nietzsche, too, that we owe the concept of the "last man." His "last man" is an obituary on the unitary and sufficient Self produced by a proud bourgeois and industrial civilization. Dostoievsky's Underground Man is an analogous figure. Atheism, rationalism, utilitarianism and revolution are signs of a deadly sickness in the human soul, in his scheme of things. The lost Selves whose souls are destroyed he sees as legion. The living soul clearly discerns them. It owes this illumination to Christ the Redeemer. More optimistically, an American poet like Walt Whitman imagined that the single Self and the democratic mass might complement each other. But on this side of the Atlantic, also, Thoreau described men as leading lives of quiet desperation, accepting a deadly common life. The individual retires from the community to define or redefine his real needs in isolation beside Walden Pond.

Still later a French poet tells us "*Je* est an autre." Rimbaud and Jarry launch their bombs and grenades against the tight little bourgeois kingdom of the Self, that sensitive sovereign. Darwin and the early anthropologists unwittingly damage his sovereignty badly. Then come the psychologists, who explain that his Ego is a paltry shelter against the unendurable storms that rage in outer reality. After them come the logicians and physical scientists—people like Bertrand Russell and the late P. W. Bridgman—who tell us that "I" is a grammatical expression. Poets like Valery describe this Self as a poor figment, a thing of change, and tell us that consciousness is interested only in what is eternal. Novelists like Joyce turn away from the individualism of the romantics and the humanists to contemplate instead qualities found in dreams and belonging to the entire species—Earwicker is everybody. Writers like Sartre, Ionesco, and Beckett or like our own William Burroughs and Allan Ginsberg are only a few of the active campaigners on this shrinking front against the Self. One would like to ask these contemporaries, "After nakedness, what?" "After absurdity, what?" But, on the whole, American novels are filled with complaints over the misfortunes of the sovereign Self. Writers have inherited a tone of bitterness from the great poems and novels of this century, many of which lament the passing of a more stable and beautiful age demolished by the barbarous intrusion of an industrial and metropolitan society of masses or proles who will, after many upheavals, be tamed by bureaucracies and oligarchies in brave new worlds, human anthills.

These works of the first half of our century nourish the imagination of contemporary writers and supply a tonal background of disillusion or elegy. There are modern novelists who take all of this for granted as fully proven and implicit in the human condition and who complain as steadily as they write, viewing modern life with a bitterness to which they themselves have not established clear title, and it is this unearned bitterness that I speak of. What is truly curious about it is that often the writer automatically scorns contemporary life. He bottles its stinks artistically. But, seemingly, he does not need to study it. It is enough for him that it does not allow his sensibilities to thrive, that it starves his instincts for nobility or for spiritual qualities. But what the young American writer most often appears to feel in his *own* misfortune. The injustice is done to *his* talent if life is brutish and ignorant, if the world seems overcome by spam and beer, or covered with detergent lathers and poisonous monoxides. This apparently is the only injustice he feels. Neither for himself nor for his fellows does he attack power and injustice directly and hotly. He simply defends his sensibility. Perhaps the reason for this is the prosperity and relative security of the middle class from which most writers come. In educating its writers it makes available to them the radical doctrines of all the ages, but these in their superabundance only cancel one another out. The middle class community trains its writers also in passivity and resignation and in the double enjoyment of selfishness and good will. They are taught that they can have it both ways. In fact they are taught to expect to enjoy everything that life can offer. They can live dangerously while managing somehow to remain safe. They can be both bureaucrats and bohemians, they can be executives but use pot, they can raise families but enjoy bohemian sexuality, they can observe the laws while in their hearts and in their social attitudes they may be as subversive as they please. They are both conservative and radical. They are everything that is conceivable. They are not taught to care genuinely for any man or any cause.

A recent novel like Philip Roth's *Letting Go* is a consummate example of this. Mr. Roth's hero, Gabriel, educated to succeed in this world and to lead a good life come hell or high water, is slightly uncomfortable in his selfishness. But nevertheless he wants his, as the saying goes, and he gets his. But he feels obscurely the humiliation of being a private bourgeois Self, the son of an unhappy but prosperous dentist, and he senses that a "personal life" with its problems of personal adjustment and personal responsibility and personal happiness, its ostensibly normal calculations of profit and loss, safety and danger, lust and prudence is a source of shame. But Gabriel's middle-class parents sent him into life to make the grade and that is precisely, with tough singlemindedness, what he does. His shame therefore becomes a province of his sensibility, and it is something he can be rather proud of as he does what he was going to do anyway. Roth's hero clings to the hope of self-knowledge and personal improvement, and he concludes that, with all his faults, he loves himself still. His inner life, if it may be called that, is a rather feeble thing of a few watts. Conceivably it may guide him to a more satisfactory adjustment, but it makes me think of the usher's flashlight in the dark theatre guiding the single ticket holder to his reserved seat. We are supposed to feel that Gabriel is unusually sensitive, but what we find is that he is a tough young man who cannot be taken in and who will survive the accidents of life that madden or kill genuinely sensitive young men.

I would like now to list the categories suggested by my reading of current novels: the documentation of James Jones, the partially Christian approach of Powers, the sensibility of Updike, and the grievance of Philip Roth. I do not retract my earlier statement that in American novels—for I have decided rather arbitrarily to limit myself to examining these—the tone of complaint prevails. The public realm, as it encroaches on the private, setadily reduces the powers of the individual; but it cannot take away his power to despair, and sometimes he seems to be making the most of that. However, there are several other avenues commonly taken: stoicism, nihilistic anger, and comedy. Stoicism and comedy are sometimes mixed, as in the case of the late German dramatist Bert Brecht, but our own contemporary American stoicism comes from Hemingway, and its best American representative at present is Mr. John O'Hara.

Mr. O'Hara is properly impatient with people who suffer too intensely from themselves. The characters in his latest collection of stories, *The Cape Cod Lighter,* for whom he shows a decided preference, appear to be bluff, natural people, who know how to endure hurt and act with an elementary and realistic sense of honor. When Ernest Pangborn in the story "The Professors" learns that he has misjudged his colleague Jack Veech and understands at last that Veech's behavior has been decent and manly, he is moved to say something to him but does not know what to say. "A compliment would be rejected, and a word of pity would be unthinkable. Indeed the compliment was being paid to Pangborn; Veech honored him with his confidence and accorded him honor more subtly, more truly, by asking no further assurances of his silence." The emotion we feel here is made possible by long reticence, by the deep burial of self-proclamation or self-assertion. We recall the pure decencies of schooldays, and the old chivalrous or military origins of these. These, surely, are virtues of silence and passivity. We endure. We are rewarded by a vision of one another's complexities, but there is no possibility of a flourish, or of rhetoric, of anything that would make an undue personal claim. This is no longer the sovereign Self of the Romantics, but the decent Self of Kipling whose great satisfaction it is to recognize the existence of a great number of others. These numerous others reduce personal significance, and both realism and dignity require us to accept this reduction. Such stoicism of separateness is the opposite of sensibility with its large claims for the development of internal riches.

But the O'Haras are curiously like the Updikes in at least one respect. They are scrupulous craftsmen and extraordinarily strict about their writing. Nothing unrealistic, unnatural, or excessive (as they define these qualities) is suffered to appear. O'Hara insists upon a hard literalness in his language which reminds one of the simple crystalline code of his characters. There is a roughness in O'Hara which may make the writer of sensibility feel like a dude. O'Hara's self-identification is obviously with the workman, with the average, with plain people. Or perhaps he feels himself to be a part of the majority, which is to say, of the crowd. Certainly he does not merely react against what he judges an incorrect definition of the individual; he hates it violently. And conceivably he hates it in himself. His view of sensibility or of an intricate and conceivably self-indulgent privacy is, like Hemingway's (in *The Sun Also Rises,* for instance), entirely negative. He sees the romantic Self with the eyes of the crowd. And the crowd is a leveller. The average it seeks is anything but Whitman's divine average.

The absolute individualism of the Enlightenment has fallen. Contemporary writers like Brecht, or Beckett, or the Beats, and recently and most atrociously William Burroughs in his *Naked Lunch,* have repudiated it in a spirit of violence. Some have been violently comic at its expense, others ruthlessly nihilistic and vengeful. Among them there are some who gather unto themselves more and more and more power only to release it destructively on this already discredited and fallen individualism. In this they seem at times to imitate the great modern consolidations of power, to follow the example of parties and states and their scientific or military instruments. They act, in short, like those who hold the real power in society, the masters of the Leviathan. But this is only an imitation of the real power. Through this imitation they hope perhaps to show that they are not inferior to those who lead the modern world. Joint Chiefs or Pentagons have power to do as they will to huge populations. But there are writers who will not reckon themselves among these subordinate masses and who aim to demonstrate an independent power equal to the greatest. They therefore strike one sometimes as being extraordinarily eager to release their strength and violence against an enemy, and that enemy is the false conception of Self created by Christianity and by Christianity's successors in the Enlightenment. Modern literature is not satisfied simply to dismiss a romantic, outmoded conception of the Self. In a spirit of deepest vengefulness it curses it. It hates it. It rends it, annihilates it. It would rather have the maddest chaos it can invoke than a conception of life it has found false. But after this destruction, what?

I have spoken of complaint, stoicism, sensibility, and nihilistic rage, and I would like to speak now of recent American writers who have turned to comedy. It is obvious that modern comedy has to do with the disintegrating outline of the worthy and humane Self, the bourgeois hero of an earlier age. That sober, prudent person, the bourgeois, although he did much for the development of modern civilization, built factories and railroads, dug canals, created sewage systems and went colonizing, was indicted for his shallowness and his ignoble and hypocritical ways. The Christian writer (see Dostoievsky's portrait of Mr. Luzhin in *Crime and Punishment*) and the revolutionary (see Mr. Mangan in Shaw's *Heartbreak House*) repudiated him and all his works. The First World War dealt a blow to his prestige from which it never recovered. Dada and surrealism raised a storm of laughter against him. In the movies René Clair and Charlie Chaplin found him out. He became the respectable little person, the gentlemanly tramp. Poets of the deepest subversive tendencies came on like bank clerks in ironic masquerade.

The trick is still good as James Donleavy has lately shown in his novel *The Ginger Man*. His hero, Sebastian Dangerfield, a free-wheeling rascal and chaser, presents himself with wickedly comic effect as an ultrarespectable citizen with an excellent credit rating, one who doesn't know what it is to hock other people's property for the price of a drink, the gentlemanly sack-artist.

The private and inner life which was the subject of serious books until very recently now begins to have an antique and funny look. The earnestness of a Proust towards himself would seem old-fashioned today. Indeed, Italo Svevo, a contemporary of Proust, in *The Confessions of Zeno*, made introspection, hypochondria, and self-knowledge the subjects of his comedy. *My* welfare, *my* development, *my* advancement, *my* earnestness, *my* adjustment, *my* marriage, *my* family—all that will make the modern reader laugh heartily. Writers may not wholly agree with Bertrand Russell that "I" is no more than a grammatical expression, but they do consider certain claims of the "I" to be definitely funny. Already in the 19th century Stendhal became bored with the persistent "I–I–I" and denounced it in characteristic terms.

524

Perhaps the change that has occurred can be clearly illustrated by a comparison of Thomas Mann's *Death in Venice* with Nabokov's *Lolita*. In both stories an older man is overcome by sexual desire for a younger person. With Mann, however, this sad occurrence involves Apollo and Dionysus. Gustave von Aschenbach, an overly civilized man, an individual estranged from his instincts which unexpectedly claim their revenge, has gone too far, has entered the realm of sickness and perversity and is carried away by the plague. This is a typically Nietzschean theme. But in *Lolita* the internal life of Humbert Humbert has become a joke. Far from being an Aschenbach, a great figure of European literature, he is a fourth- or fifth-rate man of the world and is unable to be entirely serious about his passion. As for Lolita's mother, the poor thing only makes him laugh when she falls in love with him—a banal woman. To a very considerable extent Humbert's judgment of her is based on the low level of her culture. Her banality makes her a proper victim. If her words about love and desire had not come out of a bin in which the great American public finds suitable expressions to describe its psychological and personal needs, she might have been taken more seriously. The earnestness of Mann about love and death might be centuries old. The same subject is sadly and maliciously comical in *Lolita*. Clare Quilty cannot be made to take even his own death seriously and while he is being murdered by Humbert, ridicules his own situation and Humbert's as well, losing at last a life that was not worth having anyway. The contemporary Aschenbach does not deny his desires, but then he is without the dignity of the old fellow and is always on the verge of absurdity. Wright Morris in his new novel *What a Way to Go* explicitly makes comedy of the *Death in Venice* theme. His American professors in Venice, discussing *Death in Venice* all the while, seem to feel that there is small hope for them. They decline to view themselves with full seriousness. They believe their day is over. They are unfit, and dismiss themselves with a joke.

We must carefully remind ourselves that, if so many people today exist to enjoy or deplore an individual life, it is because prodigious public organizations, scientific, industrial, and political, support huge populations of new individuals. These organizations both elicit and curtail private development. I myself am not convinced that there is less "selfhood" in the modern world. I am not sure anyone knows how to put the matter properly. I am simply recording the attitudes of modern writers, including contemporary Americans, who are convinced that the jig of the Self is up. What is the modern Self in T. S. Eliot's *Waste Land?* It is the many, crossing the bridge in the great modern city, who do not know that death has already undone them; it is the "clerk carbuncular" taking sexual liberties of brief duration with the "lovely lady" who, after she has stooped to folly, puts a record on the gramophone. What is the Self for French novelists of the first postwar era like Louis Ferdinand Céline, or for writers like Curzio Malaparte or Albert Camus in the second postwar era? Man in a book like *The Stranger* is a creature neither fully primitive nor fully civilized, a Self devoid of depths. We have come a long way from Montaigne and his belief in a self-perfecting, self-knowing character.

Recent American comic novels like *Lolita*, or *The Ginger Man,* or Burt Blechman's *How Much?*, or Bruce Friedman's first novel *Stern* examine the private life. It is as if they were testing the saying of Socrates, that the unexamined life was not worth living. Apparently they find the examined life funny too. Some cannot find the life they are going to examine. The power of public life has become so vast and threatening that private life cannot maintain a pretence of its importance. Our condition of destructibility is ever-present in everyone's mind. Our submission seems required by public ugliness in our cities, by the public nonsense of television which threatens to turn our brains to farina within our heads, by even such trifling things as Muzak broadcasts in the elevators of public buildings. The Self is asked to prepare itself for sacrifice, and this is the situation reflected in contemporary American fiction.

As for the future, it cannot possibly shock us since we have already done everything possible to scandalize ourselves. We have so completely debunked the old idea of the Self that we can hardly continue in the same way. Perhaps some power within us will tell us what we are, now that old misconceptions have been laid low. Undeniably the human being is not what he commonly thought a century ago. The question nevertheless remains. He is something. What is he? And this question, it seems to me, modern writers have answered poorly. They have told us, indignantly or nihilistically or comically, how great our error is but for the rest they have offered us thin fare. The fact is that modern writers sin when they suppose that they *know,* as they conceive that physics *knows* or that history *knows.* The subject of the novelist is not knowable in any such way. The mystery increases, it does not grow less as types of literature wear out. It is, however, Symbolism or Realism or Sensibility wearing out, and not the mystery of mankind.

Edwin Arlington Robinson:
A Reappraisal

Louis Untermeyer

Presented at the Library of Congress April 15, 1963

ACKNOWLEDGMENTS The texts for Robinson's poems are taken from the *Collected Poems of Edwin Arlington Robinson* (New York, Macmillan, 1946). "Ben Jonson Entertains a Man from Stratford," "Bewick Finzer," and "Eros Turannos," copyright 1916 by Edwin Arlington Robinson, renewed 1944 by Ruth Nivison; "Mr. Flood's Party," copyright 1921 by Edwin Arlington Robinson, renewed 1949 by Ruth Nivison; "Karma," "New England," and "The Sheaves," copyright 1925 by Edwin Arlington Robinson, renewed 1953 by Ruth Nivison and Barbara R. Holt. Reprinted by permission of The Macmillan Company. "The Master" and "Miniver Cheevy" are reproduced by permission of Charles Scribner's Sons.

DURING the so-called Renascence or New Era of American Poetry in the 1920's, the names of Edwin Arlington Robinson and Robert Frost were continually linked. They were considered the chief interpreters of the spirit of New England and, to a large extent, the rest of the country. Although Robinson has not been forgotten—current anthologies continue to give him considerable representation—he has been underrated and largely over-shadowed because of Frost's ever-growing popular appeal. Even when he was most talked about, Robinson did little talking; he was not a performer in any sense; he shunned the public platform. Since his death his poetry has been neglected as something somehow old-fashioned and outmoded, too passé for permanence. It is time for a reappraisal and, perhaps, rediscovery.

Let us start with the facts of his life. There was little drama in them. There were no spectacular events, no love affairs, no marriages. Robinson had only one career, the sedentary, quiet, but hazardous career of a writer. Third son of a man past fifty, he was born December 22, 1869, in the little Maine village of Head Tide. Less than a year later, the family moved to Gardiner, a river town of a few thousand, where the future poet was to

527

live until he was twenty-seven and which was to give a title to one of his most characteristic volumes, *The Town Down the River*. His father, at one time a ship's carpenter, was a storekeeper who made far more money selling timber and investing in property than he did across the counter. Worth $80,000, he was planning to retire when Edwin was born. The boy grew up with two older brothers, Dean and Herman, but, since they were four and twelve years older, Edwin found playmates of his own age across the street. He was particularly drawn to the Jordan children, whose father was a yarn-spinning sea captain; together they made up games. At ten his favorite sport was collecting large words, and his favorite game with the Jordans was finding out who could come up with the longest and queerest names, names from the Bible or ancient myths. The origins and their significance didn't matter as long as the names made an impressive sound. Years later he remembered the game, and wrote a short poem which he entitled "Two Men":

> There be two men of all mankind
>   That I should like to know about;
> But search and question where I will,
>   I cannot ever find them out.
> Melchizedek, he praised the Lord,
>   And gave some wine to Abraham;
> But who can tell what else he did
>   Must be more learned than I am.
> Ucalegon, he lost his house
>   When Agamemnon came to Troy;
> But who can tell me who he was—
>   I'll pray the gods to give him joy.
> There be two men of all mankind
>   That I'm forever thinking on.
> They chase me everywhere I go,—
>   Melchizedek, Ucalegon.

Even as a child Robinson carried the tradition of the laconic New Englander to the point of taciturnity. It was so hard to make him talk that that a neighbor taunted him, saying, "The boy has no tongue"; whereupon he stuck his tongue out as a reply. It was a reply his writings were often to make to a world whose values he despised.

At eleven he balanced words with rhythms, fitted them with rhymes, and decided he would be a poet. At the foot of his bed he hung a portrait. It was that of a poet who was the antithesis of New England propriety: the intractable, nightmare-haunted Edgar Allan Poe. The neighbors decided he was a queer boy. Even his parents, contrasting him with his common-sense brothers, were troubled. "I'm not worried about Dean and Herman," said his mother, "but I don't know what will happen to Edwin."

He was thirteen when he went to high school. His father, who had no use for the "higher learning," insisted he take the practical instead of the traditional classical course; so the future poet studied typing and stenography along with mathematics and chemistry and, somehow, managed to pick up a little Latin. At sixteen he translated one of Cicero's orations into blank verse and found it came easily, although he also found it was still easier to write in rhyme. At eighteen he began experimenting with all kinds of verse—lyrics, sonnets, ballades, villanelles—and dreaming of a better education than he could find in Gardiner. Things were going badly at home. His father was ailing, broken in health as well as in business; his older brilliant brother had failed as a country doctor and was a drug addict, a permanent invalid sustained by morphine. Only Herman seemed to have established himself; he was a businessman and, when Edwin appealed to him, Herman saw to it that his young brother went to Cambridge.

He entered Harvard at twenty-one, submitted a dozen poems to the *Harvard Monthly,* had them all rejected, managed to get a couple of French forms and a sonnet in the *Harvard Advocate,* and, at the end of two years, quit college. He had never been more lonely. At twenty-three he was, if not a misanthrope, a misfit. He lived in solitude and derived a bitter satisfaction from it. "Solitude," he said, "tends to magnify one's ideas about individuality; it directs attention to neglect and sharpens one's sympathy with failure. . . . It renders a man suspicious of the whole natural plan and leads him to wonder whether the invisible powers are a fortuitous issue of misguided cosmos, or the cosmos itself, everything, is a kind of accident." He met other men besides those of his family who were living lives of quiet desperation, and, without quoting Thoreau, he knew that what is called resignation *is* often confirmed desperation. He had known a man in Gardiner who seemingly had everything the world desires, who "glittered when he walked" and was the envy of every one, but sank into the worst kind of shabbiness. Years later Robinson dramatized his end and gave him a name, "Richard Cory."

RICHARD CORY

Whenever Richard Cory went down town,
We people on the pavement looked at him:
He was a gentleman from sole to crown,
Clean favored, and imperially slim.

And he was always quietly arrayed,
And he was always human when he talked:
But still he fluttered pulses when he said,
"Good-morning," and he glittered when he walked.

And he was rich—yes, richer than a king—
And admirably schooled in every grace:
In fine, we thought that he was everything
To make us wish that we were in his place.

So on we worked, and waited for the light,
And went without the meat, and cursed the bread;
And Richard Cory, one calm summer night,
Went home and put a bullet through his head.

I have referred to the French forms Robinson was writing at this time. He was fascinated by the effects that could be obtained by the repeated lines and echoing rhymes in these strictly ordered patterns. He recognized their artificiality, but he also realized that, like the sonnet (another severely limited form), their very structure gave them a curious and even memorable music. In "The House on the Hill" he used the echoing repetition of a villanelle to project a sense of nostalgia linked with loneliness.

THE HOUSE ON THE HILL

They are all gone away,
  The House is shut and still,
There is nothing more to say.

Through broken walls and gray
  The winds blow bleak and shrill:
They are all gone away.

Nor is there one to-day
  To speak them good or ill:
There is nothing more to say.

Why is it then we stray
  Around the sunken sill?
They are all gone away,

And our poor fancy-play
  For them is wasted skill:
There is nothing more to say.

> There is ruin and decay
>   In the House on the Hill:
> They are all gone away,
>   There is nothing more to say.

There was ruin and decay in the Gardiner home to which Robinson returned after the fiasco at Harvard. Mills had shut down, banks were closing, four million men were out of work, and Coxey's "army" of the unemployed was marching on Washington. Robinson's father had died, and his savings had been dissipated by bad investments. Herman, who had seemed to be an efficient businessman, had been cheated in a real estate deal and was drinking heavily. Dean, struggling with hallucinations, was a tragic case. Edwin, who had never recovered from an early mastoid infection, was in physical agony much of the time; he said that the only thing that stood between him and insanity was a thin membrane. The three brothers were living in the Gardiner household, and all were living in a variety of torments. "I have lived nearly twenty-four years," Robinson wrote to a friend, "and I am thankful that I haven't to live them over again." He felt that he should go to work—any kind of work—but he was helpless "in what the world calls business" (he pronounced it "busyness") and confessed that the very word nauseated him. He tried to alleviate his misery and, at the same time, repair the family's finances by writing short stories. They were about "the humble, the forgotten, the unknown," and they remained unknown, for they could not find a publisher. The editor of the *Atlantic Monthly* let Robinson down with a patronizing note saying that, although he could not use the sketches, they "showed an effort at telling something worth while." It became clear to Robinson that he had no gift for anything except the making of verse and—although he attempted to write a couple of plays later in life—no luck in delineating people except in poetry.

He felt justified as a poet when an editor or two showed a little interest in his work. He was gratified when a journal called *The Critic* accepted a sonnet, but the acceptance was not sullied with anything as coarse as money; instead of a check he received a year's subscription to the magazine. "The House on the Hill," now one of Robinson's most quoted poems, was rejected by a dozen magazines until it was printed in *The Globe,* an inferior quarterly—again without payment. *Lippincott's Monthly Magazine* did somewhat better; it paid seven dollars for a sonnet on Poe—and kept it, unpublished, for twelve years. Seven dollars was all Robinson had earned by the time he reached his twenty-seventh year. "You cannot conceive," he wrote, "how cutting it is for a man to depend on his mother for every cent he has and for every mouthful he swallows. The world frightens me."

Frightened or not, he faced the world with the only thing he could do: the making of poems. The world obviously did not want them. Rejection slips piled up; he thought of papering one side of his room with them. He put together his unpublished lines and a few of those that had, somehow, got into print and found he had a book of one hundred pages. It expressed, he said, "something wiser than hatred and something better than despair." He entitled it *The Torrent and The Night Before* and, with the usual misgivings, sent it to a publisher. The misgivings were justified. The book came back. It went out again, and was again rejected. Finally, an uncle who was connected with the Riverside Press paid fifty-two dollars for three hundred copies which, since no publisher would issue them, were printed privately. The collection was to be a surprise for his mother, a token of appreciation for her support in every sense. She died while the type was being set.

The book appeared when Robinson was twenty-seven, and it contains some of his most characteristic writing. There are several portrait-sonnets, such as "Aaron Stark" and "Cliff Klingenhagen," as well as "The Clerks," a summation of "the shopworn brotherhood," commonplace symbols of monotony who are in the same company as poets and kings, "the clerks of Time." There is the haunting "Luke Havergal," which no one quite understands but which everyone likes to hear, and which begins:

> Go to the western gate, Luke Havergal,
> There where the vines cling crimson on the wall,
> And in the twilight wait for what will come.
> The leaves will whisper there of her, and some,
> Like flying words, will strike you as they fall;
> But go, and if you listen she will call.
> Go to the western gate, Luke Havergal—
> Luke Havergal.

Two of the sonnets are remarkable for their differences and their varied use of the form. The first is a tribute to the eighteenth century English poet, George Crabbe, who was considered harsh and uncompromising, and whose unpleasant honesty kept him not only from popularity but almost from being read.

GEORGE CRABBE

Give him the darkest inch your shelf allows,
Hide him in lonely garrets, if you will,—
But his hard, human pulse is throbbing still
With the sure strength that fearless truth endows.
In spite of all fine science disavows,
Of his plain excellence and stubborn skill
There yet remains what fashion cannot kill,
Though years have thinned the laurel from his brows.

Whether or not we read him, we can feel
From time to time the vigor of his name
Against us like a finger for the shame
And emptiness of what our souls reveal
In books that are as altars where we kneel
To consecrate the flicker, not the flame.

The other sonnet is a condensation of Robinson's personal philosophy, a courageous stoicism that never wavered. Reproached for being a pessimist, he denied the charge of gloom. Harry Thurston Peck, the *Bookman*'s literary editor, praised Robinson's "yearning spirit," but condemned him for presenting the world as "a prison-house." To which Robinson replied, "The world is not a prison-house but a kind of spiritual kindergarten where millions of bewildered children are trying to spell God with the wrong blocks." In "Credo" he said it in another way.

CREDO

I cannot find my way: there is no star
In all the shrouded heavens anywhere;
And there is not a whisper in the air
Of any living voice but one so far
That I can hear it only as a bar
Of lost, imperial music, played when fair
And angel fingers wove, and unaware,
Dead leaves to garlands where no roses are.

No, there is not a glimmer, nor a call,
For one that welcomes, welcomes when he fears,
The black and awful chaos of the night;
For through it all—above, beyond it all—
I know the far-sent message of the years,
I feel the coming glory of the Light.

The reviews of Robinson's first book were polite, perfunctory rather than hostile; although they showed little perception, they were not too discouraging. They failed to see that Robinson was quietly but clearly announcing a revolt against the pretty and sentimental as well as the turgid and pompous verse of the period. He was protesting against the artificial inversions, the current stereotypes and rhetorical ornaments which were the fashion of the day, and was trying to replace them with a direct, clean-cut communication. Instead of cloudy abstractions, he was offering vividly concrete statements; instead of calling upon the Muse to inspire him with lifeless celebrations of capitalized Beauty, Love, Liberty, Life, Death, et cetera, he called the reader's attention to the life and the people he knew, workmen, clerks, butchers, tramps, drunkards, and poets. At a time when Whitman was regarded with suspicion, Robinson hailed the old bard's "democratic wisdom" with a poem which begins:

> The master-songs are ended, and the man
> That sang them is a name. And so is God
> A name; and so is love, and life, and death,
> And everything. But we, who are too blind
> To read what we have written, or what faith
> Has written for us, do not understand:
> We only blink, and wonder.

Nevertheless, there were responses to *The Torrent and The Night Before,* and there were indications that Robinson might win a wider audience. Richard G. Badger, one of the first of the "vanity publishers" who dignified his piratical ventures with a handsome format, offered to reissue the volume with additional poems for the proverbial "modest fee." A friend advanced the required sum, and *The Children of the Night,* a literary landmark, was published in Robinson's twenty-eighth year. The poet was now ready for a larger encounter with the world. With the few hundred dollars that had come to him from his father's estate, he went to New York.

In New York Robinson was one of the millions of anonymous newcomers, jobseekers, opportunists, drifting hopefuls. He made little impression on the people he met, for his was not an impressive figure. He looked like countless undistinguished others; his forehead was high and already faintly lined, his mouth was small and tightly set, his eyes were inconspicuous and primly spectacled. He might have been a bookkeeper, a bank clerk, a teacher of mathematics. He was not much of a talker; he had to drink himself into a conversation. He had a few friends and met others who were inclined to be friendly, but Robinson was a man who lived *among* men rather than *with* them. The death of his brother Dean, whose brilliant beginnings had so sordid an end, confirmed him in the belief that life itself was a vast irony.

Nothing, however, could impede the flow of poems, and nothing, it seemed, could persuade the publishers to print them. Robinson completed a long seminarrative about a nondescript garrulous old fellow who dreamed his life away in a New York garret. It was originally called *The Pauper*. Robinson changed the title to *Captain Craig* and sent it off to Scribner's. When that firm rejected it, he mailed it to the Boston firm of Small, Maynard. Nothing was heard from them for months. Inquiries brought only the response that no trace of *Captain Craig* could be found in the office. This was not strange, because the editor in charge of the manuscript had left it in a brothel and had forgotten all about it until a later visit, when the madam asked him if he still wanted it. Once more *Captain Craig* went the rounds, and once more nothing happened. After the sixth rejection Robinson added some shorter poems, and finally Houghton Mifflin agreed to publish the book if it were subsidized. A few well-wishers supplied the cost of an edition of five hundred, and *Captain Craig; A Book of Poems* appeared in print. It was Robinson's third volume; he was thirty-three, and the only money he had earned from writing was the seven dollars he had been paid for the sonnet on Poe.

The reviews of the book were, if not enthusiastic, not too damning. They ranged from protests against the poet's "obscurity" to dubious commendation for his "promise" and small praise for his exposure of brutality and for the plain speech used to attack the prevailing materialism. Discouraged but not defeated, Robinson managed to hang on. Undernourished, he frequented saloons where, with a dime for a glass of whiskey, he could live on the free lunch. On one occasion a bartender offered to lend the hungry man a couple of dollars. Friends helped him occasionally with money, which he humiliated himself to accept. Once in a while he met important figures in the literary world, but he had to refuse invitations to their clubs because his clothes were too shabby. He moved from one dingy rooming house to another. He had lost what little money had been left from the inheritance, but he had not lost his sense of humor. When he was close to starving, he wrote facetiously to a friend: "The first duty of man is to like beans. I wish you could get into some other sort of slavery, but don't for heaven's sake get into my sort unless you have a bean vineyard in your own name."

Reduced to a stale roll for lunch and a glass of beer for supper, unable to pay his rent, Robinson saved himself from complete starvation by getting a job in the New York subway which was being constructed. He worked in the murky and sometimes dangerous depths as a timechecker, keeping track of the men's time and the loads of material excavated. He worked ten hours a day for twenty cents an hour, two dollars a day. "I was a tragedy in the beginning," he wrote, "and it is hardly probable that I shall ever be anything else. What manner of cave I select for a time is of no real importance. . . . Sometimes I feel that I ought to go and drown myself for cherishing the thought of succeeding in anything, but then I get over it."

Robinson got over it by drinking intermittently, and then, for a long time, steadily. Every evening, emerging from his hole in the ground he made a round of the saloons before going to bed. His plight made him sympathetic with all the dreamers who had taken to drink, from Poe to the nameless derelicts he saw every night. What is perhaps his most often quoted poem is about such a lost dreamer, "Miniver Cheevy."

MINIVER CHEEVY

Miniver Cheevy, child of scorn,
    Grew lean while he assailed the seasons;
He wept that he was ever born,
    And he had reasons.

Miniver loved the days of old
    When swords were bright and steeds were prancing;
The vision of a warrior bold
    Would set him dancing.

Miniver sighed for what was not,
    And dreamed, and rested from his labors;
He dreamed of Thebes and Camelot,
    And Priam's neighbors.

Miniver mourned the ripe renown
    That made so many a name so fragrant;
He mourned Romance, now on the town,
    And Art, a vagrant.

Miniver loved the Medici,
    Albeit he had never seen one;
He would have sinned incessantly
    Could he have been one.

Miniver cursed the commonplace
    And eyed a khaki suit with loathing;
He missed the medieval grace
    Of iron clothing.

Miniver scorned the gold he sought,
    But sore annoyed was he without it;
Miniver thought, and thought, and thought,
    And thought about it.

Miniver Cheevy, born too late,
    Scratched his head and kept on thinking;
Miniver coughed, and called it fate,
    And kept on drinking.

Later Robinson expanded the theme in a somewhat larger picture. There are few poems in American literature more ironically tender, more unsentimental and yet more touching than "Mr. Flood's Party."

MR. FLOOD'S PARTY

Old Eben Flood, climbing alone one night
Over the hill between the town below
And the forsaken upland hermitage
That held as much as he should ever know
On earth again of home, paused warily.
The road was his with not a native near;
And Eben, having leisure, said aloud,
For no man else in Tilbury Town to hear:

"Well, Mr. Flood, we have the harvest moon
Again, and we may not have many more;
The bird is on the wing, the poet says,
And you and I have said it here before.
Drink to the bird."   He raised up to the light
The jug that he had gone so far to fill,
And answered huskily: "Well, Mr. Flood,
Since you propose it, I believe I will."

Alone, as if enduring to the end
A valiant armor of scarred hopes outworn,
He stood there in the middle of the road
Like Roland's ghost winding a silent horn.
Below him, in the town among the trees.
Where friends of other days had honored him,
A phantom salutation of the dead
Rang thinly till old Eben's eyes were dim.

Then, as a mother lays her sleeping child
Down tenderly, fearing it may awake,
He set the jug down slowly at his feet
With trembling care, knowing that most things break:
And only when assured that on firm earth

It stood, as the uncertain lives of men
Assuredly did not, he paced away,
And with his hand extended paused again:

"Well, Mr. Flood, we have not met like this
In a long time: and many a change has come
To both of us, I fear, since last it was
We had a drop together. Welcome home!"
Convivially returning with himself,
Again he raised the jug up to the light;
And with an acquiescent quaver said:
"Well, Mr. Flood, if you insist, I might.

"Only a very little, Mr. Flood—
For auld lang syne.   No more, sir; that will do."
So, for the time, apparently it did,
And Eben evidently thought so too;
For soon amid the silver loneliness
Of night he lifted up his voice and sang,
Secure, with only two moons listening,
Until the whole harmonious landscape rang—

"For auld lang syne."   The weary throat gave out,
The last word wavered, and the song was done.
He raised again the jug regretfully
And shook his head, and was again alone.
There was not much that was ahead of him,
And there was nothing in the town below—
Where strangers would have shut the many doors
That many friends had opened long ago.

After working for nine months in the subway Robinson was let go. Facing another period of starvation, he confessed that he envied men who ran peanut stands or swallowed swords for a living; but, he added, he knew that, if he were running a peanut stand, he would burn more peanuts than he sold, and, if he were swallowing swords, he would not learn to enjoy the process any more than he did the subway.   One of his faithful friends heard that a department store was looking for someone who would write advertisements for a minimum salary.   Robinson took the job; it kept him alive.

He was barely living when something of a miracle occurred.   A fourteen-year old boy at the Groton School was looking through the library for something "different."   He found—or was helped to find—a book of poems, *The Children of the Night*.   The boy was so fascinated by it that he ordered a few copies from the publisher and sent one of them to his father.   His father happened to be the President of the United States, and

Theodore Roosevelt appreciated his son Kermit's taste so much that he wrote to the indigent poet and invited him to Washington. Robinson had no clothes suitable for a call at the White House and evaded the invitation. Roosevelt understood, and offered him an inspectorship at Montreal or in Mexico. When Robinson intimated that he would like to stay in this country, preferably in New York, Roosevelt saw to it that he was installed as special agent in the Custom House at a yearly salary of two thousand dollars. "I want you to understand," said Roosevelt, "I expect you to think poetry first and your work in the Customs House second." Robinson's reaction was characteristic. "Now," he wrote to a friend, "I can not only write poetry but own two pairs of shoes at the same time."

Robinson never forgot what he owed the President. Years later, writing to Kermit Roosevelt about the novels he had attempted and had abandoned and the plays with which he was still grappling, Robinson wrote—and his letter is one of the many treasures in the Manuscript Division of the Library of Congress—"I don't like to think of where I should be now if it had not been for your astonishing father. He fished me out of hell by the hair of the head. . . . I hope sincerely that I have made him understand that I know this." The protean Roosevelt not only rescued Robinson physically but called attention to him as a poet by reviewing his poems. Besides being an unusually energetic leader of the nation—he made our language more active with the word "strenuous"—Theodore Roosevelt was one of the first of our presidents to establish and extend a new cultural frontier.

In 1908 Robinson sent a poem to *Scribner's Magazine*. At the same time he wrote a letter to Kermit Roosevelt—another document now among the Roosevelt family papers in the Manuscript Division of the Library of Congress—a letter which reveals not only his modesty but his wry self-effacement. "You will find," wrote Robinson, "the enclosed in the February number of *Scribner's*. Rather a foolish thing to undertake I suppose—but I have discovered that folly and wisdom occupy the same hut on Parnassus, and that wisdom is not always at home. In this instance you will form your own conclusion." The poem Robinson enclosed was called "The Man Who Came." We know it now with another title, "The Master," a poem which has become one of the classics of modern American poetry.

Robinson never specifically indicated who "The Master" was or what his mission might have been as "The Man Who Came." But he added a subtitle which read: "Supposed to have been written not long after the Civil War." The speaker is obviously a man—presumably a political figure—who made fun of the Master and then realized what a colossal mistake in judgment he had made.

But soon the name was everywhere
To be reviled and then revered.

The name is never mentioned in either the title or the poem; but, as the poem gathers strength and definition, it is clear that it can refer to only one man: Lincoln.

THE MASTER

A flying word from here and there
Had sown the name at which we sneered,
But soon the name was everywhere,
To be reviled and then revered:
A presence to be loved and feared,
We cannot hide it, or deny
That we, the gentlemen who jeered,
May be forgotten by and by.

He came when days were perilous
And hearts of men were sore beguiled;
And having made his note of us,
He pondered and was reconciled.
Was ever master yet so mild
As he, and so untamable?
We doubted, even when he smiled,
Not knowing what he knew so well.

He knew that undeceiving fate
Would shame us whom he served unsought;
He knew that he must wince and wait—
The jest of those for whom he fought;
He knew devoutly what he thought
Of us and of our ridicule:
He knew that we must all be taught
Like little children in a school.

We gave a glamour to the task
That he encountered and saw through,
But little of us did he ask,
And little did we ever do.
And what appears if we review
The season when we railed and chaffed?
It is the face of one who knew
That we were learning while we laughed.

The face that in our vision feels
Again the venom that we flung,
Transfigured to the world reveals
The vigilance to which we clung.
Shrewd, hallowed, harassed, and among
The mysteries that are untold,
The face we see was never young
Nor could it wholly have been old.

For he, to whom we had applied
Our shopman's test of age and worth,
Was elemental when he died,
As he was ancient at his birth:
The saddest among kings of earth.
Bowed with a galling crown, this man
Met rancor with a cryptic mirth,
Laconic—and Olympian.

The love, the grandeur, and the fame
Are bounded by the world alone;
The calm, the smouldering, and the flame
Of awful patience were his own:
With him they are forever flown
Past all our fond self-shadowings,
Wherewith we cumber the Unknown
As with inept, Icarian wings.

For we were not as other men:
'Twas ours to soar and his to see;
But we are coming down again,
And we shall come down pleasantly,
Nor shall we longer disagree
On what it is to be sublime,
But flourish in our perigee
And have one Titan at a time.

Four years later Roosevelt was no longer in the White House, and Robinson lost his position in the Custom House. He was forty, by no means financially secure, but no longer in desperate straits. The more intellectual critics had sniffed at the President's championship of one whom they considered a rather mediocre versifier; nevertheless, Roosevelt had stimulated talk about the poet, and Robinson began to attract not only attention but an audience. Magazines that had rejected his verse now asked for it; book publishers, who had not thought of him except as a commercial calamity, offered to issue his future work, *The Town Down the River,* perhaps his richest single volume, was published and was followed by a dozen other collections in little more than a dozen years.

Recognition did not change Robinson's nature. He was rarely at ease with people; tongue-tied, he could not lose his distrust of most men and practically all women. Women frightened him. Isadora Duncan, the fabulous seductress who had danced her wild way through the world, somehow got him alone, tried to seduce him, and, instead of rousing him, only embarrassed him. He needed a long evening and a large bottle to break down his resistance to anything like conversation. He hated to stir from his room. "I don't want to visit even my friends for more than a few days," he said in one of his letters. "I don't want to travel unless I can see a bottle of Scotch at the end of my journey." A good part of his aloof philosophy is woven into the poem "Ben Jonson Entertains a Man from Stratford," in which Jonson tries to explain to one of Shakespeare's fellow-townsmen the enigma of Shakespeare's retirement. In this long monologue, one of the most sensitive portraits of the great dramatist ever drawn in verse, Robinson indicates his own sense of estrangement and seclusion, a rejection of the world that so often had rejected him. Here is a striking and significant passage:

Not long ago, late in an afternoon,
I came on him unseen down Lambeth way,
And on my life I was afear'd of him:
He gloomed and mumbled like a soul from Tophet,
His hands behind him and his head bent solemn.
"What is it now," said I,—"another woman!"
That made him sorry for me, and he smiled.
"No, Ben," he mused; "it's Nothing. It's all Nothing.
We come, we go; and when we're done, we're done.
Spiders and flies—we're mostly one or t'other—
We come, we go; and when we're done, we're done.
"By God, you sing that song as if you knew it!"
Said I, by way of cheering him; "what ails ye?"
"I think I must have come down here to think,"
Says he to that, and pulls his little beard;
"Your fly will serve as well as anybody,
And what's his hour? He flies, and flies, and flies,
And in his fly's mind has a brave appearance;
And then your spider gets him in her net,
And eats him out, and hangs him up to dry.
That's Nature, the kind mother of us all.
And then your slattern housemaid swings her broom,

542

And where's your spider? And that's Nature, also.
It's Nature, and it's Nothing. It's all Nothing.
It's all a world where bugs and emperors
Go singularly back to the same dust,
Each in his time; and the old, ordered stars
That sang together, Ben, will sing the same
Old stave to-morrow."
When he talks like that,
There's nothing for a human man to do
But lead him to some grateful nook like this
Where we be now, and there to make him drink.
He'll drink, for love of me, and then be sick;
A sad sign always in a man of parts,
And always very ominous. The great
Should be as large in liquor as in love,—
And our great friend is not so large in either;
One disaffects him, and the other fails him.

Robinson's spells of isolation and his sense of "nothingness" increased to such an extent that his friends became alarmed. One of them, the poet and critic Herman Hagedorn, who became Robinson's first biographer, brought him to Peterborough, New Hampshire, to the growing circle of artists and writers known as the MacDowell Colony. Robinson intended to try it for two weeks. Instead he spent all his summers there and found something like a home. He was free now to write anything he wanted to attempt. He attempted two plays, *Van Zorn* and *The Porcupine;* when no one would produce either, he turned *The Porcupine* into a novel which no one would publish. Reluctantly accepting the fact that he was neither a playwright nor a novelist, he returned to what others besides himself knew he could write. In the midst of new and unusually condensed lyrics he chose one of the oldest subjects: the Arthurian cycle. Leaving for the moment the American scene, he plunged into a theme whose subject and setting were ancient English; yet the turn of thought and the twist of phrase were as distinctly modern American as Tennyson's tea-table version, *Idylls of the King,* was recognizably Victorian. The cycle consisted of three book-length narratives: *Merlin,* written when Robinson was forty-eight, *Lancelot,* which appeared three years later, and *Tristram,* which was published when he was in his late fifties. To everyone's astonishment, *Tristram* was selected as a book-of-the-month, widely distributed by the Literary Guild, and Robinson became a vogue. It is doubtful that most of the people who received the book read it, but it brought the poet a measure of fame as well as what to him was a fortune. Too integrated to permit self-contained excerpts, *Tristram* has a dramatic unity; it has been performed both as a reading and as a dramatized series of scenes recently given at the Poetry Center in New York and, staged by Arnold Moss, in the Coolidge Auditorium in Washington in 1960.

Tristram is a surprising product for one as peculiarly inhibited as Robinson. It is a curious spectacle, the ascetic Puritan venturing into a glamorous territory and losing himself in confused romanticism. The thoughts are his but not the emotions—the conflicting passions were disturbances he either did not understand or could not master. Perhaps the most fascinating thing about *Tristram* and the two other Arthurian poems is Robinson's cerebral entry into passion and his efforts to direct or diagnose his way out of it. For this very reason the trilogy was an important and even essential part of the Robinson canon.

Nearing sixty Robinson was noticeably tired. Weary but not wornout, frightened by the failures of his past and fearful of an adverse future, he pushed himself into a frenzy of creation. "I used to write for pleasure," he told me, "now I write for an income." Each year for seven years, up to the very month of his death, he produced another volume. Several of these works—*The Man Who Died Twice, Cavender's House, The Glory of the Nightingales, Matthias at the Door, Talifer, Amaranth,* for example— show strain in their nightmare content and melodramatic contrivances. But such a late collection as *Dionysus in Doubt* is full of Robinson's old power; among other excellences, it contains three of his most effective sonnets, "Karma," "The Sheaves," and "New England." The first is packed with concentrated bitterness.

KARMA

Christmas was in the air and all was well
With him, but for a few confusing flaws
In divers of God's images. Because
A friend of his would neither buy nor sell,
Was he to answer for the axe that fell?
He pondered; and the reason for it was,
Partly, a slowly freezing Santa Claus
Upon the corner, with his beard and bell.

Acknowledging an improvident surprise,
He magnified a fancy that he wished
The friend whom he had wrecked were here again.
Not sure of that, he found a compromise;
And from the fulness of his heart he fished
A dime for Jesus who had died for men.

The second is as near a lyric as a sonnet can be. It is, incidentally,

built around one of Robinson's most beautiful images and one of his few
purely sensuous ones.

THE SHEAVES

Where long the shadows of the wind had rolled,
Green wheat was yielding to the change assigned;
And as by some vast magic undivined
The world was turning slowly into gold.
Like nothing that was ever bought or sold
It waited there, the body and the mind;
And with a mighty meaning of a kind
That tells the more the more it is not told.

So in a land where all days are not fair,
Fair days went on till on another day
A thousand golden sheaves were lying there,
Shining and still, but not for long to stay—
As if a thousand girls with golden hair
Might rise from where they slept and go away.

The third sonnet caused a great deal of comment—most of it unpleasant—in the northeast corner of the country. Its combination of ironic
wit and light banter was considered not only undignified but insulting by
the self-conscious mentors of propriety.

NEW ENGLAND

Here where the wind is always north-north-east
And children learn to walk on frozen toes,
Wonder begets an envy of all those
Who boil elsewhere with such a lyric yeast
Of love that you will hear them at a feast
Where demons would appeal for some repose,
Still clamoring where the chalice overflows,
And crying wildest who have drunk the least.

Passion is here a soilure of the wits,
We're told, and Love a cross for them to bear;
Joy shivers in the corner where she knits
And Conscience always has the rocking-chair,
Cheerful as when she tortured into fits
The first cat that was ever killed by Care.

This, of course, was teasing, for Robinson never abjured New England. When he was not in New York, he divided his time between Boston

545

and the MacDowell Colony in New Hampshire. In his midsixties he weakended perceptibly and had to forgo travel of any sort. At sixty-six he was in great pain, because of a growth on the pancreas. He was taken to the New York Hospital, but it was too late to operate, and he died there on April 6, 1935.

Although often requested to do so, Robinson refused to write his autobiography; he was even chary about furnishing ordinary biographical details. Yet in the Lewis Chase Collection in the Manuscript Division of the Library of Congress, there is a particularly revealing letter. Chase, professor of English at the University of Wisconsin, was compiling data on the lives, works, and theories of contemporary American writers; somehow he was able to draw out unusual information even from so reluctant a correspondent as Robinson. Nearing fifty — on July 11, 1917, to be exact — Robinson replied to Chase with something rare, a long letter summarizing his attitude toward himself and his writings.

"I find it rather difficult to answer your letter," he began, "I am handicapped at the start in having no biography and no theories. As for my work, I have hoped that it might speak—not very loudly, perhaps—for itself. Ten years ago I was called a radical, and most readers looked sideways at my work on account of the unconventional use of so-called simple language. I suppose that I have always depended rather more on context than on vocabulary for my poetical effects, and this offense has laid me open to the charge of oversubtlety on the part of the initiated and of dullness on the part of the dull. Whatever merit my work may or may not possess, I fancy that it will always be a waste of time for any reader who has not a fairly well developed sense of humor—which, as someone has said before, is a very serious thing—to bother with it. . . . When I was younger, I was very much under the influence of Wordsworth and Kipling, but never at all, as far as I am aware, under that of Browning, as many seem to believe. . . . I began the writing of verse long before I was old enough to know better, and I fancy that my style, such as it is, was pretty well formed by the time my first book was published. . . . As for my methods of work, there does not seem to be much for me to say. As a rule I see the end of a thing before I begin it—if I don't see it then I am likely never to see it—and the rest of the process is simply a matter of how the thing goes. . . . When occasionally I have become disgusted and throw an unfinished poem away, it is always because I had really nothing to write about. . . . I imagine, however, that the worst poetry in the world has been written in the finest frenzy of inspiration; and so, probably, has the best. . . . I thought nothing when I was writing my first book of working for a week over a single line; and while I don't do it any more, I am sure that my technique is better for those early grilling exercises. In fact, I am inclined to believe that the technical flabbiness of many writers is due to the lack in earlier years of just such grilling. . . .

Robinson then goes on to mention the poems of his which seem most suitable for reading aloud. It is an odd list, and I should mention that it differs greatly from mine. For example, he says in an almost deprecating tone, "The end of 'The Master' might possibly give pleasure."

Since I have mentioned our differences in taste, it might be interesting to mention some of the authors Robinson liked and a few of those he loathed. He dismissed John Donne as "dogmatic, and hardly to be considered apart from his period—which to my mind is sufficient damnation for any writer. Donne doesn't seem to me to interpret much more than a sort of half-mystical sexual uneasiness and a rather uninteresting religious enthusiasm." Most of Browning left him cold. "I dislike 'Rabbi Ben Ezra' so much that I haven't read it in something like thirty years." Of his immediate predecessors his favorites were Rudyard Kipling, A. E. Housman, and the forgotten William Vaughn Moody. He admired only a few of his contemporaries. He spoke well, though briefly, about Frost and MacLeish, but he had little praise for most of the others. Sandburg was an exponent of "blood and guts . . . a sweet singer in Amy Lowell's jazz band." Edna St. Vincent Millay was "an eminent little critter . . . her book is a remarkable business, and yet it seems to me in some ways more literary than alive." He concluded that Elinor Wylie "is to John Donne what The Millay is to Shakespeare—if you care to figure that out." He thought the Imagists were too self-conscious and exclusive to stand the test of time. The poetry of Santayana seemed to him "like something written by a highly sophisticated corpse." He could make nothing whatsoever out of Joyce. "Maybe you can read the Joyce thing," he wrote a friend, "I can't." Auden and Spender were not for him, he said, but "for the youngsters."

Robinson was decidedly not for the youngsters of his day, and perhaps not of ours. He lacked everything that might have made him popular. He had absolutely no talent for publicity. He never shone at parties; indeed, he could seldom be induced to go to them. He would not—in fact he could not—lecture. I only heard him read his own poetry once, and he read it badly, read it as though he were reading a particularly depressing stock report in the *Wall Street Journal*.

I have already implied that he was a poor conversationalist. It took half a bottle of Scotch to start him talking, and the end of the second half restored him to silence. I was with him often at my own home and in the company of others, but I remember nothing he said that was memorable. His remarks were not, let me say, remarkable. The brilliance was in the writer, not in the tightlipped talker. I do remember, however, an after-supper dialogue at the MacDowell Colony. We were speaking about unfinished poems, and Robinson said he had tried several times to complete a poem on the inexhaustible whippoorwill, the bird whose energy caused the colonists many sleepless nights. Robinson said, "I got the first line—it goes like this:

> Thou iron-lunged, incessant bird of Hell!

—then I stopped. I found that I had written the entire poem. That line said it all."

It was quite an evening, for it was the occasion of the only pun I ever heard Robinson make. We were discussing Masefield, Gibson, and other Georgian poets who were then making a considerable noise. Robinson, who had not offered a word about them, suddenly spoke up. "No one," he said, "has mentioned Kipling—and he's a better man than they are with all their din."

Apart from the bad pun, the contribution of opinion itself was unusual. He disliked talking about poetry. He claimed that any such discussion killed the spirit of the poem; he would have writhed at the explications, studied involvements, and probing ambiguities of the New Criticism. He was outraged when one of the artists at the Colony tried to read an ambiguous allegory into one of his most plain-spoken sonnets. " 'Calvary' " he said, "means just what it says, nothing less and nothing more." One of the bitterest religious poems of our times, it is a counterpart to the Christmas poem, "Karma."

CALVARY

Friendless and faint, with martyred steps and slow
Faint for the flesh, but for the spirit free,
Stung by the mob that came to see the show,
The Master toiled along to Calvary;
We gibed him, as he went, with houndish glee,
Till his dimmed eyes for us did overflow;
We cursed his vengeless hands thrice wretchedly,—
And this was nineteen hundred years ago.

But after nineteen hundred years the shame
Still clings, and we have not made good the loss
That outraged faith has entered in his name.
Ah, when shall come love's courage to be strong!
Tell me, O Lord—tell me, O Lord, how long
Are we to keep Christ writhing on the cross!

It has become the fashion to laud the experimenter and to belittle whatever seems traditional. Robinson never objected when he was called a traditionalist. True to the tradition, he was a poet who worked with the skill of the confident craftsman. There are, in his poems, practically no loose images and blurred abstractions. The outlines of his verse are firm and sharply defined; the nuances are delicate but always precise; the inner content is clearly, immediately comprehensible.

It is true that Robinson was somewhat too fond of a paradoxical balance of words. Sometimes, also, he fell so much in love with the suggestion of a phrase that he let it run into mere sonority, a rich but sometimes hollow rhetoric recalling Swinburne—as in the final verse of "Eros Turranos":

> Meanwhile we do no harm; for they
>   That with a god have striven,
> Not hearing much of what we say,
>   Take what the god has given;
> Though like waves breaking it may be,
> Or like a changed familiar tree,
> Or like a stairway to the sea
>   Where down the blind are driven.

Another paradox is Robinson's use of tinkling measures for serious purposes. Many, if not most, of his stanzas are built on forms as airy as the lightest of light verse. The "plot" of "Richard Cory" is grim, but the technique, the verse pattern, is similar to that of The "Babs" Ballads by W. S. Gilbert. This is illustrated throughout Robinson's work, notably in one of his most pathetic portraits, "Bewick Finzer."

BEWICK FINZER

> Time was when his half million drew
>   The breath of six per cent;
> But soon the worm of what-was-not
>   Fed hard on his content;
> And something crumbled in his brain
>   When his half million went.
>
> Time passed, and filled along with his
>   The place of many more;
> Time came, and hardly one of us
>   Had credence to restore,
> From what appeared one day, the man
>   Whom we had known before.

The broken voice, the withered neck,
   The coat worn out with care,
The cleanliness of indigence,
   The brilliance of despair,
The fond imponderable dreams
   Of affluence,—all were there.

Poor Finzer, with his dreams and schemes,
   Fares hard now in the race,
With heart and eye that have a task
   When he looks in the face
Of one who might so easily
   Have been in Finzer's place.

He comes unfailing for the loan
   We give and then forget;
He comes, and probably for years
   Will he be coming yet,—
Familiar as an old mistake,
   And futile as regret.

Robinson was the first to acknowledge that he was no innovator, that he had no theories, no understanding of the creative impulse. He did not explore new methods of writing or new ways to be new. He felt instinctively what the ancient poet felt that, as C. M. Bowra pointed out in *The Greek Experience*, tradition dominated classic poetry "without hampering its freedom in the smallest degree. Indeed, just because it laid down the manner of art expected from a certain kind of poem, it left the poet free to show his skill without troubling himself to invent new forms or manner of approach."

In an introduction to a long posthumous poem, *King Jasper*, Robert Frost put the matter succinctly. "Robinson stayed content with the old-fashioned way to be new. . . . For forty years it was phrase on phrase with Robinson, and every one the closest delineation of something that *is* something. . . . His theme was unhappiness itself, but his skill was as happy as it was playful. . . . The style is the man. Rather say the style is the way the man takes himself. If it is with outer seriousness, it must be with inner humor. If it is with outer humor, it must be with inner seriousness." (Incidentally, this last dictum applies not only to Robinson but to Frost himself.)

Characteristic of Robinson's style was his handwriting, miniscule, almost microscopic. It would not need the services of a professional chirographer to read Robinson's character in his tight, finely etched characters. Here, as Frost says, is the way a man takes himself; modestly definite but unassertive, reserved, restrained, and reticent to the vanishing point.

A lonely man, loneliness was his leading theme, loneliness and the strength one acquires from being alone. Today many poets, in common with painters and sculptors, have discarded beauty and harmony as inappropriate to the hideously inharmonious world in which we live. To reflect the temper of our times, they have relinquished sensuousness for force, shapeliness for violence. For music they offer a maze of ambiguous meanings; they abjure sentiment and rely on hate, anger, and tension as substitutes for communication, or dispense with communication altogether. Tension and outrage are by no means absent from Robinson's poetry, but they are shaped, controlled, and fashioned in forms which interweave music and meaning, vision and vitality. The sincerity of his poems is their sadness; Robinson met adversity with a probity that refused to soften circumstance with hypocrytical moralizing and easy answers. His pervading sympathy was with the wrecks of our greed-driven society, the tragic Richard Corys, the dream-frustrated Cheevys, the ruined Bewick Finzers, the outcast Mr. Floods, a whole world of bewildered misfits. He made every reader understand not only the discarded and the dispossessed, but also the unbeaten humanity of these failures. Speaking for them he spoke for himself and, through his poetry, wrung a triumph out of defeat.

Hidden Name and Complex Fate:
A Writer's Experience
in the U.S.

Ralph Ellison

Presented at the Library of Congress January 6, 1964

In *Green Hills of Africa* Ernest Hemingway reminds us that both Tolstoi and Stendhal had seen war, that Flaubert had seen a revolution and the Commune, that Dostoevsky had been sent to Siberia, and that such experiences were important in shaping the art of these great masters. And he goes on to observe that "writers are forged in injustice as a sword is forged." He declined to describe the many personal forms which injustice may take in this chaotic world—who would be so mad as to try?—nor does he go into the personal wounds which each of these writers sustained. Now, however, thanks to his brother and sister, we do know something of the injustice in which he himself was forged, and this knowledge has been added to what we have long known of Hemingway's artistic temper.

In the end, however, it is the quality of his art which is primary. It is the art which allows the wars and revolutions which he knew, and the personal and social injustice which he suffered, to lay claims upon our attention; for it is through his art that they achieve their most enduring meaning. It is a matter of outrageous irony, perhaps, but in literature the great social clashes of history, no less than the painful experiences of the individual, are secondary to the meaning which they take on through the skill, the talent, the imagination and personal vision of the writer who transforms them into art. Here they are reduced to more manageable proportions, here they are imbued with humane value; here injustice and catastrophe become less important in themselves than in what the writer makes of them.

This is *not* true, however, of the writer's struggle with that recalcitrant angel called Art; and it was through *this* specific struggle that Ernest Hemingway became *Hemingway* (now refined to a total body of transcendent work, after forty years of being endlessly dismembered and resurrected, as it continues to be, in the styles, the themes, the sense of life and literature of countless of those who write). And it was through this struggle with form that he became the master, the culture hero, whom we have come to know and admire.

It was suggested that it might be of interest if I discussed here this evening some of my notions of the writer's experience in the United States, hence I have evoked the name of Hemingway, not by way of inviting farfetched comparisons, but in order to establish a perspective, a set of assumptions from which I may speak, and in an attempt to avoid boring you by emphasizing those details of racial hardship which, for some forty years now, have been evoked whenever writers of my own cultural background have essayed their experience in public.

I do this not by way of denying totally the validity of these by now stylized recitals, for I have shared and still share many of their detailed injustices—what Negro can escape them?—but by way of suggesting that they are, at least in a discussion of a writer's experience, as *writer,* as artist, somewhat beside the point.

For we select neither our parents, our race, nor our nation; these occur to us out of the love, the hate, the circumstance, the fate of others. But we *do* become writers out of an act of will, out of an act of choice; a dim, confused, and ofttimes regrettable choice, perhaps, but a choice nevertheless. And what happens thereafter causes all those experiences which occurred *before* we began to function as writers to take on a special quality of uniqueness. If this does not happen, then, as far as writing goes, the experiences have been misused. If we do not make of them a value, if we do not transform them into forms and images of meaning which they did not possess before, then we have failed as artists.

Thus for a writer to insist that his personal suffering is of special interest in itself, or simply because he belongs to a particular racial or religious group, is to advance a claim for special privilege which members of his group who are not writers would be ashamed to demand. The kindest judgment one can make of this point of view is that it reveals a sad misunderstanding of the relationship between suffering and art. Thomas Mann and André Gide have told us much of this, and there are many critics, like Edmund Wilson, who have told of the connection between the wound and the bow.

As I see it, it is through the process of making artistic form—plays, poems, novels—out of one's experience that one becomes a writer, and it is through this process, this struggle, that the writer helps give meaning to the experience of the group. And it is the process of mastering the discipline, the techniques, the fortitude, the culture, through which this is made possible, which constitutes the writer's real experience as *writer*, as artist. If this sounds like an argument for the artist's withdrawal from social struggles, I would recall to you W. H. Auden's comment to the effect that:

In our age, the mere making of a work of art is itself a political act. So long as artists exist, making what they please and think they ought to make, even if it is not terribly good, even if it appeals to only a handful of people, they remind the Management of something managers need to be reminded of, namely, that the managed are people with faces, not anonymous members, that *Homo Laborans* is also *Homo Ludens*.[1]

Without doubt, even the most *engagé* writer—and I refer to true artists, not to artists *manqués*—begin their careers in play and in puzzlement; in dreaming over the details of the world in which they become conscious of themselves.

Let Tar-Baby, that enigmatic figure from Negro folklore, stand for the world. He leans, black and gleaming, against the well of life and remains utterly noncommittal under our scrutiny, our questioning; starkly unmoving before our naive attempts at intimidation. Then we touch him playfully and before we can say "Sonny Liston!" we find ourselves stuck. Our playful investigations become a labor, a fearful struggle, an agon. Slowly we perceive that our task is to learn the proper way of freeing ourselves, to develop, in other words, technique.

Sensing this, we give him our sharpest attention, we question him carefully, we struggle with more subtlety; while he, in his silent way, holds on; demanding that we perceive the necessity of calling him by his true name as the price of our freedom. It is unfortunate that he has so many, many "true" names—all spelling chaos; and in order to discover even one of these we must first come into the possession of our own names. For it is through our names that we first place ourselves in the world. Our names, being the gifts of others, *must* be made our own.

Once while listening to the play of a two-year-old girl who did not know she was under observation, I heard her saying over and over again, at first with questioning and then with sounds of growing satisfaction, "I am Mimi Livisay? . . . I am Mimi Livisay. I *am* Mimi Livisay . . . I am *Mimi* Li-vi-Say! I am *Mimi*. . . ."

And in deed and in fact she was—or became so soon thereafter, by working playfully to establish the unity between herself and her name.

---

[1] From his essay "The Poet & The City" in *The Dyer's Hand* (New York, 1962), p. 88.

For many of us this is far from easy. We must learn to wear our names within all the noise and confusion of the environment in which we find ourselves; make them the center of all of our associations with the world; with man and with nature. We must charge them with all our emotions, our hopes, hates, loves, aspirations. They must become our masks and our shields, and the containers of all those values and traditions which we learn and/or imagine as being the meaning of our familial past.

And when we are reminded so constantly that we bear, as Negroes, names originally possessed by those who owned our enslaved grandparents, we are apt, especially if we are potential writers, to be more than ordinarily concerned with the veiled and mysterious events, the fusions of blood, the furtive couplings, the business transactions, the violations of faith and loyalty, the assaults; yes, and the unrecognized and unrecognizable loves through which our names were handed down unto us.

So charged with emotion does this concern become for some of us, that we have earlier the example of the followers of Father Divine, and, now, the Black Muslims discarding their original names in rejection of the blood-stained, the brutal, the sinful images of the past. Thus they would declare new identities, would clarify a new program of intention and destroy the verbal evidence of a willed and ritualized discontinuity of blood and human intercourse.

Not all of us, actually only a few, seek to deal with our names in this manner. We take what we have and make of them what we can. And there are even those who know where the old broken connections lie, who recognize their relatives across the chasm of historical denial and the artificial barriers of society, and who see themselves as bearers of many of the qualities which were admirable in the original sources of their common line (Faulkner has made much of this); and I speak here not of mere forgiveness, nor of obsequious insensitivity to the outrages symbolized by the denial and the division, but of the *conscious* acceptance of the harsh realities of the human condition, of the ambiguities and hypocrisies of human history as they have played out themselves in these United States.

Perhaps, taken in aggregate, these European names which we bear (sometimes with irony, sometimes with pride, but *always* with personal investment) represent a certain triumph of the spirit; speaking to us of those who rallied, reassembled and transformed themselves and who, under dismembering pressures, refused to die. "Brothers and sisters," I once heard a Negro preacher exhort, "Let us make up our faces before the world, and our names shall sound throughout the land with honor! For we ourselves are our *true* names, not their epithets! So, let us, I say, Make Up Our Faces and Our Minds!"

Perhaps my preacher had read T. S. Eliot, although I doubt it. And in actuality it was unnecessary that he do so, for a concern with names and naming was very much a part of that special area of American culture from which I come, and it is precisely for this reason that this example should come to mind in a discussion of my own experience as a writer.

Doubtlessly, writers begin their *conditioning* as manipulators of words long before they become aware of literature—certain Freudians would say at the breast. Perhaps, but if so that is far too early to be of use at this moment. Of this, though, I am certain: That despite the misconceptions of those educators who trace the reading difficulties experienced by large numbers of Negro children in northern schools to their southern background, these children are, in *their* familiar South, facile manipulators of words. I know, too, that the Negro community is deadly in its ability to create nicknames and to spot all that is ludicrous in an unlikely name or that which is incongruous in conduct. Names are not qualities, nor are words, in this particular sense, actions. To assume that they are could cost one his life many times a day. Language skills depend to a large extent upon a knowledge of the details, the manners, the objects, the folkways, the psychological patterns of a given environment. Humor and wit depend upon much of the same awareness, and so does the suggestive power of names.

"A small, brown, bow-legged Negro with the name 'Franklin D. Roosevelt Jones' might sound like a clown to someone who looks at him from the outside," said my friend Albert Murray, "but on the other hand he just might turn out to be a hell of a fireside operator. He might just lie back in all of that comic juxtaposition of names and manipulate you deaf, dumb, and blind—and you not even suspecting it, because you're thrown out of stance by his name! There you are, so dazzled by the F.D.R. image—which you *know* you can't see—and so delighted with your own superior position that you don't realize that it is *Jones* who must be confronted."

Well, as you must suspect, all of this speculation on the matter of names has a purpose, and now, because it is tied up so ironically with my own experience as a writer, I must turn to my own name.

For in the dim beginnings, before I ever thought consciously of writing, there was my own name, and there was, doubtlessly, a certain magic in it. From the start I was uncomfortable with it, and in my earliest years it caused me much puzzlement. Neither could I understand what a poet was, nor why, exactly, my father had chosen one for my namesake. Perhaps I could have understood it perfectly well had he named me after his own father, but that name had been given to an older brother who died and thus was out of the question. But why hadn't he named me after a hero, such as Jack Johnson, or a soldier like Colonel Charles Young, or a great seaman like Admiral Dewey, or an educator like Booker T. Washington, or a great orator and abolitionist like Frederick Douglass? Or again, why

556

hadn't he named me (as so many Negro parents had done) after President Theodore Roosevelt?

Instead, he named me after someone called Ralph Waldo Emerson, and then, when I was three, he died. It was too early for me to have understood his choice, although I'm sure he must have explained it many times, and it was also too soon for me to have made the connection between my name and my father's love for reading. Much later, after I began to write and work with words, I came to suspect that he was aware of the suggestive powers of names and of the magic involved in naming.

I recall an odd conversation with my mother during my early teens in which she mentioned their interest in, of all things, prenatal culture! But for a long time I actually knew only that my father read a lot, and that he admired this remote Mr. Emerson, who was something called a "poet and philosopher"—so much so, that he named his second son after him.

I knew also that, whatever his motives, the combination of names he'd given me caused me no end of trouble from the moment when I could talk well enough to respond to the ritualized question which grownups put to very young children. Emerson's name was quite familiar to Negroes in Oklahoma during those days when World War I was brewing, and adults, eager to show off their knowledge of literary figures and obviously amused by the joke implicit in such a small brown nubbin of a boy carrying around such a heavy moniker, would invariably repeat my first two names and then, to my great annoyance, they'd add "Emerson."

And I, in my confusion, would reply, "No, no, I'm not Emerson; he's the little boy who lives next door." Which only made them laugh all the louder. "Oh no," they'd say, "you're Ralph Waldo Emerson," while I had fantasies of blue murder.

For a while the presence next door of my little friend Emerson made it unnecessary for me to puzzle too often over this peculiar adult confusion. And since there were other Negro boys named "Ralph" in the city, I came to suspect that there was something about the combination of names which produced their laughter. Even today I know of only one other "Ralph" who had as much comedy made out of his name, a campus politician and deep-voiced orator whom I knew at Tuskegee, who was called in friendly ribbing, "Ralph Waldo Emerson Edgar Allen Poe, spelled *Powe*." This must have been quite a trial for him, but I had been initiated much earlier.

During my early school years the name continued to puzzle me, for it constantly evoked in the faces of others some secret. It was as though I possessed some treasure or some defect, which was invisible to my own eyes and ears; something which I had but did not *possess*, like a piece of property in South Carolina, which was mine but which I would not have until some future time. I recall finding, about this time, while seeking adventure in back alleys—which possess, for boys, a superiority over playgrounds like that which kitchen utensils possess over toys designed for infants—a large photographic lens. I remember nothing of its optical qualities, nor of its speed or color correction, but it gleamed with crystal mystery and it was beautiful.

Mounted handsomely in a tube of shiny brass, it spoke to me of distant worlds of possibility. I played with it, looking through it with squinted eyes, holding it in shafts of sunlight, and tried to use it for a magic lantern. But most of this was as unrewarding as my attempts to make the music come from a phonograph record by holding the needle in my fingers.

I could burn holes through newspapers with it, or I could pretend that it was a telescope, the barrel of a cannon, or the third eye of a monster—*I* being the monster—but I could do nothing at all about its proper function of making images; nothing to make it yield its secret. But I would not discard it.

Older boys sought to get it away from me by offering knives or tops, agate marbles or whole zoos of grass snakes and horned toads in trade, but I held on to it. No one, not even the white boys I knew, had such a lens, and it was my own good luck to have found it. Thus I would hold on to it until such time as I could acquire the parts needed to make it function. Finally, I put it aside and it remained buried in my box of treasures, dusty and dull, to be lost and forgotten as I grew older and became interested in music.

I had reached by now the grades where it was necessary to learn something about Mr. Emerson and what he had done, such as the *Concord Hymn* and the essay on *Self-Reliance,* and in following his advice, I reduced the "Waldo" to a simple and, I hoped, mysterious "W," and in my own reading I avoided his works like the plague. I could no more deal with my name— I shall never really master it—than I could find a creative use for my lens. Fortunately, there were other problems to occupy my mind. Not that I forgot my fascination with names, but more about that later.

Negro Oklahoma City was starkly lacking in writers. In fact, there was only Roscoe Dungee, the editor of the local Negro newspaper and a very fine editorialist in that valuable tradition of personal journalism which is now rapidly disappearing; a writer who, in his emphasis upon the possibilities for justice offered by the Constitution, anticipated the antisegregation struggle by decades. There were also a few reporters who drifted in and out, but these were about all. On the level of *conscious* culture, the Negro community was biased in the direction of music.

These were the middle and late twenties, remember, and the State was still a new "frontier" State. The capital city was one of the great centers for southwestern jazz, along with Dallas and Kansas City. Orchestras which were to become famous within a few years were constantly coming and going, as were the blues singers—Ma Rainey and Ida Cox—and the

558

old bands like that of King Oliver. But best of all, thanks to Mrs. Zelia N. Breaux, there was an active and enthusiastic school music program through which any child who had the interest and the talent could learn to play an instrument and take part in the band, the orchestra, the brass quartet. And there was a yearly operetta and a chorus and a glee club. Harmony was taught for four years and the music appreciation program was imperative. European folk dances were taught throughout the Negro school system, and we were also taught complicated patterns of military drill.

I tell you this to point out that although there were no incentives to write, there was ample opportunity to receive an artistic discipline. Indeed, once one picked up an instrument it was difficult to escape. If you chafed at the many rehearsals of the school band or orchestra and were drawn to the many small jazz groups, you were likely to discover that the jazzmen were apt to rehearse far more than the school band; it was only that they seemed to enjoy themselves better and to possess a freedom of imagination which we were denied at school. And one soon learned that the wild, transcendent moments which occurred at dances or "battles of music," moments in which memorable improvisations were ignited, depended upon a dedication to a discipline which was observed even when rehearsals had to take place in the crowded quarters of Halley Richardson's shoeshine parlor. It was not the place which counted, although a large hall with good acoustics was preferred, but what one did to perfect one's performance.

If this talk of musical discipline gives the impression that there were no forces working to nourish one who would one day blunder, after many a twist and turn, into writing, I am misleading you. And here I might give you a longish lecture on the "Ironies and Uses of Segregation." When I was a small child, there was no library for Negroes in our city; and not until a Negro minister invaded the main library did we get one. For it was discovered that there was no law, only custom, which held that we could not use these public facilities. The results were the quick renting of two large rooms in a Negro office building—the recent site of a pool hall—the hiring of a young Negro librarian, the installation of shelves, and a hurried stocking of the walls with any and every book possible. It was, in those first days, something of a literary chaos.

But how fortunate for a boy who loved to read! I started with the fairy tales and quickly went through the junior fiction; then through the Westerns and the detective novels, and very soon I was reading the classics—only I didn't know it. There were also the Haldeman-Julius Blue Books, which seem to have floated on the air down from Girard, Kansas; the syndicated columns of O. O. McIntyre, and the copies of *Vanity Fair* and the *Literary Digest* which my mother brought home from work—how in light of the effect of these on my own life could I ever join uncritically in the heavy-handed attacks on the so-called big media which have become so common today.

There were also the pulp magazines and, more important, that other library which I visited whenever I went to help my adopted grandfather, J. D. Randolph (my parents had lived in his rooming house when I was born), at his work as custodian of the Law Library of the Oklahoma State Capitol. Mr. Randolph had been one of the first teachers in what became Oklahoma City after having been one of the leaders of a group who walked from Gallatin, Tennessee, to the Oklahoma Territory. He was a tall man, as brown as smoked leather, who looked like the Indians with whom he'd herded horses during the territory days. And while his status was merely that of custodian of the Law Library, I was to see the white legislators come down on many occasions to question him on points of law, and I was often to hear him answer without recourse to the uniform rows of books on the shelves. This was a thing to marvel at in itself, and the white lawmakers did so, but even more marvelous, ironic, intriguing, haunting— call it what you will—is the fact that the Negro who knew the answers was named after Jefferson Davis. What Tennessee lost, Oklahoma was to gain, and after gaining it (a gift of courage, intelligence, fortitude, and grace), used it only in concealment and, one hopes, with embarrassment.

So let us, I say, make up our faces and our minds!

*   *   *   *   *   *   *

In the loosely structured community of that time, knowledge, news of other ways of living, ancient wisdom, the latest literary fads, hate litera- ture—for years I kept a card warning Negroes away from the polls, which had been dropped by the thousands from a plane which circled over the Negro community—information of all kinds, found its level catch-as-catch- can in the minds of those who were receptive to it. Not that there was no conscious structuring—I read my first Shaw and Maupassant, my first Harvard Classics, in the home of a friend whose parents were products of that stream of New England education which had been brought to Negroes by the young and enthusiastic white teachers who staffed the schools set up for the freedmen after the Civil War. These parents were both teachers and there were others like them in our town.

But the places where a rich oral literature was truly functional were in the churches, the schoolyards, the barbershops, the cotton-picking camps; places where folklore and gossip thrived. The drugstore where I worked was such a place where, on days of bad weather, the older men would sit with their pipes and tell tall tales, hunting yarns, and homely versions of the classics. It was here that I heard stories of searching for buried treasure

560

and of headless horsemen, which I was told were my own father's versions, told long before. There were even recitals of popular verse, "The Shooting of Dan McGrew," and, along with these, stories of Jesse James, of Negro outlaws and black U.S. Marshals, of slaves who became the chiefs of Indian tribes, and of the exploits of Negro cowboys. There was both truth and fantasy in this, intermingled in the mysterious fashion of literature.

Writers, in their formative period, absorb into their consciousness much that has no special value until much later, and often much which is of no special value even then perhaps, beyond the fact that it throbs with affect and mystery and in it "time and pain and royalty in the blood" are suspended in imagery. So, long before I thought of writing, I was claimed by weather, by speech rhythms, by Negro voices and their different idioms, by husky male voices and by the high shrill singing voices of certain Negro women, by music; by tight spaces and by wide spaces in which the eyes could wander; by death, by newly born babies, by manners of various kinds, company manners and street manners; the manners of white society and those of our own high society; and by interracial manners; by street fights, circuses, and minstrel shows; by vaudeville and moving pictures, by prize-fights and footraces, baseball games and football matches. By spring floods and blizzards, catalpa worms and jackrabbits; honeysuckle and snapdragons (which smelled like old cigar butts); by sunflowers and hollyhocks, raw sugarcane and baked yams; pigs feet, chili, and Blue Haw ice cream. By parades, public dances and jam sessions, Easter sunrise ceremonies and large funerals. By contests between fire-and-brimstone preachers, and by presiding elders who got laughing-happy when moved by the spirit of God.

I was impressed by expert players of the "dozens" and certain notorious bootleggers of corn whiskey. By jazz musicians and fortunetellers and by men who did anything well; by strange sicknesses and by interesting brick or razor scars; by expert cursing vocabularies as well as by exalted praying and terrifying shouting, and by transcendent playing or singing of the blues. I was fascinated by old ladies, those who had seen slavery, and by those who were defiant of white folk and black alike; by the enticing walks of prostitutes and by the limping walks affected by Negro hustlers, especially those who wore Stetson hats, expensive shoes with well-starched overalls, usually with a diamond stickpin (when not in hock) in their tieless collars as their gambling uniforms.

And there were the blind men who preached on corners, and the blind men who sang the blues to the accompaniment of washboard and guitar; and the white junkmen who sang mountain music, and the famous hucksters of fruit and vegetables.

And there was the Indian-Negro confusion. There were Negroes who were part Indian and who lived on reservations, and Indians who had children who lived in town as Negroes, and Negroes who were Indians and traveled back and forth between the groups with no trouble. And Indians who were wild as wild Negroes, and others who were as solid and as steady as bankers. There were the teachers, too, inspiring teachers and villainous teachers who chased after the girl students, and certain female teachers who one wished would've chased after young male students. And a handsome old principal of military bearing who had been blemished by his classmates at West Point when they discovered on the eve of graduation that he was a Negro. There were certain Jews, Mexicans, Chinese cooks, a German orchestral conductor, and an English grocer who owned a Franklin touring car. And certain Negro mechanics—"Cadillac Slim," "Sticks" Walker, Buddy Bunn, and Oscar Pitman—who had so assimilated the automobile that they seemed to be behind a steering wheel even as they walked the streets or danced with girls. And there were the whites who despised us and the others who shared our hardships and our joys.

There is much more, but this is sufficient to indicate some of what was present even in a segregated community to form the background of my work, my sense of life.

And now comes the next step. I went to Tuskegee to study music, hoping to become a composer of symphonies, and there, during my second year, I read *The Waste Land* and that, although I was then unaware of it, was the real transition to writing.

Mrs. L. C. McFarland had taught us much of Negro history in grade school and from her I'd learned of the New Negro Movement of the twenties, of Langston Hughes, Countee Cullen, Claude McKay, James Weldon Johnson, and the others. They had inspired pride and had given me a closer identification with poetry (by now, oddly enough, I seldom thought of my hidden name), but with music so much on my mind it never occurred to me to try to imitate them. Still I read their work and was excited by the glamor of the Harlem which emerged from their poems, and it was good to know that there were Negro writers.—Then came *The Waste Land*.

I was much more under the spell of literature than I realized at the time. *Wuthering Heights* had caused me an agony of inexpressible emotion, and the same was true of *Jude the Obscure;* but *The Waste Land* seized my mind. I was intrigued by its power to move me while eluding my understanding. Somehow, its rhythms were often closer to those of jazz than those of the Negro poets, and even though I could not then understand it, its range of allusion was as mixed and as broad as that of Louis Armstrong. Also, there were its discontinuities, its changes of pace, and its hidden system of organization which escaped me.

There was nothing to do but look up the references in the footnotes to the poem, and thus began my conscious education in literature.

562

For this, the library at Tuskegee was quite adequate, and I used it. Soon I was reading a whole range of subjects drawn upon by the poet, and this led, in turn, to criticism and to Pound and Ford Madox Ford, Sherwood Anderson and Gertrude Stein, Hemingway and Fitzgerald, and "round about til I was come" back to Melville and Twain—the writers who are taught and doubtlessly overtaught today. Perhaps it was my good luck that they were taught at Tuskegee, I wouldn't know. But at the time, I was playing, having an intellectually interesting good time.

Having given so much attention to the techniques of music, the process of learning something of the craft and intention of modern poetry and fiction seemed quite familiar. Besides, it was absolutely painless because it involved no deadlines or credits. Even then, however, a process which I described earlier had begun to operate. The more I learned of literature in this conscious way, the more the details of my background became transformed. I heard undertones in remembered conversations which had escaped me before, local customs took on more universal meaning, values which I hadn't understood were revealed; some of the people whom I had known were diminished, while others were elevated in stature. More important, I began to see my own possibilities with more objective and, in some ways, more hopeful eyes.

The following summer I went to New York, seeking work which I did not find, and remained there, but the personal transformation continued. Reading had become a conscious process of growth and discovery, a method of re-ordering the world. And that world had widened considerably.

At Tuskegee I had handled manuscripts which Prokofiev had given to Hazel Harrison, a Negro concert pianist who taught there and who had known him in Europe, and through Miss Harrison I had become aware of Prokofiev's symphonies. I had also become aware of the radical movement in politics and art, and in New York had begun reading the work of André Malraux, not only the fiction but chapters published from his work, *The Psychology of Art*. And in my search for an expression of modern sensibility in the works of Negro writers, I discovered Richard Wright. Shortly thereafter, I was to meet Wright and it was at his suggestion that I wrote both my first book review and my first short story. These were fatal suggestions.

For, although I had tried my hand at poetry while at Tuskegee, it hadn't occurred to me that I might write fiction, but once he suggested it, it seemed the most natural thing to try. Fortunately for me, Wright, while on the verge of his first success, was eager to talk with a beginner, and I was able to save valuable time in searching out those works in which writing was discussed as a craft. He guided me to Henry James' prefaces, to Conrad, to Joseph Warren Beach, and to the letters of Dostoevsky. There were other advisers and other books involved, of course, but what is important here is that I was consciously concerned with the art of fiction, that almost from the beginning I was grappling quite consciously with the art through which I wished to realize myself. And this was not done in isolation; the Spanish Civil War was now in progress and the Depression was still on. The world was being shaken up and, through one of those odd instances which occur to young provincials in New York, I was to hear Malraux make an appeal for the Spanish Loyalists at the same party where I was to first hear folksinger Leadbelly perform. Wright and I were there seeking money for the magazine which he had come to New York to edit.

Art and politics; a great French novelist and a Negro folksinger; a young writer who was soon to publish *Uncle Tom's Children;* and I who had barely begun to study his craft. It is such accidents, such fortuitous meetings, which count for so much in our lives. I had never dreamed that I would be in the presence of Malraux, of whose work I became aware on my second day in Harlem when Langston Hughes suggested that I read *Man's Fate* and *Days of Wrath* before returning them to a friend of his. And it is this fortuitous circumstance which led to my selecting Malraux as a literary "ancestor" whom, unlike a relative, the artist is permitted to choose. There was in progress at the time all the agitation over the Scottsboro boys and the Herndon case, and I was aware of both. I had to be; I myself had been taken off a freight train at Decatur, Alabama, only three years before while on my way to Tuskegee. But while I joined in the agitation for their release, my main energies went into learning to write.

I began to publish enough, and not too slowly, to justify my hopes for success, and as I continued, I made a most perplexing discovery; namely, that for all his conscious concern with technique, a writer did not so much create the novel as he was created *by* the novel. That is, one did not make an arbitrary gesture when one sought to write. And when I say that the novelist is created by the novel, I mean to remind you that fictional techniques are not a mere set of objective tools, but something much more intimate: a way of feeling, of seeing, and of expressing one's sense of life. And the process of *acquiring* technique is a process of modifying one's responses, of learning to see and to feel, to hear and observe, to evoke and evaluate the images of memory, and of summoning up and directing the imagination; of learning to conceive of human values in the ways which have been established by the great writers who have developed and extended the art. And perhaps the writer's greatest freedom, as artist, lies precisely in his possession of technique; for it is through technique that he comes to possess and express the meaning of his life.

Perhaps at this point it would be useful to recapitulate the route—perhaps as maze-like as that of *Finnegans Wake*—which I have been trying to

564

describe; that which leads from the writer's discovery of a sense of purpose, which is that of becoming a writer, and then the involvement in the passionate struggle required to master a bit of technique, and then, as this begins to take shape, the disconcerting discovery that it is *technique* which transforms the individual before he is able in turn to transform it. And in that personal transformation he discovers something else: He discovers that he has taken on certain obligations, that he must not embarrass the form, and that in order to avoid this he must develop taste. He learns—and this is most discouraging—that he is involved with values which turn in their *own* way, and not in the ways of politics, upon the central issues affecting his nation and his time. He learns that, from its first consciousness of itself as a literary form, the American novel has grappled with the meaning of the American experience; that it has been aware and has sought to define the nature of that experience by addressing itself to the specific details, the moods, the landscapes, the cityscapes, the tempo of American change. And that it has borne, at its best, the full weight of that burden of conscience and consciousness which Americans inherit as one of the results of the revolutionary circumstance of our national beginnings.

We began as a nation not through the accidents of race or religion or geography (Robert Penn Warren has dwelled on these circumstances) but when a group of men, *some* of them political philosophers, put down, upon what we now recognize as being quite sacred papers, their conception of the nation which they intended to establish on these shores. They described, we know, the obligations of the state to the citizen, of the citizen to the state; they committed themselves to certain ideas of justice, just as they committed us to a system which would guarantee all of its citizens equality of opportunity.

I need not describe the problems which have arisen from these beginnings. I need only remind you that the contradiction between these noble ideals and the actualities of our conduct generated a guilt, an unease of spirit, from the very beginning, and that the American novel at its best has always been concerned with this basic moral predicament. During Melville's time and Twain's, it was an implicit aspect of their major themes; by the twentieth century and after the discouraging and traumatic effect of the Civil War and the Reconstruction, it had gone underground, had become *understated*. Nevertheless, it did not disappear completely, and it is to be found operating in the work of Henry James as well as in that of Hemingway and Fitzgerald. And then (and as one who believes in the impelling moral function of the novel and who believes in the moral seriousness of the form) it pleases me no end that it comes into explicit statement again in the works of Richard Wright and William Faulkner, writers who lived close to moral and political problems which would not stay put underground.

I go into these details not to recapitulate the history of the American novel, but to indicate the trend of thought which was set into motion when I began to discover the nature of that process with which I was actually involved. Whatever the opinions and decisions of critics, a novelist must arrive at his own conclusions as to the meaning and function of the form with which he is engaged, and these are, in all modesty, some of mine.

In order to orient myself, I also began to learn that the American novel had long concerned itself with the puzzle of the one-and-the-many; the mystery of how each of us, despite his origin in diverse regions, with our diverse racial, cultural, religious backgrounds—speaking his own diverse idiom of the American in his own accent—is, nevertheless, American. And with this concern with the implicit pluralism of the country and with the composite nature of the ideal character called "the American," there goes a concern with gauging the health of the American promise, with depicting the extent to which it is being achieved, being made manifest in our daily conduct.

And with all of this there still remained the specific concerns of literature. Among these is the need to keep literary standards high, the necessity of exploring new possibilities of language which would allow it to retain that flexibility and fidelity to the common speech which has been its glory since Mark Twain. For me, this meant learning to add to it the wonderful resources of Negro American speech and idiom and to bring into range as fully and eloquently as possible the complex reality of the American experience as it shaped and was shaped by the lives of my own people.

Notice that I stress as "fully" as possible, because I would no more strive to write great novels by leaving out the complexity of circumstances which goes to make up the Negro experience and which alone goes to make the obvious injustice bearable, than I would think of preparing myself to become President of the United States simply by studying Negro American history or of confining myself to studying those laws affecting civil rights.

For it seems to me that one of the obligations I took on when I committed myself to the art and form of the novel was that of striving for the broadest range, the discovery and articulation of the most exalted values. And I must squeeze these from the life which I know best. A highly truncated impression of that life I attempted to convey to you earlier in this paper.

If all this sounds a bit heady, remember that I did not destroy that troublesome middle name of mine, I only suppressed it. Sometimes it reminds me of my obligations to the man who named me.

It is our fate as human beings always to give up some good things for other good things, to throw off certain bad circumstances only to create others. Thus there is a value for the writer in trying to give as thorough a report of social reality as possible. Only by doing so may we grasp and convey the cost of change. Only by considering the broadest accumulation of data may we make choices that are based upon our own hard-earned sense of reality. Speaking from my own special area of American culture, I feel that to embrace uncritically values which are extended to us by others is to reject the validity, even the sacredness, of our own experience. It is also to forget that the small share of reality which each of our diverse groups is able to snatch from the whirling chaos of history belongs not to the group alone, but to all of us. It is a property and a witness which can be ignored only to the danger of the entire nation.

I could suppress the name of my namesake out of respect for the achievements of its original bearer, but I cannot escape the obligation of attempting to achieve some of the things which he asked of the American writer. As Henry James suggested, being an American is an arduous task, and for most of us, I suspect, the difficulty begins with the name.

American Poet?

Karl Shapiro

Presented at the Library of Congress January 27, 1964

For about a quarter of a century I have been putting together lectures and talks about poetry, criticism, modern literature, politics, religion, and culture. Most of these have ended up in journals or books. I have always written these pieces with gusto and sassiness, with the delight of an amateur filling in. I do not think of myself as a critic or a litterateur or a "spokesman" but merely as someone who responds to an invitation. I rise to the bait.

Now, for the first time, I have been stumped. Roy Basler asked me to speak here, following Ralph Ellison, on what would appear to be the easiest subject of all—myself. All at once I was tonguetied. I hardly ever write about anything else and seldom conceal the fact, yet a head-on confrontation with myself threw me out of gear. Perhaps I had never written about myself after all. I began to have the anxieties of a man who hears himself on a tape recorder or watches himself on television for the first time and thinks—My God, am I that phony!

The suggestion, of course, was not to regale you with my autobiography but to discuss my writing in relation to my milieu. But my writing *is* my milieu, and insofar as I am I, this is the only I, I know. A student said to me the other day, "I enjoy the way you deliberately mispronounce French." I was flabbergasted. And once a woman came up to me before a lecture I was about to give on anarchism and said, "I don't believe a word you are going to say, and I don't think you do either." I am a prey to rudenesses like this, but having an easy disposition, I blame myself for these intimacies. I wrote a glowing panegyric about Henry Miller a few years ago and have been asked a million times how much of it I meant to be taken seriously. People who disagree with me tend to consider me a liar. High-powered critics consider me a clown. A religious magazine once called me the Mort Sahl of criticism. I took this as flattery though it surely wasn't meant that way. I am a member of a sect sometimes called anticritics and I cannot in good faith expect to be treated with the dignity accorded to an Aristotle or a T. S. Eliot. It is part of the program of my sect to laugh criticism out of business, to play practical jokes, and in general to harrass and demoralize the enemy. It is serious play.

I began this lecture about six months ago and have worked on it steadily and with an increasing feeling of failure. I filled three medium-sized note-books with small script and typed about a hundred pages trying to develop my ideas. Only a minute quantity of this matter remains. It is more or less what I go through in writing a poem. I will write a poem many times and one day throw it all away and write a completely different one. But the "different" one could not have been written without the wrong ones. This is the process of getting at oneself. Only, in this case, I am not sure I succeeded.

Now it is absolutely of no interest to you how much time and waste of time go into a man's poem or essay and I think it is ill-mannered for a writer to brag about his herculean efforts, but on this particular occasion I think the subject calls for it. For the subject here is that I do not know what the subject is. I have never asked myself what I am in relation to my poems. I am afraid to. The answer might turn out to be—nothing. What if I am no more than the sum of poems? What if the poems are not worthy?

Eventually I made a pattern of my notes and found I was trying to get at myself from several directions. One was "racial" (I debated about whether to put that word in quotes, and finally did). Another was auto-biographical. A third had to do with my withdrawal from the Serious World into poetry. A fourth was an account of how I returned to the Serious World after having gained a reputation. To me this return signified the surrender of the prodigal wandering of my mind. And finally my pres-ent direction, which I am not sure about.

These are the things I am going to talk about, personally and in the abstract. I will apologize for "that frightful quantity of I's and me's" later.

Let me get the race business out of the way first. Anthropologically I would describe myself as an American Russian-Jewish Southerner. I think I have the items in the correct order. The word *Jew* in the Western World is certain to make anyone's skin twitch, including a Jew's. Some years ago I collected all the poems I had written having to do with this word and called the volume *Poems of a Jew*. The title aroused indignation from Jews and Gentiles alike. My chief reason for the book was to make people and myself say the word without any feedback. It would be a word like any other.

Now when Ralph Ellison and I received the invitation to speak in the Whittall series we both had a slight attack of anxiety. At least he phoned me from New York to ask what I was going to do. I think we both experienced a fleeting fear that we were about to revive the minstrel show, with a Negro novelist and a Jewish poet as the end men. A perfectly innocent and gracious come-on can produce a severe attack of shyness.

I read *Invisible Man* again. It is not only the best novel about the American Negro, it is probably the Great American Novel itself. Ellison has got it all down. The Negro is invisible and that is his grief. He is not a single separate person but only a member of a category. The applicable expression, the significant folk prejudice about other races, goes: They all look alike to me. One refuses to recognize the other race except as a phylum. The individual is not to materialize, under any circumstances. I have an aunt who as a child walked from the white side of a Virginia town to the black side to hear Booker T. Washington speak from the back of a train. She was the only white person in the crowd. Her father, my grandfather, was a Russian Jew. Somewhere in this incident was a recognition of a visible Negro. For this I am proud.

But as visibility goes, the Jew is the opposite of the Negro. The Jew is always and only the individual and is so recognized. Jewish culture in modern history, as well as in the mythology, is the triumph of the visibility of the one self. In the West, only the Germans evidently have persisted in seeing the Jew as a collectivity. This might account for the fact that Germany could produce super-Jews such as Marx, Freud, and Einstein, while the Jewish mass was fated for obliteration. The German technique of nonrecognition by obliteration is only the logical development of the technique which white people in Europe and America have carried out for centuries against slightly discolored people whom they do not wish to see.

It is practically impossible for a white person to understand the training a Negro must undergo to conceal his individuality. The Negro who made himself distinct, much less distinguished, was asking for the rope. For years I puzzled over the absence of Negro poetry in this country. The Negro had created jazz and jazz poetry, which had revolutionized music the world over. But he had no poetry with a capital P. What Negro would so assert himself or debase himself to write the Poem, that white and sacred object which sanctifies the white book? All we had was the Negro spiritual, the weakest example of Negro art—Uncle Tom on Sunday.

But with me visibility was a curse. I was raised as a middle-class Jew and underwent the formal training of a bar mitzvah, after which I lost all interest in what I had learned. My family was observant but only sporadically and without fanaticism. Fundamentally, religion was for old people and Europeans. As we know from American-Jewish novels, a generation ago the children of immigrants were pulled away from the old culture by the breathless and somewhat mindless opportunism of the New World.

The new acculturation had to wait for a third generation, my generation. The formula has been stated often and applies to me. All of my uncles and my father are business people. Almost all my cousins are professional people. And my children and their contemporaries have a strong leaning toward the arts, perhaps even by encouragement. What will happen to the fifth generation I don't know. According to writers like Philip Roth, there is a strong possibility of character degeneration as a result of too much material or professional success.

Anyone writing about himself who says, "I became a writer because," and then enumerates causes, is guessing. But I guess about myself that I became a writer for some of the following reasons: a lack of interest in study (I went to three high schools and two universities and am without a degree); a hypersensitivity to my Jewishness, aggravated by complex social distinctions in the South and in Baltimore; a sense of inadequacy to face the street; boredom; self-pity; eroticism; lack of seriousness; bad memory; fear of lightning and dogs; love of impressions and hallucinations; a tendency to speak in analogies (which perhaps led to a love of rhyme); a love of the obscure and esoteric; and a desire to impress by being witty or profane or irreverent. I have said nothing about a love of poetry, for such a thing could hardly be more than a sum of a great many causes. All I know is that by the age of seventeen I spent most of my time and all of my money in secondhand bookstores. The poetry shelves were the ones I searched most closely. I stole a rhyming dictionary from my high school in Baltimore and also a beautiful edition of the *Odes* of Anacreon in Greek (which I could not read).

In my family's circle of friends there was no literary atmosphere, yet my father encouraged my older brother to write and perhaps even to become a writer. My brother won a literary reputation while still in high school. A poem of his won a state contest in Virginia, and he read it at the University in Charlottesville, where he later distinguished himself in every field of study he undertook. I tried to impress him once by showing him a book I was reading. It was a psychopathic study of Poe—that was perhaps the subtitle—and was my first introduction to the pathology of poets.

Yiddish, a rich Chaucerian language, was not taught to us, although my parents spoke it sometimes as a private language or with elders. I was not aware of a Yiddish literature until long after I had become a poet. The cultural attitude among our class of people was generally that of middle-class people everywhere—that culture belongs to the leisure class. As far as culture for Jews went, that belonged to the German Jews, who were somehow culture aristocrats. Culture in my mind was vaguely associated with Germany and in its negative connotations still is.

These few facts and observations scarcely add up to a vita. I am at present attempting to write a kind of novel in which I will be able to deal with realities regardless of the facts. Unimportant details are often the most significant for our understanding of a man's life and work, and I think that a novel itself is some such construction; whereas the autobiography of a writer is liable to be lusterless and wooden, when not full of misinformation. What poets have written well about themselves? Yeats' friends complained about his *Autobiographies*. Yeats himself in one of them catches himself in a lie and then asks, "Why did I tell that lie?" Yeats is not the best example, however, with his psychology of the mask, his ritualistic posing, and his sad love life. I suggest that poets cannot write well about themselves because what they consider important in themselves, the Serious World considers trivial. Furthermore, poets have difficulty distinguishing between reality and fantasy. This sometimes, rather frequently in fact, makes the poet a clinical case. I have never quite believed that rigamarole of Coleridge's about Kubla Khan, but it is as good a "truth" as any about the poem.

Saul Bellow, speaking here last year, quoted the well-known line from Stendhal's autobiography: "that frightful quantity of I's and me's!" In a new book of poems I have coming out I use three quotes from this book, the one mentioned and also: "How many precautions are necessary to keep oneself from lying!" And a third: "What! is it nothing but that?" Stendhal was always being surprised by his disappointment in experience. He says about his love affairs and about the Battle of Waterloo—"What! is it nothing but that?"

Stendhal's real name was Henri Beyle, but in writing his autobiography he didn't call himself either Beyle or Stendhal but Henri Brulard.[1] It is the typical act of the artist, who knows less than his neighbors who he is. The world is about to celebrate the birthday of Shakespeare, yet after four hundred years the world still does not know who he was. We do not even know *that* he was.

It is a social convention of immemorial standing that only certain people are permitted to speak of themselves in public. Artists fall in this class, as do comedians, criminals, and alcoholics. But on the whole, society and the guild of artists are content to leave this area of expression to a very few Augustines, Rousseaus, Gandhis, Cellinis, and now and then a Stendhal. Moreover, there is a strong tendency in literature today toward the "veridical"—the novel that tells all and the poem that expresses sentiment. But no one is any the wiser about Henry Miller or Allen Ginsberg for having read their books. I think it was Keats who said that the poet is without character. It is even something of a platitude that the artist is a man in search of

---

[1] See his *Vie de Henri Brulard* (Paris, 1890) and later editions.

himself. For that reason, I am always suspicious of the poet who has found himself and who has delineated himself clearly and unmistakably to the world. Yeats, Eliot, and Baudelaire are such poets. Sartre felt the need to write a "pathography" of Baudelaire, which he calls an existential biography. He completes Baudelaire's personality, a necessary service in the case of a poet who invented the man called Baudelaire. Sartre coldly ferrets out the mother love of Baudelaire, his fetishism, and his inability to surrender to any experience except the peripheral. It is a study of the poet as onanist. We do not need a biography of Shakespeare, even if all the facts were laid before us. We definitely need one or many about the self-invented poet.

The writer's apprenticeship is a long and lonely affair from which he emerges cured of his loneliness, if he is fortunate. But in that case he may be cured of his writing as well. The density and unintelligibility of much youthful poetry is caused not so much by lack of skill as by the fear of communicating. The theory of poetic hurt has always been with us since ancient times—the lame foot and the cherished wound. "Mad Ireland hurt you into poetry," says Auden in his elegy for Yeats. And something or other does hurt the poet always "into" his poem. The youthful poet may withdraw first from the vision of ugliness which he sees everywhere around him; he would and does remake this world that wrongs the image of beauty. This is the typical withdrawal of the poet and is the world's explanation of what he is. This same hurt poet may later become a passionate public poet, a man of ringing ideals or a revolutionary. A good example is Swinburne who graduated from Our Lady of Pain to the Statue of Liberty. Byron is the most celebrated poet of this kind.

I am talking about the poet, not about poetry. Modern criticism has made it a taboo to talk about the poet and has taken the poem out of context so completely that little or nothing remains of it but its sensibility. It is perhaps the triumph of the wound theory of art. And modern society being what it supposedly is, the enemy of the individual, the poet and all other artists inherit the wound. Sometimes I think we should call them the poets of the Purple Heart.

But an ancient distinction was made also between the poet with a happy gift of nature and the poet hurt into madness. Of the poets with a happy gift of nature we have few. We are not ready for that. Poetry as celebration we have little of. Our joys are carefully disguised, so as not to offend the canon.

I went through all the ritual stages of anger and denial and enjoyed a long and lonely apprenticeship during the Depression. The Depression was a fine time for me; it substantiated my anger and prevented me from getting a job. My family was not poor. It was the time for young Com-

573

munists but I was saved from them in several ways. I detested meetings, I hated majority opinion (and so pretended to be a Trotskyite), and I carried on a private flirtation with Catholicism. In those days of political involvement I studied piano and had myself tutored in Latin.

But the only activity I pursued in good faith was writing poetry, or trying to. When I was twenty-one, I published a book of my poems. Like most such volumes the less said about it the better, yet it served the purpose of getting me a scholarship to a university. That was not the intention of the book but was the only form of recognition it received. The poems were imitations of William Carlos Williams and William Shakespeare. The Shakespeare ones were terrible, the Williams pieces much better. Over the years, Williams has superseded Shakespeare in my taste. I don't mean that he is the greater poet but that he speaks to me still. I was attracted by Williams' simplicity and his obscurity, the way he would let a piece of a poem stand for a poem, and the way he loved typography. But it was many years before I understood his theory of the object. The New Critics were beginning to take hold in the journals and I was infuriated by the theorizing without understanding it. I hated to think that Williams had a theory. No one was more opinionated or more given to generalizations that I, yet I could not bear the opinions of others who were more entitled to have them. I still think I am right in this denial of the equal rights of criticism. It has always seemed to me that good poetry is obviously good and the discussion of it qua poetry is a waste of time. The career of a poem, on the other hand, has always intrigued me—how far it goes in the world.

In the midthirties, Auden and Spender began to be printed in this country, and it was through them that I learned what I needed to know about writing my own poems. I could imitate Williams but not proceed beyond his style. The big Pound-Williams influence later helped form the generation of Beat poets, but I have always failed to be Beat, no matter how hard I tried. I went on a trip to Tahiti and took with me Spender's 1934 *Poems*. They were the hardest, clearest, loftiest, and most hurt lines I had ever seen in modern English. For me they were a textbook I had been looking for. While I was in Tahiti, the Spanish Civil War broke out. I returned home, not to join the Abraham Lincoln Brigade but to sun myself on the beaches of Atlantic City and write.

Auden, as every poetry professor knows, remade the whole fabric of diction for poets. He did the necessary and the seemingly impossible job of bringing poetic language up to date. Because of him poets today can use the language of technology and the theoretical sciences at will and without the self-conscious overtones of a word like *gramophone* or *motorcar* in Eliot. A line like "Here is the cosmopolitan cooking,/The light alloys

574

and the glass" had the same impact on me as "For God's sake hold your tongue and let me love" had once had. Auden presented modern English to poetry.

When he came to this country in 1939, I wrote him a long letter explaining carefully that New England is not a part of the United States. I forget what this was about. He replied with a beautifully written postcard that said succinctly, "Thank you."

I continued my retreat, which ended with two years of undergraduate study in Baltimore. Ostensibly I was to enter graduate study in English, though in the back of my head was a plan to study classics. I never got to that stage of the game but was drafted into the Army about a year before Pearl Harbor. There was a one-year conscription law, my name was drawn from a hat, and there was no deferment. But by that time, A.D. 1940, I was beginning to publish poetry in national magazines and could carry this vice with me to the barracks.

The Army was a kind of echo of my Depression years. In the Army one is totally isolated as a person. Soldiers can only lead fantasy lives, with a few brutal hours or days of freedom in between the shouting and the ritual of training. The din is so great and so incessant that it acts as a silence. One can write because everyone writes in the Army. People who have never put pen to paper spend hours composing letters. I found I was in a Writers' Colony. And because I was in Virginia, in a strange way I felt I was home. By the time I went overseas, I had had published my first large group of poems in a volume of new poets. It was well reviewed by well-known reviewers and I felt my first gratification for my years of effort. Just then my orders came through to be shipped to Australia; I was almost insane with fury.

During the space of three years in the Pacific, I published four books, which must be some kind of record for a foot soldier. That term doesn't sound quite right. I was a company clerk in the Medical Corps and something of an adept at goofing off to write poems. It had long since become expected of me in my outfit, and I do not recall ever having suffered any abuse because of my "hobby," as it was thought to be. Until the time I reached home I received very heady praise from the critics. The tide began to turn when F. O. Matthiessen praised one of my books written in New Guinea as perhaps the most important literary achivement to come out of the war. The review was on the front page of the *New York Times Book Review,* and a large Signal Corps photograph showed me sitting on the wooden steps of a tropical tent reading one of my own works. I would like to say a word about this book, which was widely resented by poets and critics alike, perhaps because Matthiessen attached such great importance to it.

My outfit was one day informed that we would be deactivated for ninety days preparatory to going to the Dutch Indies. I sat down and sketched out a critique of poetry which I wanted to write in verse. I would write about thirty lines a day (which I did) and at the end of three months have what I wanted, a kind of 20th-century neoclassical treatise on the art of poetry. The book was divided into three parts called The Confusion in Prosody, The Confusion in Language, and The Confusion in Belief. Everything was going to be straightened out. As the subject was contemporary poetry, I had to use contemporary poets for my examples. The foreword opened with a salvo against criticism in general. It then announced that 20th-century poetry is a kind of zoo. The whole work was two thousand and seventy lines long; I numbered the lines to make them look incontrovertible. It was my initial anti-intellectual essay, one of a long series to come, and I neither remember why I wrote it nor why Matthiessen, who had written one of the definitive books on T. S. Eliot, praised it. William Carlos Williams has an essay about it in which he is generously ambiguous. But to most of the poets my age, I had announced myself as a Philistine.

The fact is that I had never had any ideas about poetry but only overpowering predilections and prejudices. My antipathy for criticism was almost constitutional, though I did not begin to read it seriously until I became a professor several years after the war. My last retreat occurred in this library. The books I read here when I was poetry consultant were esoteric and mystical books, the Kabala, theosophy, Jung, Ouspensky, Plotinus, and so forth. Orthodox philosophy did not attract me.

I taught modern poetry for three years at Hopkins, awkwardly, for I had never taught. I wrote out vast dull lectures on Francis Thompson and AE and the Georgians, thinking I would work my way up to the interesting stuff but somehow never quite got there. I fiddled around with prosody a lot. At the first opportunity, I left the University and went to Chicago to edit *Poetry*. I have taught in universities off and on for twelve years but have never felt at home in what cultural symposiums call the academic atmosphere. Like most writers of today, I have written my share of criticism about the Academy and its literary produce, but I doubt if I have contributed any solution to the argument about the effect of teaching on writing and writing on teaching.

In any case, I breathed a sight of relief when I gave up my professorial role and sat down in Harriet Monroe's old chair. *Poetry* magazine was going on forty years old when I got there and was about as formidable a literary institution as any in the country. More than that, one had the feeling that if it collapsed, the entire city of Chicago would crumble into

576

dust. That was the impression I got from the mighty personages of the town who guarded over it spiritually, while keeping it on a starvation diet. I have never understood the marriage of wealth and culture, but I soon discovered that my real job was not editor but money-raiser. I am about as good a money-raiser as I was a soldier. Once I passed Tony Accardo on the street, and the thought flashed through my mind that perhaps the Syndicate would help support *Poetry*. I didn't follow that up, but in the end we founded a drinking club on the premises and that promised a solution until the whole thing unaccountably blew up, the *Poetry* offices were banished to the attics of the Newberry Library, and I went West. I once again became a professor and am likely to remain so.

So much for literary adventure.

Randall Jarrell gave a very courageous talk here a little over a year ago in front of the largest collection of live poets I have ever seen. In this talk he played the schoolmaster and gave all the American poets of the modern anthology a name or a grade. When he got to me he said I was neoprimitivist. Or rather he said my poems were like neoprimitive paintings. I must say I was pleased. I paint, not on Sunday, but whenever I find paint lying around. And in my paintings, which I find always make people laugh, I am ashamed to use shadow or perspective. I feel there is something dishonest about shadows and distances, but then I have never learned to draw. Nor do I wish to learn.

In poetry, I dislike shadows—"without any confusion or profundity of atmosphere," as Jarrell put it. Over a long period of time I have been charging quixotically at a huge shape called Culture without ever knowing whether I have scored against the leviathan. These tilts have taken various forms: against mythic form, symbolism, the Tradition, and so on. It is a kind of guerrilla warfare in which I am not the only assailant. Still, the battle against the Tradition and the continuity of culture and the presentness of the past, and so on, has become tedious. In the long run, criticism can't change anything. Only new works of art can do that.

American poetry is in a unique situation. At least I know of no other poetry which has its particular problems. I am referring to the English language. We have the language of England more or less by accident, for we might, giving and taking a battle here and there, be French- or Spanish-speaking people. Be that as it may, we have the language of England without the culture of England. The culture of this country is so multiplex that it is indescribable. In my state, for instance, there are dialects of German spoken which no longer exist in Germany. But the question is deeper than dialects. It is one of contents. There is also the fact that most Americans are descendants of uneducated populations and that whatever cultural aristocracy existed here in the 18th century has long since been swamped by wave after wave of subcultures. As poetry goes, we are precultured.

A century ago one man tried to create an American poetry with his bare hands. He did not succeed in that, but he did succeed in writing our greatest poems or some of them. The great literary works of America are predominantly prose, political works, fiction, even criticism. And in a sense the same thing holds in the 20th century. The attempt to impose the European mythos on our poetry has in part determined the character of what we call modern poetry, but this had to be done by missionaries, such as Pound and Eliot. And it had to be done through the agency of the American university. Pound's criticism consists of innumerable epistles directed to what he calls the Beaneries, our institutions of higher learning. Eliot's essays, the most formidable body of criticism in modern literature, helped set in motion a practical school of criticism which revolutionized the literary sensibility in our universities. (Eliot disclaims too great an influence here, though he is commonly thought of as the originator of the New Criticism.) And in turn this criticism affected not only the pedagogy of poetry but poetry itself. Many people, myself included, nowadays speak of university poetry. The battles, or rather skirmishes, between university poets and street poets have occupied our attention in the past few years.

All of this is related to something like a class conception of the art. The missionaries or exiles were addressing a newly arrived educated class, not a small elite but a vast army of Ph. D.'s or graduate students in literature. And these people by and large are themselves critics, instead of scholars, and frequently poets or people who want to write poems. And they have developed an expertise in the techniques which makes it sometimes impossible to tell who is a real poet and who is a technician.

I won't annoy you by trying to define Real Poet. Everybody has his own criteria. And I see no reason why there can't be poets, actual live ones, in the university or in the nightclub or on the assembly line. But I think that the poet is always nostalgic for the street, since he has become so urbanized that that is his only alternative to the university.

The most recent lecture I've given was called "Is Poetry an American Art?" The answer was: probably not. Some people asked why *American* poet; why can't one just be a poet? The answer is that you can't. A poetry is part of the character of the place. The place is inherent in the language. All of which is stated in the philosophy of Dr. Williams, who fought against the European influence on our poetry all his life and who said that *The Waste Land* was to modern poetry what the atom bomb was to mankind. (It was a necessary exaggeration.)

There is a legend that Apollinaire once stole the *Mona Lisa* from the Louvre. And there is the artist who decorated her with a moustache.

They were trying to pry this criterion off the wall. It had become an idol, practically in the religious sense, though it is the opposite of a Madonna. Masterpiece or not, this picture had acquired the power to judge all other pictures.

I sympathize with the thief of the *Mona Lisa* and with the artist who added to her charms. The motto of such poets is: let the past take care of itself. Everything is new.

It appears to me that American poets have begun to admit that the English influence is dead and that it never really obtained in this country as poetry. As an English professor, I foresee as a side effect to this discovery the withering away of the English department. (The fact that English departments are at present the largest in most universities indicates some kind of sickness.) More and more poets, even of the educated variety, have begun to drop the mannerisms of the conventional poem and to play with the more intricate rhythms and tonalities of prose and speech. In a way, we are back to where we were when the new poetry began in the second decade of our century, back to the image, the cadence, and the statement without embellishment. And we have discovered the new poetry of the Old World and not simply the classics and the metaphysical poets. We are closing the gap between prose and poetry.

To allow standards to take root in this country, we have had to devalue the standards of the past. Someone or other is everlastingly trying to impose a literature a thousand or two thousand years old on a nation that is less than two hundred. Thus most of our poetry has been as rigid and unoriginal as the architecture of banks. But we find poets now arguing in favor of "bad" poetry. I am one. Bad is in quotation marks. Bad means good. It means not great or major or monumental or mythic or epic. Poets in my situation, poets who have withdrawn from the high culture, are more interested in the art of children, the untrained, the hallucinated, even the psychopathic and the criminal. I think this is true of most artists today except the poets of—if I may use the well-worn word—the Establishment. And if one works himself clean through the poem and comes out on the other side, into empty space, and finds himself poem-less, what then? I sometimes think I have done this.

It has been about five years since I wrote what I used to think was the best kind of poem I could write. That was the poem with a beginning, a middle, and an end. It was a poem that used literary allusion and rhythmic structuring and intellectual argument and the works. I had written for years for a famous New York magazine which one sees on cocktail tables the world over (I don't know why I am being coy about it, but at one point I was practically the poet laureate of that publication). One day I shook myself and said, "No more." I think it was because I started to collect those poems for a book and found too many I didn't want to see in a book.

So I began to backpedal. I worked for several years trying to break the style I had become habituated to. Eventually I came up with something more free which I could use. I had always been a fan of those D. H. Lawrence epigrams called *Nettles* and *Pansies* and especially those glowing bunches of poetry called *Birds, Beasts and Flowers*. My new rhythm, however, sounded too much like Lawrence and I knew I had not gone far enough back. Then I started reading French prose poems, Baudelaire, Rimbaud, and the *Éloges* of St. John Perse. While I was at this library Perse had once seen a prose poem or two of mine and hinted that that was the technique that mattered. But I had only written one or two such poems and waited a long time before I was ready to tackle the thing in earnest. This sounds like I am about to present the great American prose poem, but all I mean to say is that I finally felt at ease in the form. What I was searching for was a medium in which I could say anything I wanted—which for poets is something like finding the philosophers' stone or the elixir vitae. For one thing, I wanted to be able to use the ridiculous, for another the nonsensical, for another the "obscene." I wanted to be as personal as I liked, as autobiographical when I felt like it, editorializing or pompous, in short, to be able to drop into any intensity of language I liked at any time. None of this was particularly original, but it was new to me. I wrote a huge stack of these poems, the form of which was governed by the size of a sheet of paper in the typewriter. When the publisher saw the manuscript he commented dryly that the only limits to the book seemed to be physiological. And not wanting to violate the fashion of slenderness for volumes of poems, we cut it down to about twice the size of the usual seed catalog.

It is as important to learn how to lose one's skills as to acquire them in art, and just as difficult. The kind of poem I am talking about may be indistinguishable from that of the high school composition or the worst polyphonic prose of Amy Lowell, but that is inevitable. The writer must learn from his underlings as the painter learns from the billboard or the composer from the trombonist blowing the blues. This is what I think has been deficient in so much modern poetry—a fear of coming to grips with the raw material. That and too much attention to stock intellectual attitudes. The modern artist and sculptor are fascinated and delighted with the industrial world, but the poet has not yet heard of it.

On the last day of a Creative Writing class of mine last week—I have taught myself to say Creative Writing without wincing; nobody would ever think of saying Creative Painting or Creative Music—after we had gone through the last purple stack of mimeographed student poems and had once again demolished the split-level house, bombed the second car, the streamlined church, and the powder room; Freud having been buried with the air conditioner and the last corybantic prose poem in praise of sex or LSD analyzed, I gave a valedictory. It was a little talk about the *Oxford Book of English Verse, 1250–1900,* and I contrasted it with the modern anthology. I hadn't thought of the *Oxford Book* or looked at it for many years, but it all at once crossed my mind that this book had been my bible when I was the age of my students and that in all probability they had never heard of it or anything like it.

It is true that this famous anthology is the product of Victorian taste, yet it would be difficult to imagine a much different version of the seven hundred years of English poetry. The Quiller-Couch *Oxford Book* (he did many of the Oxford anthologies) begins with the fresh and beautiful "Sumer is icumen in," dated around 1250, and ends with a muggy religious poem or hymn called "Dominus Illuminatio Mea." This final poem is anonymous, and one senses the editorial hand in this concluding work or benediction.

But in between the "Sumer is icumen in" and the "Dominus" poem there are seven centuries of the greatest poetry of the European culture, even with the omission of the great plays, narratives, and epics. And in all that poetry there is scarcely ever more than a suggestion of philosophical despair. It would be a tour de force to compile a minority report of the centuries, gleaning a darker side of the English creative spirit, opposing Rochester's ode "Upon Nothing" to Milton's faith in order and Providence, or paying more attention to the satanic Swinburne than to Tennyson or Alice Meynell. But such an anthology would tell nothing, for until the magic year 1900, English poetry as we know it is essentially joyous. It is true that the Oxford editor would not even include "Dover Beach" and could see nothing better in Whitman than "O Captain, My Captain"; nevertheless the book is triumphantly representative and great.

By now there are several generations of students, at least, who began the study of poetry with the 20th century, that is, with the proclamations of failure, the failure of love, the failure of history, the prophecies of imminent darkness. *The Waste Land* is probably the first classic that impinges on their minds; however it was intended or has since been reinterpreted, it embodies the modern poet's code of the banality of modern existence and the evil of 20th-century man. And if not this poem, then one of a dozen others. The 20th-century reader of poetry must regard any poetry before our time as something as far away as the poetry of classical Greece.

I am not expressing a preference for the Oxford collection or suggesting a compromise. I am merely making the observation that the 20th-century anthology has closed the *Oxford Book,* perhaps forever. In this country, at least, we have broken the circuit between the poetic past and the poetic present. And I do not see how it can be otherwise with us.

What does this do to us as poets and to our poetry? American literature in a quite real sense is a boy's literature. From Fenimore Cooper to Salinger, it a literature of youth. I was given a complete copy of *Moby Dick* as a child because it was a boy's book, and I read it as a boy's book, though it had some tough passages. And poetry was always something far away and long ago; Americans couldn't write poetry. There was one American poet, Edgar Allen Poe; one didn't press the point too far. I do not recall the name of Whitman from public school, though my memory may trick me. I think I discovered Whitman on my own.

The American poet has from the beginning been faced with a choice, whether to accept or to reject the *Oxford Book,* using that term as an oversimplified symbol. And in modern poetry the choices have been made. Of our four greatest 20th-century poets, Pound, Eliot, Frost, and Williams, two went abroad to repair the fences of the Tradition and to create, intentionally or not, a criticism which became a pedagogy which became a poetics. Frost refused to believe that the fences needed mending and quietly amassed a wealth of poems which all but proved that English poetry was still solvent. Williams nearly lost his mind watching these antics.

American binary psychology lends itself to poetry as to politics. We have in our century created two poetry parties called whatever anyone wants to call them, Paleface and Redskin, Academic and Beat, Classic and Romantic, or Republican and Democrat. And it is unfortunately true that the Redskins are pink with rage and the Palefaces blue with indignation. And it is also true that these two literary parties end up in the same anthologies—in one big unhappy family of poetry.

So many times have the characteristics of these parties been described, at least to those who read the literary journals, that there is nothing more to say about them descriptively. But there is much to say otherwise. I will stick to the usual nomenclature of Academic and Beat to avoid confusion.

The Beat professes Innocence, with or without a capital I. The Academic professes Guilt with a capital G. The Innocence of the Beat of course identifies him with American literature, even though the Beat chants hymns to Castro. The Beat extracts the quality of rebellion and revolution from American literature and then sits back and waits for the police to prove his point.

The Academic gaily assumes a metaphysical guilt, possibly a Christian guilt; in any case a kind of mandarin Hollywood guilt which presumes the nature of literary violence and destruction on the part of the Beat. The Academic forgives and protects the Beat. The Beat is overwhelmed by the failure of success.

This kind of nonsense seesaws back and forth. But modern poetry never seems to escape this biparty system, this wrangle over precedent and originality. In reality, both parties are literature-centered (to invent a typical vulgarism of our speech); and because literature is the center of value of both schools, neither can know much about anything except literature. Beat poetry is as academic as the Academic. Academic poetry, which has become noticeably gamy, is as gossipy (you might say "subversive") as the Beat. And both end up as a variety of social criticism, but of such a hieratic style that only the highly trained in poetry would even care to notice it. Both Beat and Academic, however, subscribe to the 19th-century hope, the hope of the *Oxford Book,* that in the end poetry will reinstate human virtue or national virtue or the virtue of oneself.

Modern poetry is a kind of lobby. It has something to sell, it is not sure what, yet it knows it has a corporation of power behind it, either a thousand years of reputation or the idea of genius or sainthood. And it knows that this power is real, for Culture, with whole armies and navies behind it, has said so.

It is only with the greatest effort and charm that the Beat can convince us of his assertion of innocence; and only with the greatest diplomacy and wit that the Academic can convince us of his culpability.

Possibly poetry in America is obsolete or not yet born because it is literature-centered. This is precisely the thing that has always separated poetry from the other arts of writing. Even in this country one distinguishes between the poet and the writer—I am always pleased to be confronted with the question at those Nabokov-like places called Writers Conferences: Are you a writer or a poet? Poetry has always been the ultimate enemy of literature, and if poetry is good for anything, that is what it is good for.

And yet, how, in a nation where books are as plentiful as food, or more so, can the poet escape literature? How, where literature is also an industry, can poetry breathe? Here, where the latest literary movement is put on sale after the first manifesto is written, where every writer (and poet) hopes to be "controversial" in order to rise above the din of the linotype, how can the poet ever dream of such a thing as an audience when the audience is rejected both by the Beat (as bourgeois) and by the Academic (as bourgeois). For the Beat pretends to be the proletarian and the Academic pretends to be the aristocrat. And both—whatever bourgeois is supposed to mean at this late date—share in this bourgeois sensibility and morality. Both kinds of poetry are in a secret alliance to uphold Literature.

All I am saying is that, for me, American poetry has long since ceased to hold my attention, because it seems to me to aspire to a place in society. That is, the poet-in-residence in a university is no different from the poet-in-Skid Row. Both are on Culture Relief. Both are trying to prove to themselves that the fate of nations is bound up with their personal fates. Both, in the back of their minds, think in the way that Pound and Eliot and Yeats thought: *that poetry will tell people what to do.*

One can forgive poets for these hallucinations. It is harder to forgive governments for egging them on. I said earlier that I could never understand the marriage of wealth and culture. Even less can I understand the marriage of government and culture. I know I am standing at the moment somewhere on Capitol Hill, but I have always tried in a little way to keep State and Poetry separate. This is not in the Constitution. I hope the Constitution will never have occasion to think about such things as institutionalizing Poetry.

There was a fine young British poet killed on the battlefield in the First World War who wrote the famous line: "The Poetry is in the pity." He was referring to the pity of War. He was too late for the *Oxford Book* and a little premature for the 20th-century anthology. Wilfred Owen came into that no man's land between the end of the old poetry and the beginning of the new. He said that he was trying not to console but to warn; he went so far as to apologize for telling the truth about war. But the true poet must be truthful, he said.

The 20th-century poet is not so embattled except ideologically. He has somehow earned or inherited an intellectual leisure which has made him a parvenu of sensibility. The 20th-century poet cannot locate the poetry, either in the pity or anywhere else. He locates it, or tries to, in vague and anxious dissatisfactions within himself or within what he thinks are the crimes and sins of society. He can't decide whether to be a peacock or a phoenix or an ostrich and takes turns trying to be each.

I mentioned Wilfred Owen to paraphase him. With us the poetry is not in the pity, but the poetry is in the situation. As the *Oxford Book* failed the situation of war, for example—it would have ended with Rupert Brooke's "The Soldier" if it had had to face the trench war of 1914–18, and could not have ended with an antiwar poet without spoiling the whole illusion of the great tradition. Everyone at the turn of the century had the premonition that time had run out on the Tradition; it is extraordinary how many writers knew in their bones that what lay just ahead would be unlike anything that had ever been known before.

When Yeats later put together his *Oxford Book*—the *Oxford Book of Modern Verse, 1892–1935,* he enshrined the *Mona Lisa* on page one, taking a famous prose sentence from Pater, a bit of high mystification about her, and turning it into a piece of free verse. And there she remains, the patron saint of Academic poetry. And the Beat has failed to pry her off the wall.

American poetry is irrelevant. It does not pertain to our situation. It pertains only to language and literature and sensibility. It pertains only to form and to "philosophy" or to the personalized anguish of the socially angry. America is more than a campus, I am convinced, and more than a picturesque and disaffiliated slum. What it is is for the artist to reveal in every way he can. And, as I have said, all our artists have been busy revealing our world, with the exception of the poets. The modern poet has closed his eyes to life, as it has long since closed its eyes to nature. To the modern poet, nature may sometimes provide a bestiary, and, in fact, we have written the finest allegories about moths and ants, praying mantises and flies. But all the apples are dead, except the Genesis apple. People in the modern anthology are dead or somnambulatory. The modern anthology might just as well be copyrighted on the moon. I forget the date of the death of the moon.

Perhaps I haven't progressed at all from the time I wrote my verse critique in the tropics. I still wait for the poetry of the situation. Our poetry has everything to do. It has to escape from itself first of all. It has to liberate itself from literature before it can do anything else. Most poets, I think, have agreed that poetry is not an art of language and not even an art. It is one of the techniques of revelation, one of the powers through which we control relationships and conciliate nature. The sculptor who drives to the junkyard, who makes beauty out of trash is performing this function. Poetry has been making trash out of beauty for the most part. This is tempting fate. Or if I am exaggerating, let us at least concede that it is the function of poetry to propitiate, to quiet the anger of things. I am not talking about affirmation and negation; that is a question of circumstance. I am talking about the poet in situ. If he is in place, he is where he belongs. Whitman had a long recital of things in their places, small things and cosmic things. Williams took the least likely objects for poems—least likely for the *Oxford Book*—a piece of brown wrapping paper rolling in the street or a rotten apple. These poets revealed things in their situation. There is something like this in the Marquis de Sade who says that in Tartary there is a people which creates a new god for itself every day. This god has to be the first object encountered on waking in the morning. If by chance it happens to be an object of great revulsion, that thing is still the idol of the day.

Our poetry has been so industrious manufacturing values that it has practically forgotten how to do anything else. That is why it must empty its mind of its moral and ethical contents and of its esthetic contents as well. When it does so, it will be in a position to experience the world as our painters, our musicians, and our novelists have experienced it.

For myself, I have solved the problem of the racial wound, which drove me into the various retreats where I could assert myself and create myself. But it is too late for me ever to be assimilated into the Serious World.

I can only play at responsibility. I am yet to be conviced that those who make the decisions by which we live are not play-acting. I hope that this sense—or perhaps gift—of amazement will never leave me.

Ways of Misunderstanding Poetry

Reed Whittemore

Presented at the Library of Congress October 12, 1964

I HAVE A BIG PROGRAM for you. I'm going to praise spiritual drifters (with appropriate reservations); I'm going to propose a simple but revolutionary reform in the Library of Congress—elimination of the Poetry Consultant; I'm going to redefine positivism; I'm going to recommend an old movie called *Bridge on the River Kwai*. And I'm also going to talk about poetry. So although I'm not going to talk very long it will probably *seem* long. It will seem especially long when I explain, in passing, philosopher Alfred North Whitehead.

I wouldn't try such an ambitious statement if I hadn't found that ambitious statements are expected of poetry consultants. On one of my very first days here this September a reporter asked me if I thought the world was getting better or worse. I said I didn't know, which was disappointing to her. One must learn not to disappoint the press, and the press, like the rest of the world, seems to expect of its poets and poetry consultants information not available elsewhere. This is perhaps one of the basic misunderstandings about poetry, and one that the poets themselves have cultivated. I was very flattered to be asked whether the world was getting better or worse.

Which reminds me of a poem I wrote this summer, a poem that never got past the first draft but is appropriate here.

TODAY

Today is one of those days when I wish I knew everything, like
   the critics.
I need a bit of self-confidence, like the critics.
I wish I knew about Coptic, for example, and Shakti-Yoga.

The critics I read know them, and they say so. I wish I could say
    so.
I want to climb up some big publishing mountain and wear a little
    skull cap and say so: I know.

Confidence, that's what I need—to know—
And would have if I came from California or New York. Or
    France.
If I came from France I could say such things as, "Art opened its
    eyes on itself at the time of the Renaissance."
If I came from California I could say, "Christianity was short-
    circuited by Constantine."
If I came from New York I could say anything.

I come from Minnesota.
I must get a great big book with all the critics in it
And eat it. One gets so hungry and stupid in Minnesota.

This poem, aside from its own great merits, suggests another and
opposite view of the poet: far from being the source of most worldly
wisdom the poet is somebody who writes poems because he has failed at
everything else. You may recall that Robert Frost was fond of describing the jobs he didn't make a go at. He was a failure as a student and
a millworker and a farmer and a conchologist and a newspaperman. He
did fairly well, but only briefly and without much staying power, at
teaching school and raising poultry (why do you suppose poultry and
poetry sound so much alike?). Furthermore, while in the poultry business (poetry with an "l") he displayed one of the weaknesses most
commonly assigned to poets: ignorance. He wrote a piece for a magazine called *Farm-Poultry* in which he said that healthy geese are apt
to roost in trees in the winter. Since geese of the garden variety, healthy
or unhealthy, apparently don't do that, Frost suddenly found himself
in the same boat with John Keats who had stout Cortez discovering the
Pacific when he should have had stout Balboa. (You may read about
Frost's further exploits with poultry—with an "l"—in an eccentric book
called *Robert Frost: Farm-Poultryman,* turned out at one of the institutions Frost didn't make a go at, Dartmouth.)

    It occurs to me that this view of the poet as an all-thumbs nincom-
poop, since it is so prevalent, might well be made into law, in which
case the mysterious office I am so lucky to hold this year might actually
come to perform a serious administrative function. It would issue a
poetic license to each poet, and no poet would be allowed to practice
in the pages of our literary journals before he had been accredited as
an official fool. The interviews which I and my successors might con-

duct would themselves be instructive: we would ask such questions as "What is the Third Law of Thermodynamics?" or "What is a goose?" and throw the candidate out if he could tell us.

Actually this process is already in operation in many of our provinces, though it hasn't reached the Library of Congress. For example, one of the chief qualifications for admission to some of our creative writing classes and schools would seem to be an inability to pass freshman English. No more of that.

Why do we entertain these two contradictory views of poets, that they are great repositories of wisdom and that they are ignorant and ineffectual? One answer is perhaps Professor Whitehead's, that one of the views is just wrong. He had little but contempt for the values of poetic knowledge—for prophets, seers, and the like. He said, "the world's experience of professed seers has on the whole been very unfortunate. In the main they are a shady lot with a bad reputation. . . . The odds are so heavily against any particular prophet that, apart from some method of testing, perhaps it is safer to stone them, in some merciful way." I tend to sympathize with Professor Whitehead, though in doing so I am betraying my profession; that is, I am not persuaded that there is anything unique about poetic knowledge. Think of the essence of so many of our most familiar poems, which tell us that life is real and earnest, or that death conquers all, or that love is best. One doesn't need a poetry consultant to tell the country such things; and that is why I recommend that my post be abolished (after I leave, of course). Yet not all wisdom contained in poetry and poets is of such a banal sort; and rather than rejecting entirely the image of poet as prophet or wise man I would like to suggest a simple way of reconciling our apparent contradiction between wisdom and ignorance. What we need to do is to change the key words and *not* say that the poet is both ignorant and wise, but that he is frequently dissatisfied with certain conventional kinds of knowledge and peculiarly susceptible to other kinds. Thus in the case of Mr. Frost we might say, though there are many who would argue with us, that Frost made a poor student because he was suspicious of what Dartmouth and Harvard wanted him to learn, and that he made a good poet partly because of his suspicions and partly because he was open to all sorts of information from elsewhere, that is, from birches and ovenbirds and stone walls and so on. So if one were to chart Mr. Frost's knowledgeability, one would come out with a large grey patch covering a whole continent of human and natural affairs, whereas his nonpoetic academic friends would be restricted to little black spots here and there on that continent. Frost probably knew no areas of experience as well as some of his black-spot

589

friends knew them, but there was more that he partly knew, and more that he wanted to know. He was a man who wanted to fit a lot into what I will call, for lack of a better word, his cosmology. But as thanks for his cosmological ramblings he has been called, by Yvor Winters, a spiritual drifter.

Philosopher Whitehead once said, in a quite different connection, that a cosmology should be adequate. Pithy was Whitehead. He was talking of ways of looking at the cosmos, and therefore of ways of looking at man's place and role in it; but in context he was primarily complaining of the many ways man had discovered of avoiding looking at it, particularly the way of the positivists. He was thinking primarily of scientific positivists—mostly chemists and physicists—who eschewed metaphysics on the grounds that it was not relevant to their immediate concerns, but he also had a few words of scorn for positivist humanists, that is, those who concoct great philosophies of man and society without thinking it relevant to put man in his natural and cosmological setting. Now I am only a fourth-rate metaphysician, and you won't catch me talking at much length about the cosmos, at least tonight. Yet it seems to me that the phrase "a cosmology should be adequate" is one that a poet can ignore only at his peril; or in other words that positivism in all its various forms is the great modern ideological trap the poet must seek to avoid.

What is positivism? Says *Webster* (second edition):

> A system of philosophy originated by Auguste Comte. It excludes from philosophy everything but the natural phenomena or properties of knowable things, together with their invariable relations of coexistence and succession, as occuring in time and space. All other types of explanation are repudiated as "theological" or "metaphysical."

Let me now convert that definition into the sense of this occasion and say that positivism is what we have here in America at almost all levels of thought and action: a philosophy of exclusion, exclusion of all knowledge that, as in intelligence circles, we do not need to know to get through the day and perform our respective duties efficiently. Specialization, departmentalization—these properly maligned components of our society—are simply products of the positivist philosophy, and we know them well; yet we do not, I think, pay enough attention to their effect upon our arts and our artists. We do not, I think, since we are all positivists by trade if not by inclination, consider sufficiently the almost insuperable problems of fostering a great art or literature in a positivist society.

But there are those who will say that I am quite wrong here and point to the great concern constantly exhibited by modern American

590

writers and artists for the evils of positivism around them. My opponents will cite the familiar fact about a great deal of American literature, that it expresses alienation from the American Way; and they will perhaps quote me a few thousand poems in which the limitations of our American social and spiritual vision are harped upon, poems decrying our inability to see beyond the immediacies of our restricted and regimented daily lives, to see beyond our 8–to–5 commuters' jobs, our supermarkets and bathtubs and Christmases, in short our inability to find other than immediate social and economic motivation for anything we do. One could start perhaps with T. S. Eliot's poem about the readers of the *Boston Evening Transcript:*

> The readers of the *Boston Evening Transcript*
> Sway in the wind like a field of ripe corn.

And go on to Cummings on the Cambridge ladies:

> the Cambridge ladies who live in furnished souls are unbeautiful and have comfortable minds . . . they believe in Christ and Longfellow, both dead.

Or to Pound with his description of a woman dying of emotional anemia, and of artists enslaved by a botched civilization. Or to a good bit of that rather neglected poet Kenneth Fearing. Or to dozens of others. The guiding spirit here is perhaps Thoreau. Thoreau was complaining, and I certainly sympathize, against a positivism which finds irrelevant all but the conventional properties of thoughtless community living. Our modern writers follow in his footsteps and continue to bellow against the full purse and the empty spirit with the ineffectiveness we have earned the right to expect of art.

I can hear these bellowings too, of course. I have even bellowed myself and will probably continue to do so, though, as I will soon indicate, I think some of these bellowings are themselves positivist. Furthermore I am persuaded that it is impossible in our society not to be positivist in some measure. Positivism, you know, is a way to money and bed and board, as well as to power. It is also a way to knowledge, knowledge within the closed circle or circuit the positivist chooses. And the kind of knowledge and control and power that positivism brings is in certain areas essential just for survival. You can't even drive downtown in Washington, for example, without being something of a positivist, that is, a being with detailed special knowledge. You have to know at what times of day what roads go which way, and how it is possible to get where you are going without ever turning left. A spiritual drifter like Frost will drift over into the sovereign State of

Virginia almost every time. I sometimes wonder how many people crossing the Potomac really want to.

Now in poetry too a certain amount of positivist knowledge is essential for survival—survival in sophomore English, or survival in the tiny literary circles which make up our poetry world. It is true, as I have already suggested, that a good many know-nothings pose as poets, persons who know little about grammar and rhetoric and less about the formal properties of traditional verse. But I do not think the real know-nothings will survive, can survive. One has to be a craftsman to be a poet—that is, a sort of specialist—and there is finally no substitute, not even pornography, for a certain minimal skill with words and forms. But that kind of skill, in modest doses, is not the kind of positivism that bothers me. Nor is it the kind of skill that, of itself, leads to power. To make the distinction I want I must refer to the movie I promised to mention, *Bridge on the River Kwai*, where two kinds of positivism are quite eloquently set before us. You may remember the movie: unlike the River Potomac the River Kwai has no bridge over it, and the problem is to make one so that the Japanese Army can drift over it. To make the bridge the Japanese employ about a battalion of British prisoners of war, mostly engineers, headed by a positivist British colonel, played by Alec Guinness, who is so interested in building bridges and observing the international rules for prisoners of war that he takes great pride in building, in record time, the best damned bridge ever made out of old bamboo. That he is building it for the enemy is not a relevant consideration for him, not at least until the very end when, with a bullet in his back, he allows his cosmology to become adequate.

The two kinds of positivism here are the technological positivism which gives the British the knowledge and power to build the bridge well and fast, and the ideological positivism which makes the colonel think that building for anybody is all right. It is the latter form of positivism, as it appears in poetry, that bothers me; we could well use more poetic engineers—and for the survival of the art we will need them—but we do seem to be building a lot of bridges for the enemy these days. The enemy is cosmological inadequacy, which is death to poetry—poetry in the largest sense of that difficult word. Let me elaborate.

I would have you consider the various ideological views of poetry that our alienated poets put forth. I will be cavalier and assert that there are three: (1) that poetry must be pure; (2) that poetry must take man back to the simple natural world around him; and (3) that poetry must oppose, deny, subvert the whole culture and somehow salvage the individual. Obviously the three are related, but they are discussible separately for they do tend to produce three different kinds of verse.

Pure poetry. I wish someone in the back of the room would mutter "art for art's sake" for me, for no poetry consultant should descend to it even though it is appropriate. There are a number of ways of characterizing poetic purity. A poem which said nothing would be pure, but I have yet to see one. A poem which said nothing capable of being generalized upon would also be pure—and lots of objective descriptions and accounts are frequently so classified, though here again I would question the possibility of real purity. And finally—here is the conventional loose use of the phrase—poems which demonstrate little or no social-political "engagement" are pure. There are lots of these, and perhaps Ezra Pound's identification of the genre with the work of Sextus Propertius may serve to characterize them. In Pound's Propertius poem Propertius is represented as hoping that he will be able to bring a few lines of verse "down from the hills unsullied." Those few lines, if he can achieve them, will last after all the emperors and generals and other men of the world, together with their works, have gone with Ozymandias into the sand. It is a familiar if constantly discredited thesis, and in our time it does not even need to be associated with the notion of the immortality of art to be espoused. The word for it now, or at least one of the words, is autotelic. A poem stands alone; it establishes its own conditions for being and can only be judged by them. Now the autotelic principle became popular in our time in the classroom, and it was in its beginnings not so much a principle as a classroom expedient to make students actually read the poems they kept saying they were reading. I. A. Richards and then Brooks and Warren discovered that people weren't reading poetry so much as using it for a mirror; what a poem meant, what they got out of it, and what they thought of it depended entirely upon them, not upon the poem. The poem was thus merely an occasion for introspection. Or, if not that, it was an occasion for browsing about in the lives of the poets: read a bit of Shelley and then have a good cry about his death. Richards and Brooks and Warren—and of course a good many others —set about to change this softheaded view of poetry's function, and you know the results: books and books, courses and courses in close reading, in microscopic examinations of all the possible components of the world's poor struggling quatrains.

But from these researches emerged a full-blown principle about verse, that each poem is a little world with its own citizenry and streets and traffic laws and parking meters; and that anyone who enters that world—that is, any reader—is bound to live by its laws and mores.

Now here, surely, is purity; here also is a most virulent positivism. I see no substantive difference between the poet or critic who adopts such a view, and the chemist or physicist Whitehead was complaining about who holes up in his laboratory and refuses to consider the metaphysical implications of his physical discoveries on the grounds that such considerations are irrelevant—or in other words refuses to believe that one needs a cosmology to live and work in one's own particular corner of the cosmos.

That's all I will say here about the ideological defects of theories of poetic purity, though obviously one could talk about them interminably. I should mention, though, briefly, a few of the practical consequences of such theories. In publishing, for example, we see a number of literary magazines, or exclusively poetry magazines, which are turned out under purity's banner. They profess to have no politics, no social or cultural views, they are merely there to print the good and the beautiful. Looking at them—and I have been looking at them for a long time—I am reminded of the center of Washington: all those monuments, all that turf, all those inscriptions, all those marble pillars and steps and busts—and not a delicatessen for miles.

Enough. Now let me turn to the second notion of poetry I wish to explode, that it must take man back to the simple natural world around him. Here also of course I am treading on sacred ground, even Frostian ground, and I do not wish to be misunderstood as wishing to discard the birds and the birches. I spent a wonderful month this summer with the birds and the birches in New Hampshire, and they were invigorating. I even wrote an immortal bird poem, which I will not burden you with. The first line is "One can't do much in these woods without a bird-book" and has later as one of its best lines simply a bird noise: chrrr-k, chrrr-k. So you can see that I'm in favor of birds. Furthermore I think it is true, as I have already indicated, that one of the most effective poetic ways of opposing the positivism of our society is the way of Thoreau. You may be familiar with a modern Thoreauvian book about Washington itself, called *Spring in Washington*, by Louis J. Halle, who is one of our best social-political journalists, and also, though I don't know that he has published any verse, a poet. In *Spring in Washington* he says many of the things I have been saying about positivism. For example:

It has been said before that a fundamental aim of education is to enable men to live in time and space beyond the present and the immediate. The majority of uneducated men and women appear to lead entirely somnambulistic lives, never pausing between the cradle and the grave to look up from the immediate task in hand, never raising their heads to take stock of the long past or to survey the plains and mountain ranges that surround them.

Or:

> Any ape can deal with his immediate and momentary environment by instinctive reaction—as when he brushes a fly from his eyes—or even by figuring things out. That capacity to live in the universe . . . is man's alone.

Now what could be more germane to my thesis here than these remarks? Yet they arise from one intelligent man's daily confrontation of the birds and fauna down along the Potomac here. In view of such remarks how can I possibly say that poetry should not undertake to remind man of the natural world around him? Obviously I cannot. Let bird and birch poems thrive. Yet in Mr. Halle's last remark, where he distinguishes between the ape and man, I find the kernel of my complaint, a complaint not against the *expanded* vision the natural world may provide us with, but against the possible limits of that vision. For when the Thoreauvian cries out, as Mr. Halle does, against the full purse and the empty spirit, he is in danger of doing what Mr. Halle does not, in danger of proposing some simple natural life like the ape's life as a proper life, full-time, for man. This is not expansion but withdrawal. Now he may do this in discouragement with man's life, as Frost does in his poem "Directive," where he recommends climbing a mountain and putting a sign up on the road behind: Closed. But to do this in the expectation that a man will be made more fully man by such an operation—this seems to me to be dangerous, except maybe on weekends. Over my library desk in the past few weeks have come a couple of dozen books of translations of primitive poetry, for example. I am not complaining about such poetry when I assert that it is very fashionable now. Some of it, particularly from Africa, may be explained away by saying that the literature of certain primitive countries is now being published for the first time because the countries are now in the world's eyes for the first time. But we also find much primitivism in our own American poetry, even in the work of very sophisticated poets. In one of Theodore Roethke's last poems, for instance, he suggests, though a bit sardonically, that he would like to become an Indian, preferably Iroquois. I like the Roethke poem, just as I like Frost's poem "Directive"—and I know that I can find in my own work plenty of withdrawal symptoms. Who does not want to withdraw after a few rounds of Washington traffic? The subject is current; the impulse is important, human, modern; so we can only be pleased that it appears in our poetry. And yet if that impulse is not balanced by other impulses —if in other words it becomes the whole blooming cosmology of a poet —then, it seems to me, it becomes a positivism in reverse, a negative positivism, still essentially positivist in being a philosophy of exclusion.

A primitivist philosophy in a nonprimitivist world is a philosophy of exclusion. When Whitehead said that a cosmology should be adequate he was being, as I understand him, deliberately relative. Such a question as "adequate in relation to what?" he would have answered culturally and historically by pointing out, shall we say, that the cosmology of a primitive Iroquois Indian would not be adequate for a modern American, Indian or not. Now that modern American may of course be a poet—that is, one of the ignorant cusses I have already described—and in that event the cosmology adequate for him will almost surely not be Whitehead's. Yet my humility here as a poet is not unlimited; I suspect that even for me the Indian's cosmology is sure to be inadequate. To become positivist in despair and settle, not for an adequate cosmology, but for no cosmology, or a primitive cosmology, or a deliberately restricted cosmology, and then go about one's noncosmological business as if that business were in no way affected by the cosmos as it is now known to the best minds in the culture—this seems to me profoundly wrong, as well as softheaded. I am assuming in other words, with Whitehead, that there is at any historical moment a sort of minimal cultural-cosmological adequacy which no responsible mind can sink below and be satisfied. In sweeping and crude terms this means that adequacy in our time would have to take into account cosmologically the new occult in science, which hardly gives us back God, but hardly gives us a materialistic, mechanistic world either, and have to take into account culturally Marx, Freud, Darwin, an industrial, technological, increasingly nonrural and nonregional culture, and so on. Obviously I can't even tick off here all the diverse parts of our muddled and complicated lives that we would fit neatly together if we were all the sensible, tough-minded, cosmological poets I am suggesting that we ought to be; to do so would be as hard as telling the reporter whether the world is getting better or worse. Yet I think you can see, without my doing further ticking, the direction in which I think our poetic minds ought to move. And that direction, that right, general, impossibly difficult direction is not being moved toward in primitivist poetry.

Nor, I think, is it being moved toward by those poets who entertain the third view of poetry I mentioned, the view that poetry must oppose the culture at all costs to salvage the individual and his freedom. Most of what I have said about nature poets applies here also, but I am not talking about nature poets, I am talking about a variety of other literary anarchists. Karl Shapiro, who is one of them, and one I happen to respect, thinks this category includes all American artists. He says:

Almost to a man, American artists are in full-fledged opposition to the American

Way of Life—that is, life according to Business, Politics, Journalism, Advertising, Religion, Patriotism and Morality. . . . And almost to a man, they revere the primitive America which claimed freedom of action for all men.

I don't agree. I think you will find near unanimity in the artistic community on *some* of the issues that our anarchists are constantly faced with: at the moment, for example, the issue of obscenity. The anarchists are constantly being hauled into court for obscenity, and they delight in it—some of course because it means fame, sales, money —but most of them because they see a principle at stake: they want to get at the moral positivists who would protect us from ourselves. The good poets of this breed Shapiro has called "authentic obscenicists," and I doubt that you will find a single committed artist in this country who would not go into court to defend their work. The freedom of all artists is crudely and blatantly at stake in such cases, the freedom, indeed the obligation, of artists to speak honestly, truly. But there is more at stake than freedom. Behind every aspiring D. H. Lawrence or Henry Miller—at least every one I am familiar with—is a theory about human nature that I do *not* think all artists share. There are all those Socialists and Communists, for example, who do not share it; what they call socialist realism is an anti-anarchist aesthetic of considerable import in the world; and surely there are plenty of artists on our side of the curtain who, while not social realists in the communist sense, still retain a notion of the reality of the social macrocosm in artistic endeavor. The theory of human nature which my third group of poets entertains is simple latter-day Rousseauism, with the genitals rather than the heart at the center of things, and with the human mind and all its rational accomplishments socially, scientifically, philosophically, artistically—with the human mind still relegated to a subordinate place in human affairs.

I have several angry speeches on this subject, one for instance about the word "reason" in which I point out that the very word has come to be identified with apathy and the status quo—or in other words with the "squares." Just so long as rationality is identified socially with the normal, the responsible, the positive, the healthy and so on—that is, with the administration whether the administration be that of a college or a country—just so long will our rebels find themselves standing for the irrational, the abnormal, the irresponsible, the negative, the sick. Yet surely to deny society, and to deny the mind, is simply to cultivate another philosophy of exclusion. I won't go further into this lest I get overwrought and lose touch with my subject here.

My subject, you remember, was "Ways of Misunderstanding Poetry." I have described, loosely, three ways, and I have even prophesied grimly the death of poetry if the misunderstandings are allowed to continue. I apologize for the prophecy. Somebody is always looking for an audience so that he can prophesy the death of poetry; meanwhile poetry, though limping badly, does go on, and most of those who are having anything to do with keeping it on its feet have been guilty of one or more of the misunderstandings I have cited. From personal experience I can report the difficulty of avoiding these misunderstandings; I know that I haven't consistently avoided any of them myself. There is entirely too much to be a rebel against, to withdraw from or to be purified of in this country of ours for most artists to have anything but sympathy for the misunderstandings I have cited. Perhaps then the word "misunderstanding" is wrong, and I should substitute something else like "dismal understanding." My title then should have been "Three Ways of Understanding Poetry and Being Dismal."

Actually I am not sure which title is appropriate. Nor am I sure, as I come laboriously to my message for this evening, exactly what the message is to be. If I take the position that the misunderstandings are really dismal understandings, then I can hardly propose that the poets take a new look at themselves and try to clean house; I must admit instead that they have already looked and found the house uncleanable, and then acknowledge the impossibility of a reformist poetry, a poetry of engagement. Proposals for a poetry of engagement are apt to be easy and shallow anyway; and they've been made so many times, and their sponsors have been disillusioned so many times, that one can hardly stomach the thought of another pitiful charge on the barricades. As Allen Tate has said somewhere, the prospect of an effectively political poetry is like watching Percy Shelley set a fleet of paper boats forth on the waters of Hyde Park. No poet is going to become effectively engaged simply because he makes a New Year's resolution to that effect or because some critic makes the resolution for him. His reformation will take place, if it takes place at all, only as his whole cultural being suffers some slow sea-change away from the positivism to which he has been bred up. For the poet is, as poet, pretty well stuck with things as they are. He may spend fifteen hours a day in class or in some office trying to reform the world or reform the sentences of illiterate freshmen; but when he sits down to his poems he is not so much a reformer as an observer, a recorder. And if what he observes is a world in which the creative intelligence has no role in the world's affairs, then he will record that observation and go to bed.

To put it differently, before the poem can be reformist in spirit the world of the pre-poem must be reformist. It is back there with the pre-poem, I think, where all the trouble is. Somewhere back in the mists of the brain before the poem emerges and gets written down is where poetry is dying, somewhere back there where we are all potentially poets, all potentially capable, like gods, of moulding and making sense of the world, the whole world, in which we find ourselves. For it is back there, alas, where we all seem to be deciding—right along with the professed poets—to be pure, withdrawn, disengaged, softheaded. How sadly, back there, we misrepresent the world to ourselves. The small is big. The big is invisible. All our petty grievances and tiny triumphs shake us to pieces; we have no emotional or intellectual resources left for the really shaking. We can't live with the world, much less the cosmos, but just barely with our families, our bank accounts, our meager selves.

Now if we are like this back in the pre-poem part of our culture, we can hardly expect the poem part *not* to be like this. Or so I say to myself when I would blame not the poets but the culture. I am reminded of an analogy A. J. Liebling once drew between journalism and an insane fishing industry. Perched on the shores of the ocean, he said, was a tremendous industrial fish-processing complex which unfortunately had as a source of supply only a few leaky dories manned by drunken fishermen dangling rusty hooks into the brine. The fishermen were of course the reporters, a pitiful few who had been made responsible for feeding the mighty presses of journalism. Now to transform the analogy, imagine our whole culture with all its machinery as that fish-processing plant, and imagine its workers looking wistfully out to sea for the great catch they confidently expect from the deep; and then turn your eyes seaward with them and note that the leaky dories are still the only boats out there, and now they are manned by drunken or otherwise disabled poets. My metaphor is becoming comically unwieldy, but I am trying to say that a sane culture has to have a good portion of its ablest and most intelligent members out in the boats fishing or there won't be much of a catch. Positivism keeps everybody on shore or sends them out so poorly equipped that they might as well not go out.

So at least runs my argument when I want to blame the culture and not the poets. Then I think of a poetry of engagement as nonsense. Yet at other times I think: why hold the culture responsible?—for that is the same as having nobody responsible. One can grant that the culture has done its bit to alienate its artists—it has not only censored many of them or taken umbrage at them, but also ignored them or put them in little magazines (which is almost the same thing) while elevating to various states of social grace hordes of frauds. The culture has done its bit but it has not done it in one simple sweeping motion as so many of the sociological accounts of our culture's love affair with mediocrity and fraudulence suggest. What is forgotten in these accounts is that the culture is a big culture, a broad culture, perhaps best described as many cultures. It still has plenty of the kind of room in it that Whitman, for one, was always celebrating. Furthermore its roominess is tacitly acknowledged by most of our poets themselves in their daily lives; they simply won't admit to it in their poems as they enjoy it and participate in it. Their stubbornness or blindness here is what finally leads me to accuse them of misunderstanding rather than dismal understanding and finally to believe that the various philosophies of exclusion around us *can* be combated in some measure by the artists themselves if they will only try. Living in the woods with Thoreau, in Paris with Henry Miller, or in Yale's Hall of Graduate Studies with René Wellek—these are not the only livings available to the poet these days. And though each of these livings may be said to have its peculiar virtues, each has as well, as I have tried to indicate, limitations for which I am persuaded that the artists share at least part of the responsibility. In a way the poets have sold themselves on their own positivism—poets from Ezra Pound to Allen Ginsberg—and now that they've got it they've also got an art that is about as central to our world as stamp collecting.

So. I have given you a polemic. Now what? What proposals for reform can I send you off home with? Would it be appropriate, for example, for me to suggest that our judiciary in its wisdom label our poets anarcho-individualists and parasites, haul them into court, and sentence them to some honest work? The Soviets did this recently with one Michael Brodsky, a poet who as an anarcho-individualist looks like Snow White compared with most of his American counterparts, but who was nonetheless found guilty of parasitism and sentenced to 5 years in Siberia shoveling manure. In fairness to the Soviets I should add that after a short manure term Brodsky now appears to have been let off, and to be back in circulation as a parasite. We need to remember him and his like, however, when proposing reforms. I, for example, with secret administrative yearnings in me, might, if I had the power, suddenly issue an edict prohibiting poets from writing verse, requiring them to write in the "living language" only, that is, in prose like Karl Shapiro. Or I might advocate the abandonment of literary quarterlies as now conceived and executed—"executed" is the word—or, more drastically, the abandonment of the literature departments of our colleges, on the grounds that these distinctive activities merely serve to enforce the deadly positivism of literary exclusion. I might even go about ordering poets to become physicists, journalists or—imagine—librarians. For

600

sometimes I wish such reforms *could* be imposed on the literary world, wish there were someone in a position to impose them.

But of course nobody is in such a position. Nobody, not even a Soviet tribunal, has any effective long-term powers over literature, except maybe the power to stamp it out. For the nature of literature makes inevitable that literary reforms come from *inside* the makers of literature, not outside. Our poets and pre-poets—all those hopefully good, tough minds—have to be tolerated, even encouraged in their driftings; they have to make the decisions, do the persuading; and they have to do these things not because it would be illiberal and un-American for anyone to keep them from doing them—though that's a reason too—but because no outside administrator or critic has any essential authority over creation. The created thing on the page grows much the way a living thing grows in the bushes, by its own internal logic and history. Outside forces can kill it; outside forces can eventually make it modify some of its characteristics—but that is all. Nobody has ever successfully converted a rose into a skunk cabbage, or vice versa, by executive decree.

Which leaves us, perhaps, stuck with our skunk cabbages, at least for so long as the skunk cabbages choose to remain as they are. And since neither skunk cabbages nor poets are noted for their capacity to transform themselves, we may well be in for a long era of skunk cabbages.

Yet let me suggest, in conclusion, a more optimistic way of looking at the difficulty, by quoting a scientist who will doubtless be astonished to hear himself thus used. He is Cyril Stanley Smith of M.I.T. A friend of mine here in Washington got for me a piece by Professor Smith having to do with all sorts of structural or formal problems in science above the level of atomic structure.[1] At the end of his piece he observed that the need in science now "is for concern with systems of greater complexity, for methods of dealing with complicated nature as it exists;" and then he added: "The artist has long been making meaningful and communicable statements, if not always precise ones, about complex things." How pleasant to have somebody in the enemy camp think this! And how pleasant, if confusing, to hear him conclude as follows: "If new methods, which will surely owe something to aesthetics, should enable the scientists to move into more complex fields, his area of interest will approach that of the humanist, and science may even once more blend smoothly into the whole range of human activity."

[1] Cyril Stanley Smith, "Structure, Substructure, and Superstructure." *Reviews of Modern Physics*, XXXVI (April 1964), 524–532.

Now I say this statement is confusing because, if you have been listening to me at all you may have gotten the impression—I certainly intended you to—that the arts, at least as represented by much modern poetry, are hardly blending smoothly into the whole range of human activity. Confusing or not, Professor Smith's statement seems to me an appropriate one here, appropriate because it serves to remind us that the arts have at least a *reputation* for ranginess, and perhaps even that in past eras they have almost, on occasion, earned that reputation.

Why then can we not say that ranginess is *already* a part of the poetic organism, a now submerged part? If we do, our problem becomes not one of trying to change the organism, or trying to persuade or force the organism to change itself, but merely to encourage it to come out of the bushes and remember to *be* itself.

☆ U.S. GOVERNMENT PRINTING OFFICE : 1973 O—470—477